What If ?

for sweet Jane
with love

Jack

To order additional copies, please contact us.
BookSurge
www.booksurge.com
1-866-308-6235
orders@booksurge.com

Visit the website:
www.thewhatifproject.org

Cover art by:
Ray McDaniel
www.artofraymcdaniel.com

What If ?

A Beginners Course In Exploring The
Quantum Question Of Consciousness

By Jack McDaniel

Buffet of Contents

Instruction Manual

Beyond this page, this book contains no commas and employs periods only as markers for paragraph endings. Instead you'll find these (-) and these (~) with an occasional (or actually numerous) one OF these (=) thrown in. The first (-) a hyphen or dash, replaces the comma but it's not just a replacement, it exaggerates and extends the usual job of a comma, which is a momentary pause, often barely noticed, to a specific road sign that says - go slow. The intention = Is exactly that - to slow you down - to mark a rhythm - that gathers the full meaning - of each word - especially - particular words - and so - to do what commas are generally too quiet to do - which is - make - you - notice - the pause.

The deliberate timing of such a device - could - appear - as though - I thought I was writing for an audience of idiots. The truth - is entirely the opposite. I'm asking you to squeeze the language - for its full power of expression - by giving the words the space they need - to grow - into understanding - a process that requires one of the most obvious indicators of intelligence there is = Patience.

Which is also - why - the period has been replaced by these things (~) which in mathematics represents the word - which represents the concept = Approximately ~ They do mean basically the same thing as a normal period - a full stop - the end of one action - or idea - in order to separate it - from the next ~ The difference is = A full stop - recognition - of that space ~ Nothing approximate about it ~ Because = The gap - the silence - between words - is the fertile ground in which they do their work ~ So - this road sign (~) doesn't just mean stop - it means - look both ways - before proceeding ~ In other words - you're only approximately ready to move on to the next sentence - as you ask your self = Did you pay attention - to what you just read? Not that you won't get used to it in no time and be ignoring these suggestions as much as normal punctuation ~ So don't worry - it's easier than it looks

As for these (=) I wouldn't bother explaining what they mean - since = I think you already know - but = Just to avoid any possible confusion = When one of these (=) appears - it means = This idea equals - moves into - or is answered by = This new one ~ Their use - is not governed by exactly the same (semi precise) - grammatical replacement formula as the others - and instead = Are more in the category of methodically rogue deviations - with a certain measure of whim involved in their placement ~ And yet = I think you'll still find them = Just as simple as $1 + 1 = ?$

I have other reasons - for this messing with - your relationship - with punctuation ~ But - for now - I'll let you try to work those out on your own (although if you really can't stand the mystery - or the punctuation - you can turn to the end of class three and see if the explanation you find there helps) Some of you might find it easier - if you use this sentence structure - as what the voice-over narration script for a documentary film would look like - if it was laid out according to timing - and then think it - in your own speaking voice (what you might call - reading aloud silently) Some of you super fast readers - it will just irritate no end - because = It works = It will slow down your reading ~ The point is = That's the point = Take your time ~ Read each word - as though - it were important - to the meaning of each sentence - because = It is ~ If - you find it very uncomfortable = Good ~ That means - you're pushing a part of you (that we'll get around to talking about - eventually) - which - may very well be of great service to you to push ~ If - it's not uncomfortable - that's good too ~ There'll be other parts to do that pushing job ~ Either way = If you think about the punctuation - you'll miss the meaning of the words = So don't ~ Just use it the way I've told you and you'll get along just fine.

Mixed up - with that theme of timing pauses - is also - the pause - of timing - or - how you take these classes ~ And - in a world ruled by time = Timing - is everything ~ My suggestion is = One class at a time - with a break of two days between each ~ You could stretch that to more days - or narrow it to fewer ~ Of course you'll still do whatever you like - but - my suggestion remains the same ~ Then = Each class ends with an assignment ~ No = Nothing difficult - yet - requiring time - to sink in - but = Not so much time - that distraction washes it back out again ~ Plus = There is a second book - within this one (pregnant - you might even say) - and timed - between each class (disguised as Notes from a Parallel Universe - chapters one - two - three - and so on) - to be read as a part of that assignment - that - a day or two's pondering - not to mention - rereading - wouldn't hurt.

So - there you go - two books in one ~ If nothing else - you got a bargain ~ Of course - there is a reason for that as well - which perhaps you will - reason out - for yourself ~ But - don't worry about that either - there'll be plenty of clues.

Plus = The whole thing is salt and peppered with distracting little inserts and extras (sort of mini essays for the most part - that begin [[[[[[[[[and end]]]]]]]]] like this) - which = Are intended to extend and enrich your understandings and experience of the whole - which really means - three books in one (those bargains just keep coming) Some of those seasonings - may seem a little obscure and out of context ~ Pay no attention to that ~ And instead = See if you can work out how they do connect ~ I suggest (very strongly) = That you first ignore them when you come across them - and then = Return to them - when you've finished reading that particular section ~ Up to you of course - but = Don't forget to give each idea the time it takes to do that sinking in thing - which = May mean regularly rereading portions (there's that rereading word again - because - it's important - repeat after me - reread - reread) - before - moving on ~ In fact = See if you can turn your old habit - of just reading on regardless of whether you understood what you read or not (those of you who do that) - to a scientific process - a glance over your shoulder type of making sure where you stand - one piece at a time ~ Ultimately - this is an experiment ~ You'll recall the title mentions exploring a question? Well = That's - what an experiment is = Exploring a question ~ Rushing the results - will only prove = You were in a rush.

And (that's - AND) = Check the facts ~ This course - is an invitation to learn about just about everything (in a certain sense) - and so = Since it can't do the whole job on its own - it's also an invitation (inspiration - polite poke in the ribs - suggestion) - to follow up and dig around - on your own ~ Much of it lays on the sharp edge of that realm called controversy - where the brand new - and the brand old - are mixed up in that endless process we call change ~ Facts (by that definition of new and old) - also change ~ Therefore = Play your part ~ Look things up ~ Ask questions ~ You can doubt - believe - reject - or embrace what ever you like - but = Participate ~ That's the trick ~ The one thing this course will never claim to be - is on its own - and in that = Neither are you.

Most importantly - once you've remembered all that - remember this = Have Fun.

Class One - Introduction?

The first thing I'm going to do - is introduce myself ~ So = Hi ~ I'm called Jack.

I say called - because it's not actually my name ~ I've gone by several names during my life - and certainly been called a few you may have been called yourself ~ I've settled on Jack - because = It's not just a name - it's a word - an extremely versatile word - that describes lots of practical devices - people - and actions - at least the ones that are in the dictionary ~ And - in a sense - it covers everyone - connects them you might say ~ At least the males of the species (much like that word Dude does) Then again = There's that word mankind - which is meant to do that job in an equally single gender kind of way ~ So - you might also say = It's really a matter of perspective ~ But go ahead - look up that word Jack ~ You'd have difficulty finding a more useful name.

The point is - I'm not Jack ~ I'm not any of the - names - I've ever signed ~ They are strings of letters - that symbolize sounds - that symbolize meanings ~ In the case of personal names - the original meaning is generally disregarded (like Paul means humble and Robert means bright flame) - so their current meaning - is really just that person instead of the other one ~ In other words = Words ~ The word - chair - might help direct you where to sit - but - it's not what you sit on ~ Words aren't - the things - they talk about ~ Names aren't - the people - they identify.

But - you knew that.

So - the reason I point this out - is that - one - of the obstacles to complete communication among humans - is - words themselves ~ Not to say - they aren't also - one - of the best tools we've got going for that endeavor - but = By definition - words - are limitations = They have their own separate meanings ~ They're set up that way - for the very practical and obvious purpose - of knowing what someone else is talking about ~ The trouble is - that's not always enough to accomplish the job (of knowing what someone else is talking about) - or even being able to talk about - what you do know - particularly = When you encounter opposing definitions of the same word ~ You know - like the big ones - Truth - Justice - Freedom - Wisdom - Consciousness ~ Of course - on the surface - that list of communication obstacles might appear much longer than just words ~ Especially when people are killing each other over them.

But - defining obstacles is not the objective ~ The objective - is slipping around the words - that limit by definition - the word in question in this course - which is =

2

Consciousness ~ That one's a definition with some pretty fuzzy edges ~ Especially the deeper you examine it ~ In fact - you might say = It really has no edges at all - or = You might say the opposite ~ If you ask ten people - to really define it - almost definitely = You'll get ten different answers - that range - from somewhat different - to totally different ~ With that difference of course - being reflected - in words ~ Again = I don't mean to be defining an obstacle ~ It's just not like that word - chair ~ No matter how many designs of chair you might describe - it's purpose (though not perhaps it's deeper reality) - is still a place to rest your butt.

Then - there's that word = Quantum ~ It's a measurement word - like quantity - being a specific amount of something ~ It's usually mixed up with Physics (or the science of matter and energy) - when it gets trotted out for general use - where - it means = The smallest unit of energy going ~ And then = Continues on to more meaning - in how that energy behaves - like a quantum leap - and quantum mechanics - which = Is the set of theories trying to explain why something - like a quantum leap (which we'll get to) - could take place among charges of energy - so small (we're talking the world of stuff smaller than atoms here) - and so fast - no one has ever actually seen one in action ~ Very tricky stuff ~ Which means - that basically - the majority of people using the word - probably - have only a limited understanding of what it means ~ Even - if they know - what it means - they still have their limits ~ Which is why the word - theory - is in there ~ However - they do know (the people that have been studying such things) - after miles and miles of mathematical equations - years of experimentation - and volumes of evidence to support those theories - that the ideas involved - are concerned with the fundamental construction of our reality - and how we interact with it - and = So am I ~ So - that's why it's in the title.

[[[[[[[[[**Quantum Theory:**

Quantum theory (just to give you a taste) - first began to be formulated in 1900 by the German physicist Max Planck (and friends) - as a result of his work with thermodynamics (the physics of heat and other forms of energy in relationship) - where the idea (extremely simplified) - that electromagnetic energy travels - or exists - in very tiny amounts - or quanta - appeared to explain certain functions that previously made no sense ~ As the theory progressed - it went on to predict (among other things) - the strength of interactions between electrons and magnetic fields (no - you don't have to understand what that means yet - only that it's referring to some of the most fundamental features of physical reality - as we understand it so far) - which = Has been confirmed accurate to a precision of two parts in a trillion - which means (other those miles of complex mathematics and diligent experimentation involving impossibly miniscule things - that aren't really things - which - we'll do our best to translate into simple terms as we go along) - that = These physicists are truly onto something big (regardless of how small) - which = At the core of that big - is the other aspect - of that all but proven theory - that = We can no longer assume ourselves - as observers - to be separate - from what we observe.]]]]]]]]]

But - it's still just a word - and so is consciousness ~ They all are ~ Words that is ~ Fact is - due to that very inadequacy of language to describe consciousness - this course is also about becoming more conscious - of language (which is another reason for the wacky punctuation - and - why you'll sometimes have to work a bit to follow along) Therefore (or perhaps in spite of) - the most important idea to keep in mind throughout this course - is not so much what words get used - as it is - what you experience - because of them - and how you judge - and react - to those experiences ~ That - is one of the key defining functions - of coming to a broader understanding - of what - why - or - how - consciousness works.

Here's an example ~ Just see what it - feels - like.

What if - consciousness - is the fabric of experience - the means (or capacity - ability) - by which - we know we are experiencing - and (at the same time) - the means (or resources - support - raw material) - by which - there - is - something - to experience? To put it another way = What if - consciousness - is like the light in a movie projector - and what we take for reality - is what happens on the movie screen - while in fact - what reality really is - is that light - or = Consciousness?

Big question = Yes ~ Perhaps a bit too big ~ But - again - those are just words ~ In your head - maybe they go Ding - maybe they go Flop ~ The question - is not whether those questions are on to something that is true - or if you understood them - or - if they make any sense at all ~ The question is = What did they do? Meaning = What - did - you - do with them? {{Rereading them might help to fill in that response}}

See = Paying attention to - YOU - or - what goes on in you - is the beginning of paying attention - to consciousness ~ Even though consciousness is much larger than anything I just said - or will say ~ At least - according to what - I mean - when - I say - what I just said.

Still - an entirely amazing thing just happened.

In order for you - to know your version - of knowing what I'm talking about - your brain/mind (I say brain/mind from the point of view - of = Have you considered that your brain may be only a very small part of what - your mind - or - a mind - or simply just mind at all - actually is? Anyway - your brain/mind) - has to sort through all the past reference layers you've accumulated - for the particular word symbols mentioned - then analyze how they stick to each other - to create a recognizable pattern - also according to your own past experience (which is why the word recognizable is in there) - before it arrives at - and delivers - to your feeling thinking self - the meaning - it decides on - and = All this - while it monitors huge amounts of data gathered from your five senses - plus deals with any other distracting thoughts or reactions you may be having at the same time ~ In other words = What - you have to be - is conscious - or - alive - on the tip of the iceberg - of consciousness.

Luckily - most of that stuff takes place in a tiny space of time - that few people ever really consider - simply because = We don't have to ~ At least that's what seems to be working for the majority ~ The question is (one of them at least) = How well is it

4

working? If you are a regular viewer of the evening news - you may have some doubts about the accuracy of our collective decisions on how to - best - use our consciousness.

What I'm going to ask you to do - that - perhaps you've never been asked to do before = Is to pay attention ~ No - no = Not the way you've been asked three million - give or take a hundred thousand or so - times before ~ The attention I mean is = To explore that mind of yours - to pick it apart - sit in the middle - and feel the whole thing.

See - the real introduction - I'm interested in making here - is - you - meeting your - self ~ This Course is jammed with practical tools to do just that ~ But - because of those fuzzy edges I mentioned = Some of them - may look pretty fuzzy themselves ~ I assure you - they are as practical as the word/name - Jack ~ You don't have to believe me though = Try them for yourself ~ After all - you - are what this course is really all about ~ Fact is = I'm not asking you to believe a single word of what I say ~ Not that I don't want you to listen ~ Instead = I'm asking you to question what I say ~ Not the kind of question that says = That's impossible ~ That's not a question ~ I mean the kind that asks = Is it possible? Examine - test - explore - dig in and roll around in your own - not knowing ~ You may find - what you think you know - no matter what it is - is only a tiny portion - of what knowing really is - and = You may find - what's beyond even that.

Yes = Those are also - only words - and the sense they make - is what sense - you want them to make ~ And yet = Where do they lead? Where are you open? Where are you closed? All they can ask is that ~ Invention - discovery - breakthrough - only occur - where there is space - to allow them to occur ~ The word - question = Describes a doorway to that space - and = Consciousness - is a word - for what's in that space - and = That space = Is in you ~ Not that - IT - really concerns itself with boundaries of - in or out ~ IT - just - is ~ Without consciousness - the you - behind the you - that thinks - you're you - would not - be ~ To Be - or exist - would not - be ~ At least the way we are accustomed to experiencing it - and perhaps - even in ways we are not.

If you look in a dictionary - the first definition of the word conscious (which is the present tense of the word consciousness) - goes something like = Having an awareness of ones own existence ~ Well - if you are aware enough to know you exist - then the general rule is = That you'll have a preference - about what you want that existence to feel like ~ Is it enjoyable? Is it rotten? Which do you prefer? That's where - one of the other reasons - for this whole study of consciousness kicks in ~ Which is = What part - does that you - that thinks it's you - play in all this fuss we make about success and happiness? What are we doing with it? What are we - not doing with it? What's in it for us?

Those are the kinds of questions we're going to look at ~ There's a great deal of mystery involved - a lot of unknown territory to explore - which = Requires pioneers with courage and determination ~ Do you - want to be one?

||||||||| Doctor Dude's Dictionary - word one - Integral:

There's a word you might consider integrating into your vocabulary - in the interests of establishing completeness ~ The reason is = Integrating - and completeness - go a long way toward defining the word = Integral ~ It's meaning - is about wholeness - or - all the parts intact - together ~ An integral part - is an important one - a necessary one - an essential one - one - which - when it is missing - means incompleteness - or you might say = Not one - broken - fragmented - into parts ~ To integrate is to bring together - unite - join - or paste up to make one thing ~ Integrating a conceptual knowledge (or a set of ideas gathered through experience) - with an active skill - is what makes up any job - and = That knowledge - and that ability - are integral parts - of completing that job ~ Integral is just an all-around essential addition to any vocabulary - because = A vocabulary's just not complete - without it.||||||||||

This course is an invitation (just one invitation after another - what fun) - to that frontier (the unknown territory one) It may be - that you are someone that will change the course of history ~ It may be - we are all that person put together ~ Because = What if - history - is the story of consciousness - exploring - interacting - and discovering - itself - and = There's not one of us - that isn't taking part?

Remember = The driving force - behind a great mystery - is not finding the answer = It's - wanting - to find the answer ~ So - allow me to solve one mystery right off the bat - by putting you onto another.

You won't find the answers in this course - you'll find them - in you.

What do I mean by that? Well - I'm not going to tell you ~ I am - going to ask you an awful lot of questions ~ I know - the word - awful - was in there - right next to the word - question ~ Which may be exactly how you feel about being asked questions ~ These aren't the kind of questions you're used to ducking though ~ I don't care if you did your homework - or cleaned your room - or where you're going with your friends ~ I'm not even expecting an answer ~ Answers aren't the point = The questions are ~ The space - that questions are - is what I'm asking you to enter - and = I'm going to ask it very seriously ~ Not because it's not enjoyable ~ Enjoyable - is really what it's all about ~ But - because = If you do - truly enter - that space I'm talking about - you can't return ~ Not the same - you - anyway ~ The ground - you're used to standing on - will be changed - and you won't be able to change it back ~ That's what I mean by serious ~ What I mean by - enjoyable - is - you won't want to be the same ~ But - it's up to you - 100% ~ All of it - is - you ~ That's the real point ~ The real question - is = Do you want to know - what that is?

There's an expression going around - in an underground kind of way (even if it is in plain sight) - that's based on an element in a book - written more than a hundred years ago - that - in that light - you'd have to wonder what the author of that book would think of how it's being used today ~ Personally - I think that - Lewis Carol - who wrote - Alice in Wonderland - would be very pleased by "How far down the rabbit hole do you want to go?"

Have you read the book? Some very strange goings on - go on - in it ~ You might say - the message - woven through it's pages in the disguise of nonsense - is = Reality is not

6

what it appears - and = What appears to be reality - is not Real ~ Which may sound like saying the same thing twice - but = Is it?

Alright then - this first class is going to be short ~ Actually - they all will be (although it's possible you may have a different opinion of that measurement - and - you may very well be right) This stuff takes some digesting - and - some practice ~ So = Short is good ~ The secret though - is this class = Is really just the introduction ~ Because = Quite often - people are apt to skip the introduction - thinking - it's not important - and sometimes - they're quite right ~ The important part though - is - your first assignment is contained in it - and - in a sense - it's the most important one ~ It's spelled out in that - rabbit hole - question ~ It's (that is - I'm) - asking you = Do you want to change? Change meaning = Pull apart your foundation - of how - everything works - in order - to find out how - everything - works.

That's your assignment - that question ~ No - not the pulling apart bit ~ That comes later ~ I'm asking you - to ask you = Do you want to change? And - no = I don't want the answer = You do ~ Because = It's what you feel - that's the answer ~ What you feel - about - what it's like to be you = Is it enough? Is it complete? Is it limited? Is it free? Yes? No? Then maybe you want to chase some rabbits ~ Maybe you don't ~ First - you're going to have to ask the question ~ Then = You can continue - and - of course = You can stop whenever you like - although it may be too late - and = If you do stop - you really won't have the full picture of what is offered here ~ Either way - that's not a sales pitch = It's simply the truth of it - because = The purpose of the information presented here - is to assist you - to learn about - the whole you - and - the full power of what's hidden there ~ But - again - because of that - you have to remember = The whole answers - are not in - it - they're - in you.

By the way - this might all sound like a lot of drama ~ Pay no attention to that ~ Or to what all those uses of the word - you - might mean ~ You'll - find out ~ The drama is just for fun - and - fun - is whatever - you - want it to be.

And another = By the way = How's that punctuation working out for you? Is it irritating? Is it enjoyable? Does it make sense? Keep it up - you're doing great.

See you soon..... Jack

THE PERCEPTION PAPERS - number one

Seeing Is Believing:

What perception is = Is the experience of awareness - that is at the end of the line of a process (officially known as transduction) - by which energy from outside the body (light - sound waves - textures - flavors - and so on) - is converted to an electrochemical form of energy - which is recognizable as information to our brains - that then = Flows through all the judgment filtration systems we've established through life experience - in order to become = That experience of awareness just mentioned ~ In other words = Our sensory experiences - blended with our thought experiences - are = Our perceptions.

Perception - is our first interface (meaning - point of contact - boundary surface - shared border) - with the physical world - and as such = It often tends to be regarded as what consciousness is (or the reason consciousness exists) - but = What if - perception - is really just the beginning - or the first interface - with an infinitely larger world of consciousness - the same as - or as compared to - how little of the planet your eyes are seeing in this particular moment?

Whether or not - the true definition of consciousness - extends no further than we can reach - or just begins there = Without question - our senses are an active part of it - and = Learning how to use them - in a more complete way (which is to say - make conscious use of the astounding amount of information they are feeding us every waking second - or try) - is the first - and most obvious tool at our disposal for exploring this consciousness thing.

Therefore = This is the first in a series of five short detours (not to mention several other little twists and turns in the road) - intended to inform you about - and assist you in experiencing - the hidden workings (meaning - backstage crew) - of those familiar five navigators ~ Which = As you can see (provided you paid attention to the title of this section) - begins with the sense - generally regarded to be our most dominant (not that that's true for everyone) = Vision.

Take a look around you ~ I mean = Really - look around - up close - faraway - in between ~ Turn yourself in a circle - walk past something - watch things pass you ~ Isn't it just completely amazing how you are putting together all that information (that is - if your eyes function relatively normally - my apologies to those of you whose eyes don't) - all those colors - shapes - depths - shadows - movement - and - you making complete sense out of it all? And then = It's so consistent ~ As you move toward something - it gets larger - clearer - more textural - more detailed ~ As you move away - the opposite happens ~ If it wasn't so absolutely taken for granted = You'd call it a miracle.

Looking - at the process then = Just like those stars you see at night (a concept that will be explained shortly) - it's not things you're seeing = It's light ~ You've noticed of course - that you can't see things if there's no light present ~ It's light - bouncing off things - which enters our eyes - that allows us to see ~ That light passes through the lens at the front of our eyes - which inverts it (flips it upside down) - and projects it (like a movie projector) - on to the retina (specialized cells at the back of the eye called rods and cones - for the hardly surprising reason - they look like rods and cones) - which convert all the parts of that incoming information to electrical signals - that are then sent along the optic nerve to the visual cortex at the back of your head (which is why you - see stars - if someone whacks you there) - where = Those signals are separated into at least four different elements of vision - or - motion - form - color - and depth - and = Forwarded onto the parts of the brain responsible for working out what they mean (and flipping them right side up again of course) Apparently (and in a way - not surprisingly) - an entire third of our brains (according to the conclusions of certain types of research which have attempted to narrow down such things) - are devoted to sorting out what our eyes are taking in.

But = It's not just those four parts of vision we're - looking for - when we use our eyes - it's = Meaning - that we want ~ Perception (as previously defined) - is not a data gathering function alone = It's really more an analytical one ~ Seeing - involves a constant process of comparing memory - or learned through experience information - with what it is were looking at - in order to identify - what it is were looking at ~ And - to say the least = It's an incredibly complex process - that works at super fast speeds (perhaps we're back to that miracle idea) - which = Is not even mentioning - that we process movement in black-and-white (possibly - because it's faster than color - and so speeds up our response time to potential danger) - and - paint this perception picture of a world (in so many colors that no artist could ever even approach reproducing a small fraction of them in a life time) - from the three single color signals our eyes are capable of registering - red - green - and blue ~ If it's not a miracle (and who is it that's deciding?) = It certainly is impressive ~ And = It couldn't do it - without you.

We - are active participants in our seeing process - far beyond just keeping our eyes open ~ We make mental corrections all the time - about - what we're seeing - which fill in the gaps in what our eyes are actually supplying ~ Objects - which are partially obscured by other objects - poorly lit - or dimly see in smoke or fog = Our minds - complete ~ In those instances - we are literally - seeing - our mind at work - which = Is hardly breaking a sweat for it - when you consider that there is a blind spot in each of our eyes that has to be compensated for in much the same fashion every time we open them ~ It's called the optic disk - and = It's the area in the middle of the retina where the optic nerve (that transduction TV cable to the brain) - connects to the eye ~ It's a hole - in that there are no receptors there (rods and cones) - but - like I say = Instead of having an actual blank spot in our vision - the brain (which seems to play a key role in that experience we call perception) - simply makes up what's there - by borrowing from the surrounding information like an option in Photoshop.

Having said all that = We persist in - seeing - the process of vision - as an information exchange on the level of the physical evidence we know something about measuring ~ When quite possibly = It actually functions at a level (somewhere between physical - and not) - we are only beginning to truly recognize - which = Is the world of subatomic energy waves - or frequencies ~ We don't see what's - out there - in here (like a movie projected inside our heads) We see it - out there - where it apparently is - despite the action of doing so - is - all in our heads ~ That means = Sight - is a kind of virtual reality - constructed somehow (out of frequencies perhaps) - to allow us to interact in three dimensions - with (or is that - in) = Our minds.

It's all part of living in the - image-I-nation - of your head - because = Seeing - is all in our heads ~ We cannot separate our thoughts and feelings and memory and beliefs - from what we're looking at ~ The phrase - seeing is believing - says it all ~ What we recognize (and it is an amazingly long list of stuff we do) - and therefore make sense out of - is what we believe to be out there - according - to what we've - seen - before ~ Toss in an alien or two - maybe a sea monster - or a ghost - and the first thing anyone would do - is blink to clear away that something that - shouldn't be there - which - they might later describe as = I couldn't believe my eyes ~ The reason (which is not saying those things are real - nor is it saying otherwise) - is that = Seeing - and believing - are - the same thing to us.

So - try this = Use your eyes = Really - really - really - notice what you're seeing - and how - you're separating those things from their background ~ Look at color - marvel at it - see how bright colors fairly shine a light on you - and pale colors are much more complex than you ever thought they were ~ Pay attention to how shadows and shading - inform you of shapes - and the distances between objects ~ Watch motion - feel your eyes follow it ~ Flick your focus back and forth from the horizon - to your hand held up in front of you - the wall a few feet away - to the page of a book you're holding ~ Note how fast it works - how instantly focus takes place ~ Just plain explore that sense like you can't believe your luck at getting it for your birthday (which of course - you did) Play with it - squint and stare and swivel and = See - what you've been missing.

Notes From a Parallel Universe - Chapter One - Deep Space?

Let's begin at the end - shall we? Why waste time? What I mean is = The frontier - the edge - the pushed to the point of who knows what's beyond it location ~ What I'm about to describe - is a starting point - to seek beyond - and - an ending point - to look back from ~ And so - by those rights = Belongs on either end of this course with equal validity ~ The question (and there'll be plenty of them) - is = What - makes that point - that location - valid - or - of value? (Remember I just said - validity - about which end of this course - that frontier should appear - in case you're already confused) The answer - which is of course - another question - is = What - are we using to decide - where we are - and - what we know? In other words = What - establishes that frontier - what makes - it - the edge? Or = What in the world is this guy talking about? The edge of what?

Alright - it begins by visiting the place where one of humankinds oldest questions was raised ~ Follow me down this hallway - out this door - and = Here we are - the most ancient - awe inspiring - location on the planet - the backyard.

Not that a rooftop - or a field - a street - a mountainside - or a vacant lot won't do just as well ~ The point is - to get free of walls and ceilings for a moment ~ Not to say those aren't very practical structures all of us have made use of as protection from cold - hot - wet - wind - predators - insects - and each other for thousands of years ~ The trouble is = They're in the way ~ Just the same as many of the things - we think are meant to protect us - are in the way of our seeing beyond our limits ~ Where we need to be - is what has rather oddly become known as - outdoors - despite the fact it was there apparently billions of years before doors were invented ~ Just the same - that's the place ~ And the reason is = So we can see the night sky.

What do you see - when you look up there?

Just for the sake of argument = Let's say - it's clear weather - away from a lot of tall buildings and street lights.

Stars?

What if - I told you - you were wrong?

What if - I told you - what you are seeing - is the history of the universe?

See - what you are looking at = Is light (this is that star concept I mentioned) Light that may have been traveling for millions of years ~ Some of those stars - you think you are seeing - may no longer even exist to generate that light ~ Basically = All we are doing - with these eyes of ours - is receiving the information - that the space we are looking out at = Is unimaginably vast ~Those twinkling lights (the twinkling is caused by our having to look through our own atmosphere to see them) - have been traveling at 186,000 miles a second (yes - that's a second) - for hundreds of thousands - and - yes - even millions of years ~ Which means = Distances and time our human experience really can't relate to very well ~ Of course - then there are the numbers of them - which are equally boggling ~ Galaxies comes first - each containing hundreds of thousands of stars - and then - there are thousands of millions of galaxies ~ Which means = There are trillions of quadrillions of gazillions of stars out there - in a universe that may be only one of who knows how many.

To reduce it to just slightly more manageable = Our own sun is one of those stars ~ It's hanging on the outskirts of what we call - the Milky Way - our home galaxy ~ It would take a flash of light approximately 100,000 years to travel from one end to the other of that Milky Way ~ And remember = That's at the speed of circling the equator of the earth nearly seven times in the time it takes to say - Mississippi ~ The word big - certainly doesn't work to describe it ~ The Pacific ocean is - big - and most of us would consider that a small word for it ~You could try hugely giagunda enormous mega-totally colossal - and still fall pitifully short ~ That is if you're still talking about the Pacific - say - from the point of view of sitting in a life raft in the middle of it - never mind what you might feel like if you were adrift in a broken rocket ship somewhere in outer space.

[[[[[[[[Inventory:

Stop right there ~ Just stop (after you read this section actually - I'm just emphasizing a point is all) - and = Take an inventory (you know - like a store owner counting the stuff on the shelves) What are your senses taking in? What do you see? What do you hear? All five of them - what are they up to? Notice ~ Review them ~ Pay attention ~ What's going on around you?

Then = Close your eyes ~ How do you feel - physically? Go over your body - part by part ~ What does it feel like? Feel it - the whole thing.

How about - emotionally? What kind of feelings are you having? Not judgments of good or bad - just the feelings themselves - what are they? Spend a few moments in them = Feel them ~ Are they clear? Are they floating in a fog of undefined mood? Are they right in your face - or at the back of your mind? Again = What are they?

And thoughts = What have you been thinking about? What's your attention been on - in the sense of = What have you been following in your head? To be sure - if you're really doing what I'm asking = Then that's what you're thinking about - but = You haven't yet - and = You may not even be paying attention to this ~ So = Witness those thoughts ~ What are they? What ideas are you attaching to what ideas? What are you thinking?

Can you do that? Can you get a clear picture of all that information? Did you try? Are you going to?

Okay = Just asking.]]]]]]]]]

But - okay - okay = What's that got to do with you - right?

Well - you're thinking about it - that's a start ~ So - I'll give you a bit more to think about.

Back in 1996 - the Earth orbiting Hubble space telescope - snapped a repeated exposure photograph that took 10 days to complete - and - it was of a subject so small - one tiny spot of space - that you might get a feel for its size by holding a grain of sand at arm's length and seeing how much of the sky it covers ~ Pretty exciting huh? No?

Well - if you were to see the result - you might feel differently ~ Especially - if you were an astronomer ~ That sand grain size piece of sky - contained over 1,500 galaxies - some of which - have been streaming light toward us for 13 billion years.

Okay = That's pretty cool - but = Since then - they've topped it = They've done the same kind of thing - only this time - it took three months - and = It displays an estimated 10,000 galaxies - and = Peers hundreds of thousands of millions of years further back in time than the first photograph - which = Is only a relatively short 3 million years or so from the theorized (that's - Big Question) -beginning of the universe - known as the Big Bang - which maybe you've heard of already.

So - that's all very interesting - but - again = What's it got to do with you - or consciousness for that matter? Any ideas?

Yes = Space ~ Specifically - that space of question - you may remember hearing about more recently.

When ancient people stood in their - backyards - and looked up - they questioned = What is out there? And then - most of them - went on about the business of surviving ~ Well - we've seen a glimpse now of what - is out there - or (more accurately - what was out there) - and so - in some form - still is ~ And - because of it = We are changed forever ~ We can go right on with the preoccupation of survival and ignore all that mystery as having nothing to do with us - but = It's really too late - it's wormed it's way in ~ A new question - or more like the old question - seen through different glasses - is = What is our relationship - to all that infinite possibility - that just seems to keep getting bigger? And - the other question is = Why the question? Why are we asking? (Which is actually two questions) Well - because = We - are a part of it = We are each of us - one of those possibilities.

What if - the change - in being humbled by such immensity - is to see our conflicts as a species - fighting over what we think we know - or must control - or keep from being controlled = Are tiny? What if - we are called by that change - to recognize ourselves -

globally - one planet - one people - because - we - now - know - how small minded it is to think otherwise?

[[[[[[[[Are Your Thoughts You?

What I mean is = Do you identify with your thoughts? Or - in other words = Is your personal world - your self - your identity - the thoughts you think?

What I'm getting at here - is the question of = What is identity? Compared to = What is thought? One end of that question is = Are we experiencing - who - or what - we are - through our thinking - and in particular - what we agree with in our thinking? Or = Are we just experiencing what the power of thought - creates?

As you may have noticed = We can think anything we want ~ We can create the perfect romance - or the perfect crime - with that thinker of ours ~ The thing is = Thinking - and - the Real World around us - do not seem to be required to represent each other at all ~ Meaning = The world seems to be there whether we think about it or not - and - what we think about - doesn't (again - seem to) - have to ever play out in the world we see (at least in the way it plays out in our minds - such as possible crime and romance for instance)

At the same time = The - requirement - to have an identity - or an outward (and inward) - representation - or agreement - of who and what we are - does look like a lineup (or again - an agreement) - between our name and appearance and other such physical and historical reference kind of things - and - what we think - because = What we do - and when and where and why - we do what we do - is because = We think what we do - and do what we think - which - is all about agreeing - with what we think.

But - the question remains = Do we have to identify - with what we think? Or - to put it another way = Is - what we think is true - truly - who we are - or = Are we more than that?

In defining the word - identify - what we're looking at - is a set of characteristics - or conditions and relationships - which remain basically the same - and so - are recognizable ~ Therefore - given that definition = Do your thoughts change? Do you learn new things? Do insights - inspirations - and invention - create questions and doubts and new perspectives - on old ideas?

It follows then = That thoughts - and identity - are not the same thing (so long as you are willing to have new ones) Does it follow that following then - that = If thoughts can continuously change (and thoughts are the medium through which we perceive - recognize - and measure identity) - then - identity (particularly our own - self identity) - could be just as fluid a thing as thinking - provided we are willing to think about it that way?

In the end = Is this thing we call identity - just the result of all the things we've thought in the past - that - we're apt to go on thinking in some form or another - into the future? What would happen then - if - you were to suddenly discover that everything you ever believed in - was not true? Which is to say = You were forced to disagree - with who you had always been - with your self ~ Would you still be you? Who are you? Are you your thoughts? What do you think now?]]]]]]]]]]

The question - for you - is = How - do you - want to think - and feel - and behave?

The conditions - of how we choose to do those things - are based on what we have decided - we know ~ To contemplate a photograph of 10,000 galaxies across nearly 14 billion years of time forces us to consider - that our real knowledge - meaning the kind that's mostly dependent on words for describing - may be very nearly zero.

It is simple enough to recognize - what we - do not know (rather closer to home) - with the shortest effort of examination ~ We don't know how to cure HIV-AIDS (which now infects hundreds of millions of people and is the major cause of death in Africa) Cancer continues to baffle us ~ Autism is on a frighteningly steep rise ~ Then = There are the issues of war - terrorism - pollution - hunger - poverty - over population - global warming or climate change - and the long list of human caused destructive effects on the environment - all of which = Contribute to the statistic that all (other) living species on the planet are in a state of decline (which means slowly - or quickly - dying)

When actually - in a sense - we do know how to solve (or alter the course of to some degree - climate change is with us for keeps now) - all of those problems ~ That sense being = A complete rearrangement of our priorities and huge cooperative actions undertaken on a global level ~ Only - it would take such drastic sweeping changes to accomplish such a thing - that we don't know how to do that ~ So - it may sound like we have enough problems - without staring awestruck stupid into the vast unknown reaches of the universe ~ But = What if - the real problem - is our habit of rearranging old ideas - in the hopes of arriving at new results? Or - rearranging the deck furniture on the Titanic - as a popular saying puts it (one of my personal favorites - I might add) - which means - quite simply = Forever treating the symptoms (or effects) of the disease - rather than - its cause.

What if - the key to curing all those problems - is the same - as discovering the secret of interstellar travel? What if - that key - is creating - the space of a question - to receive the answer?

What if - it is not in - knowing - things - but - for a moment - in not - knowing - anything - and - in that same moment - knowing with all our hearts - there is a part of us - that does know? (Or not = That's just how questions work ~ You have to ask them)

What if - it (it being one response to the set of questions just asked) - is like - stepping away from the walls and roofs of limited knowledge - long enough to understand - that what we think - is safe - may be comfortable - but = It is always small - and constantly in need of defending? A rather well known character - by the name of Albert Einstein - once described such conditions in words something like = You can't solve a problem - by using the same thinking - that created the problem in the first place.

16

|||||||||| **Measure This:**

The scientific structure of belief - which declares = What constitutes - or makes up - the ingredients - or functions - systems - and purposes of - Reality = Are only those things that can be measured by - or experienced through - the data collected by our five senses - or the technology designed and made use of by those senses (in other words - perception alone) = Is - according to that same system of examination and verification - proven = Inaccurate.

So - after you reread that last sentence a couple of times - it means = There is a contradiction at the very core of the belief structure just described - because = There is no way to apply that same technique of scientific measurement to - the truth - of that belief structure ~ Perception (the sum input - and mental use of sensory data) - can only prove = That perception happens - within the context of perception ~ It's a case of = The evidence is only about the evidence = It doesn't solve the mystery = It merely defines what the mystery is ~ A reality - outside of - or beyond perception - is not proven impossible because it cannot be recognized by perception ~ Perception only proves = That perception is only capable of recognition - within the particular range our senses operate in ~ It's just the same (metaphorically speaking) - as looking up in this moment and trying to see radio waves passing by ~ The fact - that you cannot - obviously (to us that know about them) - does not disprove their existence (although it certainly would to someone 500 years ago) - it just illustrates the limits (in this case measurable) - of that particular sense.

By that measurement = Accepting (or a step further - defending) - a scientific proof (perception) - based reality - as the only possible - reality (not to say that it isn't completely up to you - and what science can measure expands all the time) - is not unlike believing - that English is the only language capable of forming a sentence meaning = Get a clue.||||||||||

So - what has the Hubble ultra deep Field photograph got to do with you?

Well = It's sort of like a blink at - everything - and you - are a part of everything - and therefore - represent everything - and = What if - your consciousness - or consciousness itself - knows that - and it's simply waiting - for you (which means us) - to catch up?

Class Two - Oxygen?

I'm going to assume - that - since you're here - your answer to the first assignment is = Yes = Because - if it isn't = You're still here - which has to mean = You're at least a little willing to find out - and = That's really all I'm ever going to ask of you.

Alright ~ Everyone stand up - if you would please ~ I'm serious now ~ Come on - come on ~ That's it - all the way to your feet ~ Yup - both feet ~ You can do it ~ Very good.

Now - I'm going to show you an exercise ~ No = Not that kind of exercise (at least not strenuously so) This one is all about the muscles of consciousness - and = By our standard method of locating consciousness in our heads - it's centered on = The brain.

What you do is = Take your left hand - and grab your right earlobe between your thumb and forefinger with the back of your thumb facing out and squeeze gently ~ Then = With your right hand - do the same with your left earlobe ~ Yes = It looks a little silly - but never mind that ~ There's some powerful stuff about to take place.

Now = Press your tongue to the roof of your mouth just behind your teeth - and = As you smoothly squat down (a deep knee bend kind of action) = Inhale through your nose ~ Really pull the air into your lungs by pushing out your belly as you inhale - which pulls down on the diaphragm (the membrane of muscle that separates the lung cavity from the abdomen) - and fills those babies much more effectively ~ Then = As you stand up again = Exhale through your mouth (contracting your belly now) - tongue still pressed firmly to the roof of it (weird as that may feel) - and = As you do = Make an AAAHHH sound.

Go ahead = Try it.

Good - good ~ Now repeat the whole thing - inhale - squat - exhale - stand - fourteen times in a row ~ No - no = I'm not kidding - and = I'm entirely serious about this being a very powerful exercise for your brain - and perhaps much more ~ Of course you don't have to do it - or you may have some physical reason why you can't (the hands and breathing part can be done sitting down however - and may not even reduce the effect) In that case = You'll be fine without it - but = If you are capable of it (and I mean - standing up and all) = How will you find out - what it's capable of - without testing it out?

Alright = Ready? Here we go = One.............................

Great ~ Let's sit down.

So = Why did we just do that?

I'll make one part easy for you = Anybody here using oxygen? What happens when you stop? Yup = If you stop long enough - you die ~ How about if you stop temporarily - like if I were to choke you - but not long enough to kill you? Right = You'd pass out ~ You'd go - unconscious.

So - what is this course about again?

That's right = Consciousness.

Well = What is Consciousness?

Remember in the introduction - I gave you the start of a dictionary definition of the word conscious? What was it? Yeah = Awareness was in there - and existence ~ So = What does awareness mean? Okay = It's like knowing what's going on around you? Like the weather - other people - sounds - movement - action? What about - what's not going on - in the sense of being - inactive - like being - aware - of where the post office is? But = That knowing - is an action as well - isn't it? When you bring it to mind - that is - when you're actively aware of it? So - you may - know - where the post office is - but - you're not really knowing it - or being aware of it - until that moment of calling it into awareness? Does that mean that consciousness - is a kind of action?

Alright - you obviously know the word unconscious ~ Are you - aware - of what's going on - if you're unconscious? And = What happens if you starve your brain of oxygen?

Do you think oxygen has something to do with the action (at least in a body) - of being conscious then?

So = We just did that breath and movement exercise - to make what happen? Right = To pump our blood and deliver oxygen to our brains ~ I see yours is working ~ But = Why do that? Yes = The pump and deliver bit does create more efficiency in there - that's exactly right ~ Our brains love that oxygen stuff ~ Just in normal use - they demand 20 to 30% of our blood flow (by way of delivering that oxygen) - when they are only about 2% of our body weight ~ But still = Why would we want that boost (which - by the way - includes more than just increased oxygen when you do this weird bobbing up and down) - of efficiency? Okay ~ Those are good reasons ~ Now - I'll give you mine.

We were preparing ourselves to look for answers - in the place most people are only used to looking in part of - for answers ~ Where do you suppose that place is?

Absolutely = Consciousness.

Now - I don't mean the kind of asking - like = What do we know - or - what does experience tell us - and how we stick one thought to another to come up with an answer - like some history test idea of consciousness (which of course - is that part of the idea just mentioned) What I'm talking about - is the place - where we - don't know - and we let ourselves - not know - in order to let some other part of ourselves - that we don't usually listen to - answer ~ What if - the reason most people aren't listening to that part of themselves - is because = They don't know it's there to listen to ~ Which of course opens up the question = Is there such a part?

I know I'm talking in - what might seem - a mysterious kind of way ~ The reason is - the way into this consciousness stuff - is = Being in the mystery of it ~ Which may also sound a bit strange as well - if not - make no sense at all ~ But - I think you'll catch on.

So let's do it again ~ That is = BREATHE.

{{By the way - whenever it says - BREATHE (and it will at the beginning of each class) - please repeat the breath and movement exercise described at the beginning of this one ~ I know = You might not want to ~ You might think - it doesn't matter - or - who's going to know if you don't ~ But = What if - it does matter? Again = How would you find out? Of course - I'm also going to tell you more about it as we go along - but = As a direct hint = You'd be really smart to take it on full fledged - as well as do it on your own - say... when you get up every morning}}

[[[[[[[[[The Breathing Belly:

Conscious use of the diaphragm (the thin membrane like muscle that divides the chest cavity from the abdominal cavity - by way of repetition) - while breathing (which means involving your stomach muscles in the act) - will expand the lungs to capacity - and - supply the blood vessels in the lower sections of the lungs with the oxygen they don't get when shallow breathing is the case ~ Otherwise = In order to compensate for inadequate - or shallow breathing - heart rate and blood pressure are forced to increase - the whole cardiovascular system is placed under stress - which = Means the whole body is also under that same stress - and = In time - a long list of oxygen deprived cellular problems can be the result - including = The growth of cancer - which thrives in such conditions ~ That is not to say - you are in danger ~ It is to say = The simple act of regular deep breathing - is = One of the strongest medicines there is.]]]]]]]]]

So = What did you notice - about yourself - while you were doing that?

Light headedness?

Do you suppose that's your brain getting more oxygen than it's used to? Or - telling you that it is? What else? Did you notice yourself being present? What does that mean - present? So = It's like - paying attention - to the present moment? If you're not present - what are you doing? Right = You're somewhere else - either physically - or mentally - but either way = Not there.

Okay = How about this = Do you have to tell your heart to beat? How about your stomach to digest food? Are there any processes your body does - inside you - that you have to think about - in order to get done? What about breathing? Yeah = That one is different - isn't it ~ We can control it - or - let it do its own thing - right? So is your body always present? In other words - does your heart wonder if you're going to get enough exercise today - or your large intestine think about the pizza you had last week? No? They just do their jobs - no past - no future - just what's going on right now? Yes = That's exactly what happens ~ So = What do you think is the quickest way to get present? Excellent guess = Be - in your body.

So = How do you do that?

||||||||| Made of Food:

Have you thought about nutrition? I mean - really thought about it? Sure - you've heard about it - learned some things about it - but = Have you thought about it?

The first thing to think about nutrition is = The first thing the word means - is not - what foods you should eat ~ The first thing it means is = How your body works.

Our bodies are made of hundreds of molecular compounds (combinations of atoms - that join to make molecules - which join to make compounds) - which perform thousands of functions ~ Nutrition - is the chemistry - which describes the supply and demand relationship - between those compounds - and their functions ~ Or in other words = What's needed to do what (in particular - be healthy) Where what you eat comes in - is the supply end - because = Every single last molecule of your body (excluding toxins - implants - steel hardware for broken bone repairs - or other foreign objects) - is made of = Food.

You are what you eat - is not just a catchy saying - it's (as far as the word - you - being used in relation to your body goes) - a 100% accurate statement ~ Therefore = It's not just important that - you - eat = It's absolutely essential - that you eat what your body requires to provide the services it does for - you.

As for cutting close to the bone = There is a very strange blind spot in our American culture - when it comes to food - which - is probably illustrated best - when you compare it to that other great American obsession = Technology.

Do you own any machines - like say - a car - a computer - a bicycle - an iPod - a refrigerator? It's a very long list - all those gadgets we take for granted - or wish we could afford - or... whatever way you would complete that sentence ~ But = Just take one - that car for instance = Let's say - you like to work on your car yourself - so = When you go to change - or top up - any of the fluids it needs (oil - transmission fluid - brake fluid - power steering fluid - coolant) - do you just use anything that's handy - like vegetable oil or hand lotion? Do you buy those fluids according to what they look like - smell like - the picture on the packaging - the speed in which you can get your hands on them? Or = Do you buy and use - exactly - what the manufacturer says you're supposed to - because otherwise = It would mess up that car that's so important to you?

I know you're smart enough to have worked out the point I'm making ~ Yet - just to hear it spelled out = There is no longer much mystery - about what the essential nutrients are - which human bodies require to thrive ~ There does remain some controversy about which foods - or supplements - are the best ways to deliver those nutrients ~ But = The information is out there - and = Growing more thorough and precise all the time.

The very sad fact (perhaps more accurately - dangerous fact) - is that the majority of Americans - remain happily (or unhappily) - ignorant - or all together deaf to that information ~ Even the training of new doctors - a form of education one would simply expect to fully appreciate the importance of nutrition - barely touches on the subject = Despite the FACT - that all healing - all cellular reproduction - the immune system - the organs and tissues and blood and bones - which oxygenate - nourish - filter - cleanse - hold up - and move around the body - are all = Made of food - and = If that food is deficient in what is needed - or works counter to those needs (otherwise known as poisonous) - they (every last one of those things) - are weakened ~ Wouldn't you say = That hardly seems an intelligent approach to health?
What's your approach?]]]]]]]]]]

Okay ~ Our bodies are busy being alive physically - right? What does being alive require? Yes = Energy ~ Does energy ever sit still? No = It wouldn't be energy if it did ~ So = Being alive is always some kind of - action? When you are doing something - are you doing it - in the past? The future? Right = You could have done something - or will do something - but = When you - are - doing - something - when is it? Exactly ~ So = What was the one essential physical action our bodies need - that we can control? Yup = The oxygen our breathing gathers ~ So = What do you think is the easiest way - to interrupt your thinking - about the past - or the future - which is to say = Bring it back from something that you are not actually doing right now? You got it = Breathe.

We'll add another word to it = Consciously breathe ~ Or - in other words - think about - be aware of - put your attention on - feel = Your breathing ~ You've all been told to take a deep breath and count to ten when you were upset or causing trouble - haven't you? Well - that's why = It works = It interrupts the tape - looping round your mind - just long enough to be present in a different action ~ Do it enough - and you will feel different ~ It may not solve the problem - but = It will - affect - how you go about solving it.

[[[[[[[[[**Doctor Dude's Dictionary - word two - Intuition:**

Knowing things - is generally regarded as the end state of a gathering process ~ We collect experience and information ~ We accumulate data ~ We store facts ~ We remember the reasons why one thing leads to another - and = When we rub those reasons together - in order to work out how or what or why something does or doesn't or might happen - we call that process = Reasoning.

There appears to be another reason for knowing things - which is the reason - why there is a word for that reason - even though it has nothing to do with reason (which is the noun form of reasoning) That word is = Intuition.

Intuition - is that talent of the mind (traditionally considered a trait stronger in females than males - which may be due to the alpha brain wave pattern being in slightly higher daytime use by women than men) - where a kind of knowing just appears - without benefit - or reliance - on the standard information gathering processes we normally use (meaning sources of information we consider - outside of us - or that figure things out employment of reasoning just mentioned) Which = Is not to say that there is no gathering process involved in intuition - just that the information source being tapped - is better described by the word = Irrational ~ Of course that word is usually reserved for questioning a person's sanity (which describes another traditional viewpoint about intuition) But - what it really means is = Other - than rational ~ And rational means = Exercising the ability to reason ~ So intuition - when it's accepted as valid - is allowing a strength that doesn't require exercise ~ In a way - that strength is written right into the word ~ It begins already having arrived - since it starts out as - in - which is that strength - in place - available in-side ~ And then it declares itself already paid for - in-tuition ~ The fees - or tuition (like what it costs to go to college) - are in - they're paid up ~ And then - within the roots of that word tuition - is the older meaning of guardianship - which has even older roots in a Latin word meaning - to watch - look at - protect.

All up - what the word intuition is describing - is a reason - to trust what we know strongly - without knowing why we do - because = Just maybe - what's really looking out for us - is already - in us.||||||||||

Now - why would I tell you this? Do you suppose it has something to do with consciousness? Good guess = Yes = Conscious breathing is one of the easiest points for the exploration of consciousness to begin from ~ It's like getting in your car in order to go on a trip ~ You haven't driven anywhere yet ~ You haven't even turned the key ~ But = You've decided to ~ You can't do any of it - without doing that first.

Well then - there you go - that's your next assignment ~ Breathing ~ Yup = Breathing ~ I'm betting - you're probably pretty good at it ~ But how good are you - at paying attention to it? Because = That's the full assignment = Breathing = Consciously ~ In other words = Being conscious of your breathing - actively aware of your control over it - paying attention - to - what is happening - how it's happening - how it feels - mouth - nose - throat - lungs - head - the sound of it - temperature - texture - chest expanding (don't forget that belly) - chest deflating - the whole experience of breathing - and = Only that ~ See - I don't want you to just walk around and take a few deep breathes - and that's that ~ I'm talking - sit down - relax - and spend a full minute doing it ~ Yeah = A minute doesn't sound like much - and that's because = It isn't ~ But - do that first minute - and see for yourself ~ Then - do three minutes more ~ Then - another five ~ If you can - throw in one more for an even ten ~ If you really like it - don't stop till you feel like stopping ~ If you stopped at one minute - do something else for a while ~ Then - try again ~ But - like I said - only conscious breathe ~ Meaning = don't think about other stuff ~ Yes - other stuff will turn up ~ It always does ~ But - go back to your breath ~ Think about (which really is to say - don't so much think about - as just be with) - your breathing.

The other thing - I forgot to mention - is = Inhale - and exhale - through your nose (provided your nose isn't blocked for some reason - in that case breathing through your mouth is fine) - and = Don't pause at either end of the cycle = Fill your lungs = Empty your lungs = One - two - one - two - a smooth even circular kind of motion - like a piston rising and falling - only without effort or force - especially on the exhale ~ Calmly draw the air in - then just allow your lungs to empty like water flowing from a jug ~ If you find that your mind keeps wandering off - then keep pulling it back ~ It doesn't matter that it wanders ~ In fact - you can expect it to ~ It matters - that you notice - and - return to your breath ~ It matters - that you - do - the assignment ~ Not for how long ~ Or how often ~ Though the more often and longer you do it - the more you'll learn from it ~ Because = If you - don't = You won't ~ That's the point ~ It's not a point of being right or wrong ~ It's just simply - the point ~ Okay? Breathe away.

{{{So = Have you been thinking about why I chose to do the punctuation this way? Do you still have to think about it? What do you think about it? What sort of effect is that thinking having? Have you thought about that? Okay - I was just wondering.}}}

24

N.P.U. - Chapter Two - Galileo?

Science = Now there's a word we've all used from one end to the other of its possible meanings ~ Sometimes = That's done with great trust in an ability to expand our understanding of wondrously complex nature in a vast universe - improve health - extend lives - increase productivity - comfort - convenience - and even entertain us ~ While at other times = It's a cold mechanical enabling process that tortures animals - builds weapons - and poisons environments - as it scoffs at the great mysteries of being and brushes aside the strange and unexplained as so much ignorant superstition ~ It is - very obviously - a word with controversy for a shadow - because = It describes - in our general use of it - a way of thinking - rather than specifically - what is being thought about ~ While at the same time - it has come to mean - exact - accurate - precise - and - absolute ~ And yet = We seldom use it that way ourselves - who are not scientists ~ More often we use it the way we might use the word - roof (or technology for that matter) We realize - there are considerable variations among roofs (and technologies) - but - when it's raining - most of us rely on the first available one - and so = Group them together as - more or less - the same thing (That being said = Technology and science - are not the same thing - despite their being so closely connected - which = Is just something to keep in mind)

||||||||| Mind Event:

What if - the mind - is really an evolving event - rather than a fixed substance - or container?

Now = I'll break down that question into its parts.

What I mean by - evolving - is = Actively changing - developing - accessing more - more experience - more ability - more energy ~ By - event - I mean = An action - a verb - a movement - a happening (questionable English that that is) - in short = An event ~ Then - in contrast (indicated by the word rather) - by using the phrase - fixed substance - I mean = Not solidly one thing - like say - a squash or a vacuum cleaner ~ A squash can grow - can be food or seed or compost - but = It's a fixed - stable - unchanging - thing (except as governed by its own - fixed - range of ability to change) - established by its being a plant ~ And then - to conclude - by - container - I mean = A bowl - a refrigerator - a suitcase - something you can put things in or take things out of - which on its own - is just that - a container - a limited space - for storage.

Of course - what the whole question really adds up to is = What - is - a mind?

So - in stretching one end of that question = If - mind - is an evolving event - then - there is a fluid quality to it - just as there is to any event - one action flowing into another = The band steps on stage - the crowd roars - the first note is followed by the next - and the next - and the whole concert cuts lose ~ That's an event happening ~ Does an event have boundaries? Or - does it flow into all other events - never a pause - time without end? Is your mind like that? Can you watch it happening? What is it that's watching? Is it more of your mind? How much more is there?|||||||||||

So = What does science mean?

Well - for the past 500 years or so - it's most consistent description would have to be - systematic measurement ~ Which is to say = Carefully recording observations of the behavior - changes - contrasts - sizes - requirements - and energy - of objects - and organisms - their parts - construction - environment - and interactions - by figuring out - or employing - ways - or systems - to measure those things.

The key to - or strongest argument for - accepting the conclusions of - Science - is held to be - repetition ~ Which means = Reproducing the same results - repeatedly - by following the same steps of experimentation - and of course - observation - in order to state = This is a fact (the opposite - or achieving different results - concludes = This is not a fact) In other words = If you were to find an elephant that could sing "Old Man River" in Swahili - you might have a real moneymaker on your hands - but = You would be laughed out of the scientific community if you were to publish a paper - on the scientific fact - that all elephants can sing ~ That is - without producing several thousand more with the same talent - if not the same taste in music.

Alright - that being said - let's take a quick - very quick - look at one of the foundations of our modern use of the word science.

Back in the year 1609 - an Italian gentleman by the name of Galileo Galilei - inspired in part by the work of an earlier Polish gentleman named Mikolaj Kopernik - better known as Copernicus - made certain observations of the relationship between the sun - the moon - the Earth and other planets - and determined (through - yes - measurement) - that - the sun - did not (as it was very determinedly believed) - revolve around the Earth ~ He realized (as did Copernicus before him) - that in fact - the case was entirely the opposite - with the Earth - orbiting the sun ~ It was (as you might imagine) - a revolutionary moment in humankind's understanding of our world - and the solar system - it does all that orbiting in.

So - revolving - around that discovery - Galileo made his name as one of the founding fathers of modern scientific method - or systematic measurement ~ What's more he became one of its heroes ~ Not so much because of his - admittedly - well argued - but still shaky proof of Copernicus's heliocentric theory ~ Helio meaning - sun - and centric meaning - center ~ In other words = The sun stays put and everything else goes spinning around it ~ No = That was really more of a sideline to his work with telescope development - astronomical observation - the laws of motion - the speed of light - and all kinds of other tedious measurements he had such patience and enthusiasm for ~ The reason the business with the Sun and Earth took a kind of center stage (that is - centric) - was because = He got into all kinds of hot water over it.

See - there were certain people in power in those days - which means there were certain - ideas - that had power over - other ideas ~ To disagree with those powerful ideas - no matter how much proof you could present for your own - was - to put it plainly = To mess with that power.

Power - in a social political sense (and perhaps - in every sense) - requires - agreement - that - it - is - powerful ~ That agreement might be demanded at the point of a sword or by a blue flashing light on the highway ~ Either way - there tend to be problems when - the ideas - that power bases its power on - are pointed out to be wrong.

Note - I use the word - wrong ~ I did not say - incorrect - or mistaken ~ There is a rather large difference - and that difference - is in the eye (that is - mind) - of the power holder ~ Galileo - being no dummy - must have known this ~ However - he believed - in his methods - in his measurements - and - in himself - and - had such faith in all three - that = He assumed anyone else - with the power of reason - would be convinced as well ~ That assumption in hand - in 1610 - he published a book titled = The Starry Messenger ~ In it - he laid out all kinds of interesting sights he'd seen floating around space - like the moons of Jupiter - and the first glimpses of other galaxies - and - of course = The proof for Copernicus's theory ~ He was excited - he thought everyone would be - or at least the people who could read and take an interest ~ In that - he was incorrect - or mistaken - which - of course - added up to = Quite wrong ~ The short of it is = What with all the controversy generated - by 1633 he had to face a trial - that was rather heavily stacked against him ~ So - in a time when being roasted on a fire in public was - both - a punishment – and - a spectator sport (granted - there wasn't much sport in it) - he got off rather lightly with being forced to recant (that is - deny the truth of his writings) - which were banned - or made illegal - as well as any he might write in the future - and - he was sentenced to house arrest (not fun - but - a huge improvement over real prison) - for the remainder of his life - which turned out to be about nine years.

[[[[[[[[[Heliocentric History:

Galileo's concept (which of course - expands on the work of Copernicus and Kepler) - of a heliocentric - or sun centered solar system (which is why it's called a solar system) - was actually first proposed nearly 2,000 years earlier in the third century B.C.E. - by one Aristarchus of Samos (a Greek - in case you didn't notice) - who obviously was quite a smart guy - but - more or less slipped through the fingers of historical notoriety - by basically being ignored.

More proof - that there's nothing like being arrested - to get your name in the headlines.]]]]]]]]]]

Alright - you're wondering - no doubt - as usual - what this has to do with you ~ Well - being one of the few billion people clinging by gravity to the surface of this planet as it - orbits the sun - it's got to be at least vaguely interesting that someone had to figure that out for you ~ But - the real reason is = The power of ideas.

There was some other - systematic measurement - observed - much more recently - that describes the reaction to Galileo back in the 1600s - in a light - shall we say - that shines on all of us ~ And no = It's not the sun ~ It's really more like a card trick.

A group of scientists scanned a deck of cards into a computer program ~ Simple enough ~ Then - they changed the color of a few of them - so that - the nine of hearts was black rather than its customary red - the jack of spades was red rather than black - and so on ~ Remember - not the whole pack were changed - only half a dozen or so ~ Then - they asked volunteers - one at a time - to identify what cards they were seeing - as they were flashed on a computer monitor in front of them ~ At first - they were flashed by so fast - no one could accurately identify each card ~ Slowly - the amount of time - each card - was displayed - was increased ~ And so - as you'd expect - the accuracy of identification increased accordingly - But - the fact - that some of the cards were the wrong color - was not - recognized - by any - of the volunteers - until the exposure time was increased to nearly a minute - and even longer for some ~ However - what did occur for nearly all of the volunteers - was a rising feeling of anxiety - and the sense (in some cases so extremely powerful that they refused to continue) - that something = Was wrong.

They (scientists of course) - have coined a phrase for that state ~ It's called = Cognitive dissonance ~ You might - recognize - the word cognition (which is the noun from which cognitive comes) - in the middle of the word recognition - because - basically - that's what it's about ~ Cognition - is the act - or process - of learning - or - knowing ~ To recognize something - is to remember - you - know - it ~ So - cognitive - is about the ability - to do that ~ Dissonance - you might say - is what's getting in the way ~ It's - usually a sound word - a harsh sound - out of harmony with other sounds ~ In other - words = A disagreement ~ Like the alarm clock shaking you out of a tropical island dream in order to get you to school on time - it has a feeling connected with it - and definitely - not the one you were having on the beach a moment earlier.

So = Have you put the two parts of the story together yet? That is - Galileo - red spades - black hearts - and you?

Alright - it is a little bit of a sideways technique of making a point ~ But - the point is = There appears to be a part of our consciousness - that - recognizes - when we are - mistaken - or - blocking - in some way - information - we - know - to be true ~ Even though we can see what is in front of our eyes - such as the card experiment - when there are other ideas - you might want to say - in front of behind our eyes - we can't see - or know - what we are looking at - even though - in another sense - we do ~ And since that is probably confusing = You could also describe it as = When you're feeling unhappy - yet keeping a smile on your face - that part of your consciousness - just mentioned - does know - what's really true - and so - either it all ends up in tears - or - you actually do become happy ~ It would seem - we're just plain incapable of doing both at the same time without something happening internally to attempt to align us with what's really going on.

The pope (who was leading the power struggle with Galileo by the way) - was no dummy either - just a bit narrow minded ~ He could probably - with a little training - or a lot - have just as easily - repeated - Galileo's observations and seen for himself what the evidence indicated ~ The problem was = It was not - a question ~ It was not about - new information - or evidence ~ It was seen as a direct assault on - the agreement - of being - RIGHT - which had to mean = WRONG ~ And that - just would not do.

That's where the alarm clock breaks in ~ That's where the card trick experiment volunteers get upset ~ A part of them - knows - something - the rest of them - doesn't seem to yet ~ The knowing - information - is trying to get through - but - it's blocked - by some other idea of knowing - and - the friction of those two information sources - is interpreted - as an upset - that makes people want to quit the experiment - or organize a little torture session ~ History is packed with such upsets - and - history - is still going on.

So - that word - Science - as I said earlier - has come to mean for many of us - exact - accurate - precise ~ However - it also means - measurable ~ The sticky part between those definitions is = Weird stuff - that goes on - repeatedly - that - so far - has been unable to be measured - and so = Upsets - scientists - or science minded people - who have determined that - their ideas - are right ~ Are yours?

SPECIAL BONUS EXERCISE - number one

Observing Beauty:

There is a word we toss around with such casual regularity - that one might be apt to think there is some built-in standard we are all accessing that determines its use ~ Well - that might be the case with miles and meters and the names of the days of the week - but = Not with beauty ~ What is beautiful to one person - may be little more than mildly appealing to another - or even entirely repulsive ~ There really is no fixed standard for beauty - because = Beautiful - is not what something is = It's a feeling - an experience - a set of internal actions - that both respond to - and create - more internal actions.

Perhaps - at the level of brain activity - you could assign a scale of measurement - that could be matched and averaged out with other people's experiences - that would then define whether or not you were having an experience of beauty - and = That might be scientifically interesting (and in fact - is) However - the real point - is the experience itself - and - its effects (also very scientifically interesting - but - if we really need a scientific study to recognize that beauty effects quality of life - then - we really are in trouble)

What this exercise is about - is not what defines beauty - but = What beauty feels like - and - learning how to more completely experience that feeling.

Now - by beauty - I'm not just referring to faces and bodies - or art and sunsets - or even necessarily experiences based on eye sight at all ~ Not that I am excluding any of those categories either ~ What I mean by beauty (in this case at least) - is a sensitivity to what inspires admiration - wonder - awe - struck stupid staring - or in short = Joy ~ And = A focus on the specific senses involved - which is (you might say) = How beauty out there - gets in here (go ahead - point at yourself)

The actual case I'm pointing at however - is the opposite - or - cause and effect reversed - which means = There is no beauty out there - only your recognition - of the feeling within yourself - you register as meaning = Beautiful ~ Which is not to take away from what you judge to be beautiful ~ Actually - it's meant to enhance that judgment ~ Or - more precisely = To use that judgment - to pass beyond judging - and enter the pure experience - that is the reason behind the judgment.

Enough introduction then ~ Here's what you do.

Choose one of your senses ~ You know the list - taste - touch - hearing - sight - smell ~ Then = Locate something - you use that sense to experience - that - you would describe as beautiful ~ Maybe it's the odor of something cinnamon baking - the sound of wind chimes through the window - a piece of chocolate melting on your tongue - anything - that pinpoints a particular sense ~ And then = Experience - that thing - through that sense ~ Place every bit of focus you can on that sense at work ~ Don't name it - describe it - or compare it to any other thing with your mind - just fully live the experience of that sense delivering its information to you ~ Do it for a minute - two - eight and a half - however long you can ~ Don't worry if your attention wanders to other senses or thoughts - just notice that happening - and return to the sense in question.

Next = As you move through your day - your week - repeat the same thing with each of your senses.

Then = when you've got the hang of that - try the same process of full focus experience - with any (that's - any) - sight - taste - smell - sound - texture - that you come across ~ Stroke the chair leg - breathe the burnt toast - soak up the traffic - just experience the sense involved ~ Do it enough - and you might find that the list of things you think of as beautiful - just gets longer and longer.

Class Three - What If?

BREATHE (You remember = Crossed arms to your ears - left hand first - tongue to the roof of your mouth - inhale on the way down - exhale coming up - AAAHHH = That's it ~ Fourteen times now ~ No skimping ~ If you find you lose count = You can write large numbers on a piece of paper - tack it to the wall - and focus on the number you're on as you go through each repetition.)

So = What about that assignment? Did you get enough oxygen? What was all that breathing like? Boring? Peaceful? Sleepy? What? Did it change how you felt - compared to - before you started? How long were you able to do it? How often? Did it feel different each time? How did you feel about doing it? Would you keep doing it?

So - let me explain a few things about this journey we're beginning together.

First off = Why have I called this course - What If? Any ideas?

Well - there are three reasons actually ~ The first = Is a description of a very particular kind of space ~ This room is a certain kind of space - right? How about your pockets? If we were to seal off all the windows and doors of this room - then pump it completely full of concrete - would it still be a space? Actually - technically speaking - it still would be a space - but one with no space in it.

The space - I'm talking about - is quite different ~ If - IT - is full - then - IT - doesn't exist ~ The reason is = Because - IT - is a mental space = A question ~ Basically - it's an invitation (another one of those) - like come to my party - the door is open - which = Is the starting point of all invention and discovery ~ It's the place where - Ah Ha!! - is welcomed in.

So = What is - IT?

Of course = It's the question = What if.......?

Now - those aren't always the exact words ~ Especially - if you speak Chinese - or something other than English - or even just English - because = It's not so much what form the words take - but = What ideas - form the words ~ So - the words can change - yet - the principle remains the same = There must be a question ~ Like say = What if - we could travel back to the 14th century? That sort of thing ~ Often such questions already seem to have an answer - like = It's impossible to travel backwards in time ~ The point is = If the answer - we've heard - read - or picked up somehow (including - made it up ourselves) - makes sense to us = We don't ask the question ~ Therefore = That space is filled ~ There is no space ~ And so = Yes - it's impossible to time travel ~ But - the other side = Is the open space = What if - it is possible - to travel backwards in time? Perhaps it's still impossible ~ Perhaps it's not ~ It is a rather extreme example - but = Either way - a new opportunity for discovery is opened - which might lead who knows where - simply by asking the question - because = Space - allows things to happen - or - grow ~ Perhaps not - grow - what you expected - but (around we go again) = The same is true - when you - expect - a certain - or exact - result - to any question ~ Do that - and you haven't really opened any space ~ It's like planting a seed in concrete ~ Not a very successful gardening practice.

That time in question - by the way - to travel back to (or history - as it's better known) - is punctuated over and over with brave minds willing to do just that - which is = Question - what is - or isn't - possible.

I'll give you an example ~ That is - a kind of backwards one.

What if - back in 1901 - Wilbur Wright (You've heard of him? That's it = He was one of the Wright brothers - inventors of the airplane and all - or - the first one that really flew with some measure of control ~ Anyway = If Wilbur) turned to his brother and said "Hey Orville - reckon we could build a machine that people could fly in?" And Orville said "Nah - only birds can fly. Let's start a chain of hamburger restaurants. Now that will fly".

So = How much space - is available there for invention? Not much on Orville's part - is there? (For flying machines anyway - that other idea has certainly met with a fair amount of success) But = What about the other question - the What if one - about both brothers having that imaginary conversation? That's right = History would be different ~ Actually - there were several people tinkering on flying machine designs at the time - particularly the French - so the airplane was bound to turn up ~ There's no way to know for sure what effects taking the Wright brothers out of the invention picture would've had ~ But (you knew it was coming) = That's what the space of question is all about ~ As long as we hold that space open - any story is possible.

Fact is - old brother Wilbur himself actually said to someone in 1901 - that he doubted mankind would master flight in his lifetime - if not in the next thousand years ~ Luckily (at least from the point of view - that airplanes are good things) - master - and try - were two very different things in his mind.

The trouble is - we humans don't like those kind of spaces ~ The kind without answers ~ The reason we ask questions - is because we want answers ~ We want solid ground on which to walk ~ Space under our feet makes us nervous ~ No wonder Mr. Wright had his doubts ~ But it's the same for the rest of us as well ~ Even in the most normal of circumstances.

[[[[[[[[Conscious Cabbage:

Back in the 1970s - some Russian scientists conducted an experiment on the conscious perception of plants - by using a pair of those plants so dear to Russian cuisine - cabbage to be specific - and - one of those machines so dear to organizations like the FBI - a lie detector ~ They began by placing the two potted plants about 3 feet apart on a windowsill in an otherwise empty room and attached the lie detector to the leaves of one of them ~ For the following week - a group of lab workers - would individually - in pairs - or what have you - walk through the room - in random sequence at random times - several times a day ~ All the workers were identically dressed in white coats and head covers - and none of them had any interaction with the plants aside from being in the room with them - except the one whose job it was to water them.

At the end of the week - one of the workers entered the room - and proceeded to hack up the cabbage plant which was not attached to the lie detector with a knife (he had been instructed to do this of course) - and then left the room and the chopped up plant behind ~ The lie detector readout on the surviving plant - was a leaping scribble of intense distress ~ Which of course (difficult to believe as it may be) - supplies obvious proof that it had perceptually registered what was being done to its comrade cabbage - and by extension - was reacting to the implied threat to itself.

Ah - but then - there's another - probably far more surprising - twist to this story of the cabbage murder.

For two days - no one entered the room - excepting the usual lab assistant - who watered the monitored cabbage and removed the coleslawed remains of the other ~ After that stretch of time was over - the regular round of random visits by lab workers began again - and went along quite normally (from the cabbage's point of view) - until - the attacker returned to the scene of his crime - at which point = The cabbage freaked (on an electronic level that is) - until the man exited the room again.

Aside from the conclusion = That humans are constantly terrifying the vegetation = It appears that something as seemingly unconscious as a cabbage - has both the abilities - of memory - and - ~~identity~~ recognition - operating at a level which could only be explained as perception (in some electromagnetic way at least) Unless it could be explained some other way ~ Either way - which is to say = One way or another - what we're talking about here - is some form of = Consciousness.]]]]]]]]]

Let's say - you say something to someone - expecting a reply - and - they don't say anything back ~ Do you immediately begin to make up what they are thinking? Don't they understand? Are they stupid? Do they think you are? You know the story ~ You've done it ~ We all have ~ We don't want questions ~ We want answers ~ Ah - but = What if - that is why - we know so little about our own consciousness?

You see = What if - that space - that is a true question - that isn't stuffed full of the first answers that come to mind - is the same space - required - to create a doorway to our

*PATTERN

deeper consciousness?

Let me draw you a picture ~ This is your awareness = @

What is in it? What are you - aware of - right now?

Okay = You're aware of your surroundings? What your five senses are telling you? What you are thinking? What about a sense of time? So basically - that's the information you go on everyday to get through life?

Alright ~ What if the relationship between your awareness and consciousness (their relative sizes - so to speak) - could be represented like this = Here is your awareness again = @

Now = Take a look around you at everything you can see ~ Go outside (if you're inside) - and look off as far as you can see - all the things - the ground - the plants - buildings - people - animals - and = The sky itself - in all its immensity - clouds - moon - stars ~ Even if you can't see them in daylight ~ They're there ~ That (as compared to @) - is = Consciousness.

Fact is - I've portrayed it this way (or you have - by being it) - only out of a lack of room (or rather - perspective) - to make consciousness larger - much larger ~ What if - consciousness doesn't even have a border? And = What if - indicating one - in any form - is like filling that question space in the usual human way - of wanting solid ideas to stand on - by using old ideas - rather than floating precariously on curiosity - or patience - or - space - for new ones? What if - consciousness - has no beginning - and - no end?

What does it feel like to think about such an idea - no beginning - no end - no boundaries? Try to feel what really happens inside you when you do ~ How does your mind react? Do you allow that space - or do you fill it? What do you feel?

[[[[[[[[[Doctor Dude's Dictionary - word three - Whole:

We all recognize the difference between - a whole apple - and a hole in an apple ~ The same as we distinguish - that apples is theirs - from - that apple there ~ Spelling of course - clues us in - sentence structure - and context - or the collective meaning of the other words used ~ Then - there are visual clues - if it is spoken sentence - like someone actually holding the apple itself - maybe a finger pointing - plus inflection - or the way a voice emphasizes particular words or syllables ~ Not to mention - understanding the language (a very key point there) There's all that - but not (in the case of such words) - a difference in the sound of the words in question to prompt our understanding ~ In order to get around that little obstacle - we have to have gotten around all the rest.

It's not often we tease apart all the workings of what seems to be such a simple action of understanding ~ But = Like the huge contrast of meanings between the words mentioned - the difference between a partial understanding - and - a whole understanding - weighs entirely on what we're paying attention to - and why - or = It might pass by - just as unnoticed - as a hole - in their apple.

It's that word - whole (the one that looks like whale with a hole in it) - that's there to describe the kind of attention that arrives at understanding - because - it means = All the parts put together - one unit - one system - working as such - not divided - or disjointed - or separate - but = Whole ~ An amazing word really - in that it always views things as complete ~ There is no need - no lack - in the word whole ~ When a body is whole - it's healthy and thriving ~ If it's made whole - it's restored to that state - it's healed - recharged and ready for use ~ If you walked - the whole way home - you still made it there ~ It's done ~ Even if you spent the whole time complaining - or lost the whole bag of groceries ~ There are no half measures in whole - no doubts or inconsistencies ~ It's an honest word ~ Not because of some moral superiority - but because it cannot help but consider all the evidence - the opinions - causes - effects - and possibilities - and arrive at a whole result ~ If you expect whole to take sides - you've missed the whole point.

The point is = Nothing happens - that does not affect something else ~ Nor does anything happen - that is not the result of many things happening ~ Looking at - or for - the whole picture - always requires effort ~ Yet even so - it's really that effort - that makes the whole thing worthwhile.|||||||||

Let's try a visual exercise that will help you expand your ability to allow that space to stay open.

Sitting up straight - pick an object - or a spot on the wall - directly in front of you - on a level with your eyes ~ Not up or down - just level with your eyes ~ Now - raise your hands in front of your face - so the palms are facing each other about six inches apart ~ Stare at what you picked - through the gap between your hands ~ Now - slowly - move your hands away from each other - still looking straight ahead - but - maintaining an awareness of seeing your hands ~ Move them until they reach the very edge of where you can still just see them ~ Don't move your eyes - they're still looking straight ahead ~ Now move your hands - very slowly - until they disappear.

This spot - where they disappear - is called the edge of what?

That's right = Peripheral vision ~ What happened to the object you chose to stare at? It went a bit fuzzy? What else happened? What did it feel like?

That - is a demonstration of your visual awareness field ~ Of course - you can turn your head and look - up - down - all directions - but still - that peripheral vision edge remains the same ~ The thing is - that most of the time - our vision - is focused on only the narrow center of what we see ~ That's what we - mean - by focus.

But = Remember what happened to the object you were staring at? Right = It - lost - its focus ~ So that's what happens when we do this with our eyes - which represents a certain problem for doing particular things - like driving or fixing things and such - but (again - But) = What if - our whole consciousness - is very different from - just - our eyes

- in that = It can see - everything - in all directions - including inside us - all at once - and - in focus?

Okay = Whether that's true or not - how will this business - with the hands and eyes - help you?

Let's do it again ~ Pick a spot ~ Stare at it - and move your hands till they're gone ~ Only this time - keep seeing that way ~ Try to push the edges of what you see on the sides further back ~ Turn your head one side to the other - without changing how you are witnessing your whole visual field ~ Don't focus on single things or people - try to see - everything your eyes are seeing - all at once.

Great ~ Does it feel strange? Kind of uncomfortable? It's not the way we are used to using our eyes ~ But = We can ~ What if - there are lots of things - we can do - and even are doing - we just aren't paying attention to them? What if - the reason we aren't - is because = They don't feel like what we are used to feeling - so we label that uncomfortable - and don't do it? Or don't think we are?

What are you doing to your brain when you practice this exercise? Could it be = You are telling it - you want to experience more of what you are? Could it be = You are telling something (that is - a different part of you) - possibly - much larger than your brain (larger in the sense of ability rather than size) - the same thing?

Either way - I will guarantee - that if you do this several times a day (see if you can do it while walking around as well) - for the next week - something inside you - will change ~ What will change? Well - you'll just have to wait and see what the change is yourself ~ In fact - it's your assignment to find out.

I have another assignment for you too ~ You know that name you call yourself = What is it? Okay - the homework isn't quite that easy ~ What - I want you to find out - is = What does that name of yours mean to you? Is it you? Do you like it? Is there another one you would prefer? Is your name the one you use when you talk to yourself inside your head? Do you use a name for talking to yourself? I want you to carefully consider all the questions above ~ Decide on a name for yourself - if it's not the one you've got ~ Then = Have a conversation with this person - that you're calling by that name ~ Do it silently - or out loud - doesn't matter ~ Ask them who they are - what they think - feel - want ~ Get to know them - the way you would anyone else ~ Ask questions ~ Answer questions ~ Ask more questions ~ Do it at least twice a day until the next class - or - as often as you like ~ Maybe after you practice a little conscious breathing ~ That might help ~ Okay? See you then.

||||||||| Punctuation Decoded:

I told you I would give you some time to work out on your own the other reasons for punctuating this course in this way - and = I have (not so very much time it's true - unless you're thinking the opposite) Which also means = Have you? (Given that question some time to stew that is) Though perhaps - it's not something you've done (how else can I put it but) - consciously ~ I do however - guarantee - that you have been working it out in another part of your consciousness ~ So - in the interest - of both - bringing that part to your awareness - and possibly - making the whole process more appealing to participate in (just in case it's been having a very different effect) - I'll do some explaining.

Learning - is a process of connecting new dots to old dots - to create a pattern - that is no longer separate dots - but a whole (or relatively whole) - picture ~ The process requires three parts - or stages - to set up ~ First = A stimulus - meaning = A cause - a need - a reason - and above all - a desire - to seek new information or acquire a new skill ~ Second = A means to that information - or = A teaching source - words - demonstrations - observation ~ You know the drill ~ Third = To be in possession of enough related information - to be able to recognize how the new information holds together - and can be made use of ~ And - in very simplified terms - 1 - 2 - 3 (excluding the fourth step - which is practice) = You've learned something.

The word - stimulus - is the real reason for this little detour - because = It - is the main "other" reason for the punctuation you've been so delighted by ~ It is - admittedly - a bit of a sneaky kind of stimulus - in that - it's not a direct study choice you made - like = Now it's time to learn to speak Russian - or rebuild a transmission - or... something ~ What it is = Is requiring your brain - to reorganize previously learned systems - the way brushing your teeth with your left hand (or your right - if you're left-handed) - stimulates an internal scramble to lay down new connection routes between brain cells (known as neurons) - to get the job done ~ Right there - you're taking all three steps of the learning process in one big bite on your own - simply - by pushing yourself to do something uncomfortable - and = By doing so - actually increasing your ability to learn - by the action of that elasticity of neurons trying to compensate.

As for completing the list of reasons = The same process - because it's new - demands at least a slightly higher degree of attention - or focus - than your standard expectations of punctuation do - and so = A level of concentration - you might not ordinarily dedicate to the subject matter - is occurring despite you ~ And then = Because the same system is continually repeated - you've moved - relatively effortlessly - right into the fourth step - or practice - where you're intentionally (well - perhaps not quite intentionally - except at the level of neurons) - constructing accessible routes to potentially positive new ways of being - because = You're not just observing presented ideas - but - having a new experience - which = Is much more stimulating to curiosity and experimentation than having the same old oatmeal for breakfast again.

Yes = All that from a few dashes and squiggles = Who knew?||||||||||

N.P.U. - Chapter Three - Remote View?

Alright then - here's a look at some attempts - by scientists - to measure some of that - other - scientist upsetting - weird stuff that goes on - to see what kind of results turned up.

But first - there's an element of the nature of human culture that would make sense to witness in this moment ~ It was stamped all over the Galileo story - not to mention thousands of other stories before and since - so it should be pretty easy to - recognize - at least as a kind of re-occurring trend in societies of the past.

The trick is = To suddenly discover yourself standing in the shoes of a 16th century mind - that just happens to be surrounded by 21st century stuff - because = In certain ways - we continue to operate under influences that have really not changed that much since then - or even further back - despite all those high tech gizmos we've got wired all around us ~ See - the cultural thing I'm referring to begins - or appears - to begin - by involving only certain individuals - like say - the pope and Galileo - but = It actually includes - draws energy from - and fuels - the entire culture.

Let me ask you a question = Do you have any trouble with the idea that the earth revolves around the sun - rather than the other way around? No = I didn't think so ~ How about - the idea - that crimes can be solved by people with the ability to see actual events in their minds - that - their own eyes - were miles - or even continents - weeks - months - or years away from - when the crime was committed?

Okay - that's a rather different kind of response ~ Some of you said - definitely not ~ Some said - maybe ~ Some said - of course ~ And - a whole lot wavered around - unsure.

Why do you think that is?

Exactly = The idea of psychic crime solvers has been floating around our culture in the form of a - popular idea - for some time now ~ It's in books ~ It's in movies ~ It's on the TV - and - not just once a week - or on one particular channel ~ Not to mention - all the other psychic stuff - that has nothing to do with crime - offered in all those same places.

What ties those two ideas together - Earth orbit - and - psychic cops - is = A decade or two after Galileo's death - the idea - that the Earth orbited the sun - had gone through a truly significant change = It had become a popular one ~ Just like - in our time - the use of psychic detective work and espionage (which has been going on - mostly very quietly -

for several decades now) - is still - upsetting for some - but = The idea - is slowly becoming popular - and thus = Normal.

||||||||| Normal?

Normal means… you know… normal.

Yeah - right ~ Now there's a word whose meaning remains the same about as much as the chance that gasoline will cost 25 cents a gallon next week ~ If next week were in 1961 = Sure - but = It probably won't be - at least under - normal - circumstances ~ Plus = Next week - when you say - this week = You won't mean the same thing ~ Normal - is fluid - it flows ~ Just like water - it takes on the shape of its container ~ It was not normal to be sitting in front of a computer while talking on a cell phone and listening to a CD when your pizza got delivered in the 14th century - any more than it's normal to be nervous about your neighborhood being wiped out by the Black death today.|||||||||

But - hang on = What is this very quietly going on business - I just hinted at? What is going on?

Well - if you were psychic you'd already know ~ Since most of us aren't - or haven't realized we are yet - there's the next best thing - the Internet ~ All you have to do is log on to your favorite search engine and type in the words "remote viewing" ~ Of course - you'll only get about 923,000 possible results (partly because those two words make a rather useful phrase for other meanings as well) - so try not to be disappointed by the lack of information available ~ If you want to get straight to the heart of the matter - you can sign up for one of several courses offered in how to do it yourself - some of which are presented by individuals acknowledged to be masters in the field by no less well-known organizations as - the Pentagon and the CIA ~ And no - that's not the Culinary Institute of America ~ Although the technique probably would be a great way to steal secret recipes.

{{{Just in case you've ever wondered why the word - google - has entered the language as a verb for a certain form of information gathering (aside from the reasons that are probably already obvious to you) = Is the word - googol (pronounced basically the same) - which stands for the number 10 raised to the power of 100 - or - a one followed by 100 zeros ~ In other words = A very large number - shall we say... at your fingertips}}}

So = What is - remote viewing? And as usual = What's it got to do with you?

The first answer = Must be limited to an outline of the results of remote viewing - because = How it actually works - no one knows yet ~ Though you can bet there are some lively theories floating around ~ What happens is this = The viewer (in circles such as the Pentagon - this would be a person that had exhibited a strong natural talent for what I'm about to describe) - works him/herself into a kind of light trance - or a very calm even breathing state of relaxation characterized by a particular brain wave pattern ~ In this state - the viewer - begins to describe and/or sketch - the images that occur to them - while mentally focusing on a specific distant location - event - person - or object - usually referred to as a target ~ Afterwards - whatever information was produced by the viewer - is compared to what is known about the target - and so - exact - or strongly similar descriptions are registered as - hits.

All sounds harmless enough I know - like some ESP party game - where lucky chance and cheating stand better odds than any kind of skill - but = The actual results tell a very different story.

[[[[[[[[[E.S.P.:

We've probably all heard the abbreviation E.S.P. - which stands for = Extra Sensory Perception ~ And means = The ability to gather information about other people and events - seemingly from nowhere - which is to say = Using the mind alone - or - an extra sense - we generally don't regard as existing - or don't all have the ability to access.

If there is such an - extra sense - then = How many more extra are there?]]]]]]]]]]

First - you have to notice who was sponsoring the early research into this hocus-pocus - which = Over a period of about three decades - dropped more than 20 million dollars into its continued investigation ~ That's right = It was none other than that famous - internationally active - err... nonprofit organization - the government of the United States of America ~ Not that they were the first ~ The inspiration came from uncovering the secret doings of another equally well-known real estate interest (that has since gone out of business) - called - the Soviet Union ~ Which - in the early 1970s - when the program began - was considered the chief competition for world domination and therefore could not be allowed to achieve the upper hand - no matter how bizarre the tactics involved ~ So - we're not talking about just flaky do-gooders who will believe most anything ~ We're talking some seriously dedicated black-and-white thinking self styled realists - possibly rather intolerant and paranoid to be sure - but not people inclined to swallow outrageous notions without extremely strong persuasion.

The reason was = That persuasion was very much present ~ One of the early sessions quite accurately described the structure of a Soviet building - spies on the ground had been unable to penetrate ~ It went on to detail the unusual welding techniques and shape of segments under construction - of what later turned out to be parts for a giant nuclear submarine (or rocket parts for a manned Mars mission - depending on your information source) - and - all located thousands of miles from some cozy little room at Stanford University in California where this describing was taking place.

Other early cases involved sneaking around foreign embassies and locating their code rooms - as well as the same in American installations - whose accuracy to detail could be more easily (not to mention legally) - verified ~ Again - all undertaken without going anywhere near the target sites ~ There were years of experiments - targets of all kinds - in the next room - across town - another state - hundreds of meters under water - identifying where certain people were - what they were wearing - looking at - carrying in their pockets (there was even a report of the strange - and completely unexpected - rings around Jupiter - which were later confirmed by the NASA Pioneer 10 as it flew by that planet) Of course - there were many inaccuracies - and plenty of object comparisons and impressions too inexact to count as hits ~ Yet overall = The evidence continued to build a case for something spy agencies like to term "operational possibilities".

And why wouldn't they? Invisible intruders reading secret documents - hunting through heavily guarded laboratories - examining weapons systems - deciphering codes - eavesdropping on conversations - with no chance of being caught - no physical danger - no risk of international incidents - not even coughing up plane fare - just a bit of time behind a desk and then go out for lunch ~ A whole new era of espionage appeared to have opened up - where 20 million gets you a real bargain.

Well - something happened that closed down - Stargate - as the CIA had poetically codenamed the final stage of the program ~ Why that occurred - what might have taken its place - and the whole ball of wax - of exposures - disclosures - secrets - and cover-ups that obscure the core of that business - are part of that 923,000 Internet locations you're free to go clicking your way through ~ For my part - it's enough just to tell you about this strange human ability - that - you - might - have ~ Because = We may all have it ~ It may be related to that peculiar sense of - been there done that but don't know how - called déjà vu ~ It may be the same as picking up the phone - certain of who it is on the other end - before they say a word ~ It may be a skill as natural as remembering where you left the car keys - and forgotten - just as naturally as those same keys ~ Either way - all those websites may not prove it's real - but = They do prove - something - is going on out there - and - without question = Popularity - is one of those things.

|||||||| Psi:

There is a phrase in popular circulation - which is used to reference certain strange experiences ~ Experiences - in fact - that apparently are so basic to the greater human experience = That every language on Earth contains words meaning the same thing.

That phrase (in English) - is = Psychic phenomena ~ There is another term - meaning the same thing - in common use among scientists and other interested parties - coined (or invented) - for the sake of neutralizing some of the negative reactions (or - that's hogwash) - to the word psychic - that are generally more popular among scientists ~ The term in question (which is the 23rd letter of the Greek alphabet) - is = Psi (pronounced - sigh)

Psi - as a sound - and as a root meaning - or derivation - turns up in such words as - psyche - psychology - and psychedelic - all of which are referring to the realm of the mind - and the experience - of consciousness ~ Another reason for using the term Psi - is as a label for the study of that realm of - strange experience - where the laws of reality - as we've generally agreed upon them - meet the observing eye of science - in order to test out why all those languages agree there should be such a word.

So - whether or not - you agree - that Psi - or psychic phenomena - are a reality - or a

superstition - the concept is represented by a real word - or actually hundreds of them - so = If nothing else - we all have something to talk about.‖‖‖‖‖‖

Just by way of demonstration of that popularity = Remote viewing has - quietly - moved into police work - into medicine - mineral exploration - psychic research - and the locating of lost objects ~ During the 1970s - a Russian military plane was lost in a heavily jungle covered area of Africa ~ Agencies of several governments searched for it with no success ~ It wasn't until a pair of Americans - known to be highly skilled as remote viewers - were asked to - find it - that it was ~ Even the president of the United States (who was Jimmy Carter at the time) - went on record to endorse and congratulate the success and - possibilities - of employing such skills.

Another element of remote viewing to consider - is its apparent disregard for what we consider the laws of time ~ Meaning = Time follows - only one - fixed course - from the present toward the future - one moment - at - a - time - and so = We are never able to witness - either what has already taken place - or - what will ~ Over and over - remote viewers - have broken those laws - in both directions - the past - and the future ~ Such as = In an experiment attempting to determine if a - viewer - could accurately describe the location - where the driver of a car - instructed to drive in a totally random pattern for a certain amount of time - would stop (the driver - of course - was completely out of communication with the viewer - or any other person involved with the experiment - until they returned with photographs of their destination) Repeatedly - the details - seen by the viewer - unquestionably matched the stopping point - long before - the driver had arrived at that spot - or even turned in its direction ~ The same is true of - seeing things - buildings - objects - trees - at target sites where they no longer existed - which seemed to score those sessions as strikeouts - but = Were later found to have stood exactly as described.

Yup - that's some pretty cool stuff - or - a thorough going delusional state - if you prefer ~ But = What about - mentally - traveling to the future - and (now this is cool) - returning with the plans for technologies that haven't been invented yet? Could it be done? Has it been done? Will you be the one to do it?

The point is = It's not remote viewing that's the point ~ It's really a personal question = What does the - popular culture - in - you - look like - feel like - represent? What are you willing to investigate - to question? Remote viewing is only one - of a huge library of the mysterious - the unknown - the unexplained - the unwritten (give or take a few million websites - books and articles) There is a common human tendency however - especially in our - modern scientific world - to disregard - or reject - those reports - or even personal experiences - that do not fit within the boundaries of what - familiarity - will explain ~ There are even clubs and societies - boasting large numbers of members - whose sole reason for organizing - is to debunk - discredit - disprove - de-ride - delight in - fixing the boundaries of their world in the - facts - of the past ~ That is their pleasure - their sense of safety - and every right they have to it ~ But = That is a space - that's already filled ~ Meaning = In such a court of thought - most often - the jury does not want to hear the evidence - only - the law ~ Which is not to say - such thinking is wrong ~ Skepticism - is one of the great working tools of exploration ~ It's more a measure of = How far must limitations be argued - before - it is seen - that the arguing itself is a much larger limitation.

There are cases in China - sought out and supported by the Chinese government - where people are performing impossible feats - moving objects through space by no visible means - appearing in locked rooms without having physically entered - causing hundreds of flowers to bloom simultaneously with a single command ~ Does the fact - that you do not speak Chinese - have never been to China - not seen or heard of such events before - and certainly not on the evening news - mean = They're not true? Or - even if you do speak the language - and have lived there for years - the same question?

See - this really isn't a question - of what is true - or what you think is true - or what might be true - or how others weigh what is or might or definitely could not be true ~ It's a question of why - you think - the way - you do ~ It's only what your judgments and curiosity - do - with the information I've just given you - that is the point in this moment - not its reality - because = What if - the points beyond (meaning the future) - are chosen - by present judgment (or curiosity) - and the limits set there (meaning now) - or expanded there (also meaning now) - are not about what the universe - is capable of (since quite possibly - it's capable of just about anything) - but = What you - are capable of? In other words = Does the way we think and believe - create - the future?

|||||||| Left-Handed:

According to a study conducted by the Institute of Noetic Sciences in California in 2003 (involving a relatively limited number of people it must be noted) - a character profile (meaning a list of behavioral characteristics) - of the type of person most apt to have psychic experiences - was built up from the data collected ~ Among several particulars of temperament observed to fit into that profile (which you might expect - due to their potential for - well... weirdness) - such as - anxious - introverted - artistic - and spiritual - the specific qualification turned out to consist of being = A left handed young woman. Sorry all you righty guys.||||||||

Class Four - Happiness?

BREATHE (There you go = Jump right up = That's how it's done ~ It's working ~ Your brain is being stimulated to new heights of function - and = I haven't even told you the rest of what's going on with this weird little exercise - but = I will ~ So - keep it up.)

So = How did the assignments go for you? Did you do them? How often? Did you do anything in particular to remember to do them? Did the vision exercise become easier with practice? How does your name feel to you now? How did it feel when you conversed with that person as your self? Did you discover new ways of understanding yourself? Did you enjoy doing one or the other or both? Did you observe any changes in your thinking? Your vision? Your sense of yourself? Can you describe those changes?

Well done.

So - I didn't finish explaining the reasons for the name - What If - last time - did I ~ I mean - here it is the fourth class - and I'm still explaining the first one ~ How slack is that? Or - is it?

Any of you ever ride in a car - before - you learned how to drive one? You haven't learned yet? Well - either way - think about that for a bit = We'll get back to it ~ Meanwhile = I'll get on with the explanation ~ But first = Can anyone summarize what the first reason was? Yes = The question space thing ~ And that goes = Without space for a new answer - only old answers are available? Do you suppose that describes all learning?

Reason number two = Is the simplest one (at least to describe) Basically - it stands as = It's up to you - to decide - what's true ~ So - in the future I might say = What if - this set of ideas is true? Or = What if - that set is not? Many of these ideas - will be ways of looking at life - you may never have considered before ~ In the end - it doesn't matter what I say ~ What matters = Is how - you - think - and feel - and choose - among the subjects we cover - and = Come up with the truth that best suits your own experience - that then = You can go on to question further ~ All I ask = Is that you join me in that active space of question - and = When the judgments of your past experience leap to fill it = You consider the possibility - that those judgments - may be incorrect ~ I'm not saying - they are ~ I am saying = Test them - experiment - explore ~ In the simplest terms = Question what you think - and then decide = What else to question ~ What if - it makes the most sense to remember - that = Deciding completely - what is true - before

46

experiencing - every crack and corner of what might be true - could be - to shut the door on the possibility - of having what you truly want.

[[[[[[[[[Bending Body/Mind:

There are many ideas in circulation - around influencing - or controlling - different bodily functions through the use of mind alone ~ It only makes sense - that this very visible body thing - that apparently houses the very invisible mind thing - which = Is constantly deciding how to move around that body thing - should = Be in communication in such a way that all physical functions would be subject to the same decision-making power ~ After all = Our bodies know what's going on inside them ~ But = Picking your nose - and dispatching white blood cells to an infection in your toe - are more like descriptions of life on different planets - than existence in the same body - and = Imbalanced as that may be - we tend to accept it as = The way it is.

There are - however - two extremely simple indications - that that's not - how it has to be.

The first = Is the well documented - fact - that focusing your attention on any one particular part of your body - increases blood flow to that area (and no - I don't just mean - that - area) - by a small - yet still measurable amount ~ It's also been found = That by visualizing a part of your body (such as your hands) - as slightly larger (about an inch or less - more than an inch - and the trick won't work - your body isn't stupid) = Will momentarily trick your circulatory system into supplying extra blood to that - extra area.

You can test this out on a cold day - by going outside (or not - it's your body temperature that matters - not where you are) - and doing exactly as I've described - or (in more detail) = Touch your hands to your face and notice their temperature ~ Then = Take a good look at them (so their image is printed in your mind) Then = Close your eyes - and visualize what you just saw (peek again if you have to - until you get a clear image) - or = Do what ever it takes to fully tune your awareness into your hands (the image isn't necessary - the focus is) Then = Imagine them larger = Feel them being larger - pulsing - changing color - glowing even ~ After a couple of minutes of that = Touch them to your face again ~ Have they warmed up? You can attempt precision - by holding a thermometer between your fingers - before - and after the experiment ~ Although - just by performing the before part - you will influence blood flow.

Your results will reflect several variables (air temperature - health - duration of time spent - level of concentration - willingness - belief - etc.) - and may appear to prove nothing (unless you're trying to prove it doesn't work - which - a minute or two's lack of real interest should cover nicely) - but = I guarantee - that you - will - increase the circulation to your hands - and = With some practice (should you be willing) - eventually - you will get very clear evidence of that guarantee.

This imagined expansion - is also an extremely beneficial practice for expecting mothers (or more specifically - their babies) - if they (or you - should you happen to be one) - regularly spend a number of minutes a day imagining that pregnant belly to be that much larger - and thereby = Increasing the flow of oxygen and nutrient rich blood to the growing child inside.

The second mind/body communication trick = Has to do with pH levels - or that measurement of alkalinity versus acidity - that is such a specific balance issue to the health of our bodies ~ Lemons (it turns out - despite the idea that they are acidic) - have a very strong alkalizing affect ~ Drink the juice of one lemon (that's - lemon juice - not lemonade) - and instantly = Your pH level becomes more alkaline.

The amazing thing = Is that imagining yourself to be sucking on a lemon (I mean - really imagining it - until you actually get the full pucker up sour reaction going in your mouth) = Will - also raise your pH as though a real lemon were involved.

Of course = There's another list of variables involved (though the mental dedication ones remain the same obviously) - and - it's slightly more complex to measure the results ~ However = It is possible to accomplish a much more precise measurement - than was the case with hand temperature exercise (barring having all the proper equipment) - by using litmus paper strips that test the pH level of your saliva ~ To achieve a significant color (meaning pH) - change however - is no simple matter.

But then = Perhaps the simple matter of - the way it is = Is not quite so simple either ~ It appears - that absolutely everything we eat or drink or just be around - has an effect on pH level ~ Music can be acidic - loud noises - unfriendly interactions ~ As well as the opposite - of alkaline music - sounds and interactions ~ In particular though (as just pointed out by the two - tricks - mentioned) - are thoughts themselves ~ How we think - and thus feel - produces immediate chemical reactions ~ It is a very simple matter to say = Being healthy - feels good ~ It may in fact - be just as simple (and true) - to say = Feeling good - is - healthy.]]]]]]]]]

Which brings us directly to reason number three = The final - and in a sense - most important - motivation behind the name = What If.
Who can define the word motivation?

Right = Inspiration - is another good word - for what moves - that is - motivates - us to do what we do ~ Although it tends to more often be used on the passionate side of motivation - than say - being motivated to go to work just to avoid being fired ~ In other words = What we're talking here = Are the reasons - behind what we do - the purposes - the goals - and yes - the inspirations = Those - are motivations.

How about the word acronym? Anyone know what that means?

I'll show you (at least the backwards method of producing an acronym) First = We take a word - or a phrase - like say = What If ~ Then - when we use each letter of that phrase - as the first letter of another word - we get - that is - you could get - and more accurately - I get = We Have a Totally Important Function.

That's an acronym.

It's also a rather intriguing idea.
What function do you suppose that totally important one might be?

Let me see if I can help you out.

What is - the single - motivating force - behind - everything - human beings - do?

I know = That's not an answer = It's just another question ~ But - think about it = What does everyone want? That's where you'll find the answer.

Okay - sure = Those are things people want ~ But = Why do they want love and money and sex and stuff? Why do you? How do they make you - feel?

That's it = Happy.

What if - the reason - we do everything - no matter what it is (I repeat = No matter what it is) - is because = We are trying to be happy?

What do you think? Could that be true?

Alright ~ Good question ~ Why would someone kill another person? Yes = Those are reasons why someone might want to kill someone ~ But = Why would they do it? Do you think it would make you happy to kill someone? Well - maybe some part of it would ~ But = Is killing people - a happy kind of thing to do? So - it looks like maybe the happiness theory is blown out of the water immediately ~ Ah - but let's dig a bit ~ Remember those reasons you gave for killing someone? So = If your family was murdered - or someone stole all your money - how would you feel? Do you like how those feelings feel? Are they - unhappy - feelings? Do you want them to change? What do you want them to change to? So = Does that mean - you are - motivated - by wanting = Happiness?

It would be easy enough to find people that say that happiness isn't the bottom line for why we do the things we do - instead = They might say - survival - is the reason ~ Okay = What does the word survival mean? Right - it's all about - going on living ~ But = Why do we want to survive? Sure = People can be afraid of dying ~ But = Do we - want - to survive to spend our lives in prison - or have some terrible disease? Right = It's much more like - we want to survive - through those things - to something else ~ So = Why do we want to survive? But - but - but = It's not that simple you say = There's the survival instinct = We can't help ourselves = We'll fight to stay alive = Sure = That's true = But why?

What if - We Have A Totally Important Function?

What could it be? Oh lots of things - sure ~ But...... That's it - that's the one I'm after = TO - BE - HAPPY.

Not that it matters - that's the one I'm after (meaning - me - a single individual - trying to influence you to want what I want) What matters is = What if - that is - IT? What if - that's - our purpose - our meaning - our defining point - our function? What if - that's why we're here - why here is here - why - what - when - where - and how come - is here? Could it be? Is our function - happiness? Is that why we all want it? Yeah = We don't all have it - or have it all the time - but = What's that got to do with the question - except another reason to want it more ~ Again = What if - we have a totally important function - and - happiness = Is it?

[[[[[[[[[Doctor Dude's Dictionary - word four - Dynamic:

Here's a word for you = Dynamic ~ It's an action word - which is so much about action - it basically means action - and yet = It's almost more active than action - because = It's about the relationships between energy and force and motion and change - and - the intensity of all them - all - at the same time ~ It's really a very dynamic word ~ It's there to explain the exchange of information - dominance - submission - harmony - effectiveness - and influences between people = When we say the dynamics of a group ~ It means powerful and inspiring = When we say = She was a dynamic speaker ~ Or - it's stimulating and energizing = When music is dynamic ~ A dynamic force - is one that causes lots of action - especially change ~ The dynamic of a situation - is where action is produced - or blocked - or some combination of both - by the forces - or personalities - involved in that situation ~ In the end = No matter how you use the word dynamic - what you're really talking about = Is energy doing things - and = That's exciting - because = Energy doing things - is what excitement is.]]]]]]]]]

Okay - I know this sounds like trying to funnel a big complex world into one small word - so - we'll add another dimension to it = What if - what everyone is doing all the time - is trying to achieve particular feelings? In other words = What if - every time - we choose what to do next - our choice is based on - what we want to feel? After all - everything we do - feels like something ~ In that sense - maybe you prefer a word different from happiness ~ Maybe you want to feel angry - or joyous - or content - or frustrated - or any word that stands for a feeling ~ Maybe it's really just feelings we're after ~ But = What is the core one? What is driving us to go through all those others? Could it be = Simply a state of well being we're after - and the word that does the job simplest - is a very simple one = Happy?

So = What is Happiness?

An emotion? Sure ~ A state of mind? A mood? A condition? Yeah = All that ~ But - at the same time - happiness does seem to cover a broad range of feelings associated with different interactions ~ Feeling powerful could be one ~ Just as giving up your power could also be one - depending on the reason you identify with - to achieve that state ~ So = What - is - it?

I know - it's hard to pin in words ~ You have to feel it - don't you?

So = What if - the simplest explanation is = Happiness is Happiness? And = What if - the simplest terms you could put it into is = Feeling good?

||||||||| **Is Happiness What We Are?**

What such an obscure sounding question means - is = If - we go searching for the core nature of our being - the goal of all self inquiry - investigation - observation - physical - mental - and energetic discipline = Will we discover there - that happiness (or an electromagnetic frequency we describe our recognition of - as happiness) - is what that core nature is?

When I say - core nature - I'm referring to what I'll call = The source signal ~ By that - I mean = Like radio or television stations broadcasting their programs out to the cosmos - they do so at a particular wavelength - or frequency ~ The content of those programs can change and range anywhere in the A-to-Z bandwidth of our human experience ~ But = It's the unchanging frequency that carries them that is their - core nature - or - source signal - the power on which they depend to be perceived (which is to say - to be tuned into - by listeners and viewers like ourselves) So = What I'm saying - is = If - what we are as humans - is a range of wavelengths being broadcast by consciousness (I know - big stretch that idea - but) = Could it be - our core nature - is one particular frequency - and that frequency = Is happiness?

To repeat that idea another way = The programming carried by those radio or television waves - may have no obvious connection to the fact - or the story - of their being an electromagnetic frequency ~ In other words = They never describe themselves as frequencies (much like ourselves) While at the same time = There would be no ability to be a witness to that programming - without the action fact - that that's what they are - which = As applied to ourselves - and everything else being frequencies (this being a preview of ideas to come) - describes the action of perceiving life in form - which = Is only possible through the action of the quantum field - which = Is really just the action of energy - in vibration (which is what a frequency is) - which = You may or may not believe or agree with (or have any idea what I'm talking about) - which = Is fine.

Therefore = Removing this concept from analogy - and scientific theory - and placing it square onto us = The reason I use the word - Happiness = Has two inspirations.

First = Is the idea - that our prime motivator in life - is = The pursuit of happiness ~ Which of course - is also that famous phrase from the Declaration of Independence - coined (supposedly) - by old Tom Jefferson - but = Not because it was some new idea - but because = It is basically obvious - as being the mode of human operation - when a systematic dissection of everything we do gets to the lowest common denominator of what the thing is - we are all pursuing.

And secondly = Because - everyone that has ever made a long serious and concerted effort to search out the core nature of themselves (which - by extension - means all of our selves - as being the same type of creatures) - and then reported back on their findings = Has described the experience in words such as - joy - rapture - bliss - and = Happiness.

Not that you have to agree with their experience - if it isn't yours ~ It does raise the question however - of = Why are we so attracted to happiness? What is the reason - those seekers - experienced bliss? What is - happiness?

Could it be = That vibration - wavelength - frequency - signal - getting jiggy with possibility thing that's going on at the subatomic quantum field level (don't worry - we'll get to explaining that last bit soon) - and as such = Is broadcasting our reality onto the screen of particles where we interact with it (again - we'll get to that - and - the beginning of this sentence is still = Could it be) = Happiness? And = If - it is - then = It's not just the answer to the four questions I just asked = It's = What we are.]]]]]]]]]

So = Where does it come from? Is it outside of you getting in somehow? How does it work? What happens when you just want to be happy? No = Not want something to change in order to be happy = Just want - to be happy = Are you? Think about that one - can you just choose to be happy? Sure there are challenges to it - but = Can you?

Is happiness a way of being then? What does - being - mean? Like Human Being? So = That's being human - not being something else - like a plant or an elephant? Alright = Then - is - being - a choice of what you want to be? Like being president? Yes = It's true = You're not being president - until you are president - and that's not very easy to do ~ But = What about happiness - do you have to get elected to it? Who is it up to? So = If you decide to be happy - can anyone stop you? Oh they can certainly try - that's for sure ~ But = Is it up to them?

What if - the true secret to happiness - is - simply - deciding - to be happy?

Could it be that simple? Yeah = I know it doesn't seem like it ~ But = What if - it is? How would we learn how to do it? What would we have to change?

By the way - remember me asking you - if you'd ridden in a car - before - you learned how to drive? Have you thought about that? Any ideas? Yes = Excellent = Experience ~ Part of the learning - has already taken place - if not more than half of it ~ Had you just taken the wheel - without ever having been in a car before - you'd probably be hopeless - as well as terrified - at least in traffic ~ But - no = You've gone hundreds - maybe thousands - of miles in the things ~ So - there are very few surprises - just a bit of technique to practice.

And that = Was my point ~ You've been around the block - as they say ~ You've experienced happiness ~ No matter how short a time - you've still created some reference point - for what happiness - feels like ~ So - just like taking the wheel for the first time = It's getting the responsibility into your own hands that's the leap - and maybe the scary part - but = It just takes a bit of time - a bit of familiarity with the territory = You've already done the leg work ~ The very same - as turning 16 and getting your learners permit = You qualify ~ All you really had to do = Was be alive until this point

Alright - This is what I want you to do ~ For an assignment - that is ~ I want you to feel happy ~ No - it's not some fuzzy Hallmark moment ~ Though I do hope you get plenty of chances to test it out ~ I mean = FEEL - what happiness - feels like - in you ~ Next time you feel happy = NOTICE ~ Go there in your mind = I feel happy ~ And = Ask yourself = So self - what does happiness feel like? Then = Just hang around in there - feel it ~ Don't question why you're happy - or if you're going to stay happy ~ Totally - simply - just - experience - what - happiness - feels like - to you ~ Talk to yourself about it ~ You are anyway ~ So - notice - that as well ~ What kind of stuff are you saying about this happiness thing? How does that affect the feeling? Then = Feel that ~ Okay?

And = While you're at it - do some of that breathing - the conscious kind ~ Do a lot of it - in fact ~ Especially = When - you - feel - happy ~ Then again - when you don't - it could be just the thing - to change that.

N.P.U. - Chapter Four - Mars?

Have you ever wondered if it would be possible to colonize Mars? No? You're thinking has been more in the range of = Will you ever be able to afford to live in Southern California? Well - believe it or not - a lot of people - have spent a lot of time - energy - and money - on doing just that (working out how to colonize Mars that is - Southern California is the same but that's not what I'm talking about) What's more - they not only think it's possible - they think it's inevitable (meaning - just plain bound to happen) According to them - humanity is headed for the stars - and Mars - is just a natural step along the way.

There are (as you've already imagined) - a few difficulties to overcome ~ Just getting enough people and all the stuff required - to a place over 35 million miles away (at it's closest - and about seven times that distance when it's furthest away) - is the first obstacle ~ But - that's relatively simple compared to the second one ~ Mars - as you more than likely are aware - has a very limited atmosphere ~ No = I don't mean the wrong kind of decorations and lighting - with no little candles and flowers on the tables ~ I mean = Air ~ There's hardly any oxygen - far too much carbon dioxide - so little water vapor there's hardly ever a cloud ~ Not that clouds would be much protection from the killer solar radiation the place is subject to ~ In short - it means = Plants - animals - and people - can't survive there ~ You've got to admit - that makes the cost of living in Southern California that much easier to accept.

Anyway = Those people in favor of emigrating to our nearest neighbor in the solar system - clearly - understand those problems - and - all that time - energy - and money (I mentioned before) - has been spent on solving those problems - or at least trying to ~ And - you guessed it = Some truly amazing technologies are in the works to bring the possibility (of you becoming one of the first human Martians for one) - closer to reality ~ One of them - and possibly the most large-scale and successfully tested here on earth - is called Biosphere II ~ Perhaps you've heard of it - or even driven by on Highway 77 South of Phoenix Arizona - while taking the scenic route to Southern California ~ What it is - is a big glass bubble of a building that is designed to produce - and sustain - its own ecosystem - meaning = The whole interconnected system of atmosphere to breathe - water to drink - food to eat ~ In short = Habitable conditions - where they did not exist before ~ Yes = Such conditions do already exist in the Sonoran Desert of Southern Arizona - so = The experiment (which was conducted to see if the theories worked) - required sealing off the big bubble - just as it would be on Mars - from the outside environment - and = Because it would not function without humans to operate it - eight of them were also sealed in for the experimental period of two years.

Well - it worked ~ Mostly anyway ~ It produced oxygen from plant life - water from that oxygen - food from both - and life (or the human necessities of life - which of course include the parallel needs of a broad range of other species) - from all three ~ Aside from a few technical difficulties - it was basically a resounding success ~ Almost.

There was one flaw - a rather major one - if not the greatest problem facing humanity's efforts to sustain life where ever they might be (or go) = The people = Did not get along ~ They disagreed - they argued - they chose sides - ignored each other - avoided each other - even hated each other on occasion ~ Which is not to say - that was the entire picture - but = It was enough of the picture - to claim = That Biosphere II - despite mostly being a scientific success - was - a social - failure.

Alright - yes = Here's that point again = What - has all this got to do with you?

Well - perhaps it causes you to rethink that vacation on Mars you've been considering ~ But - beyond that = It exposes a giant gap in the priorities of our systems of preparation - or that training - known as education - we consider so important in our society ~ To simplify that = Could it be = The choices of what's important - in how we learn - what we learn - and what we - do - with what we learned - are missing the central point in our own mission (both biologically and philosophically) - which is = The successful - happy - survival of our species?

You see - some of those people - that volunteered to spend two years in Mars Arizona - were experts - highly trained individuals with years and years of extra education stuffed between their ears - and some of them = Weren't - but = All of them - were the product of (so-called) - Western culture ~ Not to say - there's just something naturally wrong with that - or to suggest there's anything wrong with any of those people ~ Yet = What had they been most successful - in learning - from that system of training do you think? Sure = How to run sophisticated technology and understand complex concepts ~ But = What about the kind of basic operating program behind it all? Could it be = What they learned best - was = How to compete?

Of course - there are some would say = That competition is the natural order of things - the first design principle of that very thing we call - Nature - and = They are correct - to a certain level ~ Plants compete for water and nutrients and sunlight ~ Animals - insects - fish - fowl - and even single cell organisms - all compete for food and territory and all that - but = If competition were the whole picture = Then nature would have competed itself right out of a job billions of years ago ~ The fact is = The longer a natural environment - or ecosystem - exists = The more diverse the life it supports becomes (known as biodiversity) Were it the other way around = The dominant species (the winner - as it were) - like say... humans - would no longer have a life support system (food - water - oxygen - and all the microbes and bacteria that aid in the breakdown of nutrients and waste) - on which to live ~ Close up - the natural world looks like one great struggle for survival - but = A couple steps back - and that whole picture turns to one of an intricate fabric of = Cooperation ~ A point - on which the entire working design of Biosphere II was dependent.

If - one day - a group of earthlings arrives on Mars equipped to establish a colony - do you think their ability to harmoniously cooperate with one another - would be nearly as important - as their ability to produce oxygen? In fact - might even be what that oxygen production - was dependent on - and so = More important?

So = Why - did people who are smart enough to design - build - and operate such a thing as Biosphere II - not think of that?

[[[[[[[[[**Dubrovnik:**

About 800 years ago - in the tiny Balkan country of Croatia (go ahead and look it up - it's in the southern part of eastern Europe just above Greece on the Adriatic Sea) - the walled city state of Dubrovnik outlawed warfare and territorial expansion ~ Its council members also chose to design a government without kings and queens - or - long-term rulers of any kind ~ To be governor of Dubrovnik - meant being absent from your regular job for a mere 30 days - which = Effectively discouraged abuses of power based on personal agendas - and instead - seems to have grown from - promoted - and succeeded in supporting - a belief in upholding the well-being of society as a whole over the interests of private business and the cultural economic control of small groups or individuals - which seems to plague the politics of most every other place.

All sounds very lovey-dovey and high-minded and all - but of course - the question is = Did it work?

The answer - in short = Is yes ~ That is - if you accept over 600 years of peace on a continent that witnessed wars - both large and small - nearly every generation of those passing centuries (if not more often) - as a qualification for that = Yes ~ Nor are we talking some little out-of-the-way place that no one was interested in anyway - but = A thriving seaport engaged in broad international trade - which = Established diplomatic embassies in 50 other cities.

The reason - for pointing out the example of Dubrovnik - is not to say = That's how peace is achieved and maintained ~ But instead - to say = When peace is what we choose = We get it.]]]]]]]]]

Well - most likely - some - if not all of them - did think of it ~ The problem was - or is = The skills required for deliberate harmonious cooperation - presumably - were not included in the training ~ At least not as a high priority - or simply - just as something - they - or you - or me - and everybody else for that matter - were supposed to absorb along the way - as needed - from family and classmates and culture as a whole ~ Well = Did you?

Alright ~ If there is such a gap - such a central point missing from earthling training - then - clearly - it's a kind of blind spot - or something we're not seeing - clearly - despite its results being all around us ~ What is it? What's at - the core - of our misunderstanding ourselves?

In order to think clearly - about this lack of clarity - let's stand for a moment - on the surface of Mars - and consider - its core ~ A few deep breaths would be of great help - but remember = Up here - that will kill you ~ But why = Why is the atmosphere of Mars - the way it is? Well - as close as - science - has worked it out so far (and they could be wrong) = About three and a half billion years ago - Mars had a very different atmosphere - possibly even resembling our own ~ At least as far as moisture and heat are concerned ~ Then - a crisis occurred = Deep inside the planet - the super hot turmoil of molten iron that generated its magnetic field (the same as our own planet - as far as we know) - had cooled to a temperature - where that field fizzled - sputtered - and stalled out ~ This meant that - the magnetosphere - a kind of outer shell of protective force surrounding the atmosphere - which was helping to keep - that atmosphere in - and bad stuff - like cosmic rays and solar radiation - out - also blinked off and was gone ~ Now Mars - only a little more than half the size of Earth - never had much of a gravitational pull to keep its atmosphere at home in the first place - so = Those two factors (plus a stack of other scientific complexities) - spelled doom for any kind of Martians - animal or vegetable (if they existed) - as it was goodbye warm and wet and potentially breathable - hello freezing desert zapped by radiation.

[[[[[[[[[Inventory Time:

You'll likely recall being invited to take an inventory of your perceptual state early on in this little journey we've undertaken ~ Did you do it?

If not = Try doing it now (you can refer to chapter two for the full instructions if need be) If you did do it = Then do it again ~ Get yourself squarely on the page you're on right now ~ Go ahead - I'll wait.

The reason - for taking such an inventory - is not unlike the purpose a store owner has in counting their goods = It's about seeing where you stand - what you've got to work with - what you need to pay attention to - to look for - change - organize - or celebrate (it's a long way from being just about seriousness)

The first place to look for consciousness - is in what you're conscious of ~ It's that state we call - awareness - where the senses - and the interplay of thoughts and emotions - which add up to perception - are arrayed on the screen - the movie - your (our) - observer mind (consciousness) - is watching ~ Being aware of awareness - is not about - what - you're aware of = It's about experiencing - being aware - of the things you're aware of.

This inventory business – is (as I've already strung the analogy along) - an integral feature of business - your business - your work ~ Checking in with the state of your awareness - is a way to track how much of the stuff you've got going - and = To feel that awareness taking place - to observe it - especially = As you expand it - to an awareness of all its parts - working in concert together to produce what that movie of consciousness is for you this very moment.

Therefore = I'm going to remind you from time to time - that its = {{{{Inventory Time}}}} Which means = Stop - and review your awareness ~ What are your senses and thoughts and emotions - communicating - to that observer you call your self - right now? It needn't take long - a minute - a few seconds even - just long enough - that you touch them all - nostrils to negativity - itches to inspiration - and be aware - of all that awareness.

That's it - simple as breathing ~ And just like that breathing = If you're not paying attention = It's probably pretty shallow.||||||||||

Okay ~ Back on Earth - where you'll be pleased to start breathing again - we can still count on our good old magnetic field - compass needles firmly pointing north (or close enough - at what's known as magnetic north) - to keep those - life supporting conditions - right where we need them ~ For the moment anyway.

I'm afraid there is a small problem = Our magnetic field is changing - it's showing unmistakable signs of being about to do one - or both - of two possible options ~ Which are = Reverse polarities - where South takes over the control of compass needles - or = Go out altogether - hopefully temporarily - perhaps not ~ The good news is = It's happened before - often in fact (option number one that is) - or - magnetic pole reversal ~ We - know that - from studying ancient lava flows and pottery ~ Which might sound like visiting a gift shop in Hawaii - but it's really a way of looking at a kind of Polaroid of earthly magnetism at work ~ You see - at the moment lava cools from a liquid to a solid - its iron particles are arranged according to the direction of the Earth's magnetic pole ~ Exactly the same thing is true of iron particles - present in clay - at the moment they are fixed permanently in place by firing ~ By comparing different ages of pottery - or - lava flows - layered one on top of another - a very clear illustration of the flip-flopping of that field is laid out for all to see.

One of those illustrations - is a picture of magnetic polar shifts - occurring on an average of every 250,000 years or so ~ Since the last one happened about 750,000 years ago - we're good and overdue for the next ~ Which also means = We have really no idea what to expect - beyond certain navigational problems - and maybe some migrating birds turning up in Greenland rather than Brazil ~ Of course - then there is - option number two - perhaps coupled with the effects of global warming - with the possibility of continent splitting earthquakes - tsunamis - supercharged electrical storms - massed tornadoes - hail the size of basketballs - and of course - total incineration by solar flares ~ But don't worry ~ Not because such things can't happen - might happen - or will happen - but because = Worry won't do any good ~ What may do some good = Is recognizing - that you yourself - at your core - also - generate a magnetic field - and perhaps - that field - and the Earth's - are connected.

Yes = I know = Connected seems like too… well… connected - a word ~ Obviously we're all here moving around on Earth - held down by gravity - using the same air - and so on ~ You could call that connected - but = It - appears - to be a loose kind of connection - like - all librarians are connected - or people who have won the lottery are ~ Remember though - what we're talking here are magnetic fields - which vary in a broad range of measurable ways - but - at the same time = They all - share one inseparable connection = They are all - the same thing.

By - the same thing - I mean (other than meaning - the same thing) = Magnetic fields are the result of - one - of the four - forces - that govern (according to currently agreed upon science) - the physical universe ~ That - one - particular force in question - is (you guessed it) = Electromagnetism ~ It's responsible for useful stuff like - light - electricity - magnets ~

That cell phone - you won't put down - wouldn't work without it - and = Neither would you.

The question is = Why do you generate a magnetic field? What does it do? How does it do it? And = Is it possible that it could be - at the heart - of getting along with your fellow Martian colonists - as well as changing life as we know it here on our own planet?

SPECIAL BONUS EXERCISE - number two

Babble:

Communication occurs at many levels - both conscious - and unconscious ~ Blocks to communication are the same - in that = Regularly - we consciously hold back - or modify - what we put out or take in - in the way of communication - and more often = We unconsciously enclose ourselves in the shell of our individual selves - where sending and receiving communication is reduced to a narrow band width.

The following exercise - is both a chance to experiment - and - to play with opening that sending and receiving ability - in a way = That will quite possibly surprise you at several levels ~ Those levels - I'll leave you to define - or discover - for yourself.

What you do is = Babble ~ Which - if you look the word up in a dictionary - will be described as = Uttering foolish or meaningless words and sounds ~ Only = The way you will be doing it - will be neither foolish nor meaningless - because = The intention = Is to communicate.

There are two ways to proceed ~ First = Is with a partner ~ Which is actually much more effective (after all - like I told you - the exercise is about communication) But = You can also practice it alone - just to loosen up the systems involved - and = Explore your own communication with yourself (which cannot help but affect your communication with others)

Therefore = With a partner - or alone - describe your innermost hopes - desires - pains - frustrations - needs (in a word - feelings) - in babble - or gibberish - which means = In your own made-up language of words and sounds that represent - as close as you can come up with - the flavor of the sounds you make - what those feelings are - and - how they feel.

Yes - you may - feel - foolish doing such a thing - but = If you can push past that - and really focus your energy into expressing those core parts of your self - as well as applying that same - full energy - to listening - both - to that partner (who is also getting over feeling foolish) - yet - even more importantly = To yourself (which means listening to your own listening) Because - like I said = Communication occurs at many levels - as do its obstacles ~ The more complete a witness we are to those levels = The more complete - is communication.

Class Five - Electricity Now?

BREATHE (Good = Cross your arms like that ~ What you're doing is connecting the two hemispheres of your brain - which govern opposite sides of your body - through a kind of energy pathway located in each earlobe - rather like completing an electrical circuit ~ Now do the rest = Off you go)

Well - did you - FEEL - happy? What was it like? Was it the first time you ever really noticed? Is looking around in your head changing the way you look around - outside your head? Has it made - choosing happiness - any easier? How do you feel right now? Can you locate any of that happy feeling you found going on before - going on - now? Where do you feel it? Does locating it - help - it - grow stronger? Do you want it to grow stronger?

Okay = 500 years ago - could you walk over to that corner there - and flick on the light? Well - yes - that's true = This room didn't exist then ~ But = Could you flick on one anywhere? (On Earth that is) So = What makes the light work? Was electricity around 500 years ago? No? What about lightening - and static electricity - weren't they around? So = How about the physical action itself - of walking over there and turning the light on - what powers that? Yes = Certainly you telling yourself to do it is a big part ~ But = How does that work - what kind of energy is involved? Exactly = Electricity ~ The action of our nervous system - commanding our muscles to contract and move us around - is electrical (Yes - it's also chemical - but never mind that for the moment)

So = Could people move their muscles 500 years ago?

Let's get this straight now = 500 years ago - none of these things that work on electricity - that we have now - existed? Why? Right = People hadn't figured it out yet ~ So = They hadn't figured it out - but - at the same time = Everything they did with their bodies - was using electricity? (Fact is - everything about bodies or objects of any kind involves electricity - but we'll talk about that later on as well) So = This amazing power was inside them all along - they just didn't know it? Has it been there throughout all of history?

What if - a situation - exactly like that - is going on today? What if - there is a power inside us - right now - capable of doing more than electricity - or any other form of energy - ever could - and = We just don't know about it?

Is that possible?

What could it be?

What if - it is consciousness itself? (Whatever that is)

How would we find out? Where would we look? What if - we were to look - in our happiness? Yeah = I know that doesn't sound like it makes much sense ~ But remember = We're talking about something invisible - or = Energy ~ Is happiness visible? Ah = But - are smiles and laughter - the thing itself - or just a result of it?

Alright - that still leaves the whole question - of - how to find out - rather foggy - doesn't it? Let's see if we can narrow it down some.

I need a volunteer.

Okay ~ Everything behind Janice here - is the past ~ Everything in front of her - is the future ~

Alright Janice - show us how time works.

So = What did you notice about Janice as she walked across the room? Was she in the past? Was she in the future? Where was she? Yes = The present ~ What is a three letter word for the present? Absolutely = Now ~ Are we in the past now? How about the future? So when are we?

Okay = When you got out of bed this morning - at that exact moment - what part of time were you in? Right = It was a present moment - it was a - now ~ How about when you go to bed tonight - what part of time will that be? Yes = Another now ~ So = Is it always now? Ah = But isn't remembering a previous time - or thinking about a future time - something that can only happen - when you're present - in the now - that is happening now?

Again = Is it always now?

Is that how time works - an endless stream of nows? Does that mean that time doesn't really exist = Only now does?

Tricky sort of question - isn't it? Let's dig into it a bit more.

How about that word - being - is that kind of like another word for now? When you are - being something - what part of time do you use? Would you say - I'll be being late today? That's not very good English - is it? Why? Of course = Because - being - only happens in the present - and - the language has that much going for it - that it locates the time it's talking about pretty well.

So = What about happiness - is it the same? Yes = Happiness is a now thing ~ You either are happy - or you're not ~ Maybe you've - been happy - or will - be happy - but when you - are happy - it's a now - isn't it?

So - Again = What if - time doesn't actually exist - there's really only - now?

I know - there seems to be a flow of connected - being - involved in things happening (such as breathing - to name one of the simplest) - where that - happening - follows a seamless line of this stuff we call time - and = In the midst of that - we remember events - and expect more to happen (exhaling is a good one) - but = But = Where - are - those events? Can you see them? Yes = All of these things - the furniture - the building - seem to prove a link to the past - but = How do you know they were here ten minutes ago? Okay - you - were here ten minutes ago - but = How do you know? Remembering - yes ~ BUT = When - are you remembering that time ten minutes ago? Exactly = Now.

[[[[[[[[[Doctor Dudes Dictionary - word five - Paradox:

A contradiction is an action of some kind - such as - words spoken - behavior participated in - or information circulated - that is opposite - to some previously agreed upon or understood or reported intention or purpose ~ For instance = If I were to tell you that I can't stand people who gossip and I never chew gum - and then = I proceeded to tell you about how Bill lost his job because they caught him stealing - with a big wad of gum in my mouth = You could say - that was contradictory behavior - and = You'd be correct.

Now that we've got that straight = There is a type of contradiction - where = Despite the fact - that two ideas of action appear to contrast - or oppose each other (which generally means one of those actions is right - or true - and the other wrong - or untrue - at least as compared to each other through the ideas in play ~ Now go back to the beginning of this sentence and skip this stuff in parentheses) - the actual case = Is that they are both true ~ Of course - such an explanation probably makes little or no sense - but = That's what a paradox is = A seemingly contradictory explanation - or statement - that may nonetheless - be true ~ It's a tricky little notion to understand - essentially because it goes against our usual means of understanding - but = Perhaps the closest example of a paradox we can access now - or any time - is now itself.

To explain that - or attempt to - would be to say = There is only one now ~ Indeed - there appear to be an endless string of nows - but = As you well know - we can only ever experience - one at a time ~ Therefore = There - is - only one.

Told you it was tricky ~ Also told you = It's a paradox ~ What I didn't tell you - is that the word paradox - can only get you to the edge of one - where you may understand the two sides of the issue in question - but = Not necessarily experience the understanding of how they can both be true simultaneously ~ That experience generally goes beyond the use of words ~ But hey = That's a paradox too.]]]]]]]]]]

We can't actually prove there's time - no matter how much geology - photography - or - records of change you produce as evidence = We can only prove - there's now - because

62

= Whenever we interact with ideas about time - we can only do it - in the present ~ That doesn't mean that evidence doesn't exist (seemingly) - or that we don't just go along with it as all the proof of time we need ~ And still = The now business holds true - right now - and right now - and.........

Do you remember that partial definition of the word conscious - I mentioned at the beginning? That's it = Having an awareness of one's own existence ~ Is the word - conscious - the present tense - of the word consciousness? So = To be conscious of the existence of say... that desk in the corner - would it have to be happening right now? Did that desk exist a week ago? How do you know? Ah = That memory thing again ~ So = Is a week ago happening right now? Is your memory of that desk then - a part of your present consciousness - that you're accessing right now? Ah - we're starting to expose this consciousness thing a bit aren't we?

What if - time only exists - as a part of our consciousness - but = Because - we can only be - conscious in the present moment - then all of time is going on right now - and so - by extension = All of consciousness is going on - right now = Does that mean - that that's what consciousness is = Time? Or in other words (actually just one) = Now

Yes = That's a twisty one ~ I don't expect you to make sense of it instantly though - because = Most of our - thinking - about time - works like clocks and calendars ~ But - I do expect that you can make sense of this next idea - which might help with the other bit.

When you are unhappy about something - what parts of time are you thinking about? (By parts - I mean - past - present - and future) Yes = That's right ~ The answer is = The past or the future = Even (I might add) - when those times - we're thinking about - are so close to the present (like seconds - or even fractions of seconds) - as to appear to - be - the present (such as when we're in great pain) But why? Sure = We're usually unhappy about something that - has happened - or something - we don't want to happen - right? But - are the past and future happening in the present - even - like I said - as one second to the next? So = What is preventing you from being happy right now? Yes = Those things that caused you to get unhappy in the first place ~ But - again = Are they going on - right now? So = What is it you're doing - now - that keeps you from being happy - now? Bingo = Thinking - about the past or the future ~ Or - perhaps more precisely = Choosing to make the past or the future - more important - than the present.

Remember - being happy - is a now thing ~ So = Is being unhappy - also - a now thing? Does that mean - it would make sense - to examine what's going on in our thinking - now - to see if that's where the cause - of that unhappy present - is (meaning - the influence of thinking about the past or future - the cause - right now) - in order to work out - how to cause a different feeling - right now?

So = What is going on right now for you?

[[[[[[[[[**What's in it for me?**

Now (and all that aside) = We do tend to haul around a concern for the future - which also tends to effectively distract us from the present moment - with some regularity ~ But - what can I say - we do ~ And - it often looks like the question = What's in it for me?

For all such a question seems to demonstrate thoroughgoing selfishness = It's also a standard operating procedure for all of us on a fairly constant basis ~ It's not that we humans are not capable of - and regularly do perform - acts of altruism - or selfless giving ~ It's just - hey = You know you're looking out for number one = It's what we do - what we expect - what we consider natural.

So = The question - right here - and right now - is the same = What's in it for you - to take this course?

Well - (if you want my opinion) - for one = This course is predominantly concerned with bringing to question - what we do - what we expect - and what we consider natural - for the purpose of potentially - personally - replacing those conditions - with ones (meaning understandings) - that are better suited to fulfilling our natural yearning for = Happiness.

Secondly = There's a lot of stuff in here (meaning - the results of research - experimentation - observation - studies - and theorizing - not to mention the practical applications threaded through that exploration) - which to know about - is to possess the fuel to start a fire under your old ideas - and cook up some new ones - that just might - taste better (even if the digestion process is a bit tricky at times)

And thirdly = What - do you think? What is in this idea of an examination of consciousness - that will benefit - you? You've gotten this far - so = There must be something - some set of ideas - some interest - curiosity - desire - some - something ~ Is it possible = That if you were to identify the set of ideas you possess - that identify - what you think is (or might be) - of benefit to you - it (it meaning - the action of acquiring that benefit) - again = It - might be that much more beneficial to your achieving that effect - with or without this course - say… now?]]]]]]]]]

Okay = Now - that you're looking around inside yourself - I'll put the same question to you again - in different words = Does that mean - when you are unhappy - you are comparing how you want to feel - to how you do feel - because of something that's happened - or is planned to happen - or might - happen to you? So - is - happy - how you actually want to feel? So why would you be - unhappy? Yeah = It goes right back to the original - assumed (again meaning that past or future you're thinking about) - cause of unhappiness again - I know ~ Which = Repeats the same question = Where is that cause (the one you're blaming for making you unhappy) - in the past - or - the future? And = Is it happening - now? Oh sure = Pain can be a major cause of unhappiness - which is - apparently - exactly in the present ~ But = Even then - that same comparison is going on with the past and the future - meaning = Focusing on the cause of the pain (the past) - or the dread of it continuing (the future) - right now ~ This idea could go round and round like that for days - because = It will always arrive back at the same point - which is = What do you want to feel - right now? Is there a word you might use to describe that point? Yes = That's very true = That point - is a now ~ But = How about this word = Choice.

When you realize - that what is making you unhappy - is not - what's going on in the present - or = Even if it is going on in that - one second to the next - present = What is the choice - you are presented with regardless? That's it = How you want to feel ~ Again = Is that choice - going on all the time - no matter what? We could break that down even more by asking = What is the other choice we are - always - presented with by the present moment? Good one = What do I do now? Is thinking a type of doing? If you are unhappy - what kind of thoughts are you having? So = What is the other choice - the present asks of us? Exactly = What - to think.

Do you remember how we got started on this whole discussion? Right = There was all that stuff about time and now and all ~ What came before that? Yup = That's it = Electricity and 500 years ago ~ So = What was the thing about people and electricity? Yes = It's in us - always has been ~ And = That led me to ask what question? That's it = The possibility of another more powerful force hidden inside us ~ And = What did I suggest it might be? Our own consciousness = That's right ~ And = Where might we look to find out? Ah - you are paying attention aren't you = Our happiness.

Let's add this business up and see where we got then = Janice proved what to us? So = If we are - being - or - doing - something - it must be taking place when? Does that mean - that being conscious - can only take place - now? Would that mean - that being conscious - that we are conscious - is the way to interact with our consciousness? What was that state of being we all want again? Is happiness something we can only experience in the present? Is life easier when you are happy? Does being happy effect other people's happiness? So = Is consciously choosing - to be happy - a powerful thing to do? In order to choose to be happy - what - do you have to think? But = Would the center of those happy thoughts have to be - simply - what - you want - is - happiness? So = Are your thoughts powerful? {{Now - read that paragraph again - only - slowly this time}}

What if - our thoughts are more powerful than we can imagine?

What if - they are what the world is really made of?

Your homework this time - is to practice - NOW ~ How do you do that? Well - there are lots of ways ~ But - this time - I'm not going to tell you ~ I want you to think about it yourself ~ How - do - you - do it? Is it possible? What does - NOW - feel like? Plus (yes - there's a plus) - I want you to do it - while you have a conversation with yourself ~ No - not just any conversation ~ I want you to talk to your self - about choosing happiness ~ How are they connected - this - now - choice - happiness - trio? I know we've talked about them some ~ Now - I want you to feel them ~ And - there's more = Try to - feel - talk - choose happiness - at the same time as you use that peripheral vision thing ~ Yeah = That may sound like overload ~ But - try it - and see - if it takes you right to the place you're looking for (which is now - in case you forgot) And then again - if not - where does it take you? Of course - while you're at it - Breathe.

[[[[[[[[[Look Where You're Going:

There is a very interesting lesson to be had - from observing one of the fundamental rules in mastering the seemingly totally different skills of motorcycle riding - and skiing - when - you apply the same rule to the skill of = Happiness (in an abstract kind of way that is)

The rule is = Look where you're going.

Well - duh - you might say - but = There's more to it than just seeing what's coming at you ~ Both motorcycling and skiing - are balancing acts (you might say happiness is as well - but anyway) Surprisingly - or not - our eyes are a major part of maintaining that balance (check out the difference between standing on one leg with your eyes open - and the same thing with them closed) The same balance - applies directly to steering the bike - or the skis - where you want to go - in that = The route you take - follows the line your eyes do ~ That doesn't mean that glancing to the right instantly whips you in that direction ~ It does mean - that negotiating a path between two obstacles - requires looking at the space between them - rather than at the obstacles themselves - or in the direction of the curve you're taking - rather than straight ahead ~ Even driving a car or walking - which can be pulled off with relative safety while very nearly asleep - still demands something of the same attention ~ And = That is where happiness comes in.

Mastering the skill of happiness (after all - it really is more of a skill than anything else - given how often we are tested on it) - requires keeping your eye on it ~ Which is to say = Knowing that's where you want to go ~ You may pass over some very rough ground - and dodge all kinds of rocks and trees and traffic - but = If you don't place your complete (this moment defines everything in my life) - attention on those things (those things being the unhappy obstacles) - and instead = Keep your inner eye - or ultimate desire attention - on where you want to go (that being happiness) - there's far less chance of crashing into - unhappiness.

Of course - this is all a metaphor - trying to simplify what appears to be a far more complex ride through life ~ But - it does have one thing going for it = It's a good one.]]]]]]]]]

N.P.U. - Chapter Five - Biosphere Too?

Okay = What - is a magnetic field?

Well - the full answer gets kind of long and technical - so - we'll go with the short - no ambition to become a Nobel prize-winning physicist - answer ~ Of course - if you do nurse such an ambition - there are plenty of resources out there that would be happy to - fully - inform you.

Anyway = A magnetic field - is the area covered by the invisible force of magnetism - in which = Its influence - or effect - is strongest ~ That effect - is most easily witnessed - by placing a piece of paper over a magnet - then - sprinkling iron filings on the paper - and - seeing what happens ~ Good chance you've already seen this - or a picture of its results - somewhere back in that - western culture - schooling of yours ~ What's happening is = Those filings are conforming to - or being arranged by - the lines - or pattern - a magnet's magnetic force flows in from one end of the magnet to the other - which = Are called - positive and negative poles ~ This flow - is always the same ~ Just like a stone dropped in still water will always create a predictable ripple (as defined by the size of the stone - the strength of impact - water density - temperature - that kind of stuff) - so - also = Are magnetic fields - predictable - according to the - matter - that is generating them - which - generates the question = How do they do that generating?

The answer basically (very basically) - is = They do it by = Excitement ~ When you excite atoms a certain way = They generate a magnetic field ~ No doubt - you've passed through a metal detector at some point ~ Well - that's how it works = Its magnetic field excites the atoms of any metal you might be concealing - which in turn = Give themselves away by generating their own field - which = Broadcasts back to the detector - and = The alarm goes off ~ The other side of that answer however = Is that atoms - are combinations of subatomic particles - whose very being - is a state of excitement - and hence = Generators of magnetic fields.

Now - it does appear as though this magnetic field business (in the form of magnets) - only associates itself with metal ~ After all - trying to pick up the box of tacks you spilled - with a handful of cornflakes - is just a waste of perfectly good cereal (even if you don't like cornflakes) But = If you remember - I mentioned previously - that you = Generate a magnetic field ~ You're doing it right now ~ There - is - iron in you - it's true ~ You'll find it listed right there in the ingredients on that box of cornflakes - because = There are definite health problems associated with not having enough of it in you ~ But = Is that why you produce that field?

In order to answer that = I'll give you a simple experiment to perform = Take a balloon - blow it up - then securely tie the open end closed ~ Now = Vigorously rub it on your shirt for a few seconds ~ Then = Press the side of the balloon you've been rubbing against you - against a smooth wall - and = Let go.

It stuck there - didn't it? If it didn't - try it again = It will ~ That's because = The force of magnetism - is allied - connected - intertwined - kinda sorta - and entirely - the same - as = Electricity - which = Is what you just produced - in the form of - static electricity - and = By now - you may have even recalled that term we used last time = Electromagnetism - or = The electromagnetic force.

What this means - in regard to your ability to produce a magnetic field - is = Your body is a lousy source of iron - to a mining engineer that is - but - to an electrical engineer - it's one of the best rechargeable batteries on the market ~ Every move your body makes is directed - and executed - or performed (since the word executed may sound a bit drastic) - by electrical charges ~ It's a walking dynamo ~ For that matter - it's also - a sitting dynamo.

[[[[[[[[[Electrons at First Sight:

Across a crowded room their eyes met - and for a moment - it was as though time stood still...

Magnetic attraction is obviously something built right into our understanding of the world (certainly our romantic fantasies about it) We are continuously attracted to things - food - colors - scents - clothing - art - music - entertainment - and each other ~ It's one of the simplest mechanisms of survival - the way it powers the species to continue being a species - which = Constitutes biological drives spiced with imagination and flavored by diversity - and yet = It also seems to serve - a higher calling (as they say - according to our scale of philosophical measurement) - of drawing us to states of being - ideas - appreciations - feelings - attractions to - beauty - beyond smooth skin and plates piled high with fragrant delicacies - which = Powers a parallel continuation - of change - of evolution - of = Mind.

We are pulled by an irresistible force - to know the mystery (again) - the beauty - of our consciousness ~ Not that everyone responds to that force the same way (some of us will fight to the death to prove they know all that is needed) Nevertheless = All of us - are pulled.

The reason is (or some small crack into that reason - is) = Magnetism - is part - of one of the four forces of the universe (as counted by physicists that is) - which = May actually be different angles (like looking - one at a time - at the sides of a box) - of one unified force ~ That force (of which magnetism is part - as though you could actually separate it) - is of course = Electromagnetism ~ And = In the case of electromagnetic fields = It has no boundaries = All electromagnetic fields - overlap - touch each other - interact ~ The strength or weakness of that interaction - is governed (at least to some degree) - by proximity (or how close one object is to another) Just the same = There is no containing that force - because = What an electromagnetic field is = Is really a mystery (aside from the spin and movement of subatomic particles that's known about - otherwise - it's an abstraction made up by physicists to explain influences at a distance with no substances involved) - other than = We (that collective we - that was generally dependent on someone else) - know (or think - we do) - the electromagnetic force - in the shape of a field (being a region of space sharing a certain physical property) - is a property of (a trait - characteristic - quality - possessed by) - space (told you so) - and = Space - is in contact - with everything.

{{Now that last bit is definitely a reread ~ Can't expect me to do all the work and make it easy for you all the time ~ Fact is = There are times when I will deliberately do the opposite in order to get you to feel that thinker of yours in action ~ But - in short - it means = Space - and electromagnetic fields - are kind of the same thing}}

According to that property of space then = We - are sharing particles - or charges - with everything around us - or = A subatomic electrical exchange - as direct as being plugged a socket – which = We have only just begun to question (a far cry from truly comprehend) It's been a question a long time in coming – if = You consider it began a few thousand years ago near the Greek city of Magnesia = Someone (the legend states it was a rather simpleminded goatherd) - noticed that iron was attracted (physically pulled) - by a type of stone (possibly iron ore which had been struck by lightning) - which came to be called - loadstone (who knows why - when they had a perfectly good name like magnesia handy) The ancient Chinese made the same discovery as well - and = It was them - about the year 1000 - who found that if you rub a steel pin on such a stone - then suspend it by a thread = It will orient itself (point) - in a north-south line ~ Obviously - the compass - was the innovation which sprang from this connection ~ However = It took another 600 years before an English physician - named William Gilbert - told the Queen that the Earth itself was probably one big magnet - and = He was right (after a fashion)

Two hundred more years passed - and a Danish scientist named Oersted - noticed that the flow of electric current through a wire - influenced the movement of a nearby compass - which = Was followed by more experimentation - mathematics - repetition - and the diligent head scratching of great minds - which = Has gotten us to our present understanding (and use) - of electromagnetism - which = Could be easily confused with - fully understanding the stuff ~ However = The compass needle of all those previous discoveries (whose very virtue of building one on another) - does point rather eloquently toward (that so very attractive compulsion of) - learning more - more - more - about this experience we find ourselves conscious in - if = We keep looking.]]]]]]]]]

So - can you guess where - the heart - of your strongest magnetic field is generated?

Excellent ~ How did you guess? Yes = It's your heart ~ Surprisingly - or not - your heart's magnetic field - is 5000 times stronger - than your brain's - with 60 times more electrical amplitude - which = Is a measurement of - frequency - which = Is the length - height - and depth - of waves of energy ~ You might think of the measurement tool as a ship rising and falling in mid ocean ~ The amplitude = Is the distance between the highs and lows of the ships movement (meaning - up and down - or vertical measurement) - and wavelength = Is the distance traveled between the peak of one wave to the next (meaning length - or horizontal measurement) Although - that's really just a two dimensional means of understanding ~ In true three dimensional space - a frequency = Is a spiral.

That technicality laid out then = The difference of the two magnetic fields we're talking here (the heart and the brain) - if measured by the crew of that ship = Is between a gently breezy day - and a hurricane ~ Also - this field of yours (meaning everyone's) - extends several feet in all directions - and = Is easily detectable by sensitive machines designed to do that ~ However - by extends - I mean = The area in which it's influence is measurable - or (like our short answer to what a magnetic field is) = Where - it is - strongest ~ Magnetic fields - don't actually have edges - or boundaries - their energy - extends indefinitely into space (but then - you may have already read something about that) They simply - are strongest - nearest their source - and weaker and weaker - the further away from that source you travel (according to our current measuring abilities that is) - like - say… Earth's magnetic field - on your way to Mars ~ Even Mars - which stopped generating a magnetic field billions of years ago - still has detectable remnants of that field floating around its surface ~ So - the question is = What is that magnetic field of yours (mine - and everyone else's) - up to?

Well - for one = They're moving really fast.

Back around the time Americans were murdering each other in droves over the issues of states' rights and slavery - a Scotsman by the name of James Clerk Maxwell - managed to fill in some of the blanks which had accumulated in the work of his aging English friend Michael Faraday - concerning the connections between electricity - magnetism - and light ~ Faraday - had come to recognize through experimentation - that electricity and magnetism - were somehow - interconnected ~ It was he - that coined the term - electromagnetism ~ And what's more = Conjectured (or took a really brainy guess) - that light itself - is an electromagnetic vibration - occurring at a particular frequency (remember that ship in mid ocean) All this - led Maxwell - in a fury of mathematics - to eventually describe - quite beautifully - how that force - his friend had named - works.

Imagine - if you will - two strands of wire - twisted together ~ One is electricity - the other - is magnetism ~ The end of this wire - facing away from you - is growing - by a kind of cooperation between the two strands - or - in other words = Electricity produces magnetism - which moves it through space - which produces more electricity - which produces magnetism - which produces electricity - and on and on and on ~ Ah - but it doesn't end there (as much as that on and on doesn't seem to end anyway) The conclusion of these equations - is = This electromagnetic force is doing all this - at about 670 million miles an hour - or - fast enough for energy from your electromagnetic field - to make 19 roundtrips to Mars - when it's at its closest to Earth - in 60 minutes (usually known as an hour) - or = The speed of light.

Some time later - it took another man - a German this time - named Hertz (you may be reminded - for good reason - of the measurement megahertz) - to finally prove Faraday's - guess about light - to be completely accurate - when his (Hertz's) - experimentation produced a low frequency electromagnetic radiation - that behaved exactly - other than the shape of its waves - as light does - now known as = Radio waves.

So What does this tell you about your magnetic field?

Well - not only is your body an electrical generator - it's also = A radio tower - broadcasting to the universe ~ And = What is it broadcasting? Why - your feelings - of course ~ At least that's what the findings of some recent research (conducted by a group called Heartmath) - seem to point at (as well as a variety of other - rather less scientific - sources) So let me tell you about that research - and see how it effects that radio station you're the DJ of.

We'll start by defining the word - coherence ~ That is = Define it as it's applied to physical systems - like - respiration - immune function - blood pressure - you know - the stuff your body is always up to ~ Essentially - it means = In sync - in tune - or = Patterns - that mirror each other - and so = Work smoothly together ~ In other words = Patterns that agree to - or support - an overall healthy kind of condition ~ Its opposite is = Incoherent ~ It's what you'd expect - with that - in - in the front of it ~ It means = A disability - out of sync - out of tune - an interference (such as drunkenness or exhaustion) - to healthy function - and = As the research I'm referring to has found dramatic evidence of = Another contributor to such a state (incoherence) - is = Bad feelings - or = Not - what we do - but = What we think.

Now - I'll describe two measuring tools - in common use in hospitals - that are the key components of how this research was conducted ~ The first is = An electrocardiogram - or - ECG (also commonly known as an EKG for its German spelling - elektrokardiogram) Its purpose - is to measure - and plot out as a graph - the electrical activity of the heart ~ The second is = The electroencephalogram - or - EEG ~ It does much the same thing - only = Its focus - is on the brain ~ By employing these two machines - and comparing their results - it's possible to directly measure - the amount - of coherence - or - incoherence - of the two frequency patterns they record - and so = See - printed out in black and white - how well the heart and brain are cooperating ~ In other words = Is your day a smooth voyage - or - a rough one?

[[[[[[[[Berger's Brain Waves:

The inventor of the brain wave measuring device - called on electroencephalogram - or EEG (by way of repetition) - was a German scientist named Hans Berger ~ That information in itself is precise - though hardly unusual (you'll find several inventive Germans mentioned in this course) - but = The inspiration - for his dedication to the study of the human brain - is.

While attending University in the early 1890s - with the intention of becoming an astronomer - instead = He became disenchanted with city life and decided to join the cavalry for his year of compulsory military service - and - since it was peace time = Have a bit of fun riding horses in the country and such ~ One day - during a training exercise - he was thrown from his horse and narrowly missed being trampled by a team of artillery horses pulling a field gun ~ All in a military days work of course - but = That night he received a telegram from his family urgently inquiring about his well-being - due to the fact - that his sister (whom he described as being quite close to him) - had been overcome by a terrible dread for his life at the very moment of his near fatal accident.

Puzzled - yet intrigued by this event - as soon as Hans completed his year of service he returned to University - intent on studying medicine - and - getting to the bottom of how - what he termed psychic energy - could travel from one brain to another - as it did between his sister and himself.

It took Berger many years - of mostly solitary work - but he finally developed a system of recording - Berger rhythms - or what we now call brain waves ~ It was the first time that electrical brain activity (a phenomenon already known to occur) - was witnessed to be connected to - or produced by - different states of mind.

Meanwhile - psychically driven Hans - conducted hundreds of experiments on telepathy (or mind to mind communication) - with subjects in states of hypnotic trance ~ Unfortunately - he never succeeded in proving much in that direction ~ Nor were his brain recordings looked upon with much more than skepticism and distrust by contemporary scientists.

In the end (or 1941 - a difficult year for millions of other people as well) - having suffered a long illness and a terrible skin infection - the much misunderstood scientist took his own life (An odd turn of phrase don't you think - as in = Took it where?) Too bad for poor old Hans though - that he was not psychic himself - or he would have realized that his work had revealed the basic brain mechanisms that would later be used in medical imaging devices - such as the PET scan and MRI - which = Are now relied on by hospitals around the globe - not to mention how his remarkable EEG has been put to use in further studies of the brain - and of course = Psychic abilities ~ One can only hope = He's receiving the message now.]]]]]]]]]]

Okay - that makes for an interesting set of data on its own - but = It's relatively useless - without investigating - what causes - those patterns - to match - or not ~ Therefore - since the study was inspired by an investigation of = IF - the heart's function goes beyond being just a mechanical pump = The natural choice - for pinpointing those causes (or what makes those patterns - printed out by those machines - look the way they do) - was to test the effects of different emotional states ~ After all - for thousands of years the heart has been considered to be - the seat of emotion - and - as it turns out = There may have been a very good reason for that belief.

So - they hooked people up to their machines - and - gave them the assignment of producing different feelings - or emotional states in themselves ~ Then = They stood back and watched the readouts ~ What they saw - was both - astounding - and somehow - really not surprising at all ~ For the negative feelings - rage - frustration - anxiety - terror (the list goes on) - the two graph patterns - basically - only resembled each other by the fact they were both graphs ~ When it came to - the positive feelings - love - admiration - fascination - and - you guessed it - happiness - there were strong and obvious -

correlations - or resemblances - or = Coherence ~ Added up - it appears to be - clear evidence - that in those states we're inclined to label positive - the heart and brain cooperate with each other far more harmoniously than they do - under the stress of - so-called - negative emotions.

But - the math didn't stop there ~ With the addition of other machines - and physical reaction measurements - a much broader view of other body systems - and their relationships with each other during different emotional states - was graphed - and compared - and tested - and retested (like good scientists will) - until - it became solidly obvious = That the higher the level of heart/brain coherence - the stronger and more efficient - all other systems function as well ~ Which means = The more time spent - in a positive emotional state - the better your cells are supplied with oxygen and nutrients - the quicker your immune system deals with intruders - your blood pressure regulates - hormones travel faster - tissues regenerate - even your hair looks better ~ Clearly = They were on to a good thing.

So - they didn't stop there either ~ They began experimenting with ways - to entrain - that coherence - or synchronization - of electromagnetic waves between head and chest (but first - a short detour) = If - you've ever read Army orders from the past - you'll know the word entrain meant = Everyone get on the damn train ~ Well - that's exactly the idea here = Trains go to one place (at a time that is) You don't see a train - with an engine coupled on either end - and both trying to pull in opposite directions ~ They don't do that ~ But - we do (figuratively speaking) Anyway = Those experiments produced more of the same - positive results - when - very particular - yet very simple - techniques were followed ~ Such as = Maintaining an awareness of the area of the heart - and - thinking appreciative thoughts - like gratitude and admiration ~ In the process - they discovered - that such techniques had a strong influence on increasing cognitive (remember that word) - abilities = You know - learning - understanding - retaining information ~ They also showed significant results in reducing anxiety around testing - and other performance related stresses ~ The math - at this point - is very easy to follow = Positive plus positive - equals (or is in coherence with) = Positive ~ Perhaps you know some astronauts that might benefit from this study?

[[[[[[[[[Feel This:

So - what's with this word - feeling - I keep chucking around as though it always means the same thing - like a basketball means = A basketball.

Well - obviously - there's much the same problem with any word that describes a set - or range - of things - grouped together under one word - such as plants or buildings ~ Big difference between an oak tree and a geranium - a skyscraper and a chicken coop ~ Same thing - when you are comparing a bee sting to a broken heart ~ Those are both feelings - but - they require more words - to arrive at their specific meaning.

Therefore = I'll give you my specific meaning for the word = Feeling ~ In the context of this course that is.

First off = I'm not talking about - physical sensation that is the direct sensory result of a physical interaction - such as crashing your snowboard into a tree - or yanking splinters out of your feet - or the good ones either - like stepping into a hot bath - or getting a massage ~ So - forget about that type of feeling (at least in the context in question here) - because = Physical sensation is involved in what I'm talking about - but = Of a variety - that is produced by an interior interaction - a friction - knock together - rub up against - what have you - of two non-thing things (whose non-ness may appear a bit confusing after using so many physical specifics - but =) Those two things are - emotions - and - thoughts - and they = Are complexities all on their own - which one word sign posts can't do much more than wave in the general direction of either - but = That's where the word feeling - narrows down to a more precise definition.

Feelings - are the point of impact between an emotion - let's say - surprise - and - a thought - like = I know just what to do with the bonus I got in my paycheck today - which then generates = A feeling (an electromagnetic energy - to be exact) - which in that example = Probably falls in the happiness category - and = As often as not - is accompanied by a physical sensation (an electrochemical response) - meaning = Some type of bodily signal - peculiar to that particular intersection of thought and emotion - such as sensations of tightening - loosening - lightness - heaviness - falling - rising - you know what they're like.

A feeling - is a whole experience - layered up with information - cause and effect - reasons and responses - that can be mined for insights - understandings - and general mirror like reflections of who we are (which is to say - how we think and behave - according to the results of our past learning) - provided = You are paying attention - or are willing to ~ Either way - focus or distraction - we're all producing the things - and = Experiencing that combination of perceptual forces which result in - feelings - right now.

So = How does that feel?|||||||||

Let's go back to those astronauts for a moment then - even if they're not quite astronauts (I'm referring to those Biosphere II volunteers - of course) But - let's look at them - from the point of view - of electromagnetic fields.

There is yet another element to this systems coherency business - and - we can approach it through the more standard use of the word - coherence ~ Which is = Coherent - and its opposite = Incoherent ~ Not unlike the earlier use of the word = They are centered on levels of successful - or unsuccessful - communication ~ If you were just slapped awake at 4:00 a.m. - after a night of heavy drinking - and ordered - in some obscure language from the Brazilian rain forest - to explain the pile of underwear on your motel room floor - chances are - you will not find those orders very what? Of course = Coherent ~ Which might mean = That your own reply would be equally = Incoherent.

Well = It's the interaction - or communication - between magnetic fields (that same Heartmath study shows) - that seems to play - a hidden - yet extremely significant role - in whether or not communication - between people - is coherent.

See = Everywhere we go - we are at the center of a whirling force field - whose area of strongest influence is - 3 - 4 - 5 feet in all directions (not to mention dwindling off to the far reaches of the universe) - and = This field - appears to be telling - or attempting to tell - anything within that range - how we feel.

Returning to our EEG and ECG machines = It was found - that someone - practiced - in entraining their own heart/brain fields to coherence - would often cause the EEG readout (or measured brain wave pattern) - of another person - to come into sync - or similar pattern - with the ECG (or measured heart frequency) - that person (the practiced one) - was producing ~ To simplify that statement = One person's heart - was affecting - another person's brain ~ The obvious question is = Is that what we're doing - all the time? The somewhat less obvious question is = Is it better to - entrain - your systems coherency - by appreciating Betty - because you want to happily survive on Earth (never mind surviving on Mars) - or - to hold a grudge against her - for hogging the chocolate pudding?

Class Six - YES?

BREATHE (That's right = Up you get = All the way = That's it = Get that tongue touching the roof your mouth ~ What you're doing with that - is activating another energy pathway - or acupressure point - that connects other circuits of energy moving upward from your lower body to your head ~ Provided you believe that ~ Let me remind you though = That you're busy finding out what to believe - by doing ~ So - don't let me stop you = Do)

So = Can you tell me about how the assignment went? Did you find yourself smack in the middle of now? Did you have any great revelations about how to choose happiness? Did you want to? Did you try? Did you feel happier? What did you feel? What about your vision - have you noticed any changes? Are you becoming more aware of what's around you? Are you becoming more aware of what you think about yourself - or how you feel? Do you notice ways that the three activities -connect? What does that feel like?

Let's look at a way of connecting those assignments - plus a good many other things - possibly = Everything ~ Which = I'm thinking would warm up nicely with an = {{{**Inventory Time**}}}

What do you think - is the most powerful word - in the English language?

Yes = Those words have their power - but = What could be the most powerful one?

What if - one of the simplest words you can imagine? What if - I told you the word is the one I just used a moment ago? What if - that word is = Yes?

That's true = It doesn't sound very powerful ~ But (again) = What if - it is?

I'll demonstrate something to you ~ You see this ball? Alright = Catch ~ Now - when I hold out my hand - closed in a fist like this - and keep it that way - what do you think will happen - when you throw the ball back to me? Alright = Throw it back ~ So = Did what you think would happen - happen? Sure = I couldn't catch it that way ~ So – let's say my closed fist - represents the energy of = No ~ Okay? Catch ~ Now - when I hold my hand like this - with the fingers open palm up - it represents the energy of what? Right = It's Yes ~ So = What do you think will happen - when you throw it to me this time? Okay = Go ~ Were you right? Sure = It had to be an accurate throw - and myself coordinated enough to catch it ~ But = What's the difference - between the two?

Look at it again ~ This is my hand as No ~ How would you describe what No can do?

This is my hand as Yes ~ How would you describe what it can do?

What are the feelings associated with No? How about Yes? Which are more enjoyable? Ah = There can be enjoyable things about both - can't there? Interesting point that ~ I'd store that thought for later.

Here's another demonstration.

You hold the ball ~ Close your fingers around it tight now ~ You're not going to let any of us have it ~ Okay? Is that a kind of No energy? What happens if we all want the ball? Right = We'll try to get it ~ We could ask for it - but = You don't want us to have it ~ So = What do you do? Of course = You say = No ~ Then what's apt to happen? Yup = You'll have to defend it ~ There are games that use exactly this kind of no of course - and they can be great fun to play - but = Do they work - if only one player controls the ball all the time and won't let go no matter what? Or - can another player catch the ball with their hands closed? So is a team - a type of Yes energy? Which makes the game more fun to watch or play (in a team work kind of way that is) - the Yes energy - or the No? Which one wins the game?

So = Why does it work that way?

Do you know what the word - prefix - means? You know - from your English class ~ That's it = It's certain letters - that come at the beginning of a word - which modify - or change - its meaning ~ What does it mean to put the letters - a-n-t-i - at the beginning of a word then? Right = It means - against something - like - anti-drugs - or - anti-war ~ How about the letters - p-r-o? Yeah = They're the opposite meaning ~ Meaning = For something - like pro-war - pro-drugs ~ Are - anti and pro - Yes and No energies?

Let's see if we can pull them apart and find out how they work.

What's the example I just gave - of both a pro and an anti position - about the same thing? Right - I did give two such examples ~ Just checking to see if you were paying attention ~ But - let's look at the war one = If you are pro-war - what do you do? Yeah = You support war ~ You vote for it ~ Pay for it ~ Fight in it ~ In other words - you - want - war? So if you want war - you must think what about it? Sure = You'd have to think it was the right thing to do ~ What feeling would you be trying to get from it? What was that one we're all looking for? That's the one = Happiness ~ Of course - war - where the fighting is at least - seldom makes people happy ~ But - that's not the point.

Okay - so what about anti-war - what do you do then? Right = You do things to try to stop war ~ Like what? Have marches - demonstrations - make speeches - write articles? Sure ~ Are people who are anti-war angry about war? So = Are they fighting against war? What do you do when you go to war? Exactly - you fight ~ So = Are people who are anti-war having a war against war? Does it work? Yes? No? Sometimes? When does it work? Right = When enough people agree - there shouldn't be a war ~ What is the opposite of war? Of course = Peace ~ Do you think war's end - because people don't want war - or - because they want peace? Indeed - the majority of war's end - because one side gives up ~ But - they don't have to - they could go on fighting till they're all dead - and yet = That almost never happens ~ Still - that's not the point here ~ What we're talking about here - is that difference between pro and anti ~ So - think about it now = If you are fighting - against fighting - are you really - against fighting? And what is a war? Fighting - yes ~ So = Would that mean that anti-war is really pro-war? I know it sounds like twisting an idea around to try to simplify something that seems complex - but = What if - it really is that simple? What if - the reason any action that is anti something - works - is because of the part that is - pro - something else?

[[[[[[[[[Doctor Dude's Dictionary - word six - Gestalt:

Now here is an excellent word = Gestalt ~ It's pronounced like the ge in guest - the st in stop - and the alt in salt ~ It was a German word originally - but now crosses all kinds of language barriers just as easily as its meaning puts other invisible barriers in the mental blender ~ What that meaning is = Is a unification (meaning - a fusion - an agreement frappecino) - of physical (senses) - psychological (ideas - beliefs) - and symbolic references (words - images) - that make up a whole response - or reaction - to a place - event - situation or relationship - which = Any one of those references alone - would not describe sufficiently {{Now reread that last sentence and ignore the bits in parentheses}}

So = What I'm saying is - you walk into a room - and inside you - a system of information gathering - sorting - weighing - recognizing - and imagining - kicks in (not that it wasn't on already) All the relationships present - between sensory input - emotions - ideas - purpose of objects - interaction of people - animals - atmospheric conditions - the whole soup of perception - settles on a kind of thinking/feeling/sensory tone - which describes (or perhaps more accurately - is) - the whole experience in that moment for you ~ And that = Is a gestalt.]]]]]]]]]

Let's keep cutting up the pro and anti-war idea - because = It's possibly the easiest place to see the difference I'm referring to.

So = Why would someone be anti-war? That's right = All kinds of terrible suffering and destruction are the result of war ~ Are people happy - who are suffering and dying and having their property destroyed? So = Does that mean - people who are - anti-war - are really - motivated - by wanting happiness for other people and themselves? Well = It would seem that way - wouldn't it? Ah - but = Do they get it by shouting and cursing and hating politicians - or maybe throwing bricks and blowing up government buildings? Not likely - no ~ So = How do they get it? There it is = By doing things that are pro-peace - pro-happiness.

What about anti-drug laws - do they work? Well sure - there are thousands and thousands of people in prison for breaking drug laws ~ But = Do people still use them -

including plenty of those people actually in jail? Do any of you? So = The laws don't stop drug use? What is the opposite of being on drugs? The word - sobriety - covers all that - doesn't it? What do you think would be the best way to prevent - or draw people away from - drug use then? Bingo (fun to say that word isn't it) = Bingo = Do - things - that are pro-sobriety.

We'll talk more about that word sobriety another time ~ It has even deeper roots than you might think ~ Let's link up some ideas here first.

Remember how we talked about choosing happiness - and its relationship with time? When is it - that happiness happens again? So = Where is your attention - when you are unhappy? Exactly = On the past - or the future ~ And = That's because the cause of your unhappy ideas - comes from one or the other? Where do you have to place your attention in order to - choose - happiness then? Right again = On - happiness itself - right now ~ So = If you are anti-war - where is your attention? Yup = On war ~ And = You're against war - because you want peace? So = Where do you think - you would have to put your attention - to experience peace?

[[[[[[[[Popular Violence:

Have you ever noticed - that when someone is hurt or injured in a public place - just about anyone that happens to be nearby will rush to help that person? Or perhaps - you haven't witnessed such things ~ Or in fact - have witnessed the opposite - where people are deliberately hurting someone - or are afraid to go to the assistance of another - for fear of being harmed themselves.

There is a distinction - between those opposing reactions - that brings to question what the true nature - of human nature - really is ~ In other words = Are we compassionate beings at heart - or - dangerous savages only civilized on the surface?

By way of answering that question - at its most direct personal core measurement = What is your preference? Meaning = Do you prefer to go about your life - in a setting where people are courteous and peaceful and basically non-threatening - or - in a war zone subjected to constant danger where fear and suspicion and violent behavior are the norm?

Well - duh = Of course the first choice is preferable - or certainly easier ~ But then = Maybe you have a secret fantasy of testing your mettle in that war world (which is not an exclusively male fantasy anymore - girlfriends) You read books about war and violence - watch movies about it - play video games - stare off into space during geometry class imagining yourself as a powerful warrior hero who is armed to the teeth and trained to split second deadly reactions with every weapon imaginable.

Okay - cool - so = Why?

But - before you answer - let me ask another question = Have you ever grown a garden - or kept houseplants - or just been around people who do? How about = Owned pets - or raised livestock - visited a zoo - a farm?

Yes = That was several questions ~ But = If - you answered yes to any of them - then = You probably understand that there are certain conditions required (such as nutrients - water - the correct temperature range - you know the list) - for any of those organisms to thrive - or more importantly (at least from a basic survival measurement of importance) - to remain alive at all ~ Are there similar conditions required for your survival - your well-being?

Again then = Why - would anyone nurture a fantasy of a warrior lifestyle - when nothing about that lifestyle (meaning - the conditions that dictate such a lifestyle) - nurture well being?

Don't get me wrong now = I'm not questioning your intelligence - or anyone else's (at least not as directly as all that) I'm questioning something deeper ~ I've galloped around on those fantasies in the past myself ~ We all entertain dreams of grandeur and heroism - geniuses or idiots alike (though granted - it does tend to be a more exclusively male preoccupation in the way of statistical grouping) - but = The question remains = Why violent ones?

Why is it = That when you (or I) - go into a video rental place - at least a third of the pictures on the covers - are of actors holding some kind of weapon (again - a good many of them are female) Are a third of the people you encounter on the street - holding weapons? Why do we love those guns and swords and grim expressions so?

Why is it = That those individuals - who are most apt to display flags and declare themselves patriotic lovers of their country - are also most likely (as a very generalized statement) - to take pride in things military - support military solutions to questions of foreign policy - and identify the military and the country - as the same thing? Do they want wars in their own neighborhoods? Do they want to fight in wars themselves?

Even - if those answers are = Yes (because sometimes they are) = Is a battleground a good place to raise food - or children - small businesses - stable economies? Are gang members - who protect their fellow gang members - by killing members of enemy gangs - heroes? Why are soldiers - called heroes? Sure = There's bravery and self sacrifice and all - but = Mostly - soldiering is numbingly dull - or intensely terrifying - among young people who would rather be somewhere else - and = Isn't murder illegal? Is there a good reason why it's illegal? What makes us support that contradiction?

There can be any number of judgments assumed to be behind these questions (and of course - there are) - but = The real question is still = Why? Indeed = There are plenty of learned minds - that have thought and taught and published books on the subject - but = I'm not asking them = I'm asking = You = Why?

Why - do we (that's essentially everyone in the world by the way) - prefer peace - require peace to have enough to eat - to heal injuries - maintain sanity - basically support all levels of health in all ways - and yet = So many of that - we - romanticize past - present - and future wars? Why do we make laws to ensure peace - enforce those laws - are protected by those laws - simply assume that others around us will follow those laws -

and yet = Maintain (meaning - think - act - print bumper stickers) - that the way to uphold those laws - in matters of dramatic disagreements between nations - is to break them? Why do we measure strength in its potential for violence - pride in enduring suffering and loss - and security - in our ability to destroy lives and property?

And then (I mean really) = Just think about the amount of money that's spent on all that - strength and pride and security - billions and more billions - tens of billions - hundreds of billions - by the day - the month - the year ~ Did you know - that if you had a job - which paid you one dollar every second - and - you were always at work - 24/7 - 365 days a year - it would still take you 33 years to earn a billion dollars ~ Have you ever considered = That if this nation were just a single individual (or a small group of individuals) - and that person (or persons) - spent the same proportion of their huge income on weaponry and security systems as this nation does - that = We'd be talking about a dangerously insane mind.

Might you say = That perhaps - we are a bit confused - when it comes to our own best interests? Might you still wonder = Why?||||||||||

Pretty simple huh? (If you agree) That thing with the ball was pretty simple as well - wasn't it? Too simple - you might say ~ And the rest of this as well maybe ~ But = Look at this next idea - and try to put off that decision a bit longer.

In reference to the closed hand thing = Is - No - a defensive position? So - does that mean = No - is limited in what it can do? Would that mean = Closed to new possibilities? How about change? Yeah = That's a biggy = No - is very much against change ~ Do things in this world change all the time? So = Does that mean - that if you say no to change - and things change anyway - that you are in pain? How about alone? Is a closed hand any good for shaking? What kind of touching does a fist usually do?

So how about the Yes hand - what kinds of limits does it have? So = Whatever possibilities are open for a hand - are open for it? What about change - is the open hand capable of adapting? How about being helpful? Friendly? Kind?

Sure - it's simple - but = Does it make sense? Is it possible = That differences between thoughts and actions - could be that simple?

Ah - you're thinking - aren't you.

It's true = Sometimes - No - is a positive thing (you'll remember saying that earlier when I asked which one - Yes or No - feels better) But = Look deeper ~ Which energy is really at work - when No feels good?

Say you said = No - I won't steal that - or = No - I won't have sex with you ~ Are you really saying - yes - to some strength in yourself?

So - of course - the other way around as well = Yes - I will kill him = or = Yes - I hate those people too ~ It's not really the words is it? What is it then? That's it = It's the power represented by the words ~ What is it that again - that powers things?   Yup = Energy.

As far as words go though - consider this one = Vibration ~ What if - the energy - of Yes and No - work as vibrations - like guitar strings do? You've all heard the phrases - good vibes - and bad vibes? Obviously - vibes is an abbreviation - for vibration ~ Well - maybe that word explains far more - than you may have given it credit for ~ What if - the vibrations you create - echo back to you - like a bat navigating through the night - and so - what you find to eat out there (so to speak) - are the same kind of vibrations - of Yes - or No?   In other words = What if - how you vibrate - is what brings you - your experience?

Let's go directly to some vibrations then (not that we can ever really get away from them) But first = Stand up - if you would - and let's do that - BREATHE - thing ~ Come on now ~ It won't kill you ~ How many times have you heard that one? I know - but humor me ~ I guarantee - something interesting will happen.

Okay = Deep breath..............

Great - but don't sit down yet = I have a question ~ Yeah = I know - that's not surprising.

The question is = Do you want to be happy?

Alright then - on the count of three - I want everyone to shout that answer as loud as they can.

YES!

That's not loud ~ Again.

YES!!!

Once more and really mean it this time.

YES!!!!!!

Excellent ~ Go ahead and sit down.

It's time for your next assignment ~ Anyone guess what it might be? Yes = Exactly = It's - noticing - that Yes energy - at work - and working it - vibrating it - like we just did ~ Of course - one way to do that - is to notice - No energy - at work - by way of contrast ~ But - I think we'll stick to Yes this time - because - it's more fun ~ So this is what you do = Notice - when - you - agree ~ Someone asks you to do something - and you say yes - notice that you did - then = Notice what it feels like ~ Or - when you agree with someone

- about anything = Notice - what that feels like ~ Then = Agree with your self - for agreeing = Feel - the yes in there = Really - allow - it - to be complete - an accomplishment - an achievement - a reward - a total = Yes ~ And = Notice - if that - Yes - is the same - as your - happiness ~ Meaning = A feeling ~ Of course - you'll have to get in there - and really feel it - to find out - but - after all - you - are - in there - already.

Another thing you can do - to get that Yes energy flowing - is exactly what we just did ~ Shout it ~ Answer your question about your own happiness - with what you want = YES!!! But don't stop there = Go there = Experience it = Feel it = Spend time with it ~ What else are you going to do with your time? Oh I know = You've got plenty on to take up your time ~ But - that's the beauty of happiness = You can do it at the same time - as you do anything else - without interfering - with what you're doing ~ Except maybe - being unhappy ~ And - best of all - you can do it - while you're doing what? That's it = Breathing.

THE PERCEPTION PAPERS - number two

Sniffing around the right words:

When you smell things - you are actually drawing tiny bits (molecules - to be specific) - of those things into your nose (disturbing as that may be) - where they quickly dissolve in the gooey mucus which covers your olfactory epithelium (a couple of dime size spots located just north of the bridge of your nose and slightly behind your eyes at the top of your nasal passages) - where = A whole bunch (many millions) - of olfactory receptor neurons (a specialized type of nerve cell) - receive those molecules - and relay their specific odor information (out of about a thousand different recognition possibilities) - to the next link in the smelling chain = The olfactory bulb - which is a part of your brain.

Molecules - of course - are more than very tiny things ~ They are really - really - really tiny things ~ Like everything else though - they vary in size ~ Water molecules - that familiar combination of hydrogen and oxygen atoms (H_2O) - are one of the smaller varieties ~ A single drop of water can contain something like two million quadrillion (that's a 2 with 21 zeros after it) - molecules ~ Different molecules - behave differently as well ~ The molecules of gases - such as hydrogen and oxygen (when they are not combined as water - which means all sliding around with each other as a liquid) - are separate - and constantly in motion - often at speeds of hundreds of miles an hour ~ At those speeds - as well as slower ones - gas molecules are slamming into each other all the time and bouncing all over the place.

But - again = When you smell something - it's because = That something allowed some of its molecules to escape (which is called - volatile) - to get knocked around in that chaos of bumper car gases - which = Deliver those escapees to your nose pronto - where = That first process of olfactory information gathering (I described a moment ago) - does its thing ~ The completion of the - what's that smell - identification - and working out how to react to it - takes place deeper in your head however - in the area known as = The limbic system ~ That part of your brain - occupies itself with several survival oriented functions - such as - telling you when you're hungry or thirsty or should sweat or shiver or really get down to flirting ~ It's also = Where emotional responses originate - which = Is why odors - aromas - scents - stinks - and stenches - can trigger so many different emotions (memory is also more closely linked to the sense of smell than any of the other senses) - as well as the instinctive reactions - of come closer - or run away.

Thing is = All of our sensory processing overlaps - includes - is a part of - or integrated with - our judgments and memories and adopted personality traits - which = Are all emotional to one level or another ~ The exercise - I'm about to describe - is a way of investigating - and expanding your awareness of - those relationships - from an angle we've all touched on - yet seldom scratched very deeply into (unless of course - you're in the perfume business - or some equally aromatic calling) - because = What you're going to do - is describe - what you smell.

When I say describe = I don't mean - identify - like = I smell lemons ~ I mean = What do lemons smell like? Do they smell - pointy - bright - active - clean? Is there a picture that comes to mind? Again - not a picture of lemons = A picture - the scent of lemons - pops into your head = Maybe a memory - a place - a person = Or a feeling ~ Now we're getting somewhere = What does the scent of lemons feel like? Vibrant - contracted - busy? What color is it? Yes = Lemons are yellow - but - the feeling = What color is that? What texture? What is it? What's the smell - picture - memory - color - texture - feeling - sound like - in language?

So = When you are walking somewhere - waiting somewhere - whatever it happens to be you're doing - when = You smell something strongly - or even just barely = Snuff it up - taste it - roll it around in there - really examine it - then = Describe it to yourself ~ Is it smoky fungus earthworm wet leather staring down a cobwebbed cellar stairs full of secrets? Or maybe - slippery cold bite of slushy March morning with a touch of sweet sad and low clouds? Is that what the newly plowed field across the road and a bag of crushed aluminum cans - smells like to you?

Go ahead - sniff around - use that sense - pay attention to it - and = Feel how it bubbles up - all the other stuff it's connected to in your mind - especially = Those words ~ No need to wax poetic now - don't trouble yourself over choosing the words - just breathe in - and see what comes out ~ It's especially fun - when you encounter an odor you can't identify = There aren't constricting specific names then - it's just your nose - and a whole paint box of textures and colors and feelings - and of course - molecules - just waiting to melt into your imagination ~ So = Describe them.

N.P.U. - Chapter Six - Philosophy?

So = If - you are the generator of an electromagnetic radio beacon broadcasting into space = What's all that energy - doing - out there?

Well = What if - it works the way sonar does? In other words = Could it be - that energy of yours (meaning - all of ours) - rushes out there - and - bounces off some - other energy - then returns to you a message - or a response - to the message - your energy was carrying - and - that response - is - the world you (or we) - see?

What I'm getting at here (as well as repeating - if you recall a certain reference to bats looking for dinner I made earlier) - is a question - that's often on the lips of - popular culture ~ What it is - is = Do we - create - our reality?

Before we go scratching around for answers = There is a distinction that should be made ~ It concerns the differences and feeding habits - of two - often competing - yet just as often (when you crawl under the surface) - difficult to separate creatures called = Philosophy and Science ~ We've already spent some time describing - the customs - of science ~ So bear that in mind - as we track down - philosophy ~ First though = The following - is a general rule of thumb - for identifying the tracks of one - when mixed up with the other = In the case of science = Belief - is a question of - enough evidence ~ Whereas with philosophy = Evidence - is a question - of enough belief.

The trouble is = The edges of these tracks are often rather blurred and run together ~ Questions arise in both - that look to the other for answers - as do the answers - that create more questions ~ Of course - what we call answers - or understanding - are always connected to - couched in - or described through - familiar references - which means = A type of parallel with the thinking - that considers the deciphering of ancient writings - by translating them into modern English use and definitions - to have arrived at the same meaning - which = Given huge differences in belief - technology - customs - and day to day life = Just can't be true ~ But - enough of the confusion = Let's look at some stabs at definition.

If you look in a dictionary - you'll find a long description of the word philosophy broken into a dozen parts all pointing at studying - something - that = If you were to trace a kind of theme through what it is philosophy is studying - you'd probably settle on a word like - knowledge - or wisdom - something you'd do in your head - that you wouldn't need other body parts for - aside from maybe turning some pages - or writing your own ~ Philosophy - is a world of intellect - invisible - personal - yet touching the underlying essence of - every - thing - by way of mental understanding (some intolerant scientists might say - mental oversitting) - rather than mechanical means - like dissection or excavation.

Science - on the other hand - more often than not - requires those body parts - particularly hands ~ While - at the same time = The two share the path of investigating - the why and how - of bodies (and nature) - being - here - as well as - what - here is - for bodies (and nature) - to - BE - in ~ You can tease science away to run on its own track - thumbing it's dirty nose at philosophy for having its head in the clouds - only to find them intersecting again - a short distance away - as science scratches its chin over which way to turn - and philosophy grows fatter on a diet of science.

What you could say for certain - is = What I just said - is far more philosophical than scientific ~ Unless of course - you break it down and analyze it for motivations - double meanings - rhythmic patterns - and potential responses to heavy-handed subtle humor ~ The point is = Statements that solidly divide - science and philosophy - into two armed camps opposing each other - just plain have their backs turned to the lively trade passing between the two of them ~ The truth of the matter is = Certain elements of both disciplines have recognized their investigations to be running in parallel courses ~ Which means = Either they'll be politely waving at each other indefinitely - or - eventually = Arriving at the same destination.

The name emblazoned on one such philosophical train is = Metaphysics ~ Admittedly - many scientists would claim there is no such train - only a fog shrouded station - with no timetables - where = If there are trains - they neither go in - nor come out ~ That's because - metaphysics - is the branch of philosophy that deals with - the mystical - the great mystery of being - and = Ultimate reality ~ It's - what comes after - or beyond - the physical - and - the physics - that tries to explain - how the physical works (at least in the sense - that physics hasn't managed to do all that explaining yet) So - to repeat that sense = Metaphysics - points the way for physics to follow - meaning - it - supplies the big mysteries - to attempt the solving of ~ Not that all physicists would agree with that statement - any more than they would consult fortunetellers to design their next experiment ~ Which is not to say - that a philosopher necessarily would either ~ Just the same = Those two branches of - inquiry - more and more - are finding themselves on either side of a very flimsy partition - talking about - the same thing ~ That same thing - of course - is a question ~ That question is = What is the source of this experience - this interaction - with stuff - with ideas - with feelings - with possibility - we call life - or = With that observer of life - we call = Consciousness?

|||||||||| Metaphysical:

As a word - metaphysical - breaks down to two parts - which describe one idea - or active function (sound electromagnetically familiar) Those parts began with - meta = Which means - a sort of odd mixture of locations - somewhere between (which includes - in between) - with - beside - after - beyond - and - changing ~ Then there's - physical = Which means - physical - or - having to do with form - physically existent things - in relationship with the laws that govern physical things (otherwise known as physics) Put them together = And you get a process of investigating the nature of reality - which = Is - a neither here nor there - beyond where - beingness - of physicality.

If that doesn't make sense = That's because it's a word about a different means of making sense - then adding up what makes sense in a purely physical sense of making sense out of physical things.

In that sense = Metaphysical - is beyond our five senses operating in time - beyond perceptual abilities to determine what the laws of the physical universe really are - and yet = Metaphysical - loves to talk - and speculate - and generally roam around in big ideas ~ You could call it a mind game - or a game of mind - and = It's such narrow distinctions of language - such slipping through the cracks of meaning - where metaphysics (that branch of philosophy which is described as metaphysical) - is a hairsplitting (you know - shaving ideas down to their tiniest parts - in order to compare them to each other) - form of reasoning - which = At the same time - operates on such a grand scale - it can stack up universes like the pages of a dictionary.

What we're talking here = Are measuring tools - which discard measurements as the final word ~ The fact is = If you're looking for a final word - metaphysics - is unlikely to provide it ~ Unless of course - you count the word - infinity ~ Although that's hardly a narrowing down to one thing kind of word.

The beauty of metaphysics - is kind of like - the beauty of beauty = It's an experience - a feeling of understanding - which remains = An open question - and = An invitation to more ~ Experience - is the byline of metaphysics - because = It never stands still - it slides one now to the next ~ Physics (without the meta bit) - is all about standing still ~ Even as it describes movement - it employs fixed measurements - weight - distance - time - density - numbers - numbers - numbers ~ It's when physics goes quantum - that the edges of the two become ever so slightly blurred (not that physicists are inclined to let on - especially when the blur is distinctly blurry) - and there = Is the reason for this brief scratch into the word metaphysical = You want to truly understand = You have to feel ~ You want to truly feel = You have to question ~ It's there - where you get into new words - like - metamorphosis (look it up if you need to) - and - all that crawling around = Pays off.|||||||||

A big question - yes ~ No wonder it's so much easier - just to wonder why the idiot in front of you is driving so slowly ~ But - it's that word - wonder - in there - that all of it seems to spin out from ~ Wonder - is that movement of mind - that is curiosity - doubt - suspicion - surprise - awe - marveling - journeying down paths of speculation - weighing different outcomes - knocking against the barriers of the - known ~ While that same action of mind - in language form (or the other half of the definition) - is the reason for its leaping into action - the wonder of child birth - of a clear night full of stars - whales spouting - mountains rising into the clouds ~ We're drawn to the gravitational field of that big question - like magnetism - and = Like magnetism - it generates the electricity - of seeking answers - which generate more questions - which….

Let's narrow it down some then - by placing it in the hands of another word = Inspiration ~ The first word - the dictionary I looked in - used to begin its definition of inspiration was = Stimulation ~ We all know that one ~ We go looking for it regularly ~ The local café would do a poor business without it ~ No coffee - no sweets - music - art - newspapers - conversation - and - members of the opposite sex - the same sex - and any idea of sex in between? Stimulation - is what makes - action - active.

Okay ~ That same definition goes on to use the word = Faculties ~ Are we talking a bunch of teachers here? No = It's mind - these faculties hang out in - and direct - and = Are (or at least - are - part of - since the word faculty means the powers or capacities possessed by the mind) So - what's this - stimulation - doing - to those - faculties? Well - it's raising them to a higher level of - feeling - and - action ~ Which clearly means = That our mind - that gang of student teachers - is a movement - through time and space - of actively feeling - and - actively thinking - intertwined - supporting each other - generating each other - creating - an electromagnetic field.

So = What is it that's doing - this inspiring - this stimulating?

That takes us straight back to the - Big Question (the one about - the source - of this conscious life) - doesn't it? Oh sure = You can trim down inspiration to - seeing an apple fall - and so - work out how gravity functions (to a point at least) - or watching a mountain range at sunset and be driven to paint it ~ A simple - one plus one - explanation - works - until you get to more complex - which came first - the chicken or the egg - kinds of equations - like = When - an inspiration - is larger than the sum of its parts ~ In other words = When - the idea - that just comes to you - is more information - than the amount of information - you had to work with - can account for.

That's - when we reach for another word = Revelation ~ It - does just what it sounds like = It reveals - it opens up a whole new landscape to view ~ But = Where - does that great idea - that just came to you - come from?

Let's go back to our first question ~ Not - The Big One - that is - the Huge Big One about source ~ I mean the other big one = Do we create our reality? (Which - is apparently assuming we can separate the two - but never mind that for the moment)

Ah = But - in order to move - in the direction of an answer - we have to do that thing - that intertwines physics and metaphysics ~ Which is = Consider how our ideas - about what reality is - effect - our relationship with it ~ Which means = To look at the two methods we employ - to come to our understanding - of whatever we understand - which = Are also choices of how to interact with - what we call reality ~ First = There's the reality of objects - known as = Objective reality ~ And then = Ideas - which = Usually get filed under different subjects - hence = Subjective reality ~ So - again - we've reconstructed that boundary between science (objective) and philosophy (subjective) - and - also again - defined that boundary - as - the same thing - which = Is a question = What is reality?

||||||||| Understanding:

There is a tricky little function of the mind that is defined by the statement = I don't understand.

There are different levels - of course - to a lack of understanding - such as = I don't understand the word you just used - compared to = I don't understand how nuclear submarines work ~ The function - I'm pinpointing here - is not about - what is not understood - but - about a state of being - where understanding - is blocked - by the idea - of not understanding.

The difference - is one of attention - specifically = Where is it? Is your - not understanding - happening in what we'll call - a mental location (meaning - where your attention is focused) - like - annoyance - distress - not caring - feeling stupid - being preoccupied - tired - hungry - in love?

The point - is not that those are wrong - or right - places to put your attention ~ The point is = If -your attention is busy not understanding - then = Your chances of understanding - are pretty low.

The real question is = Do you want to understand? Straight up now - an honest yes or no - to whatever the understanding issue is - not right or wrong again - but - yes or no - because = If it's no = It ain't gonna happen ~ If it's yes = There's another question.

Are you willing to accept - that you don't understand? No = It's not a question of where your understanding can go - but = Where it is in that moment - because = What if - you're not understanding - is not about understanding - but about - resisting understanding? What if - when you place your attention - where you really are right now - which is to say = You understand to the level you do - and you don't understand beyond that - and - you accept that - then = You're ready for the next question?

Which is = What - do you understand? In other words = Put your attention on understanding - even if it's limited to = Submarines are boats that are capable of traveling underwater ~ That's hardly complete information about nuclear submarines - but = It's still an understanding = It's a reference point - a place to start - and - an opening to the next question.

Do you want your level of understanding to increase? The answer to that question - is the decision - to move from one place - to another ~ It's where the key turns in the ignition ~ Or not ~ In fact - whether you pick up that key consciously - or unconsciously - your mind has no choice = If - it's going to discard that obstacle idea - of not understanding - and so resume movement toward - understanding ~ The benefit - of making that decision deliberately - or consciously - is discovering the choice is yours = You own the key.

It will take more action than just starting the engine of course - to travel down that road (for example - rereading the chapter this is in the middle of - or some such thing) - but - just knowing that key is in your pocket... Well = Who knows where you'll go.**|||||||||**

The question - of course - that follows in the shadow of all those questions (I've been knocking you back and forth between - for which I'd apologize - except there's a reason for it - so I won't) - is = How - do you find the answer? Maybe that's even the - BIGGEST - question.

The thing is = What if - we've been doing it already? (Meaning = Here comes the reason)

Just like the electromagnetic force - the vibration of learning - is the result of two equal parts - of one force - working together - to extend that force = What if - we move - toward - or in - the creation - or absorption - of knowledge - by employing - both sides of that boundary (that knocking back and forth) = The physical - and - the metaphysical - because = They are - in reality - the same thing? After all - I'm sure you've heard the phrase = Seeing the light ~ Which of course = Is the combination of two physical (meaning - form types of phenomena) - function words - seeing - and light - which = Are all about - nonphysical - realization ~ In other words = Mind.

Alright ~ That's an interesting arrangement of words - perhaps even poetic ~ So = What does it mean? Better yet = How - do you - do it?

Let's look at the example of a few characters from - the history of science and invention - to see how they crossed that - border - and what they brought back with them.

Speaking of how = How about we start with Howe? That's Elias Howe - inventor of the sewing machine (more precisely - one - of the inventors of that machine - but definitely the first to patent one) One night back in 1845 - he dreamt of being hotly pursued by cannibals - whose spear points - he somehow managed to notice despite his terror - had neat little holes - just like the eye of a needle - only = Bored near their sharp tips - rather than the usual blunt end ~ A moment or two after he burst awake - gasping and sweaty - he realized = That's exactly what he needed to do with his sewing machine needles to finally make the blasted things work properly.

A similar - dream revelation - occurred for the German chemist - Frederic August Kekule - when he was trying - unsuccessfully - to formulate the structure of the benzene molecule ~ Having spent hours mentally wrestling snaky chains of atoms - he dozed off in front of his fire - only to find those same chains transformed into real snakes - that twined and twisted as he watched - until = He noticed one of these atomic serpents swallowing its own tail ~ That was it = He awoke with the realization - that the atoms of benzene form a closed ring.

Then there's Thomas Edison - who probably needs no introduction - due to the fact that among his 1,093 patented inventions - were several electric light bulbs ~ But - did you know he was a terrible student in his youth - even considered stupid - with his own father among those doing the considering? Perhaps he was just practicing what he later became famous for among his friends - which was - napping ~ Since he considered spending most of the night sleeping - a great waste of time - he always kept a bed in his laboratory - to which - after hanging a sign on the door which read - Important experiment - Do not disturb - regularly retired - at odd times of day (if you can get away with saying both regular and odd in one sentence) - to refresh his inventiveness.

Now - I'm not suggesting that sleep is - The - gateway to that borderland of revelation - only = That it's one of the more familiar locations were apt to spend time in - where strange mental occurrences are relatively acceptable.

Of course - as far as relativity and familiarity go = There's also the example of Albert Einstein's brain to inspire us ~ And in that - I'm being entirely literal ~ In 1955 - when old Albert died - the surgeon who happened to be on duty at Princeton hospital that night - and so - was the one to conduct an autopsy on the body - gave in to a strange temptation = He stole Bertie's brain ~ In the years following - that organ was finely sliced and diced and microscopically peered at in hopes of discovering the physical secret of genius ~ About thirty of those years later - a neuroanatomist (a fancy word for brainy brain dissector) - named Marian Diamond - obtained a few chunks of the professors thinker herself - and through her work - the secret was at last revealed ~ Or - at least more revealed than it had been ~ And perhaps the true credit - not to discredit the good Doctor - is really due to the generous rats who sacrificed their freedom - and their lives - for that scientific leap.

The secret was - lots of glial cells - which = Act as a kind of electrochemical conductor glue between nerve cells - or neurons (at least according to the very limited and theoretical understanding of the things we have so far) Which means = They (glial cells - which come in half a dozen different forms) - seem to perform the double task - of being cement - and - telephone wire - as well as several other functions - at the same time ~ Their importance (particularly in certain areas of the brain) - is the importance of having the right tools for the job ~ We do all have them - generally outnumbering those other brain cells - neurons - by about ten to one ~ But (like I said) - its numbers - in the right place - that are - part of - what count (and - as that suggests - there are other cellular factors which also count) One of the places those numbers got counted (other than Einstein's brain) - was in the brains of the two groups of rats Diamond had been experimenting with ~ One group - lived a life of bare jail cell boredom - and the other - in a playground world of - stimulating - toys and rodent exercise equipment ~ It's easy enough to guess which group had the higher developed brains ~ But - just in case you're feeling a little fuzzy on that point = Stimulation - is definitely the key.

Okay = You're right = By comparison - it doesn't sound - very stimulating - to go lay down for a nap ~ So - there's obviously more to it than that ~ We're going to have to dig deeper - that's equally obvious ~ But - for the moment = How about - we just sleep on it?

SPECIAL BONUS EXERCISE - number three

Bed Time Review:

There is a moment in every day - that has a much larger effect on your life than most people ever consider ~ Often in fact - even if they do consider it ~ That moment - is the one just after you've arranged yourself physically for sleep (got into bed - turned the light off - closed your eyes and all that) - and - just before you actually fall sleep.

You may have noticed - that piece of time - is unusual (compared to other times of day that is) - for what goes on in your head ~ We're talking = Weird stuff - mental visuals - thoughts - story lines that are more like dreams - even though you're still awake - that go flitting and flashing and generally jumping around in there.

Whether you've noticed those peculiarities or not - that time - is what's called - stage one sleep (by sleep researchers at least) It's also called - the hypnagogic state (hip - like hip - na - like nut with no t - goj - like god with a j - completed by - ick) It's - the transition point - where beta brain waves - stretch out to become alpha waves - and = Although it has long been of great interest to mystical minded and creative people = It remains the least scientifically understood of the stages of sleep ~ Either way = You'll probably find - that sort of mildly hallucinatory experience - is especially apt to happen - if you lay on your back - and = Pay attention ~ Maybe you've done that ~ Maybe you haven't ~ Maybe it doesn't work like that for you at all ~ But = I'm betting that next time - you will pay more attention - to what does go on ~ And = If you follow this exercise - you'll be deliberately influencing those goings on - plus = Much more - as I've already hinted at.

Sleep - is far more than just rest ~ It's a busy process of cellular reconstruction - hormone secretion (in order for the growth hormone - HGH - to be discharged into the bloodstream - the brain must relax into the delta wave pattern of stage three sleep) - and of course - that psychological processing adventure we call dreaming (a state which also includes more important physical functions than - don't meet the eye) Actually = It's really not fully understood what the entire sleep experience is all about ~ Which is to say = What our consciousness does - while we're not conscious ~ However = According to many traditions - disciplines - and a certain amount of common sense - the time just before sleep - is an ideal moment for setting the tone - of what that regeneration process - regenerates.

Therefore = the exercise in question - is designed in a very simple way - to isolate - and promote - everybody's favorite tone = Happiness ~ It works like this.......

When you arrive at that interim (moment separating two events) - between hitting the pillow and out for the count = Close your eyes - and ask yourself = What made me happy today? And then = Answer it = Review your day - and pick out all the pleasurable moments - all of them - big - little - hardly worth the notice ~ It could be as simple as - getting in the door before it rained - or - being able to put off doing your laundry for one more day ~ And so = Notice them - acknowledge them - admire them - relive them - delight in them - feel the satisfaction of them ~ But - above all = Be grateful for them ~ Pour that on ~ Cover the memory of those high points in the rich gooey syrup of thank you - thank you - thank you.

You don't have to be thanking somebody - or something ~ Although - being grateful to the people who assisted you to your happy moments - certainly won't hurt ~ And of course = You're welcome to take on that gratitude directing part however you choose ~ The idea - is really more of a vibrational tuning - a personal electromagnetic broadcast - which declares = That's what I like - because = Gratitude - has a way of turning that dial right to the clearest signal ~ What we're happiest to receive - is always what we're most grateful for - and = What the target is here = Is happiness itself ~ And the point is = To fall asleep in that state of mind - that vibration - that attraction - to more happiness - while = Deliberately offering to your nighttime regeneration system - your eagerness for the learning/training process of getting that mind of yours into the habit of = Being - happy.

Class Seven - 100% Know?

BREATHE (No - no = Don't just look the other way like that ~ You know what to do ~ Though you may still be wondering what exactly it is you're doing ~ So = You're activating - or energizing - or stimulating - or whatever word you like - electrical amplitude in your brain ~ Particularly (according to EEG read outs) - in the parieto-occipital region at the back of your head - where sensory information integration (or sorting out what you see and hear and so on) - takes place ~ That sound like a good thing to you?)

Alright = Let me hear you shout it ~ You know what I'm talking about ~ Come on now ~ You call that shouting? Again ~ Once more ~ Now that's a Yes ~ So = Can you tell me about the - feel - of it? Is your happiness connected to that feeling? What about agreement - what did that feel like? Are they all the same? No? How are they different? Are those really different feelings - or are they ideas - about different feelings? Can you identify a single feeling underneath them all? Can you describe it? How about a single idea? Did you notice how - your ideas about agreement - influenced - your feelings - about agreeing? How do you feel right now? Is that a yes or a no feeling?

Since you're half way there already - it sounds like the moment for an = {{{**Inventory Time**}}}

Okay = I used the word adapt before ~ What does it mean? So = In its simplest terms - it means change? Can you give me an example? Excellent = Adapt to living in a new country ~ That means - you'd have to learn new things? Sure = A different language maybe - customs - how to get around ~ What would be the purpose of learning those things then? Right = To go on living and - be happy.

Are you the same as when you were five? Is your world the same? What are some of the changes you've had to adapt to? Were some of those changes harder to accept than others? Why? So they were harder - because = They were things you didn't - want - to change?

Remember in the closed fist example of - No = How we agreed - that No - is a painful place - when it comes to changing? So = Are those difficult changes in your past - because of - that No energy (or vibration) - that closed fist to change?

Remember the whole business about the space of question - and = Keeping it open in order to learn? Does that fit the word adapt? So then = To learn a language - customs - the names of streets and where they go - is that using that same question space? Is that space a - Yes - energy?

What does the word willingness mean? Right = It means = Agreeable to doing something ~ So = Is that a Yes kind of word? Would you say that the sentence = Yes - I'm willing - to adapt = Represents the whole power - behind - successfully changing - to suit conditions?

||||||||| Hand Full of Change:

The action of change - regardless of how well it is recognized to be a desire - or even a necessity - is often slowed - postponed - dragged out - or stopped altogether = By lack of a reference point for what life would be like beyond - or on the other side - of the change required ~ In other words = It may be clear what's not wanted - but not = What - IS - wanted ~ Such a condition - describes exactly the difference between those pro-and anti and yes and no energies - in the very personal form of = I want to be different - but = I'm not.

What if - the answer - is a question = Who would I be - if - I were different? And the trick is - to find out - to observe - to imagine - visualize - to create a model - a kind of location that exists in your mind = In order to be that person - that could be you in the future - right now - and then = Believe it.

Okay = Never mind that it's not true ~ In fact = What if - you were to accept - that you think that fantasy future is not true - and = All the reasons why you think it couldn't possibly come true = You accept them as well? What would happen - if you didn't resist those negative ideas - those limiting beliefs - in the way of becoming the new you - and instead = Just recognize that they are there - you've got them - and all the evidence you've built up for them - and okay - you accept that? And then = Go back to imagining yourself transformed.

I know = It seems like the wrong way to go about it ~ Like giving up to the obstacles - before you've even started ~ But = What if - what I just described - is exactly the opposite? What if - what held you back (or any of us) - all along - is resisting those negative ideas - fighting them - wanting them to be different - wanting to slip around them? In other words = What if - you've been giving all the power of your effort (paying - your attention) - to dealing with the ideas of what can't be - rather than the ideal - of what could be?

What would your life be like = If it was the one you want it to be? Can you imagine it? Go ahead = Imagine all the way down to your toe jam - and enjoy yourself = Why not? And = If there is - a reason - for why not - for not doing that imagining = Then try accepting that reason - and then = Doing it (the imagining bit - that is)

What it comes right down to (and that's the spot we're trying to hit) = We don't actually ever change who we are = We grow - new versions - of being - who we are.|||||||||

Let's look at a kind of picture of the human mind.

Here's a nickel = How many parts of a dollar does it represent? Okay = This dime - how many parts of a dollar is it? How about when I put them together? Okay - if we were talking in percentages - what percent of a dollar would the nickel be? Right = Five % ~ And the dime? And both?

According to a kind of popular myth (built up over the past thirty years or so) - many people say - and believe = That the average human uses somewhere between - 5 % and 15 % (most often quoted as 10%) - of their brain ~ After all - there are claims by microbiologists - that as much as 97% of our DNA is unused - so = How does that translate to our brains? However = Neuroscientists (or brain studiers) - have caused severe doubt - of that being an actual fact (the 10% brain use one) - if not reversed - that conclusion all together (even if - less than 10% of people know that yet) The new - fact - is = We - physically - use the whole thing ~ That 10% idea - could really be based more on how we - observe - each other using it - and = A certain general lack of respect governing that observation you may have noticed yourself participating in ~ It also (that low percentage use) = May be true = In the sense of - what the thing is actually capable of doing - or = Its potential ~ Or perhaps = That 10% thing just reflects a case of bad organization - like messy files - the information is all there - but = We haven't worked out how to coordinate our access to it properly ~ Yet why (proven or partly proven incorrect - or misunderstood for whatever reason) - that myth (or misrepresented truth) - exists = It still makes sense - to investigate the idea - since = If there is the possibility that an unused potential is hidden up there (or wherever it's hidden) - wouldn't you like to learn how to use it?

So = What does that word potential mean? Yeah = What's available - what's possible to use (at least as the most direct physical definition) So = If - you had ten pounds of bananas - you have the potential - to eat ten pounds of bananas? Okay = What does this mean about - our brain potential? That's right = It looks like - potentially - there might be a lot of brown bananas up there.

So = If our brains have a dollars worth of potential - every time we use them - how much of that dollar would we be spending - that is - if those 5 to 15% ideas we're right? How much can you buy for fifteen cents? (Notice I'm allowing you the higher percentage) Not much huh? Yeah - it's true = You can't get much for a dollar either ~ So let's say our brains are worth a hundred dollars ~ What's 15% of that?

What if - you went to the store - and they told you - your money was only worth 15% of its face value? Would you be upset? Sure would be ~ So = Why not about your brain potential? Don't you use it - for absolutely everything?

[[[[[[[Doctor Dude's Dictionary - word seven - Subtle:

Have you ever examined the word subtle? It's a clever little word really - often in a sneaky sort of way - that has a talent for pointing out minor differences - which = When multiplied out to a big picture view - have huge effects.

Subtle - started out as a Latin word - meaning thin or fine - and has come down to us the same - in the sense of = Being able to slip between the cracks unnoticed ~ It's - what's there right in front of us - but not immediately obvious ~ It's the part - that takes some noticing - something more than a casual look - where a larger attention is required ~ It's also - that very narrow distinction - that fine point - that divides two things - which are apparently the same somehow (say - viewpoints - or understandings) - and declares them to actually be = Entirely different ~ Subtle - is a powerful action in a quiet unobtrusive way = A behind the scenes intrigue - or = The slight turn of the wheel - that would never show up as obvious a mile at sea - but = Causes the ship it steered to make landfall 1000 miles off course a week later ~ Subtle - is a way of being - a way of communicating - observing - and changing ~ It's not loud - because that's what makes it subtle.

The real beauty of the word subtle - is how it describes some minor piece of information - that when brought to notice - is what tremendous revelation hinges on ~ Now that may sound as though I'm describing something entirely different - like discovery - but actually = The difference - is really rather subtle.||||||||||

Let me draw you a picture to make this brain potential idea clearer ~ Which is to say = You're going to do the drawing - that I direct.

First = Draw a small circle a little to the left of the center of a blank sheet of paper ~ Or use a scrap of old envelope or something - a chalk board - a stick in the dirt ~ No sense wasting paper - which = Is another whole side of consciousness.

Okay - this circle - is the stuff you've experienced - or - what you've learned - and believe - to be true ~ Go ahead and label it (inside the circle) - L - for learned.
So = What kind of stuff is in (meaning - represented by) - this circle? What do you know how to do? Where have you been? What have you seen? What do you expect to happen if I drop this piece of chalk? Yeah = All - that stuff.

Now draw another circle - the same size - an inch or two to the right of the first one.

This next circle - is the stuff - you're aware - you could experience - or learn about - but = You haven't = You just know it exists ~ I'd label it - P - for possible

So what's in that circle? Anybody here know how to fly a jet? Anybody been to Antarctica? Speak Chinese? Can perform open heart surgery? So = You get what I mean?

Now = Draw a larger circle that encloses both the smaller ones.

This circle = Is uncharted territory ~ This is what - IS - that we don't know - IS ~ Or - what we haven't found out - that we haven't found out.

In fact = Most people know so little about the possibility of this - IS-ness - that they don't even consider - it - could be real - and pay no attention to finding out - if - it - IS ~ Therefore = We can't even label it.

There is - it's true = A certain amount of sense - in paying no attention to this circle ~ What do you think it is?

Let me help.

Say - someone in Indonesia - works out a chemical process that dyes cotton fabric a certain shade of blue - much quicker and cheaper than previous ways of doing it - so that = When the jeans - that are the final product of that process - reach a store in the US - they cost less than other brands ~ At that point = You - go in that store - and (after a few trips to the fitting room) = Decide to buy the cheaper jeans - because = They're obviously just as good - and - they're cheaper.

Are you concerned about what caused them to be cheaper?

That's kind of the situation with that unused part of our - so called - brain potential = We can get away without using it ~ We think - we have enough information already ~ What we're used to - is that 15% or less (brain use or access or whatever) - and - it seems to work okay ~ At least according to what we can judge - using 15% or less.

But = What if - we are mistaken - and that missing information (or what ever it is) - could really be immensely more useful than - we think - not like that Indonesian dye at all? (Unless - you plan on going into manufacturing blue jeans)

Let's say - if you had never seen a dollar - or a picture of one - or ever been told that paper money exists - would you recognize the value of one - when you did see it? No = How could you?

That's our problem with that missing 85% = We can't understand its value - if it's a big blank ~ It's like those people 500 years ago - carrying around all that electricity that can do so many things - things that they couldn't have even imagined in those days - like refrigerators - hair dryers - stereo systems - computers - and they didn't have a clue it was in there (which is not to say that such things have made people any happier) It's a bit tricky - knowing - what you don't know - isn't it? Especially - if you don't know you don't know there might be something more you could know.

Well - what if you could? Let's look at it - from the opposite direction - so to speak.

What do you suppose we could - do - with the full 100%?

You've heard of having a sixth sense? What does that mean? Ah = Psychic abilities ~ So = Knowing things - beyond what our five senses tell us - or what physical conditions - like distance and solid obstacles - would ordinarily limit? Does that sort of thing go on - out there in the world? Okay = You've heard about it - but = That doesn't make it true? Fair enough ~ Well = What if - that sort of thing - would be totally normal - to a 100%

brain user? What if - there are more senses - seven - eight - ten - more? We don't - really - know - do we? Or do we - think - we do know?

When you go to the movies - and watch the previews for other movies - do you know what the whole movie - they're advertising - is like - completely? Some of them tell you more than others - it's true ~ But = Do you ever know? I mean - again = Completely?

Why do they have previews? Sure = To get you to go see the movie ~ What if - the life - we're looking at - through our limited percentage of potential use now - is more like a preview - than a whole movie? What if - it's even really no more than a poster - for the real movie - we're capable of living? Do you think 100% might be that different from 15%? Doesn't seem like it - does it? After all - the planet would be the same - gravity - the need to eat and sleep and make a living - all that.

But = What if - the ability to use 100% of brain potential - actually changed all our relationships - with all those things as well? What if - with complete use of our brain potential - or - instant access to everything that potential might be capable of doing - those things even ceased to be real to us? In fact = What if - what we have to do here - is stop using the word brain - and substitute the word - I've really had in - mind - the whole time = Mind - or - whole mind - or even (who would have guessed it) - consciousness?

Alright- enough of theories and questions and balancing words with other words (for the moment anyway) But yeah = How do we find out? How do we do it? How do we use more - brain/mind/consciousness - potential.

[[[[[[[[[Sleep on it:

You've probably heard = That we spend approximately one third of our lives asleep ~ And - if you haven't = We spend approximately a third of our lives asleep.

But = Why? It seems like such a waste of time ~ Got to achieve - achieve - you know how our culture is ~ I mean - a third of your life? How lazy is that? Course - then there are those who would just assume spend only a third of their time - awake ~ Either way - driven by ambition - or happily couldn't care less - we all need to sleep - and - there's still that big = Why?

So - by way of answer - first off = Sleep is not just rest for tired muscles and brain cells ~ At least not in the sense of your body just lays there and does nothing - in order to feel revived in the morning ~ Oh no = It's just a change of shifts = You fall asleep - and that's the whistle for the night crew to get to work.

There are five different stages to sleep (as categorized by sleep research science) - which = Are distinguished from one another by the brain wave patterns - and particular physiological functions - that occur during them ~ Stage one = Is that - just got comfortable - eyes closed - drift from the daytime working beta wave pattern into the longer slower alpha wavelength - where logic tends to loosen up and flow thoughts into blends - that would not make sense at noon - but now just run smoothly together right over the edge of...

This first stage - generally lasts two to five minutes - with maybe a few involuntary muscle twitches - sometimes a sudden waking as you doze into falling off an imaginary roof - or a momentary paralysis - which also passes back into the dreamy downstream zzzzzzz.

This is the hypnagogic state (you may be remembering something about from another part of your waking experience) The root of the word - is in the name of the Greek god of sleep - Hypnos (pronounced - hip - noss - rhymes with boss) The same as the word - hypnosis = Another reference to an apparently sleeping state of consciousness - that still only makes so much sense to us.

Sleep - has often been characterized in the past - as an existence somewhere between waking and death ~ But = It is most certainly nothing like death - as measured physically at least - and so = Enter - stage two…

Complex learning - meaning = Multilayered coordinations of information and motor control relationships - such as - learning how to drive - play an instrument - decorate a wedding cake - pole vault = All require (or at the least are sped up and improved by) - a type of shutdown and reboot (kinda sorta not really but still) - like a computer needs to do to complete installing some programs ~ Stage two sleep - is where this happens ~ The wave outputs now show sudden spikes of activity - which = Are organizational adjustments - being made between what neurons (nerve cells) - are connected to other neurons - a kind of information access grid (you'll be hearing more about later) - that's being fine-tuned with the data you've accumulated during the day ~ You might think of it - as more efficiently arranging the shelves for the next day's business with those new gadgets you just received ~ Of course - that's the kind of thinking that fits better in stage one weirdness ~ So = On to stage three.

Slow wave sleep (SWS) - a long smooth delta wave - is the steady rhythm now ~ The so-called stress hormone - cortisol - has disappeared entirely from the bloodstream - and instead = Human Growth Hormone (HGH) - is being pumped by the pituitary gland like a free buffet to hurting tissues all over the body ~ HGH - is one of the biggest whys for spending all that time asleep - it -performs all kinds of essential services - like promoting muscle and bone growth - breaking down fats (particularly cholesterol) - and carbohydrates for cellular use - and = Helping to move the remnants out of the body - as well as assisting in the complex structuring of proteins the body is constantly demanding = If you don't sleep = You age faster.

Another process occurring in the slow rolling depths of SWS - is a kind of brain clean up - where stored - but seldom accessed or confusing information - is disconnected from those grids mentioned earlier ~ It's like selective pruning in an orchard- which is intended to encourage the trees to grow stronger and more productive - thus = Another efficiency booster- most simply described as = Clearing your head.

Stage four = Doesn't stand out for additional processes - as it's apparently continuing the ones set in motion by stage three - instead = It's distinguished as the deepest sleep stage - throbbing a low low delta wave ~ It's also the time of the most thorough physical system shutdown the rest of the body experiences during the entire cycle.

Where does consciousness go in those sluggish moments? Do you know?

Then = There's REM ~ Sound familiar? (Or did you just dream it?) The fifth stage - is the most fun - or possibly the most scary - but certainly - the most memorable = REM (named for rapid eye movement - or the swiveling around our eyes do in that state) - is of course = The dream state ~ I say it's the most memorable - not because of remembering dreams (even though that's the only part of sleep we seem to be capable of remembering) - but because = That's where short-term memories - are transferred to long-term storage (so to speak anyway) It's a kind of learning consolidation period ~ And - because of that = Is actually required (in other words - gotta have it) - to retain certain kinds of memorization learning ~ In that light = Taking a nap after math class - or after studying your lines for the play you're starring in - is not only = NOT a waste of time = It's a very sensible course of action.

Another advantage to REM activity (which - on an EEG readout - is all over the shop - and far more like the waves generated during waking hours) - is emotionally oriented ~ Which means = Positive emotional memories (you know - like happiness) - are solidified (sort of locked in cellularly) - while negative ones - which are no longer productive - are eliminated ~ What could be more useful than that?

Plus = REM sleep - appears to have some connection with pain management ~ At least as inferred from the results of studies - which conclude = People deprived of REM - suffer a higher sensitivity to physical pain ~ Take two aspirin and call me in the morning - may not have been such bad advice after all.

These stages (excepting stage one - which only happens the one time in a sleep cycle) - repeat over and over through the night (or whatever time you're sleeping) - with about half the overall time in stage two - about 20% in REM - and the rest in three and four ~ A full cycle averages around 90 to 100 minutes ~ And that = Is at least partly why - we sleep so much ~ And - most definitely why = You'd want to do it on a very regular basis.|||||||||

Do you remember - when you were still less than a year old? But - you were alive then = So why don't you remember? Okay = When you were that age - you lived - in a state of consciousness - that basically - just absorbed information ~ More information - by the way - than you ever have been capable of absorbing since ~ So = Why don't you remember it?

The simplest way of putting an answer to that question is = There was nothing to stick memories together with ~ Two things were missing ~ Do you know what they are? Alright = They were - a sense of time - and - a habit of judgment ~ What you were doing then - was floating in a soup of nows - that you couldn't tell apart from other nows - because = There weren't - reasons - in your mind - about why you should.

Any of you been around very young babies? Not that they aren't all very young - if they're called babies - but = I mean less than a year old ~ Anyway = So you know how they can be completely absorbed by the smallest thing - or distracted by another? And when they cry - and then get what they want - what do they do? Yeah = They're fine again ~ They don't sulk or complain about how long it took you to do what they wanted? Pretty simple really - huh? Just reacting to exactly what's on in any given moment?

So = Why did you stop brain growth - and absorbing information - the way an infant does? Yes = It does appear to be the natural thing ~ But = What if - it's because you started deciding things - picking out what was possible - and what wasn't - what was true - and what was fantasy? Oh sure = You had plenty of help = Everyone was in on it ~ But = What if - that's why? I mean = What if - it wasn't that you couldn't absorb and grow the same way - but = That you were beginning - to direct the show yourself - and not looking - in all directions wide eyed - just the one direction - you chose - and therefore = Created that limitation yourself?

So = Even if that were true - what would it have to do with learning how to increase your brain/mind/consciousness (we'll call it BMC) - use?

Do you suppose there's something we could learn - about such learning - from little babies? How is it that they relate to time? Do they judge what's happened - or is going - to happen? So = If you were to do the same - do you think a new part of your BMC use might open up? Yes = You're right = There's only one way to find out.

So here's your assignment - Everyday this week - as often as you remember - for as long as you can {Hang on - here's a helpful tip - or it is for me = When I want to remember something important - I often will take a pen and write it on the back of my hand ~ You know - like - Annie's phone number - or - buy toilet paper ~ Anyway} = I want you to look around you - as though you had never seen this world before ~ Use the peripheral vision trick - alternate between narrow focus and wide focus - talk to yourself - and choose happiness - all at the same time ~ Which - again - does sound like too much all at once - but = Take a lesson from the one year old you once were - and make it all simple - by just being willing - to be in the present now - without judgment - eyes wide open - and take it all in ~ Okay? By the way - don't forget to breathe.

N.P.U. - Chapter Seven - Number Three?

We still haven't worked out - what all that electromagnetic field we're generating - does - after - we generate it ~ One - possibly good reason for that is = There's yet to be - a single - 100% agreed upon - explanation of that phenomena in circulation among humans that declares something unquestionable like = Peanut butter - is made from peanuts ~ Which is not to say - that no one - has the complete answer - just = Most of us don't (depending - of course - on how you define the phrase no one - or the word complete - or answer for that matter - or who - what - and where - the holder of such an answer might be)

Let's not let - that - stop us though - There are plenty of - incomplete answers - left to consider ~ So - this time - instead of a word - to balance our attention on - we'll use a number ~ It's one of the ten most famous numbers in the world - it's the number = Three.

First (that is - number one) - we'll tidy up a bit and complete the story of Herr Einstein's brain.

You'll recall - that Dr. Diamond - isolated a portion of Albert's brain - known as the left parietal lobe - which = Functions like a search engine in contact with other search engine areas of the brain ~ In that site - she found a particularly high concentration of glial cells (or neuroglia - if you want to get technical) - which are = Those bits of protoplasm - which it looks like - hold together communication up there - both literally - and figuratively - plus - support the action of nutrition - and generally help regulate the conditions of the physical brain environment ~ Obviously - very handy little things.

Now - if you're wondering why - you don't - recall all that = It's because I just gave you more information than I did before - and perhaps - your own glial cell growth would benefit from a bit of - stimulating ~ The beauty of this project is = That - is - what we're doing (stimulating your brain - in case you needed it pointed out) The question right here is = How did Einstein do it?

Well - as he himself described it = It - was because of his slow development as a child ~ Up to and throughout his early education - he had been faced with certain - language learning challenges ~ Because of this - until the age of seven - he was in the habit of softly repeating everything he said (or tried to say) - under his breath (as the expression goes) The result - of these challenges - also according to him - was = He arrived late - at questions of space and time - that most children had put aside and moved on from - by the age he came to asking them ~ Presumably meaning = Those other children had - accepted - what they were told by adults - in the way of answers - whereas he (the

108

youthful Einstein) - had not ~ In part (as pointed out) - because he had not asked those questions ~ Actually - he was notorious for paying no attention at all to teachers - or their subjects - where he had no interest ~ A habit - it's not my intention to advertise as necessarily profitable ~ The advantage Albert had - in that lack of interest - was knowing exactly - what - he was interested in - and applying - not just his thinking - faculties - to that pursuit - but his entire sensory awareness ~ Daydreaming - for Einstein - was a vivid experience of imagery and sensation - including - or more accurately - riding upon - emotion ~ He didn't worry the pencils of his thoughts down to a nub with words and numbers = He saw things = He felt them ~ The - details - of expressing them - came later.

Another bit of information (your glial cells may be helping you to recall - about glial cells) - is that research involving rat brains - which much of this business about the professors brain hinges upon ~ The rats - who lived a life of ongoing educational stimulation (at a rodent level at least) - produced a far higher concentration of the cells - than their stir crazy cousins ~ They also lived a good deal longer ~ And - in case there are any neuroscientists in the room = Yes - the size of their brains was larger - and - the branching tangle of dendrites and axons (the skinny treelike connector tissues that transmit electrochemical signals from one neuron to another) - was far more dense and evenly distributed ~ The short of it (or the long - depending upon your attention span) - is = The conditions of your birth (meaning - where - when - health - ancestry - and what your parents are like) - definitely determines much of how your brain will turn out ~ But = It's what you - do - with that brain - that (according to new research) - outweighs all the rest of those influences put together ~ Excepting of course - the different varieties of damage those squishy Jell-O molds behind our eyes are vulnerable to ~ But - again (with an echoing bang on the table) - that means (or certainly very much could mean) = The greater part of genius - is a choice - and = I don't think I have to remind you - who - is making that choice.

[[[[[[[[No Brainer:

If - these brains of ours are the required physical mechanism - for thoughts and learning and all that other brainy stuff to happen - how can we possibly explain = How a first class honors student of mathematics at Sheffield University in England (with - I might add - a reported IQ of 126) - was discovered - during a set of routine tests for some minor ailment - to have (what was described in a 1980 issue of the journal - Science) - virtually no brain?

What's meant by - virtually no brain = Is that his cerebral cortex (or - the outer layer of brain tissue - where in - supposedly - all the thinking function under your hair takes place) - had been reduced to a thickness of less than a millimeter - by a disorder called hydrocephalus (otherwise known as - water on the brain - where an accumulation of fluid compresses the brain the way a brick can compress a fly)

But again - the remarkable thing = Was that he suffered no impairment of his mental or physical processes - and was - by all standard measurements of the phrase - a really smart guy ~ In the end - all one can say is = Huh?]]]]]]]]]]

How about that number three then (forgot that did you) - and what (you must be wondering) - could it possibly have to do with this brain dissection we've got going on here ~ Alright (even if you're not wondering) = Three - in this case - is a simple form of mathematics - which only makes sense = If you ignore the usual rules of mathematics ~ It takes place when you add one thing to another - like say… electricity to magnetism = From the point of view - that electricity is one thing - and - magnetism is another - and therefore = They both have the numerical value of one ~ Which - of course - looks like - 1+1=? Okay? Now - standard math demands what answer? Sure - if it were a question of - objects - like handguns - or subjects - like opinions about handguns = The answer would be exactly as you'd expect ~ But - like I told you = This isn't that kind of math ~ The real answer is = Three ~ Because - electricity - and - magnetism (in this example) - are not the same thing - until you add them - and then - you have a third - entirely different - thing - that stands on its own - which means = Its value - is one ~ So - our equation now looks like - 1 +1 = 1.

As you can see - the number three - as I've just used it - is not a firmly defined measurement - like good old number two (since it didn't actually show up in the written equation as the answer) That's because = It's an action - a fluid - a thing - that in order to be itself - has to move ~ You might also see (if you're an exacting kind of mind) - that - since electricity and magnetism - can't - technically - be separated - they only - appear - to be two different forces - but are really - only one - then - the three - never really existed - as part of the equation - except - as a means - to get back to one ~ Which is = My point exactly.

[[[[[[[[[**Three = two ones:**

You may find it interesting to note - that in the binary number system of ones and zeros that make up a computer's operating language (or essentially - how a computer communicates with itself) - the number three - is represented - by two ones.]]]]]]]]]

So = What is - the point of this point I'm trying to point out? Of course - I just tried again to explain it - but using the word point - three times - to arrive at - one meaning ~ But - if that flew past like so much cloudy weather = I'll give you some other examples - which might do the trick more effectively ~ I'll also give you a reason - to pay attention to this foolishness ~ Which is to say - inspire you to consider = This may quite possibly be of more use to you than you presently think - and in fact - might reverse - what you presently think - into something - you think - is foolish ~ Or not ~ Anyway - that's the reason - or enough of it to chew on - to keep you chewing ~ Don't worry = They'll be more.

Remember now - this three - that equals - one - is always in motion ~ In fact = Moving at the speed of light ~ Since that's a bit too quick for most of us - we'll stick - for now - with apparently slower things - but = It's still movement - were looking for ~ Therefore - the word equal (or the symbol =) - in our equation - stands for = Results in - or = Resulting movement.

110

Okay? Here's an easy one.

You have a problem in mind - you don't know the answer to (Otherwise it's not a problem is it?) Alright = That answerless problem - is one (as in 1+) Next = You're willing to find out the answer ~ No = That's not two = That's the other - one (to complete 1+1) Did you notice - by the way - that both these - things (a problem in mind - and a willingness to find an answer) - are already actions? Now - when you add them together (1+1=) - you get a third action ~ Which is -seeking an answer (represented by the symbol =) - which = Could be as simple as just having a question pop out of your mouth ~ But - you see - that's where - the third thing - turned the two things - into one ~ Which is = A question - or - to spell it out = A problem - plus - wanting an answer - equals - a question.

Yes = That does seem like - over complicating a simple action - that doesn't need to be ~ The thing is = It's not complicating it - it's slowing it down - in order to see - how it works.

I'll add another taste - of the big reason for doing this = To pry open - how - every - thing - works - or - why - everything - is - the way it is ~ Big order - I know ~ But = Big stuff - is what a lot of small stuff - adds up to ~ If you can get a handle on the small stuff - you'll often find - the big stuff - is just more of the same ~ So - on to the next example.

You're in possession of a concept - or a mental explanation of how something works (this - one plus one make three return to one concept - for example) So - just like before - this mental action of a concept (it's an action - because - in order to reference it in your own mind - you have to re-explain it to yourself - even if that only takes a millisecond) - is the first - one ~ Okay - then (for a moment) - you give up your doubt - about this concept being true - and allow (for that moment) - that it may be possible - that it is true ~ That (as you've guessed) - is - the other - one ~ So then - you add them ~ Which - of course - you've already done ~ And = It happened again ~ A new action - transformed two things into a third - that made them both = One.

Do you know what that action was? It was an = Experience ~ It clicked ~ You felt it ~ Yes = It made sense ~ Or - that's what's being described = An experience of sense being made ~ Whether the example made sense to you - is another question {{If not - try reading the last bit over again}}

So - again - from the top = An unknown - added to a willingness to know - moves into seeking an answer - and becomes one thing - which is = A question ~ That - is the first part (but you knew that) - which - by the way - also adds up to = An understanding - or a concept - of how a question arises ~ And now - the second equation - which followed on the first - took that first concept - added allowance of it being true - which equaled - or resulted in = An experience - of it being one thing - which is = A true concept - or simply = True.

To be sure - you may disagree with that last statement - and every right you have to ~ But = While you're doing that - let's follow this line of reasoning further and see where it's going ~ However - just for the sake of continuity (or an even flow of ideas) - we'll proceed as though - you do agree - that the concept outlined - is true ~ Later on you can disprove it to your heart's content.

So = You now have a question - answered by a concept - and - an experience - that has proven that concept to be true ~ To true - you add another question - like = What if - this simple idea is an explanation of much more complex things or ideas? The magic of outside the box mathematics does its thing - and - the result is = Excitement ~ Which = Is immediately cooking along at fantastic speed to whip those two things into one frothy overflowing extra-large size - thing = Inspiration.

No sense slowing down now ~ You take that - Inspiration (which is a combination - of ideas and feelings - which came from - or was equal to - a true concept - which are ideas enclosed in a secure sense of filled space - which came from - or was equal to - a question - which are ideas of mystery floating intriguingly in an empty space) - and add it to - Imagination - and = Kazzappp = The resulting vision - insight - opening - download - whatever word suits your taste - fuses inspiration to imagination and turns them into = Revelation.

You could go on and on - but = What - is that revelation?

Well - you remember that question of = What do these electromagnetic fields of ours - do - out there in the universe? What if - they're doing something - very much like - this quirky math that led us to this point?

[[[[[[[[[One of those twisty questions:

What if - consciousness is not in the body - and instead - the body is in consciousness? And - if so = We are not in the world = The world - is in us?]]]]]]]]]]

I used the word sonar before - by way of example - and comparison - in this electromagnetic question - remember? I suggested that perhaps - our energy - carrying the message of our feeling state - bounces off - some other energy - and returns to us a response - which is = Our world ~ Or - to refine that idea a bit = Our life experience of a world ~ Now - what I mean - in relation to that idea - and the action of the number three - is = Our energy field - of feelings - is one thing ~ That other field - sometimes called the quantum field - the zero point field - or just - the law of attraction (though seldom - if ever - by physicists) - is the other thing ~ That bounce - of the sonar ping - making contact between them - is their addition ~ The result - number three - is = Manifestation ~ Which blends those two fields - at the speed of light - into one thing - which is = A moment of life in the world ~ Or - of course - from the more standard perspective = That's not how it works at all - the world is just there and stuff happens - or = The answer is something else altogether.

So = If you want to consider the possibility - that something other than the - standard perspective - may be the case - it sounds like it'd be pretty key to know what that word manifestation means ~ In case you don't = It's a demonstration of existence - or the appearance - the presence - of a reality of objects - people - animals - places - stuff ~ Basically - it's making stuff - real ~ You could use the verb of manifestation in a sentence like this = All her hard work eventually manifested in a great job.

In this case (the one I've just made for the electromagnetic sonar of your feelings) - we're looking at the possibility - of making stuff - not from other stuff - but - from feelings - shaken together with - possibility.

The question is = Is - that really what happens? Do - our feelings make our life - rather than the other way around - of life - causing our feelings? Of course - everyone knows - the second part of that sentence - is true - whereas the first - is just silly ~ Unless of course - that every-one - that you are referring to - is wrong.

[[[[[[[[[Nap Time:

Have you had your nap today? No? You're standing in line for your triple shot mocha gotta go now and who's even got time for that wake up fix instead?

Cool ~ As you know = That'll do the trick ~ At least until all that caffeine and sugar has completed its initial effect - and begins to have the opposite one ~ Just like gravity = What goes up - must...

And that = Is why your body is telling you it was slowing down in the first place = It's a cycle - a very natural one - of required repair and renewal and reinforcement - which = Even though your stimulant boost will deliver you energy - now = Later - it will steal much more (which includes undesirable health effects) - than 20 minutes of sleep would have handed you on a platter = For free.

As you of course remember (from reading an earlier segment on why we sleep so much) - a whole string of health maintaining benefits are provided by sleep ~ When I say - health maintaining - and - provided = I mean much the same as substituting the word - eating - for the word - sleep - in the same sentence = You have to eat to live - and = You have to sleep - for the same reason ~ Sleep deprivation (meaning - going without sleep) - will kill you slower than starvation - but only because - your body just plain falls asleep on its own eventually ~ Otherwise - you'd probably break your neck somehow anyway - from being too exhausted to pay proper attention to what's going on.

The point is = Despite the fact - that our culture regards napping as either - childish - lazy - indulgent - or something to do after you retire - it is - in fact = An intelligent choice - and even - in certain circumstances of prolonged stress = A life saver.

Returning to what your body is telling you = You are responding to - sleep pressure - which is a natural balancing rhythm - between being awake - and the need for SWS (slow wave sleep) - with all its repair crew hormone secretion and neuron rearranging ~ Of course - there's also just boredom and over exertion - to cause sleepiness - but (generally speaking) = That afternoon low - is your body calling out for SWS.

And then = Let's say - you're a teenager ~ What that means - as far as sleep goes - is = Your needs are different from when you were younger (kids aged 5 to 13 need 10 to 11 hours of sleep) - teenagers - require less sleep (about 9 hours) - but - your (if you happen to be one of those teenagers) - natural rhythm of sleeping and waking - has changed as well ~ Your body - now wants to fall asleep later at night - and - wake up later in the morning ~ Problem is = Natural timing - and cultural timing - don't agree ~ Schools start - way - too early ~ Then = It's go - go - go - sugar - pressure - caffeine - pressure - sports - sugar - homework - and why won't you go to bed pressure ~ Adults - who need less sleep (7 to 8 hours - and often manage that need more effectively) - get up on Sunday morning - having pulled off 54 hours of a 49-56 hour ideal sleep week - and start chewing your tail for laziness - after you only managed 45 hours out of an ideal of 63 ~ What's wrong with this picture?

Well - you can try to convince your parents of their misunderstandings - or = Start snatching naps.

The same is true for any age group (so forget about convincing anyone of anything) Naps are sleep - and sleep heals ~ All the good stuff that can happen at 2 a.m. - can happen at 2 p.m. ~ And yet = Differently ~ A well timed nap - can jumpstart creativity - snap up alertness - raise your mood - clarify your thinking - boost memory - even make you look better ~ Refining that timing - is a bit of a trick however ~ 20 - 40 - 90 minutes of sleep - all have different effects - due to the amount of time spent in the stages of a sleep cycle - and = Which one you wake up in.

Many people complain of feeling groggy after napping - which is really not the fault of a whole nap - so much as it is awakening in a slow wave sleep stage - and - having to rev up all the other frequencies the waking brain runs on - out of that one steady delta throb that does so much for us ~ You're not actually - more tired - any more than you would be - more hungry - from snacking ~ It's just a kind of appetite stimulator - for something your body needs - that's kicked in ~ A bit of jumping up and down - some cold water in the face - will help with that rev up - and next time = Take a shorter nap - or a longer one ~ With a bit of practice - and you can tune your sleep stage timing to the perfect awakening.

You can also experiment with fishing for great ideas - with a sitting up nap - by holding a handful of spoons (or some such thing) - and - asking yourself the question you have in mind - or whatever it is you want inspiration for - then closing your eyes and relaxing for sleep = The moment you cross that stage one line and enter stage two (meaning - fall asleep - as well as remembering earlier references to the hypnagogic state) - your hand will loosen - and the spoons crashing to the floor will wake you up - perhaps clutching that great idea instead.||||||||||

.

The Second Quarter

Good job = You're well on your way now ~ Not to be confused with the fact = That you're actually right here.

Ah = But do you sense movement? Do you sense change? Does the word quarter - sound like change? Do two of them make 50 cents? Are you wondering what you'll get for four of them?

Yes = I am playing with words ~ But - the reason I am = Is to draw attention to a way - things - fit together in our experience.

There is a word - which is = Synesthesia ~ It's pronounced - sin (like naughty - naughty) - es (like saying the letter S) - thee (like the first part of thief) - zha (rather like slurring the first two letters in the word just) Of course - that's also playing with the way - things - particularly sounds - and the meaning of words - fit together - or connect meanings - which make sense to us then in a multiple reflection kind of way - because = Our word synesthesia - is about the sense - of senses connecting - in a similar form of mirror meanings ~ A dictionary will call it = A phenomenon - in which one type of sensory stimulation - evokes (or causes) - the sensation of another ~ For example = Catching sight of a café sign poured the taste of milky coffee over Myra's tongue ~ Or = The sound of a police siren and the instant sensation of wet clothing clinging cold all over Jimmy's skin stopped him in his tracks (which would cause one to wonder what Jimmy's been up to) It's not - touch - see - hear - taste - or smell something - then = Think of a sensation connected ~ Not to say - that thought - is not involved - just that it participates more in the form of effect than cause ~ It's a case of = Feel that sense strongly (like cold clinging wet) - while thought - is still occupied by the stimulus (café - siren) - before - thought registers a cause (memory - anticipation - etc.) - for that sensation.

It sounds very dramatic and all - but = That's just due to the examples I've chosen ~ Actually - it's a quite a regular phenomenon - involving any combination of senses - which = You may very well notice from now on ~ A phenomenon (to get that word straight) - the same dictionary will tell you - is both = Any occurrence - that is directly perceptible by the senses - and = An unusual or unaccountable occurrence - or = A marvel ~ Apparently - there are different ideas going around about what our senses tell us - that - we rather confusingly - use the same word for.

The real story (depending of course - on how you define the word - real) - is = The whole phenomenon of having senses - is a marvel ~ What's more = There really is no disconnecting them ~ All - the occurrences of our physical life - are a massive information intake - a constant flow of interior communication - about what's going on around us - and in us - where all the senses overlap to create a whole picture (a phrase we might switch to whole sculpture - or those old familiars - ball of wax - kit-n-kaboodle - lock stock and barrel) And then = What if - we don't just communicate - about the environment - but = To it - as well? For all it may not look like it = What if - it's not a one-sided conversation our senses are having with just us - but = An electromagnetic field conversation - with other electromagnetic fields of all kinds?

It's that word - communication - that is the gong dinger - because = That is the drive - that drives - our senses ~ Even the most sensory impaired body - has the force to communicate going on within it as a means to move beyond itself ~ Not because it's a body - but because = It's alive = It's conscious of being alive - because = Consciousness and communication and alive - are synonymous.

And - that's another word (which is a form of the word synonym) - which means = A word having the same - or very similar - meaning - as another word ~ It begins (as you've noticed) - the same as - synesthesia - because the syn part - means the same thing - or = Alike - with - together - union ~ The second part (of synesthesia) - basically means = To feel ~ Likely you know the word - anesthesia - and - how to pronounce it (even if you might have had trouble spelling it) It's - when a doctor numbs out some part of you - or knocks you out altogether - before an operation - so you won't - feel - pain ~ In this world - we have the option to - anesthetize - our feelings in many ways - with certain drugs - alcohol - anger - you know the list ~ They're not wrong = They're choices - and = They all offer a range of sensation and experience (and of course - consequences) - from which we can learn ~ Everything does - good - bad - and illegal - there's no denying that ~ It's what - we do learn - can learn - have learned - or want to learn - about - from - or instead of those things - that's the question - which makes that choice a conscious one.

The real question of choice - or the guidelines for a certain type of choosing (most specifically - how to treat our bodies and minds so they work their best) - are = What limits communication (and I'm talking brain cells to jail cells) = Limits consciousness - and = Limited consciousness = Limits everything.

Class Eight - Energy?

BREATHE (AAAAAAAAAAAHHHHHHHH = That's it ~ While you're at it = What are you learning about the effects of this exercise? Are you beginning to see the same surprising results that studies of students - autistic kids - and elderly adults - all performing this simple exercise have had? Are you wondering what those results are?)

Who wants to tell me about their experience with the assignment? How did it feel? What did you notice about how your thoughts worked when you pretended to see things as brand new to you? Was it difficult to stop judging and identifying everything? Did it change the more often you did it? Did you notice things - colors - objects - sounds - you hadn't noticed before doing it? Like what? Did you find you wanted to do it - or didn't want to? What are your ideas about why? Would you continue to do this sort of thing on your own - if you weren't asked?

So = Can anyone tell me what the last thing was - I reminded you to do - when I gave you the assignment last time? That's right = To breathe ~ Just like I do every time ~ Any ideas why? Yup = Aside from that whole oxygen use thing = It's that present moment thing again ~ Why do you think it fit particularly well with the last assignment? Of course = That's what the whole assignment was about = Being in the present.

Remember what that acronym - What If - stands for? Right = We have a totally important function ~ And = What was it that I suggested that function might be? Bingo = To be happy ~ So = To Be anything - you have to Be - in what part of time? Are you - being alive - right now? So = Is that what alive is - as a definition = Now?

Remember those people 500 years ago? Are they alive now? What would make them alive now? Yes - short of a miracle - or some amazing science - or - an entirely different idea of what alive really means = They can't be - they're dead ~ Let me put it this way = If they were alive - what would prove that they were? Right = You'd have to see and touch them - being alive - right here and now? Then again - perhaps - with 100% use of BMC potential - that whole idea - would also change.

But - what about time = Is it the same way? What I mean is = Can you prove time exists? How? Okay = There are books - and photos - and videos - and all the stuff that's been built - and fallen down - and grown up - and changed ~ But = When - would you have to do the proving? That's it = Right now ~ So = What have you proved then?

118

What if - the thing you've proved - is - the only thing you've ever proved = That you're alive - right now?

So = What does this all mean? (And yes = Basically - everything I just said - I've said before) Why do I keep coming back to this now thing? There's a good guess = It's about consciousness (I'd say - duh - but that tends to sound rude - so instead) Okay = How is it about consciousness? That's it = It's where consciousness - is located ~ If you want to find something - do you look where you think it might be? Sure ~ Well = If - now - is the place to look for your consciousness = What do you think you'll find in there?

Remember that diagram we drew - of the stuff you've learned and might learn and haven't found out you haven't found out there is to learn yet? Draw it again = The two small circles inside the larger one = That's it = You remember ~ Okay = What does it look like?

Of course (exactly like you noticed before) = A face ~ And = What does that make you want to add? Yup = No getting around it = You want to turn it into a smiley face = It's practically instinctive (in a modern kind of way) - but = Do you know why?

What if - what's in there (there being - that unknown unknown) - to find - is happiness?

Do you remember me telling you to look in your happiness to find your consciousness? Why would I ask such a thing? Exactly = To - be happy - in this world (this world being a limited location - as compared to this universe it's true - but anyway) - you have to - be - being - alive ~ Which all happens when? And = What happens when you experience your breath? Yes = You return to the awareness - of now ~ What also happens? Sure = Everything else ~ But - how about = You - consciously - stay alive - now - where - there's always the choice - to consciously choose - happiness - because = That's where it is.

[|||||||| Flower Power:

If you think that handing out bouquets of flowers (especially to females) - is a good way to spread happiness = You'd be right.

A variety of psychological research - unanimously agrees = That receiving flowers - creates an immediate upswing in mood - which often lasts for hours and even days ~ No doubt - there are some men out there who would be pleased to counter those statistics with the macho distain that they would never be influenced by flowers (not that you wouldn't catch them handing out flowers to get themselves out of trouble) - but = It's the scent of flowers - where the real power lies ~ Floral essences and essential oils enjoy a wide popularity - for the very simple reason = Their scents cause specific definite effects ~ The scent of violets - for one = Is known to enhance concentration and increase learning speed ~ Lavender influences brain waves to settle into more relaxed and reflective frequencies ~ Roses stimulate olfactory-evoked (meaning - odor stimulated) - nostalgia (although - almost any pleasing scent can do that - given how closely odors and memory are linked) There are any number of subtle and profound effects which sniffing flowers can produce ~ But of course = Happiness - is always right there at the top of the list.||||||||||

Remember what else it takes to stay alive? Bingo again = Energy.

So here I am going around in circles - and = Arriving at the same point over and over ~ Does it seem like we're getting nowhere? Could that have anything to do with you - thinking about the past or the future - right now?

Try this one - and see if it helps you understand my point = What - is the shortest distance between two points?

Nope = The straight line answer only works - if the past and the future are involved ~ The new answer is = The shortest distance between two points - is when you realize - that both points = Are the same thing.

See - all these key words I've been getting you to define and look at - like motivation - happy - being - existence - adapt - yes - no - perception - awareness - potential - now - and any I've forgotten - are there for the question (which is) = In order to experience them - you have to be - when? Yup - can't get away from it = Now.

|||||||||| Doctor Dude's Dictionary - word eight - Appropriate:

The appropriate use of the word appropriate - is always dependent on = Conditions ~ Which means = Distinctions - a determination of differences - a means of judging - choosing - splitting - and basically separating out what is suitable for creating a certain result - according to = All of the above ~ In that light = Appropriate - is not a particularly open-minded word ~ But - for all its pickiness - it's also a describer of harmony - like the perfect guitar chord backing up the ideal lyrics ~ Where appropriate accurately fits - it removes its own need to be expressed ~ The action in question - simply flows without obstacle ~ Unless those obstacles - are what's appropriate.

We've all heard the word - inappropriate ~ Especially paired with the word - behavior ~ What's going on there - is a type of friction - an against the grain current - where energies oppose each other ~ It might be a case of opinion ~ It might be a consideration of safety - tradition - social codes - fear - territory - one or any or more of the same that end up being the inspiration for inappropriate ~ But - there's always a feeling involved - that is opposite - to the one we would call appropriate ~ If it were an electrical circuit - appropriate would be the smooth running balance between positive and negative that keeps the ice cream frozen and the lights on ~ Whereas - inappropriate - is a breaker flipping fuse blowing short out - that = Even if it's not that dramatic - never feels right ~ Fact is - appropriate - when it's used in its highest form as symphonic agreement - or mirror compatibility - or - whatever's appropriate - is really about as close as words can get to differentiating the two sides of that judgment we call - right from wrong ~ Everything else (including most uses of the word appropriate) - are just opinions.

120

What it comes right down to - is (as opposed to wrong down to) = Appropriate functions as a tuning device ~ Which is to say = Crafting all the notes of that symphony into agreement - choosing them the way puzzle pieces mirror each other in compatibility ~ It's picky - in the sense of - the correct wrench to fit the bolt - or the boots that keep your feet dry - because - it's really about = What works best.

Then again - the darker side of appropriate is = To take possession of - or use for one's own purposes - often without permission - such as = The Army appropriated their land in order to build an airstrip ~ Yet even still - it may be appropriate to say = There is not such a great difference ~ At least when you examine the root of the word - which is = To make one's own ~ And - what is one's own - is what precisely fits ~ If we're talking - truly appropriate - that is ~ The rest (appropriately enough) - is still just opinion.||||||||

Alright ~ Let's move toward applying these ideas to something we could call = Practical ~ We need to look at a little history first.

During the last century (the twentieth) there was such acceleration - (What does that word mean by the way? Yup = Like stepping on the gas pedal - going faster ~ I repeat - such acceleration) - in those 100 years - of scientific understanding and technological development - that more change - of that kind - took place - in that time - than in the previous 5000 years combined - And = In that same 100 years - there was more advancement - in those areas of learning - in the last three decades - the 70s - 80s - and 90s - than in the whole century itself ~ If - this trend were to continue - then = What the world looks like now - and what it will look like when you are - say... 50 years older - could be as different as night and day.

That is - if you're there to see it - or anyone else is - because = That same acceleration - is the cause of some whopping big problems - some of which - are only now beginning to be recognized ~ But - we won't dwell on them - because = What we're really working on here - is the solution to those problems - in fact - all problems ~ Difficult as that may be to believe ~ So let's get on with it - if we're going to find out if it works.

What - do you think - was the biggest factor - in supporting - that acceleration I've mentioned?

True = Education has improved and been available to more people ~ However - that may be more of an effect - or a result - than a cause ~ Yes = The two world wars put some heavy pressure on technology to develop ~ Which - of course - is connected to science ~ So now we're capable of blowing up the entire surface of the globe - several times over - in under an hour's time ~ But still - that's part of the effect again ~ Shall I give you a hint? Okay = It's very much the same as one of the reasons we eat food.

That's the one = Energy.

So what do I mean - energy - like what? Right = Coal - oil (particularly OIL) - natural gas - electricity - nuclear fission.

You know those people 500 years ago - who didn't have electricity? What about the people 100 years ago - did they? Yeah = The stuff was certainly around ~ But = How many people had it in their houses? Certainly not everyone - no ~ How about now? That's right = In the USA at least - it's extremely unusual to find a house that doesn't - and that's usually way out in the country somewhere - where they've chosen not to have it ~ In fact - you may not have even heard of such places.

Anyway - it's the availability - and invention - of how to convert those resources into the power to run all those machines we're so used to now - which has been behind transforming our world so quickly (not to mention - how petroleum byproducts have found their way into every part of life from fertilizer to shampoo - plastic to polyester - pharmaceuticals to the souls of our shoes)

So = Does it look like energy is a central theme (perhaps - the - central theme) - of our world? What about our bodies? Sure enough = You plan on eating today don't you?

Is happiness a kind of energy?

Let's all just stop for a minute - close our eyes = And see if we can feel energy going on inside us ~ Okay? Go.

What happened? Did you feel yourself being alive? Where? How? What does it feel like?

Remember that word adapt? Well - if changes happen in the next 50 years - like they have in the past 50 - you will have to do a lot of adapting ~ Indeed = Big time ~ Petroleum - is on its way out (just to avoid any possible confusion - petroleum - is oil - you know - that stuff that attracts so much attention to places like Iraq) Climate change - is slowly (or not so slowly) - adding up to = Everything change (if that surprises you - I would strongly suggest studying up on the subject) - and = Nearly seven billion humans (about seven times more people than the planet has been sustaining through most of our history as a species) - all want to consume = Energy (and every other thing that goes along with it) Therefore = One of the biggest adaptations on our collective plate - is = How - on Earth - are we going to manage all that?

Remember - when we talked about people running around in the past - full of electricity - and not knowing it? Yeah - I know = Of course you do - after me repeating it so often ~ Anyway = What was the idea - that led us to in the end? Exactly = That we may still be running around - in the same condition - of having an energy source inside us - that we don't know about.

Anyone here seen the movie - The Matrix? (I'm talking the first in the series by the way - not the two sequels - in case you're a big fan) What was the energy source the machines were using? Humans = Right ~ And = How were they doing it? That's it = The machines were keeping humans alive - in endless rows of life support pods - and fooling those human minds - into thinking they were living an entirely different - normal life - that was really a computer program ~ So = What was the energy the machines were using? No = The movie never really spelled it out - did it? Was it physical energy? Well - yes = But - those people weren't moving - and the machines had to feed them ~ So - it wasn't really a direct physical - doing - kind of energy ~ Was it mental energy? True again = It was never explained ~ But = What is physical or mental energy? Is it just our trillions of cells - or that pale pink-grey Jell-o between our ears - keeping busy electrically? Is it - vibration? Is it - being alive? Is it - consciousness?

Okay = That movie - is science fiction ~ What does the word fiction mean? Right = Made up - make believe ~ Just the same - that is a remarkable film - at a remarkable time in human history - that could not have been made = If certain changes - seeping into the thinking of our culture as a whole - hadn't occurred ~ True = It is also extremely violent - which might not point to any great evolutionary leap ~ Just the same = Any guesses - what those changes seeping into our culture are? That's it = Questions ~ Questions about our relationship with technology and machines - and our use - and need of - energy ~ But most importantly what? Ah - you are thinking = Thinking itself ~ How our minds work ~ The true nature of consciousness - and = What reality - really is.

Do you know what the word matrix means? Yes = It's a word in its own right ~ It has several definitions actually - but the main one is = A situation - or substance - in which something originates - develops - or is contained ~ So = Does that mean a family can be a matrix? Or a school? How about cement? Yes = Those are all different kinds of matrixes ~ What about consciousness - is that a matrix? Do you suppose that's the one they had in mind - when they named the movie?

Where did you look for the answer - when I asked all those questions? In your brain? Does that mean - if I was to cut open your skull - I could look for the answer there myself? No? I wouldn't find it? Why?

What if - these brains are not the kind of machines we think of them to be? What if - our thoughts don't originate in our brains at all - but they are more like received radio signals? Could that be possible? Do you think it is? No? Why not? Could you prove it one way or the other? That's the problem isn't it? We know we all have thoughts ~ Science - and our own experience - tell us that our heads are involved ~ But - how they work - at least from the point of view of = Where - or how - does a thought originate? We're still guessing.

Okay = I'm going to make it easy on you this time ~ Your assignment - is to go back to the second assignment I gave you ~ Which - I'm not even going to make you remember - or guess - what that was ~ It's the conscious breathing exercise - that I've reminded you of so often - you might not even have to guess ~ But (expecting the but weren't you) - as you do it - I want you to think of your brain as a radio receiver ~ Now - think - isn't really the best word - because = Thinking is apt to distract you from the work of simply breathing ~ So - what you need to try to do - is - feel the inhale and exhale as a kind of circuit of electricity - powering that radio receiver - and - just do that - power the thing ~ After all - radios don't think about what they receive - they just do ~ The rest of it - is = See what happens - what comes through ~ Don't - I repeat - don't - interact with yourself about what comes through ~ You'll know you are - if you start sticking more thoughts to the ones you have ~ Yes - you're right = It's not that easy to do ~ Compared at least to what you're used to doing ~ The trick is - to breathe - pay attention to your breath - and wait - just wait ~ All you have to do - is supply the lungs in action - and wait ~ Who knows what kind of signal you might pick up ~ And = I don't even have to remind you - to breath.

[[[[[[[[Nutritive Values:

We (humans) - spend all of our time - in this life - inhabiting bodies ~ Everything we - do - involves some portion of them ~ Most - of those "everythings" - involve some action/intention/purpose having to do with maintaining their survival in some way = Keeping them fed - housed - clothed - fit - healthy - feeling good - and of course - looking good whenever possible - or - just getting them from one place to another ~ In this world - right - wrong - obliged or mistaken = It's all about = Bodies.

You'd think then - that we'd know everything there is to know - about how bodies work ~ We own them after all - why wouldn't we ~ But = Nope - we don't.

Take that little ache you've got going - that muscle soreness - those pimples - that itchy spot - red eyes - cramp in your foot - bit of gas you're hoping won't smell bad = Chances are - you haven't got a clue what the full story is behind any of those minor symptoms - not to mention any major ones you might be having.

Ah = But doctors know - science knows = It's all been worked out somewhere.

Is that what you think? Is that why you have medical insurance - or wish you did?

Well my friends = It's true that modern medical science has made astounding advances in understanding and treating physical systems ~ But = Is it all worked out somewhere? Another - very loud and resounding = Nope.

Fact is = Modern medicine - will patch you up lickety-split - replace hip joints - knees - sew up someone else's organs inside you - all kinds of procedures and interventions that will save your stressed behind and keep it going - which = Would have been regarded by any other period in history = As completely miraculous ~ But = Will it cure (or prevent - for that matter) - cancer - HIV Aids - arthritis - a cold? The list of diseases goes on to some length - and = I'm afraid that's another (by the exact definition of cure - which is - to fully restore to health - or - get rid of the disease - and most especially - its causes - altogether) = Nope.

Doctors and hospitals - for the most part (a part which is fortunately - yet slowly - changing) - operate as (what's sometimes termed) - a sick care system ~ Which means = You've got to be sick - to be cared for - and the majority of that care - is about controlling symptoms - keeping the body alive - and = That's about it ~ Not to fault doctors - they're doing the best they can - they just don't know it all yet - aaaannd = Sometimes they forget that.

124

At the same time = These bodies - we lug around everywhere - do know those things ~ Which is to say = They are right there - acting - reacting - fully aware of what needs doing - and = Doing their best to do it ~ Bodies are constantly putting themselves back together - sorting out microbes - flushing toxins away - balancing pH - regulating this that and the other cellular function ~ Bodies know how to heal - just like they know how to grow and digest and poop ~ It's no mystery to them ~ All they ask of us = Is some cooperation.

I mean hey = Do you keep your cat in the freezer at night in order to maintain its health?

Of course not ~ And - the reason is = You know better.

Well = What if - cooperation with our bodies - is linked as closely to learning about - understanding - expanding - happily being - Consciousness - as skin is to muscle?

The reason - I would pose such a question - is covered in the simple word = Nature ~ Our bodies are natural systems - or = A part of nature ~ Which means - just like every other natural system = They are a part of the environment in which they live - a member of an ecosystem - or - all the levels and varieties of life which inhabit - support - and maintain an environment ~ And as such = Their health and well-being - is a direct reflection - of that environment's health and well-being ~ They are also - environments - or ecosystems - themselves ~ One element of which is = We are absolutely crawling with bacteria ~ Some of which (if there are too few) - you can't live without - and some others (if there are too many) - you can't live with.

Everything that goes on inside us - is connected ~ Including = Connected to what goes on outside us - exactly as = Everything we do with our minds - is connected - inside - outside - side to side - no sides - and - anyway = As far as our bodies go = The most obvious connection - between inside and outside = Is what we put in them - and = The strongest connection between - in - out - thin - stout - healthy - wealthy - and tolerant of bad rhymes = Is what we think about - what to put in them ~ Which = You've heard before ~ But = Do you know - what to put in yours?

Do you know what the ideal pH level is - your body is constantly trying to achieve? Do you know what foods will assist that achievement? Do you know what foods work against it? Do you know what pH is? Do you know what anti-oxidants are - and how they prevent cancer? Do you know what probiotics are - and how they support healthy digestion and immune function? Do you know what proper hydration is - or how the structure of water molecules affects how they are absorbed by cells? Do you know what the effects of sugar are on the body? How about exercise? Or = Your own mental attitude?

What you should know (should - in the sense of taking full responsibility for your own health) - doesn't end there ~ But = If you don't know the answers to those questions = This - is certainly where your homework begins.||||||||||

N.P.U. - Chapter Eight - Electricity?

Have you ever experienced an electric shock? It's a very active kind of experience isn't it - a real buzz? Do you have a choice of whether it will pass through you or not? After you've touched whatever it is that's electrified that is ~ Nope = That's for sure ~ That speed of light action just plain beats the best we've got every time ~ The choice ends - the instant - we're the conductor ~ But = What's that mean? Conducting what? A symphony orchestra? A test of the emergency broadcast system? What is electricity doing? Why would it have such a strong effect on our bodies?

Alright - in order to understand how electricity moves - you have to do something - the vast majority of people - who use electricity every day - seldom - or never - do = You have to want to know how it works ~ Then - if you do that = You'll find out ~ You'll also find out - there is another whole world - tiny beyond measuring (if you're measuring with a word as giant as tiny in that place) - that's running this whole show we call a universe - and = It's all done with - electricity (kind of anyway)

So - for the sake of speeding that up = I'll outline a few of the basics for you.

A little over a hundred years ago - the basic = Was the atom ~ Early models of the atom identified it to have three parts - or particles = The nucleus - or center of the atom - are where two of those particles - the proton and neutron do their thing ~ Which is = Spin - and - wait (not really - but it's our human equivalent word for it) - for things to happen ~ One of the things happening - is what the other particle is up to = That's the electron - and = It's flying around in an orbit of the nucleus - so fast- it might not even appear as a blur - if we were able to watch - which = We're not.

Now atoms - aren't just limited to one of each particle ~ There are different numbers - for different kinds of atoms - which = Is officially described - as atomic weight ~ Nor are electrons - limited to only one orbital path in one direction ~ If you think of our solar system and the nine planets orbiting the sun (despite the fact little Pluto has been reduced to less than planet status) - you'll have a clear idea of an orbit - but = Not an electron ~ Not only can they orbit in both directions (with most atoms having an equal number of electrons doing just that - half one way - and half the other) = They can also switch - from an inside orbit - to an outside orbit - instantaneously - or vice versa - in an action known as = A quantum leap (Sound familiar?) - which = Is much like switching from the high speed lane of a highway to the exit ramp without actually traveling the distance in between ~ An impressive little trick at any scale.

As for electricity - well = It's already there ~ Two of those particles have a charge - which can be described in magnetic terms (can't forget magnetism now can we) - as polarized ~ Electrons - have a negative charge ~ Protons - have a positive charge ~ Neutrons - are neutral (as you might suspect from the name) - with no charge ~ It's the magnetic force - generated by these oppositely charged particles - that keeps the little family - more or less - together - and objects - like you - and that wall - more or less - apart ~ That phrase - more or less - is measured in electrons - and = Is also how that question of ours - the one about electricity - gets answered.

Unlike the particles of the nucleus - that are glued together by a force we'll get to by-and-by - (even if it is somewhat questionable that science really knows what it's talking about in claiming such a force) - electrons - have the option of joining other atomic families ~ When that happens - electricity (it's said) - is generated - which = Is apt to give the misleading impression - that it wasn't there - previous to its being generated ~ The truth is - that everything that's constructed of atoms (and - everything physical - is) - is - electrical - or - if you like = Charged ~ However - at our human level of relating to electricity - where it's mostly a matter of switches and motors and dials and various humming sounds - that generating is rather important ~ So - back at the level of atoms - the description goes = When an atom has a deficiency of electrons - or too few - it becomes positively charged ~ If it has too many - it's negatively charged ~ Electric current is produced - when circumstances (such as Niagara Falls turning giant turbines) - create the conditions that allow the free flow of electrons between atoms - now negative - now positive - magnetically drawn from one to the other - at roughly the speed of light - so that charge - or that electricity - that atoms are made of - can do things ~ Of course - the only thing - those electrons are ever really doing - is being themselves.

||||||||| Power Lines:

For some reason - Niagara Falls - has become a traditional honeymoon destination ~ Perhaps from nature's suggestion of - taking the leap - so dramatically demonstrated by the Niagara River's thundering plunge ~ Yet - no matter why the falls have generated that attraction - the real magnetism - takes place deep underground = Where that same river generates many billions of kilowatt-hours of electricity every year.

The unique detail of hydroelectric power (figuratively different from other techniques of generating electricity) - is the parallel - between the movement of water - and the movement of electricity itself ~ Electricity - is said to flow - in a current - the same as any river in the world ~ It also has a kind of pressure behind it - or force to move - just as when you turn on the tap and the water gushes - or trickles - out = Which is what the term voltage means = More water = More water pressure ~ More electricity = More voltage.

And then = There's rate of flow - as in gallons per hour = Which - in electrical terms - is covered by the word amperage ~ The amount of work - electricity can perform - works - exactly the same as harnessing waterpower (such as ancient water wheels or the mill wheels of the 18th and 19th centuries) - according to a combination of - pressure (voltage) - and rate of flow (amperage)

The parallel continues - in the amount of energy - delivered - by both water and electricity ~ Pump a certain amount of water in one end of a pipe - and (given there are no obstacles to it's getting through) - the same amount of water - pours out the other end ~ Electric current - mirrors that consistency precisely (what goes in - comes out) - including - how some of that energy (or ability to perform work - not the substance itself) - is converted by resistance (friction) - to another form of energy (namely - heat) - in both those cases of - juice - traveling.

When it comes to the two cooperating to generate power (back there under the falls you just tossed your bouquet in) - it's another simple matter of conversion going on (simple as a statement at least) Water pressure - at a particular rate of flow - spins huge turbines (much like the props - or propellers - that drive a boat through the water) - which turn a shaft - at the top of which - is an equally large magnet - spinning at the same rate - which = Produces a magnetic field - which - as it passes continuously by a conductor (windings of copper wire) = Induces (sort of stimulates - or convinces) - the charge of electrons already present in that copper - to leap one atom to the next as what we call electricity - and = There is the conversion - of waterpower - or work - turned into electric power - zipping off to do its work.

Of course - the differences between water and electricity - are equally obvious ~ And - that being said = Let us raise our water glasses to hydroelectric power (at least in a place like Niagara - which has an extremely low environmental impact) - and these amazing electrons - that just can't help - but go with the flow.|||||||||

When it comes to yourself - or at least your body - the reason encountering large amounts of electricity is such a shocking experience = Is because the components that make up these bodies (particularly water - which accounts for better than three quarters of the body ingredient list) - are excellent conductors ~ In other words = Like copper - those are substances in which that electron exchange can move easily ~ Very much unlike - rubber or plastic = In which that same process is pretty much contained and unable to move ~ Which - of course = Explains why all those electrical cords - plugged in around your house - are made of those oppositely functioning materials (or -copper inside rubber or plastic) - in order to conduct that exchange safely ~ Which means = Do the cooking - for you - rather than - of you - because - quite literally = That's what electricity can do to the cells of your body.

I mentioned earlier - that the atom - and its three component particles - was - the basic - a little over a hundred years ago ~ Well - clearly much has changed in that time ~ What used to be the smallest building block - is now recognized to be more like a building in its own right ~ Those three charges - plus - minus - and doesn't really care - are housing dozens more of their tiny cousins - and = Still not letting on what's in the basement.

So - to take another step toward getting a more up-to-date look at subatomic particles = Let's return to Einstein's brain for a moment ~ No = Not those gooey bits of gelatinous cauliflower preserved in jars of formaldehyde and passed from scientist to scientist for decades ~ I mean the working apparatus firmly attached to the rest of the living professors body - and - the reason is = Light.

Einstein - was obsessed with fathoming the mystery of what light is - and = Out of that obsession (or rather - in it) - something occurred in that brain of his - that altered the course of history ~ Odd turn of phrase as that is - as it seems to presume that - history - was intent on going somewhere else ~ Just the same (or is that - different) = That light - that went on in his head - illuminated - far more than a few moments of electrochemical activity between glial cells - neurons - dendrites - axons - synapses - and memories of sausages and beer - and = It's still shining on the world today ~ What's more = It fits in a neat little package requiring no more than five everyday symbols = $E=mc^2$ ~ Probably - THE - most famous equation in history ~ Even find it printed on thousands of T-shirts - right up there in popularity with - I'm with stupid ~ But = What does it mean?

Well - to simply translate the symbols - it reads = Energy - equals matter - multiplied by the speed of light - squared (or the speed of light multiplied by itself) What - that means - is = Energy and matter are not separate things - they can be converted into each other ~ What that means = Takes some explaining ~ But - it begins = With the speed of light.

|||||||| Tick Talk:

Ever since - humans began scratching and painting and carving symbols of their thoughts on rocks and cave walls (and then every other means of recording communication we've employed in the rest of that - ever since) - measuring time - has been a central feature of our interest in ourselves (or that which powers and controls our lives) - because = Time - is the ultimate measurement - of life (at least in the sense of physical form - which tends to be our rather limited definition of life)

Time - is also - one of the main measuring tools of science - and = The science of measuring time - has slowly (one of the most general of time measurements) - developed tools - which (as far as accuracy goes) = Tend to reflect the speed at which science develops ~ We now live in - the time - of the atomic clock (which is reported to be accurate to within a few seconds over many thousands of years - although - less than 50 years of use so far - does point at that being a slightly premature claim) - where = New scientific developments occur all - the time.

The first evidence - of measured time - comes from the period when the last Ice Age was retreating back toward the poles (some 13,000 years ago) - in the shape of bones and sticks carved with depictions of the phases of the moon ~ Apparently - 28 day cycles were as close to accurate as those - times - required (or at least achieved) Then = There are the stone circles of the Neolithic period (roughly 7,000 years ago) - such as the famed Stonehenge - whose astronomical alignments with such Earth axis tipping days as the summer and winter solstices - are also well known ~ Not quite as well known - are the number of such circles and standing stones across Europe - especially Britain - and the theories of alignments with invisible lines of energy crisscrossing the planet - known as ley lines.

Calendar time - or mathematically plotting out weeks and months and years - have had people staring at the sun and moon and stars for all those thousands of years as well - but = What's led to that quick glance at a watch - while running late for another meeting - began in ancient Egypt around 3,500 B.C.E. - with shadow clocks (the earliest form of the sundial) They - worked according to the lengths and direction of a standing object's shadow = Which wasn't much help in getting you to Pharaoh's palace on time after dark or on cloudy days - but = We had to start somewhere ~ Somewhere - moved more or less simultaneously (another view of time) - into water clocks - which = Work rather like the principle of an hourglass - only with very different designs of inflow and outflow - in which designs = The ancient Chinese and Arabs competed for most elaborate (not intentionally however) - and = Candle clocks - which = Are the simple concept - of a candle (whose rate of burn is known) - marked off in increments (fractions of a unit of measure) - something like hours - which = When the candle has burned down to the next mark - mark - the passing of that amount of time ~ The same concept - was used in glass oil lamps - whose dropping fuel - could be measured against the same type of incremented scale on its side ~ And then = My own favorite - the incense clock = Which worked the same as the candle clock - only smelled better.

Sundials - having been on the scene - a very long time - were useful - what with their ability to break down the day into 12 equal parts = The drawback being - those parts were shorter in the winter - and longer in the summer ~ That problem was eventually overcome by one of those amazing Arab mathematicians (we have them to thank for our Arabic numerals) - who worked out how to produce a sundial which would mark time consistently year-round (through some clever trigonometry - and a working knowledge of the Earth's axis) - in the year (another measurement of time of course) - 1371.

Mechanical clocks - had already been around (and improving slowly) - since the late 10th century ~ Monks - with their regular schedule of devotions (prayers and rituals) - were particularly interested in (or is that - devoted to) - designing and building new mechanisms - in order to more precisely maintain those daily rhythms ~ Their machines - worked by inter-meshing gears turned by the force of weighted ropes ~ It wasn't until the invention of the pendulum clock - in 1656 - that weighty technology began to be eclipsed ~ And then = The spiral windup spring turned up in 1675 (the work of the same Dutch scientist who harnessed the pendulum to time keeping) - and = We were well on our way to the Rolex = Which became universally popular (the wristwatch - not specifically the Rolex) - during the first world war - due to its convenience (compared that is - to the timing of hauling out and opening a pocket watch as machine gun bullets kick up the mud around you) The discovery - of the electrical polarizing qualities of quartz crystal under stress - in 1880 - finally produced a clock that ran on that principle - by 1927 - which = Set a new standard for accuracy - and = Forty two years later - produced the first of billions of quartz watches - being glanced at this second.

Now - you may wonder why - I've wasted your time (and mine) - on this little diversion into measuring such waste = And the reason is = As you grind at the frustration of a website taking ten whole seconds to load = Take a breath - and notice (if you can) - that all the parts of time along the way are = Interesting ~ And = In this modern world - where nanoseconds count - wonder - for just one moment of your precious supply - what all the fuss about time really is - when - all the time - there ever is - is = Now.]]||]||||]

Einstein accepted Maxwell's idea you could never catch up to a beam of light ~ It made some kind of instinctive sense to him - that - no matter how fast you go - that light would still be traveling away from you at 670,000,000 miles an hour ~ It was a concept many of his contemporaries (or people in his moment of history) - had a great deal of trouble with ~ As you might yourself - if you think about it ~ So - think about this instead = As Albert and a friend were looking at the clock towers of Geneva (in Switzerland) - and considering that same speed of light = Something happened ~ You might call it a quantum leap ~ You might say - it happened - in that brain of his ~ Then again - you might say - his brain just helped explain it to him - after - it happened ~ No matter what you say - what happened was = A connection was made between two (apparently) - completely unrelated things ~ You can't even say things - because = Even though you might use that word (as I just did) - it really doesn't fit - even if you turn on the light in order to see your watch - because = Time - and - light - were those two - things.

What Einstein realized was = That time does not govern the speed of light ~ Rather = The speed of an object - the closer it approaches the speed of light - whether that be 500 miles an hour or 650,000,000 miles an hour - governs - the speed of time ~ In other words = The faster you go - the slower time goes ~ Which means = Time is not a fixed speed - or = It's not the same - for everything - everywhere ~ Light - on the other hand - is - a fixed speed - it never varies - never changes ~ Time - therefore - is relative - or - dependent on circumstances (acceleration being the circumstance in question here) It's not the tick-tock of a constant force to which every - thing - must bow = Something else is ~ The real timer of the universe = Is the zip zap - of electricity turning into magnetism - turning into electricity - turning into magnetism ~ Catch up to the speed of light - and - you catch up to the speed of time ~ Catch up to the speed of time - and - you have located = Now.

Electromagnetism is at the core of any - and all - things (including that action in your brain that just scurried about defining what - a thing - is) Its two parts (that join to make a third - which is actually just one) - are what makes everything - one thing - just like the words - every - and - thing = Make - everything - one thing ~ It's really that simple - even if it isn't {{So read that a couple more times just to see}}

One - thing - that perhaps makes it appear not simple (other than everything - appearing - to be distinctly separate stuff) - is = Electromagnetism - is not a thing either = It's a force ~ Or - to put it in a more familiar setting of language = A word that gets used all the time - the same as we use cars - with the great majority of people driving them - hopeless at fully understanding how they work = Energy.

But – let's not just stand by the side of the electromagnetic highway waiting for the quantum tow truck to do the work for us ~ Let's ask another question = Why does energy equal - mc^2?

SPECIAL BONUS EXERCISE - number four

Changing the Past:

There is one thing that people agree on (even if they still torture themselves over it - or fantasize over how it could be different) - and that agreement is = You can't change the past.

Of course - the reason for that agreement is = It certainly seems to be true ~ The apparent fact of it - is right up there with = The past is over and done and gone and it ain't comin' back ~ But = What if - it's not true? What if - you can - change the past?

In the world of observing observation - it's long been noted - that when there are several witnesses to an event = There are also several descriptions of that event - that do not match each other ~ It's the usual case of what people focus on - their different angles of view - their relationship to the people - places - or things involved - plus a whole long list of other variables - not the least of which = Is that the majority of people are very poor observers of detail (not to mention - storing those details as memories) It has also been noticed - that as time passes (especially lots of time) - the descriptions - or stories of those events - change - or no longer match their originals.

Now you may say = The event in question - does not change - no matter what anyone reports or remembers - because = It can't = It happened just as it did - and = That's that ~ However = The effects of that event - are all defined - by how the participants responded in their minds - and = Continue to respond there ~ To be sure = There may have been plenty of physical elements as well - injuries - property damage - treasure found - pregnancy - on and on ~ But still - the continuing response is mental - and emotional - as well as physical - and all those things = Change.

The other side of the coin - is the idea that = You can't change the future ~ But - for that notion - there is almost no agreement ~ According to most of us = We change the future all the time - by the choices we make - and how we change our minds - and do what we do.

The thing is = How do you change something that hasn't happened yet? The future is really no more accessible than the past ~ It doesn't exist ~ All we are really capable of changing (which is really to say - doing) - is what is going on in the present ~ And - chiefly (which is to say - at the core of our experience) - what that changing/doing is = Is what's going on - in our minds.

The real question then - follows the logic - that our present state of mind influences the future - which has in turn - been influenced by the past ~ Therefore = Can we - in the present - use our state of mind - to change that influence from the past - by envisioning - a different past - the same way as we would - a different future - and in that way = Change - the past? At least as far as it is related to changing the present - and - the future.

Could give it a shot anyway ~ So - try this = Locate a memory in your mind - of an event - an interaction - something that caused you great difficulty or emotional pain ~ When you've settled on the memory = Picture the scene - the people - the words spoken - as clearly as you possibly can ~ Rerun it in your mind as much as you can stand - searching for details - the weather - the furniture - expressions - clothing ~ Then = Add a new detail of your own - something small - yet significant - that changes the feeling of the situation just slightly = A smile - an added word - the sun came out - there was money on the ground - a song was playing ~ Find something - that in any other circumstance would please you - and plug it into the memory ~ Then = Go about your business - until some hours later - when = You do it again = You return to that memory ~ Only now = It has a new part.

Yes = You know you put that part there - and for that reason it stands out ~ But = That's good ~ Pay attention to it ~ Allow it to be just a detail you'd forgotten - which = You remember now ~ Tie the two together - and then = Forget about it - until you remember again ~ Go on adding details if you like - but = Make sure they fit - that they slip in neatly - the way a red leaf blowing past fits into an autumn day (provided that happens where you live)

Of course - if you want - you can also make up brand-new memories as far-fetched as you like ~ You've done that kind of thing for your future ~ Why not your past? Because = What we're really talking here - is the present - and = Can the past be different there? Maybe.

Class Nine - Perception?

BREATHE (And... 14 ~ Well done ~ Have you thought about doing more - say... 21? That's the number I like ~ As well as just doing them more often of course - such as before a test - or study time - or just when you're tired and cranky or anxious and emotional or - whatever ~ Those studies mentioned earlier - all - witnessed dramatically increased academic achievement - participation - concentration - memory skills - stress reduction - and just plain happy calm ~ What do you say? Back on your feet?)

How did your receiver work? Did you pick up any aliens? No? How about your thoughts - did they feel different from your usual thoughts? Did you have to wait a longer time than usual for them to turn up? What did it feel like powering yourself like that? What did the action of mind it took to try - feel like? Have you ever waited for a thought before? Anyone have any surprising thoughts come through? Did doing the breathing this way change how you feel about doing it? Would you continue?

So - check this out = In experiments on brains - using fancy scanning machines (more accurately known as an MRI - or Magnetic Resonance Imaging - and a PET scan - or Positron Emission Tomography) - subjects (meaning people) - were shown an object - let's say... a banana = While this went on - their brain activity was mapped and measured - then = The same subjects - were asked to close their eyes - and picture the banana - in their minds ~ It was observed = That the exact same areas of the brain - showed essentially the same activity - as when they were using their minds - to see the banana - as they did for using their eyes ~ The moral of the story (if you will) - seems to be = That our brains cannot tell the difference - between what we see - and what we remember (or perhaps even imagine) - seeing.

||||||||| PET your MRI:

Positron Emission Tomography (as you've likely gathered - despite its abbreviation to PET scan) - has nothing to do with dogs and cats and goldfish ~ It is - what the medical profession (or is that - industry) - calls an imaging test ~ The general purpose being - to see - what's going on inside a body - differently from other imaging technologies (such as x-rays) - and - short of cutting that same body into pieces.

In very simple terms (we like them) - it works = By taking a biologically active molecule (active - in the sense of - it's something our body uses for its own purposes anyway) - like glucose (which is a sugar) - and adding a tiny bit of a radioactive substance to that (that - actually being many molecules) - and injecting that combination into the bloodstream ~ After some time (roughly 30 to 60 minutes - depending on the specific test) - that substance collects in tissues and organs - and emits (sends out - like light from a bulb) - a type of energy called gamma rays (which breaks down to being called - photons) - which the machine picks up (like a radio receiver) - and then (through the wizardry of computer science) = Converts that information into a 3-D picture of the parts of the body under scrutiny.

What's shown by this picture = Is both - structure (or the shape and dimensions of individual parts) - and metabolism (or the function of absorbing molecules for different cellular uses) - which = Can then be interpreted into what's going right or wrong with that organ or what have you ~ As far as the brain goes (that seeming seat of consciousness) - it's assumed that blood flow (or where blood is in highest demand) - with its essential cargo of oxygen molecules (Are you breathing?) - indicates = Which parts of the brain - are most active in any given moment of scanning.

The MRI (or Magnetic Resonance Imaging - as already pointed out) - is of course - another imaging technology ~ It - uses a strong magnetic field (much safer than radiation) - which it broadcasts at the body being tested - specifically - at the protons of hydrogen atoms (the most numerous atoms in the universe) Those protons - tend to align with that field (much like the iron filings on a piece of paper magnet trick) - until = Another magnetic field is pulsed (like a strobe light) - at them - which = Knocks those protons out of alignment with the original field - and = As they move back into alignment with that first field (still being broadcast) - they emit a radio frequency signal - which = The machine records ~ The protons of different tissues (such as muscle and fat) - realign at different speeds - and so can be contrasted as different structures in the printout of images the machine creates - which = Are like quarter inch slices of bread - from the whole loaf - that is the body being tested.

When it comes to brains (again - a central theme here) = It's that oxygenated hemoglobin (blood carrying oxygen) - that's also most important to mechanically plotting out brain activity with an MRI (not to mention - just plain brain activity - so = Breathe) It's also where the word - functional - gets tacked onto the front of MRI - because = It's a slightly different machine (called an fMRI) - which focuses on brains - from a slightly different spin - on subatomic particle spin - which (slightly - or perhaps - dramatically) = Is probably more than you need to oxygenate your brains with just now.]]]]]]]]]]

Here are some more scientific observations.

Our brains (it appears) - take in - something like 40 billion bits of sensory information every second ~ Yes - that's bits - like a computer (or sequences of zeros and ones - only - it's really a comparative measurement - rather than actual zeros and ones) - and yes = Every second ~ We (we meaning - our perception awareness) - on the other hand - consciously - and partly consciously - use - only about 2000 bits a second - according to what an invisible super fast process sorts out as immediately useful to us in relation to our bodies and the environment they're in - and = Ignores the rest ~ Our eyes - of course - are a major source of this information gathering ~ Yet - we only seem - to see - what our experience has patterned us (that is - trained us) - to see - or pay attention to ~ What I mean by that is = Our eyes take in huge amounts of detail - but = If asked to describe all that detail - we're generally lost ~ And - well = I'm actually suggesting = That there may be a good deal more - we see (meaning - take in as information) - but don't see (meaning - be aware of) - because = Our past experience - hasn't - doesn't - or for some reason is unwilling to - support that function.

Do you know what the word perception means? I'm thinking you ought to for some reason ~ But hey = How would I really know without asking?

Okay (and by way of a little review) = Yes = It's the act - of perceiving ~ Which is basically like that word - aware ~ It's kind of like what your brain and body are up to = Perceiving - a relationship - with a world - through senses - and ideas - gathered through experience of those senses - and ideas - in an attempt to understand - and so survive - that relationship - with that world ~ It's a word - to cover the whole picture - of all that going on (sort of one step up - in the language scale - from the word awareness) - because = It's meant to include - the relationships between - all types of awareness - or = What you - think - feel - and experience - about - what - you - think - feel - and experience - the world is - according - to what - you - think - feel - and experience - what - you - are {{Yup - I'd read that one again}}

So = Why do I mention it? After all - it's only a word - and words (as we've noticed) - are a bit short for such a long job.

Well - basically - because = The definition I just gave - for perception - is often - more or less - the perception - of what consciousness is (Sound familiar?) - and = There is a very important distinction to be made - which = Would - of course - include knowing the definition - of the word - distinction.

That's right = A distinction - is clarifying - or making clear - defining - pointing out - or drawing attention to - a difference.

What if - perception - is only the thinnest surface layer of what consciousness really is? Because = Perception - is based on - relationships - or - how one thing - or idea - relates - to another = Rather than - how all things - or ideas - are = Being - all at once - right now.

I know - I'm stretching human possibility to its limit ~ That is - suggesting (however subtly) - that humans might actually be able - to DO - what I just said ~ Which is = Relate - to all things - at the same time ~ But - it's like that action - of the huge amount of information we are gathering with our senses - right now ~ What if - we are throwing - most - of what we can experience - out - because = We are limiting - what we perceive as immediately useful - because = We think - our experience - can only come from our senses - as we - have previously (meaning - in the past) - understood them - and that's (our past experience) = What we think - is useful? In fewer words {{that is after you read the first bunch again}} = What if - we are - limiting - our potential - by what - we think - that potential is?

136

What if (again) - what we see (meaning - again - our visual awareness) - is even less than 15% (again) - of what sight is actually capable of (again) = Seeing?

[[[[[[[[[Digital Deception?

If you own a digital camera - perhaps you've noticed strange bright spots - floating circles of light - that look sort of like smudgy reflections - or semitransparent full moons hanging in the air of your finished photographs ~ Or perhaps = Not ~ Regardless of whether they appear in your photographs - they have appeared in thousands of others - and…..

What are they?

The answers = Cover one end of the - belief spectrum - to the other ~ There's the optical engineer end - which asserts = They can be unquestionably explained away - as the natural (that's natural - in the sense of what science - up to this point - has agreed upon as natural) - phenomenon of light reflecting - or refracting - off various objects - such as dust - water droplets - and the lens and mechanisms of the camera itself (and - in nine out of ten cases - maybe more - they may very well be right) Then - there's the metaphysical (or looking more in the direction of the unseen - and unproven - at least by the measurements of the scientific agreement mentioned previously) - community - who happily declare them to be visitations of disincarnate (not in bodies) - beings - spirit guides - departed loved ones - or any number of inhabitants of other dimensions - which = This relatively new form of technology - is allowing momentary visual access to.

No matter which side of that fence you care to plant your toes = There is no denying - that such physical evidence of - something (natural - or supernatural) - shows up in digital photos - which = Only rarely occurs with conventional film ~ One possible explanation for this = Is that digital cameras (or the CCD - charge coupled device - which takes the place of film in such cameras) - are more sensitive to frequencies of light outside - what's called - the visible spectrum (meaning - the middle part of the light spectrum - represented by the rainbow - we can see with our eyes) - particularly the infrared - or high frequency end of those energy variations collectively known as light ~ So much so in fact - that more up to date digital cameras have built in filters to solve the problems that infrared light causes.

What all that means is = Light exists as a wave of energy (electromagnetism - to be exact) - which = You could get a picture of in your mind - by tying one end of a rope to something - holding the other end in your hand - and - flipping the hand end up and down so that a wave travels the length of the rope (turning your hand in a circle at the same time will create the more precise spiral form a wave actually travels in - just so you know) A fast bumpy wave - is a high frequency (like ultraviolet - just beyond the purple end of the rainbow) A long slow wave - is a low-frequency (like infrared - just past the other - red end - of the spectrum) It's the medium waves - between the high and low - which are the ones we can see with our eyes.

Whether that makes sense to you or not - is not entirely the point ~ The point is = There is mounting evidence - that these Orbs (which is what those floating spheres have come to be called) - could very well be evidence of other dimensions interacting with our own - which = Would require a thorough rewriting of the definitions of what is - natural.

Some of that rewriting (if not all of it in fact) - is about our understanding of energy ~ No = That's not the sort of energy that powers lights and cars and such (well - that is included - but...) It's the energy - of thoughts - and feelings - in a word = Consciousness.

The connection with orbs = Is that certain states of mind - certain types of interactions - which generate certain types of thoughts/feelings/consciousness - apparently - attract the things (if you can call them things - unless you mean dust and mist and reflections) Those types of states and interactions - are ones of joy and wonder - musical - playful - worshipful - imaginative - healing ~ When those conditions are multiplied - the incidents of orbs appearing - can - also multiply ~ Which = Does not support - the belief - that they are nothing more than reflections ~ It also doesn't - prove - they are something else.

Some of the intriguing pieces - of the proof of something else evidence - is how rapid sequence shots of the same scene - often show changes in position of the same orb - at speeds - and consistency of appearance - impossible - for the natural objects thought to cause them to display ~ Some photo sequences even shown tremendous numbers of orbs swirling into a spiral pattern - which ends up looking much like a tunnel of light ~ While others - show orbs which appear and disappear between one shot and the next - as though they are not so much being caught by the camera's flash (in cases of using a flash that is) - but = As though they are using the light of the flash (storing it up - so to speak) - to make themselves visible ~ Another case of - unnatural causes? Maybe ~ Maybe not.

Whatever these digital mysteries are - or aren't = They are - an example of looking at familiar things - in unfamiliar ways - and so = Asking new questions - questioning old answers - experiencing = The possibility - of new frontiers.|||||||||

We've already played with this idea a bit - haven't we? Sure = That peripheral vision thing ~ Didn't know you were getting in so deep did you - just by opening your eyes? Ah - but that's the thing = You were already in there ~ It's just - a question of = What you're looking at ~ Kind of like getting driven around in that car you eventually learn how to drive yourself.

Let me put it a different way = What if - our eyes are capable of seeing - a far broader range of light and color and energy - than what we normally expect from them? What I mean by - capable - is = What if - they are designed - so that - they are doing those things - right now? By - doing those things - I mean = Seeing sound waves - or electromagnetic fields - or ultraviolet light - infrared light - gamma rays - just to mention some of the ones we know about = No telling what we don't know about ~ What if - we think we don't see those things - because = The ability to do so - is part of that 85% potential - we're not using - or ignoring - or insisting is not there? What if - those abilities are like software programs - already installed - that we could simply click on = We just don't know they're available? In other words = What if - that kind of information is being taken in

138

constantly - but = Doesn't show up on our monitors (so to speak) - because we haven't asked it to? Do you think - that because there is all this stuff going on - waves and rays and frequencies - that we don't see (that is - maybe just think we don't see) - there would be an advantage - to being able to see it? What kind of advantage?

I seem to be asking (several times now) = What do our eyes really see out there? But - better yet = What - do we - really see - in here? Where is your experience of the world? Isn't your entire experience of everything = Inside you?

Okay - yes = We touch - and see - and smell - and hear - and taste - a world - which seems to prove it's there - but = Where is the experience of your senses taking place? Would you say = That our minds are in a constant state - of describing to us - what we are experiencing? Does that mean = Our experience - is our mind? No? Is it our bodies then? Doesn't that circle right back to - where do we experience our bodies? Isn't it true = That no matter what happens on the outside of our bodies - our relationship with that happening = Is on the inside?

Let's look at this idea from that inside then = Close your eyes for a moment - and look around inside you = Feel yourself being = Take inventory of all your sensations ~ Yes = that does sound like an = {{{**Inventory Time**}}} = So go for it.

Anyway = Doesn't it feel like a larger space inside you - particularly in your head - than the amount of space you actually take up? Do you hear yourself - telling yourself - the story of what's going on - for you - right now? No = Not in words necessarily ~ Although - they are around in there I'm sure ~ Isn't it more like a state of constant information flow from your senses - and then = All those judgment reaction observation and interaction thoughts - about - that information? What - is - it - like - in there?

[[[[[[[[[Doctor Dude's Dictionary - word eight - Nuance:

Variation means - differences among similar things - like varieties of music or breakfast cereal ~ It's when you step past the glaring gulfs of what separates - for example - Beethoven from Bob Marley - and start peeling down those variations - splitting the hairs of description that define their differences - that = A smooth little word called - nuance (pronounced - new - and aunts - as though you were from England) - paints the subtle shades of color that pick out such things as - one cloud from another ~ Not that clouds have any direct connection to music - excepting through that word nuance of course - whose origin is in the clouds ~ Which - is really more to say = Looking at clouds - since it began its career in a word meaning clouds - that somehow drifted into partnership with another - rather similar word - meaning shades of color - and became both useful and popular with people who spent time staring at clouds - or = French landscape painters to be specific ~ And there you have it.

Exactly how nuance got its head out of the clouds - in order to get down with musicians and writers and subtle little quirks of speech - is anybody's guess ~ Excepting - obviously - that useful inspiration for language - which = Is a need to express a certain idea - separate from other ideas - so that people will know which idea you're talking about ~

The idea in question - was slight differences - or subtle variation - in meaning - in quality - tone of voice - color - decoration - or basically anything that's not quite the same as other things that are called the same thing.

For all nuance might be labeled a noun - you can't go down to the store and pick one up ~ It's much too slippery for that ~ It's an active noun - a verb like noun ~ Which doesn't quite make it a verb - more like an inspirer of action (or verbs) - that's hanging around to watch ~ You can detect nuance in a politicians speech ~ Notice the nuances of body language - of expression - or mood ~ You can respond to nuance in the choice of colors in a room - or appreciate the nuance of shifting light in that same room as the sun sets ~ You might even pick up on the nuance of just enough salt - or the perfect amount of pepper in your dinner ~ Nuance is just that smidge - that barely brushed against - that whisper of a change - that once it's identified - is no longer nuance - because = Nuance - is the moment - of that identification ~ After that - the differences - are just differences - that mean different things ~ To be sure - that might sound like slicing words down to a very thin distinction - but then = That's nuance.]]]]]]]]

So - are all those - goings on - energy - of one kind or another? What if - there is only one kind of energy - despite all the ways it can appear or be generated? What if that energy - is consciousness?

Why do you think I would say that?

Alright = We'll let those ideas just simmer for the moment - and = We'll do a couple of exercises that are about fooling those brains of ours ~ Well - not exactly fooling = More like stimulating - or coaxing - into a particular chemical response ~ Did you know - that all of our emotional responses - are communicated to our cells by chemicals? Doesn't matter if you did or not = Because - actually - there may be a good deal more to it than that at the quantum level ~ But - for the moment - the trick - is to get them pumping.

The warm up to performing that trick - is another quick = {{{**Inventory Time**}}}

The first exercise - I like to call the Buddha Laugh ~ It's extremely simple ~ All you do is laugh ~ I don't mean - laugh for a reason - like tell a joke - or try to find something funny on the TV ~ I mean - just laugh ~ Open your mouth - and make the sound of laughter - and keep doing it for a whole minute ~ Okay? You ready to try? Go.

How did it work? Were you really laughing after a while? How does your body feel? Are you holding it differently now? Doing this in a group - of course - speeds up the result - because of the humor of watching others do it ~ But - doing it alone can be just as effective ~ Provided you want it to be ~ That's the trick = Wanting it to work ~ The biggest reason is = If you don't want it to work - you won't do it in the first place.

So = What are you telling your brain - when you do this laughter thing?

Exactly = You're telling it = You're happy ~ So what does your brain do? Yup = It gets those chemicals flowing that are associated with feeling happy ~ In fact - if you truly get a real laugh in action (which would - of course - include any time you laugh for any other reason) - it acts like a flushing mechanism - clearing your brain of the chemical residues of other emotional states - and = Returning you to a condition called - neuroplasticity - where the whole system is reset - and so = Makes it better able to learn and function clearly ~ What do you suppose happens to you then? Sure = You learn and function more clearly.

The next one is a little easier ~ To get away with in public that is - so that people don't think you're some kind of nut (in case that sort of thing matters to you) It's called = Looking Up ~ For the very simple reason = That's what you do ~ Just stand up - or - sit up straight - and turn your eyes upwards ~ Our brains are trained to back up our thoughts physically ~ You may have noticed - that when you feel down - you look down - you slump - you shuffle - everything about you seems to be pulled down ~ When you do the opposite with your body - your brain is getting a different command ~ The thought - I'm happy - may not be there - or be strong - but - the thought = I want to be happy - becomes present ~ Otherwise (again) - you would not have made the first move ~ When you do this looking up thing - your brain - reads your body - as the thought - quite literal in this case = Things are looking up - and responds accordingly (creates a burst of alpha wave activity - to be specific) If you add a smile to this posture - you're reinforcing the command even more strongly (closing your eyes will also accelerate the effect) You don't have to feel it - but = If you do it - just the action - of contracting the muscles - that move your lips - immediately signals the brain - to release serotonin into the bloodstream ~ Have you heard of serotonin? Perhaps you've heard of its relationship with smiling as well? Have you tried smiling for no reason? Let's try it now.

What did it feel like? What did your thinking do? Did it change as well? Do you think it would make sense - to try these things - when you really do feel bad?

It's possible you'll find the answer to that question - with another = {{{**Inventory Time**}}}

Alright ~ Here's your assignment ~ As much as you possibly can - or remember (forgetting - by the way - is not a great excuse - that is - if you - want - to remember) = I - want - you to practice the Buddha Laugh - and - Looking Up ~ Throw in a bit of the eyes of a one year old wide open to the edges of your vision while you have a conversation with yourself about everything you're experiencing (just to liven it up) - and = Don't think about what happens = Feel it ~ Can you do that? So = What else do you have to remember to do at the same time? No = It's not to write it on your hand (although - that probably wouldn't hurt) = It's that other thing ~ Yup = That's it = While you're smiling = Breathe.

N.P.U. - Chapter Nine - MC^2?

Do you know what the answer is yet? That is - why does $E = mc^2$?

I'll save you some of that time - which = If you were traveling to Alpha Centauri (a binary - or double - star in the constellation Centaurus - about 4.4 light years from Earth) - at the speed of light - would be passing something like ten times slower than it does here on earth - which = Since you are here on earth - you might be interested in saving - by saying (remember - we're trying to answer that $E=mc^2$ question) = The whole thing - points to the conclusion that = Every bit of matter - is the condensation - or crushing down into mass - of vast quantities of energy ~ That means = If - it was possible to release - the energy - stored in that finger you were just picking your nose with - the result = Would be like the explosion of a nuclear bomb.

Alright - we'll spend a bit more of our - precious time - and see if we can make some kind of sense out of that last statement.

||||||||| **Tiny Power:**

In this world of bigger is better - in the sense of being more powerful (such as engines and rockets and muscles) - it is interesting to note = That it isn't actually true.

What is true = Is that the further down the causation ladder one goes (the ladder being the levels of what makes up what in this world) - the smaller things get - the more power they contain ~ For instance = Take the chemical (meaning molecular) - reaction - that is the explosion of a stick of dynamite - and compare it to the - atomic reaction - that is the explosion of a nuclear weapon ~ The atoms in that warhead are a million times smaller than the molecules in the dynamite - and = A million times - more powerful.

When you take another step smaller - and arrive at the vacuum - or that space between the particles of the atom (and stars and planets - for that matter) - where small doesn't even work - because = There doesn't seem to any - thing - there to compare to = There is so much energy present - that it exceeds the energy of matter - by a factor of ten to the power of forty - or - a one followed by forty zeros ~ It's been said = There is enough energy in a cubic meter of space - to boil all the oceans of the world ~ That statement's never been put to the test obviously - but = It does put that huge jacked up truck with the extra wide knobby tires that nearly just crushed your bicycle - into a different perspective.|||||||||

142

How about mass then - what does that word mean?

Well = Before Albert's quantum leap - mass - was simply a measurement of bulk - or volume - (like how much water slops over the side of a brim-full bathtub when you get in) - added to density (which is how tightly packed are the solid parts of an object) - plus (or in addition to) - the weight of that object ~ The classic physics measurement of mass therefore = Was - all those others combined - yet in the sense only - of how much force - it takes to move the object - that was subjected to all those other measurements ~ Which = Is where you encounter - Isaac Newton's first Law of motion - being = The tendency of a body at rest - is to stay at rest ~ While the tendency of a body in motion - is to follow a straight line - unless acted upon by some other force ~ Mass then - was determined - by the amount of force - it takes - to move that mass - and = It still is - where it's needed to figure out things - like getting a satellite into space - or a piano to your third floor apartment ~ Of course - the word has some other definitions - but - they don't matter here (other than maybe - a mass of words) What does - matter - is = After relativity - the same definition - didn't mean the same thing = Mass - had become something you could - divide - energy by.

[[[[[[[[[After Relativity:

When you encounter a date in a book - which is followed by the two letters - B.C. - then - more than likely - you already know that indicates a time more than 2000 years ago - because = Those letters are an abbreviation of the words - before Christ - and are based on the birth year of that rather well-known historical reference = Jesus of Nazareth ~ Which - also explains why - that particular year became known as the year A.D.1 ~ The A.D. bit - stands for anno Domini - which means (in the literal translation of the Latin) - in the year of the Lord - but - informally = Is understood to mean - after Christ ~ And also - informally - it's often used - after the date (2008 A.D.) - rather than the formal way - I just properly demonstrated (nose in the air) - with A.D.1~ Of course - some of that changed - when B.C. was altered (by some at least) - to B.C.E. (which means - before the common era) - in order to avoid offending those members of other religions - whose ideas of how history should be split up - run counter to that abbreviated distinction.

But then = You knew all that.

What you may not have known = Is that it's now fairly well accepted among scholars - that the birth in question - and so that calendar on your wall - those history books full of such two letter qualified dates - and every other document that carries a dates on it - are about six or seven years late (meaning - add that many years to the current date - to achieve a more precise historical accounting of Jesus' birth) Nor is December 25th any more accurate as the actual day of that famous arrival ~ That particular date - was chosen - most probably - as an act of co-opting (taking over - assimilating - or making your own) - a date already considered auspicious (meaning - marking fortunate or favorable circumstances) - by preceding religions (possibly due to certain astronomical events which occur at that time of year) - in order to assist in - what might be politely termed - a smooth transition - to a new religion.

Now those statements - are not intended to negatively reflect on religion - or faith - or any other matter of personal belief ~ What's under scrutiny here = Is a relationship with time - based on the - meaning - given to that time ~ In other words = The fact - that I would identify this day as Monday, August 25, A.D.2008 - only zeroes in on this day - as being this particular day - to someone who might see this page some months or years from now - who - is using (which means - is in agreement with - or at least understands) - the same form of calendar (by calendar - I'm referring to a system of tracking the cycles and seasons of the year - rather than a particular paper one hanging on my wall) A different calendar - say - the one Jesus himself would have used (which is still in use - just not in a general kind of way) - employs entirely different names and numbers - which - make just as much sense to the person familiar with that system - as we are - with our own.

The point is = We measure time (particularly our own lives) - according to - the importance- we place on events ~ August 25th - I would report as a more or less insignificant day of the year - except - that it is the first day of the second half of this year of my life = Yesterday - being exactly 6 months since my last birthday ~ The number of years that time adds up to (which I'm not going to tell you) - is an important piece of identifying information about me (according to human culture at least) - and so = Stands out for that reason ~ Any other reason for this day to stand out for you (it is a national holiday from work in Great Britain this year) - is either personal (like mine) - or cultural (like being 25 days since July 31st) - or maybe has nothing to do with this twelve month calendar of ours - such as it being nine days since the last full moon (which happens 13 times a year)

All that being said = Were we - as a culture - to adopt a new calendar system - we might be calling this year A.R.103 ~ The translation being = 103 years after Einstein's theory of relativity hit the streets (or - After Relativity) Not because - I mean to class Albert and Jesus in the same league (other than they were both Jewish) - only - that for all that Bertie's paper was a - relatively - quiet moment in history - it marked a change in our relationship with time - which = Is also a very different relationship - with reality.
Of course - the other side of the calendar (our actual personal lives) - is only ever measured in - good days - and - bad ones ~ Happiness - is still the bottom line - and in that sense = It's what our obsession with measuring time - is all about.||||||||||

Remember - $E = mc^2$ - means = Energy is equal to mass - when mass - is multiplied by the speed of light - which is multiplied by itself (or squared - as that mathematical concept is simplified in language) So - that means = The reverse - is also true ~ Or - like I just said = Energy can be - divided - by mass ~ So - that action of multiplication (or again - division - if you're going in the opposite direction) - has got some awfully big numbers involved ~ The speed of light - represented here by the letter C (for the Latin word celeritas - meaning swift) - is - as you'll remember - 186,000 miles a second - or 300,000,000 meters a second - or 670,000,000 miles an hour (mind you - these are all rounded off approximate types of numbers for the sake of convenience in conversation - which you'll now be able to have about the speed of light) When you multiply the first one by itself you get 345 trillion 965 million ~ If you want - go ahead and do the other multiplications ~ As for me - that one answer - is enough to indicate something very big -

hidden - in something very small ~ Or - not small = Every second - of every day - 4 million tons of solid mass - converts into energy before our very eyes - and - if it did not - this place called Earth - would be a very different place - or no place at all - because = The location of that nuclear reaction - is our sun.

Welllll - actually - to be a real stickler for accuracy - that last statement may not be entirely true ~ But we'll try to sort that out later.

It's in that word - nuclear - where the real proof of Bertie's genius showed up ~ Shadowed - I'm afraid - by a certain - collective - lack of genius - on the part of the greater - mass - of humanity - and = It can all be traced back to what the nucleus of the uranium atom meant to a German physicist - who happened to be a woman - and - a Jew.

Lisa Meitner - was the person so described - and described so - not because - either her gender or her religion - are important considerations in any other way - than = The times in which she lived - and = How her work - and those times - led to the most destructive power humanity has ever held in its hands.

Meitner - and a chemist named Otto Hahn - worked together for more than 30 years on the subject of radiation - centered - on the uranium atom - whose nucleus was known to leak out particles in the form of energy - or (as just mentioned) - radiation ~ That same nucleus - was also the largest known - at the time - with a total of 238 protons and neutrons ~ Their idea - was to bombard one of these nuclei (being the plural form of nucleus) - with neutrons - in the hope = That it would accept one - or more - and so = Grow larger - and - reward science with the information that provided (whatever that information might be)

This was all in the period between 1907 and 1938 ~ In Germany = That meant the first world war - followed by crushing economic depression - and the rise of Hitler's Nazi party (at least to note the more negative - from a certain point of view - highlights - in an extremely abbreviated form) It was also - a great time for radiation research ~ Bit by bit - a better time for women (Meitner became the first woman in Germany to bear the title of Professor) - but - by the end of the 30s = A terrible time and place - to be a Jew.

On the brink of breakthrough - Professor Meitner - was dismissed from her position - and barely managed to escape Germany with more than her life ~ She still managed a correspondence with Hahn however - and that Christmas of 1938 - she received a letter from him - describing certain complications within his experimentation he was unable to make sense of ~ So far - Hahn wrote - there was no evidence of the uranium nucleus growing - and instead - traces of barium (a smaller atom) - were appearing ~ Presumably - it meant a kind of contamination - like sand in your lunch - not a welcome sensation between the teeth ~ Ah = But - that razor physicist mind (despite its being housed in a Jewish woman) - underwent its quantum leap ~ With the help of her physicist nephew - Robert Frisch - and some quick mathematical calculations (most of us would be hard-pressed to make it through - with - the assistance of electronic devices) - she worked it out = The atom - was split.

You see - that uranium nucleus - was indeed - accepting neutrons ~ It had grown - as expected ~ What was not expected - was its unstable nature ~ It had become heavier and heavier - and eventually - like pouring water into a glass - it overflowed - it became two atoms ~ The barium found - had not been a sign of contamination - but of production ~ They - had produced it ~ But = How?

There was a question - of energy - at the bottom of this other question ~ If - the nucleus had split - the action of that occurrence - required - a huge amount of energy ~ Huge - that is - at the level of one nucleus ~ However - 200 million electron volts - was the number used in Meitner's math - and = That's a pretty big number ~ Where - the question continued - would that energy come from? Simple - in a complex mathematical way = The two nuclei - resulting from the split of the original - weighed less - than that original ~ Which means = Some - mass - had been lost ~ So - when you multiply the amount of that lost mass - by the speed of light squared - you arrive at (you guessed it) = Exactly the amount of energy required - or - 200,000,000 electron volts ~ In other words = $E = mc^2$.

It was less than seven years later - that the discovery made my Meitner and Hahn - tested - what their research had never intended to create - in a flash of light and a huge cloud resembling a mushroom in the sky above New Mexico ~ The war in Europe ended soon afterwards - but = It was not the - A bomb - as it was called - that ended it - as it did in Japan a few months later ~ It could have though - and what's more - it could have ended very differently ~ Those same Nazis that had driven out some of the greatest minds of their times - including Einstein - had wanted the secret - of turning a few pounds of uranium and plutonium - into a power of mass destruction - just as badly as the Americans did ~ They simply did not manage to work it out quickly enough ~ In part (you might say - though you might say many other things as well) - by lacking the help of those minds they had considered so inferior ~ Meitner herself - refused to have anything to do such work - despite repeated offers by the Americans ~ Her nephew Robert Frisch - was perfectly willing however ~ Driven as he was to see the Nazis crushed - he played a major role in the top-secret Manhattan Project - that finally produced that strange cloud over New Mexico.

[[[[[[[[[Bombs over Broadway:

The Manhattan Project (now famous - but once so amazingly secret - that three small virtual cities - housing and employing tens of thousands of people - sprang up in a matter of months in New Mexico - Tennessee - and Washington state - and no one - which included the vast majority of people employed - knew why) - was the nickname - derived from the official code name - Manhattan Engineer District (originally coordinated from an office building overlooking Broadway in Manhattan) - of the American initiative to develop and build the world's first nuclear weapon.

Shortly before the second world war - a kind of intellectual telepathy passed invisibly between scientists worldwide - as the results of experimentation with - splitting the atom - converted to the theoretical concept - of harnessing the energy released - as a means of generating electrical power - or - blowing things up like nobody's business ~ That explosive idea - is what's known as nuclear fission.

Fission occurs - when a neutron (one of those subatomic particles) - is forcibly introduced into the nucleus of another atom - which frees (or scatters) - other neutrons of that invaded atom - to go flying around and do the same thing with other atoms - which is called = A chain reaction ~ As that series of atomic events occurs - energy (as mentioned) - is released ~ In a nuclear power plant - that release is a carefully controlled (hopefully) - relatively slow process of tapping that energy as needed ~ In a nuclear weapon - it's an intentionally super fast event - of all control flung to the wind.

The difference - between a conventional bomb - or conventional fuel (such as coal or gasoline) - and nuclear fuel (uranium and plutonium) - is at least 10 million times less bang for your buck ~ That would sing out nuclear energy as the clearly obvious choice for powering this world - if = The process of producing it - didn't result in creating a deadly waste product (hundreds of thousands of tons of which have already been produced) - which remains lethal for thousands of years.

Back in the 1940s - the hazards of radiation were still quite vague ~ The hazards of a global war - chewing up millions of lives - were quite the opposite ~ So = The government of the United States (not to mention those of - England - Russia - Germany - and Japan) - were extremely interested in developing a weapon - whose superiority would put paid to the whole contest ~ The US - had the advantage of trained minds (many of which - as previously noted - had escaped from Nazi Germany) - and resources (2 billion dollars - the equivalent of approximately 24 billion today - was dumped into the project before anything actually blew up) Einstein himself - wrote several letters to President Roosevelt - urging him to press such innovation before the Germans - literally - beat us to the punch.

Not an easy thing however = The reasons for building those - secret cities - was to manufacture (in an atomic kind of way) - the necessary fuel - or - uranium 235 - and plutonium ~ The installation in Oak Ridge Tennessee (covering over 60,000 acres - and simply taken from the sparse local population for a minimal sum - often with only two weeks notice to vacate farms which had been worked by families for generations) - was the uranium 235 plant (uranium ore requires a type of purification process - called enrichment - in order to convert it into the proper atomic form) - which was consuming more electricity than New York City itself ~ Due to wartime shortages - the huge amount of copper needed (for the electromagnetic coils which performed part of the job) - was unavailable ~ And instead = 70 million pounds of silver - were borrowed - from the US treasury reserves (which no doubt disturbed a great many treasury officials) - and returned after the war.

The location in Richland Washington (which grew to nearly 1000 square miles - during the Cold War) - was where plutonium was produced = The first step taking place in nuclear reactors (essentially the same as what happens in a nuclear power plant) - where the plutonium was physically separated from uranium - by a process of absorbing neutrons - which causes other subatomic particles to start flying around (called decay) - and eventually yields plutonium ~ That was followed by a series of chemical separation processes - that further refined the plutonium to a highly pure state ~ All of it requiring tremendous electrical power - and oceans of water - to continuously cool the reacting uranium so it didn't become a nuclear meltdown with dire consequences for all concerned.

It was in Los Alamos New Mexico - where the real brain work (as well as the actual assembly of the bomb) - took place ~ And from there = That two bombs (one charged with uranium - and the other with plutonium - with different firing mechanisms) - dubbed Fat Man and Little Boy - for their relative sizes - were crated up for their journey to the island of Okinawa (recently wrested from Japanese control at the cost of 12,520 Americans - and well over 200,000 Japanese soldiers and civilians killed) - for their eventual delivery to the crowded Japanese mainland.

But = Not before they had made sure that the things would work - by detonating a third device (nicknamed - the gadget) - near Alamogordo New Mexico - just seconds before 5:30 a.m. on July 16th 1945 - with a flash and a shock wave that were seen and felt and heard up to 200 miles away ~ If not (to wax lyrical) - the far ends of the world.|||||||||

Perhaps there was - hidden in Lisa's mind - perhaps even hidden from her own knowledge of it - an equation that would describe the achievement of peace in this world - as elegantly brief - as Einstein had matched energy with mass ~ Something like = Peace equals humanity multiplied by the square of compassion - or - $P = HC^2$ ~ The pity is - we can no longer ask her (by the usual channels) - and - in that sense - we cannot know the answer to what was hidden in her mind ~ But - there is a part - of the answer - we can know - whose question begins = Why this business of - squared? Why - is that little - ^{2} - perched up there - so important?

First then = What does it mean?

The simplest visual description of the principle of - squared - is to build a wall of blocks - say - five across - and - five high - then - count the blocks it took to build it ~ 25 blocks should be stacked up in front of you - if you followed the instructions properly ~ Which probably you didn't even do - because you already knew what squared means - such as - $7^2 = 49$ or $10^2 = 100$ or $14^2 = 196$ or $18,312.56^2 = $????

But = Why - is still floating around isn't it ~ In relation to $E = mc^2$ - that is.

Okay = Possibly - you have noticed the signs along roads and highways that are printed - Speed Limit - with a number in the middle? Good = I'm reassured to know you've noticed them ~ Even though those signs are generally regarded as a - speed minimum - or a number you can safely add five to ten miles per hour to and still avoid being stopped by the police - they do represent a law - that = When we break it - is called speeding ~ However - there is a certain law you cannot break - no matter how fast you go (knowing of course you'll never get that car to go faster than the speed of light - unless of course that isn't true) - that even the great Sir Isaac Newton got wrong ~ That law states = The force required to stop an object in motion is - mass times the square of its velocity ~ What it means is = If you are driving your car at 20 mph (which is what velocity is - or - the rate of speed at which an object is traveling) - and you suddenly see a kangaroo in the road ahead - there is a definite fixed distance required for that car and everything in it - according to the weight of the car - road conditions - and a few other variables - to come to a complete stop ~ Provided - of course - the brakes are also in good working order.

148

Okay - as you sit there waiting for your heart rate to slow down again - you can ponder several things - such as = What on earth is a kangaroo doing in Wisconsin? Or = In places where kangaroos are common - there are some people who don't even consider slowing down ~ And = What would've happened - if you had been going 60 mph?

Simple math divides 60 by 20 and gets the answer = 3 ~ If the laws of motion were the same - like Sir Isaac thought - then the obvious answer to the 60 mph question would be = Three times the stopping distance would be required ~ What the actual truth is - is = Nine times the stopping distance of 20 mph is required at 60 mph - or - three times three - which of course is = 3^2

So = Einstein - obviously - knew this - and - because he was dealing with the cosmic speed limit of light - the connection was already there (although there is some new experimentation - and of course - theories - that indicate that speed limit may not be the limit) As for the rest of us = Even if that connection is still a bit vague - at least it's become somewhat clearer = Why they post those signs by the roadside ~ And even perhaps = Why - world peace still alludes us.

Class Ten - Comparison?

BREATHE (Yes = All it takes - is = Yes ~ And of course - just that little bit of technique ~ That left hand on your right ear - is activating the left side of your brain - and the pituitary gland ~ The right hand - is doing the same for the right side - and the pineal gland ~ At least that's the claim of the ancient science of acupuncture ~ Perhaps you'll have some astounding claims about it yourself soon.)

Did you do the assignment? How did it go? Did your mood change? What changed? Was it difficult to get yourself to do any of the parts? Any one in particular? Why do you think that was? What kind of thoughts did you have - about doing the exercises? Did those thoughts help you do them? Did they help you be happy? So = Were you in a - Yes state of mind - or - a No state - around the whole assignment? Is it getting easier to identify such states?

Alright ~ Remember last time - how we talked so much about the present moment - Now - and all that? What part of time are you using to remember by the way? Okay ~ So = What about that question about - if time exists or not? Do you remember? So = How does - no time but now - make sense - if - it does make any sense?

Right = It's about = Being ~ We can never - Be - in the past or the future ~ We can only - Be = Right now.

So = How does such an idea - affect your life?

Would it mean - if you really took it on = That the only thing - that was truly important - is what you are doing and feeling - right now?

Seems that way - doesn't it?

Alright ~ Regardless of all this now business - we still seem to live a life of relationships - between the past and the future - people - events - plans - mistakes - all that stuff ~ Let me show you an example - of that life of relationships = See my left hand here? Okay = How is it - you can see it? That's right = Your eyes = Your brain = The light on it ~ But - there's more ~ How - do - you - see - it?

I'll help you out = Do you see all the things behind it - in front of it - and to the sides of it? Okay = That's how = You see - it - by seeing everything around - it - that's not - it ~

That's how we work ~ We make comparisons ~ We see opposites - in order to see - to interact with - to try to understand - what we see ~ Light compared to dark - love to hate - girls to boys ~ We are comparison making machines ~ You wouldn't see my hand - if you thought it was the wall ~ We wouldn't do any of this thing - we call seeing - if we couldn't tell - what we call the differences - between - things.

Okay ~ Now remember how we have looked at - the experience of life - as an interior world - all our own? Everything we sense - react to - feel - think about - decide - know - the whole picture - is going on - inside us?

Okay ~ So then = Would that mean - that the greatest relationship - we take part in - the greatest set of comparisons - we make - is between thoughts - and other thoughts?

While you think about that one - I've got another question for you - a really big question.

What - is the most powerful idea - held by the human race - that if you could change - would change everything?

Told you it was a big one.

But think about it ~ Dig ~ Powerful idea ~ The whole human race ~ Change everything ~ What do you think?

I'll see if I can help = Remember we're talking about the whole population of the world - so = Let's take a look at our ideas about them then.

We need a volunteer.

Okay ~ Here's Jimmy ~ What do you notice about him?

How - do you notice those things? Very good = They are things - that are not other things ~ What does that make those observations then? Comparisons = Exactly ~ What other comparisons are going on? Sure = Ones with your self - with other people - clothing - that sort of thing ~ So = Do comparisons basically break down - to observing differences and similarities? It's a kind of - sorting things into groups - isn't it? We know - a book - is a book - because it resembles other books - no matter what it's about ~ Is it the same with - our reactions - to people? I mean - people are people - instead of penguins?

Alright = What else do we know about people? Like - what are they made of? Is it all that stuff - skin - muscles - bones - guts - all the same - in everyone?

That's right - the parts - do the same things - by design ~ But - how they look - and work - and develop - are different - which means = There are still comparisons going on.

Remember - we're looking for one idea - we all have ~ That means = The same idea - not different ones.

Why do you think I brought Jimmy up here - and - these ideas about bodies?

Someone said = We're all different ~ Is that the answer then? Is that the idea to change? Remember the question now? Change one idea - and everything would change ~ If we all thought we - weren't - different - would everything change? Yup = Plenty would change = That's for sure ~ But everything? Like - would it change - the differences?

Let's look deeper.

First off = Is it true? Are we all different? Let's compare ~ That's what we're so good at after all.

What are the differences?

Okay = Lots of differences.

So = What are the things - that are the same about us?

Okay ~ Lots the same.

Let's break it down then - shall we?

Like you said - we're different - in shape - size - strength - looks - health - intelligence - plus cultural ways - racial ways - languages - beliefs - the list goes on and on ~ But then again - we're all humans - with human bodies - and physical and emotional needs and desires - that = Though - they vary a lot - pretty much - they fit in a category - of being the same (not penguins) So - is = Not Different = The answer?

We've got to go deeper don't we?

Well then - how about these bodies = We've looked at the skin on the meat and bones - and the ideas we carry around about the appearance of us - and noticed the obvious differences ~ So = What about the systems in us - respiration - digestion - the immune system - nervous system - are they the same? Yes = They're meant to do the same things - but = They're not exactly the same in everyone - are they?

What about our cells?

That's right - we're getting closer to sameness ~ But = Are all my cells exactly like yours? Not really? Sort of? What does it matter? I know = But - stick with me ~ Like - what about cancer cells? Some people have cancer ~ Does that make them different?

Okay - what are cells made of? Molecules = Exactly ~ Are they all the same? No? There are many different kinds of molecules? That's right = There are an uncountable number of different molecules ~ But = That uncountable number - is made of molecules which are combinations - or compounds - of a very countable number of particular molecules - known as elements (103 known elements - to be exact) But then

152

- is a molecule of carbon (which is an element) - the same - as any other carbon molecule? Well yeah = Exactly the same (as far as we can measure anyway) - that's why they've been placed on that list of elements.

So - we've narrowed it down - to all being made - of the same - ingredients ~ But even then - if all my molecules - are made of exactly the same stuff as yours = Aren't they're still - my molecules - and not yours? So that makes us different still - doesn't it?

What are molecules made of then?

Yes = Atoms.

Are atoms - different from each other? Yes - they are = They have different numbers of electrons - neutrons - and protons ~ Ah - but = Are those individual parts - different - from other electrons - neutrons - and protons?

Welllll = That's a question that hasn't been answered to everyone's satisfaction yet ~ See - this is the place - where things - that is - how we look at things - begins to really change - and so = The very way we think - must change - in order to stay in tune ~ To start off = We can't look at atoms - because = We can't see them - they're too small - and even if we built a microscope that could see something that small = We still couldn't see them - because of how light works - and atoms behave - which = Takes some explaining - but = The key word here - is = Behave.

[[[[[[[[[Seeing Atoms:

I have to modify that - can't see atoms - statement somewhat ~ Thanks to a device called a scanning tunneling microscope (invented in the early 1980s) - and the more recent - atomic force microscope = Scientists have been looking at - the images - of atoms for some time now - as well as refining that technology to higher and higher levels of resolution (or focus if you like) However = It's not really seeing - in the sense of = Did you see that truck nearly hit that old lady? The word microscope is a bit misleading in this case = It's rather more like electronically - feeling - a surface with a sharp point whose tip is the size of one atom - and generating a picture - from the information gathered ~ Which of course - is a complete oversimplification ~ The point is = Viewing atoms is not rocket science = It's nanotechnology (nano - meaning extremely small - generally one billionth of something - like a nanosecond) - which makes rocket science seem relatively simple ~ The rest of the point is = We can get something like an imaginative still photograph of an atom - but - not a video - not the action ~ Which means = We can't see atoms - because the key word is still = Behave.]]]]]]]]]]

They're doing things - those atoms - they're behaving - which always means = Action ~ Of course bodies and cells and molecules - are doing things as well ~ Ah = But when we start to break down atoms (which are what all those other things are made of after all) - and look - at what they're doing - and - what they're made of - basically = All we find is energy - some of which is flying around at incredible speed - and the rest - is doing all kinds of weird stuff.

As for that - the rest - of what we find inside atoms - it appears - to be almost nothing but space ~ What's solid about atoms - is so very tiny - compared to even the atom itself - that the word - solid - can't really be used with certainty ~ Although - we do call them subatomic particles - because we can't help it - we have to name things ~ We don't just stop at that name either - there's quarks - neutrinos - muons - gluons - positrons - on and ons - a whole long list of the things ~ Anyway = Then = There is the way atoms are located - in relation to each other ~ If we could magnify an atom - to the size of my fingertip here (never mind that we can't - if we could) - the distance to the next atom - at the same magnification - would be many miles away ~ Yes = Miles ~ Which means = This world - we take for granted - to be more or less solid - is actually more than 99.9% space = Not solid at all ~ Which is something - that goes pretty solidly against - what most people - feel really certain about ~ And yet - when we look deep enough at these particles - that make atoms - or the subatomic world - what we find = Is a whole lot of uncertainty ~ Meaning = These guys - particles - don't behave in ways we can really pin down - and even seem to appear and disappear - according to rules of their own.

[[[[[[[[[Flea in the Cathedral:

In case you need more evidence of - space - being the main ingredient in matter = New Zealand physicist Ernest Rutherford - has maintained that - to properly understand the relative distances - or size relationships - inside an atom = The region - or space in which the electrons travel - can be visualized as the size of a cathedral - and the nucleus - as the size of a flea..]]]]]]]]]

Then - when we keep digging - we find nothing ~ That is - NO - THING ~ Which is to say = We find even more - space ~ Or that's the word - I just used - which tends to make people uncomfortable - almost as much as that word - nothing ~ So - another way to say it is - the quantum field - zero point field - wave function - vacuum energy field - the potential of all possibility ~ And of course - then there's = String theory ~ Then again - just - energy - or what some people call light - both work to fill that space - with a word - and they have their enthusiasts ~ But - in this moment = All of those words are just more words - or things that aren't things - and of course - the (that's - THE - as pronounced - thee) - word - among physicists - is = We still haven't got to the bottom of it ~ Of course - some of that same group is also working - from an agreement - that there is no bottom to it ~ That is - in our ability to describe the parts of things - as things - or - like you might say - a car begins at the radiator grill and ends at the tail pipe = In the subatomic world - it just ain't that simple

See - what I'm doing here - is simplifying - a truckload of complex mathematical equations - and learned hair pulling burning of the midnight oil - into = A few mostly one syllable words - that would undoubtedly make a theoretical physicist cringe ~ But - don't worry about that = They're used to cringing at the rest of us. The thing is = Despite all kinds of incredible thinking by very smart people - we really don't know how to describe - nothing ~ We only know how to describe things ~ So that's what we go searching for ~ And yet - this no thing - this vast space that has no things in it - except energy - which

154

isn't really a thing (in the sense of holding it - touching it - or getting a photo of it) - appears to be what we are made of - or from ~ So - that would have to mean = That everything - is made of - or - the single essential ingredient of everything - is = Space? No? You don't like that? What then? Particles? Energy? Vibration? Strings? Okay ~ What are they made of? Could it be = They are made of a no-thing - we just begin to scratch its "no surface" - by calling it = Consciousness?

[[[[[[[[[Doctor Dude's Dictionary - word ten - Mystery:

There is a very simple reason = Why mystery novels - movies - and television shows - are so popular (not to imply that reason would be a great mystery to anyone) = We love mysteries ~ Some - more than others to be sure ~ And then of course = There are those people who would admit to no such attraction ~ Still - even they would have to admit - that when a mystery really impacts them personally (meaning - not knowing the cause or solution to some important part of their life - which I'll switch directly to the personal now and say - you) - it bugs you - spins you out - or just plain obsessively drives you nuts - until = It's solved ~ Or not ~ That's part of the great mystery of being human = There's no telling what anyone's got going on in those heads of theirs.

Just the same = Mystery - is one of the driving forces in our world ~ So = What does the word mean?

In general use - a mystery is something that stimulates curiosity (or obsession) - because it is unexplained ~ Unexplained - of course - means = There's no neat little line of explanation between cause and effect that satisfies that need for explanation ~ And then = That word - satisfies - indicates the presence of a certain lack - or hunger - that is uncomfortable - that wants - satisfying ~ Which brings us back to the beginning - in solving the mystery of the popularity of mysteries - which is = Solving them.

We don't actually love mysteries = We love solutions ~ Not that - that defines the word either ~ To really define it - you have to go searching for secrets - because that's what's at the core of the word ~ It comes from the ancient Greeks through the Romans in words meaning - secret rites - or rituals and ceremonies- but most of all = Secret knowledge - that which is known to only the select few - the initiates - or those that have been initiated - that have passed through the trials and tests and teachings that qualify them to take part in those secret rites ~ It also meant (for obvious reasons) = To keep your mouth shut ~ Secrets don't remain secret for very long if you go blabbing them around the Mediterranean.

So - mystery - is really a word about knowledge - or what you know - don't know - are willing - or unwilling - to share - uncover - dig up - investigate - ponder - or torture out of someone ~ It's an oddly complete word for something that really isn't ~ When we say - It's a mystery - we really mean = I don't know ~ Unless - what we really mean is = It's a secret ~ Secret - seems a much more complete word - because it's all about boundaries - or containing who gets to know ~ But then = What fun is a secret - if no one wants to know it? To turn a secret into a mystery - there has to be someone wanting to work the thing out ~ The real mystery is = How many mysteries can you handle at once?]]]]]]]]]]

Now - I know that - no-thing - really doesn't seem to make sense ~ Or certainly not from the point of view of a seemingly solid (which I've just pointed out isn't) - world of things - that are always made of other things ~ But remember = This course is about exploring new ways to think ~ Did you forget? Or didn't I tell you? And = What more challenging thought could there be - than to think about nothing - or things made of nothing - or - nothing - but thoughts - making things?

So - just like those thoughts - in your head right now (which may be saying - how confused you are by all this - but - pay no attention to that) - that - No Thing Space - is invisible - untouchable - immeasurable - and even unable to be proved - except by its effects - which is us walking around thinking about it ~ So - it - really is - just like those thoughts ~ See - the effect of a thought - is that you can speak it - or act on it - and therefore show that you experienced it - yet = You can never produce - the actual thought - to show anyone else.

What if - this - space - we have been talking about - is directly related - to those thoughts of ours?

I know = That's basically a repetition of what I just said - but = It does seem to take some repeating ~ Let me explain = Related - both - in the sense of - being able to understand - that space - and - or - because - they (thoughts and that - space) - are the same thing?   Or - to put it a bit more simply = What if - everything - is made of - thought? Or a bit more abstractly inclusive = Mind? Or - perhaps simpler - or not = What if - everything - is - consciousness?

Okay ~ We really are going for a different way of thinking here ~ So don't try too hard ~ And = Don't tell yourself - you don't understand - because = That closes down that space of question faster than anything ~ It doesn't matter if you understand ~ It's how - you feel your way - into the understanding - and understand - the feeling - that matters ~ The trick is - to let that 85% BMC do the work - instead of your old ideas ~ Not - because I'm claiming these new ideas should take over for them - only = That they will lead you into that question space - where more are available.

Okay = Here's the assignment ~ Find a quiet spot - where you won't get interrupted for at least 15 minutes ~ Sit down ~ Lay down - if you like ~ Though this will work better sitting up straight ~ But = It's up to you - and = You're the one who'll find out ~ If you fall asleep = It's not working ~ Unless - that's what you want to happen ~ In that case - it should work quite well ~ But - remember = That's not the intention of the assignment ~ So - here goes = Get comfortable - and start the conscious breathing exercise ~ Spend a few minutes with that - until you're fully calm and relaxed ~ Then = With your awareness - move through your body - feeling all the parts of it - arms - legs - feet - nose ~ You get the picture ~ And = As you are - moving your awareness - begin to break your body down - in your mind - to flesh and bones - blood - tissues - organs = Then cells - all the different kinds - doing all their jobs = Then molecules - chains of them - clumps and clusters and patterns - busy making up all that stuff = Then atoms - little whirring blurs of energy hanging out by themselves in space - yet still a moving interacting part of it all = Then = Take a deep breath - and = Step into the space that everything is full of - and =

156

Float there ~ Just = Float ~ Take as long as you like (or can) - with this - and = Repeat it - as often - as like or can - allows as well ~ I'd remind you to keep breathing - but = You already are.

N.P.U. - Chapter Ten - Quantum?

In case you're still wondering how Einstein's theory of special relativity draws such a strong connecting thread between - things - let me connect you = With the ideas of another one of those genius Germans ~ This one preceded Albert by two centuries - yet = That thread of theoretical physics is firmly looped between the two ~ Connected in other words - and = To pluck it - results in some very interesting vibrations.

His name was - Baron Gottfried Wilhelm von Leibniz - so = We'll call him - the Baron - for the sake of speed ~ He was born three years after Isaac Newton - yet lived a remarkably parallel path of mathematical innovation with that more famous Englishman ~ By some strange cosmic timing - those two men - essentially simultaneously (though completely independently) - invented the abstract mathematical form - now known as calculus - and then spent years - distantly (though heatedly) - arguing over who was - the first - or true inventor ~ In the end - it was the Baron who had the worst of it - and died penniless and disgraced ~ But - before that = He penned an enormous amount of complex philosophical writing - based - clearly = On a far more enormous amount of - thinking ~ One of the great benefits of that thinking - is the foundation on which those machines - that now do much of our thinking for us - is dependent ~ By which I mean = The binary number system - or - the series of ones and zeros that all computer programs run on.

[[[[[[[[[Mathematical Marveling:

The fundamental theorem of calculus (or - the unifying guidelines of the mathematical disciplines collectively known as calculus) - is - in a word - complicated - and - surpasses the purpose of this course to arrive at any detailed (or perhaps none at all) - understanding of it ~ Having said that = There is a purpose in describing the design (which in this case - means - purpose) - of calculus - which - in another word - is = Function.

A function - of any kind - be it the orbits of planets in our solar system - or holding a door shut against the wind - is entirely dependent (figuratively speaking) - on the word = Change ~ A function - always - changes something ~ Even if what it changes - is the natural tendency - to change (such as the latch on that shut door for instance)

Calculus - is the study of change (or function) - just as geometry - is the study of shape - and trigonometry - the study of movement - and algebra - the study of relationships - or the relative values (comparisons) - of this to that (and this course - is the study of how to make intensely complex things - appear less so)

158

The two branches of calculus (which are connected through that fundamental theorem) - are called - integral - and - differential ~ They split (roughly) - along the lines of - a known whole value - like a kitchen table - or the number 3 (which is an integer - or whole number - same as - 4 - 5 - 6 - and so on) - and = Unknown values - like the edges of the universe ~ Yet both - still deal with the same movement in time - we call change.

Integral calculus (again - roughly) - is in the business of integration - or = When set things (like one population) - interact with another set of things (a different population) - calculus provides a means of determining - or predicting - the changes that will occur - as a result of - fixed (like locations) - and changing (like attitudes) - conditions ~ Of course - that's all done with numbers - and symbols (as well as objects - rather than people) - which represent relationships between numbers (such as the results of measurement) - which is a language far more precise - than language.

Differential calculus - is concerned with differences (particularly irregularities) - as they happen - or what you might call - the behavior of a function (such as the expansion and contraction of diverse materials) - as it changes - in relation to the forces (such as dramatic temperature variations on the surface of Mars) - causing that change ~ A derivative (the name for a particular mathematical result - or answer) - could be described as = How much a quantity (say - the influence of gravity on tennis shoes as you approach a black hole) - is changing at any given point in time.

The beauty of calculus (or any mathematical form) - as a describer of phenomena - is a purity of definition = A three - is a 3 - no matter what ~ And as such = Numerical relationships must conform to specific rules (unlike some delinquent mathematical behavior this course may indulge in) - which leave no doubt between - right - and - wrong (no questions of morality involved) The same integrity holds true - as describer turns to - theorizer = Math - has become the explorer of the universe - both large (intergalactic) - and beyond small (subatomic) Calculus (used as a kind of umbrella term here) - is the trailblazer that exploration - predicting what must be beyond the horizon - because = The equations say so ~ It's a system which seems to discard the poetry of spontaneity - or the art of fluidity - and yet = It lacks nothing for beauty - when it all lines up - sharp as a diamond hurtling through space.|||||||||

Getting back to plucking that theoretical thread with Einstein ~ There was one very obvious connection ~ Well - aside from some brilliant innovations in the use of differential equations - also pioneered by the Baron - that Albert no doubt benefited from ~ That particular - obvious connection (I've actually already described) - is the difference of the stopping distances between 20 and 60 miles per hour ~ It's - understanding = Was also the contribution of the Baron ~ Although he intended it to bear witness to something rather more invisible than keeping your car from squashing a kangaroo - which was = A thing he called - Vis Viva - meaning - in Latin = Living Force - a kind of intelligence within motion - that - among other things = Described - the beingness - of energy ~ His equation - written out in its simplest form - has a distinctly familiar look to it - $E = MV^2$ ~ Translated into English - it means = Energy equals mass times it's velocity squared ~ You know - the stopping difference between 20 and 60 - only - like I said - the Baron was frying more fish than that in his = Living Force.

For better or worse - the deeper principles that so occupied the Baron's brain have mostly been stashed in the obsolete theories cupboard - meaning = Science - has moved beyond what it considers their usefulness ~ But - if you were to wade into Herr Leibniz's maze of language - you might get the sense = That he had at least touched upon a much larger picture of reality - that = Though he painted his impression of it in the colors (meaning - ornate and lengthy language) - of his time - perhaps = He was onto the workings of some fundamental systems - that same science (the one that's stashed his ideas in the cupboard) - will eventually prove ~ After all - a guy who can invent calculus - the binary number system - differential equations - and one up Newton's understanding - of the Law of conservation of momentum = Certainly had something on the ball.

Either way = You've got to wonder - what the old Baron would think of - and contribute to - the next scientific discipline we're about to wiggle our toes in ~ Which is (at long last) = Quantum Physics.

There is an idea - in popular circulation - that says = If you are going to understand the principles of quantum physics inside out - up - down - and sideways = You'd also have to understand a long history of scientific inquiry - discovery - and argument ~ Not to mention the workings of what's called classical or Newtonian physics (named after the same Sir Isaac Newton we were just talking about of course - who was the 17th century Englishman who contributed so much to their foundations) - plus = A good dose of chemistry - biology - astronomy - electrical engineering - and enough mathematics to sink Manhattan - or at least make it disappear in a cloud of chalk dust ~ Short of all that - it would take a stack of books - roughly equivalent to three times your own height - a local source of high-grade caffeine - and an abundance of free time - let's say - a decade or two = To reach something approaching that state ~ So - whether any of that's true or not - it is pretty safe to say - it's a limited number of people that have such an understanding - and = That the people who do - are also dealing with the limits - of the understanding of quantum physics as a whole - and definitely = That listening to me - for whatever length of time - will not do the job.

But = The real beauty of quantum physics - no matter what you may or may not have to do to master an understanding of it - is = You don't have to fully understand it - to fully appreciate = The opportunity to view reality in a different way it presents - and so = Create - and practice - a new relationship - with reality.

Of course - that does stand right in the middle of the question = Why would you want a new relationship with reality?

[[[[[[[[[Democritus:

About seven centuries ago - in a section of northern Greece called Thrace - a man by the name of Democritus (who has come down through history to us with the title of - the Laughing Philosopher - presumably - because he found the troubles of human kind to be basically silly - and considered that expression of happiness a reasonable response) - scratched out on a piece of parchment a truly extraordinary statement = "Nothing exists except atoms (he used the word atomos - meaning not able to be cut) - and space - everything else - is opinion".

The atoms he was referring to - were not entirely his invention - but = He was right there on the ground floor of theorizing about them - and definitely = The first to extensively publicize the idea ~ What was really remarkable about his atomos idea (being that he wrote them down around 460 B.C.E.) - is = He was not just talking about a lot of tiny bits of stuff that add up to bigger stuff - like our modern word atom - which = We of course now know to be exactly that - with a whole list of tinier parts that make them up ~ What he was talking about = Were - those tinier parts - and = Not just super small specs but = Forces - energy - and - uncertainty (an important word - we'll get to by and by) - at (dare I say it) - the quantum level.]]]]]]]]]

Welllll = Let's look at a little history of a few fundamental principles of this quantum stew - and see how you - feel - about that question afterwards.

First = There's the atom ~ The word has been around for maybe 3000 years - but = It wasn't until 1808 that any - scientific argument - for its actual existence - was discovered in the form of an explanation for chemical reactions ~ Of course - it took another hundred years - of thinking - experimenting - and learned poop flinging - by scientists on either side of the question - before there was any - real proof - that atoms were - in fact - real (whatever real really means)

Okay - that's now part of - accepted knowledge ~ Atoms - are at the bottom of the upward causation ladder - or - what causes what - because of - what's made of what (Ringing any bells?) - or = Particles - atoms = molecules = cells = tissues = bodies (the list for things like rocks and water is slightly shorter) - and = That's how we've come to see it ~ Not that - we can actually see much of it - just walking around without microscopes and such ~ It's that - wanting - to see more of it - that drives scientists though - and - in the case of physicists = The idea - that there must be - things - that make up atoms (like the ingredients on the side of your cereal box make up cereal) - that's driven them - to dig deeper - for the smaller and smaller stuff - that stuff - is made of ~ And - as you know = They've been pretty successful ~ The most blatant evidence for which - was obviously - the instantaneous vaporization of two densely populated Japanese cities on a pair of sunny mornings in the spring of 1945 ~ Then there's the breakdown of atomic particles (you know - those zippy little electrons and that minuscule huddle of protons and neutrons those Germans managed to split in two) - into - subatomic particles - by firing impossibly tiny things down long tubes at higher and higher speeds in order to get them to collide with other impossibly tiny things - and so (something like - but really not) - photograph that collision - and (in a rough sense) = Count the pieces.

[[[[[[[[[Atom Smashers:

The chief technologies in the investigation of the subatomic world (or the sharp part of that term cutting edge) - are things called = Particle Accelerators ~ They come in many shapes and sizes and designs - but = They are all intended to do one thing = Slam subatomic particles into each other - in order to get a look at what they're made of..

Now - that may sound a bit crude ~ Like bashing rocks together to study geology (and likely will appear so a thousand or so years from now - if humans are still around) - but = I assure you - it's no simple task to achieve those close to light speed collisions - and then = Work out what the results mean ~ There is also some really big money riding on those babies by the way = Billions - with billions more in the works (excepting those places - such as here in the states - where funding has dried up - as they say) So = You can be sure (or not - since that is definitely the other option) - there is some kind of worthwhile goal going on with these atom smashers = Such as the brand-new underground facility on the French Swiss border (the largest in the world to date - with a circumference of 27 km - or 16.2 miles) - poised - in this very moment (as quick to pass as any other moment) - to begin smashing its way to the secret ingredients of the universe (in particular - the Higgs boson - the fabled God particle - theorized to be - THE PARTICLE of particles - or the smallest most fundamental power charge out there - and already mentioned for that matter)

Accelerators - though they vary in many features - are either one - of two basic shapes (provided you disregard TV sets - computer monitors - and x-ray machines - which are all simpler versions of the same working concept) - which are = Linear - or the straight line fixed distance type - which = Are rather (in the fewest possible words) - like a cannon which fires particles at a target - and = Circular - where particles go whipping round and round at ever-increasing speeds (never exceeding the speed of light mind you) - and keep going - until that crash - scientists are gambling on (as well as doing their best to influence) - happens - or doesn't (that end's all a bit chancy)

That race track movement (in either type of machine) - is controlled (which means both - acceleration and steering) - by that power of positive and negative attraction and repulsion (electromagnetism) - those little guys are so excited by ~ Which means = Energy directing energy to do energetic things ~ It's also - because of that cosmic speed limit of light - that physicists tend not to speak in terms of speed with those machines - and instead = Just use that word energy itself - and = We're talking some truly amazing energy - as well as some incredibly speedy technology = Especially at the finish line (those tiny Big Bang events) - where (in some machines) - millions of electrical events (we'll call them recording flashes) - happen in a seconds time.

That's (those flashes) = The detector's job ~ Again (the same idea of diversity) - there are as many types of detectors as there are accelerators ~ Some - are the size of a small washing machine ~ While others (not that there are many) - are the size of apartment houses - including = The one at Stanford university - which is six stories tall and weighs 4,000 tons (remember - just one ton - equals 2,000 pounds) They (detectors) - do the sorting out work - or = Sifting through all the layers of information snatched in those fractions of nanoseconds - constantly on the hunt for a particle's mass - by determining its momentum - or speed (or again - energy) Some detectors - are large chambers filled with mineral oil (the one at Fermi lab in Illinois holds 50,000 gallons) As a particle is produced (separated - freed - created - your pick) - by a collision - it travels through the oil - and leaves a bubble trail = Which can then be measured in a number of ways - to extract that all important identity information (instantly compared to all other particle information previously gathered) - ever vigilant for that new behavior - which means = A new particle = Hooray.

You may wonder why - scientists (and governments) - would go to such trouble and expense - to slam things no one will ever see - into other equally unseeable things - in hopes of measuring them - and = That's an excellent question ~ Perhaps - eventually - those activities will prove of inestimable value to the well-being of earthly life (and the universe) And - if not = At least it seems like a better thing to study than how to blow things up.]]]]]]]]]]

Meanwhile = Before all of this - practical work - was going on - another set of ideas - that had been concocted in Copenhagen Denmark during the 1920s under the direction of a man named Niels Bohr - were having their influence - and = A very significant influence that has been ~ Those ideas - for obvious reasons - have come to be called = The Copenhagen interpretation ~ Let's see if we can compress them into a digestible nut.

First = It (the Copenhagen thing) - says = There is - no - deep reality ~ Which means = Once you reach a certain point on the smallness scale = You can't break down - this form reality - or objects existing and interacting in space - to a further - or - final smallest part - like it does on that cereal box - or an illustration in a car repair manual of your engine exploded out to its last nuts and washers (or perhaps - the Higgs boson) In other words = Reality - is not a machine - or a recipe ~ The beingness of things - is - at its foundation level - not based on - a combination of smaller things (ingredients - if you will) - or parts - or one particular thing/ingredient/part - but = On an entirely different basis of being - that = Has no resemblance to what we are accustomed to witnessing - or expecting - from a form - or phenomena - based reality ~ Which - in essence - is saying {{Not that it would hurt to read that last sentence again}} = Under the surface of our world/universe reality - down there at the subatomic level = Is a creative force - that far more resembles what we would call magic - than say - a toaster factory - and = What it manufactures our world from - are not raw materials - but = Possibilities.

Okay - that doesn't seem to point in the direction of an answer - to how reality works - more like = Away from ideas of what makes up what we used to call an answer (which may not sound unfamiliar at this point) It's the second bit of the interpretation that might feel slightly more satisfying to that craving for answers we humans suffer from - because = It - overflows from the following nutshell = Observation - creates - reality.

That - means (in its simplest terms) = It - ain't there - till you - observe (meaning - pay attention to in some perceptual way) - it ~ Which is not to say = That things - or - phenomena (the action of things interacting with things) - are not real ~ It's more like saying = Things - are only real - while they are being real - to an observer - otherwise - they - are only possibilities.

Much more satisfying - wouldn't you say?

Well = Maybe not ~ But = The thing is - there are now hundreds of thousands of hours of studies and experiments and elegant mathematical equations amassed by incredibly brilliant minds as supporting evidence for the ideas I just twisted your baseball cap with ~ No = That doesn't - prove them true exactly ~ But = It does make them very attractive to investigation ~ Even if - your question is still = Why?

Because (if you want the suggestion of an answer to grind your molars on) = You - do have - a relationship - with reality ~ That's exactly what all that Danish deduction is about - or - the earlier question = Do - we - create - reality? Like I said - that relationship is in place and going on this very instant - question or no question - and = Quantum stuff (that is - the products of crazy physicists minds) - is worming its way into that relationship ~ It's becoming - popularly - accepted ~ And = Not just because of - notions - that take the sense out of what makes sense to us - but - because = Such notions - are a part of a larger relationship - pro - rather than anti - toward what makes sense - and so = Those notions are changing - that personal relationship (now I've used that word - relationship - five times in one paragraph you might be beginning to get the impression it's important) - with reality you're having - which - as a result = Could very possibly - start making more sense {{Yup - that's a "rereader" for sure}}

Any of you been to a grocery store recently? Did they scan your purchases? Well - that's a quantum technology at work - and = There's going to be lots more (possibilities at least) - such as - interactive computers - communication systems - interstellar travel - all kinds of science fiction - which (like Jules Vern's imaginings of submarines and rocket ships over a hundred years ago) - can be - could be - will be - might be - the reality of the future ~ Of course - according to Niels Bohr and company = Only while - it's the reality - of an observer - and = There is someone (or some kind of consciousness) - around - to be that observer.

What I'm telling you is = These ideas - of a question - of how reality functions - are = At the foundation of a new - relationship - of how to function - with reality ~ Not that the question is new - or quantum physics - which has pushed past a century now (portions of it at least) - is new either - but = That relating of ours - has lots of new elements to it - because of those things ~ For instance = Perhaps your view - of the true nature of the human world - most closely resembles the model of pro wrestling ~ While - at the same time (equally perhaps) - you take for granted the iPod in your ear - the cell phone on your hip - and the image quality of your satellite system 42 inch plasma TV screen (even if all those things are just sitting on some department store shelf you've only ever driven past) I'm not suggesting = That improved technology is the end result of the quantum concepts I've barely touched on so far ~ There's galaxies more to it than that ~ Instead = I'm asking a question (imagine that) = Who are you really listening to? Is it Dr. Digital - or - Boris the bone breaker? And who - do you want to listen to? Not - because there is - a should - hidden in my words - but - because = You - are already doing that listening - because = You - are the observer - and after all = It's your reality.

SPECIAL BONUS EXERCISE - number five

Qualities List:

Do you ever have to do something - or want to do something - that's very important to you - but = Scares the squirt out of you before you do - or - maybe even while you're doing it as well? Then - to top it off - you go and beat yourself up about not having done it well enough?

Well - sure = We've all done that ~ From gym class to speaking in front of a group - we all want to do well - to do great - to impress and amaze and get the big applause - the big bucks - the girl - the boy - the job ~ We know it can be done = We've seen it done = Hundreds of times in some cases ~ Trouble is (when there's trouble) - we're afraid we can't do it ourselves - were not good enough - smart enough - talented - coordinated - blah - blah - blah ~ And that = Makes it worse ~ What's more - knowing that we're making it worse - yet still not being able to stop - makes worse- even more so.

So = What do you do?

Well - first = You have to allow yourself time to learn anything that requires learning - and = There aren't many skills that don't ~ Practice - practice - practice - is the bottom line for most of us I'm afraid ~ Then - there are mistakes ~ But = Mistakes - for all they can be terribly uncomfortable = Are part of that learning ~ One of the best parts in fact ~ When you truly experience a mistake - as a mistake - and know exactly what you did - that was mistaken - next time = You're much more likely - to do something else.

That bit aside = Here is an exercise that can help in acquiring any skill you've witnessed someone else's - expertise in ~ By help you = I mean in a way that will likely surprise you - because = It's not about you ~ Not in the way you're probably used to thinking about yourself practicing a skill that is ~ At the same time - it's completely about you - because = It's your unconscious mind that the help will come from.

Okay = What you do - is write down all the qualities you can think of (which is to say - witness yourself witnessing) - that someone - whose skill you admire - possesses ~ What that means specifically - is = Say you want to be an actor = Pick one then - that you are impressed by - and = Write down what impresses you about that person ~ No = Not just their looks - their body - their voice = Look for how what they do - feels ~ Are they confident? Are they convincing as the character? Do their movements and expressions convey as much as - or more of - the story - as their words do? Are those qualities - grace - imagination - attention to detail - presence of mind? Did they achieve those skills by being observant - by being patient - dedicated? Watch them closely = What are they doing - that makes them so good? What qualities do those skills require?

You can do the same with any skill set - athletics - teaching - art - science - music - engineering - politics ~ You name it - no matter what the skill - anyone that has mastered it - has particular qualities - that have led to their success ~ Things like ambition - diligence - humor - humility - determination - on and on ~ When you look for them = You'll find them.

Now = What you - Don't Do = Is compare yourself ~ This is not a list of your qualities ~ It's a list of what you recognize - as qualities ~ It's a recognition of what you admire ~ And = It works - when you fully do that admiring - really feel it - because = What you are doing - is recognizing - what you already recognize ~ You would not admire those people - and their qualities - if you did not already contain that recognition - if it wasn't already inside you - and therefore = Yours.

Oh yeah - it might not sound particularly helpful ~ But = If you do it very thoroughly - study those people very carefully - and - really - really - really - feel what it is you admire - and then of course = You write it down - then = When you read it to yourself - or just remember it - especially right before you have to perform the skill in question yourself - you'll be accessing something very different from fear = You'll be accessing a type of certainty - which is entirely the opposite of fear ~ Provided (very - very - important repeat note) = You forget all about what you think your skill level looks like by comparison = Just do the admiring = Drain off as much of your attention as you possibly can into that - and = You'll find out what happens.

There is one more caution however ~ What we're talking here - is also a skill ~ As such - it also requires practice ~ It might not - appear - to work instantly ~ Which doesn't mean it hasn't done some work ~ It means = Keep trying.

Class Eleven - Space?

BREATHE (You have been doing this haven't you? Not waiting for more reasons are you?   Does achieving an immediate electrochemical (possibly quantum) - synchronization between the two hemispheres of your brain qualify? Does the clarity of function - such a result offers - appeal to you? Are you on your feet yet?)

I see you haven't floated off into space ~ Does that mean you didn't do the assignment? You did do it? What was it like then? What did you feel in that space? Was it peaceful? Was it active? Was it difficult to remain there? Anything strange - happen while you were floating like that? What about afterwards? What about now? Does your idea of your body feel different? What about the things you touch or see - have you been testing their solidity? Are they still solid? Are you?

I'm thinking it would make sense to check in on that solidity - by using that least solid of devices we've got going - meaning = It's = {{{**Inventory Time**}}}

Alright – let's look at this - no thing business - on a couple of different levels ~ The first being = Something I said - as a comparison - before I gave you your last assignment ~ Which is = The experience of our thoughts happening - despite the fact - that we can never see them - touch them - or put them on display ~ Yes = We can describe them - do things according to them ~ But = Is that the thought - or the effect of the thought? So = Thoughts aren't really things - are they? And yet - they are - entirely real to us - and - produce effects - all the time?

The other level - that is = Comparison - distinction - whatever - to look at = Is the space - in which - our thoughts take place.

Go ahead and close your eyes for a moment = Feel that space behind them ~ BE in it ~ What is it like? Does it feel like a space? Does it feel like an inside space - and yet - bigger than inside you? We've done this before - haven't we?

Okay ~ Again = What if - this space in you - and - the no thing space - is - the same no thing? What if - they are both = Consciousness?

How does that help with the question? Did you forget the question? Right = That's the one = The change one idea - and change everything business ~ Never did quite get to the bottom of that one ~ Well = What do you think?

168

Do you remember why - we started to break down - what these bodies are made of?

Exactly = We were looking at differences - between us - thinking - that maybe - not being different - was the idea to change ~ What did we find? Right = We found differences ~ That is - until we got to the smallest part - and looked inside - and found nothing there ~ That is - nothing we recognize - as a thing ~ While all along - the thinking we're using to investigate this stuff - is just exactly - as no thing - as the no thing - we've uncovered - or considered at least.

Am I leading you in a circle? Why would I do that? Yes = I'm trying to get you to think ~ But = Think how? Exactly - again = Differently = Beyond - what you thought was true before - has limited you - to think - is the limit - of what is true.

Anybody able to answer the question yet?

Let me take you through one more angle - of this no thing - thing - and we'll see where we get.

Okay = If it's true - that all these solid things - we see and feel - are really mostly made of space (whether it really is true or not - I'll leave you to find out on your own) - wouldn't that mean - that the space - that appears to separate one thing from another - is only more - of the same stuff?

Go ahead and wave your arm around in front of you ~ What's there? Air? Okay ~ There's also radio waves - television waves - sound waves - odors - dust - lots of things we can't see (except maybe the dust) But = What's important to your arm? Yup = Space ~ So - again = What if - it's the same as you? That space that is ~ What if - it doesn't really define boundaries - between things - because - it can't? What if - I'm using that word - can't - because = Space is doing an entirely different thing - than just (just being a no big deal kind of word) - being the stuff that's not stuff between things - because = What it's - really being = Is the same thing? What if - what space - really does (a truly big deal) - is connect everything? What if - all this talk about space - is happening - because = What we are doing - we - right here - right now - and scientists - and people who are anything but scientists - all around the globe - are discovering - is = That we are not separate? Which would have to mean = Not from each other = Not from anything ~ What if = That - is the answer to the question?

||||||||| **Space in black and white time:**

Space - touches everything - and = Everything - touches space ~ Does that mean = That everything - touches everything?

It may seem a bit repetitive - to be asking that question ~ But = There it is spelled out in black and white - where = The white - of course - is the space that makes it possible ~ The black - stands out - as where our attention goes ~ But = Take away the white = And there is no black = There's no container = No - matrix = No - connection ~ The paper (like I said) - is the possibility - of the words ~ It's what allows them cohesion - or binds them together - from individual letters to sentences to paragraphs - cover to cover ~ A scroll (you know - those rolls of parchment on which books were written long ago) - is actually a better analogy example of one continuous space - connecting all those words - no matter what their arrangement - but……..

I think you get it = The space that touches you = Touches Antarctica - touches Mars - touches every star and galaxy - out there - and = Every cell and molecule - in here - and = Stretches the distance between every subatomic particle - as = One thing

That - getting - does make room for another question though = If - space and time are one thing (as Herr Einstein theorized) - and = We employ space to travel to any other location in space - because = They are all connected = Does that mean = That all of time - is the same way - or = One continuous same thing - that = Would mean (if we could only figure it out) = That we could employ time the same way - to reach any other point in time - because = They are all connected?

Of course - you might say = That is what we're doing with time - or = Traveling from here to there in one smooth continuation of connected time - and = You'd be correct ~ Which = Also describes how space and time function as a progression of manifestation - or = Being doing its thing of being - which = Also would have to mean (according to that linear progress) = That just as each moment is new - then so must each location in space be new as well ~ In other words = You can't actually return to an old location - because = It's a new time when you do - and so = A new location

Yet still = Because of that one thing business - of both time and space - could we travel the opposite way in time? There have been experiments - where light shone out of one end of a device - some small fraction of time - before (that's before) - it was shone in the other end ~ Indeed - that's a long way from sci-fi time travel - but = It's also an extremely intriguing moment - in time.]]]]]]]]]]

What do I mean?

I mean = If - we changed - the idea - we have - that we are separate - would - EVERYTHING - change?

What do you think?

Would people go to war if they thought - other people (would they even use the word - other) - were really part of themselves?

Good answer = Some people are at war with themselves all the time ~ Does that mean we - sometimes - or even always - think we are separate - even from ourselves?

What is a self?

Okay - okay = We'll get back to that one another time.

170

So = You still think we are separate? Fair enough = Let's look at that.

What if - we - are - hopelessly separate? After all - most people think we are - and = The evidence to prove it - does appear to be overwhelming ~ What if - all that subatomic world stuff - is just a lot of baloney? What if - we looked for the answer to the question - in another way?

You do have to admit that - not separate idea - would make a huge difference - but then = We - would have to believe it - wouldn't we? So = Even if we're not connected - at the subatomic level - are there levels - where we are?

Anybody here - breathing oxygen? Do you know anybody - that's living - that isn't? Do you happen to be getting that oxygen - from a different atmosphere - than everybody else? How many planets do you live on? Anybody here - want to go on living? Anybody want to be happy? Anybody thinking? How about listening?

So = Are those ways we are connected?

Any of them important to you?

[[[[[[[[Doctor Dude's Dictionary - word eleven - Universal:

Saying the sky is blue (unless it's cloudy) - is a universal experience - even among people who know it's not really blue ~ Which of course - it isn't = The blue color is actually the effect of the electrons of oxygen and nitrogen atoms up there - which are scattering the high-frequency (or blue end of the spectrum - of white light) - in all directions (notice the colors of the rainbow - the blue and violet end is high-frequency light - the red and orange is low frequency)

But = It's not the color of the sky in question here - or even the rather complex condition - of still believing - what we know to be untrue ~ What - is in question - is that word = Universal ~ Universal means = Worldwide - or affecting everyone or everything in the world ~ Which does seem like a sizable order - so = The word can also be shrunk to fit a particular group - such as = It is universal among carpenters to own a hammer ~ To be sure - it's just a word - not a rule ~ Likely you could locate a carpenter - who for one reason or another - is temporarily without a hammer ~ And then = What does blue sky mean to someone who is blind?

The real benefit of the word - is in defining common ground - or the point at which things fit together - and the reason - for that fit ~ That reason may be a decision to manufacture plumbing fittings according to agreed upon - or - universal (meaning - standardized to the same measurements) - sizes - no matter who makes them ~ Or - it might be the clockwise orbits of the planets of our solar system around the sun ~ It's what unifies - or unites - things - forces - ideas and beliefs - that is the significance of universal - because = It is the viewpoint of a whole - according to how all its parts cooperate - to form that whole ~ Universal - is both the small connections - and the greatest natural laws at work - as they go about their business of organizing that other word - which = Despite its being the largest word (in a sense) - we have going in the language - still - only takes up three of universals four syllables = Universe ~ Which means = All existing things - or whole - entire - matter - space - aliens - you name it ~ It also (if you go far enough back into the history of its being a word) - means - in part (the second part - to be specific - which is verse) = To turn ~ Or more completely (when you include the other part - univ) = To turn into one ~ Which means = The action - of being - one thing.

So - what is - universal = Is what ties the thread between things - to perform that turning - that unification - even though by the time it reaches a sentence - that business is generally accomplished ~ Unless you were to say something like = The presence of harmony among all people will eventually be a universal condition ~ Then again - that would probably require arriving at a universal definition of the words - presence - harmony - eventually - and - condition ~ So = Be patient.]]]]]]]]]]

Okay - those are all things worth thinking about - aren't they? So = Where are your thoughts taking place again? In your head? In other words = Inside you? Do you think about other people? Are they inside you? No? But your thoughts about them are? So how do you know they aren't inside you? Ah = Because you can see them - touch them - smell them - bite them even?

But = Where - is your experience - of all those senses - going on?

Anybody here ever have dreams? I know = Some people just don't remember their dreams ~ But - for those of you that do = Do - all the people you dream about - come to your house at night - and act out all that stuff? What is the difference then - between having a dream - and thinking about what's going on around you - when you're awake? They both seem real don't they? When they are happening at least ~ So = What's the difference?

Do you remember the experiment - about looking at the banana (or was that an apple) - and then - thinking about the banana? What happened? Right = The same areas of the brain - showed the same activity ~ Do you think - it might be the same - with dreaming about something - and doing the same thing awake ~ Meaning = If - our brains - can't tell the difference - between - awake and dreaming - how can we?

Does any of this lead you to an answer to our question?

How about this = What if - the answer is still about - not being separate - but - this time = For a different reason (if you want one - not that you can really quite pull the two apart - anyway) = What if - we humans - are all sharing the same dream? What if - we're not really outside each other - we're all - on that inside - that each of us - is looking at the world from - because = It's really - the - same - inside? And = All that business - about cells and molecules and atoms and space - is just a part of the same dream?

What do you think of that? Stretching things a bit - am I?

But = How would that affect your ideas about how to be happy - if such a thing were actually the case?

Would everything change - if everyone thought that was true?

Alright = You want to know what the point of all this is - do you? Let's look at the question one more time then.

What is - the most powerful idea - held by the human race - that if you could change - would change - everything?

What is the - key word - in that question? Bingo = Idea ~ It's what the whole thing swings on ~ So = what we've been talking about here - are ideas? What is an idea? Sooo = It's like a thought - or a set of thoughts put together - about some specific - thing? Sure = Ideas describe - things - in the sense of - things to do - or - that can be done - might be done - or are impossible to do ~ In other words = Interactions - or relationships - between things - even if those other things - are just more ideas - about things ~ So - would you say = That ideas are definitions - of how our world works - and - how we work with it? Does that mean - ideas are powerful? Can you give me an example of a powerful idea? Good ones = Freedom - Success - Popularity ~ Those are all things that affect your life in some way? Are they things then - or ideas? Hmmm = Kind of both? How can they be both? Is an idea a thing? Not really? And yet all those ideas influence how you live? How you relate to - things?

Okay = When you change your mind about something - what happens? You - DO - different things? Does that mean - you are listening - to different - ideas? What happens when you - DO - different things? Ah = Different things - happen? So = Does that mean - that ideas - are powerful?

What about - believing one idea - keeps you from believing another? Is that a kind of power? Who chooses what ideas you have?

Okay ~ So = If any of the answers - we've come up with to our question - are true - do you think they would change everything? How about - some - things then? Like what? What would change?

Does all that change mean = People doing things differently? Why? Exactly = They'd have different ideas ~ What kind of different ideas - would you like - people to have? Why? Because = You - would be happier? Do you use those ideas yourself - the ones you want other people to have? Yes? No? Why not? Because = They don't?

Could it be = That those ideas (the ones you want other people to have - but don't always live up to yourself - or even if you do) - are the ideas that keep you from being happy? In other words = If your ideas of doing things differently - or the way you'd like them to be done - are based on - or in comparison to - other people - changing their ways of doing things - then = How could you be happy - unless = They change?

What if - everyone - suddenly changed their idea - that they were separate - from everyone else? Do you think that could happen? No? It doesn't seem very likely does it? Nor would it make a whole lot of sense to wait around for it to happen ~ Just like the idea we were just looking at - of wanting other people to change - that tends to slow our own changing down ~ But = What if - YOU - did? What if = YOU - took on that idea? Do you think that would change - your - life?

||||||||| **Mahatma Gandhi** - the nationalist and spiritual leader of India - whose teachings and insistence on nonviolence helped to secure the independence of that country from British rule - once said = "We must become the change we seek in the world" ~ Since then - so many people have repeated it - that it may feel a bit stale - but = It's still true. |||||||||

Alright then - that's your assignment this time ~ Try out the idea ~ Wherever you go - look at people - as though they aren't really outside you - but = Are in your head - in your space - where all your ideas about them - are (you could call it - seeing outside in) I know = They sure look like they're outside you ~ But = Remember - we're talking about ideas here - and = Where are they? That's it = Inside us ~ Plus = I want you to = NOTICE - space - because = What does space touch? Yup = Everything there is to touch ~ Look around you - feel around you - see and touch and pay attention = To what's between things ~ Try to recognize (the way a photographic negative is the opposite of dark and light) = That space - is something ~ You can't see it with your eyes (even though - in fact - we look at it all the time) - but = You can with your mind ~ See what happens - when you put your attention there - and = What that attention - feels like ~ Go ahead and use all the other techniques we've used before - to expand your experience of this idea - the vision thing - talk to yourself - be brand new to the world - and = Don't forget to what? Absolutely = Breathe.

174

N.P.U. - Chapter Eleven - Wave?

Perhaps you've been wondering about how your - seeing a world - could possibly be - why - it's there to see ~ After all = Look at it ~ There it is ~ No fuzzy edges ~ No blank spots ~ The more obvious explanation (or what you might be inclined to call - the only sane one) - is = The world is there to see - because = It was there to see all along - and = The world is not a product of our observation - we = Are a product of the world ~ And of course = That is - the correct - explanation ~ That is - for those of us - who are incapable of moving faster than 186,000 miles a second ~ Better known as? That's right = The speed of light ~ And of course = Those of us who don't want to know what in the world that last sentence is all about.

Let me introduce you to another theory ~ Another theory - I might add - that also - like the Copenhagen interpretation - has a great deal of supporting evidence to back it up ~ Not - prove - mind you ~ It's lawyers - not scientists - who are free in their use of - that word - when it comes to describing evidence ~ But - again - there is plenty of the stuff (evidence that is) - even if the theory itself - paints - stuff (which you might even say - includes the evidence we're about to look at - in a very different light) - than our usual verdict on reality ~ It's a part of (or related to) - quantum theory (or mechanics) - and it's called = Particle Wave Theory.

It all began - as an attempt to understand how light functions - at that level of its tiniest parts - because = Yes - it does have parts - of a sort ~ It's an electromagnetic radiation after all - so = It's electricity and magnetism - which = Involves a particle called a photon - which = Is really more of a force than a thing - in interaction with other force not things - and.......

Okay = So - back in the early 1800s - an Englishman named Thomas Young - designed an experiment - using a light source - a piece of sheet metal with two vertical slits cut in it - and a photographic plate ~ What he was doing = Was trying to determine if Mr. Newton had been correct - when = More than a hundred years earlier - he had declared - light - to be a stream of particles ~ As it turned out - Newton was only half correct ~ Which in physics - basically means = Wrong ~ Because = When shone through just one slit - onto the photographic plate - the light - did - behave as a particle - but = That's just the beginning.

176

||||||||| Defining Light:

By the way = You might find it interesting to note - that when you look up - light - in the dictionary = You'll find it's probably the longest list of definitions for any word in that book ~ Which = Is just a bit more evidence - of how important light is to us (though it's hardly like we need more evidence - just look around and - see - how useful the stuff is) - and then = There seems to be - an innate (naturally possessed) - wisdom = That there's far more to light - than meets the eye.|||||||||

Imagine - shooting hundreds of BBs through a narrow window - about twenty yards in front of you - at a soft wall beyond it ~ The pattern of impacts - would appear much like the shape of the window - or a vertical rectangle - when you went up close to look ~ No surprise there = However - back in Young's experiment - when the other slit was uncovered - and the light shone onto the photographic plate through two slits - the result = Was something entirely different ~ It (the result) - was a series of vertical lines - wide in the middle of the plate - and progressively narrower as they moved toward it's edges ~ What it meant = Is that light - also - behaves as a wave.

You see - if the same experiment had been conducted - with the slits half immersed in water - and instead of light - you pushed the water toward the slits - in the form of a wave = On the other side of the sheet metal - you would witness lines of ripples - called an interference pattern - and - if the top of each ripple had a way of making a mark on the wall (which would be the photographic plate in the original format) - when it struck it (the wall) - the result - would be the same - as when the light was shone through both slits (meaning - direct evidence of an interference pattern)   To cut the whole thing down to a single statement (don't worry if your understanding is still looking for a slit that makes sense) = Light - can behave - both - as a particle - and - as a wave ~ When it is a particle - or when it's many gazillions of particles - we call those individual actions of being - or particles of light - photons ~ When it is a wave - well - we just sort of wave with it.

But - first (even though it might look like way past second - since I've already used the word so many times) = What - is a particle?

Well - like I said earlier = It's really more of an action - than a thing ~ You know - a verb - rather than a noun ~ Like that electron we've talked about = It's a charge = It's moving ~ If you were to hold it still - it would no longer be an electron ~ It's also infinitesimally small and incredibly fast ~ Not to mention = Impossible to predict - its location - and momentum - at the same time - and as such = It poses certain difficulties to measurement (that being the most basic explanation of what's called - Heisenberg's Uncertainty Principle) However = The word particle - used in any of the other ways it's commonly used = Indicates tiny bits of a substance - like particles of dirt in the salad - and = That's the way subatomic particles have been looked at much of the time physics has been trying to understand them ~ From that - point - of view = A particle - is an object - a thing - a defined (and therefore limited) - object/thing - that makes up - or constructs - in its multitudes - the object/things - we see and interact with ~ Which is to say = That particles are the first step in that upward causation ladder - mentioned last time ~ Remember = atoms = molecules = cells = tissues - and so on (in the case of bodies - or living organisms at least) Particles then - come first (I'm already repeating) as the - parts - of an atom (as far as we know) And so = They represent (in the wording of this theory - and because - in essence - they are) = Everything (meaning physical stuff) Which (to clarify that) - would be like saying = If the basic ingredient of everything - was oatmeal - then = When you said oatmeal - you'd mean = Everything.

[[[[[[[[**Electrons** - by the way - have so far proved themselves to be - as small as electrons get ~ Which is to say = Despite using energy - many billions of times stronger than the energy that holds atoms together = No one - has succeeded in breaking down an electron - to a possible ingredient list.]]]]]]]]]

Okay ~ So = What's a wave?

Unlike - waves on the ocean - or in a bathtub (or even when you are causing them by stirring that pot of oatmeal you're probably glad everything is not made of) - the wave we're talking about here = Cannot be seen ~ But - like that word wave (it's borrowing the use of) = It can move in any direction - cover an area any size - split in an infinite variety of ways - and - collide with the path of any other wave - and not be destroyed - the way solid objects - or particles - are destroyed by such collisions ~ Beyond those similarities - with the liquids of our world - there are none - because = This wave - is nothing but pure potential - or possibility - or - stuff that could be - but = Isn't yet.

[[[[[[[[**Possibility Potential:**

There is an important distinction to be made - between the words - possibility - and potential ~ They appear - to be almost interchangeable descriptions of future events that may or may not occur - but = The difference between them - is a question of scale ~ Meaning = Which is the more limited? Or = Which - will stretch the furthest?

You may have guessed already - that = Possibility - is the smaller of the two ~ Possibility - is like a deck of cards - in that = There are only 52 (meaning - a limited number to any given situation) - and as such = There are only so many different hands you could be dealt in a game of poker (certainly a far larger number than 52 - but still - a finite one - a limit) Potential - even though we - limit it - by the words we trap it into sentences with - like = He's not living up to his potential - or = She has the potential to become a great artist = Does not share the same boundaries ~ It's (meaning - potential) - the big picture ~ It's - the field - where possibilities grow.

It is possible - you will come to a full understanding of quantum physics ~ Whereas - your potential - for understanding quantum physics - could be - infinite.]]]]]]]]]

So there - that's what particles and waves are (in a rough and dramatically limited way) - on their own ~ The thing is = They're not on their own ~ They are the same thing ~ What they do (at least in a time orientation kind of way) = Is take turns = First being one - then = The other - wave - particle - wave - particle - 1 - 2 - 1 - 2 ~ The reason - we can't see this going on = Is also - basically - two things ~ The first is = It happens at the speed of light ~ Kinda too fast for most of us ~ The second is = The wave - is not something - to see ~ It's not a thing remember - it's a potential thing ~ It's everything - and - no thing - every where - and - no where ~ The particle - is the where = In its state of being (rather than the wave state of being) - it's = Things we can see ~ Without it - that is - before it - or - after it = There's nothing there = There's no there - there - because = You need particles - to make up objects - to make - dirt - grass - buildings - mountains - oceans - and - every other damn thing - in order to decide (which basically means - observe the existence of) - where - they are - or = To locate them.

It's a rather interesting - language - sound - comparison - to see our word - aware - next to those two words - a - and - where ~ Our awareness (a-where-ness) - is a constant locator device - always rubbing bits of information together to decide (or work out) - where we are - in relation to - sensation - emotion - navigation - interaction - opinion ~ Our thinking locates - where we stand - with what's going on - according to - what has gone on before - or might happen - expect to happen - plan to happen - or wish would just go ahead and happen ~ Our entire world revolves around - where - things - are ~ So - that's the job of the particle ~ It's that bit of pavement the tire just rolled onto - and of course - the tire itself - the rest of the car - the landscape - the - everything ~ And then = It's the wave again.

Let's slow this down a little ~ Which means = Speed up ~ Which could mean = Start whipping around the earth at 186,000 miles a second - only = For what I want you to see = That won't work ~ At least according to our understanding of light - which is always moving away from us at light speed - even = If we were traveling at the same speed ~ Of course - we've already been over that ground ~ So - what we need to speed up - is not our bodies - but = Our perception (never mind that our perception is just not up to so speedy a job - we'll still use that word for the moment) - which = Would mean slowing down time - to what you might call - or I already have - the speed of = Now ~ At that rate - what we might be able to see = Is our world appearing and disappearing - in a kind of a strobe light effect - particle - wave - particle - wave ~ Physicists - describe this reoccurring moment with three words - superposition - threshold - and - collapse ~ What they mean is = Superposition is when - let's say - electrons - are not yet electrons - they're potential electrons - they have no location - nothing that can be measured - they are everywhere - flirting with the endless possibilities (or at least two or three) - of what they might be next ~ So - in this - wave moment - this superposition - they're not - any - thing - they're possibilities dancing in pure potential.

There's an interaction taking place however - it's our awareness (our a-where-ness) - communicating with this wave ~ It's affecting this shapeless invisible - not stuff yet - with our ideas (thrown in with everybody else's) - of what the next particle moment is supposed to - look like ~ It's (that a-where-ness) = The Observer ~ It (which is us) - doesn't think in limitless possibility = It thinks = I ordered the super duper triple deluxe extra large size not the skimpy wimpy economy size ~ And so = This superposition reaches threshold - just like stepping through a door (you know - that piece of wood or metal at the bottom of a door frame called a threshold) = The possibility range - is narrowed to just one - it (that wave of all possibility) - collapses (or you might say - implodes - an explosion from the outside in - rather than the inside out) - and = It's a particle again ~ The room - meaning location of stuff - you stepped over that threshold into - is the one that fits with your awareness ~ It's where = You think it is ~ So - you stick a straw in that super duper triple D - and give yourself brain freeze.

The funny - thing - is = If - this particle wave business is what's really going on - or - 1 - 2 - 1 - 2 - wave - particle - wave - particle - then = Both - are happening for equal amounts of time (again from that time orientation viewpoint - which doesn't actually make it true) - all the time ~ In other words = If the wave collapses to a particle - say - forty times a second - then = Every second would be broken into twice that number of parts - or = Forty events of particle - and = Forty events of wave ~ Which means = That an equal amount of time - in your life (all our lives) - is spent as a thing - as it is - as a no thing - or = As limited to what we perceive through our senses - and = As an unlimited field of possibilities.

This explanation - is of course - the simplest (even if it doesn't look like it) - just push the cruise control button description - of how the complex vehicle of quantum wave function travels the superposition highway of creating reality ~ In practice however - it could actually be - quite simple ~ After all = If that's what's really going on - then - quite simply = That's what's going on.

Either way - this explanation captures one key point - that could very well be of great advantage to us all in mastering the ability to happily steer a course through that wavy reality ~ That point - is the one I just made - which is = If - this particle wave picture of the universe is true (and there are dramatic reasons to believe it - or something very much like it - is true - unless of course you want to stick with what you think is the personally more dramatic evidence - you've gathered yourself - that it is not true) - then = We spend equal amounts of time on both sides of being ~ Which means = We are not actually confined - to just the one our senses describe to us - which is = The particle ~ It's possible = That the only - thing - that confines us there (there - being the world - or dimension - of form - or particle) - is that = That - is where - our attention - is focused.

You'll notice the word - where - is - again - the hinge - in that last sentence ~ You may have heard the often repeated advice for running a successful business is = Location - location - location ~ It can be no surprise - that the entire focus of our sensory perception world of constant comparison judgment = Is the same ~ And yet = What if - fully half our lives - we live - no - where - or - without location - and amazingly - we never notice ~ We think - the half we see (or is that the15% we see) - is the whole thing.

The question is = What happens - when we remove our attention from - the particle - and place it - on the wave? It's true = The very use of language seems to sabotage the effort from the start with words like - remove - and - place - with their definitions of location ~ And yet = Can we? And if we do = Will we become masters of the particle - because - we will know - we are only surfing - the wave?

||||||||| Forty Times a Second:

In case you've been wondering about how time and consciousness interact - at the level of particle wave mechanics (and even if you haven't) = There is a line of research - which suggests a possible breakdown/definition/understanding/theory/wild stab at that relationship and the quantum field churning out reality together - which states = Quantum computations - reach threshold - every 25 milliseconds.

What that means is = The condition of superposition - or the wave state - where potential is wide open - does its thing - its computation - or decision-making process - which means = Narrowing infinite potential down to the possibilities that are consistent with the preceding moment (like the baseball continuing to zip past the first baseman's glove) All in relation of course - to the state of the whole field of individual and collective consciousness (which may be what the wave is) And then = The whole thing collapses - or - chooses the construction of the next moment from one of those possibilities - and = Implodes - crystallizes - solidifies - becomes (for a few milliseconds at least) = The particle ~ And = It does so in 25 millisecond intervals - which = Adds up to 40 times a second (of course - you've already guessed that)

If - that is true = It may be reasonable to speculate - that every second of our lives - contains forty opportunities - for a whole new life.|||||||||

Class Twelve - Seeing?

BREATHE (According to that ancient science - on which this exercise is based = The ear corresponds - or is rather like an interactive map - plugged into an energy circulation system that connects to all other parts of the body ~ The earlobes - represent - and - interact with - and - are hubs through which energy flows to = The brain ~ Holding them the way you do - is like flicking a switch that - quite literally - turns on that energy flow ~ What are you waiting for?)

So = Are you different? Is your view of the world changed? How did it feel to see people in that way? Did it alter how you behaved towards them? How about how they behaved toward you? Was practicing the exercise different with strangers - rather than with people you know? How about with people you don't like? Could you allow them in - so to speak? Did you try? And = What about that space thing? Now that's cool - I just have to say ~ Did you think so? What effect did it have on your thinking - seeing - feeling - the world around you? Did it affect the other part of the assignment? What does space feel like - right now?

Alright ~ We need a volunteer.

Good ~ Now - this time = I want you to tell me what you observe - about Juanita here - that you observe - about yourself - observing her.

Huh what? Yeah - I know = It sounds confusing ~ So - we'll work our way into it slower.

What is the same - as Juanita - and yourself?

Yeah = Those are things - we can see ~ How about things - we can't really see - like = Can you tell how she feels emotionally? Or = What she's thinking? A little? How do you know those things? Yeah = Her facial expression = How she holds her body ~ That does tell us a lot ~ But = How do you - know - about those thoughts and feelings - when you can't see them - only those bits of evidence of them? Have you - had those thoughts and feelings yourself? So = Are you - observing her - through the lens (so to speak) - of your recognition - of what it's like - to be you?

A moment ago - I asked you to tell me - what you observe about Juanita - that you observe about yourself - observing her ~ That means = What I'm asking you to do - is not just look at her and say what you see - but = To observe - the action of yourself - doing - the observing.

Tell me then = How you'd go about doing that? Well - yes = There's simply seeing - for one ~ What does it feel like then - to see her? It's not often we think about the process of seeing - unless we're having some difficulty doing it = It just takes place ~ We don't consider that - our ideas - might have anything to do with what we see ~ On those terms = What we see - is just the stuff out there - and = We see it ~ What I'm pushing = Is seeing - the ideas - generating - and generated by - the process of seeing.

How about this then = Does Juanita see you? Sure = You can tell by looking - that she's looking back ~ But = How - do you know - she can see - you? Ah = She waved back ~ Very clever ~ Still = Are you really seeing her - seeing you - or the ideas - you have - about seeing her - and her - seeing you? Why would you assume her experience to be the same? Did you notice you were doing that? Assuming - that is ~ Are you beginning to observe yourself observing yet? Where - after all - is your experience - of seeing - taking place?

[[[[[[[[[Optical Allusions:

Since - we barely even began to peer into the amazing power of sight (when we did) - it's time to check this out = Take a cardboard toilet paper tube (without the paper wrapped around it by the way) - and = Hold it up to your right eye (you know - like a spyglass) - and then = Hold your left hand - palm open - about four inches in front of your left eye.

What do you see?

That's right = It's an optical illusion ~ Obviously - there's not a big hole through your left hand (unless there is - and in that case - there's no need for the tube - and more for a doctor) What's happening is = The information being delivered to your visual cortex - is separated into two streams - for the obvious reason = That it's collected by two eyes ~ The difference - between the two images (those streams deliver) - is called - retinal disparity - and is one of the main contributors to close up depth perception (close one eye - and you'll notice - when you switch back and forth between it being open or shut - that what you see with just one - is slightly flatter or more two dimensional looking) Of course - when you get too close - that disparity (disparity means - unequal - dissimilar - different - which in this case is the inch or two between your eyes) - still delivers the same individually accurate sets of information - but = The real thing doing the seeing (your mind) - is confused - because = When it does what it normally does - which is = Interpret - or translate (meaning - to convert one form of information into another - in order to make it understandable) = It encounters a situation - roughly parallel - to trying to read a page of text with another page printed over it.

We're not - photographing things - with our eyes - or - watching a video of our surroundings on our visual cortex = We're filtering - information - through our system of accumulated information - to create = Understanding ~ Otherwise - what would be the point? Distinction (or what differentiates one object from another - and is the bottom line of that understanding) - is a perceptual selection - between what's called - the figure (no - not hers - unless it is) - which is the object being given attention (say - words on a printed page) - and - the ground (like the white paper that is that page) An optical illusion - occurs when - the figure - and the ground - become confused - or interchangeable ~ Not because of the information observed - but = Because - of how that information is translated.

The basic automatic features of sight - are color - movement - and contrast (or light and dark) In order - to bring order - or organize recognition of those things - our minds (that's minds - not brains - a very particular distinction) - are at the receiving end of brain rules (or patterns) - for grouping - or categorizing - our understanding systems for what we're looking at ~ When we see a car - which is partially obscured by the corner of a building - we don't gape in bafflement at half a car - our mind supplies the rest ~ Just as it does = The information that the building doing the obscuring - must be closer to us than the car - or - the tiny box in the distance - houses full size people.

Eyesight then - is really visual experience ~ The physical information gathering occurs automatically - like an automatic transmission in drive - but = It's the mind that must steer to use that information (such as avoiding accidents) - which means = What we see - is constructed over time - and - colored - contrasted - and moved - by familiarity ~ Exactly the same as listening to a language - where familiarity allows us to pick out where one word ends and the next begins - including - context - importance - meaning - and - feelings = Vision (when seen as the end product of a system) - is a mental bias - a predisposition - a learned behavior ~ At its extreme = A coiled rope on the desert floor - is a rattlesnake - the redhead a block away - your long lost lover- and then = The rest of the familiarity kicks in - to accurately identify = What's familiar.

The hole in your hand - the cardboard tube exposed - is easily explained away as messing with your retinal disparity ~ But = Perhaps - the real disparity - is that everything we see = Is an optical illusion.]]]]]]]]]

Try this = Stare at Juanita for a few seconds - and then - close your eyes ~ Try to bring up as clear a picture of her as you can (in your mind's eye as they say) Is there other stuff in there as well - the furniture - the walls? How about other thoughts? Is there actually - a lot going on - that's - more noticeable - with your eyes shut? Is that stuff - interfering with - being able - to picture Juanita? Do you suppose the same stuff - or something like it - was also going on - when you had your eyes open? Could it be = That when you were looking at her = You weren't really seeing her - but instead = Were reviewing all the information going on in your head - one small part of which = Was the visual image of Juanita - but - all of which = Was in fact - your ideas - of what your eyes and other senses are telling you - all run through the filter - of what you recognize - from past experience - of yourself?

184

||||||||| Photographic Memory:

Another way you can exercise (experience - explore) - your visualization ability = Is to take a photo (any photo - although beginning with a simple one might be helpful) - and stare at it for a minute - then = Close your eyes - and bring the images in that photo to mind ~ Try to bring up (remember - visualize) - as many details as possible - before = You open your eyes - and check the photo - and then = Do it again ~ See how clear a focus you can create - how precise and detailed a picture you can scan in your head as though it were in your hand - Try different photos - more complex images - crowd scenes - landscapes ~ How many faces can you pinpoint? How many rocks and trees and clouds mirror the original?|||||||||

That's rather backwards to the way we - usually - see things - isn't it? But = What if - that's how it works? What if - we only see - what our previous experience has seen - that is = Things - formed - and behaving in some way - that are recognizable - according to how they are similar - to what we've seen or felt before? Like - metal - wood - fabric - water - or - surprise - sadness - confusion - excitement? Remember that 15% BMC use business? Could it be - that only - 15% - or less - much less - is what you see - of what Juanita - really is? How would you know?

Do you - SEE - now - what I meant - by observing yourself observing?

There's a lot of = I know this - and I know that - going on in us - isn't there? Her hair is brown ~ Her sweater is green ~ It's not a question - like = How does light work - so that brown and green are different colors? Generally - we don't - look for - what we don't know - we look for - what we do know - that is - what we - think - we know ~ And we simply = Think it ~ We don't question what we think and why ~ What I'm asking you to do here - is think - about your thinking.

What if - the way to see more = Is to question - what you see? Like = Is what I'm seeing - what's really there? Is there more to see than I do? Is what I see - not - really there? Is the world outside me - or inside me?

What do you think about those questions? What do you think about - what you think about - those questions? Why? And while you're at it - how about an = {{{**Inventory Time**}}}

||||||||| Doctor Dude's Dictionary - word twelve - Why:

The word why (which is one of the few in our language that can be an entire question simply standing by itself) - stands in a particular conceptual location - that = Divides the two sides of any question - more so than probably any other word ~ Those two sides are = Cause - and effect ~ When why is used - it's generally directed at one or the other of those two sides - rather than both ~ Meaning = We either want to know - the cause - of an event or thing to happen or exist - or = We want to know - the purpose - of that happening or existence - which is = It's effect.

The trick to arrive at perhaps a more holistic - or complete big picture answer (if you're looking for one) - is first = To be aware of which side - either cause or effect - you're looking to answer - and second = To consider them in reverse.

In simple math = You can describe a cause as 1+1 ~ The two ones - as an interaction of addition - are the cause of the answer = Two = Which is an effect ~ It reverses just as simply as 2 = 1+1 ~ In the seemingly far less simple example of a whole world undergoing cause and effect - and asking why = It actually comes down to the same thing - or = Cause and effect are equal ~ In other words = You can reverse them - or = Understand one - by examining - or coming to an understanding - of the other.

For example = Jim ran a red light and wrecked Alice's car ~ Which is reversed as = Alice's car got wrecked by Jim running a red light ~ Simple? Yes ~ Too simple? Just as yes = It doesn't seem to cover all the effects you're thinking - like - a totaled car - towing costs - insurance (no one was hurt by the way - so no medical expenses) - not to mention major inconvenience - buying a new car (two actually) - legal problems - the whole big bummer from one stupid move ~ And = That would be true - if all you looked at were the effects.

Every last one of those effects - springs from a cause - that's equal to it ~ From speed of impact - to what was in the backseat - to what was going through both their minds before they entered the intersection = There's a reason - what happened - did ~ It's all an intricate network of ideas - systems - objects - relationships - and time - that are mirrors of each other ~ It's also very simple - in that - the effect describes the cause - as the cause describes the effect ~ You narrow them down to the same thing - and = You have the answer to the question = Why? At least until your next question is = Why?||||||||

I'm digging aren't I? That's probably not what you really want to do - is it - or you'd be doing it already ~ Well - too late = You've already started ~ Ah - but = What if - that's one of the greatest things you've done in your life so far? Do you think that's possible? Who is it you'd be learning about - by observing yourself - observing the world? Do you plan on spending the rest of your life - with your self? Do you think that knowing - how you think - would change - the way you think?

Oh = You already know how you think?

Alright = What if - I was to suddenly shout at you = That you are a bunch of idiots? What would you think then? Sure - you wouldn't like it ~ You might get angry - or think = I was the real idiot ~ There's any number of reactions you might have - but likely = They'd be negative in nature ~ So = Why?

Okay ~ You're obviously not idiots ~ So = That would mean = I was wrong? What would that make you? Sure = You'd be right ~ Did you know - you wanted - to be right? Do you know why? If you know - for sure - you're not an idiot = Why - would someone calling you one - bother you?

186

It's not quite as simple as it first appears - this thinking business - is it?

What if - the thoughts we think - and the reasons - why we think them - are really the same thing? Meaning = What if - we're really just repeating - by thinking - what we've learned to think? Would - that mean = That if we're not completely aware - why we think what we do - we're really not fully aware - of what we think?

What if - our vision works the same way - that is - connected to our thoughts - and so = Is limited by what we've learned (or allowed ourselves to learn) - because = Of what we think there is to learn? In other words = What if - not knowing - exactly why we think what we do (therefore - not thinking completely) - causes our vision - to also be incomplete? By incomplete - I mean - something like that 15% I keep referring to ~ What if - the obstacle to our thinking completely - and seeing completely - and using 100% of our BMC potential - is = Our thinking itself?

What do I mean?

Okay = Do you believe your thoughts? Like me holding up this book = Do you believe your thoughts about it? Why? But - aren't those just - more thoughts - you're believing? Why do you believe them? Ah = Your experience - tells you - they're true.

Anybody here been to Antarctica? No? Do you believe it exists? Why? So = Books - maps - photos - movies - are all things you believe in? Why? You've seen them? So = Why do you believe your eyesight?

Again = What if - we are only seeing - a very small part - of what there is to see? Why would that be? Could it be - because = We are believing - the thoughts we have - so - we are not allowing new experiences to take place - that our old thoughts - are telling us = Can't?

I know = That probably sounds like a repetition of an idea we've been banging around for a while now ~ And = That's because it is ~ But = It's also subtly different ~ And = As that word subtle works - the difference may appear hidden - or only very slightly changed - and at the same time - point at an entirely different angle ~ Just like steering a ship the tiniest bit off course - will cause it to completely miss the island it was headed for a thousand miles away - if - that course isn't corrected (Another familiar concept?) Actually = I've been making such small steering corrections all along with this seeing idea ~ Not to take you to some specific island of my own choosing - but = To keep you from returning to the port of your habitual thinking ~ The idea = That we believe the thoughts we have = Was the most recent twitch of the wheel ~ The questioning of which = Is bound to make for an interesting voyage.

Alright ~ Here's your assignment = I want you to observe your self observing ~ It's simple - just look around you ~ You're already doing that ~ But = Instead of placing your attention only on what you're seeing - observe - that is - feel - your inner awareness - of seeing - itself - and - the constant action of describing to your self - what it is - you see - or - how you - relate - to what you see ~ In other words (or really just one) = Feel - what you feel - about what you see ~ Every association (that is - set of ideas connected to what you're seeing) - has a long list of references - a world - of past awareness ~ Just switch on - the awareness - of that past of being aware - when you think of it (so do try to think of it - you know - like it's written on the back of your hand) But - don't just think of it (that is - while you're doing it) = Feel it ~ Yup = I'll say it again = FEEL IT ~ You don't need to go into great detail over every detail ~ What you need to do = Is become aware of just how much - is - going on in there - and = Despite that complexity - just how simple - and clear - the emotional response - or FEELINGS - can be - to any particular thing ~ And = There you go ~ Any moment will do ~ Lots of them would be best ~ And = Breathing - will be a great help.

THE PERCEPTION PAPERS - number three

Touching Moments:

When we say - we were touched by something - we mean = Either - something physically touched us - like an object or another person - or = We were favorably influenced - in an emotional way - by the actions of another - or something our senses have been witness to ~ It's generally pretty easy to tell the two apart - such as = I was touched by Alison's letter ~ As opposed to = I was touched by Alison's letter.

Well - I did say - generally ~ And (by way of sticking to that) = That General - is in command of context - which - in the case of this case = Is the slender - yet still blatant difference of = What would be the point of mentioning that letter physically touching you - without more contextual clues?

As for having a reason - for pointing out this touching distinction = There is - from the moment of birth - a built-in feedback loop (or - cause and effect equals cause and effect relationship) - between our sense of touch - and - our physical/emotional well-being.

When touch is denied an infant - such as is often the case with babies born prematurely and confined to - so called incubators - their development is dramatically handicapped ~ The need for weight gain - is a life or death issue - as is the development of the immune system ~ What might cause a hugged and fondled baby temporary illness - is apt to kill a touch deprived premature one ~ On the other hand = When such babies are regularly touched and massaged and physically made a fuss of - their healthy development is speeded up just as dramatically.

The same kind of observations - have been made by experimenting with (which is to say - torturing) - baby monkeys and rats - by isolating them from all touch - or other contact with their species - or even another - such as our own ~ The other hand - in this case of missing hands - are the features of psychological development witnessed in such experiments - which - I'm sure come as no surprise - to be described as = Depression and anxiety and abnormal behavior of many kinds ~ In the same vein = There is hardly the need of an intellectual leap (much less - a scientific explanation) - to realize why - babies orphaned by the war in Bosnia and Croatia during the 1990s - exhibited an extremely high incidence rate of autism ~ Autism - is a mental disorder - characterized by a detachment - a kind of ignoring of people and the surrounding - reality - while living instead in a personal fantasy world - which is often violently unable to cope with this one ~ The crowded and understaffed facilities - those large numbers of desperate unfortunates were crammed into - were barely adequate to tend and feed them all ~ Touch of any kind - beyond purely hygienic maintenance - especially nurturing motherly touch - was essentially out of the question (or at least a question seldom asked) And there = Is the very simple addition - of pairing - the need - for loving touch - with its cold absence - equaling = Total emotional withdrawal.

That of course - is the bad news ~ The good news is = In the part of our minds - closest to our animal understanding of ourselves - where that craving for cuddling affection baby has never actually grown up = We know ~ We know we are meant to give that touch - just as much - as we desire it given ~ To be sure = That doesn't mean we do - but = It's in there ~ Just as certain as our skin is covered in nerve endings always poised to zip their information to our brains = That knowledge - is in there.

Of course - in there - begins at our skin - or just under it ~ Same as - outside - is the opposite (according to bodies as units of measurement at least) That's why - when it comes to touch = It's all about skin.

Our skin - has been called our largest organ - for the simple reason - it covers us head to toe - and - performs numerous essential functions ~ It's our first line of defense - cushioning impact - battling foreign objects (so long as they're not too sharp) It's several layers thick (five in fact - depending upon how you define the word skin) - with the outer layer - the epidermis - about 25 to 30 layers of dead cells one on top of the next ~ Yes - that was the word - dead (it would be your hide - if someone were to skin you) - and what it means is = Cells which are no longer nourished by the bloodstream - because = Such cells are constantly being reproduced and pushed toward the surface in their trillions (where eventually they flake off onto your sheets and down your shower drain) - and - at such a rate = That not a single one of your skin cells is more than a month old.

Returning to function = Our skin helps regulate our temperature - expanding and contracting - secreting sweat - and oils - and goose bumping up the hairs it's covered in (feminine fuzz or manly fur) - to increase its insulation value ~ It assists in vitamin D absorption - toxin elimination - and the list keeps going (not to mention keeping all that gooey stuff on the inside of us - where it belongs) But = It's those nerve endings - that all the hype is really about.

Like I said = We are covered in sensory receptor neurons (not that that's exactly what I said) - which = Are constantly - in touch - with our brains - delivering news of any outside stimuli - any friction - tickle - pain - or texture of the world around us ~ A wide spectrum of sensations - is going on right now - all over you - regardless of what you're doing ~ There's hot - cold - wet - dry - itchy - irritated - the feel of clothing - of air moving - the ground under your feet - the chair under your butt - uninterrupted contact with a whole world - but = Particularly in certain areas of skin - where the concentration of receptors is most dense ~ No - not - those areas ~ Our most sensitive skin zones - are also our most public= Our hands - our faces - and - that most keenly tactile (meaning - used for the sense of touch) - aware spot on our bodies = Our lips.

Just take something like a pen - and feel it with your fingers ~ Note how much pressure you have to use to really get all the textural information from it - such as any writing printed on it - the shape of it - edges and ridges and so on ~ Then = Rub it on your lips - feeling all the same features ~ It barely requires any pressure at all for your lips - to read - what's there ~ That's why babies - of a certain age - will put most everything they pick up into their mouths (one reason anyway) They're gathering information - feeling their way into telling one thing from another in this complex place they find themselves.

And then = There's a whole language of touch - the pat - the stroke - the grip - slap - caress - and poke ~ Our most intimate communication occurs between - skin touching skin = As does - our most casual acceptance of the intimacy of sharing space - sharing purpose - understanding - humor ~ A simple touch on the arm - the shoulder - speaks volumes in the language of agreement - of focused attention - sympathy - or pleasure ~ If you find yourself waiting on tables somewhere - you just might go home with more tip money = If you slip a casual reassuring touch or two into your interaction with the customers ~ Almost all of us are suckers for that thing the baby in us can't (or didn't) - get enough of.

So = Go out there - and touch things ~ Pick them up - explore them with your fingers - rub them on your face - your lips ~ Take inventory of all the sensations you're registering with your skin ~ Scan your whole body covering - try to count the individual sensations ~ Then = Find a smooth rock and - a rough one ~ Hold them in separate hands - while you rub them between your fingers ~ Take a walk with them in your hands - still rubbing - still scanning all those sensations - feeling the temperature - the ground - your clothing - the sun ~ And then = When you're around people - notice how - and what - they communicate with touch ~ Really - feel it - when someone touches you - or you touch someone else ~ What are the emotions - that touch triggers? What are the ones - you're trying to convey? But - most of all = Don't - lose touch - with that knowing - of the power of touch - and = Give it away (you know - politely and all) At least that way - you're apt to get some back.

N.P.U. - Chapter Twelve - Entangled?

So - let's say you - are… surfing ~ Literally I mean ~ You've just caught the big Kahuna off Waikiki and you're in the pipeline riding that baby like a dolphin's dream ~ Then = As you watch the sunlight molten blue silver through the hundred tons of water that would happily grind you into fish food (if it could only catch your flying behind) - you realize - that every atom - of every molecule - of every drop - ounce - pint - gallon - cubic-kilometer - of water - in that pacific ocean - is cooperating perfectly - to be - that ocean - and so = Give you - that perfect wave - just before = You wipe out.

Ah = But it doesn't just end there (and we're not talking hospital bills or funeral arrangements) Something else happens - at exactly the same moment - which is - in a sense - exactly the same - well… sense - only = It happens - several thousand miles away - to someone else.

Your twin sister (did you know you have one) - is driving home from work - in Detroit - at rush hour - in a snowstorm - and watching the snow swirl and spin the most intricate weaving dance through the beams of her headlights - when = She has the same extraordinary experience of watery connection (only in waters other physical state - frozen) - as she slides off the highway in a graceful looping skid - that ends - wwwhhhmmmpppfff - in a six-foot snow drift.

So = What just happened?

Yes = A remarkable coincidence ~ And yes = Some would call it a psychic experience - or - clairvoyance ~ Then there's that word - revelation - which often finds itself attempting to describe such things ~ And - of course = There's plain old blind dumb chance ~ You're free and welcome to take your pick - or add your own ~ But = If your answer falls within - or near - the ones just mentioned - then = You've been thinking some interesting ideas - but - in this case = You'd be wrong ~ Because = What just happened = Was a story ~ A compelling story perhaps - but - I'm afraid = Fictitious - entirely made up on the spur of the moment ~ After all - it was about you - and your twin sister ~ So - you know = Get real.

[[[[[[[[Galloping Spontaneity:

We all know (forgive my assumption - but...) - what spur of the moment means ~ We know - spurs - are those jingly things that attach to boots - which are intended to be jabbed into a horse's sides in order to compel it to move faster (an innovation - by the way - at least 5000 years old) - and = We know that - the moment - is that fleeting bit of time which seems to keep appearing as another opportunity for action - or = Reminds us - of actions not taken.

But = Here is a moment - to mine that phrase for its deeper inspiration - because = It's all about - taking sudden inspiration - to the level of immediate decision - where it becomes - action - or = A moment - which divides - do - from don't - without dragging along a lot of undecided moments to slow down that action.

Spontaneous - is the word kicking those Spurs - and - good - bad - hero - or villain - it's a type of moment - in a category all its own for its sudden freedom of movement - its openness to invention - improvisation - and creativity ~ Not that it can't also be the choosing of unreasonable actions (meaning - behavior - short on the power of reason) - that moment's impetus gallops into ~ Many a dire consequence is the result of dropping the reins at the wrong moment.

But = What pleasure there can be in allowing an impulse straight from the core of your truth to spur you on - and = That allowance (perhaps with a bit more practice) - may be the perfect reception to what you're 100% mind happiness radar is insistently pinging at you - which means = Telling you = You know how to act = So = Act (Or - not)

Regardless of the results = Spontaneity - is a feeling - and = Freedom - is that feeling's closest linguistic ally ~ So = Why not test out that alliance some time today - and see what kind of ride - it takes you on?|||||||||

There are reasons though ~ Much as you suspected ~ And the first of them is = We humans love stories ~ We make careers out of them - lifetimes - days - hours - or just a few moments stopped at a red light marveling at the skill of a squirrel tight roping along a telephone wire ~ Stories - are our mirror ~ They tell us about ourselves - as constantly - we tell our selves - stories about ourselves ~ By reflecting back - on what we know - through our own experience - while watching - or hearing - the experience of another - our own (experience - appreciation - understanding - comprehension - realization) - is broadened ~ It really is like looking in a mirror - where someone else's face looks back ~ Even everything I just said - is just another story.

Alright ~ As I said = That was the first reason ~ The second reason (even though it is - the real reason) - cannot help but be tied to the first - because = Where one ends and the other begins - is not actually a point that can be identified - and = If you were to attempt to identify that point - you'd probably think you had - but = What you'd only be doing is = Telling yourself a story.

Just the same = The second reason - is contained in a word - and = Illustration - is that word ~ I set out to create an illustration ~ You know - a picture is worth a thousand words and all that ~ But - instead of the picture = I tried to give you one in words (120 something words to be exact - so perhaps it's somewhat abbreviated) However - in that illustration - is the reason - beside the reason - within the reason - why = I chose that particular story ~ Which is = To feel - the concept I want to introduce next - before - you heard it - so = You will = Hear it ~ It's called = Entanglement.

To get at what this entanglement word means - or - the meaning I intend to convey (since you could become - entangled - in a fishing net and drown - which would be unfortunate - and what's more - confuse the issue at hand completely) - we'll need to look at another ordinary word - whose flip side - is really quite - extraordinary ~ That word is = Local.

In classical Newtonian physics - everything that happens - has a - local - cause ~ To get a feel for this - go in the other room and shove your television set on the floor so hard that it breaks ~ The TV - in this case - was an object at rest ~ You - are another object - that just exerted a direct - or local - force on the first object - with enough energy/mass to move that object in a straight line - until it encountered another energy/mass/object - the solidity of the floor - which stopped its movement quite effectively ~ Of course - there will probably be another event of - local cause and effect - that happens soon after performing this demonstration ~ But - at least you will have eliminated one excuse for not doing your homework.

Okay ~ So - what I'm saying (that is - what classical physics is saying) - is = Things - cause - things - to do - things ~ In other words - for a physical action to take place - there must be - a physical force - to cause - or account for - that action - which must be = Local.

The thing is = When you get down to that subatomic particle world - those rules - don't seem to explain what's going on ~ One reason = Is that we haven't quite got a totally complete look at what - the things - down there - are exactly - or = What it is they're doing ~ The other reason is = They seem to be - doing things - too fast ~ No = The problem is not that - they are - doing what they do - so fast - it's = That they shouldn't be able to ~ You'll remember - Maxwell and Einstein setting up the speed of light as a cosmic speed limit ~ Well - that means = Nothing can go faster ~ Which also includes = To go that speed - requires time - to travel any given distance - like the eight minutes it takes light to reach us from the sun - about 93 million miles away ~ Therefore - one particle - affecting another particle - at a distance - any distance - especially a huge one - should also take time - and = Involve some kind of - so called - local force.

|||||||| Speeding Ticket:

Could it be possible = That what are known as - other dimensions - begin (or exist) - just beyond the space time boundary (or manifestation speed limit) - of light speed? In other words = Could it be = That an altogether different world (different universe) - overlaps our own - which = We display the same lack of awareness of - as we visually have (that's without microscopes) - of the gazillions of microbes crawling all over us this very second - because = ITS existence - is formatted at that higher speed? Which leads to the inevitable - other - other words = Can - things - move faster than the speed of light?

There is a hypothetical subatomic particle - the characteristics of which (meaning - the math) - point toward a big (possible - maybe - likely not - can't prove - yet haven't disproved) = Yes - to that question ~ It's called = A tachyon (tacky - on) - or = A tachyon field - which is basically the energy state - in which tachyons (might) - exist.

In examining that hypothetical - existence - it's useful (or at least interesting) - to look at another theory = Which considers the possibility - that what we see (or technologically visualize) - as particles - are actually - different states (such as liquid - ice - and steam - are different states of water) - of the same thing ~ Much like the different notes - plucked from a single guitar string - are the same string - or = The same guitar - if you go on expanding the idea ~ It's possible - the speeding violation side of tachyons - is that guitar (so to speak) - or - the source - of this dimension we call home - exhibiting another state of being (or not)

Of course - all this flighty invention - goes thoroughly against the physics rules we accept as true (even including many without that acceptance) - and = One of the big ones - tachyons just might thumb their noses at - is = Causality.

Yes = That's the great cause and effect law - which says = One thing leads to another ~ And of course - exceeding the speed of light - which is the speed of time - could mean = Moving backward and forward in time - is not a problem (for tachyons) Of course - time = Is exactly what holds together that cause and effect business ~ We can't have events in the future - causing events in the past - now - can we? Unless - that's just the simple (not) - condition of parallel universes - where such interference divides time (history - or what was - what's next - and what might be) - into two distinct streams of time - one altered - and the other not.

We may be spared that infinite complexity (not that we'd ever really know) - by the math - which = Indicates that tachyons - can only exist (meaning - be created - or annihilated) - in pairs ~ Therefore = A tachyon moving backward in time - would meet itself - moving forward in time - and = Efficiently cancel its own effects out (or not)

Then - there are those intriguing fancies of warp drive - or practically instant travel between galaxies (which appears to work just fine on television) - and = That locomotion's hypothetical cousin (or possible definition) = Wormholes - between the loops and folds of the space-time fabric - Einstein himself considered possible ~ Both tachyon technologies - should we be able to catch up to them.

But = Returning to that first question - of dimensions = Could it be - the ancient legends of Faerie - that realm of immortals - whose landscapes stretch over our own world as close and invisible as oxygen molecules (yet just as real - to the inhabitants of that realm at least) where = Should you happen to be one of those rare few that find their way into that world for one night's revelry - only to discover - on your return - that a hundred years have passed and all your friends and relations long since dead = Could it be - that is the remnant of an ancient set of memories (woven by time into folklore) - of interactions with tachyon fields? Or = Then again - are Tachyon fields - what imagination is?]||||||||||

Well - guess again sir Isaac = It seems such rules were made to be broken ~ And - not just on the rare occasion - but - quite possibly = All the time ~ The extraordinary flipside to the word - local - is achieved by simply adding the prefix - non- - and suddenly = There is non-local communication between particles - even millions of light years apart - that happens - not fast - or even super fast - but = Instantly.

Alright - just for a moment - return to our - story - about you and your twin sister - and - allow your imagination - to make it truly yours ~ Which it's actually done already - to whatever level it did ~ But now - do it deliberately - consciously - and just - feel it ~ That's - entanglement - occurring - non-locally ~ It's also - still = Just a story.

The experimentation - that has witnessed this phenomenon of quantum entanglement - is also a story - but = Of the kind we like to call - a true story ~ Several actually - that once more - center on the actions of light - or = Photons - to be specific - which are the particle packages (you might say) - that the energy of light travels in (by - particle packages - I mean a unit of energy - a quantum - or one photon = one quantum) These photons spin - much the same way our planet does - only - they have a few more options ~ First = They are either - right-handed - or - left-handed - meaning = Their spin is - counterclockwise - like our planet (from a north pole point of view) - or clockwise - which = For us - if that was what the Earth was doing instead - would mean the sun setting in the east ~ Then - there's the axis on which they spin ~ Also easiest to visualize as the axis we've all seen demonstrated as a rod through a globe - that allows us to rotate it as we try to locate Uzbekistan ~ Of course - the globe example is not exactly how photons work - but don't worry about that ~ Instead = Add to that visualization - that the axis - of that photon - can tilt - either horizontally - or vertically - or any angle in between - and so = They go spinning at the speed of light - since = That's what they're carrying ~ Their energy also varies - in proportion to their frequency - like that ship riding the waves we talked of before - but = That's just so you'll know - in case anyone asks.

Alright ~ So - we've got these photons - like a swarm of gyroscopic marbles flung into space ~ Under certain laboratory conditions - namely as single photons fired by a laser (or multiple light waves - locked - into one high energy beam) - at a particular type of crystal (such as calcite) - some of those photons can be made to split into two photons - called = Entangled pairs (or twins if you prefer) They're called that because = Even though they travel off in different directions - at different polarizations (Polarization being that combination of spin direction and axis tilt already mentioned ~ Run around the room with a spinning globe to approximate this action ~ Now read the beginning of the sentence again and ignore this explanation) - the instant - one of them is - measured (meaning - observed) - to be - say… a right hand spin with a vertical axis - its twin = Does the exact opposite - as a lefty on a horizontal axis ~ You yourself can perform just this sort of - measurement - with a pair of polarized sunglasses ~ Such glasses are designed to allow only those photons - with a particular axis tilt - either vertical - or horizontal - to pass through ~ Likely - you'll have some difficulty identifying individual photons - but - essentially = That's what's going on in the laboratory ~ So - again - the instant - twin photon number one - passes the polarization test for a vertical access - and makes it to your eye - twin number two whips to the opposite polarity - and instead of passing through the glass - is reflected back into space.

Now - that may sound like an incredible amount of useless detail for no practical purpose (other than making a sunglasses purchase perhaps - if you could only figure it out) Don't worry though - even Einstein was stumped by quantum entanglement ~ That's what he was referring to when he said "spooky actions at a distance" ~ But = What if - what it really is - really possibly maybe is = Fuel for stories of unimagined proportion? What if - what we're talking about here - is not just two of the smallest things there are (as far as we know - which really isn't far) - spinning through space - with the ability to communicate instantly - but instead = A pinprick hole view - of the possibility - that everything - is doing exactly that same entanglement thing - all - the time? In other words = What if - everything - is entangled?

|||||||| Remotely Possible?

What if - all that business about - Remote Viewing (remember that?) - is really just momentarily tapping into information available through the - non-local - spooky stuff at a distance - that is the natural action of - entangled particles?||||||||

Perhaps - you might also think = That - is attempting to load a herd of elephants into a teaspoon ~ And - of course - you'd be right ~ But = Why - would you want to be?

There's more to it you see = Entanglement weaves its - counterintuitive (Counterintuitive = Counter - or opposed ~ Intuitive = What intuition or gut feeling suggests is true ~ And so - counterintuitive is the opposite of what you think/feel/expect things should be) - thread through the very heart - that is guts - of quantum theory ~ Theoretically - every bit - of atomic information - is sub-atomically - entangled - with other bits of information - therefore = Connecting them all - and = Not just as opposite spins - but = As simultaneous occurrences of the same thing - like you and your twin sister hitting the water (which was frozen in her case) - at the exact same instant.

But - you don't have to go there if you don't want to ~ Instead = You could consider the probability of quantum computers - which would be based on entanglement - and so - work in two directions at once (with more of a language than the current zeros and ones computers talk to themselves in - which of course limits them to only answers of - yes or no) - and thus quantum computers would be much closer - to being actually able to think - and = Think - really fast ~ In certain applications like cryptography (or code breaking) - they would be - what's called - many orders of magnitude faster - or (like I said) = Really fast - and = Really - really - really - tiny ~ Quantum computer chips could be absolutely miniscule ~ Then = There's tele-transportation (you know - "Beam me up Scotty") - where all the particles making up an object - are somehow split into entangled pairs (or twins) - and so - that object (like you) - is momentarily in two places at once - and then = One set of particles (the one where you started out) - is eliminated - in order for the other set - to materialize (where you want to go) Now what a story that would make ~ But = Has it ever occurred to you - that you might be doing that - every half a millisecond or so - in some parallel universe somewhere - already?

SPECIAL BONUS EXERCISE - number six

Joy Scribble:

Any of you out there enjoy feeling joy?

Well - yuh = It's a dumb question I know ~ Of course you do ~ We all do ~ Haven't we kept coming back to that idea = That happiness (joy usually being a word for its more intense expression - but certainly representing the same family of feelings) - is the common denominator of human striving ~ I repeat = We all want it.

So - if you like joy - the next question is = What brings you joy? Which is to say = What do you do - that you associate - or identify with - as bringing you joy? Since - after all - it's really you that supplies the joy ~ Those things you do or see or interact with - which bring you joy - don't actually bring anything of the kind ~ They're just the reminders of your preference for the stuff ~ Not that that's bad ~ In fact = It's great ~ It's also the action of this next exercise - which is = Reminding yourself of joy - by remembering - what reminds you of joy.

This is what you do = First = Get a big piece of paper - cardboard - mat board - or smaller pieces of the same which you can tape together or pin up ~ Next = Get some crayons - colored pencils - markers - pens - colored chalk - what ever you prefer ~ Colorful is good - but - if you haven't got those things - and just want to get down to it - any kind of writing implement will do ~ Then = Scribble out - what ever - brings you joy - anything - running - sleeping - dying your eyelashes - counting flies - eating octopus - doesn't matter what it is = So long as you associate that action with your joy ~ It also doesn't matter how you write it down ~ In other words = You can write sideways - overlapping - upside down - or in precise neat little rows (if that brings you joy)

The point = Is to record joy - and = To notice - all the things that are joyous in your mind ~ This is about your mind by the way ~ Sure = Those joy bringing things - are outside your mind (or they appear to be) - but = Joy - is not ~ So - the idea here = Is to connect them - to take the joy causing things outside your mind - represented here by words you scribble out - which of course represent ideas (basically because they are) - and = Have those ideas ~ Which is to say = Welcome them - entertain them - invite them in and offer them your full attention as you see them scrawled out right before your eyes ~ The more things you scribble down - the more ideas you'll find that you have about joy - and your willingness to feel it - and - the more you feel it - the stronger will be your invitation to feel more of it in the shape of the things you've written down.

Don't skip the little things then - the perfect temperature - birds on the window sill - a joke with a passing stranger - great music over the phone while you're on hold ~ They're not little things = They're joy.

Then of course = Hang it on your wall ~ Add to it ~ Admire it ~ Think about it ~ Think about joy ~ Let it be proof of how much joy is in your mind ~ Never mind how much of it is in your life or not ~ It's in your mind where it really comes from ~ Which of course -

is also where your life is happening - when you really - think - about it ~ So - the more you find of it in there…..

Find out = Scribble away.

Class Thirteen - Now Now?

BREATHE (Yes = That does mean right now ~ Then again - this exercise is another way of planting your attention firmly in this (or any other) - right now ~ It has been shown to increase focus and reduce distractibility (and I mean really significantly) - in kids who previously were either bouncing off the walls or staring into space ~ I'd say doing it - now - is exactly right.)

Well - what do you see? Have you started to feel what you see as much as see it? What's that like? What's it feel like in there right now? Has your awareness of your awareness been changing? Are you noticing more detail of what goes on around you? How about inside you? Are you finding feelings connected to things you didn't realize caused feelings? So - again = Has your awareness been changing? How so? How do you feel about that?

Alright - let's experiment with our vision - and - our thoughts about it - a bit.

Take your hands - and hold them as fists out in front of you about a foot from your face ~ Point just your index fingers at each other - like two pistol barrels - a couple of inches apart ~ Now - focus your sight - just above those fingers - on some object in the distance ~ Does a sort of sausage (maybe it's a cocktail weenie - I just prefer the word sausage) - of finger appear floating between your fingers? Don't forget to focus just above and beyond your fingers ~ Did you see it?

Right = You've done this before haven't you? What's that sausage bit called? Of course = It's another optical illusion ~ Kind of fun - yes - but not exactly startling I know ~ However - try this = Do the same thing again ~ Only this time - when you see the sausage - take away your hands - and maintain the same kind of focus ~ You can test to see if you're getting it right - by putting your fingers up again - to check if the sausage is still there ~ Just keep practicing this for a couple of minutes ~ Try turning your head slowly - with your focus remaining the same ~ It may take some practice - but = If you do - you'll get it ~ Then you can add the peripheral vision practice ~ Meaning = Observing your whole field of vision - with the type of focus I just described ~ You'll find the focus sensation is much the same - yet the area seen - is obviously - much larger.

Feels rather odd doesn't it? It's not how we're used to using our eyes ~ But = Do you think suddenly using a much larger percentage of BMC potential might feel uncomfortable at first as well? Why would that be? Yeah = It's new ~ Like learning how to walk as a toddler = We're anything but steady at first - and yet = The ability to walk - is built in ~ Unless there's some disability that prevents it = All of us learn to walk.

So = Why have we done this?

Right = We're looking for ways into that unknown potential ~ But why = This technique?

Well - there are people - that claim - they can see all kinds of strange things - we normally can't see - when they use their eyes this way (remember those Orb things) What if - you're one of those people? What if - we all are - with a bit of practice? What if - just like walking and talking - there are abilities in us - just as natural - that we never master - because = Our thoughts - that those abilities don't exist - are in the way?

Okay - that's certainly something to think about ~ Or not think about ~ Indeed - that thinking business - can be sticky stuff.

[[[[[[[[[Independent Thinking:

Look out the window - or - just look around you - if there are no windows between you and - the outside (Which side is the out - side?) - and visualize what that spot must have looked like 200 years ago ~ Now - try 2000 years ago ~ How about - 2 million?

How did that work out? What did you do - to put those pictures together? What information did you access? Did you just change the houses - erase them - throw in a woolly mammoth or two?

Now = Do it again ~ But - this time = Notice - where you're looking in your mind - to construct that visualization ~ What references are you using? What information - are you adding up - to fill out the picture? I don't mean = Course titles and books and page numbers - or even one clear image of the scene your inner artist is now putting the finish brushstrokes on ~ I'm talking information = What is the process - your mind employs - to do what I just asked? And = What does that doing - feel like?

Thing is = No matter what it is we think about - we are constrained (meaning - limited by boundaries) - to access our previous experience - or = What we have learned to recognize - in order to construct - new recognitions - of - new thinking ~ In that sense - you might say (or think) = There is no new thinking - only rearrangements of old thoughts - which = Is true - to a certain extent ~ And yet = We all have experienced new thinking (as compared to old) To be sure - that's generally the result of - new learning - which has been threaded into (through the same process of recognition) - the old - previously learned stuff.

The beauty of that - new learning - however - is the moment when it functions much like a chemical reaction - where = One set of molecular compounds come in contact with another - and then - a third is introduced (which is called a catalyst in chemistry - and acts as the stimulus - or cause - of the change called a chemical reaction) - and flash = A brand-new compound is created (1+1=1)

The question is = Is it possible to experience glimpses - of new thinking - independent - of our old thinking - to step - momentarily - outside that famous box we all seem to be packaged in? Can't we just receive - or generate - or participate somehow - in understanding some cosmic download of understanding - our previous understanding - doesn't possess the raw material to understand - and yet - still understand it? Is that possible? Is that - what a brainstorm is? Has it happened to you?]]]]]]]]]]

Let's return to the idea of observing our friend Juanita here for a moment ~ There was one thing - nobody mentioned - that all of us are sharing with Juanita ~ What is it?

I'll give you a hint = It's about time.

Yes = Excellent = The present moment = Now = We're all sharing that same now ~ It's a bit like breathing - in that = We're all sharing the same source of oxygen - this one atmosphere surrounding the planet ~ But = Now - is even more fundamental than that - because - after all = When are you breathing?

Remember the question about being happy - the one about - what happens - when you decide - you truly want to be happy? Right = You are ~ In that instant = You feel happiness.

So = When does that instant take place?

Exactly = You could have - been happy - or - will be happy - but = When you are - being happy - it's always a present moment - a now?

So = What's the big deal? How did we get back to this now thing?

Well - basically = We can't help it ~ It's like we're all jammed into a car called a Now ~ We pass through all kinds of countryside and experiences - but = We're still always in the same car ~ Which means (in case you missed the word - all) = Everyone and everything else - is in the same car too ~ I know = It doesn't really work as an accurate representation - but = The idea behind it does ~ We - are all sharing - now - because = We - are all alive ~ In order to be alive (at least in the way we generally define it) - what part of time do you have to be in? That's the one = Right - now.

Okay ~ So being alive is a now - and - being happy is a now ~ So = What about the act of seeing? Or thinking? Or picking your nose? Exactly = Whatever we do - when we're actually doing it = It has to be happening - now.

Alright = Remember last time when we talked about the question of an idea that would change everything? Remember the possible answer = That we might not be separate? Do you think - this now business - might have anything to do with that answer?

There you go = Yes = We're all existing now = We're connected by it = It's the - WHEN - we're alive in = Every other - WHEN - is a - was alive - or - will be alive = Really alive - is right now.

So = If everything alive - is sharing the same moment - wouldn't that mean that - that exact instant - that NOW thing = Has an unbelievably huge amount of energy in it? Yeah - I know = That's not how we're used to looking at time ~ Time appears to move ~ It never stays the same moment ~ And yet = What is the moment - that any action requires - in order to happen? Yup - it's that - NOW - AGAIN.

And again - and again - and again = This exact instant - that is now - every activity - every heartbeat - spark plug firing - seed sprouting - blink - sound - wave on the beach - and who knows what all across the universe - is using energy to - BE ~ Does this include you? So - would that mean = Now - is where all the power is? And - if it is= What an unimaginably huge amount of power that must be ~ A regular - Big Bang - you might say.

Remember that word - awareness - we've used to describe being conscious? What does it mean again? So = Being present - is in there? Ah - now there are two potent words = Being and Present - and = They can only happen when?

What if - focusing all your awareness - on the now - opens you - to all that power going on? But = All that power (or at least most of it) - is going on elsewhere you say? True ~ And yet = What if it really isn't? Where is your experience of yourself going on again? (I keep saying that don't I?) Right = It's inside you ~ That's a kind of energy isn't it? So = If - it's - energy - and energy can only - be energy - now - and all of us are alive - only and exactly - now = Then wouldn't you say - that now - is actually what all energy is? AND = The fact that we're all sharing the same now - connects us - because = None of us can actually step out of it and remain what we call - alive? AND = All of us are alive - experiencing everything we experience - inside ourselves - with that energy - that is our awareness? Wouldn't that make you want to say - that they're all the same energy - or = NOW?

Well - maybe you wouldn't ~ It's a tricky business I know.

[[[[[[[[[Interconnected Being:

What if - we are one interconnected being - and = All information - all abilities - all knowledge - are available to each and every one of us - to experience in some way - all the time - the way a whole baseball team experiences a World Series - individually - and yet collectively - because = It's the same World Series.

What if - our statements of - I can't do that = Are like the toes of a great musician saying - I can't play music? While all along = They are completely connected to the system which includes the fingers that do play the music - and so = Are that musician (in body form at least) - just as much as those fingers?

What if - what other people do - is just a part of us suited to that doing - the way teeth do one thing - and knees another?

What if - all that were true?||||||||||

Let's look at it a different way.

When athletes describe the state of being in - the Zone - what do they mean? Okay = So - it's being completely engaged in what they are doing - no other thought - only what's going on in the present moment - and performing the response - that best suits that moment? Have any of you ever experienced such a feeling? It's quite good isn't it? Does it have to be some kind of sport you're involved in - in order to feel it? No? It can be just about anything that totally absorbs your attention? Well - you've just described - exactly what I'm talking about = There's power - in being totally absorbed that way ~ Are you apt to kick the game winning goal - if your attention is on the car you want to buy? Not likely no ~ So = It's that total focus that can make the difference between being a good player - and being a superstar? I imagine you can see a certain advantage in the idea then - can't you? Well = What if - the idea goes far beyond sports - or any other human skill we know about?

Remember us talking about electricity - and people 500 years ago walking around with it inside them - without knowing? Then of course = You'd remember me saying - that we might be the same - with another form of energy inside us - that's hugely more powerful? What if - that energy is = NOW?

I think we're going to need to take a little extra time this time ~ Or - a few more nows ~ So - for a moment - lets all stand up and.....

BREATHE

What does all this have to do with happiness - you're thinking? No? You're thinking - what has this got to do with anything that makes sense? Well - what ever you're thinking - let's try a little experiment - that does connect it to happiness.

But first = Can you be happy - if you're thinking about something that happened in the past - which made you unhappy? How about = If you're being afraid of - what might happen in the future? So = Happiness - real happiness - is - being happy - right now?

Okay - okay = I know = You've got it ~ So = What about all this stuff about experiencing everything - through - or in - the world - inside us? ~ What has that got to do with happiness? Sure = That's where it happens ~ Would you call that - being in the Zone thing - happiness? Yeah = It's different from laughing and joking and opening presents ~ But - what do you think = Is it happiness? It's kind of a stretchy word - happiness - isn't it? What if - we were to define it as = Enjoying being alive = Would that work?

Enjoying ~ There's a powerful word ~ Is it an action word - a verb? Sure ~ And then = We could break it down by changing the en bit to in - to see it as = IN-JOY-ING ~ What would it mean then?

Sounds like putting joy into something doesn't it? Injoying lunch ~ Injoying work ~ That's being present in those things isn't it? Not = I wish I had something different to eat ~ Or = Can't wait to go home ~ So = If you're enjoying being alive = What do you need to be doing? Bingo = Being alive ~ So = If you were to take enjoying being alive on as being - a definition of happiness = Do you think that might make happiness more accessible? Again - after all - what would be the only thing you'd have to be doing?

Have you ever wondered what the experience of being a plant (you'll recall an experiment involving a lie detector and a pair of cabbages perhaps) - a tree - a cactus - a rose bush - poison ivy - any and all of them - might be? No? Well = What if - that experience is exactly the one I'm referring to here - or = Being entirely present in the joy of being alive?

No = We don't generally associate joy with plants - but = What if - it's true? What if - plants are in joy? I mean - just look at the way Spring throws up all that new green - and summer just covers the place - every square fertile inch alive with leaves and flowers and seeds ~ At least in the parts of the world that support such growth ~ Yet even in the driest and coldest places - a bit of wet or heat - and something alive takes advantage of it ~ What if - that advantage - is not just opportunity - but = Feeling? And that feeling = Joy? It's just a thought really - and = At the same time = It's a question - of what and how and why we think what we do - about the boundaries of happiness ~ Go ahead = Go out there and hang out with some plants - or talk to your geranium or whatever - and = Think about it ~ See what you feel ~ Even in freezing butt winter - hanging with a tree will show you it isn't suffering = It's alive - and more patient than the word patient even has time for ~ Or even better = Plant something - and see how that feels ~ What if - we are surrounded (planet wise I mean) - by green growing joy? How would you find out?

[|||||||| Doctor Dude's Dictionary - word thirteen - Rejoice:

At first glance - the word rejoice - might appear to be describing a repeat action - such as - rewrite or replace ~ But then = How do you - joice - in the first place?

Since you probably have some familiarity with the word - you're already aware that it refers to being happy about something (joyful actually) So - what's going on - when you're rejoicing is = Feeling joy ~ The cool thing about that - re - plugged in there at the beginning - is that it's what is known as - an intensifier - and that's what it does = It intensifies - or makes more intense ~ And = How does it do that? Well - turns out that first glance was correct = It's a repetition ~ It means - do again - have the same joy over - and over - and maybe a few more times ~ Rejoicing - is recycling joy - using it again for another purpose ~ Only - like other types of recycling - that new purpose is much like the original - it's still joy.

The beauty of rejoicing = Is in getting more mileage out of the joy you started out with - or - reminding - remembering - returning - repeating - responding - which all makes it more intense ~ And hey = Who couldn't do with a bit more of that action? So - next time you feel some joy = Rejoice.||||||||||

Alright ~ Let's try that experiment now?

What I want you to do = Is sit up straight in your chair - without resting your back against it ~ That position will help keep you alert ~ Now = Close your eyes (meaning - after you've got these instructions down of course) - and place your attention on your breathing ~ By attention - I don't mean thinking about your breathing - like analyzing how it works ~ I mean = Just observe your breath going on - simply feel it - inhale - exhale - inhale - relax and just - breathe - nothing else ~ When you feel good and calm and relaxed - spread your awareness into your abdomen ~ Do you feel yourself being alive there? A kind of vibration? The mildest hum? Open your awareness wider to include your legs - your chest - neck - arms ~ Can you feel all of your body as a whole - being alive? All your cells - busy with the tasks of life - like the faintest tingle of electricity radiating through you? Do you feel it? Don't worry if you don't yet ~ You will ~ Just go on feeling inside you ~ Not thinking about it - just feeling ~ I know thoughts turn up ~ Just let them pass - without following them into others - and feel the energy of your inner body ~ Think with your body ~ We'll just do this quietly for a couple of minutes now ~ Keep breathing and feel yourself being alive.

So = What was it like? What did you feel? Was it a good feeling? Some of you felt a kind of anxiety sensation? Yes = Some people do ~ If you keep practicing this - and just sit in that sensation - without running away from it (so to speak) - because it's uncomfortable = You'll most likely find that sensation changes ~ Sometimes the change is sudden laughter - or maybe tears ~ It's nothing to worry about ~ It's just a kind of energy - you've stored in your body for some reason - that's being released (or that's the simplest language for expressing such a thing) The more you do this exercise - the easier it will become - and then = You can put your awareness on that inner energy - anywhere - anytime - you want.

Ah = But why would you want to? Any ideas?

Excellent = Quite simply - it's practicing being alive in its raw state ~ And = What time does being alive take place in? That's it = It's now again (of course) What's that mean we just attempted to experience then? Yup = The same thing = Now.

Doesn't quite answer - WHY - though - does it?

Okay ~ Happiness is a now thing? So = If - what you're up to - is - consciously choosing to experience happiness - you'd have to get yourself to - Now - right? Sure = You are in now - you can't help it ~ But = Is your awareness? That's the trick.

The rest of the trick = Is - to - IN - JOY - being alive ~ That is = Put joy - in the experience ~ Vibrate = As joy.

Actually - the more you practice this exercise - the more you just might find = That joy - IS - what the feeling inside you - IS (or a word that tries to describe it) Words - as usual - really can't ~ Which is another reason to sink past thought and into feeling - because = The descriptions - that are our thoughts - describing to us what we think - are always limited - to what we think - they - mean {{STOP ~ Now = Go ahead - and read that sentence again}} You might say = That is how our past learning has shaped our relationship with ourselves - and the world - and so = Keeps that relationship from changing - because = Of the meaning we've given it.

What if - simply feeling the life inside you - will teach you far more about yourself - than thinking ever will?

Then - there are those that say that doing this will improve your health - boost your immune system - keep you from aging ~ Who knows what it may be capable of doing ~ If you really want to know = You'll have to do it yourself.

By the way - it's your assignment ~ Plus the vision thing with the floating sausage ~ Try to put them together ~ See with your whole body ~ Flood yourself with awareness - every cell - hair to toe nails - and = Pay attention to what happens ~ Remember = Don't analyze - just watch ~ Something will happen - because = It's already happening ~ All you need to do - is observe it ~ Well - other than - breathe.

N.P.U. - Chapter Thirteen - Strings?

Since the 1930s - when quantum mechanics first took root in the imagination of the physics community (no - that's not a town - it's the loosely - closely - and sometimes trying not to be - connected - population of people throughout the world paying close attention to physics) = There has been a split in that community ~ The split - is basically organized along the lines of = Big stuff - and little stuff ~ The big stuff = Is objects like star systems - planets - distances measured in light-years (and actually - right down to miles - inches - and even millimeters) The small stuff = Ts hidden in the doings of atoms - those hopping in and out of particle - particles - millions times millions times smaller than things we could balance on the point of a pin ~ But = Why? Why do the two sides seem to be traveling in opposite directions? Is it just a matter of preference - like choosing between playing golf or knitting? Are astrophysicists paid better than nuclear physicists? Are the vending machines in their buildings different?

[[[[[[[[[[Entanglement Big Bang?

If - entanglement - is true at the level of subatomic particles - could it also be true = As the description of a larger law of reality? Which is to say = Could it be - a law of nature - or physics = Like reproduction or leverage are such laws?

What I mean is = Are all events entangled - and time itself - as in past/present/future - generated - or perpetuated (meaning - made continuous) - by that entanglement?

According to the theory of the Big Bang - there was a moment of super - super - super - density - where the entire universe was contained in something the size of - well... beyond imagining how small by comparison to how big it is now and still expanding - and then = It went flying apart in all directions ~ Only - there weren't any directions ~ It contained them as well ~ Which means = The space itself - to do that exploding into - was part of what was exploding.

Whether that describes what's going on at the backside of a black hole (meaning - new universes being created) - or - what happens when parallel universes collide (more Big Bangs) - or = The educated guessing - mathematics - astronomy - fantasy - what have you - still goes on - and = So does the question = Do we begin - middle - end - and over again - entangled - with everything?]]]]]]]]]]

Well - the answers to those questions may play some role in the decision-making process of graduate students considering career choices ~ But - mostly = It's a question - of force.

You see - physicists have determined (meaning - something like a majority of them agree) - that there are just four fundamental - forces - in the universe - that govern the actions of all physical phenomena ~ They also theorize - that at the time of the old Big Bang (which is very much still a theory itself) - all four = We're all one ~ So - the Big Push - in modern physics - is looking forward (from that looking backward - over 13 billion years or so) - to the moment that those forces are once again unified - only this time - into = A Theory of Everything - or = Unified Field Theory - or = What Do We Theorize About Next Theory.

So - those forces are = The gravitational force ~ You know - gravity - or what keeps you from flying off into space ~ Next is = The electromagnetic force ~ As we've already discussed - it - controls light - electricity - and - magnetism of course ~ Turn on your TV - they're all there ~ Then = There's the strong nuclear force ~ It (if indeed it - is what's really going on) - acts as the glue holding neutrons and protons together at the center of atoms - and so = There are atoms - which means = Stuff - to exert and be influenced by gravity - and generate and be illuminated by electromagnetism ~ Last = Is the weak nuclear force ~ It - allows for radioactive decay (better known as radioactivity) - that atomic mystery that led those two famous Germans to split the atom - and - of course = Hydrogen fusion - which is how the sun (kinda maybe - or not) - keeps us warm - as well as being how nuclear weapons work (which would create the opposite effect - if we were ever foolish enough to use them) It (meaning radioactivity) - also - allowed - for another new understanding to emerge.

About 40 years ago - in the 1960s - three different physicists - independently came to the mathematical conclusion = That the weak nuclear force - which works only over the distance covered by the nucleus of an atom - and the electromagnetic force - which works over an infinite area = Are in fact - just different actions - of the one force = Electromagnetism ~ Big step - in that unification goal - let me tell you ~ It also leads us straight into talking about - the Standard Model - of elementary particles ~ However = We'll ignore that - for the moment ~ But - do remind me later.

Alright ~ You've got these forces going on ~ That's relatively simple ~ But - relative - is the word - or more like = The location - where the conflict arises ~ It's a family sort of thing - this physics of everything business - and = Just like it's fine to have your old uncle Frank around at Thanksgiving = It really doesn't work out to have him along on a hot date ~ See - back in 1915 - when Professor Einstein published his second great earthshaking brainstorm called - General Relativity - he turned Newtonian physics on its ear = By explaining - at long last - how gravity works (in a theoretical way mind you) What his logic did - was describe space and time - as one thing - a kind of fabric - that curves and warps and stretches - according to the influence of - big stuff - rolling around on it (in it - with it - it's your call how to say that) However - by big - I mean = Galaxies - stars - planets - moons - that kind of thing - but most of all - I mean = Big gravity ~ Not that it's really explained quite as easily as that ~ Still - what - it - did explain = Was how - big stuff - interacts - with smaller big stuff - like those planets - moons - asteroids - tall buildings - all the way down to the cookie crumbs in your bed ~ All very smooth actions - very organized - very predictable.

Okay = So - if everything - is subject to this - force of gravity - what's the problem? The problem (if you want to use that word - challenge - is perhaps the better choice) - is = When you go in the other direction - toward the small stuff place (the millions of times smaller than the molecules that make up those crumbs in your bed - place) - where = The rules of quantum mechanics (or - those other three forces) - are directing the show - the same rules - those of General Relativity - that describe gravity = Don't work.

But why? If those four forces are what control everything - then = At either end of everything - why wouldn't they be controlling = Everything?

Well - you can go ask your uncle Frank - or - you can ask a theoretical physicist ~ Perhaps even one that's all excited about = String Theory.

First - Dr. String will tell you = That at the level of the subatomic - that fabric of space/time - is not smooth and predictable like the moons of Jupiter circling their giant gravitational master (as Einstein described it) - but instead = Is random and chaotic ~ So - in the quantum world - things - or the events of energy that end up as things - are more like the results of throwing dice - than Sir Isaac's simple math of dropping an apple on the ground - or Albert's much more complex math of keeping the solar system in order ~ It's like I told you about uncle Frank - he's just not always welcome - and he doesn't seem to have all the answers either.

[[[[[[[[[The Big Wiggle:

What if - the universe is like one giant Jell-O mold - which = The smallest movement (or thought) - wiggles through to all points of the compass? And = If - that is so - then = What if - an experience of ESP - clairvoyance - remote viewing - whatever - of a psychic variety = Is merely a glimpse of the entangled - or consistently connected - fabric of reality - and not an aberration - or something out of the ordinary - except = In the sense of the very narrow perspective - we accept - as ordinary?]]]]]]]]]]

But - jumping back to the origins of this - Relativity vs. Quantum - quandary = Dr. String will probably tell you that Einstein spent the last 30 years of his life trying to dig his way into the secrets of the universe and come up with = A unified theory - a theory of everything ~ Well - he didn't manage to do it ~ He didn't take his own advice quite to heart for one ~ He was trying to solve a problem - with the same thinking (granted - super brilliant inspired thinking) - that = You might not say - created the problem in the first place - but certainly = Believed - there was a problem ~ He didn't like quantum mechanics ~ He didn't like - stuff - that wasn't stuff ~ He called some of its predictions "spooky actions at a distance" ~ He wanted - explainable actions - at the tip of his nose ~ Sadly for him - he died disappointed ~ However - Dr. String's excitement stems from - the possibility = That the time of that disappointment - may - be over ~ General

Relativity and quantum mechanics - may be - just maybe - unified - brought together - patched up - getting married and throwing a big party - which means = Big stuff and little - all four forces - unified - by the yet to be - experimentally proven existence - of tiny vibrating strands of energy - that may be - what elementary particles - actually are ~ And they are - quite un-poetically called = Strings.

The key point - is = These - strings - are not - points ~ The same way a length of cooked spaghetti is not a baseball ~ Which is not to say - that somehow eating spaghetti makes more sense than playing baseball ~ No = It's a simple case of - range of movement ~ A baseball - more accurately - a point - can only move in the three dimensions we're so familiar with - or - up/down - right/left - backward/forward - and of course - the forth - which is time ~ Yes = It's true that spaghetti shares those same limitations ~ Therefore = It's really just a symbolic reference here - but = When you take that fresh from the boiling water bit of pasta - grip one end between your fingers and shake it - it's immediately obvious - the advantages of shape and movement range it has over an equally shaken baseball ~ And so = The same advantage applies to these tiny strings of energy - in the sense of = Explaining the workings of the subatomic world much more effectively - than the particles are points explanation - that tried to before.

So = Did that clear it all up for you? Not quite eh.

Alright ~ May as well forge on and get all our spaghetti on the table ~ The goal here is not so much understanding - as it is = Getting a taste of why you might want to understand ~ One of the tasty little concoctions I'll temp that desire out with is = The probability of extra dimensions.

See - the usual arrangement of dimensions we have on our plate - are the three mentioned earlier - plus time - in which to do the eating ~ String Theory (that is - the math that supports it) - predicts (and so requires) - six more ~ If - you move into M Theory - which is the next step in the evolution of String - there's even another one - or = A grand total of eleven.

But - why? Why - would seven more dimensions be required to explain the four we experience? Especially = When it appears - impossible - to experience those other seven.

Well - first = Perhaps - it is - possible to experience them ~ After all - we derive great benefit from what we observe two dimensionally - words on a page for instance - photographs - paintings - films ~ It's no stretch to recognize the relationships between those dimensions of ours - like - a point on the map = Smallville = Is a single dimension = The roads pictured on that map = Which tell you to go right on Highway 3 - then left on Back-And-Forth Blvd. = Makes two dimensions = Then = Driving there itself = For a third = And = The hour and a quarter it took to get there = Makes four ~ So = We're well accustomed to moving between dimensions - But = Did you take into consideration - your consciousness? What dimension is it taking place in? Or is that = How many?

The reason the strings - of String Theory - require - extra dimensions - is room to move - to vibrate ~ Not just to - be spaghetti - but - to create the - being-ness - of spaghetti ~ You're experiencing that right now - aren't you? Well - maybe not in quite that pasta form this moment - but = Any form will do - because = What if - that - thinking - that originates in consciousness - and so - is also an entryway into consciousness - means = Consciousness - IS - what experiencing extra dimensions is? And = What if - when you begin to experience experiencing your experience - of consciousness - you will open your potential experience to experience even more - or = Other dimensions?

But - before you do that - or better - while you are = Let's return for a moment to the idea of the particles - those strings are representing ~ The Standard Model (I mentioned earlier - that you've been dying to hear about) - is based on (other than mathematics) - the results gathered from those particle accelerators (I've also mentioned) - where tiny-tiny things going very-very fast smash into other tiny-tiny things going just as fast ~ Yes = It seems an odd way of uncovering information - but = That's just what it does = It uncovers ~ For blinks of time - much quicker than you or I will ever blink - the parts of the smallest parts of the parts of parts that make up these parts - are visible ~ Or their actions - in the form of information - are - because - like I've also mentioned = They are - more like actions - than things ~ So much so - in fact - you could easily remove the word - like - from the last sentence ~ It's merely there to make the idea easier to swallow.

[[[[[[[[[Doctor of Spinology:

The term - spin - is regularly used in contemporary speech to mean - the angle - or set of opinions - an information source is attempting to uphold - or establish in - it's intended audience (such as - why killing people in other countries - poisoning the environment - and running up an immense national debt - is good for the country) It - is also the perfect word for the job - because = In this universe = Spin - is everything.

Everything (which returns to that word universe - by way of meaning the whole list of - things) - is in motion ~ And that motion - is? That's right = Spin ~ The universe itself is spinning - galaxies spin - stars spin - planets - hurricanes - even the flushing water in the toilet spins (clockwise in the Northern Hemisphere - counter clockwise in the southern - you'll be sure to notice now - next time you poop in Australia) The spiral motion of that spin is evident in the form of seashells - flowers blossoming - vines twisting round branches - the formation of crystals - the very hair on your head is arranged in a spiral pattern - as is the DNA in every cell of your body ~ And that - is because = Spin is going on in the molecular world - the atomic world - but most especially = The subatomic world.

You may not seem to be spinning ~ In fact - you probably appear to be quite still - as are most of the objects around you - but = Your atoms (including those of all those other objects) - and their subatomic particles - are hard at it - just spinning away like nobody's business.

It's in that spin - that whole new breakthroughs in physics are slowly spiraling to the surface ~ Studying the geometry - the patterns of life - has begun to form an overall pattern - a master pattern - of infinite spin - where the micro - and the macro (or - the individual parts - and the whole shebang) - are connected - and generating each other -

much like a mirror generates your reflection.

While - back here on Earth (where you don't have to worry about that last explanation for the moment) = The technological application of - spintronics - is present in a wide range of electronic devices - cell phones to computer hard drives - which = Is also all about spin - particularly that of electrons - as they are allowed to pass - or not pass - through semiconductors (the most common being silicon) - entirely according to their type of (it almost begins to sound silly) = Spin ~ Which makes all those amazing electronic memory functions (we now take for granted) - possible in this - Information Age of ours - and (good - bad - agree - disagree - or like it or not) = More is on the way - more memory storage - more electrical efficiency - more heavily slanted news - more = Spin.|||||||||

So = What are we swallowing?

Well - basically = The existence of elementary particles - but - in particular (interesting choice of word - wouldn't you say - given the subject - so again - in particular) = How those particles break down into groups (which is what the Standard Model does with them) - and then = What one - in particular - of those groups - does ~ That group - is the - Bosons - or force carriers - usually called messenger or exchange particles ~ Not unlike that same pronunciation (but spelled entirely different) - navy word - boatswain (which is the title of the petty officer in charge of the deck crew - with the very specific job - of keeping that crew - performing their jobs - properly) boson particles - are the enforcers - of the forces - of the universe ~ Well - at least to try to cram them into the box of our familiar relationship with actions ~ Because - again = That possible understanding - we're working on here - is closer to its potential understanding - by seeing these particles of force - as the action itself - rather than a thing - performing - an action ~ So - in that sense = It's not the boatswain telling the sailors what to do - it's the boatswain's authority - just being there - as a force ~ Boson particles aren't what authority does - they - are - authority.

Then again - some authority on particle physics may disagree with that description ~ But - that's the beauty of navigating in the land of Theory - the border guards are never really certain - where the border actually is.

Either way - they (the boson family) - include four members - and a yet to be proven (though strongly suspected to exist) - fifth sibling - called a graviton ~ The others are = The photon - which carries the electromagnetic force ~ Photo is apt to remind you of light - in case you need to be reminded ~ Then there's = The gluon - which does the strong force job ~ Glue - is the obvious reminder here ~ And the last two are = The W and Z particles - which are working that weak force thing - and are among the largest elementary particles known - for all there's still not really that much known about them.

The graviton - as you've certainly guessed - is the predicted carrier of gravity ~ But - since it's still just a gleam in physicists' eyes = Clearly - gravity - like old uncle Frank - is still the odd man out - in this - particular - model - of reality at work ~ But - like I told you - there's some strings attached - and what they may be attached to - is = A Theory of Everything.

Class Fourteen - Opposite Ends?

BREATHE (Up to you of course - but…)

Well = Can you describe the feeling of being alive? Is it like electricity? Does it vibrate? Did you like it? Not like it? Did you start noticing it at odd times without your trying to? Was it fun? How about the sausage sight technique? Anybody - see - anything strange? Could you maintain that way of seeing for long? Could you do both things at once?

Alright - let's look at more of - the stuff - we do with this - being - alive business.

Remember how we talked about us being comparison machines and seeing opposites in order to identify things - like night from day? Okay = Do we do the same thing with our emotions - like - angry from pleased? Frustrated from content? Happy from…..

So = If you were going to describe the opposite ends of the emotional scale - in just two words - what would they be?

That's good = Happy and unhappy ~ I see you're keeping with the theme ~ But - let's break it down further ~ Remember - what I'm asking for - are completely opposite feelings - so = They are - very strong words - with meanings - totally different from each other.

Ah = Love and hate = Now we're getting closer ~ Is that - breaking down - happy and unhappy - to what we do with them? Let's do some digging.

What is love?

Okay ~ But = Are you describing what people - do - with that feeling we call love - or - what love is? Alright - sure = We feel it for people - for things - for experiences ~ But - again - what is it?

We can't really pin it down in words can we? Is it kind of like that - happiness is happiness - definition = Love is love? Or = Is it just what feels good? Then again you might say = That love - is the real definition of happiness - or = It's what feels - best ~ Do you love to be happy? Or would you say = You happy to be love? Doesn't sound right - does it? So = If love comes first (in that sentence at least) - would you say that love - is the action of happy - like a verb? What is a verb? Right = An action word ~ Didn't we decide that happiness is also an action? So = I love to be happy - is an action in an action? Which comes first?

I know = I'm being a bit twisty there - but = Our language does the work - if you listen ~ When you're happy - you say = I am happy ~ You've got the - I - that's you - your awareness doing its thing ~ And then the - am - that's being - or now ~ So - that adds up to the present being ~ And then - happy - that's the feeling - or action ~ Actually - all of those words are actions - when you break them down like that.

Anyway = When you love something - you say it differently = I love blah-blah ~ Not = I happy blah-blah ~ See - in that sentence (the I love blah-blah one) - there's really no - thing - involved - there's just an internal action ~ There's no - am - between I and love - to locate that action as going on in time - and - nothing happens to blah-blah - or the thing you love ~ You and love - and the person/thing/whatever you love - are the same - thing - in that moment ~ If you said - I am loving cake - you might be trying to say the same thing - but = You wouldn't be ~ The language recognizes something here (that perhaps we miss quite regularly) - which is (to repeat it) = I and love - and what - I love - are not separate ~ Just the same as - I see cake - or I want cake = Where you - and the object - are - is in an action - in your mind - and that action - is seeing - wanting - or (when it is) - love - and = What that action is doing = Is connecting you - making you the same thing - where - things - are most important to you = In your mind ~ In there - you - and cake - are not separate at all ~ And - even though your reaction may be = Well - yeah - but…. THINK about it.

[[[[[[[[[Roses are Red:

Some roses are red ~ Violets - are violet ~ Unless we're talking African violets - which come in a whole range of colors - some of which have parts that are blue ~ But - The old Valentine rhyme persists ~ So much so - I don't even need to spell it out for you to know what I'm referring to (at least that's my guess)

Right alongside that persistence (you might even say - rhyming with it - in the present tense) - is the belief relationship with that word - love - which assumes - the experience that inspires the word - is governed by = Conditions ~ For example - the even more familiar phrase = Falling in love - and of course its opposite - falling out of love - describe actions in time - in quite physical language - because = Just like physically falling in a hole - we tend to see love (or its opposite) - as a reaction to things around us - rather than - a recognition - of something already inside us.

Love - may be beyond defining - in the sense of describing a universal experience in universally acceptable terms (or for that matter - in the sense of limiting it to a limited thing) - but = It is - a universal experience (with - apparently - many levels within that experience - but again - that's our take on it) - exactly as gravity is an experience ~ In those terms - love could be defined - as a force ~ It has electromagnetic qualities ~ It has gravitational qualities ~ It even exhibits aspects of the strong and weak nuclear forces - if you're willing to look that deep.

Perhaps - what love really is = Is that unifying force - so diligently sought after by those theoretical physics equations which run the length of airport runways - when = All the math they've ever really required - is as simple as = Roses are red - violets are blue - 1+1 means = No such thing - as two.||||||||||

Alright - getting back to our question = Is it kind of like - if we could dissect happiness - we'd find love in it - and = If we were to dissect love - we'd just find more love? Of course these are just words again = They're not the things themselves ~ But then again - love and happiness aren't things either = They're actions ~ And = Since they are only ever invisible actions - that cause visible actions - what they really are = Is energy.

So - why am I saying all this stuff? No = I'm not trying to confuse you = I'm getting you to feel that mind of yours - in action - because = That is what it is - an action - a verb ~ And what we're looking for - if you remember = Are the opposite ends of how it - FEELS - to use that action mind of yours ~ So = You can either love that confusion state - and - want to dig into it and figure out what's really going on - or - you can what?

Sure = Hate it.

Ah = But is hate - really the opposite of love - in a - whole meaning - sense?

What I - mean - is = Aren't they more like the two sides of one coin - and so = Connected?

You know - it's like that - we compare - in order to see idea = Light and dark - give and take = Their very differences - connect them ~ Not that any word we use won't be in some way connected ~ But = What if - hate isn't exactly the right word - because = It isn't boiled down to its simplest - defining part? Which is = What - causes - it? Could it be = There's something else - therefore = Another word - hidden in hate - that makes hate - hate?

Let's look at emotions in general for a moment.

Are all emotions a kind of action - you choose - to perform? No? Yes? They just happen to you? So = What does happen when you - have - an emotion? Is it like - having - a car - a piece of cake - a mother? No? It's a way of being? Yet - that word - being = Isn't that an action? Don't you have to be doing something - to be - being it? No? Not in the case of an emotion? What are you doing then - when you are have an emotion - like sadness for instance? Sure = You're thinking sad thoughts - and feeling sad ~ Aren't - thinking and feeling - actions? Aren't you doing something when you - HAVE - them?

Okay - okay = But - you're not choosing those emotions - is that it? Well - who is then?

What if - you looked at it like this?

216

When you - have - an emotion - does that mean - you are agreeing with it? Oh sure = You may not like the way you feel - and think it would be better to feel another way ~ But then - why don't you? Ah = Because of something that's happened to you? So - does that mean = That you agree with the emotion you are feeling - because = You think - it is the appropriate response - to what's happened to you? What if - we turned it around and said = Would you have the same emotional response - if you - didn't - agree - that was the - right - way - to feel - about what's happened to you? So = Does that mean - that experiencing emotions - is agreeing with them? Is agreement an action?

What if - I put it in these terms = Would it please you - if I gave you this $100 bill? That's an agreement isn't it? Unless of course you wouldn't be pleased by getting the money ~ What would that be then? Are there reasons why you would be pleased - or - displeased by the $100? (I know - displeased seems a little farfetched - but then - agreement - is what we're talking about here) So = Are the reasons - in your mind - what - you are agreeing with - in order to - agree - to taking it?

So = If you are - feeling - thinking - being - acting - any given emotion - isn't that a lot of action going on? And = A lot of agreement - on those levels - with those levels?

Remember our last assignment - of feeling your inner aliveness happening? Isn't that the core of all that activity we've been talking just now? What if - what we are - IS - a verb? Take away all that action and what have you got? Exactly - nothing but a dead body ~ Does a dead body have any interest in what's happening? In fact - we're not even talking about bodies - we're talking about energy - beingness - the action - of being alive ~ We don't say - alive is a body - we say - a body is alive ~ A body isn't what makes life - life makes a body ~ So = Does that mean that - what you are - is the action - of being - rather than - the thing - that's being? In other words = A verb - rather than a noun?

[[[[[[[[Doctor Dude's Dictionary - word fourteen - Celebrate:

The first two words in the definition of the word celebrate - are generally = To observe ~ What follows is = A date or event - meaning = A holiday - a birthday - a promotion = You know the story = We've all done it ~ But = What about that word "observe?" It's not observe - like look at something (not that you wouldn't) It's not study - or measure - or analyze (again - not that you wouldn't) But = It's still that verb - that action - of observing ~ As far as celebrate goes - that observation means = To follow certain patterns - rituals -ceremonies - observances - and best of all - rejoicing ~ At least as one part of the definition ~ Beyond that - it moves into public announcement - proclamation - praise (or you might say - celebrity) - as in = Ladies and gentlemen - allow me to introduce to you the celebrated author and quasi quantum physicist.....

In fact - the dictionary (or at least the ones I've consulted) - never actually mentions = Party down dude ~ Unless that's covered in = Appropriate festivity or merrymaking ~ But then = Who asked the dictionary? It's probably more - appropriate - to ask = What does - party down dude - mean to you? Popular meaning changes language all the time ~ What form of celebration - are you observing - with yours?

Let's say = If what you're observing - is modern American culture celebrating (which is to say - observing) - a holiday such as New Year's = What do you observe - music - dancing - nostalgia - resolutions - excessive alcohol consumption? After all - when it comes down to the root meaning of observe = It's all about paying attention ~ Oddly enough - the root meaning - or derivation - of celebrate - is a word meaning - numerous - or much frequented ~ When you put the two together (the way the dictionary does anyway) - you've got a meaning something like = Many popular ways of paying attention ~ The question really comes down to = What are you paying attention to when you celebrate? Or = What happens when you turn that observation on yourself = What - celebrates - you?|||||||||

Let's go back to our original question - of locating the opposite ends - of the emotional scale.

So = What about hate? If we could say - that happiness is made of love = What is hate made of?

How about = Why do we hate? Is that easier?

So = It sounds like hate - is always a reaction - to something done - to us - or just something - we don't want around - or in our lunch? Is that what hate is - a reaction? But - an emotional reaction - isn't what the emotion is made of = It's the effect - not the cause ~ So - in the same line of thinking = The event that triggered the reaction - isn't the cause either = It's really more like an invitation - to agree with a reaction - whose cause - is already in us ~ What if - there's just more to it - than reaction - and not digging deeper than just the reaction itself - is why = There is so much agreement to hate? The question is = What makes us - feel - hate? If it was a sandwich - what would be in the middle of it?

|||||||||| Virtual Murder:

Do you know how well you have been trained to kill?

If you are a regular user of video games (especially an obsessive - can't imagine anything more fun - Gamer) - then you have successfully passed the first obstacle any armed forces in the world is faced with in its training program to convert civilians to soldiers - which is = The willingness to directly fire on and kill members of an opposing force.

It might seem to you - after witnessing hundreds - perhaps thousands - of acts of lethal violence in movies and on television (never mind all the people and monsters you've blown away on video screens) - that it is the simplest thing in the world to squeeze that trigger when confronted with an us or them real shooting situation ~ Well - according to numerous studies by the military (past and present) = That's just not the case ~ It was found during the second world war (the first time such a thing was systematically studied) - that only a small minority of soldiers (15 to 20%) - consistently aimed and fired their weapons with intent to kill - while the rest = Merely pointed them in the general direction of the enemy - intentionally aimed high or low to avoid deliberately killing - or never pulled the trigger at all ~ The result (from the standpoint of the alarmed military commanders at least) - was a scramble to alter training practices - and target the psychological factors that inhibit proper military murderousness.

Those factors (just to spell them out) - are an apparently natural resistance among humans to kill other humans = Who knew?

The most immediate training change = Took place on the target range ~ Where the standard practice had been = To lay on the ground - for relatively short periods of time - and fire at target shaped targets - at fixed distances ~ The alteration = Was to place trainees in shallow cover - better known as foxholes - for many hours - on a range where - human shaped targets - suddenly pop up at random intervals at different distances and angles from the shooter ~ Modern innovations even go so far as to incorporate red paint in the targets to achieve a life like (or more appropriately - death like) - reinforcement of a job well done.

The purpose = Is to create a conditioned response - to habituate a shoot first think later reflex (sound familiar by any chance) - that desensitizes the recruit from what the actual emotional impact of shooting someone is - by sinking it under a learned pattern - a practiced skill set - no different from mastering any other athletic skill.

Another form - of the same desensitizing tactics = Is cleverly disguised by the acceptance of females as combatants ~ Which of course - also inspires a degree of gender competition from the men - both in training and real practice - which = Also contributes to the desired effect of willingly aimed fire ~ It's the enticement - that women achieve a social status of equality - by proving themselves fully capable of performing traditional male roles (and indeed they have) - that's the carrot dangled ~ However = Women in that role - are pressed (in a certain cultural deviation way) - even more so than men - to separate themselves emotionally from their natural tendency (generally - and for good reason - assumed to be stronger than in men - not that - that means it's completely true) - to preserve life ~ The military - are not interested in equality (just ask any private) If that were the case = They would be attempting to incorporate what are known as - feminine qualities - into the business of soldiering (perhaps creating - unarmed forces) They - are intent on getting the job done = The core of which = Is killing.

The other side of that equation - is the increased focus by the military - on glorifying - killing ~ Between the First World War and Vietnam - the practice of indoctrinating the would-be soldier with - kill - kill - kill - as the ideal model of the profession = Has gone from basically nonexistent - to a proud institution.

And the results are = Those alterations mentioned - plus a variety of other training procedures - have thoroughly rearranged those statistics - from 15 to 20% effective firing in World War II - to 90 to 95% in Vietnam.

Hand in hand with that increase in willingness to kill - is an equally large number of cases of - Post Traumatic Stress Disorder - or what the military used to call shellshock or battle fatigue ~ Which = Aside from being a fancier name for being mentally messed up - has the very real social effect of leading to drug abuse - alcoholism - divorce - crime - suicide - and all kinds of less dramatic - but just as unhappy circumstances.

The addition is simple ~ First = You can condition a human to blast away at a recognized form that has been labeled - Enemy (provided it presents no consequences other than numbers representing hits and misses) - until = That person is a highly skilled expert at his/her craft.

Second = You can send that person - along with the rest of their highly trained unit - into combat situations - where the standard taboo of murder has been temporarily suspended by that word long steeped in tradition and cultural pride - War - and = That person will admirably perform the task drilled in by hundreds of hours behind a trigger.

Third = Unlike training grounds (and video games) - actual combat - produces the very ugly results of bloody torn and dismembered bodies ~ Often including many - or even all - of the friends made during that period of training - and that = Has psychological consequences.

Fourth = Those consequences have long-term effects - covering a broad range of physical - mental - emotional - and social disabilities - which = Are by no means confined solely to individuals - but instead = Affect the entire society as a whole.

So - yes = On the other side of these considerations = Video games are a great hand-eye coordination practice - a concentrated focus exercise of navigating between totally clear cut rewards and consequences (conceptually at least) They are a brilliant use of creative engineering - artistry - and imagination ~ And what's more = They can be really great fun ~ But - in the end = This aside is neither about games or war or good or bad or better = It's about consciousness ~ The question is = When you scratch the surface of video game's - harmless entertainment - and wonder why they are based on the behavior they are = What is it - that you really find?]]]]]]]]]]

Let's say you know a guy - that - every time you encounter him - he's insulting and violent to you = How do you feel toward him?

Yeah = All that angry rotten stuff ~ But = Why?

Let's take the violence part = Say he's much bigger than you = He has weapons = You know he wants to hurt you = Maybe even kill you = What - is your reaction?

Let's look at that most extreme reaction = Kill him first ~ So = Are you going to? Yes? No? What will probably happen if you do? Do you want to go to jail? No? Why not? Okay - those are reasons = What is - the feeling? Can you break it down to one feeling - the one behind all the other ideas - of how lousy it would be to be in prison?

Is it fear?

Alright ~ Either way - let's say - the kill him first story - is the one you choose ~ Maybe you get away with it ~ Maybe you don't ~ Since we're making up stories - let's look at what might happen - in the don't direction.

Big Bad Guy - who you've murdered - has friends in the prison you're sent to ~ Maybe they're his girlfriends - in a woman's prison (in case you thought this was just a male story) They surround you one day when the guards aren't watching ~ What do you feel? That's for sure = You feel afraid ~ Okay - maybe you don't show it ~ Maybe you're so tough - you don't even know it ~ You killed the guy after all - you must be tough ~ But = Why are you so tough? Could it be = Because = You've always been afraid? Could it be = That's what's behind every reaction of hate you feel? Could it be = Fear - is the prison you had on your back - long before Big Bad Guy ever turned up in your life?

Break them down = With him alive - you can't go where you like - or do what you like ~ With him murdered - it's even worse = Even if you - seem - to get away with it = You'd be looking over your shoulder for a policeman for years ~ Looks like it's going to be one big unhappy life ~ Is it - fear - of those things - that makes you do what you do? Is it what you think - that makes you fear?

But = You still hate that jerk don't you?

What if - like I said before - the reason you hate him - is exactly the same? What if - it's fear? No? You hate him because of what he's like? What he does? Okay = Why? Yeah = You just told me that - but = Why? Why do those things matter to you? Ah = Because they mess with your freedom to do what you want? Like have fun? Go where you like? Walk down the street with your friends and family without trouble?

Sounds a bit like prison doesn't it?

Again = Is what we're uncovering here = Fear? Is that what hate is made of?

Sounds too simple to you? Oh - that's right = You're - not afraid of the people you hate.

Okay = When Big Bad Guy - or anybody else - calls you a moron - what do you feel? Angry? Why? Are you afraid of what other people think of you? Are you afraid it might be true? No? It's just that nobody gets away with insulting you? Okay = Why? Is it - because - if he/she did - everybody could? Then everybody could walk all over you? Why don't you want that? Because = You would be unhappy? Are you afraid of being unhappy? No? You just don't want to be? Why?

You're right = I'll keep throwing - why - in front of you - and = Why? Because = We're looking for the ground floor here ~ Actually - the basement ~ If love - is what's on the roof - what is in that dark creepy basement?

When you hate something - or someone - are you - doing - something? What are you doing? Could it be - you are defending yourself? Against what? Unhappiness? So is hatred - the armor we put up - between ourselves - and our fear - of being unhappy? Is toughness what that armor looks like? What else could that toughness be - but a defense?

Do they build tanks strong just so they'll look cool? What is that armor defending? Why?

What do you think - is fear the opposite - of love?

Okay ~ Whatever ~ What good do these words do? Isn't this course supposed to be about how to be happy? Is that what you're thinking?

Well = You're right (partly anyway) = This course is about being happy (it's also about - what that means) The thing is = One of the biggest obstacles we put in the way of - our being happy - is seeing the world as terribly complex ~ This question (the opposite ends of the emotional spectrum one) - is about making it simple - and = What if - our emotions are designed to do just that = Simply tell us which way we're headed ~ Like the lines on a road - tell us which lane we're in ~ You stay on one side of the center line = You'll make it where you're going ~ Cross over that line = You're apt to crash into someone.

What if - the simpler you see the world as being - the easier it is - to make the choice - of whether you are going to be happy or not?

If you are not feeling love - what are you feeling? Sure - there are lots of feelings ~ But don't they all lean towards one opposite or the other ~ Like - love to be happy - or - fear to be unhappy?

What - do - you - WANT - to feel?

But the world is a complex place - the argument goes - and = Who could disagree? BUT!!!!!!

What if - we did disagree? What if - we chose to see it simply as - love or fear - and then = Decided - which one - we want to agree with - which is to say = Feel - on the basis of that decision?

Remember - that basic question space - we talked about in the first class? - How does that work again?

Right = Unless - you make a space - for the possibility of a new answer = Nothing but old answers - turn up ~ And = What do old answers produce? Sure = The same beliefs and ideas - about how to deal with whatever is going on - that have been used - to deal with - the same kind of - whatever is going on - in the past - and = Guess what = Here are those same problems turning up - again ~ What if - those old ideas and beliefs - that we've used to - solve problems - are really what are - creating - the problems?

Do you think this might be one of those moments to open up such a space? What about an = {{{**Inventory Time**}}}

Good - because it's your assignment ~ What I want you to do = Is become - a radar ~ No = Not literally ~ It's just a good word for the kind of awareness field I want you to

222

experiment with ~ What you do = Is focus your awareness in your head ~ I know =
Maybe you think it's already there - but = As soon as you do - you'll see that it was more
- around you - than in one place ~ So anyway = You get it there (your awareness) - feel
yourself being there - in your head - then = Begin to look around - sensing everything - a
full circle all the way around you - 360 degrees = You're an electronic device - a radar =
Feel it = Be it = Move within that circle of awareness = Take everything in ~ What's
going on? What's the texture of what's going on? No = Not just what touching - things -
feels like = What feeling - feels like ~ Practice it ~ Switch it on and off - until - it's easy -
until - it starts coming on of its accord ~ Just do that - as often as you remember ~ In fact
- write it on the back of your hand - right now - on both hands even - maybe a foot or two
~ Or = You can use what I call the Prem alarm (named after a friend of mine for whom it
worked quite well) - where you set your watch (should you happen to wear one - and it
will do it) - to beep at regular intervals (15 - 30 - 60 minutes apart) - and when it does =
You remember ~ And then - of course - take a deep breath.

N.P.U. - Chapter Fourteen - Linear?

We need to backup here - for a moment - and look at a few more fundamentals of quantum physics - before = We go flying off into more dimensions - universes - and goodness knows what bizarre theories are being scribbled out by mad physicists with too much imagination on their hands.

Only we can't.

The phrase - back up - is just that = A phrase - words - that might make sense - if we had a moving van waiting at the curb to - back up - to the loading dock of our eager curiosity and carry in the furnishings we neglected to supply our (semi) - systematic approach to learning with earlier ~ But - no = We're already down the road - where = There is no - backing up ~ And that - (as you may have guessed) = Is really my point.

There is a word (imagine that) - that gets used - from both sides (meaning - pro and anti - yes and no - love and fear) - to describe a way of thinking (an approach - more precisely) - to seeing order - in the way things happen - get done - or are learned ~ The word is = Linear ~ It means (if you don't happen to know) = In a line - a progression - from one event - thing - conclusion - understanding - minute - hour - day - to the next ~ Linear thinking begins at A - and makes its way to Z - without reaching Q - before passing J - unless = There is a deliberate reason for doing so ~ It is basically - the standard method for viewing time - growth - construction - car mechanics - and (some might say - sadly) - education ~ There are reasons for all that of course - and good solid dependable linear reasons they are ~ However = When you find yourself trying to make sense of the quantum world - that same system of thinking (the one that wants to make sense in an orderly way) - begins to fail in its dependability ~ At least in the reference points it's depending on ~ Which are = The apparently - linear workings - of our day to day world - of stuff.

At the level of subatomic particles - there are entirely different actions - and expectations - than in stuff world ~ So therefore = An entirely different set of rules ~ This does pose a rather weighty problem - if you think about it (which obviously I'm inviting you to do) - since = Stuff world - is made of quantum world - like corn flakes are made of corn - and the rules of one - don't seem to match up with the rules of the other (meaning - stuff world sure don't look like quantum world) - then = Either corn flakes are really made from ground up alien spacecraft - or = What we think are the real rules of stuff world = Aren't the real rules.

224

So - now we'll do that backing up - just for the sake of that old saying = You can't run before you learn how to drive ~ No - no = You can't swim before you learn how to juggle ~ No - it's = You…..

Again = Linear thinking - has its purpose ~ In fact = Purpose - is what it's best at - or = Taking steps - one by one - to accomplish - a certain purpose ~ Learning how to read - for one - seems to make the most sense - by starting with individual letters - and the sounds they represent - before moving to simple words - then sentences - and so on ~ But = Since when - do the rest of our lives of learning take such a direct route? It may very well be - that the week you - learned - how to tie your shoes - you also learned how kittens are born - what the word inoculate means - that only female mosquitoes are the ones that bite - what happens when you spill bleach on the carpet - and - what your older sister does with that boy out behind the garage = Nothing linear about it (unless you make a certain conceptual leap between the kittens and your older sister)

The point is = Learning - is learning - and = Back in the subatomic world - you may have to just go bumping around randomly for a while - before its weirdness gets familiar enough - and - you relax that linear expectation of orderly progress - until = One plus one - does add up to three.

|||||||||| Ultimately Energy:

What if = Ultimately (which means - the last word - the end of the road - the outcome - beyond which there are no more - so it's one big arrogant stretch to even go near using it - but = Ultimately) - the reality of experience - or the interaction between matter and consciousness - is entirely = A matter of energy.

That's a big yes to that idea - if = You take what's often called - The New Physics - for a guide ~ So - if you do - or are willing to entertain the possibility - then = Any given experience - is real - to us - in the moment that it is - because = The verb - Energy - is being itself = It's moving - it cannot stop - and still = Be ~ Only perception - seems - to be able to do that - because = Perception (meaning - the energy - that is perception - which means - it can't stop either) - is designed to react - to gather information and inform awareness - after (again - that's after) - events of reality (energy) - take place ~ Therefore = You can perceive yourself - and other things - to be standing still ~ However = At the level of energy (which is what they really are - in that new physics way) - no thing (which is to say - no energy) - ever - stands still.

To break that down = The particles - that make the atoms - of your body standing there - are not the same particles - that make it up when you walk over here ~ Not that you have to move for that to happen ~ It's happening all the time ~ It's energy ~ It's changing constantly.

What that means - for explaining perception - is = Your experience is more like a television broadcast - delayed just slightly by the time it takes to reach your awareness ~ What you/we are watching - touching - smelling - experiencing - is = What energy has finished doing - and = Has already moved on to doing something else.

In that sense = Perception's - reality - is no more real - then that live TV show - is live (meaning - no matter what - it takes time - to get to you) - or = To put it in its simplest terms = All we ever experience through perception is = The past.]]]]]]]]]

Let's look at some of those rules in comparison then.

You'll recall hearing somewhere (wonder where) - that this - seemingly - solid world of ours - is actually (at the subatomic level) = Nearly 100% - space ~ Right there - the rules - get pretty shaky ~ And = Even if you take that idea - and say = Okay ~ Cool ~ I'll accept that = The habits of familiar expectation - linear as a bullet - from your solid floor to your solid feet about to get out of bed - still are saying = Nope = Can't be ~ Not that I blame you ~ That bed was also plenty solid enough - in a soft comfy way - and a lot warmer than that solid floor ~ But still = That space thing = Is - true ~ And then = There are those bits of energy called electrons whizzing around - as the definitely not solid - shell of those atoms were talking about ~ Of course - the thing they're doing that whizzing around - you'd think - would give us some reassurance of solidity ~ But - oh no = No substantial solidity there either ~ Plus = The size of that nucleus floating in that electron orbit defined space of an atom - might just keep you in that bed for good (not that it'd do any good) It's been said (to kind of quote myself paraphrasing someone else) = That if - that electron orbit defined space of an atom - were the size of a cathedral (you know - those huge carving covered churches mostly built in the Middle Ages) - then - the nucleus - would be the size - of a flea (sound familiar?) In other words = One billionth the space of an atom ~ So yes = When we're talking about nearly 100% space - we're talking about - nearly 100% space.

Alright - a little more of that backing up then.

You'll also remember (if you do remember) - the double slit experiment - where = Light was shone through - first just one - then two slits in a sheet of metal - onto a photographic plate - and the result was = The discovery that light functions - both - as a particle - and - as a wave ~ But ~ just saying that = Doesn't describe - how truly against the rules - that action is ~ It also doesn't describe = How another experiment was performed - using electrons - instead of photons - in a similar kind of way - in that = They also created an interference pattern (which is the tell tale signature of a wave) - which means = Not just light - but matter - also behaves - both as a particle - and - as a wave ~ Which means = Single particles - are not - choosing - things like which slit to go through (as one of those BBs you were firing through that window we visualized were) = They are actually - going through both slits - at the same time ~ Go ahead = You do that.

See - what we're seeing here - is = At the quantum level (unlike the football level) - an objects motion - follows many paths - to complete one path - whereas a quarterback - seemingly - has only one chance of getting the ball to the receiver in the end zone ~ What - that - means - is = The fans - are only really seeing - the tiniest fraction - of what went into that touchdown.

Does it matter?

||||||||| Vertical Time:

Time (Which is really just the infinite imagination of a single now - as if that makes any sense to thinking organized around clocks - but = What if - it is?) - appears - to be broken into the three familiar parts of - past - present - and future ~ Every action we take - every relationship with objects - people - and ideas - plays out that familiarity in exactly the - one - two - three - of the linear expectation we're used to - which means you'll be late for the movies if you don't step on it.

There's absolutely no contesting - that time (mixed up with space - of course) - in that linear format - is solidly responsible for the context in which those other three dimensions of our reality move and adapt and progress and change ~ And yet = There's nothing solid about time at all ~ Even those clockwork expectations of ours - are not completely rigid ~ We've all experienced time drag - during a boring wait - or time fly - when there's too much to do and not enough of the precious stuff in which to do it ~ And still = Time is the basis (not discounting space again) - by which we both - interact with what we call reality - and = How we make some kind of sense out of that interaction.

There is a concept (or a theory - if you prefer) - that's apt to challenge that sense making habit (if you allow it) - but = You've already been prepped for that challenge - by your consideration of the fact (yes - that's fact - and no getting around it) - that the present - is the only time there is ~ Therefore = What's called - Vertical Time - is actually - the next logical step.

The concept of vertical time - is based on the quantum mechanical idea - that reality - when it is expressed as the wave - is pure potential - or - infinite possibility in superposition (meaning - the whole buffet of choices that have not been chosen yet) Every instant - at the speed of light - that infinite buffet is offered as the wave - then plated up (selected) - as the particle - again - and again - and again ~ In our linear time world - those particle choices are consistent with (or match and reflect) - the previous moment = So that - something like a car - travels forward some tiny fraction of a mile in the next millisecond - rather than - leaping forward 100 miles ~ In vertical time = All that changes.

You perhaps recall a sidebar (you know - a distracting information insert like this one) - that described the concept called = The Hundredth Monkey? (If not - that's because = In the linear process of reading - you haven't reached it yet ~ So - turn to - **Monkey mind 101** - in chapter 18 - and check it out) In that (theoretical) - function of consciousness = When a certain percentage of a population (also called - critical mass) - learns a new skill - suddenly = The entire population - acquires the same skill ~ Vertical Time - is essentially the same thing - only = With the added dimension - of altering memory to suit the new present that has suddenly appeared.

What that means (other than science fiction invading your brain) - is a timeline - like your own life (say... kindergarten to high school) - arrives at 3:33 p.m. August 16th ~ All the events - that you remember - leading up to that moment - are consistent with each other - in that they are a progression of linear results - or - 1+1 - 2+2 - 3+3 ~ Then = Because a critical mass - of people (or something) - have been changing ideas - questions - desires -

intentions - consciousness = A whole new set of possibilities (from that infinite buffet) - gets chosen - and click = Something (perhaps everything) - changes - including all the memories that support what the world is like at 3:34 p.m. - for = Everyone.

Yes = That is an imagination stretcher - and does sound unlikely - if not ridiculous - given our previous experience of time and the world ~ But = How would we know?

What if - such events - governing small changes - or gigantic ones for that matter - happen all the time? What if - they are so fast - and so complete - with every last timeline of memory - in everyone's mind - tailored to fit so perfectly - that the transition is absolutely seamless - completely unnoticeable - then = How could we know?

Could it be = That certain types of what we call insanity - are just the effects of noticing such - glitches in the matrix? Could it be = That playing a willing witness to such an idea as - Vertical Time - has just created an episode of it?||||||||||

Well = No ~ And then again = Yes ~ It's a question of perspective really ~ And - of course = The perspective of a question - must be - not knowing the answer - or - it's not a question ~ So - a true question - is not - a linear thing - it's = A field of possible outcomes ~ Therefore - a quantum question = Is in - superposition - or = Wave function.

Alright - I'll stop - backing up - your memory - by playing with words previously defined - and settle on one - that hasn't been ~ That one is = Field.

The quickest way to start wrapping that cap of yours around - quantum field theory - is to go to that classic comic book fantasy power of - a force field = Bang - our hero (which is us) - slams up against an invisible barrier - just sort of - being there - in space - and that's it = A field ~ A field - is an action - taking place in a region of space - without form - that either - influences form - like our force field example - or (to access a more familiar experience) = Is the gravitational field that's keeping your chair on the floor ~ Or = A field - is pure potential - that - collapses - into particle - or form - by being - measured - meaning observed (remember our discussions of the Copenhagen interpretation and particle wave theory) - by you - or me - or Bill the bartender - who decides to shut you off on account of you're talking such crazy stuff.

The difference between - a field - or field function - and - say - Bill's tip jar - is much the same as - the difference between - a wave - and a particle ~ The wave - has no fixed boundaries - it cannot hold Bills tips - because - a place to store those tips - and - the tips themselves - are still just potential - invisible - formless - thoughts that could be - or are yet to be - or won't be thought - in the minds of Bill and his customers - and = Anyone (anyone over 21 at least) - all over the planet - is potentially - one - of those customers - and that = Is a wave ~ Of course - this means that = What ever Bill is going to take home in the form of tips - on any given night - is always - and forever - governed by - uncertainty - until he goes home ~ Which brings us - most certainly - to the next key word in the workings of quantum mechanics ~ Which is = Uncertainty.

The - Heisenberg Uncertainty Principle - is the product of yet another inspired German physicist - Werner Heisenberg ~ In 1927 - Werner was struck with the certainty - that when it comes to the measurement of - certain actions - of particles - like where an electron is located - and - how fast it's moving = The closer to accuracy you get in determining one measurement - say location = The further you get from accurately being able to determine the other measurement - which is speed - or velocity (That ring any bells?) What this means - in quantum world (which - by the way - is very thoroughly backed up by experimentation) - is = There is no such thing - as being in a particular location - at a particular speed - for electrons - or any other particle ~ As far as stuff world goes = If such uncertainty applied to traffic on the freeway = Then driving - would be considered a suicide technique.

What I'm driving at (if I haven't actually arrived there yet - it's really only you that can measure that with any kind of certainty) - is = We are faced with a dilemma = We live and interact - in our ordinary world - where the laws of nature - as we assume to understand them - appear to be - the limits - to our experience ~ While - at the same time = We now have a definite peek - at the underpinnings of that world of ours - where = What passes for ordinary - is so opposite - to our linear reasoning - that there is hardly any choice but to declare = That one - or the other - must be - absurd.

The simple beauty of that absurdity however - is the wonderful mystery it presents - where the space of question - is not some kind of poverty of knowledge - but an untapped well - of unknown riches.

SPECIAL BONUS EXERCISE - number seven

The Winning List:

This exercise - you could describe as a kind of self-confidence neuronet builder (don't worry your linear little head about what those two last words meant - we'll get to them by and by - and - by then - you'll already have some practical experience of the concept behind you) You could also describe it as = A self integrity test - or a bridge repair between intention - and action ~ Of course - describing it - is not doing it.

So - what you do is = Make a list of everything you're going to do tomorrow ~ I mean = Everything - you - are - going - to - do - tomorrow ~ By everything - I don't mean the stuff you hope to get done - or would feel good about getting done - but the stuff - that's just about guaranteed to happen= Like getting out of bed - dressing - going to the bathroom - walking downstairs - whatever it is - to what ever level of detail you like ~ Go ahead and include those good to get done things if you want - but only = If you really are going to do them ~ Otherwise - you'll defeat the purpose of the exercise - which is = To cross that list off = To broadcast to yourself - a clear and strong message of accomplishment - and = In that conscious action - begin to create a new system of neural connections (some of that brain stuff we'll get to) - that support the belief - that you are a winner - a doer of what you set out to do.

It's entirely simple ~ In fact - the simpler the better ~ You can even do a form of the same practice in a moment by moment way - by saying to yourself = I'm going to walk into the bathroom - then = Do it = Walk into the bathroom ~ I'm going to squeeze toothpaste on my toothbrush = Do it ~ It doesn't matter what the action is = It matters that you accomplish it ~ It matters that your brain stores - in its neural connection maps = Going to do something - with = Did that something.

Doing this will not change your life overnight of course ~ You'll have to keep it going some time ~ But = Will it change your life?

All I can say is = It's your life - find out.

Halftime

Well done - you've made it halfway.

Half way where - you might ask = And well you might - because it's really not halfway anywhere - it's = Right here ~ The reason - I call attention to this moment (other than the fact it is an actual approximate physical location - according to one particular form of measurement) - is to direct that attention to another form of measurement - which is = Feelings - that are a response - to placing a value - on a goal - or unfulfilled desire - that defines a half way point - as unhappily not being at that goal - or desire - rather than - happily progressing toward it.

In other words = If you were on a road trip between New York and San Francisco - arriving in Oklahoma City - would not in itself be a reason to turn back - or have a nervous breakdown - just because that's where you were instead of San Francisco ~ Not to say those aren't available choices in Oklahoma City (though I would point it out as the location of some of the lowest prices for gasoline in the country - however it's still about a hundred miles short of being half way between New York and San Francisco) The point is = We forget - the going - is what we do here in the world ~ Because = Whenever we arrive - we begin going somewhere else.

It isn't that it's not satisfying to arrive - or preferable - in the sense of a feeling of accomplishment - in comparison to unfulfilled longing ~ The difference is = There's another angle - from which to view the location - of not being in the location - you think you'd prefer to be in - and = We've been talking about it from the very start ~ It's = That space of question ~ It's = learning - knowing you're learning - inviting learning - wanting learning ~ No = It's not often comfortable ~ But - the why - or the reason for that discomfort - can regularly be traced to a not trusting in learning - and = The mad idea - that despite the constant condition of change we witness all the time - we think - things - will - or could - remain the same.

So = Here is one of those points of change - and - it's a question (as if that would be a surprise) = Why - do feelings - or emotional states - exist? What good are they - other than being the hoots and dingers of a pinball journey through life that only register reactions like nerve endings respond to the jab of a needle?

Well = What if - they are a navigational tool - a kind of internal guidance system - installed for the purpose of keeping track - of where we stand - in relation - to what our thoughts and beliefs - are causing our journey through life to look like? What I mean is =

On that one way trip to our desires - we're all traveling = What if - there is a natural energy - or a set of natural laws - that is the power - of this alive right now speed of light action of being - that provides us all - with the exact and immediate energy resources (meaning an alignment of connections with other people's minds and lives) - we need to accomplish those desires - the moment we desire them - every instant? And - to continue that - IF = The reason we receive our desires (or do not) - is because = Our thoughts and beliefs - their history and consistency - are either = In tune with the actual desire - we think we are having (meaning - having a true dedication to it) - or = Are in tune with opposing that desire (meaning - holding some other thought/belief in the way - such as unworthiness or victimization) - and - that's AND = Our feelings - are there to inform us - of the state (meaning - being in one - or the other) - of those attunements? {{Alright - read that last paragraph again - then I'll say it a different way}}

What I mean is = What if - The Universe (to put - it - in a popular phrase) - or - The Quantum Field (to use another) - responds instantly - to everything - we ask of it? And = By ask - I mean again - desire - or place a strong attention on ~ In other words = Think about a lot ~ And = What if - that instant response is always based on supporting our - well being? (At least from a big picture point of view of what well being means - which is = Infinitely - more complex than how we're apt to define it - since it includes a complete awareness of every thing and every event and everybody else there is and ever has been at the same time)

So = What if - our feelings - swing toward those love or fear ends of the emotional scale - because = They are informing us - of how we are lined up - in our minds (our thinking - believing - relationship with past experience) - with our ability to receive that instant response of energy - and it's line of results - or well being? Or - even more simply = What if - good feelings tell us how to get what we want (meaning being properly tuned in to it - like a radio station - and after all - good feelings - are really all we want out of anything we do want) - and = Bad feelings are the opposite?

I know = It - or our lives in the world - don't seem to look like what I just described ~ Especially in such simple sounding terms (not that - that big picture point of view of everything is exactly simple) Then again - the floor you're standing on - and the feet you're using to do it - don't look like 99.99% space either ~ So - I'm not saying = What I just proposed is true ~ I'm saying = What if - it is?

Class Fifteen - Attention?

BREATHE (Fill those lungs all the way = Up you go - that's right = AAAHHH ~ Good job ~ It's beginning to work isn't it? Are you paying attention to how your mind is working? Think about it ~ Start keeping track of the things you do that require concentration and deliberate focus on learning - or just interactions with others ~ Has any of that gotten easier? Pay attention from now on - and = What about trying to practice the exercise more often? Or not - but = Keep it up ~ The kids studied certainly didn't want to stop when they realized the benefits ~ Why would you?)

How's that radar working? What does it feel like? Do you like that feeling? What did you do with your new ability? Did it change how you felt about the things around you? Did you notice how present you became? Did you find that you could feel what was behind you as soon as you switched it on? Can you switch it on right now? Have you already?

Okay ~ Let's look at those words - Love and Fear - from another angle this time.

I'm going to tell you what to think ~ Okay?

You now think = That boiled monkey brains are your favorite food.

How did it work? Is that what you crave for dinner now? No? Why?

So = Can anyone - make - you think something - you don't want to?

Alright = Is deciding to be happy - something that takes place inside you? Okay = If the decision - takes place inside you - where does the result - of the decision take place? Yeah = Stuff happens on the outside - the way you act and look and the reactions you get - but = Is happiness (your happiness) - outside you? So = What are you doing in there? Yeah = Right now ~ What's going on inside you - right now? By inside - I mean = In your awareness ~ Not digesting lunch - or having to pee ~ So = What is it? In other words = {{{**Inventory Time**}}}

Okay = You're thinking stuff - feeling feelings - processing all of that sensory information that's coming in - judging this - weighing that - deciding what to do - or not do?

So here's the really big question ~ What - are you paying attention to? In other words = Out of all that mental activity - what is most important part to you in this moment?

There's some interesting language in that phrase - paying attention ~ When you are paying something - what is it you are usually doing? Sure = You're spending money ~ So = When you're spending money - you're buying something - you want - or need - or are required to? So = Does that mean - you're deciding - or defining - what's valuable to you - by what you are willing to pay for?

Now - if you were in the military and someone shouted - ATTENTION - what would you do? Yeah = You'd stop whatever you were doing and put all of - your attention - on standing up straight and stiff in the proper way ~ Would you say - that's a way of bringing all your awareness into the present moment? So = If we put those two together - could we say = That paying attention - is valuing - what's present - for you - in your mind - right now?

So again = What - are you paying attention to - right now? What part of your experience are you placing the most value on? Which also means = {{{**Inventory Time**}}}

What happens - when you pay attention - to paying attention?

See - this is the spot - where those love and fear extremes - come into play.

When you're experiencing a particular emotion - what kind of thoughts are you having? Right = Thoughts that go along with the emotion - that support it - in some way ~ So - again = Don't all emotions - lean in one direction or the other? That is - more toward love - or more toward fear?

Think about it ~ Which - is another way of saying = {{{**Inventory Time**}}}

Here's a simple way to test it out ~ Do you love to be sad? Or = Are you afraid of being sad? I don't mean shaking in your boots ~ I mean = An underlying sense - of comfort - or discomfort ~ How about - do you - love or fear - to be - excited - irritated - thrilled - lonely - content - bored? Which way do your - feelings - within your feelings - lean? I know = Some feelings - like bored - seem more neutral and not something that's fearful - just dull - like there's nothing going on ~ But = Do you like being bored? Do you avoid it - or want to be bored? What is - going on? Why?

Fear isn't always scary ~ Often - it's just like wearing a seatbelt in a car ~ You're probably not terrified of having an accident (that is - it's not what you are thinking about all the time) - but = Some tiny voice in your mind is concerned about it - or of getting a ticket for not wearing one - or maybe you're one of those people who refuse to wear the things at all ~ What's with that?

What I'm saying is (and it's not some judgment about seatbelt wearing) = What - are - you paying attention to? That's what it comes down to - because = You are - paying attention to something.

[[[[[[[[[Doctor Dudes Dictionary - word fifteen - Sublime:

You could say - you had a sublime moment gazing at the sunset ~ You could call the sparkle of early-morning dew sublime ~ Or the same for the effortless grace of a hawk soaring - maybe the far-off drone of a foghorn in the middle of the night - or the light streaming through a stained-glass window ~ You might even refer to a chocolate cake as sublime - and still be within the definition boundaries of the word ~ Which is all very nice - but = What does it mean?

A first look - at the word sublime - might indicate something that was underneath - or lesser than - a lime ~ Which would not be so terribly far off - if you forget the fruit and look at the word - limen - which means = The threshold - or entrance location - of a physical or psychological response ~ In other words = The beginning of an experience ~ Still - the sub part remains a bit confusing ~ That is - when you realize what the whole thing (sub and lime together) - translates into (or is covered by such words as) - noble - majestic - unexcelled - supreme - lofty - moving - awesome - and - the ultimate (which also identifies it as an adjective - or a descriptive word) - which = Seems to be describing anything but a - lesser - experience.

The truth is = It's really a verb - disguised as an adjective - because = It is an experience - an action that takes place internally - and so = Can only be described after the fact (or after the experience has occurred) - by being hung up before - or under (meaning sub) - what caused it ~ Which is to say = A sublime sunset - is not like saying - a fiery sunset - or a golden sunset ~ It's saying = What the sunset felt like - what the experience of being a part of that sunset was - inside the experiencer - which may very well = Be you.

And then = There's the sublime experience itself - as a category of what's out there (actually - in there) - as available to be experienced ~ Which means = When you add up the list of words used earlier - that began with noble and ended with ultimate - you come up with a range of feelings that result in the word sublime - but = What's actually being described - is the action of = Expansion.

What is sublime - is what stretches boundaries - what removes for a moment - however fleeting - the framework in which we operate - and for that moment - a little bit of infinity blows through where the roof used to be ~ Of course - there's a range - or a scale of measurement - for that expanding ~ Such as the difference between that chocolate cake romancing your tongue - and watching the sun rise from Mount Everest on your 70th birthday ~ Unless - that's not true - because = It isn't ~ Sublime - is just a word for crossing those boundaries - what we do beyond them - and when - how - or why we come back - is up to us.]]]]]]]]]]

So = In looking at those thoughts you're having - aren't you - deciding - whether to be happy or not - with them? No? Aren't they what's in control - of how you feel? No? So who's controlling your thoughts? How did you arrive at them in the first place? Did someone force you to think them? Oh sure = Big Bad Guy - or a bowl of boiled monkey brains (your favorite) - certainly have their effect ~ But - remember = This whole experience - of happy or unhappy - is going on inside you ~ So = Who is it - that's in there? And = What is he/she - paying attention to?

So again = Why - this idea of love and fear - as a scale of measurement?

It's simple really - and = I already said it = Which one - do you want to feel?

Do you think - if you really began to pay attention to what's going on inside you - you'd start to see - what thoughts are connected to which feeling - and which feeling to what thoughts? Do you suppose there's a pattern to it all - a kind of repetition - you fall into by habit? How would you find out? Yeah = You'd have to pay attention - which means = {{{Inventory Time}}}

So = How do you do that?

[[[[[[[[[Emotional Impostors:

If you experience a resounding whack to the head - four things can happen ~ One = It hurts like cursing anything - but = That wears off - maybe a headache for a while - nothing terrible ~ Two = You suffer what's known as a concussion = A somewhat generic diagnostic term - also known as a mild brain injury (unless it's a severe concussion) - where a blow to the head actually bounces your brain around in there - and causes a variety of temporary drunken like symptoms = Such as blurred or double vision and poor balance (provided it was in fact - in the mild range) Three = Some part of your brain is damaged - and so = Some part of what your brain does - doesn't work the same way any more ~ Four = You die.

That's a very simplistic list of course - and yet = As a set of outline headings it covers it all quite neatly ~ It's number three - which requires the longest list of subheadings though - simply because = Our brains do so many things - and = Some really weird things can happen - when you mess with the usual circuitry.

One of those oddities - is what's called - the Capgras delusion (that's cap - like the hat - and grah - like - well - bra with a g) Its story goes = When someone whose whack to the head has damaged them in a certain way - that person functions normally - but = Even though such things as family members - places - pets - and other closely associated things and people - appear - to look exactly the same as they did before the brain damage occurred = A delusion has replaced that certain recognition - with the conviction - that the person or thing they are seeing - is in fact - an exact copy or imposter.

As you can imagine - it's a bit of a bummer when your girlfriend/husband/mother/brother (and so on) - insists you're not who you claim to be - despite = Being the spitting image of that person ~ Or - the reverse of course = If you're the one doing the insisting.

But = Why would such a thing happen?

As it turns out - there are two pathways in which visual information travels in our heads ~

One of them - streams information to the visual cortex (the part of the brain at the back of your skull which sorts out what things look like - previously mentioned a couple of times now) That processing center's function resembles the action of a camera - in that (and only in that) - it is only concerned with delivering a picture to you - and not - deciding what the picture means ~ That information - is processed elsewhere ~ Part of that processing - is accomplished by the other immediate receiver of visual information - which is the amygdale (a - mig - duh - la) - the entrance to the limbic system - or the emotional centers of the brain.

The apparent purpose - engineered into this two-lane roadway to Recognitionville - is to simultaneously inform you (your mind - your awareness - whatever it is you want to call the thing which is observing the sum of all this information) - of the color and shape and contrast of what you're seeing - AND = How you feel about what you're seeing ~ The surprising conclusion (which cannot be avoided under such scrutiny) - is that we are seeing emotionally - as much as we are visually.

As for the - this is not my beautiful wife - sufferers = The reason they are undergoing such confusion - is because those pathways to the limbic system have been damaged - and what used to be recognized by certain strong emotional information - in conjunction with visual information - is now incomplete = It doesn't feel the same ~ And because - it doesn't feel the same = How - could it be the same?

All that being said = You might want to take good care of that head of yours ~ But - what's more = You might want to understand - that our sensory perception - is integrated with our imprinted (or built up through experience) - emotional/intellectual/memory systems - and so = What we take in - is equally a matter - of how we are conditioned to judge - as what it is - we're taking in - is being what it is.]]]]]]]]]

You remember me saying = What happens -when you pay attention - to paying attention? Well = What happens?

Any of you play an instrument - or sports - or video games - or build things - draw - paint - write stories - sew - cook - or any other creative activity or skill? So = How do you get better at it? Exactly = You have to practice ~ Do you make time for that practice? Have a schedule? Take classes? So = Are you paying attention - to getting better at any of those things? Well = That's - how you do it.

Paying attention - is the game - THE PRACTICE IS = Paying attention - to paying attention.

What if - practicing the measurement of all your thoughts and feelings - against the scale of love and fear - would make it simpler and simpler - to choose to be happy - until you were = Happy - all the time?

All my thoughts and feelings? I don't know ~ That's a lot of work ~ But - happy all the time? That's impossible ~ Can't be done.

Is that what you think? Why?

Yeah = Experience of life in this world certainly points in that direction ~ Even happy - part of the time - can be a big stretch for many people - and nonexistent for some ~ So you wouldn't have much trouble finding people to agree with you ~ But = What if - it is possible - to be happy all the time? What if - our belief - that we can't - is - why - we're not?

Would it be boring to always be happy? Indeed = That's another idea a lot of people have ~ We are lovers of drama and conflict = That's for sure ~ Look at all the movies - TV - books - magazines - newspaper articles - and just plain conversations - that center on the stuff ~ But = If - we are lovers of drama and conflict - and - there's so much of it going on - then why = Aren't we happy about it?

What if - secretly - we are happy about it? Such a - well kept secret - in fact - WE - don't even know about it?

Yes = That does sound a bit wacko - I know ~ But = What if - the reason we're not happy all the time - is because = We don't really understand what happiness is?

What if - we only recognize a very narrow band in the center of happiness? Or - not even near the center - more like = Only what we have defined as pleasing - that's kind of over in the corner somewhere - and yet we call it - the whole of happiness - when = Happiness is really - a far wider possibility of pleasure - if = We simply employed a different set of tools (meaning - ideas about what it is) - to measure it?

||||||||| Happy as Larry:

The Australians have an expression (British in origin actually - and a colloquialism - to be precise) - which goes = As happy as Larry ~ What it means is = Really bloody happy mate ~ Now - who Larry was (the expression has been around for quite some time - so presumably - the original Larry is long gone) - and why he was so happy - and just exactly how happy that is = Is all a matter of anybody's guess ~ It does bring to question though = How we measure this thing we call happiness - and = Why we do it.

You might be happy - the car flying through the yellow light did not hit yours ~ That - makes the scale at relieved ~ You may be happy - the dental checkup was quick and painless with no sign of cavities ~ That - hits the notch at glad ~ You may be happy - the birthday card from uncle Frank had $10 in it ~ That - hovers at pleased ~ You may be happy……

Happily by now = You've got the point ~ The scale of course - continues to rise toward - content - excited - gleeful - joyous - overjoyed - blissful - ecstatic - with various categories and subdivisions in between - but = What is it - we are measuring?

For one = We're measuring where our attention is - according to how we measure the expected results - of placing our attention there - and = While we're doing that = Is number two = The corresponding wavelength of energy we generate - in response to our measurements of attention and results - which = Tops out our level of happiness - as directly equal - to that calculation.

Therefore = What we're measuring in the end - is a willingness - to be happy - and = That scale can easily be influenced - by taking control of one variable - which is = Noticing - happiness - and = Being happy - about being happy - whenever - you feel = Happy.||||||||||

Yup = It's a twisty idea - I know ~ Let's see if we can straighten it out some.

When you get involved in a drama - be it an argument with a schoolmate - or an action thriller on the big screen = Does it consume all your energy and attention - at least for the moments you're not distracted by something else? So = It's (the drama that is) - very important to you in those moments? Is there a difference between - it - being your fight - or someone in the movies? Okay - sure = If it's happening to you - rather than someone else - it's your body involved ~ So = Why - is it so fascinating - to watch on the screen? Yeah = It just is - isn't it? But again = Why?

Could it be = We've got those - love and fear opposites - mixed up - and = We love fear - and fear love - because = It makes for all kinds of exciting = Drama? What if - that attraction to conflict - really isn't any different - between it being your fight - or one you're observing on the screen? (Other than the obvious differences of the consequences involved) No = That's not the way we usually see it ~ But = What if - we just don't see - all there is to see? What if - we're not paying attention - to paying attention? What if - when we are engaged in drama - we're getting what we want - because = We love drama? Doesn't it please you to get what you want?

So = Why not be happy about drama? Oh = It isn't what you want? So = Why do you have it then? Ah = You - didn't - choose it?

What if = You did choose it?

What if - we choose - everything - that happens to us - exactly the way it happens?

No way? You didn't choose your bike getting stolen - or your toe broken - or the stupid stuff the lady down the street yelled at you?

But - again = Just for the moment - try to empty that space of question - we've talked about ~ Take out the - I knows - and turn them over to = I don't know - regardless that you think you do - and see what happens.

Yeah = It's not so easy in this case ~ No one consciously chooses bad things to happen to them ~ Unless - somehow - those things fit into some plan they have - like = If I get wounded they'll let me go home from the war ~ But = What if - the choice - I'm talking about (the we choose everything one) - doesn't quite exactly - happen - in the part of your mind you're conscious of? What if - it happens in that mysterious land of the missing

85% - and that part interacts with all that no thing space (the Universe - the Quantum Field - Zero point energy) - everything - is made of - and it = Creates what happens?

Okay = What if - that is true? Or - if - it's not? So what? What good does it do? Everything is still the same and drama goes on? Is that what you're thinking?

Well - there's a point there ~ But (always have one of those - buts - don't I) = What if - that's the point that keeps us from looking in there? Meaning = Looking beyond - those pesky old ideas - of how reality works - according to our past experience - again.

So = If - we - ARE - choosing bad things to happen to us = Wouldn't you like to know? Wouldn't you like the option to change that - to just good things - happening to you?

Okay - okay = It's - what if this - and what if that ~ Where does all this questioning come to rest on something solid to chew on? That's the real question isn't it?

Alright - here it is = What do you think about? What do you feel - about - what you think about? What do you want to feel? What are you paying attention to? What are you paying attention to paying attention to? Is it love? Is it fear? Which one does the rest of your life look like? That's it ~ It's also another = {{{**Inventory Time**}}}

But = Those are just more questions aren't they? Yup = But who are they about? That's right = You = It's your life - your happiness - your consciousness - you're investigating here (which just happens to include everybody else's) - isn't it? So = Where else would you look?

What if - the more you chew on these questions - the more flavors you'll find in yourself - and = The hungrier you'll become to taste more.

I know = That's describing ideas as though they were food ~ Well = What are ideas? Oh no - that's another one to chew on ~ But = What does your body do with food? Absolutely = Energy and growth ~ Isn't that what we're talking about?

Meanwhile = Your assignment this time - is to turn that radar awareness back on ~ But this time = Close your eyes and turn it inward - and = Pay attention to paying attention ~ Examine your thoughts and feelings - while you're having them ~ Meaning = Don't go looking for them - just watch the ones that are there - the way you might watch someone you really want to be friends with - but - you're not quite sure they feel the same way about you ~ Feel your way into them ~ Do they love you? Do they fear you? Yes - they - he - she - it - are you (or a part of you – more precisely) But then again = Who is the one - paying attention?

You may find the practice of that assignment a couple classes back - of feeling the alive energy of your body - helps you to practice this one - and - vice versa ~ Put the two together - and expand that radar field all the way to your toes ~ Or not ~ The key is in the attention itself ~ The question is = What's really going on in there? And then - there's the one about - if you're breathing.

N.P.U. - Chapter Fifteen - Levels?

We seem to have left a few loose threads laying around ~ Or is that strings? Or - is that = We've done our best to untie most everything we had so well lashed down with - our rules of ordinary reality ~ Or - maybe not ~ The - thing - thing is = There are levels to this reality business ~ Mind you = Levels is just a word - and - as usual - a word can have many meanings - or levels for that matter ~ So - let me define my use of it here.

When I say - levels of reality - I mean = Just like the floors of a multi-story building - there are definite - divisions - between each level of what makes up this world (floors being - quite literally - the dividing points in a building) - where different rules apply - say with atoms - or cells - or members of Congress - and - at the same time = It's (meaning all those levels) - still the same building ~ So - levels - is not a case of better or worse - superior or inferior - it's a case of = Which limitations - are governing what part of the show.

See - rules - are nothing more than limits ~ Some of them - are obviously chosen (or made up) Like no gum chewing in class ~ Where others - appear - to be beyond choice - like breathing - or dying ~ In that tradition - each level - has its own limits ~ Molecules change and reproduce - in definite ways - according to set limits for molecules - as do cells - as do humans - and so = Each group - is - definitely - different - in how they deal with those things - because = Their limits are different ~ Therefore - you can say - with perfect certainty (and what's more - even be right) - that our rules of ordinary reality - in the midst of our ordinary reality - are true.

But (knew that was coming didn't you) = It's still - the same building ~ All those levels - or floors - are part of - one reality ~ So - when we narrow our view to just one floor (or even several - but not all) - and the sets of rules - or limits - governing that floor or floors - and then declare those to be the only rules - then = All we are doing - is trying to enforce limitations - on all the floors - which (from the point of view of the building seen as a whole) = Are not true - and so = Cannot be enforced {{Yeah - I'd read that one again myself}}

The most powerful limit going - is our habit (crusted over into unquestionable expectation) - to think - and so - govern our lives - within the boundaries - of limits ~ Even when we know about all those other floors - and even (even) - know that they are the features of only one building - we still = Are mostly convinced that our experience must be isolated to the floor in which we live - where the furthest we can stretch - is to peer down at the floors below - and philosophize about the ones above.

Now - I'm not saying - this tyranny of limitation is not true ~ I am saying = What if - it isn't?

||||||||| **Multi-Universe Experiences:**

Exactly like the concept - that you can see this pen - because = It's not the things around it = Experience - may be experienced - in the order in which it is perceived - because = It's not all the other possibilities of experience which are being played out in an infinite number of universes that are constantly generated by an infinite number of possibilities.

Of course - that is a concept beyond any human mind to fully embrace ~ And yet = To entertain it for a moment - is a mental sensation fully worth experiencing - because = What if - these human minds - are capable of embracing far more - than finite experience - is apt to give them credit for.|||||||||

With that in mind - let's visit one of those floors we've just barely glanced at the rumor of ~ Though granted - it's one of the most poorly furnished - and hardest to see in - which = Is partly because it's the deepest most basement - where only a limited number ever visit - and even most of those visits are only mathematical ~ This floor - is the land of = Branes.

But first - we have to prepare a tiny bit more - by spending a moment on one of the floors just above ~ Well - at that depth - the floors may be a bit difficult to distinguish - without a theoretical physicist along as a guide - and yet = We'll know we've found the one in question - when we begin to see - quarks.

Alright = Obviously (or not) - what we've returned to here - is subatomic particles ~ However = Did you happen to notice - how - we went about doing it? That's right - we imagined our way here ~ We employed a familiar - limited experience - of floors and buildings - and allowed their limitations - to become fluid ~ In fact - we really didn't have to - do anything - to accomplish that transition ~ In fact (in fact) - the only real choice - of doing - was whether or not to resist that imagining - because = It is the most natural thing going - to slip between the levels of limitations - we otherwise very strictly behave according to with our bodies - by doing so - with our minds ~ And = Since our experience of these bodies - takes place - in our minds - it only stands to reason - that we have - every reason (based on that experience of fluid mind) - to question - whether the limits of our bodies - exist (meaning - really are limitations) - only in those locations - where our minds - cease to be fluid ~ In other words = Are limitations - only our beliefs - in limitation?

Okay - I'll stop interrupting as we try and see what quarks and such have to add to this - potentially liquid - architecture of experience.

In the early 20th century - the atom was worked out to contain those three particles we've talked about - electrons - protons - and neutrons - all neatly modeled as the little solar system that one of your science teachers probably dusted off at some point ~ Then - in the 1930s - scientists studying cosmic rays - came across a new set of particles they dubbed = Muons ~ It doesn't seem to make sense to say - discovered - when the things are regularly bombarding Earth in their mega zillions ~ But so they are - and - where there is one - thing - there's usually more - which = Led to predicting - and then - discovering - the neutrino - in the 1950s ~ Now that was a real feat - since nothing stops these little guys ~ There are hundreds of billions passing through you this instant and the Earth under your feet - or in the other direction if it happens to be night where you are - because = It's the sun's nuclear furnace (supposedly) - flinging them into space that's causing this intrusion (on a sort of local scale anyway - the rest of the galaxy is doing its part as well)

Of course -finding things - inspires more looking - and - methods of looking - and in 1968 = Quarks - came on the scene with the refinement of those atom smashing accelerators we've given the nod to a couple of times now ~ Ah = But not just quarks = A whole family of quarks ~ One by one they turned up - and down - I can't help but say - because - they were the first = The up and down quarks ~ It turns out - that a proton consists of - two up quarks - and a down ~ Whereas a neutron is the opposite - with two downs - and an up ~ And then = Out of all these ups and downs - came four more quarks - top - bottom - strange - and charm ~ If quarks were a breakfast cereal - they'd come in six different flavors ~ Not that it would matter - because = As soon as you got them in a bowl - they'd have disappeared.

[[[[[[[[[**Nuclear Sun:**

Now that I told you that the sun is an atom splitting nuclear furnace - flinging out neutrinos with more abandon than the Defense Department spends money - I have to point out a small inconsistency.

Apparently - it's not true (that is - it might not be true - or - anyway) If - the sun's heat were the result of a nuclear reaction (as we understand such things) - there would be even more neutrinos - lots more = There aren't.

The sun is a nuclear furnace - is what's known as = Conventional wisdom ~ Which - at its furthest stretch means = Artificial wisdom ~ Even though - we - have known about the neutrino lack for some time now - we - haven't been able to work out what really is going on up there.

Is the Sun a hole in the energy field of the galaxy - allowing cosmic energy (whatever that is) - to stream through? Is it... well - there aren't even many good theories (that I've come across at least) - to plug that knowledge gap (unless of course it's a nuclear furnace)

So = How the sun works (and that presumably includes every other star out there) - remains both - an uncomfortable conjecture (for some) - and - a mystery.]]]]]]]]]

It's no simple matter (note the word matter) - getting a peek at these particles ~ The results of the - high speed - or high-energy - collisions (in particle accelerators) - I've used the word - uncover - to describe - is a bit misleading ~ The particles - uncovered - weren't really there ~ They were - produced - by the collision - from the wave state - they were really in - and the picture - of particles produced - is a process - of working backwards through time - represented by the results of the result - of that impact = Kind of like - determining the original position of all the billiard balls on the table at the beginning of a game - from the point of view - of only knowing who won.

You've got to wonder how people figure all this stuff out ~ Especially - if you're one of those people who had difficulty assembling the shelving unit you bought - and - you had the instructions.

The thing is = They do.

The question is = What is it - they're figuring out?

Well - it goes further (of course) = More particles - groups of particles - sub-groups of particles - and then - anti-particles - or anti-matter ~ It's been found - that electrons (those zippy little orbiters of all atoms) - have an opposite number out there called = The positron ~ The electron - as you'll possibly remember - carries a negative charge ~ The positron - as you might expect - a positive charge ~ Slam these babies into each other - and instantly - they cancel each other out in a burst of energy (sounds a bit like that one plus one equals three business - doesn't it) - and = It's not just electrons - with evil twins ~ It appears - as far as appearances can be proven - that all particles have them ~ Not that good or evil applies - that's just trying to put it into recognizable terms ~ Which of course means - believing - in recognizing - terms like good and evil.

[[[[[[[[Dark Matter:

Centuries ago - before the planet had been thoroughly explored and mapped and photographed from space and all that global positioning system pinpointing exactly where you are at the push of a button accuracy we now take for granted - didn't exist = There were empty spaces on maps ~ Sometimes - by way of compensating for those gaps in knowledge - those empty spaces had such things written across them as = Here be dragons ~ Or = Terra incognita - which is Latin - and translates basically to = Land unknown - or (more honestly to the people using it) = We don't have a clue what's out there - but = We know - something is.

Since we've basically taken care of that terrestrial (located on earth) - cartography (map making) - and have begun to direct our explorations skyward - as well as into the subatomic realm = Our new knowledge maps - are also riddled with blank spots ~ However = More and more of those maps - at least have a new phrase scribbled in the margins = Here be Dark Matter - or - it's even more extensive phantom cousin = Dark Energy.

Now - this dark stuff is not some wild Gothic sci-fi fantasy concocted by rogue astrophysicists ~ It's more like a repetition of the - haven't got a clue what's out there - but something is - response ~ Only = Whatever that something is - there seems to be more of it than everything else put together - and - multiplied many times over.

How do we know?

In simple terms = It's a question of math and movement ~ While observing galaxies - far - far - away - it was noted that their movements - and speed of rotation - compared to their calculated mass - just did not add up ~ They shouldn't be able to do those things ~ There had to be something - unseen - to make up for the discrepancy ~ Something - which influences - or cooperates in some way - with gravity - but = Does not interact with the electromagnetic force (which is what accounts for it being - Dark - which - again - is really more a dragon kind of word)

It's now theorized - that the total energy density of the universe ($E=mc^2$ - and all that) - consists of only 4% of things we can see - like trees and rocks and galaxies - plus molecular - yet invisible things - like gases (out in space - gases are spread so thin - it's estimated that you'd find only one hydrogen atom - the simplest and most abundant atom in the universe - in a cubic yard of that space) That leaves a whopping 96% - something else ~ Which = Is considered by many imaginative astrophysicists - to break down to - roughly - 23% Dark Matter - and - 73% Dark Energy - which (unlike that badly lit matter stuff) = Dark energy is diffused (or spread out) - through space everywhere.

Just like those maps that now say things like - North and South America - Australia - Antarctica - and so on - one day - possibly soon - we'll be able to fill in what that - nothing space - really is ~ Perhaps - it will even turn out to be = Consciousness.||||||||||

The thing is = Forget about recognizable terms ~ Unless you're a theoretical physicist who speaks higher math fluently - you'll only - recognize - so much of what's going on down here ~ Therefore - in order for you to - understand - what we're talking about = I'd suggest - you give up - right here - right now - on understanding it - and instead - feel it.

But = How do you do that?

Simple = See that space in front of you? No - not the table and chairs over there - or the floor they're on = The space ~ I know - you don't see the space - you see through it ~ Just the same - it's there ~ Go ahead - wave your arm around in it - be aware of it - feel - your attention on it ~ Perhaps for the very first time in your life (or maybe the second - if I'm not mistaken) - encourage that space - to be something - almost as though it were a liquid - but = A liquid with practically no resistance to it ~ Let your attention flow into that liquid - and feel - when it does - that it has no boundaries to it - even when it meets with walls and ceilings - they don't interrupt it - they're filled with space themselves - and beyond them - there's more - endlessly more ~ That feeling - of moving into - joining with - that space - is a way to leave the particle - and be the wave - to understand - not in words - or numbers - any more than the balance you practice effortlessly when you master bicycle riding is something you need to describe to yourself to understand how to do it = Just do it ~ Pour your attention into space - until = You feel it ~ And then - take that feeling - along with you as we descend into that deeper basement - I hinted at before

- and your understanding = Will be as effortless as peddling downhill.

Now - that doesn't sound very scientific - I know ~ Not like vast underground particle accelerators and super mainframe computers churning through data ~ But = What if - it is? Just like the first time - anyone - ever rode a bike (meaning - the invention of the bicycle - when it hadn't been done before) = That - felt like something - that breakthrough - and - in such a moment = The invention - and the feeling - are the same thing.

There's an idea - that science - has no feelings - or that feelings - are not scientific - and are more like a hindrance to investigation - rather than an investigation in progress themselves ~ But - when we do finally have a look around - the land of Branes (which is short for membranes - just so you're not confused with the one in your hed) - make no mistake = What we're really doing - what physicists - or scientists of any kind - are doing - what everyone is doing = Is seeking a certain feeling - from what we're doing ~ The question always is = Which feeling - are you seeking?

Class Sixteen - One Thought?

BREATHE (Okay - everyone now - on your feet (or sitting down if you have no choice) = That's right = Left hand - right hand - tongue in place = And = Deep breath through your nose…..)

How did the assignment go? What did that radar energy do when you turned it on your self? Was it harder to make it go in that direction - rather than outside you? Did you recognize any particular relationships between specific thoughts and feelings? Did it help you to alter your thinking in any way? What way? Did paying attention to feelings make them stronger or weaker? Did the distinction between love and fear make more sense to you afterward? Did doing this have any effect on how you responded to events or other people? Do you think it will - if you continue?

Okay = Who can tell me a thought - that has no connection - to any other thought?

Good - you're thinking ~ But it doesn't work - does it? Every thought - does - have a connection to other thoughts ~ Just the thought - of searching for such a thought - connects it to the thoughts - that are searching for it ~ We can think thoughts - that seem - to have nothing at all to do with each other - like = The Salvation Army has no guns - added to = Donuts don't have to be round - and = Gasoline makes lousy mouthwash ~ Those are some pretty distant thoughts from each other ~ But = Who would put gasoline in their mouth? Much better place for a donut - which = The Salvation Army has handed out by the hundreds of thousands.

Any one thought - requires only one other - to connect it to every thought that is - or ever could be - and you might say = That thought - is the thinker itself = You.

You've heard the phrase - train of thought? So = What does it mean? Sure = Hooking one thought to another - coupling on cars of related ideas - as it were - and = Following - or creating - a track toward some point - some destination of thought - the cargo of that train add up to - rather than = Just looking out the window at what passes (so to speak)

So = What role - do you play on that railroad?

Well - you might say - you play all of them = Owner - stock holders - engineer - brakeman - conductor - not to mention station master - porters - and all those people laying the track - repairing the engine - coupling the cars - washing the windows - and - being the passengers ~ That train - just won't run without = You.

Remember that idea - about people not actually being separate - the subatomic world and the no-thing space - and all that? And then = Do you remember the bit about coming to an understanding - that is - connecting - to that space we all share - by recognizing our thoughts = To be the same invisible no-thing action - of creating?

What if - we are not separate - because = We are all connected - by our thoughts?

But no one - knows - what anyone else is thinking ~ Is that what you say? Or - is that - what you - think?

[[[[[[[[[Reality Bytes:

What if - reality is constructed of information - rather than the reverse - which = Is generally assumed to be - information - is constructed of reality? What if - all that stuff - in front of you - behind you - in every direction you can see - and then beyond the beyond of that - all the way to the edges of the universe (if it does have edges) - is like the picture on your computer screen - meaning = Digital information? You see a picture there (on that screen - when you do) - many pictures - text - videos - which = All look like - pictures - text - videos - and yet = They're not = They're information - coded into numbers.

What if - that's what the world - the universe - reality itself - is = Coded information? What if - we could break that code? What if - the first step in breaking it = Would be realizing - it is a code? What if - the second step = Would be recognizing - that same code - is operating as you - your mind - your body - and therefore =Your consciousness - which = Must arrive at = The third step - or = Deducing - that - that same code - must also contain - the means - to its own decoding?

What would be the fourth step?]]]]]]]]]

So = How about looking at the real ground floor idea then? Or = Why - do you think - people - are separate?

Okay = You - see them - hear them - feel them - and sometimes smell them - feeling and doing things - that your body - isn't?

But - again = Where is your experience - of all those things?

Can you see a thought? Touch one? Yeah = We've been there before haven't we - but = Can you? Oh sure = There are fancy machines that can track electrical activity in the brain - but = Is that a thought being made - or the response to one? And = Can any of those machines tell you what the thought is? (Indeed - there is some machinery being developed which can track brain activity in such a way that - types of thinking - can be generally identified - according to how and where in the brain that activity takes place ~ But = Is that mind reading? No)

So = How do you know they (thoughts) - are not all shared?

Well okay - there's a point = Because = People - disagree.

But = Didn't we work out - that all thoughts - are connected to other thoughts? Yeah - I know = You took that to mean in your own head - not between heads - except in the most general sense ~ But - hang in there a moment with me = If - all thoughts are connected = Does that mean they have to agree with each other? Like how are ice cream and nerve gas in agreement? So = What connects them? Exactly = You do.

Alright ~ We'll take it another step = Is your behavior - or - the actions you use to interact with - the world outside you - outside you? Yes and no? You mean = Your choices of behavior - are inside you - but = Your actions - and their effects - are an interaction with things - outside them - meaning - your body? So = It's kind of both? Okay - that works for the moment ~ But = What happens to that moment - when you ask = What is your behavior based on? Right = Thoughts - feelings - beliefs - and all five senses working together ~ So = Where is all that - going on?

Yeah - yeah = You've heard it before = I know ~ But = The answer is still the same - isn't it? It's all going on inside you - and so = In seeing it that way - wouldn't you say = That your behavior - is how - you connect your thoughts - to the world - you're thinking about - and so = Thoughts - and behavior - are really the same thing - the same interior world of experience?

Yeah = I see you're getting the point - and yet still thinking = So what - that's just words in a circle - not life in the world? But - stay on the train a bit further - and think about = And then = There's everyone else's behavior - isn't there? Aren't they doing the same thing - of expressing their thoughts - through their actions? In other words = Living in - and through - their minds - so that = Behavior interacting with behavior - is really = Mind meeting mind? Or = Apparently - exterior experiences - happening in interior worlds - which perhaps = Is really the same world - as much as (or even more so - than) - that exterior one - is one world? Or = In fact - that interior world - is the true (or real) - shared world - and that other = An Illusion - generated by the idea - of being separate?

Okay sure = You can see it working that way ~ NOT ~ So - again = So what? Your thoughts are still in your head - right? They're not shared - are they?

Alright = How about those other people then? Do they behave more or less - the same? Yeah = Some of them do strange things - or violent things - all kinds of weird stuff ~ But = It's still recognizable - what people do - isn't it? I mean - they don't turn into monsters or puffs of smoke? Basically - they're moving around like the rest of us - eating - sleeping - living in the world?

What if - that's because we're all thinking the same stuff?

No = I don't mean exactly the same thoughts - at the same time ~ More like = What if - we're all - ordering off the same menu - so to speak? The kitchen is the same ~ The ingredients come from the same shelves and refrigerators ~ It's just one big restaurant of thought without walls and tables (except - that is - for all the walls and tables there are to think about) - and = The way we recognize what's going on - is because = We've all (once we reach a certain age or level of experience) - had at least a tiny taste off everyone's plate.

Yeah = There I go talking about weird stuff as though it were food again = I know ~ But - follow along a bit further.

Let me put it like this = What if - the human species all act and interact (that is - behave) - within a certain range of recognizable patterns - because = All the information we use to decide how to behave - has the same source - like one big library? No = I don't mean actual books ~ What I mean is = What if - there is only one mind - and = We're all using it?

What do you think? Could that be true?

Yeah = You're right = The evidence - of what we see - as people thinking separately - out there - doesn't support such an idea ~ But = What if - we're reading the evidence wrong? What if - we're reading the evidence - through - what we already believe to be true? Rather than = As something to be questioned?

||||||||| Doctor Dude's Dictionary - word sixteen - Transcend:

To climb a set of stairs from one floor to the next - is to ascend those stairs ~ To take the elevator - is to transcend the need of those stairs.

What I'm getting at here (or rising to the challenge of) = Is an examination of the word = Transcend ~ It's a verb - quite unlike the majority of its active family - in that = It's movement - is always invisible ~ Yet - the nature of that hidden movement - is so real to the person experiencing it - that the two syllable parts of the word are drawn from sources meaning = Entirely visible activity - or = Trans - which begins such words as transport and transfer - means = Travel - change - over - across - beyond ~ Trans-action and trans-late - turn one thing into another ~ Just as exchange and trade - trans-form - a demand - into a supply ~ All measurable movements ~ All quite visible ~ The second half - which is - scend (pronounced the same as - send - a letter) - although it's one letter short of getting to the top of those stairs - as ascend (which also means that trans and it share an s between them) - is still that climbing thing - a-scending that ladder - that mountain - a-scending to the throne - or the heights of stardom ~ Together - those two parts move beyond the meaning of themselves - and their limits - and become - the action - of doing so - or = To rise above limits - to surpass - exceed - leave behind - to step into another way of being - and so become = Transcendent.

The real point of the word - is to establish a contrast (as really most words are pointed) - or describe something - to differentiate it - from another thing ~ In the case of transcending to transcendent as it moves into transcendental - is to step up that distinguishing - one meaning from another - to a contrast - that well... transcends - the contrast of one thing to another - and opens to a knowledge beyond the limits of material world experience ~ That transcendence - strips away the importance of a sensory-based existence (perhaps even denies the reality of it) - and = Experiences another realm of being - where contrast and limits and words are merely the descriptions of inadequacies to describe such an experience.

What we've found here - is a word gesturing at something far beyond words - which of course = It cannot accomplish on its own - because = It's still just a word after all ~ It does supply that tricky little bit of linguistic testimony however - by being the evidence of its own existence ~ Which is to say = If someone went to the trouble of making up such a word = There must be some good reason for it.]]]]]]]]]

Okay = True or not true - what is the word - in the last - what if sentence - that describes the obstacle to examining our experiences differently.

Bingo = It's = Believe ~ When we believe something - is - TRUE - we don't question - if - it is ~ As far as we're concerned = IT IS TRUE ~ It's = THE TRUTH.

So let's look at this belief thing = We need three volunteers.

Alright ~ Lucy = You have two minutes to convince us that bathing in the winter will kill you.

Ricky = Your job is to prove the Earth is flat.

Fred = Tell us why - if humans travel at speeds higher than 50 miles per hour - the pressure will kill them.

Ethel = You time them.

So = Anyone believe Lucy? How about Ricky? Fred?

Well - they did have the disadvantage of not actually believing those things themselves = So - you do have to give them quite a bit of credit for trying.

Were all those ideas - things - people used to - think - were true? Yup = Sure did ~ Do you suppose - that since they believed those things - they must have believed in other things - that were equally untrue? So = Were those people - using those ideas - to decide - how to live in the world - and = Interact with each other? Do you think they thought they were - Right - to believe such things? What about you - is everything you believe - Right? So = Are you also - using your beliefs - to work out how - you should live and interact? How are you different from those people in the past? Ah = Your ideas - ARE RIGHT ~ But = Isn't that exactly what they thought? Yes = We've learned a lot since then ~ The Earth is definitely not flat - and = I'm sure you've all bathed in the winter -

and = Traveled a good deal faster than 50 - and = Here you are quite alive ~ So - you're right about that much.

Any of you ever studied history? Do you know why Columbus called Native Americans - Indians? That's right = He believed he'd landed in India ~ Had he?

So = Have you noticed that through the centuries - all kinds of beliefs have changed - as new ideas - and new discoveries - took the place of earlier ones? Have you also noticed - that very often = People have defended their beliefs to the point of imprisoning other people who did not agree with them - and = Even killing them - in fact = Killing them by the millions? What does that tell you about people? Yeah = They can be terribly stubborn - blind - and cruel ~ But - it's more like what drives them to it - that I'm asking about ~ What did they think about their own beliefs? (Those people doing the killing - that is) That's it = They were RIGHT = What they did - made sense to them = It was the right thing to do = That's what they = Believed.

So = Why do you think I'm pointing out this history of being RIGHT?

Very good = We all do it ~ Mostly we don't kill people over it ~ But - the majority of people operate on the belief - that most of - if not all of - what they think - is true ~ What effect - do you suppose - such a belief has on people settling differences between each other - or - between nations? That's right = From arguments - to full scale wars - the results - cause a lot of problems.

What if - everything - we believe - to be true - about this world - actually - is not true? That is = What if - everything - we think we know - is false?

Yeah = That's a big one ~ What does - such an idea - make you feel like? None of those feelings are particularly comfortable are they? Of course - some people are very comfortable with thinking things like = How stupid is that? But - the question is = Can - you - go there? Can you entertain the possibility - that everything you think - is -false? What would it mean - if it was? There'd be nothing solid to stand on (so to speak - though I hardly need to point it out) - and we humans don't like that kind of thing.

Ah = But this is the spot we've been talking about all along = It's that space of question = It's the no time but Now - the mystery power hidden in us like electricity used to be - the internal world - the missing 85% - the no thing space - the limits of our vision - the energy of being alive - the payer of attention paying attention to paying attention ~ This is the spot where = What we believe to be possible - meets = What's possible to be possible.

The real (REAL) - question is = How far do you want to go - in the exploration of consciousness? Or shall I say = The Rabbit Hole? Because = What if - the borders of possibility - are guarded by our beliefs - and we cannot pass beyond them - until we disarm them? Remember how well armed some beliefs in the past have been? I'm not saying = You have to believe - that everything you know - is false ~ I'm not telling you what to believe - or not believe ~ I'm saying = Ask the questions = Find out ~ What if - your happiness (your constant happiness) - is waiting - beyond those borders - of believing you can't be happy all the time? Oh yes = There is fear to pass - when the ground is shaky - or not there at all ~ Isn't that the reason - we want answers - instead of open questions? Isn't that why - we fill our minds with - KNOWING - things - to keep fear - of the unknown - far away?

What if - we are all connected in one great super mind? What would keep you from wanting to know if that was true? Or = From finding out?

|||||||| Beyond belief:

The word history - does not mean a long chain of events (even if it does) What it really means - is = Change ~ Time - is change ~ Movement - is change ~ Any movement in time (event - interaction - conflict - discovery - eating a bowl of oatmeal) - changes something ~ So = Like I said = History - is change.

The most powerful dynamic in (human) - history (as well as it being the measuring rod of change) - is how the flow of accepted ideas (beliefs) - continuously alters course - as it's towed reluctantly along behind the flow of expanding knowledge ~ The two currents of that belief stream (as if you could actually separate them into distinct channels without running to volumes of description) - travel the parallel courses of = What is believed to be possible - and = What is believed to be morally (and so socially) - correct ~ A case in point being = The witch hunts of the 16th And 17th centuries - where uncounted thousands (perhaps even millions) - of people (vastly more women than men) - were executed (most were burned at the stake) - for allegedly practicing witchcraft ~ The - possibility belief - was in spells - curses - demons - and magical powers ~ The moral belief (at least in its simplest terms) - was that torturing out confessions - and then making a public spectacle of excruciatingly painful deaths - was a form of doing good.

What we're talking here - are world views - or = Individual and collective - frameworks of belief - on which are hung the ideas of how the world - does - or should - function - and (to slap it down in front of you again) = They change.

It's easy to call the conviction - that you should not wash your baby's head for the first year of its life - in order to protect it from bad luck = A superstition = Or - that a bird entering your house - means someone in the house is going to die - is another.

But = It's hardly as simple to dismiss the nearly universal belief - that germs cause illness - or - that sun exposure is the main cause of skin cancer - as being more of the same superstitious dread ~ And yet = Some number of years from now - that may be exactly how such - taken for granted truths - are described (especially as those two particular examples have already attracted some serious doubt)

Then = There are the - scientific truths - of the ancient Greeks - who looked up at the vault of Heaven (a kind of rotating bowl of sky - above the never moving Earth) - quite happily in the - knowledge - that nothing up there ever changes - and = Looked around at the objects and creatures of the world (matter) - certain they were all combinations - or rearrangements - of the four elements = Earth - Air - Fire - and - Water.

Quaint - you might say ~ Or at least some kind of start (maybe even correct) But = Will the future see our probing for new subatomic particles - and - hopelessly slower than the speed of light space programs - as equally backward? Will our medical science be classed with the long out of date practice of bleeding people (intended to forestall fermentation of the blood) - which = More than likely hastened the death of Mr. George Washington (just to do a little name dropping) - or = Shelve Chemo therapy (that technique of treating cancer with intensely toxic chemicals) - with the miasma - or the bad air - which = Was believed to carry such things as cholera and yellow fever over the roofs tops of 19ᵗʰ Century London?

In the year 1900 - Lord Kelvin - a member of the famed Royal Society (a very exclusive club of science minded English gentleman) - very publicly declared = "There is nothing new to be discovered in physics now" ~ You have to imagine - he'd like to retract that statement - now = Clearly - he'd missed the very rigorously tested conclusion - that = Only nothing - does not change.|||||||||

Could it be - your belief - that we're not connected - that would stop such a question? Or = Your beliefs about - the importance - or what it means to be an individual? What if - Columbus - or Thomas Edison - had been stopped by such an obstacle as a belief in the impossible? (True enough - in the case of Columbus - that may have been a good thing - at least for those people that were called Indians for so long)

Something to think about - isn't it? Well = How about - not think about - because = That's your assignment.

I'll explain = See - basically - we're always busy reacting to what's going on ~ We're having opinions - judgments - ideas - and - right in the middle = Beliefs ~ Which - of course = Are powering the rest of that stuff ~ What I want you to try doing - is = Spend some time - not - doing that - meaning = Letting it (that stuff I just listed) - sort of slide through you - without reacting to it ~ For example - say you're watching someone do something you think is stupid - or you feel uncomfortable around someone - shy - disapproving - awkward - annoyed ~ First = NOTICE - how you feel - then = Just feel it = Don't react = Don't say anything - or walk away - shake your head - anything ~ Just let that feeling slide through you ~ It will probably be uncomfortable at first - but = Try to just hang out there in it for as long as you can ~ One trick to accomplishing it (as well as distracting yourself and calming down from any upset or concern) = Is to count to five as you inhale - and the same as you exhale - and = Keep doing it - five in - five out - until another feeling arrives (or you have to run away or something) You can do it for any feeling - any time ~ Doesn't matter what the feeling is ~ Doing it - is what matters ~ Remembering to - also matters ~ Me - I like writing on the back of my left hand ~ But that - doesn't matter ~ Not the way breathing does at least.

[[[[[[[[[Number One:

Seems an appropriate moment to consider the concept of = Ego.

The word itself - is taken from the Latin - meaning = I myself ~ Its usage in modern speech began in a paper written in 1920 by Dr. Sigmund Freud (whom you've no doubt heard of as the famous founder of psychoanalysis) - only = He used the more direct German = Das Ich - or = The I ~ What he was describing = Was what he saw as the three parts of the human psyche - or mind - as it goes about the business of living ~ That breakdown included = The Id - which = Is the (so called) - lower animal end of mind - where the biological survival and pleasure seeking drives run the show ~ The opposite end = Is the Super Ego - which = Does the high-minded critical thinking - the moralizing - that better be good or else conscience guy sitting on one shoulder job (which places the Id on the other of course) In between = Is the Ego - which = Attempts to steer the two along a path of responsibility and social delicacy - sort of moderating between crime and conscience - to get the job done of looking out for number one - without attracting too much of the wrong kind of attention - or missing out on too much of the fun.

That's the nutshell then - of Sigmund's three-part harmony (or is that disharmony) Doesn't mean that's actually how it all works - or what any of us mean when we use the word ego ~ Mostly - when we do = We mean a self-important (or egotistical) - view of one's identity ~ A big ego - is that on stage - look at me - listen to me - cuz I is just so much cooler'n you thing - that tends to rub our own egos the wrong way so irritatingly.

But - that's the thing = You can break down the experience of mind to three parts - or a hundred = It's that - number one (as I just used it a moment ago) - that's the true culprit = It's that insistence on a separate self - a separate identity - in competition with all those other egos out there - that's the real defining of - das Ich.

Of course = That doesn't take away - or intentionally degrade - the endless fascination and analysis of the experience of mind - which = At the level of perception - is quite separate - but = It does simplify it ~ What ever word gets used to point at a distinct identity contained in a body with all its history and preferences and personality = It's the unquestioned boundaries of that containment - where all the friction amongst our species (we take so for granted) - takes place ~ The question is = What does your ego think of the possibility - that those boundaries - only really exist - in your mind?]]]]]]]]]

N.P.U. - Chapter Sixteen - Branes?

Now - to reach - those branes - there is a direct route - but = It's not actually as clean cut as descending from one floor to another - like from cells to molecules ~ There are complications ~ Luckily - those complications - for all they are dauntingly complex - are also - simple = They're theories ~ Mathematically - they are maps of beautifully precise logical directions ~ Experimentally - they are - looking for Atlantis with Elvis riding on a unicorn ~ Still - their beauty is - they make sense - and = They could - tie relativity and quantum theory neatly together - but - most importantly = They stretch our imagination in both directions at once - where = The unimaginably small (strings smaller than electrons) - can also be - the unimaginably giant (strings stretched to the size of universes) - and so = Unimaginable - has to eventually tear somewhere - and = Allow some new experience - to get in.

Of course - as you've guessed = We've returned to the realm of - String Theory ~ Strings - more or less - exist right there on that same floor as subatomic - or elementary - particles - because = That's what they're describing ~ However = Those strings still have a rather dark corner to themselves - due to the fact = They remain in the entirely theoretical category ~ So - the flooring in that section is a bit touch and go for confidently walking on ~ Plus = It's somewhat tricky making the distinction between whether these strings (or vibrating strands of energy) - are what subatomic particles - are - or = What they're made of ~ Kind of like - is your bowl of oatmeal made of one oat - or many (the difference being - we've managed to figure out the answer for oatmeal)

Regardless - of that rather subtle difference = The big difference (as noted somewhere back there) - is the one between - spaghetti and baseballs - or points versus strings - as a way of - regarding - these subatomic goings on ~ Vibration - is the key word however - and = That word - key - opens the most familiar relationship we have - with understanding - vibrations working together - which is = Music.

When a guitar string is plucked - it vibrates - and - its vibration = Creates sound ~ When you add other vibrating strings to that first vibration - you create chords - which - if done properly = Are pleasing sounds ~ When you - cooperate - with those vibrations - by creating more vibrations - on other instruments - you create even more pleasing sounds ~ That is - of course - if those other vibrations are what's called - in key.

|||||||||| Talking Entrainment:

Entrainment - is not just something that occurs as the result of conscious effort ~ Instead - more often than not = Its activity - is entirely unconscious ~ In fact - the action of harmonizing energies - may - be one of the great unwritten laws of the universe (which is using the term - unwritten - in the sense - that human beings - have not universally recognized it as such) Take - for instance - the amazingly harmonious movements of flocks of birds and schools of fish = Groups that number in the hundreds - and even the thousands - will suddenly all wheel and turn and change course with the precision of digital animation (as if computers could outdo nature) - and not a single individual colliding or missing a beat.

Of course - humans are seldom inclined to see in nature a reflection of themselves ~ So - for us - there are research projects with sophisticated electronic devices to get us to notice what happens - naturally ~ In one such study - where conversations between different people were filmed - and then analyzed at slow speeds for indications of entrainment (meaning - some sign of attunement - or harmony of behavior - posture - inflection - expression - anything that would hint at energy interacting in a state of agreement) - it was found = That there were definite synchronizations of the body movements of the listener (call her - subject A) - to the sound of the speaker's voice (subject B) - a kind of physical mirror of rhythm and pitch - no matter which person took which role ~ Even examining the film at speeds as low as one 40th of a second - there was no lag time - no hesitation of response catching up - but instead = A sort of instant marionette string connection between the two subjects - as though they were actually just one - subject - including = When those two people had been complete strangers to one another previous to the filming.

Another conversational study was done - where the participants were wired to EEGs - and while they spoke = Their brain waves were recorded and compared for signs of entrainment ~ Tellingly enough (for all tellingly is not a proper word) = The subjects only produced the same patterns - during - what they later reported as - good conversations.

Then = There are findings of synchronized heart rates between psychiatrists and their patients ~ Plus = Babies breathing in rhythm to lullabies they've fallen asleep to ~ And = Many - many - demonstrations of physiological systems (breath - blood pressure - heart rate - and so on) - conforming (entraining) - to changes in tempo - harmony - and melody patterns in different kinds of music.

Fact is (to hazard the use of the word - fact) - what we are dealing with here - on our planet - in its corner of the universe = Are systems of vibration - whose natural tendency = Is to achieve harmonious synchronization (otherwise known as entrainment) The broader our understanding of how such energy relationships work = The more astounding are the possibilities that open to us - and = Our shared happiness.

After all - what is the act of trust required to share happiness with others - but = Just another type - of entrainment.||||||||||

Now - this is where that parallel - between music and String Theory - takes two different paths ~ The first is = If - String theory is correct - then = The physical universe (in those particle moments when it's being the universe) - is produced by an orchestra - of an immense - possibly infinite - number of vibrating strings - the same way = A symphony flows from the vibrations the musicians create with their instruments ~ In that sense - being in key - makes no difference ~ The music is played - whether the orchestra gets the record contract or not - because = The orchestra - is - the record company ~ The completion of that scenario then - drops in as = There is also - the possibility - perhaps - the probability - or even (forgoing all doubt and hesitation) = The absolute certainty - that at the level of strings - there is no such thing as - out of key - there is only = A perfect harmony - of creation orchestration.

The other path - is the one (also generally regarded as theoretical - when it's regarded at all) = That we can - consciously choose - to vibrate in key - with portions of that orchestra - or even the entire orchestra (seeing as how it may not be possible to actually separate one part from all parts) - in that emotional state - we call happiness ~ Or even = It may be - that is in fact = What we are doing in that state (meaning happiness) - whether we are consciously choosing it (happiness again) - or not. {{Yes - read that paragraph again}}

So = What about gravity?

Remember - that the reason string theory - has evolved - is in an attempt to - unify - those four forces of the universe - into one (so to speak) - and = Gravity (according to Einstein - even without him being around) - continues to frustrate that purpose.

Well - along comes this theory (String theory to be exact) - suggested - inspired - and constructed by mathematics - that = Subatomic particles - may take a form quite different from the world of momentary dots - seen - merely as information - that's gathered by ultra sensitive detectors in particle accelerator collisions ~ This realm of - logical imagination - went on to predict - mass-less (that's no weight - volume - or bulk = No mass) - particles - and speeds - faster - than the speed of light - and - at the same time = Didn't balance out - couldn't glue those forces into a cooperative whole - no matter how the equations were arranged - rearranged - stacked - and scrambled ~ Then = The idea turned up (as they do somehow) = That maybe - what the math was describing - was gravity itself ~ Perhaps - this phantom mass-less particle - or even this warp drive speed - is the (like a photon is the messenger particle - or force carrier - of electromagnetic energy) - force carrier - of gravity - the long sought after = Graviton.

Let's examine gravity a moment then.

At this very - moment - you - me - and everything else on the surface of this planet - are traveling through space at roughly 900 miles an hour (depending where on the globe you live) Without gravity - this action - would undoubtedly cause problems ~ However - we do have gravity - and = That intense force - that traps planets in their orbits and moons to those planets and influences every other physical movement in the universe (as far as we know) - works in such a way - that you - and all that other stuff covering the surface of the planet - doesn't have to cling on for dear life.

Okay = Now raise your arm - then = Pick something up - like a book - or a chair ~ So = How did you do that? This huge force - that holds everything down (even at 900 miles an hour with never a let up) - is that easy - to overpower? How can that be?

As it turns out - gravity - for all its strength - is really the weakest force going of those fundamental four ~ In comparison to the electromagnetic force - gravity is a number with 40 digits in it - weaker ~ That's why a big electromagnet can pick up a car as easily as you can pick up a crumb with a moistened fingertip ~ Not to mention - the electromagnetic energy in your body that allows you to do that = Is also - getting around all that gravity.

[[[[[[[[[Up vs. Down:

The graviton - is that elusive subatomic creature (which means - hypothetical particle) - the eventual (or never) - finding of which - will balance out the four great forces - by assigning a messenger (or mediator) - particle to each of them (just to put that in different words than the ones you've already been over) There's already the photon - for electro-magnetism ~ The gluon - for the strong nuclear force ~ And the W and Z bosons (for some reason there are two) - for the weak nuclear force (just to remind you of all that as well) - but = Old gravity (the first force to be recognized) - still remains free of such an authority figure - and so = Is one of the strings attached - to string theory ~ In other words = Find the graviton - and make leaps in proving all that stringy math.

As regards those strings - and their relationship with gravity - there's a certain question of - shape - at stake ~ There's the open ended string - like a worm - and - the closed loop string - like a donut (probably a gluten free - fat-free - and sugar free variety - that does not go well with anything but the theory that coffee is bad for you) When you connect the hypothesis of branes (rather like a sheet of plastic - that folds and ripples and takes on any shape at any size) - to those strings = It's the open ended ones - which have a means to connect (turn that worm into an inchworm with suctioning legs at either end) - while those diet doughnuts - just roll right off.

It's possible - that gravity (in the shape of the mysterious graviton) - is the closed loop variety - and just doesn't stick to those - backstage of everything - branes (think of sand sliding off a plate) While the other force particles - do stick (think of chocolate syrup oozing across a plate) That might account - for why gravity can affect universe size interactions - yet still allow us to run and jump and fly airplanes - because ultimately = It's a weak force by comparison - because = Maybe it just doesn't hang around - the way the sound of a car crash doesn't stay in one place - but = The wreckage does.

Another side of gravity (or gravitons) - is what's called = Gravitational waves ~ G waves - are a kind of radiation - or fluctuations (ripples - if you will) - in the curvature of space-time ~ The fabric of space-time (not so very different from the plastic sheet brane analogy I just made - but don't tell a string theorist) - is what Einstein described with his second relativity theory ~ Curvature of this - fabric (caused by big objects - like planets -

rolling around on it) - is what gravity is (also according to Albert) G waves - are an agitation in those curves - which are caused by certain celestial movements - such as two black holes orbiting each other - or a matched pair of stars (called binary stars) - which go flipping end over end - like a giant dumbbell - through space.

Now - these waves - have not been exactly proven to exist either ~ There is indirect proof however - or = Other cosmic activity points at them being out there ~ As for why it's worth mentioning in the first place = Apparently - these gravitational waves - move (or theoretically appear to) - differently than other forces through the universe ~ They are not slowed down - or altered - by objects of any size ~ If - they could be harnessed to some human application (we do like to do that) - one option - might be a type of communication device between galaxies = A gravity phone ~ Another - may be a way of seeing (or imaging) - distant things in space we have never glimpsed before (or perhaps - even suspected of being there) - the way radio telescopes (devices which - see - the radio frequencies emitted by such things as neutron stars - rather than the light that conventional telescopes look for) - have vastly expanded the horizons of our ancient habit of gazing off into space.

One day (maybe soon) - we'll answer those questions ~ Meanwhile = Perhaps gravity - is just a rogue force that can do as it pleases - slipping between dimensions - parallel universes - controlling everything - yet = Freeing everything at the same time to express an endless variety of life - or = Not.|||||||||

So = What's really going on?

Well - the thing is - we - really don't know (Interesting that - we - so often employ the collective - we - when talking about information gathered by people - we - generally regard as - knowing - more than ourselves - but = I've mentioned something like this before haven't I?) Gravity - for all - our - study of it - remains mysterious ~ But = String theory - has some very interesting possibilities up its imaginative sleeves ~ You might be tempted to say - completely imaginary sleeves ~ But then = You'd be the one imagining sleeves - and where would that get us?

Anyway ~ For a time - this string thing - was so imaginative that there was not just one theory - but five ~ The trouble was - a unified theory of everything - is hardly unified - if there's more than one - let alone five ~ Then - along came one of those people - we - are using that collective we - to depend on for - knowing (or trying to know) - the rulebook of the universe - and = He - helped straighten up that bit of muddle - or at least - added a new dimension to look at it from.

His name is Ed Witton - and - that's exactly what he did ~ He added a new dimension to that list of 10 - you might remember from when we first started comparing spaghetti to baseballs ~ Actually - that dimension wasn't his original idea - it had been floating around as a quantum mechanics theory for some time already - known as super gravity ~ But - he added it - from the perspective - of recognizing a new dimension - within the problem - of having five competing theories - which = Was entirely original = What he saw mathematically - was not five descriptions of five possible universes - but = Five ways of looking - at just one - and = In that expansion - strings expanded into potentially universe sized surfaces - or = Membranes.

So - at last we've reached - the land of Branes ~ But = What in the name of photons are they?

Okay - maybe - like many people - you do some of your best thinking in the bathroom ~ Picture yourself there then - on the best seat in the house - and = You've just run out of toilet paper ~ As you consider other alternatives (the shower curtain - bath mat - etc.) - to this taken for granted fixture of modern life - you are relieved to discover a fresh roll under the sink - and instantly = Determine to always check that supply at the start of future natural functions ~ So - as you replace the bare cardboard roll with the fluffy new fat one (like the good household member that you are) - you suddenly feel your mind traveling in many directions all at once = The whole history of the human bowel movement - and ways of hiding it - containing it - processing it - talking about it - and - cleaning up after it - swirl in the bowl of your mind - with plumbing made from clay - from lead - iron - copper - plastic - directing the digestive discards of the masses into the subterranean architecture of vast sewer systems - which flow into streams - rivers - the sea - while other thoughts steer off to huge multinational paper companies and virgin rainforests ready to supply toilet paper rather than oxygen - WHEN = You look at the cardboard tube in your hand and remember - String theory.

Well - technically - it's M theory we're on to now - but only just - because M theory - is still in the process of discovering itself.

Nevertheless = You're holding that tube in your hand - and looking at it end on ~ If you hold it just right - it's hardly a tube it all - but more like a circle - a thin ring - that = If you were to slice about a millimeter off the end - would make a very handy representation of - a string ~ That is - if you go for the closed loop variety ~ There are the other options of course - but - we'll stick with this one for now ~ Then = From the two-dimensional view of a circle - you turn the tube in your hands - and = It transforms into a three-dimensional object ~ Which means = Your perception - has smoothly entered another dimension ~ The idea of membranes - is exactly that ~ That single strand of spaghetti - a string - which already has all those extra dimensions to wiggle in (six extra to be exact) - now moves into another - by stretching itself - like rubber - into a cylinder - or the elongation of whatever shape it was in - and becomes = A membrane - or (a word with fewer gooey pink visuals connected to it) = A brane ~ And (just like that revelatory expansion of mind you underwent after finding the new roll of paper) = This brane - can expand - to any size there is to expand to - because = Just like those thoughts in your head - it's = Invisible - energy.

SPECIAL BONUS EXERCISE - number eight

Heart Listening:

Our hearts (it's been estimated) - contain something like 40 to 60,000 neurons (which are nerve cells - that - we will investigate further before long) That being the highest density of such cells anywhere in the body - aside from the brain - which (apparently) = Are contributors to an electromagnetic field broadcast - that rivals that of the brain - by being (something like again) - 5,000 times stronger.

It's also interesting to note = That the very first cells of the human body to form after fertilization of the egg - are the ones that become the heart - which = Begin to beat - long before the brain has begun to truly form ~ Obviously - the heart plays an immensely important physical role in our lives - pumping our blood and all ~ When that action stops - so do we (as far as bodies go at least) And yet = Could it be - that the heart plays a much larger role than we - think - it does? Could our hearts be - as much as (or even more than) - a thinking mechanism - as our brains? Which is to say = Thinking - in a manner different from - the sorting information kind we usually give our brains credit for ~ Meaning = A variety of thought - we more commonly label = Intuition.

This exercise - is both an experiment about - and a practice in - developing that sixth sense we call intuition - as well as - an observation of a kind of energy in action - simply referred to as = Heart.

What you do is = When you are interacting with someone - speaking - listening - or simply sitting in silence with them - maintain part of your awareness - on the area of your heart ~ Touch your chest if that helps - or let your breath filling your lungs keep reminding you of that area ~ It's not important how you remind yourself to keep your attention there - just that you do ~ If your attention wanders - bring it back ~ But - again = Just a portion of your attention is all that's required - about as much as you would need to walk down a street without bumping into things ~ No strain of concentration - or focus - or distraction - just keep in touch with that part of you - and = See what happens.

Another form of this exercise - is to deliberately cultivate thoughts of appreciation for the person or people you're with - at the same time as you gently maintain that awareness of your heart ~ While you do - pay attention to how your responses are influenced - or - if the response to you changes ~ What are all those heart neurons up to anyway? Why not see - if you can find out.

Class Seventeen - Believe?

BREATHE (Oh yeah = I think you're finally getting the hang of it ~ And - just so you know = This is called - super brain yoga ~ You know what super and brain mean I'm sure - but = The word yoga - means union - or connecting to a much larger sphere of being - or - consciousness ~ You do that = And no matter what you believe = It only makes sense you would get smarter.)

Well - could you do it? Could you let those reactions just slide through? A little? A lot? What did it feel like? Was it a kind of friction - like something actually passing through you? Was it very uncomfortable? Did that make you stop? When you did manage it - did it alter the behavior you would usually have chosen to act out in such a situation? How so? Were you more accepting? Did you stop caring so much about the opinion you were having? Can you do it right now?

Alright ~ Let's rope those wild ideas - of interconnection and one super mind - down to a more manageable size - and see how you're doing managing that reaction.

The first question is = What do you believe about yourself?

What I mean is = Are you smart? Are you good looking? Are you successful? Are you likable - honest - witty - interesting - trustworthy - dependable - prompt - athletic - generous - hard working - respectful - talented - kind?

That's quite a list - isn't it? You said yes to them all - didn't you? No? Why?

It's the same old story - isn't it? The past - says so ~ Comparison - says so ~ Judgment - says so ~ But = What was the key word in - what I called - the first question? That's right = Believe ~ So = Doesn't it come down to - the most important thing is = Belief - says so?

What would you say the culture we live in - believes - about the qualities I just listed? Sure = They're what we call - good ones - or - positive desirable ways of being ~ Okay ~ So = What would you say that same culture - thinks - about the majority of us measuring up to those standards? Yeah -= Pretty poor huh? So = Right there - do we have two beliefs - basically opposed to each other? What I mean is = We believe - that people should be one way - and at the same time - don't believe - they are - or can be ~ What kind of effect does this have on you?

That's a good one = Mixed messages ~ What does it mean? So - it's kind of like saying = I don't want you here - but you can stay? Duality is another word that fits - or - dualistic ~ When a big pickup truck has dual wheels in the rear - what does it mean? Sure = They're double - or in pairs on the same axle ~ Duality is much the same thing - in that - there are two ideas connected to the same action - only = They're headed in opposite directions ~ That wouldn't work out very well in a pickup truck - would it? Do you suppose it works out very well in anything? How about in you? Is there a conflict between your thinking and feelings about = How you - should behave - and = How you - want to behave? Is it because - you're believing - two things - at the same time?

Let's take school - for instance ~ Maybe you hate school ~ Maybe you think it's a waste of time and no fun at all ~ Maybe you want to quit ~ But - at the same time - you've seen people who quit - that have lives - that you think - are a waste of time - and no fun at all - that you - definitely don't want yours to look like ~ So = What's your decision making process feel like in a place like that? Right = It's in conflict ~ Can you do well in school if you feel that way? Can you quit school without fear?

Well = That's duality (or one side of it anyway)

You've probably heard the statement = Nobody's perfect ~ Probably heard it lots of times in fact ~ Do you believe it?

What if - it isn't true? What if - we (meaning everybody) - are - perfect?

You don't seem to like that - do you? Does that mean you don't want to be perfect? Oh - you just can't be? But you'd like to be? So = If you'd like to be perfect - how could you ever be - if you don't believe - you could be? Because it's impossible? But = Isn't that just continuing - to describe the same belief - in opposition to the belief - you'd he happier - if you were perfect? Isn't that = Dualistic?

[[[[[[[[[Affirmation Negation:

There is a transformative practice (you'll find filed under the heading of self-help over near the new age section with the inspirational speakers and life coaches) - which sounds like a great idea - and in fact - is - but = It has one rather glaring handicap ~ Aside from the bit of self amusement I just slipped in (between a pair of parentheses) - to make a subtle point about our culture (that's really not important to my larger point - or maybe not that subtle) - the practice - of repeating positive affirmations - has enjoyed wide popularity (or at least the idea has) The handicap I mentioned however - is akin to the condition of cognitive dissonance we discussed some time ago.

But first - in case you don't know what a positive affirmation is = It's simply the repetition of a declarative sentence (such as - I like my body just the way it is) - for the purpose of creating a positive outlook (and outcome) - and = The accompanying transition to happiness (or the electromagnetic frequency) - that outlook (and again - that word outcome) - provides - which = It most certainly will (at least the outlook bit) - if - you provide the true willingness and dedication.

The trouble is = If you are telling yourself something - the majority of your belief/thinking does not consider true - then - in essence = You are lying - and = You know it - and that = Is not a positive frequency.

What is really needed - to boost the potential power of affirmations - is evidence of the truth of the statement being used - which = Since the use of such techniques tends to be inspired by wanting to change something you don't want - to something you do - it generally takes some deliberate focus to collect that evidence ~ The thing is - which is to say - the encouragement is = It's there.

If there's something about you - or your life - you want to be different - then = There is some model of the outcome you want - that is a part of your experience already - even = If it is just an idea ~ Which makes sense really - when you note that what we are talking about here - are the power of ideas ~ As for something like - liking your body the way it is = What do you like about it? Does it function well - breathe - digest - contain all your senses? How about the fact - that it is constantly changing at the cellular level? Yes = That change does seem to be reproducing the same looking body - but = Change is change - so = If it's changing (and it is) - then it can be different - and = Isn't that what you actually want? At least in the context of the example I'm making.

The point - I'm poking that body of yours with - is = In - some part - of your mind - your affirmation is true ~ It's accessible as a truth ~ It's not a lie ~ And - by extension = A whole new field of vibration becomes available - when you are accessing the certainty of that truth - rather than = The nose thumbing self abuse of catching yourself in your own lie.

Again = A positive affirmation - is a statement {Although - there's no reason why it can't be a question as well - such as = How come that test was so easy? And in fact = May be the more powerful technique} - around which to build - and create the results of - a new belief structure (or neural net - which we've almost arrived at the explanation of) - but = Getting the old one to support that process in some way is the real trick ~ The way to it = Is to design an affirmation - according to the outcome you desire - and then - answer the question = What's true about that outcome already? It might take some imagination - and some time - practice - attention - but = Part of that outcome - is already in your life ~ Find that part - and you're on your way.||||||||||

Okay = So what if it is dualistic? I know = The beliefs are still there ~ That's the way it is - right?

Again = What if - that's wrong? What if - we are - perfect?

Yeah = I get that you think we're not ~ But = What are your ideas around this word - perfect? Do you think it would be boring if we all were perfect? Yeah = Just a lot of Barbie and Ken super achievers - right? But = Isn't that just fashion and cultural standards? What has perfection got to do with how you look and act - except as ideas - of how to look and act? Is it - that you - believe - we're not all perfect - or = You believe - the ideas you have - about what perfect - means - or is supposed to be? How deep do those ideas go? Do they include an entire universe functioning as a whole - or just a lot of magazine covers - professional athletes - and imaginary bank accounts?

Here's another angle = When you are - being you - when - are you doing it? Yup = Right now (Didn't think I'd let you off on that idea - did you?) So = How is - right now - connected to - not being perfect - yesterday? Sure = Memory and ideas of time ~ But = Is yesterday - happening right now? How about last year? Or when you were four? No = Of course not = Now is now - and that's it ~ But = What about all those ideas of what it means to be perfect = Have you gathered them all up and brought them along to this present now? Are they making you happy? So = Why are you keeping them? Because they're true? So = That means you won't be perfect in the future either? How do you know? Same thing isn't it? A belief from the past projected onto the future? Sounds a bit like running in circles - doesn't it?

What if - you were to look at it like this = Would you want to be the only one with a cell phone? What if - sharing perfect - is what makes more of it - spreads it around - uses the parts that everyone contributes? What if - that's what perfect actually is - meaning = Perfect communication?

Anyway - backing up a bit = What does that word - projected - mean? Yes - exactly = It's like a movie projected on a screen ~ Is the movie the actual action taking place? No = We're all fully aware that it's a recording from the past ~ What if - then = That's what we're doing all the time? That is = Projecting the past - on the future - and repeating therefore - the same movie - right now? Not because - it is the same - but because = We can only - see/understand/make sense of - what we - believe - it to be - according to what we've gathered as information from - before? Like - say - that word perfection? Would everything be perfect - right now - if you didn't make any comparisons with - ideas - of how - it - should - be? Yeah - even if = Bad painful stuff - was going on? Isn't it only bad - as a comparison - to something else?

Okay = You get the idea (especially since it's not a new one) But = We don't work that way do we? How come? Wouldn't we be happier - if we did? Maybe we should examine something about these brains of ours - for a moment - in the hopes of understanding - this belief business - a bit better.

These - brains of ours - have all these cells in them that are called neurons ~ A salt crystal size piece of brain - contains about 100,000 of them - with maybe a billion connection sites to other neurons distributed between them (It's all about connection up there) That means = Our heads are full of a fantastically intricate road map of these connected - electricity conducting cells - that fire away like strings of flashing Christmas lights - whenever = We have a thought - a memory - a reaction - or sensory input of any kind ~ Basically = They're the physical mechanism in place - to respond to any kind of stimulus - or information - that requires sorting in that cauliflower between our ears - as well as = Being the same types of cells (nerve cells) - responsible for reporting back and forth between the brain and the rest of the body (called - obviously - the nervous system) - which snake their way to every inch of us - excepting (oddly enough) = Our brains themselves ~ If we were to open up your head and poke you in the brain = You wouldn't feel a thing ~ Other than the actual opening part of course.

[[[[[[[[[Doctor Dude's Dictionary - word seventeen - Unique:

When you perform some acrobatic feat - that no one else has ever achieved - or discover a species of deep-sea creature - previously unknown to science - maybe witness some bizarre thing fly over your house - that even the letters UFO don't make any kind of sense of - or just wake up in a mood you've never experienced before - then = You've arrived at the opportunity to make proper use of the word = Unique.

Unique means = One-of-a-kind - no other like it - unparalleled - without equal ~ It's not a kinda sorta maybe type of word ~ It's really designed stiff as concrete = Unique means unique - not rather unique - or somewhat unique - only - totally - completely - without question = Unique ~ Same as the word pregnant = You either are pregnant - or you're not = Nothing halfway about it.

Now - that doesn't mean the word doesn't get used improperly ~ Probably eight times out of ten - that's exactly how it does get used ~ And = Why not? It's our right to use words however we like ~ It's actually one of the beauties of the fluidity of changing language - that we have - and practice - that right ~ So - we're not talking some unpardonable crime of linguistic abuse here ~ After all - the incorrect use of the word unique is so common - as to be anything but unique - and thereby = It still performs its communication function just fine - in that = What's being said - is also being - understood.

The picky bit - in attempting to stick to the formal definition of unique - is the advantage of possessing a word - which expresses the uncompromising stance of pointing at the single example of something - and saying = That is the single example ~ Otherwise = What's being expressed - is just an opinion.

Not that there's anything wrong with opinions (provided they don't disagree with our own too drastically) And then = There's the condition of all things - and ideas - existing in an interconnected system of dependencies on interconnected systems - and - in that sense = There is no such thing as unique ~ But - what it all comes down to - is you - and I.

We (meaning human beings) - for whatever reason governs such things - and despite the fact of all our similarities - dependencies - connections - and ultimate interconnectedness = While we are busy in bodies being human - are each of us = Unique ~ In this moment - there has never been a person exactly like you - thinking - feeling - and behaving in every detail exactly as the circumstances of this particular moment appear ~ That you - right there - right now - no matter how you're trying to blend in - fit somewhere - consider yourself hopelessly dull - unnoticed - or anonymous - are solely - singly - and without exception - one-of-a-kind - and that's it = That's - unique.]]]]]]]]]

It's the - BELIEF - learning - process - I want to look at here (an extremely simplified version at least) We'll call it - Tick Tack Go ~ It looks like this = That is - what you are about to draw is what it looks like.

So = Get a piece of paper and a pencil - a crayon - a marker - whatever you prefer - and =

Draw a line of five zeros ~ Under that = Draw another line of five zeros - and another - and again twice more until you have a box of zeros five across and five down (that being a graphic illustration of the number Five squared) You know - like tick tack toe - only with fives rather than threes.

These zeros you've drawn - represent inactive neurons waiting for information to process ~ Remember - this is a simplification (and we're talking really simple - like the difference between a spoon full of mud - and the New York Metropolitan museum of art) It actually takes billions of neuron connections for such work - but = For our purposes this will do.

So along comes an event - Let's say you're three years old and you see a ten dollar bill on the kitchen table - that - for some unknown reason (unknown to you at least) = No one will let you play with ~ You've created a memory package - images - textures - ideas - feelings - ready to be plugged into your growing knowledge of such things - because = All those other bits of information (kitchen - table - other people - etc.) - are already accessed - or recognized - for you to identify what's going on.

To represent that on your diagram = You cover a line of three or four zeros - somewhere in that five by five box of them - with Xs - which = Illustrates the beginning of a neural pathway (as it's called)

After that - you see more ten dollar bills ~ Each time - you strengthen the connection between those particular neurons - that deal with - the image - of a ten dollar bill ~ Meanwhile = Other events are getting connected to the original memory package = Purchases you've witnessed - other bills - ones - twenties - things you like - things you don't like.

Now the pathway - strengthened by repetition - gets some more Xs added to your drawing - however you'd like to place them - so long as they touch each other - plus = Darken up the original Xs.

Then one day - when you're five years old - you find a ten dollar bill on the sidewalk in front of your house ~ It's very exciting ~ You rush in the house to tell your mother ~ But - she doesn't believe you found it ~ She thinks you stole it - and even if you did find it - you're not smart enough to spend it responsibly ~ You'll just waste it on junk food ~ So she takes it away from you ~ You're devastated ~ You're angry ~ It's unfair ~ It's wrong ~ But - she's the authority - and = You did want the junk food ~ Maybe - if you had just left it where you found it - the owner would have recovered it ~ In that sense - maybe it was stealing ~ Either way - it's disappointing and confusing - and feels - bad.

The pathway now has a new section - with a strong emotional connection = So - add two or three more Xs that intersect the original line of Xs - and darken them up so they stand out.

So the years go by ~ All kinds of experiences with money take place = As they do - but = That one experience keeps turning up - as a feeling - around money - because = It's available - as a reference point - a kind of proof - for having been the strongest feeling - and = Because it seems to prove something - it acts like a magnet - looking for more of the same proof = It attaches other - unhappy ideas - about money - because = They feel the same way - they prove the same thing - they agree ~ That agreement - becomes part of what money (remember now - money is just a symbol - and that's how it's being used here as well) - feels like - and so = Means - to you = Something you don't deserve - or have to hide away to keep ~ A belief has been built ~ A belief not just about money - but about yourself - and = How others see you - which of course = Connects to other beliefs - because = All thoughts (which includes beliefs) - as you remember - are connected (entirely literally - in the case of your brain) But - what's more = An actual physical structure - has also been constructed - that supports that belief - just as constructing a building supports an architect's drawing - and then = No longer requires the drawing - because = It's been built.

Now make an X over all of the zeros - and darken them all up - and = Stand back and look at it = You've just drawn a picture of your mind (kind of anyway - perhaps more like a map of the world that only has your street on it)

Of course - you're not aware of all those layers of reinforcement when you step up to the ATM to withdraw money from your bank account ~ Maybe you don't even remember the incident with the ten dollars you found ~ But = It's there - and = Involved in your decisions around money every time - your thoughts - go near the stuff - because = You're that architect ~ You directed that particular structure to be included ~ You just didn't realize - that was what you were doing.

Okay ~ So I'll repeat again = This explanation - is boiled down to the bare bones of how a neural net gets laid down ~ That's what a system - of experience connected neurons - is called - a neural net - or neural pathway ~ That is - when we're trying to break it down to the most manageable concept size ~ A neuroscientist - would probably wring their hands at my description - but - at the same time = Would have to agree = That it (more or less) - describes the fundamental set up of the basic function ~It's also - a story (and a rather negative one at that) - about you - which is absurd ~ Unless you happen to recognize yourself in it ~ The thing is = Beliefs come in all shapes and sizes - positive - negative - pro - anti - love - fear - but = One shape they never come in - is = Neutral ~ No such thing as an indifferent belief that doesn't care one way or another ~ If you believe something - you have a fixed neural map - that goes there - and nowhere else (excepting the fact - that it's also connected to thousands of other neurons)

Then = There is another point ~ And that is = To relieve the discomfort you may be feeling - at the idea of = Oh no - I'm stuck with my painful ideas forever - which is = They can change = If - you want them to ~ It's how you interact with them that makes the difference ~ It's kind of like muscles = The more you work them - the stronger they get ~ And the opposite = Don't work them - and they get weak ~ The choice is = What muscles do you want to build? In other words = Enough mental exercise - in a new direction - will create new neural pathways - and the neurons - that used to fire together - because of a certain mode of thinking = Won't anymore ~ But - just like body building - the catch is = It takes time ~ After all - it was - time - or what went on in time - that created them in the first place ~ The good news is = It doesn't have to take - that much time.

272

Ah - there is that time thing again ~ So = Whenever you are - thinking anything - when - are you doing it? Yup - can't get away from it = Now is the spot ~ The point is = That's also - all you really have to pay attention to - if you want to change - a habit of being that's keeping you from happiness ~ What I mean is - asking yourself the question = What's happening - right now? Of course = You first have to recognize - that such a habit (being a set of thoughts that no longer serve your best interests) = Is in place ~ That's where paying attention to paying attention comes in ~ That's not to say - that you have to dig up all the details of your past and analyze them microscopically - like what happened to you when you were five ~ No = It's just observing - that leaning - toward love or fear - that happens in each of us - and = Noticing - what kind of ideas - that feeling of love or fear - happen around ~ The result = Is finding the places (that is - ideas - beliefs - and their neural nets) - that hold you back ~ The beauty of being - present in the present - is = That you don't have to be concerned - about what held you back in the past - or = What might hold you back in the future ~ What's important - about right now - is = What's going on - right now ~ And = That's where you can do - the real - work of change - because = You're not - changing - something - you're = Choosing - something else.

You see - trying to - change - something like a neural net - is like repaving an old road ~ It may get smoother - but = It still goes to the same place ~ What you want - is a brand new road - that goes somewhere else ~ Unless of course - that's not what you want.

The thing is = We all know what we want ~ At the core of all of us is the same desire = We want to feel good ~ The beauty of that - or it's result - is = We - all - have some reference point - some experience - no matter how short - that identifies that good feeling as possible ~ While the majority of people - have lots of such reference points ~ What that means - in reference to neural pathways - is = Those experiences - can provide a blue-print - from which = To build that new freeway to happiness - in your head.

[[[[[[[[[Robot I:

The central mechanism (as well as the core difficulty) - of designing and engineering that great sci-fi fantasy (or inevitability) - known as robots - is what's known as = Artificial intelligence ~ The process of A. I. development (which has been busily trying to do just that for well over half a century now) - began - and continues to operate = From the one key question whose answer lies at the heart of the system they are trying to reproduce = How does - real intelligence - work?

The neural networks in your brain - and the neural networks being engineered to - think (in an R2D2 Star Wars kind of way) - really have only one thing in common = Information processing - and = That commonality - has been made remarkable use of - it's quite true ~ Certain explicit (meaning - definite this is this not that) - sequential (A = B = C) - information juggling tasks of enormous complexity - can be worked out by machines at speeds our brains are hard pressed just to fully grasp what the commands mean in the same amount of time ~ But = If you - ask a machine to ride a bicycle through heavy traffic on a pot holed road whose edges are swarming with impatient pedestrians = It will probably be a pile of twisted metal in the first few yards - and/or = You will be involved in a law suit.

Cognitive modeling - which is formulating a simulation - or mathematical map - of how information processing in biological systems functions (such as in - fruit flies - rabbits - and you) - is the scientific groundwork for transferring that - how does - question - into a working robotic device ~ Out of that mathematical maze have come such things as - voice recognition software and digital image analysis - or = From interactive answering machines - to MRIs - to satellite surveillance systems ~ The basic networks in use (really - really - basic) - are of interconnected units - or nodes - which resemble neurons (at least as a word) - in that they receive incoming information from more than one connection - sum that information (add it - 8+4=12) - and pass that fused information on to other connected nodes (much like the work of a synapse) - where more of the same repeated process continues to build up a complex whole (function - picture - or programmed response) - through the recognition - and relationship blending - of separate pieces of information.

Such systems - capable as they may be - are not = Intelligent ~ Which of course - demands a U-turn right back to that key question of = How does - intelligence - work?

Therefore = We can put together a definition of intelligence - as = An ability to learn and apply that learning as a basis for conduct ~ But (again) = How does it work? That requires an answer that is as mechanical as a robot - which = We don't have (otherwise - you could probably get your robot to write that paper on comparative religion) We know - we are looking at a kind of complex statistical processor (statistics being - the gathering of data - the categorizing or sorting of that data - and the tabulating or relationship graphing of that data) - possibly with many parallel circuits - or systems along which different types of information are processed then integrated - which = Includes billions of pattern recognitions (from an applesauce covered spoon - to subtle sarcasm) - and implicit (implied - suggested - hinted at - entangled in) - instructions - of how to act according to all that recognition - which = Doesn't answer the question either.

How intelligence works = Is how it's working right now ~ What it does ~ What it decides ~ What it feels like ~ Intelligence - is capable of brand-new behavior - despite - that behavior going counter to patterned or habitual behavior ~ How it works - can't really be pinned down - because = It is a system of constant change - and = What constantly changes - is never - the same machine.||||||||||

That brings us to your assignment ~ I want you to sort through those memories of yours - and = Find one truly shining example of happiness ~ It could be a whole day - an hour - or just thirty seconds ~ The amount of time doesn't matter ~ The strength of feeling does ~ So - seriously now = Find that feeling - really look - don't settle on the first - good one - you come across ~ Find a great one ~ It's in there - especially if there don't seem to be many ~ That lack - of many - might appear bad in other circumstances - but = For this assignment - it will only make it easier - and in fact = Is an actual advantage to being able to focus ~ So keep looking.

Okay ~ Once you've got your happy memory pinned down = I want you to name it ~ No = Not like naming a baby ~ Take some element of the memory - like - beach - or - rain -

Webster street - satin - touchdown - hot fudge - 100 miles an hour - or someone's name if they were there and absolutely uniquely key to that memory (otherwise other memories of that person are apt to interfere) This name needn't be poetic - or sound perfect - in fact = The more common a word it is - the better ~ It just needs to represent the happiness at the center of that memory - because = It - is going to become a tool for returning you to that center.

Now = Feel - that memory ~ Get in there - and have it 100% - don't stop till you do ~ Then = Roll that name around on that feeling - cinnamon - puppies - gear oil - Gwendolyn - double crust = Connect the two - like shoe means shoe - until = That feeling - has - that - name ~ Alright?

Now do something else ~ Look at the clock ~ Retie your shoes ~ Jump up and down ~ Anything - that sends your thoughts elsewhere ~ Give that a minute ~ Then = Repeat the same process ~ Do it three more times - then give it a break for an hour or two - and = Do it again ~ Remember - the point = Is to really - I mean REALLY - FEEL - that feeling - and = Connect that name to it - that's all you have to do ~ Other than keep breathing of course.

N.P.U. - Chapter Seventeen - Universes?

So = What do you do - with these fantasy toilet roll membranes the size of universes?

Well - you can flush them down the toilet of impossible to prove nonsense that just won't pay the rent ~ Or - you could expand the borders of that space of question (the toilet response clearly wants relief from) - by considering - the possibility - that what this - relativity - quantum - string - M theory - jigsaw puzzle is describing = Is not a physical universe - but = A universe - of consciousness.

Or = Not.

One thing at least - is quite easily proven (should you happen to be looking for proof) = If - you allow that space of question to expand - to hold - in a loose kind of way - the possibilities of an overlap - of physicality - and consciousness - that blends them into one and the same thing = You will - feel - different ~ No = I'm not saying - what it is you will feel - only = That it will be - different - from what you will feel - if you do not allow that expansion.

Therefore = I'll ask you to direct your awareness - to the physical emotional response - that occurs - when you become conscious - of this next idea - which is = Parallel Universes.

What if - exactly like the pages of a book exist next to each other - yet are distinct from one another - though still - make up one thing (which is a book - in the literal case of a book) = There are universes - in uncounted numbers - just as close to us - as the pages of a book are to each other - we just can't see them - touch them - or consciously interact with them? And = What if - there is also the possibility - at the same time - that we do affect these parallel universes - and they - affect us? In fact = What if - parallel universes - are what truly explain what a quantum leap is leaping - or = Why it is impossible to measure - the location - and the speed - of a subatomic particle at the same time - and = What all the other superposition possibilities contained in the wave do when they're not the particle we see? Could it be = There are an infinite supply of universes - like endless television channels all being broadcast simultaneously - it's only the matter of a tiny fluctuation in frequency that dictate which one we're tuned into?

So = How does that - feel?

More nonsense headed for the toilet? Great plot for a science fiction novel? But = Are

276

those feelings? Or - is a vaguely anxious pleasure at the top of your guts - that's got you radaring the space around you - a feeling?

Again = I'm not saying - that's the one you should be having ~ I'm saying = What feeling - are you having?

But = Why am I asking such a thing? I mean about your feelings - never mind parallel universes.

Well - first off = Because it's that feeling you're having = That will determine whether you are willing to investigate the idea of parallel universes any further ~ And secondly (more directly to illustrating the consciousness idea - rather than the response to it) = Feeling - is where that overlap - between physicality and consciousness - is - or = Is - where we feel it anyway ~ Which is to say = The same thing ~ Feeling - is physical - no matter how subtle an emotional state (like patiently waiting) - or severe (like a broken heart) - we register it as physically happening - or = A present experience - we undergo in our bodies - consciously - and so = It is a physical experience - of consciousness.

You see = In the end - it comes down to the question = Are we physical things - having an experience of consciousness - or = Consciousness - having an experience of physical things?

Now - the same question - posed to physicists - will likely separate out the same as that uncle Frank division between relativity and quantum mechanics making up two different camps ~ With the probability being = The greater number will be in the physical seeking physical proof of being physical camp ~ But - that doesn't make it true ~ Any more than brilliant mathematical reasoning to describe parallel universes makes them true ~ What is true - beyond question = Are the feelings - generated - by either side - or smack in the middle - of such a question - which (to pinpoint again) - is = Is it (this life in a body business) - a physical interaction with consciousness - or - a conscious interaction with physicality? Which = Leaves us in the same spot = What is consciousness?

|||||||||| **Afterglow:**

There's generally a correlation (a connecting relationship) - between the words - consciousness - and - living (a simple enough idea - when compared to the word - dead) Particularly - when that word - thing - is thrown in - as in = Living thing ~ Add another word (or - the option to take this upcoming - other word - and substitute it for - living - and perhaps even - thing) - which is = Communication - and = Those dots are all lined up as - the activity - which defines their being.

What I mean is {{Other than perhaps reading what I just said again}} = To be a living thing - no matter how isolated from other such - things - requires (or again - is defined by) - communication ~ An interior communication - occurs in all organisms ~ All physiological systems are forms of communication = Cells communicate within themselves - molecules do - atoms - electromagnetic fields - and = In the case of animals (to some yet to be accurately measured degree) - particularly we human animals - that internal dialogue we call - thinking = Talks to itself all day long.

That then = Is a simple enough determiner of rudimentary consciousness (being - a capacity to communicate with self - especially when self is defined as a physical thing) - but = Is it possible - that the real - defining nature - of consciousness = Is how - its communication - extends beyond the boundaries of an interior set of systems - and = Interacts with other - apparently exterior - systems - or - consciousnesses - or even - seemingly unconscious inanimate objects - like rocks and laser printers?

According to the work of German physicist - Fritz-Albert Popp (and replicated by many others) - living things (amoebas to presidential candidates) - emit a constant tiny glow of photons (or light) - which varies and changes according to its - interactions - with other light emitting - things ~ Popp's experiments with Daphnia (a type of water flea - of all things) - observed the emitting and absorption (or sending and receiving) - of light between fleas - which = After reception - was returned - by the receiver flea - in the form of an interference pattern - as though the information received - had been modified or updated somehow - which = Resembles (also - of all things) - a conversation ~ Even algae - an extremely simple form of single cell plant (generally speaking) - which grows in colonies (also generally speaking) - seem to communicate with nearby colonies of the same algae - and = They even exchange information with their surroundings (including other types of algae) - such as with their microscopic food sources (come to mama)

A similar form of - light detection - has been applied to human subjects as well ~ Extremely sensitive CCD imaging (or charge coupled device - such as what replaces film in digital cameras) - has very clearly shown streams of photons being broadcast by a "healer's" hands - while engaged in a healing session ~ The same process - has recorded the results of - healing intention - focused on plant samples - to cause (or perhaps more accurately - facilitate) - the alteration of the photon emissions of those samples.

Light (for many reasons - to which the preceding examples lend their point) - is sometimes used as another substitute word for consciousness - which = When you observe everything (bananas to big ideas) - as electromagnetic energy occurring (which is to say - manifesting) - at the speed of light = It's a perfectly reasonable word to use ~ Not that - that defines what light actually is = Anymore than it nails down what the controversial phenomenon called an - aura - is - which (in case you're unfamiliar with the term) = Is a field of luminous radiation emanated by the body - which people (of a certain open nature) - have claimed to - see - for centuries - if not millennia ~ A rainbow of colors - are said to be present in these emanations - which (are believed to) - indicate anything from personality traits - to the health of certain organs - to levels - or states - of consciousness = A veritable personal aurora borealis (Northern lights) - of energetic information.

All that being said = True - is another word - we tend to hook to things - or wall them off from one another with - when it comes to being busy with our consciousness - but = No matter how you choose to dole out that sacred word = It's definitely true - that when we encounter someone - or something - we love - it's no surprise = That we light right up.||||||||||

Again - however = What if (just like that leap of a physicists mind that realized what all that stringy math might really be describing - was gravity) - all these wild theories - of vibrations in extra dimensions creating universes - might really be describing = Consciousness?

There is a tendency - to discount - ignore - or entirely reject - consciousness - from the scientific equation - of what makes the universe tick - or - manifest itself ~ Especially among scientists ~ That tendency - appears - perfectly reasonable - from the point of view - that no matter how long you stare longingly at your punctured bicycle tire - it will not re-inflate itself ~ In that sense - consciousness - is merely a reactor to reality - or a tool for navigating our way through it ~ But - that is only observing a fragment of the whole picture ~ The rest of the picture = Is the whole experience - of a world and beyond - that includes your flat tire - which would not exist - without the rest of that world - which only really exists for us - through - or as = Consciousness.

See - without this matrix of consciousness - we have no - what - we - call - awareness of reality ~ Which of course - opens up those questions of whether reality exists - without our awareness of it ~ Which moves into questions around the difference between being alive or dead - or even - whether or not - we are truly individuals - and not a collective energy experiencing itself in fragments ~ Not that you've probably been losing a lot of sleep over such questions ~ And - you might even ask why you would bother troubling your sleep over such things - when it's all a bit like swimming in oatmeal - with no - real answers - beyond the seemingly unable to prove ones - that can be discarded by others - as opinions.

The thing is - in the end - it's not how you explain - things (not that - that will stop anyone from trying) - it's how you feel - because = That is the core of experience - and = The reason - we feel - we need to explain things ~ Again = Feeling is the location - where - physicality and consciousness rub up against each other ~ It may also be = Why - they do - and = How - the physical plays out the way it does ~ Which is to say = They may not be - two things - distinct from one another ~ Just as Einstein pointed out - that mass and energy are interchangeable - or Maxwell mathematically wed electricity to magnetism = Consciousness and physicality (or form - to slice it down to one syllable) - may also be - one thing ~ Because (as I've already pointed out) = Feelings - are at the core of our experience - and = At the core - of that core - is an electromagnetic generating plant - which = We can also call (if we're willing to feel that way) = Our feelings ~ At the quantum core of all form - or mass - are particles - or strings if you like - which are also - energy - in action ~ What if - the only difference is = We - think - they're different?

[[[[[[[[[Plowing the Field:

When the term - zero point field - is used in conversation (as I'm sure it's often on your lips) - its meaning - tends to straddle the fence between philosophy and science ~ Which is fine ~ So long as you are aware of that (or not - who am I to judge) The reason for that uncomfortable position - is that what you would be (or are) - talking about = Are the underpinnings of the universe - and = That is a type of framework - where the nails of theory and belief are doing pretty much the same job of holding up nothing more than ideas.

But again = That's fine ~ And this time I really mean it - because = There are some pretty exciting ideas growing in that field.

Technically (in the simplest terms possible) - the zero point field - is the background energy (background - like what's behind or under something) - which fills the vacuum of space ~ The - point - in the middle of the phrase - zero point field - is a location ~ In the sense of where a change takes place - rather than an address ~ That location - is what's called - the ground state - or point of lowest energy ~ In measurement terms - it's located at absolute 0° on the Kelvin scale (which translates to -273.15° Celsius or -459.67° Fahrenheit) - where molecules have so little energy - they are unable to do much more than exist ~ Beyond that (so to speak - as well as theoretically) - lies an infinite sea of electromagnetic radiation - which is uniform (all the same) - and isotropic (the same in all directions) This lack of asymmetry (or - no imbalance - no variation - no differences) - is what makes - the field - so hard to detect (and therefore - prove) Its differences - or change - that our sensory world of comparison requires to - measure things ~ Place you in a room - where the temperature and air pressure never change - and = You are unable to move - or breathe (your blood is being mechanically oxygenated somehow) - and = You would have no way of detecting the air present.

To describe swimming in this - limitless inexhaustible Sea of Energy - gets Long (meaning - requiring many) - or - short (meaning - there aren't accurate ones) - on words - because = That conversation is about - infinite potential - the vacuum field (which is synonymous with zero point field - where emptiness contains all possibility in its latent state - or - lying hidden within - unrevealed - dormant - in other words - potential) In a sense - it's (that field) - an ocean of information - constantly in contact (through the comings and goings of subatomic particles) - with the universe ~ It's the recording medium for all actions - the matrix in which actions are formatted for delivering to the actions themselves - the past and future absolutely balanced in an infinite present - which = Are fun words - if - you can squeeze them for a meaning that pleases you.

Otherwise = We're talking a view of reality - where all things are held up (meaning - supported) - or held together - and kept track of (meaning - organized and recorded) - by a single source of energy - which = Interactively generates us (us being everything) By interactive - I mean = A participatory universe - where our consciousness - or the sum of all our thoughts and feelings and beliefs (as well as the much larger aspects of consciousness our perceptual selves are not aware of) - communicate with this field - this whole energy - to order (both in the sense of - menu - and - as organization) - the shapes of our lives.

We are only just beginning to crawl - when it comes to examining such a cosmology (meaning – a theory or philosophy of the nature of the universe) But = It has begun ~ The measuring tools are slowly coming on line ~ Experimentation is being developed - tested - and put to use ~ And - of course = The mathematics go charging ahead.

Ultimately = Talking about the zero point field - is hardly the point ~ But = If we could really know - really - really - know - that we are all dancing with - it - to make this place together = Now - that - would be more like singing.‖‖‖‖‖

We also think baseballs and spaghetti are different ~ So - in order to relieve - the gravity - of this consciousness controversy - let's slip back to the land of brains.

Yes - that's brains - with an i ~ And - of course = It's that - I - that self I-dentity - we usually center on - which is (that is - we I-dentify as) - our thinking ~ And - in that identification - as a cultural majority - most people - think - the center of our thinking - is not just in our brains - but = IS - our brains ~ Well - there do seem to be some pretty good reasons for that = Sure feels like the center of our awareness is in there = And then - there's those EEGs - MRIs - CAT scans - and other wonders of science and medical technology that measure and graph and blink and buzz and generally pry around for the secrets of what goes on up there (not to mention having made great progress in that pursuit) Nor can we discount - the very obvious evidence = That damage to these jelly doughnut calculators of ours - results in extreme changes of ability and function that can turn a life around in a fraction of a second.

But = Are they us? Or are they no more - us - than the hammer in the hand of a carpenter - is the carpenter? Which is to say = Nothing more than a tool - we can use however we like? Well sure = I do mean = Within the range of its capabilities ~ It's not like you'd use that hammer as a telephone - or a telephone as a car ~ So - as far as a tool goes - the question is - and always has been = What are the capabilities of these brains of ours? Are we limited by their design - or - is their design - limited by us?

Let's examine for a moment - that fabulous creation packed and tangled in its billions of connections in that head of yours - not to mention stretched to the calluses on your toes - without which = These words would make no more sense to you than ancient Irish poetry does to an ironing board = The neuron.

A neuron - is a nerve cell ~ While such a simple definition does them little justice - it's still true = They are the fundamental parts of the nervous system - whose largest concentration - is in the brain ~ What they do - is transmit information - not unlike telephone wires do ~ How - that all works out - to being able to picture the ceiling of your childhood bedroom while bilingually reading a menu in a French restaurant and arguing politics - is another story that is still - being worked out ~ But - how neurons work - mechanically - or simply as transmitters - is - largely understood (Well… if you avoid certain new ideas about quantum level cellular communication)

Neurons are essentially broken into three parts = The nucleus - and other standard cell components which maintain health and functionality = Then - those specialized parts - unique to neurons = Axons - which are the output channels - or message sending wiring - and = Dendrites - which are the input channels - or message receiving areas.

So - these axons extend - both tiny distances to other cells - and = Up to several feet - to control the movement of our limbs ~ Decide to wiggle your toes - and neurons - that sit just behind your forehead - lightning that command - through their axons - to the dendrites of the motor control nerves - somewhere near the base of your spinal column - which of course are also neurons - that extend down to your feet ~ Then = There's a whole other set of sensory nerve wiring for sending messages in the other direction ~ It's all a map of one-way streets this nervous system ~ That way - the motor control areas of your brain - tell your muscles what to do - rather than the other way around - and also = So the message that you just stepped on a tack - doesn't have to wait until you've finished walking before it gets to motor control central.

The location - at which these messages leap from an axon to a dendrite - is a tiny gap between the two - called a synaptic space ~ So - naturally - the electrochemical one-way transmission that occurs there - is called = A synapse ~ This synapse - is both - a flow of electricity - and - a set of chemicals - called neurotransmitters (thus the word electrochemical) These neurotransmitters - float across this - space - which is liquid filled (like a warm bath - rather than air filled - like room in the cupboard) - and cause the next neuron down the line - to send an electrical charge - that stimulates chemicals - that sends electricity - that stimulates chemicals - and all so quickly - that the idea - wiggle toes - and the action - toes wiggling - appear virtually simultaneous.

Having described all that = If - this synapse stuff seems too slow - to account for that apparently instantaneous and consistent action that is awareness - then = That might be true = It may very well be closer to - the truth - to describe that activity as occurring at the quantum level of vibrational fields - within what are known as - microtubules (or microscopic cylinders which form the frame work of cells) - inside neurons ~ It's possible (meaning - cellular research has been a witness to at least part of it) - that photons (or light) - traveling along these constantly reforming tunnels - at super high speeds (they are light particles after all) - are responsible for how neurons actually do communicate throughout the entire brain - in a simultaneous (or close enough for us) - form of coherence ~ And = Perhaps - what that really means = Is communication - with the zero point - or quantum - field (that being the information memory storage cyber space brain - if you will - of the universe) - is the real - real - interaction of brain function.

Very amazing - yes ~ But - returning to a simpler (yeah - right) - physical brain business = Just realizing that there are as many as 100 billion neurons in your head (or at least once were) - and = Each of those neurons has between 1000 and 10,000 synapse spaces - or connections to other neurons - is apt to - well… make you shake your head in wonder ~ Yet - even though we are each carrying around a personal version of the most complex structure on the planet = That none of us could ever physically match for speed or information carrying capacity (if you thought of it as a filing cabinet to lug around and sort through) = We're still the ones - that have taught it everything it knows.

Yes = It's true = We did have the cooperation of our brains in doing that - and yet = As we learn - as we choose to learn - participate in learning - and - agree with learning = The physical structure of our brains - changes - not because = It - wants to - but because = It's there to serve us - to accommodate our needs - to take on - what we - give it ~ It's designed to make navigating through life easy - so = It constantly tries to establish maps on which to depend - and then - sort of drives along those established routes ~ In fact - the simplest way to describe the function of a brain - is as = A navigational system - or - a cartographer = A map maker ~ The big question is = Will the set of maps you're using - get you where you want to go - or = Is it time to draw some new ones?

[[[[[[[[Left or Right:

It's interesting (just because it is) - that our brains are separated into two hemispheres (or halves) - and that our bodies are - wired - in a cross over pattern (so to speak) - with the left hemisphere controlling (meaning - processing and responding to the information input of) - the right side of the body - and the right hemisphere - governing the left side (something you've been playing with all along with the breath and movement exercise - you've of course been diligently practicing)

On either side of the brain (roughly in the middle) - are two vertical strips of tissue and neurons - which = Are basically circuit boards (kind of like an electrical map - not that they resemble a recognizable picture from above - the way maps usually do) - that each - keep the what and where it's happening - of the opposite side of the body - organized ~ Amputate a limb - such as the left arm - and the corresponding information area - on that right brain map - begins to be annexed (or taken over) - by another portion of that circuitry - so that eventually = A touch on the left jaw line - feels - like a touch on the missing left hand.

Having shared that information (by way of an immediate tangent to make a certain point) - the real point is = The same dichotomy (die-cot-a-me - meaning - division into two halves - parts - or pairs - such as inside a seed) - applies to the broader information processing functions of the two hemispheres as well - which = Is often over generalized by popular belief - to appear like two very different personalities in the same head - which = Are generally broken down to = Logic (on the left) - versus Intuition (on the right) The actual condition = Is a cooperative correspondence - between hemispheres - with particular processing activities divided amongst them - which = Arrive at whole functions (meaning - understandings that support thoughts or behavior) - together.

For example = Language recognition - is divided as = Vocabulary and literal meaning - in the left hemisphere - and = Intonation (or up and down speech patterns) - and context - in the right ~ While = Emotional information - is the - HOW - an emotion affects us - from the right side - and the - WHAT - that emotion is labeled as - by the left.

Obviously = There are particular - slants - to right and left brain processing orientations - and = Our modern culture - is often criticized as being prejudiced toward left brain education and productivity - which = Is easy to see is true enough (certainly from a right brain perspective) -when you note the emphasis placed on math and science - as opposed to art and music - our educational system promotes - and = That is an imbalance - which = Has certain predictable consequences - but = As for us personally = We have choice ~ We have whole brains - not partial brains (barring injuries and such) - plus = Consciousness - which = May have no more to do with our brains - than movie theaters have to do with making movies - so = Whole brain use - is not about favoring a particular side- out of some judgment about the kind of results which are most appealing (which it took the cooperation of both sides to arrive at by the way) - any more than being right handed - means you shouldn't use your left hand.

What it comes down to = Is a question of balance - of feeling - the artistry of logic musically voicing precision in a big picture filled with details that are imagining invention as it creates the exactly perfect beauty of infinity - and = Enjoying it (perhaps I might add = Breathing it)

While you're at it - by the way = You can (also) - produce coherency (or balanced communication at an electromagnetic level) - between the two hemispheres of your brain (at least temporarily) - by clapping your hands in a regular (meaning - evenly timed) - beat - directly in front of you - or the center line of your body ~ Go ahead = Try it for a minute or two ~ See if you can tell the difference ~ Mix up the beat after a while ~ Get a rhythm going - and = Breathe ~ Try it when you're stressed and need to think straight - before that test - that interview - that - whatever ~ Close your eyes - roll them back like you're looking at your own forehead - put a smile on - pay attention to your breath - and = Clap your way to who knows what great things.||||||||||

Class Eighteen - Practice?

BREATHE (Like… now?)

Well = Did you find that powerful memory? Did you manage to get in the middle of the feeling that was in it? Did getting to that feeling get easier as you practiced it? Did you remember to practice it?   What is the name you gave that memory?   Has using that name/word changed the meaning of that word to you? Have you noticed people using that word? What happened when you heard them use it? What does it feel like when you use it now? What feeling do you want right now.

Okay = Good.

Let's look at - the idea - of what happens - when you - practice - something - anything - a game - an instrument - a language - a skill - an = {{{**Inventory Time**}}}   What do you think they have in common?   Ah = You - are - paying attention ~ Yes = They all work with and reinforce - neural nets ~ Meaning = They shape what your brain looks like - or (in somewhat imperfect grammar) - what it works like.

That word - practice - what does it mean?

Right = Basically - all it means - is to repeat an action - or set of actions - in order to improve your ability - to perform it - or them - well.

Do you think you can do the same thing with being happy? I mean - practice - being happy? But = Wasn't that what the last assignment was all about? Yeah - you're right = I didn't tell you it was about that ~ It's starting to make sense though - isn't it? You chose a memory ~ You chose a name for that memory ~ You chose to feel it ~ Then you did it again and again ~ So = Are - choosing - and - practicing - really different practices? I mean = If you're practicing something - aren't you repeatedly - choosing to do it? Well - seemingly not - if you're being forced to ~ Though - can anyone ever really force anyone else to do what they don't want - if that second anyone is willing to withstand whatever abuse that force consists of? But - never mind that = I mean = Practicing in the sense of - if you want - to practice something ~ Isn't - that - wanting - just a continuous - choosing - to practice that thing? Otherwise - don't you stop? Provided that force issue isn't - in force?

How about this then? Any of you play the bagpipes? You've heard bagpipe music

286

though? Do you like it? Okay - it's not exactly your favorite ~ But - you know what it sounds like ~ So = Do you think you could pick up a set of bagpipes - and just play them like an expert? Not likely eh? So - what would you have to do - to be able to play them? Exactly = Learn how - and = Practice ~ Again = Do you suppose - it could be the same with happiness? Yeah - I know = Happiness seems to be dependent on getting what we want (which - by the way - tends to be happiness) - but = What if - it isn't - dependent on that? What if - it's - entirely - completely - absolutely - up to us - choosing - to practice it - or not?

Okay ~ Let's say - just for the sake of argument (which is a funny use of language to say - let's not argue - anyway - let's say) - it's true = Happiness is up to us ~ So again = Any of you play the bagpipes? Okay ~ Any of you ever felt happy? Alright = How many times have you felt happy? Lost count did you? Well - it sounds like you've had some practice then? Do you think that could be to your advantage? At least compared to learning how to play the bagpipes? You don't really have to learn happiness do you? So = What would you be doing - if you were practicing happiness? Sure those are all actions to expand the experience of happiness = Laughing - giving - playing - creating ~ Definitely a type of practice going on there ~ But - what I mean - beyond physical action - is = Paying attention to an interaction you're having with yourself - something you recognize - because = It's already a skill ~ You already know how to do it - that's the trick ~ You just might not have thought of it that way before ~ The difference is = Choosing it ~ Which doesn't really mean learning something new ~ It means = Working at improving a skill - you already have?

||||||||| Doctor Dude's Dictionary - word eighteen - Paradigm:

If you were to pick an example of a lifestyle - meaning = A certain way of living in the world - and all the parts of that way - such as - education - work - housing - types of relationships with environments - people - animals - food - furniture - you know - plus all the beliefs that add up to creating and maintaining that way of life - you could label that example = A paradigm.

Of course - you'd also want to know how to pronounce it properly ~ Which comes out adding - para - the way it sounds in paratrooper - to dime (you know - 10 cents) - the way the word sign sounds - only with an m instead of an n.

So basically - what you're ending up with - in using the word paradigm - is a model - or a kind of multidimensional picture of a way of being ~ It's not just confined to lifestyles either ~ It means any set of conditions that make up a context - like a Chinese restaurant or a football stadium ~ And = In that context - there are certain expectations - such as paper napkins and flush toilets - types of clothing and beverages ~ If - you were to travel to the depths of the Brazilian rain forest to take up residence with a tribe of people who have rarely encountered outsiders (such as yourself) - you would have entered a different paradigm ~ If - you took the set of expectations - you were using in that Chinese restaurant before going to the football game - up the Amazon with you (that river that runs through the Brazilian rain forest) - and continued to expect them = You'd have problems.

Now - that last statement - is not some kind of travel tip (for all it would be useful as such - if it weren't so obvious) What it is - is a reference to the human handicap of not being able to gracefully move between paradigms ~ That shortcoming - is due mainly to that condition of hanging onto the sets of expectations - that determine what a paradigm is - and = Not easily adapting to new ones ~ At the same time of course = That's why the word exists = Since one of our strongest expectations from language - is to describe how certain things are the same - because they are different from other things ~ Although that may not be the greatest set up for harmonious global relations - it seems to be - the paradigm - we've got going.||||||||||

Let's look deeper at the word practice

According to that process of firing neurons we talked about last time = What is happening - when you practice thinking about something? That's it = You're reinforcing connections between neurons = You're defining a pathway - just like you would across your backyard - or through the snow ~ The more often you walk that way - the more clearly defined the path becomes ~ You've heard the phrase - being in a rut - haven't you? Well - without knowing it (maybe we do know it on some deeper level) - that phrase describes quite well the creation of a neural pathway ~ A path used continuously becomes rutted and worn.

Now - that isn't what happens in your brain ~ We're not talking erosion here ~ It's more like a building up - a kind of growing rigid - than a wearing down ~ What we're talking here - is creating - automatic behavior = An extremely useful talent - when it comes to that range of every day actions - from walking out the door - to understanding what's said to us (given it's in a language we understand) We depend on it all the time ~ The only draw back to this recorded learning process is = When situations occur - which resemble the reasons for responses - or thoughts - we've chosen so often in the past - then = We tend to follow the old patterned thinking - and no longer concern ourselves - with the choice - of what to think ~ Our brains are very good at recording repeated information - and unless we interfere in that repetition - they will serve up the decisions on how to react - that information - has trained them to serve ~ Habits of belief - or judgment - are like regular customers at a restaurant that always order the same thing ~ They walk in the door - and the waiter knows what they want - the cook knows how to prepare it - and = There it is barely a moment later on the plate in front of them - a patterned response behavior - that tastes - more or less - the same as it did the last time.

Now - I'm playing with words here - analogy actually (Or is it food?) Do you know what an analogy is? That's right = A story of a parallel type of relationship - between objects - ideas - or emotions - that helps to clarify what you are talking about - even though - they are not the same thing - as what's being talked about ~ The reason I am - is = So you'll get the idea ~ Do you get the idea? Do you recognize yourself ever walking into that same old restaurant? Such as - what makes you angry? That's always a good place to start.

288

[[[[[[[[[Fight or Flight Poison:

No matter how you slice up that emotion - we call anger - for reasons - results - and repercussions of a mental nature = To our bodies - it's just plain - STRESS - pure and simple.

The so called - fight or flight response (for which anger is one of the triggers) - is the purely natural function of revving up our adrenal glands (two glands which are located on top of the kidneys) - to start pumping out the hormones - adrenaline - and - cortisol ~ The purpose of adrenaline - is to increase the body's metabolic rate (which means - the speeding up of nutrient absorption by the cells) - and - as a kind of messenger signal - to divert blood away from areas like the skin and digestive tract (which are not involved in the save your behind now reaction) Cortisol - works with other hormones - to release fats and sugars and proteins from tissues - in order to fuel and sustain that emergency energy need ~ It also shuts down the immune system - to conserve more energy - for the same purpose.

When all that sugar hits the blood - insulin is released by the pancreas (situated just behind the stomach on top of the small intestine) Insulin's job - is to tell the liver how much sugar is moving around - and - signal the cells to allow it in (sugar - in this case - means the broken down parts of carbohydrates - not just candy bars)

Long-term stress (like being ticked off all the time for one - not to mention - the corresponding dangers of high sugar diets and lack of exercise) - maintain levels of all three hormones in the blood - which = Fills cells with sugar ~ The pancreas - has to dump more insulin into the bloodstream - in hopes of getting those cells to accept more - but = The over sugared cells - can't take any more - which = Eventually results in pancreas failure - and = The destruction of insulin production - as well as the loss of digestive enzymes the pancreas secretes into the small intestine.

Meanwhile = If adrenaline and cortisol are still flying around (which means - various tissues are literally being strip mined for nutrients) - so is sugar - which = Is stored as fat in fat cells ~ If fat cells are filled up - and blood sugar levels are still out of control = Type II diabetes sets in.

Of course - the immune system has also been operating on low power through all this - so = All kinds of potential health complications - are not being properly attended to ~ Then = There is the reduced blood flow and efficiency of the digestive tract - which means = It's unable to provide proper cellular nourishment (provided it's even receiving such food in the first place) All that added up - and - in short = Stress - is killing you.

Now that you know all that - I'd suggest = Taking several deep breaths.]]]]]]]]]

Alright then - tell us something - that other people do - that you hate.

Okay - that's a nice simple one = Michael here - hates it - when people call him Mike ~ So Mike = Why does that upset you? Ah = Because it's not your name - and - those people are assuming a familiarity that's false - since - if they really knew you - they'd call you by your real name ~ Fair enough ~ But = Why does it upset you? No = You haven't already told us - why = You've just told us why - you don't want them to call you Mike ~ Nope = They're not the same thing.

See - there's an underlying - belief - that's the real upset ~ If that belief wasn't there = It wouldn't matter if they called you Alice = You wouldn't get upset ~ Unless - of course - you had some negative belief about being called Alice.

Here - look at it this way = When you get upset - about someone calling you Mike - who is upset? Sure = You are ~ How does that feel? Does feeling bad change the fact that you were called Mike? No? Then why do it? Because they called you Mike ~ Okay ~ Again = Does it change anything - to get upset about it? So = Why get upset?

Alright ~ We've gotten to a point - that looks like - going nowhere in a circle ~ Which it would be - if = We didn't plug in the real question ~ Which is = What is - the belief - that's causing the upset? What do the rest of you guys think?

Yeah = Maybe - things happened in the past - around the name Mike - that were painful - or - just the way people have treated Michael by not bothering to get to know him = Sure ~ Or other stories like that - piled one on top of another ~ We could go on and on making them up ~ And so could Michael for that matter.

So - let's look at the response itself instead ~ What is it? Right = It's anger - resentment - annoyance ~ Okay = If I were suddenly to throw a rock at your head - what would you do? Duck? Sure = Why? Yeah = That would probably protect your head - if you did it fast enough ~ So = Do you - believe - ducking to avoid getting hit with a rock - is the way to protect your self? Does that mean - that ducking - is a belief? No? It's just a reflex - an instinct? Well - that's right = It is an instinct.

Okay ~ Would it make you - angry - if I flung a rock at your head? Especially - if I hit you? Probably? Is that an instinct at work? Yes? No? Maybe?

What if I said = No = It's not an instinct to become angry ~ Would that surprise you? No = I didn't think so ~ It is - an instinct to become upset - in a certain sense = There is a threat present = The fight or flight adrenalin flow kicks in = A definite chemical change occurs ~ But anger - especially sustained anger? No = That is a learned behavior = It's a belief (and actually - a different chemical response - that can be just as addictive as a narcotic) - such a strong belief actually - that we often can't separate it from instinct (in our own minds that is) - and = Will even resort to excusing it as a semi-instinctive kind of entitlement - or right - we claim - as part of what is called - human nature ~ Now there's a whole stack of beliefs.

Let me add something right here - for the sake of clarity = I'm not trying to say = Anger is Bad ~ Not that I'm saying it's good either ~ But - just condemning anger across the board only makes people feel guilty about being angry - which = Tends to also make them - angry ~ Sometimes - anger is even a positive step = When it's the first step out of depression or despair for example ~ It's what follows anger - in that case - such as decisiveness or larger understanding - rather than just more despair or violent behavior - that defines what sort of step it really was.

The big question though - is = Does getting angry - change the fact - that I chucked a rock at your head?

So = Why do we do it?

What if - I were to say = We get angry - because = We do believe - it will change what's happened to us?

Take Mike here - for example - he gets angry when people call him that - because = He thinks - he'll feel a certain way if people call him Michael instead ~ So = What way of feeling is that? Exactly = Happy ~ So = Does that mean - that what he wants - is to feel happy? Why does he get angry then? Yes = Because someone called him Mike ~ But = Is that really why? Ah - now there you go = It's because he wants to be happy ~ He gets mad - BECAUSE = He wants - to be happy.

What if - that's it - we get angry - because - we - BELIEVE = That is the way - to get happy?

We've been over this before - haven't we? Could it be = It's hitting a little closer to home now? Are you reminded of parts of your life that look like - well… being called Mike?

What is the part of our lives - we have - apparently - no power to change? That's it = The past.

|||||||||| Counterclockwise:

You'll of coarse remember a bonus exercise somewhere back there (following the close of chapter eight to be specific) - where we talked about - altering the past - by deliberately manipulating memories - which = Is really about - living in the present - according to conscious choice.

Now - it's time - to consider a quantum twist to that time relationship we take so for granted (meaning - cause precedes effect - or the temporal order of Monday - Tuesday - Wednesday) - which is called = Backward causation - or retro-causality ~ What it's about = Is the flow of information - or energy (no actual difference from a quantum perspective) - traveling backwards in time - or = Effect preceding cause.

The idea - obviously (or maybe not) - is a crazy quilt of theories and philosophical musings - both scientific - and wildly imaginative - yet = Entirely compelling (or interest stimulating) - if you go in for that sort of thing - and = Why not?

This very moment's examination of the idea - may be a future causation's effect - looping the result - of a past intention to question such things - with a future understanding of them - into = A present unfolding of the new information which will lead to that eventual outcome ~ There's no way (in the generally accepted uses of mind that is) - to actually be certain whether that is the case or not ~ Which means = How would you ever know? {{And also probably means - reread that as well}}

Regardless of - knowing - or not = There has been a great deal of theorizing on the subject (which means miles of math) - by minds that are very good at that kind of thing ~ Among them - is the late great physicist Richard Feynman - who = Proposed the possibility - that the positron (the definitely proven to exist antimatter opposite of the negatively charged electron) - is actually an electron traveling backwards in time ~ He went on to suggest = That there may not be many electrons (many - being an obviously inadequate word - at least until you get to the end of the sentence) - but - only one = THE Electron ~ Rather (but not quite) - like the representation of a single force - such as = The Photon - representing the electromagnetic force - which is light.

All of these - learned musings - are immensely complex of course (at least in adding up all the various components of thinking and experimentation involved) - and as yet - are unable to be proven - but = The question - is a simple one = Is - the flow of time - always and forever - one way? Is - what we intend (not plan - intend - two very different things) - a kind of energy circuit - which connects - or opens to a communication received in the present - that has traveled backward in time from a possible future - to become the cause - for its own effects?

Yes = That second question wasn't quite as simple as the first ~ There is something to this time stuff however - that wants such questioning - since = The simple - answers - just line up as - nine - ten - eleven - lunch ~ While at the same - time - all the stops along the way (not that they ever do stop) - are all nows - or = Single present time ~ In that sense = The same as Feynman's one electron idea = Time - may very well be a single whole - represented as separate moments - but = Only for the purpose of experiencing such an expression of reality (the way brushstrokes in a painting - are only parts of the whole) - not because they are - different moments - separated by time - but (like I just said) = Because they are only - one moment - which is - the whole energy - of time.
And (after you've spent a moment pondering that last idea) = What - is the purpose - of that experiencing? Now - there - is a question.]]]]]]]]]

So = If we can't change the past - why do we get upset about it? Does getting upset ever change what's happened? Sure = It can certainly influence what will happen ~ But - again = Does it change what - has happened?

What if - we humans - have an insane belief = That getting angry will change the past?

Take revenge for instance ~ Have you noticed how many movies have revenge as a theme? Stuff like = Mom and the kids get blown up - so dad goes off to gun down the killers ~ And = When he does = We're all satisfied somehow ~ After all - the bad guys were really low down no good scum bags who deserved it - weren't they?

But = Why - did the hero (and of course us - because we like the hero) - want to get revenge? Yup = He wants to be happy - and = So do we ~ Is he going to get his family back by slaughtering the bad guys? No = Not much chance of that ~ But = He was happy - when his family were around? Well = At the times he was - he was = Right? So does that mean = That in his mind (and of course ours as well) - he has identified his happiness - as coming from his family? So in other words = His family made him happy?

Is that true? Was his happiness up to them?

So = Is what we are uncovering here - a belief = That some people can give us happiness - and = Others can take it away? Or maybe - the same people - do both? So = Do we believe that happiness - is not up to us - it's up to others? What do you think Mike?

Actually - while you're thinking about it = What do you suppose would happen - if - the next time someone calls you Mike - you appreciated them for it? Which of course - goes for all you not Mikes as well - in whatever way you can turn a minor upset into an opportunity for = Appreciation.

How does appreciation work by the way? Isn't it one of those - pro - vibrations? Doesn't it - feel - completely different - from say - irritation? Either way - the question still remains = What - do you think - would happen?

Okay - your assignment this time is to do some experimenting with how happiness moves between people ~ It's quite simple ~ What you do = Is give it away ~ How do you do that? You smile = You say hello = You compliment people = You thank them = You give them what they want ~ Hardly anything surprising in that - is there? The surprising bit comes when you really pay attention to that giving - when you look for opportunities for it - when you - feel - what happens to = You ~ There are no boundaries to who you can give happiness to ~ Everyone wants the stuff - even cops - gang leaders - and high school principles ~ So - notice - who you - don't - want to give it to ~ And - notice how that feels ~ Or - when someone gives to you - however small - pay attention - feel it - don't just slide it off as small (so what they held the door) No = Reward them with your smile - with your attention - with your happiness ~ And - while you're at it - use that word you named your happy memory = Feel it ~ Use it in your mind = Feel it ~ Slip it into conversation = Feel it ~ Enjoy the fact of its secret meaning to you alone = Feel it ~ But don't keep that feeling to yourself - give some of it away - and = Do a lot of breathing.

THE PERCEPTION PAPERS - number four

Acquired Tastes:

We eat to survive - but = We taste - because = We can.

Flavor - is at the forefront of the great compelling experiences of life in a body ~ Simple - complex - addictive - repellent - the palate of flavor - is a consuming obsession among our species (particularly in these overfed United States) - quite simply because = Of that need to eat - in combination with - the fact - that = Food - has flavor.

Just think about the number of restaurants out there = Millions of them ~ And cookbooks = Millions of them ~ And all those grocery stores with their shelves stacked and packed with different varieties of - say - breakfast cereal ~ In that same - United States - there is such a thing as - the cereal aisle ~ A whole aisle (or at least one side of one - though we are talking the great American grocery store - where such a thing is a considerable amount of space) - dedicated to nothing but - different flavors - of cereal ~ To be sure - the main flavoring involved - is sugar ~ But still - think about it = Whole countries are identified by their cuisine - or what their food is made from - and so = Tastes ~ We say things like = How about Chinese tonight? The same for - Mexican - Italian - Vietnamese - Thai - you name it.

Fact is = We identify ourselves with flavor ~ We measure feelings by it = This would be a really sweet moment (so savor it) - if things don't go sour - and we end up bitter ~ Why - just ask a salty old character like me - and I'll tell you = We don't just love to eat = We love - to taste (which - should be noted - also involves the sense of smell - and the chemical irritation - or feel - of such things as hot chili peppers - or carbonation)

One of the amazing things about this ability of ours - to taste food (aside from the straight up fact - we can) - is that = Regardless how complex the flavor combinations of a particular food or drink are - those flavors break down to the single four types of information our sense of taste is capable of registering and reporting to our brains = Sweet - sour - salty - and bitter ~ Aaaaand… just maybe a fifth - named umami (you - mah - me) - which is sometimes called - savory ~ It was named by the Japanese - and seems to identify the so called - brothy flavor - present in much of their food - such as miso soup.

Our tongues (plus a couple of spots at the top and back of the mouth) - which are at the center of this taste sensation - are covered in little bumps - called taste buds (or - more technically - three variations of papillae - which contain taste buds) Those bumps are each onion shaped bulbs of up to 100 sensory receptor cells ~ It's their job - to detect one of those four (or five) - flavor components - convert that information into an electrochemical signal - and send it rocketing off to a very specific location of the brain that just deals with that one ingredient of the flavor recipe - so that = The instant - you bite into that mango anchovy pizza with extra feta cheese - it seems like (even though it really isn't) - the same instant - you taste it.

Food is art to us - it's seduction - indulgence - naughty - decadent - blissful ~ Of course - it's also habit - routine - and the same old thing for dinner again ~ But = What drives the two ends - and the middle - of that appetite for judgment - is how it tastes ~ When you study a menu - it's not categorized as - proteins - carbohydrates (complex and simple) - fats - vitamins and minerals - even if that is what those dishes contain ~ We didn't go there to get healthy ~ We went there for the entertainment value - as much as the nourishment ~ Not that we weren't hungry - and - even decided in the end - not - to order the double fudgey triple-decker chocolate paralysis sundae - because = That entertainment - is based on taste - and taste - is what we like - and what we like - is what the other side of taste - is all about - or = What we think.

Good taste - bad taste - poor taste - no taste - that other use of the word taste - really means = Opinion - which also means - preference - which just spins back around to - like or dislike ~ The same thing goes for what you choose to put in your grocery cart - as it does for how you decorate your apartment = It's the flavor of your growing up - your family - and culture - and friends - and/or = How you've distanced yourself from all that and chosen other models (along with one or two chemical and genetic distinctions) - that defines = Personal taste.

We are all choosing off the menu of what the world has to offer ~ We add to it as well - but = More in the way a clever chef combines ingredients which may have never been in the same pan together before - yet still - were available somewhere ~ Our tastes - are the layers of influence and memory - spiced by new experiences - and simmered in lifetimes of built up habits - with maybe a pinch of experimentation now and then - that we plate up every day as = Identity ~ If you're going to describe - someone else's behavior - as being in bad taste - just get yourself to a buffet restaurant - and watch the people's plates as they return to their tables ~ Each of those people - were presented with exactly the same choices - but = Not a single one of those plates of food - will look exactly the same - and = Some of them - might even put you off your own feed ~ That's not - bad taste ~ That's just = Taste.

There is a physiological reason (meaning - physical - of course) - why some of the differences between peoples food choices (may) - occur - and that's = Their tongues ~ The number of taste buds - on any given tongue - is unique to that person - the same as fingerprints have only one owner ~ Some people are what's known as - non-tasters (by tongue testing science) They - have far fewer taste buds (to be specific - the fungiform papillae - mostly clustered on the tip of the tongue) - than the opposite end of the human buffet - where = Super-tasters - are picking suspiciously at their food ~ It's not that non-tasters can't taste ~ It's just that they're probably just as happy with the cheap bottle of wine - and are nowhere near as finicky about what they'll eat ~ They are the part of the definition of - omnivore (creature able to digest both meat and vegetables) - which is perfectly willing - to eat almost anything.

Then = There are those - tastes - we are said to - acquire ~ Some of them - like a tolerance for bitter flavors - are an actual physical change - which happens as our bodies mature toward adulthood ~ The rest - are the result of cultural practices and traditions - or interest in - or relocation to - the countries of those cultural origins ~ That's the territory - where ideas - and flavor - blend ~ Take a 12-year-old blended Scotch whiskey for instance ~ It's a valuable experience of distinct and subtle complexities to some - but - to someone with no idea of the culturally approved effects of alcohol - or the ancient traditions of Highland distilling = That stuff might just as easily be confused with paint thinner ~ It's a set of ideas (which of course - are strung together experiences - judgments - and beliefs) - that inspire - acquiring - such deliberate appreciation of what our tongues instinctive reaction to is a poison signal (I mean - let's face it - it doesn't actually take much alcohol to kill you - compared anyway - to something like orange juice)

It's in that blend though - of ideas affecting flavor - where another angle to this experience of taste arrives at the table ~ That angle = Is examining your own taste ~ Swishing it around in your mind - and quite literally - in your mouth - while you ask yourself = Why do I like this? What are the parts to this flavor? How do they connect to ideas? Is it pleasure I feel? What do I feel? What do I think as I feel it? Why?

It's not just the sense of taste - in your mouth - we're talking either ~ It's your larger sense of - you - liking - approving of - choosing - what you want around you ~ What are the reasons? What are the feelings? Why - do you choose what you do?

And lastly = Pick some food you don't like - but = You know is good for you ~ Broccoli for instance (I love the stuff myself) - and = Learn about it - research what's in it - find out why - it's good for you ~ And then = Eat some of it - just a little - and really taste it - examine that taste - chew it (lengthy chewing - by the way - significantly aids with digestion) - feel it - think about it being beneficial to your health - and then = Notice how your reaction to that food changes (or doesn't) - over time ~ Who knows what your diet might look like a year from now ~ We'll do lunch sometime - and talk about it.

N.P.U. - Chapter Eighteen - Brains?

So - I've vaguely dangled parallel universes in front of you (not that you could see them) - and = Ended up in your brain - as though that was the most natural thing in the world to do ~ Well = What if - it is? What if - it's this view of brains - as containers - of consciousness - separated by identity - as well as skulls - that makes parallel universes of us all?

Have you thought of it that way? How have you thought of it? What is - it?

Let's get something straight here = The purpose of this course = Is to mess with your head ~ That's right - in a very literal sense = When you reach the end of this book - not to mention - the end of this chapter - your brain will look different - it will be - physically changed.

Now - that's not intended to be threatening ~ Why would it be? The same thing goes on all the time ~ It's called = Learning ~ It's what that galaxy of neurons behind your nose is up to ~ They're making maps - rearranging maps - accessing maps - adding to - coloring - shading - cross-referencing - maps ~ Of course - it's not really maps that are being created ~ Even your specific memories of maps - aren't actually maps - unless you could map the network of neurons that re-create them ~ But = Maps - is probably the easiest day to day reference available - because = Brains are all about getting us - from point A - to point B ~ That's their entire concern ~ They don't tell us what to think = They tell us what we've thought before - in order to recognize - where - we are - in relation to - what we'll think next ~ They're like dictionaries - encyclopedias - tourist guides - and owners manuals rolled into one amazingly complex highway system for electrochemical maintenance vehicles to speed around - in order to tell us = Where we are - and what just happened - and the possible reactions we've used in similar circumstances before - and = They're always changing - updating - reinforcing - or pruning the unused into the forgotten bin.

What brains can not do - obviously - is tell us exactly (meaning - Exactly) - what's going to happen in the future - or even = What's happening - exactly now ~ There's always a delay - a tiny one - a matter of milliseconds maybe - but enough = So that we are always one fraction of a step behind ~ No matter what - what we're dealing with - on a physical perceptual recognition level = Is the past (especially if you're considering the speed of light particle wave potential condition of reality) Our brains - know this - in a genetic chemical instinctive kind of way - and = That's why - they're always constructing maps of that passed over territory - we call our experience - in order to have some means of anticipating what will happen in the future - so as not to get caught off guard by such things as saber tooth tigers or tailgating drivers.

Does it work?

Well - in many ways - it works quite flawlessly ~ Take actual highway systems for an example = Every day - in the United States alone - hundreds of millions of motor vehicles - collectively travel many trillions of miles ~ And = Are there accident demolished cars littering the roadsides every few feet? No ~ Perhaps (the polite way of saying - definitely) - our choices of how to power those cars - hasn't been particularly farsighted - but = In the vastly overwhelming majority - the experiential training - of the brains of those drivers - delivers them safely to their destinations.

The question remains though = Are these brains - us - or a tool - at our disposal?

[[[[[[[[[**Brain Gain:**

The moment - you shifted your attention to a focus on this section = You held your breath.

Don't worry = You couldn't help it ~ Unless you deliberately chose not to do so - which = We have the option to do ~ Otherwise = You did exactly as I said = We all do = It's - more or less - involuntary (the less part being - that volunteering not to - which - takes such constant vigilance as to be next to impossible to control - if you want to think about something other than breathing all the time that is)

The same thing happens - when we are about to engage in some physical effort (such as lifting a heavy object) - or sustaining concentration on some task (like filling out a job application) Sometimes to the point - where our bodies begin to protest (dizziness) - and our thinking ability suffers (stupidness) Our brains - being the largest individual consumer of oxygen in our bodies - are what's behind those reactions - and as such = There's a built-in reaction mechanism in place - to help compensate for when there actually is (or at least - the brain considers there to be) - a real lack of oxygen threatening its supply.

When excessive carbon dioxide (the stuff we exhale in exchange for inhaling oxygen) - builds up in the blood = The carotid (ka-rot-id) - arteries (the two major arteries in the neck which deliver blood to the brain) - expand - to allow a larger volume of blood to pass through - and thus = That much more oxygen.

Those short interruptions to breathing - which shifts in focus claim - are not generally the kind of stimulus to trigger that reaction ~ They do run counterproductive to smooth brain function however (which leads one to wonder why they occur) - and = Being aware of them - and so = Prompted to take the opposite course - and consciously override that habit (meaning - breathe instead) - is = Quite productive.

That being said = There are also ways to turn that oxygen depletion response - to productive advantage - by deliberately denying - your brain oxygen.

If you happen to like swimming = You're in luck ~ Or - even if you don't - but live near a place you can (and are willing) = Swimming underwater - and holding your breath for as long as possible = Is likely the best means there is (due in part - to the overall increase in blood flow to all parts of the body) - of expanding those arteries - and (if practiced enough) = Turning that increased blood flow into a more (meaning - still requiring some attention) - permanent condition.

The same results can be achieved (while remaining quite dry) - by breathing into an enclosed space (such as a paper bag) - which quickly increases that carbon dioxide level - by the simple procedure of inhaling your own exhalation of it ~ Do that - for 30 seconds every half hour or 21 days - and = Your brain will be in high gear for years ~ But (that's BUT) = Only (that's ONLY) = If you are super healthy - and have no respiratory complications of any kind ~ This is about being smart - not dead.

The simplest way to swell those arteries = Is to lay on your back on the floor - with your legs bent at the knees and resting on the seat of a chair - or any other object which does the job ~ Due to that increased blood flow = This position is also ideal for practicing any of the exercises in this course (which don't prescribe or require some other posture)

Of course any vigorous exercise will increase carbon dioxide levels in your blood - and = Move that blood around more effectively (so come on - and one - and two) - which = Means oxygenating all your cells - but particularly = Getting it to any parts of your brain - that are being neglected - which = Means saving those cells - from the regular die off of unused neurons that's going on all the time ~ Other than that = It never hurts = To breathe.||||||||||

There's nothing else for it but to cut one open - and look around.

The first thing an exposed brain describes about itself - is that it is basically made of proteins - or amino acids - and the rest - is essentially fats and water ~ It's highly possible - that a major portion of your lunch - contained exactly the same ingredients ~ Which makes a certain amount of sense = Since - we are required to provide our cells with the materials that fuel - rebuild - and re-hydrate - if - we want to remain alive and healthy ~ Of course - a more detailed description of that lunch - would determine how health supporting it actually was ~ Just the same = What we're looking at - from the eyes of any other carnivorous (or meat eating) - animal (and sometimes even including other humans) - is just another form of lunch (of course technically - we are omnivores - which means we'll eat just about anything - which also allows a good deal of room for vegetarianism - but getting back to the point) - which is to say = Our brains - are meat.

Now - the fact - that they are meat - doesn't take away from - the fact - of their remarkable abilities - but - it does mean = They are essentially useless (aside from their nutritive value to hungry carnivores) - if - they are not powered by this mysterious force - we call life - which = We both solve - and complicate - the mystery of - by describing - as consciousness ~ In other words = It's really the invisible power animating the brain - that defines its usefulness - despite what it's capable of doing - much like = The most sophisticated computer in the world - is useless - until someone plugs it in - and switches it on ~ Not to mention = Asks it to do something.

So - returning to that densely packed city of neurons you're carrying around = As I'm sure you've seen illustrated somewhere - a brain is a double handful of spongy tissue - all dimpled and folded like soft ice cream extruded in twists and turns one on top of another ~ The neurons form the top six surface layers of those dimples and folds - and = Because they - and their dendrites - are a darker color than other tissues of the brain (predominantly glial cells) - they are often called - gray matter (despite the fact - they are a shade of pearly pink when they're alive - the use of gray comes from dissecting dead brains - which take on that color) The (so called) - white matter of the brain - are the spindly branches of the axons - interwoven through the (pink) - gray matter - like the branching roots of some well-nourished fungus ~ One reason for this color difference - are the glial cells (known as the myelin sheath in this glia variation) - that contain and insulate that wiring system - much as rubber and plastic - sheathe - the wiring plugged in around your house - and in that way = Assist the current of electricity to travel direct without short-circuiting ~ At least - that is one - of the scientific suspicions - about myelin glial cells - and may be only a minor role - among the possibilities - of what those amazing cells are capable of ~ Which of course - your neural nets have already reminded you.

Then of course - the thing is split into two halves - or hemispheres - the right and left - and lobes - or quarters (not that they are evenly sized) - which = Are also split down the middle - same as the rest - with a fifth one tucked up underneath - and = All sitting on the little fist of tissue called the cerebellum - with the brain stem - which keeps us breathing and pumping blood - perched at the top of the spinal column ~ Throw in some very specialized glands - the optic nerves - a list of Latin sounding names - and there you have it = A human brain (not that - that explains its workings any better than explaining the operation of a car - by calling it a blue sedan)

It's that frontal lobe though - at the front of course - above our eyebrows - that seems to set us off from other brain toting creatures - because = Of ours being so much larger - in comparison to body size - than theirs (porpoises and whales being our closest proportional competition - unless you take in the fact that they do not engage in organized warfare against their own kind - which perhaps sets us back some in that competition - no matter what the size issue may be) It's in that front bit though - where our decisions are worked out - or where our rubbing together of data - meaning = Sensory input - combined with memory printed - maps - comes up with = What to do next ~ I imagine - this very moment - with the smallest bit of concentration - you can feel your own frontal lobe working.

Okay - there's slightly more of a picture - of part - of this saber tooth tiger happy meal we wear hats on - but = In this case - the picture - about 400 words - does not describe - the thousand words - racing around in there to register in recognition - all the images and associations required to make sense of those 400 words ~ The reason is = We're talking about - a whole system - here ~ A super athlete - broken down to bones and muscles - is just more Tiger bait ~ It's what energizes that system = That makes it - a system - not - just the sum of its parts ~ Which is not to say - the parts - are not part of the system ~ But = In the case of our nervous system - and the workings of its juicy brain - the connection - between energy (or life and consciousness) - and - tool function (or - navigational abilities through physicality and information) - is a state summed up in one word = Neuroplasticity.

Neuroplasticity - in its simplest terms - means = Neurons able to connect freely to other neurons ~ Now - why that might appear to be a desirable state - can also be summed up in one word = Learning.

[[[[[[[[[Monkey Mind 101:

The hundredth monkey - is a phrase that has come to symbolize a type of quantum leap in knowledge - transferred instantly to all members of a population - when a certain number of that population (in particular - monkeys) - have acquired that knowledge on their own.

To run that by you in steps - as well as detail the reason it originated as a concept - begins on the small Japanese island of Kashima in 1952 ~ It was there - when a team of Japanese scientists - who were studying the local population of macaque monkeys - witnessed a new skill spreading among the younger generation of those monkeys ~ That skill - was the washing of sweet potatoes in water before eating them ~ No = Not exactly an impressive skill - it's true ~ Especially considering that the way the monkeys were acquiring the potatoes was through the tradition of locals feeding them by throwing food onto the beaches from small boats - where of course - it would get covered in stand - and naturally - it would make sense to rinse it off in a place that is surrounded by water ~ But hey = They were monkeys - and a little grit didn't seem to bother the majority of them ~ Still - the new habit of washing continued to spread - until suddenly = Monkeys of the same species - on surrounding islands - completely cut off from Kashima by miles of open ocean - began washing their sweet potatoes - where before - none of them - ever had.

The assumption - deduction - guess - or theory arrived at - was that somehow - collective monkey mind had reached an information tipping point - where the new skill was learned through shared consciousness - rather than a continuation of the one monkey at a time action of observation it had to go through to reach that tipping point.

To be sure - the study itself - and certainly - the interpretations of its results - have been hotly debated - contested - and often as not - rejected ~ That is - if you don't take into account the growing popular circulation of the idea by - non-scientific culture ~ The question itself remains however = Do such invisible information transferences occur? And if so = How? And then of course - there's why - when - and how often? Not to mention the ever popular = Who knows what's possible in the invisible world of consciousness.]]]]]]]]]

See - there's a sentence in neuroscience (that being the scientific study of neurons and the brain in general) - which describes how a neural net becomes a fixed habit (so to speak - the addition of which phrase - may be one of those habits) It goes = Neurons that fire together - wire together ~ What it means is = The more often a certain set of ideas are repeated - like = Doughnuts are bad for me (while you're picking up a couple dozen) = The stronger is the connection between those neurons that carry that message ~ Which is sometimes referred to as - hardwired - same as the outlets in your house - meaning = That's where the juice goes - because = That's where the wires go ~ But then - we've been over that ground already ~ The state of neuroplasticity - is the opportunity - or ability - to rewire - or quite literally = Move those axon terminals into contact with new (meaning - other) - dendrite spines - or synapse spaces - and = Think (that is - access when you think) - new (meaning - different) - information - than the old net was accustomed to accessing ~ To be sure - thinking = Doughnuts are good for me - may not be quite enough to accomplish that transition - since it goes directly against the original pathway's foundational data ~ There are ways to deal with that complication - but = What we're still dealing with here is just the state of neuroplasticity itself.

So = How does IT work?

Well - first - there's the fact - that it does work ~ Again - it's the physical action of learning ~ The more we challenge ourselves with learning - the denser - and more diverse - those connections of axons and dendrites grow and change - because = Its growth - that's going on - or cellular reproduction - same as building muscles - and healing injuries ~ No matter what age you may be - the process is available - as well as its reverse = Use it or lose it ~ We're still talking meat here remember? When people say = Your brain is a muscle = They're not saying something biologically accurate exactly - but = Figuratively speaking - that statement = Is spot on ~ The same as exercise helps maintain physical health - learning maintains mental health ~ The added attraction being = Mental health - benefits - all - other systems - especially - when consciously directed to benefiting those systems.

Then - there's laughter = Yes = Laughter.

Because the communication system between neurons is chemical based - as well as electrical - there are a lot of chemical residues floating around in there - that end up - either reabsorbed for future use - or carried away in the bloodstream as waste ~ Laughter - especially a sustained event of serious laughter (if serious laughter - is a reasonable phrase) - acts like a flushing mechanism - which washes out all that chemical residue - and = Resets the whole system for efficient use again ~ In other words = Returns to a condition - of neuroplasticity ~ That means = Humor - is actually one of the most potent devices for assisting learning there is - because = It helps to maintain an active - adaptability - a kind of clean sheet of paper on which to take notes ~ Ah = But particularly = It corresponds to an emotional state - that you might term - stickier - to the learning process - in that = It's more attuned - to allow - information to stick - because = It's keyed into that strongest of drives we're all bent on fulfilling somehow = Well being - or = The pursuit of happiness ~ Which - again = Can be boiled down to one word - especially from the electrochemical point of view of your brain = Pleasure.

||||||||| Rodent Rapture:

There is a portion of the brain - which neuroscience has officially labeled - the nucleus accumbens (located just behind your nose) - and unofficially nicknamed = The pleasure center ~ It's a part of the limbic system - those survival and emotional processing circuits which represent much earlier evolutionary brain development than say... the cerebral cortex - which is at the top front of your head and associated with awareness - attention - memory - or those conscious of being conscious processes we call thought.

The pinpointing of that (we'll shorten it to) - N.A. location as the ace happy spot - comes compliments of rats with wire electrodes implanted in that section of their brains - who = When they pressed a lever in their cages - were delivered a mild electric current - which = They just could not get enough of ~ Those pleasure junkie rats would press that lever over and over - hundreds of times in an hour - ignoring food and water and other rats until exhaustion set in and even killed them.

Rats - of course - are not humans - and yet = Such an experiment - performed on humans (for some reason we think it's an okay thing to do to rats but not us) - would likely produce similar results - just a higher (or at least longer) - survival rate - on account of our superior planning abilities (not necessarily our intelligence) No doubt - if you could produce and market a device that would do the same thing (there has been some experimentation with the idea as a treatment for severe depression) - you'd make (what can I say but) - a killing.

Pleasure drives us like tractor-trailer trucks two days late ~ Which is to say (generally speaking) = It's a dominant feature in our motivations - a kind of press to get there - that bombards our culture from all angles - advertising - broadcasting - cleavage - and = That's just the first three letters of the alphabet ~ As for our brains = The allure of food - sex - drugs - laughter - and reward stimuli of all kinds appear to move through that cluster of neural connections behind our noses ~ But then = So does the action of rhythmic timing and the emotions induced by listening to music (at least some more recent experimentation points at that being the case) Does that mean - that a few chemicals - some hormones - neurotransmitters - or specifically placed electrical currents - are - what happiness is? Or - perhaps more simply = Is pleasure - what happiness is?

It seems - like a very thin line which divides the two - or = A thick one - clear as different encyclopedia volumes if you carve them up for cause or effect ~ After all = Since when - has happiness killed anyone?|||||||||

And then = It's Monday morning - early - and you've been sleepily in the school building less than five minutes - when = You look up to find - your very not young grandmother - in a zebra striped leotard - locked in a passionate embrace with your - very young - homeroom teacher - who also happens to be a woman - and what's more - a burstingly obvious pregnant woman - when she had been in no such state the day before - and you = Have just entered a state of dynamic neuroplasticity (or the alarm next to your bed hasn't gone off yet)

That's right = Surprise - is also a major stimulant to neural action = Instant rapid fire search voltage goes desperately flashing through all possible links to help you choose what to do next ~ Because = So completely bizarre a situation - is apt to register - at the neuron level - as a kind of code red - or life threatening situation - which (many people would argue) = Is why our brains have developed as well as they have - by making full use of that built-in design advantage - apparently - in place to help us master this career we call = Survival ~ The other side of that argument might just as well be = We like - excitement - extremes - surprise - and the challenge of instant adaptation - because - they are another source of = Pleasure.

Once more - the question surfaces (or goes on a wild tangent) = What puts together this reality in the order it shows up in? How does the wave become the particle? Is the brain the writer of thoughts - or just the publisher - and the library to look the old ones up in? Or is it a kind of mobile terminal connected to cosmic cyber space? And then = Are such questions pleasurable?

It's that word pleasure - that sticks - as a central theme in our motivators - our purposes for action - and as a result - in our neural wiring ~ It could hardly be a mistake - and in that sense - no surprise - that our reproductive drive is centered on pleasure ~ What better way to ensure a continuous crop of new humans? It's also why - addiction - is both - a cultural disease (as it is often termed) - and = An accepted standard functioning modality - from chocolate to gossip - coffee and cigarettes to road rage ~ Therefore - in reference to that earlier question = How does the wave become the particle? Is it possible - that addictions - as well as that same active desire for pleasure that molds our dreams and ambitions - are also a kind of personal gravitational field - that draws experiences - fitting that addiction - or desire - out of the subatomic wave of possibility - and into the particle of satisfaction - or its opposite number = Lack? Could that be how it works? Of course - such a setup would have to include all the interconnected results - interactions - consequences - and on and on - that tag along as part of a whole system in interaction with itself - in other words = A world? {{Yup - that's a re-reader}}

Perhaps - that's stretching the habits of your neurons a bit too far ~ But - there is a gland - in the middle of your head - that's reflecting that idea - on a small - or - personal - chemical - emotional scale - this very instant - that you could say = Is a physical out picturing - of the very same thing.

SPECIAL BONUS EXERCISE - number nine

Neural Newness:

The understanding of the neural net building process (which is to say - understanding that such a process takes place - rather than - understanding the complete physiological breakdown of how it takes place) - can be used to accelerate the process itself ~ At least - that's what a series of studies indicate - where students were taught about the condition of neuroplasticity (which you will remember - is the ability of neurons to alter the location of connections with other neurons) - and prompted = To participate in it.

So = The following exercise is based on the working procedure of those studies - which quite simply adds up to = Paying attention to the fact that neural net building is happening when - it is.

Here's what you do = Next time - you study - read something - watch a movie - a television program - have a conversation - or even - torturous as it may be - listen to your teachers = The instant you recognize - that you are receiving new information (or repeating the old information that's potentially important to you - such as when you sit down to that chemistry exam tomorrow) = Feed yourself a reminder - that your brain is doing its thing - its building neural connections ~ Or at least it's willing to ~ Your own willingness is what's truly key at this point ~ Which - yes = Does sound as though I'm implying that you - and your brain - are separate beings ~ However - the distinction here - is much the same as making the comparison with your willingness to lift weights - and your muscles to go along with it ~ Like you may have heard somewhere else = Use it or lose it.

So = Cooperation with your brain = That's the point ~ Which is to say = That's the exercise - because = It is exercise = It's strength building - and = All the work you have to do - is know - your brain is doing the work = You - are just feeding it the information - and = If you've ever fed - say… a baby by hand = Then you know - that you have to pay a certain amount of attention to the process ~ You can't be focused elsewhere when you line up that spoon with that dribbley mouth ~ In fact = If you think of your learning process as merely getting the proper nourishment into that brain baby of yours - in order to see it grow up strong and healthy - you'll be doing something that comes naturally to nearly every species of animal on this planet of ours = Parenting.

A parent provides the food - the attention - the behavior model - the love (not every parent of course - but that's the general job description) What they don't provide - is what the child does - grows - develops - creates with those things - which = Is the same as you and your brain (in a manner of speaking anyway) Ultimately - it's you - who are in control of your brain - such as what you choose to think with it - and the places you cart it around to ~ But = Its organizational mechanism - or structure (it created out of what you've fed it from your relationship with the environment around you) - is a different story = In the sense at least - of whether or not you've been consciously - or unconsciously (the difference being entirely about - attention) - feeding it what to grow on ~ Trouble is = Your brain can produce habits - that you - might not want to reinforce -

given the chance of recognizing that they are there ~ The idea in question here - is about = Taking the responsibility - of choosing - which habits you actually want to reinforce - before - they are habits.

So - again - try feeding your brain - consciously ~ BE - the architect - the builder - landscaper - pool boy - whatever it takes to = Be aware - that that's what you're doing - when you are ~ Plus - your brain is using its system of neural nets - every time - you have a thought ~ Which means = You can potentially always be aware of its building process - and = Constantly feed it new building materials ~ So = Try out some new materials ~ Dig into some new study you've never looked into before - and = Notice - what kind of old knowledge it's using to stick to ~ Test yourself on your new knowledge ~ Practice it ~ Tell someone some thing you've learned recently - and = All the while = Be aware = You're drawing those neural maps = What fun.

Class Nineteen - Anger?

BREATHE (Chances are you're not autistic ~ Basically - because most of us aren't ~ It does appear to be a condition that's on the rise though (as they say - and myself previously as well) - affecting more and more people - including those who live with and care for such individuals ~ This exercise we've been doing however - has been of huge help to kids living with that condition ~ That being the case = Imagine what it might do for you - without that handicap.)

Were you successful? Did you give away lots of happiness? How did people react? Were their reactions fun? Was your own? Where is that happiness coming from? Does it come from giving? What does giving come from? Do happiness and giving come from the same place? Does that make them the same thing? Is it a kind of loop? Does it - connect you - with other people? What does that feel like?

Let's continue from that same point then - meaning = Is happiness - up to us alone?

Okay ~ Yes = It's true - that people appear to influence each other all the time - and = Do lots of unhappy things to each other - and yes - of course = Do happy things as well - as you've just seen ~ In fact - maybe = There are actually more happy things going on - than the opposite (despite what the evening news considers important for us to know) After all = We do all want the stuff ~ And then again - there's that drama idea - that maybe we don't - but = Again (again) = Who - is it really up to in the end?

See - this is a truly key spot - for examining what you believe - about happiness ~ Because = What if - what you believe about IT - determines completely - how much of IT - you will experience?

Tied in - of course - is what you might call - the other belief structure - that we've been looking at - the anger one - because = They're really the same structure - same as the bathroom and the kitchen share the same structure of being in a house - except = In the house of our minds - what goes on in the kitchen sink - and what goes on in the toilet - have a much closer connection.

But = How do you do it? How do you - uncover - beliefs?

Well - for a start (if not a middle) - you could ask yourself questions - like = Do I believe - that anger changes things?

Okay sure = You've seen plenty of anger - and the result = Was often change of some kind ~ That means = There's experience there - that you've built from ~ The question is = How - have you used that experience? What have you constructed from it? Does it mean = That you - use anger - to try to change things - you don't like - back - to things you do? Do you use it a lot? So = What is it - you believe - anger will do for you? Is it a useful tool? Is it the right thing to do? When someone does something to you - that you consider - you absolutely don't deserve - is it your - right - or even - your duty - to be angry at them? How about at parents - teachers - police - politicians? And then there's = Bullies - thieves - terrorists - not to mention - brothers - sisters - friends? Have you ever been angry at any of them? Why? Could it be = That you - believe - that anger - is a way of protecting yourself - or what you consider yours - or - by extension = Your family - your town - your political party - your country?

The question remains = What - do - you - believe - about anger?

[[[[[[[[[[1914:

On a warm Sunday morning in late June of 1914 - jowly faced old Franz Ferdinand - Archduke of the Austrian-Hungarian empire (a title which sounds more politically powerful than it actually was) - and his wife Sophie - the Duchess Hohenberg - arrived by train in the Bosnia-Herzegovina capital city of Sarajevo (not so very far from that Dubrovnik place) - where they were scheduled to make a - basically routine (ho hum) - state visit ~ As it turned out = They both died of gunshot wounds before the morning was over - and thus = The major events of the 20th century (really major - like the deaths of maybe 100 million people) - were set in motion.

Now - that's not to say - that those events would not have happened - or weren't already like a bomb with the fuse lit just waiting for an excuse to be thrown - had - that morning's story gone differently ~ But - speculation aside = The story went as it did - and centers on the actions of one unhappy young man - who suddenly found himself at the center of one of those chance (got to wonder if that's really the accurate word) - moments of history - where his beliefs about himself - caused a personal decision that still echoes today.

Gavrilo Princip - was just a month shy of his 20th birthday that famous June day (the 28th) He was the son of Bosnian peasants (raised in poverty and never a particularly healthy specimen of Slavic youth) - who had gotten himself involved with a revolutionary organization known as - Young Bosnia - which = Was being armed and trained by another militant group called - the Black Hand ~ The revolutionary intention behind these underground movements - was to see certain Southern Austrian-Hungarian provinces broken away from that empire - and united with a greater Serbia - or Yugoslavia - for many reasons (the dominant one revolving around Slavic ethnicity - Slavs being one of the racial groups in that area of eastern Europe - and Serbian Slavs - separated by those contested borders)

It wasn't going well for young Princip though = He had been thrown out of school in Serbia for his politicking - refused entrance to a school in Belgrade after failing the entrance exam - and what's worse (for his image of himself as a revolutionist) = Rejected - not once - but twice (due to his short stature and overall physical weakness) - by a Serbian guerrilla force he'd attempted to enlist in ~ He had managed however - to involve himself in a small group of fellow Black Handed Young Bosnians - who were intent on assassinating the Archduke during his visit to Sarajevo - and so = Was one of that number - interspersed among the crowd that day - awaiting their chance.

Their chances came and went - as did several misjudgments and blunders ~ One of which - was a tossed hand grenade - that rolled sputtering behind the Archduke's car - and wounded a pair of city officials and a dozen spectators instead ~ After that - rather too warm welcome - the driver sped along the street - intent on presenting a more difficult target - but = In his hurry - he made a wrong turn - and = While reversing - in order to turn around = There - was that chance moment - the wars of the 20th century hinged on.

The street the Archduke's car turned on - was off the planned route of the motorcade - as was - Gavrilo Princip - who had given up on the assassination venture for the moment and gone in search of lunch ~ But = There he was - standing only several feet from the overdressed Austrians - and the rest = Is history.

Of course - that history involves the ensuing diplomatic demands on Serbia (who were blamed for the shooting) - by the Austrians (who were allied with the Germans) The Serbians tried to smooth matters as best they could - without actually giving their country over to complete Austrian domination ~ The belligerent Austrians - started massing troops on their border with Serbia (by way of backing up their seriousness) - which = Got the Russians (who were the neighbors to the east) - all in a nervous heat (they also happened to be allied with the French - just in case of such Austrian and German rumblings) - and they - also began to mobilize their army - which in turn = Inspired the French to do the same - which = got the Germans hopping troops to their French border - where = They (the Germans) - invaded France - by way of Belgium - which = Dragged in the British (which included Australia - New Zealand - Canada - and India - as parts of the British Empire) - due to their alliance with the Belgians - and = Soon enough - the Turks and Italians got involved (on opposite sides - the Turks siding with the Germans and Austrians - the Italians with the French and British) - which = All eventually drew in the Americans (not to mention - countries all over Africa - the Middle East - and even Asia) - and = Four years later - approximately 22 million people had lost their lives - with another 20 million wounded = The Russian Revolution had established communism in Russia = the Treaty of Versailles set up the conditions which brought Adolf Hitler to power - and = The second World War that followed = Nor - by any stretch - do the ripples end there - but - I'll leave that addition to you.

Now - we can't exactly place responsibility for the willingness of so many nations to fling an entire generation of young men into a war (which in the end - proved little more than our specie's ability to wage one) - on the bony shoulders of one misguided teenager with a handgun and a grudge ~ But = We can take note - that poor undersized Gavrilo's actions - were guided by a need to prove himself an equal in the eyes of others - and wonder = Is it really worth thinking that way?|||||||||

310

How about the other end of it then = Do you like it when anger is directed at you? Are you afraid of others anger? Have you witnessed - or been the object of - angry violence? How did it affect you? Do you believe that kind of anger is a good thing? A productive thing?

So = Are you finding you contain two - very different beliefs - about anger? Or - are they connected - meaning = The same belief?

What I mean is (other than - all thoughts are connected - as we've observed before) = Anger - is a very powerful energy in this world ~ We've all felt it - both - in ourselves - and = From others - and = Been witness to the effects it has (some of us - of course - far more than others) The thing is - that in being that witness - to both sides of anger - we can't help but recognize the kind of power - it seems - to have - whether we think about it - or not ~ So = Is what we are talking about here (or more like - what we are believing about here) = Power?

Now - the actions - of struggling for power - the beliefs of others seem to produce - may often = Appear stupid ~ Even our own actions - we sometimes recognize as sharing that label ~ But - beliefs - just on their own - aren't stupid - because = They - are based on reasons ~ The reasons themselves - may be the work of people and circumstances and judgments - you might still be tempted to call stupid (and you may have some pretty reasonable reasons for doing so) - but still = The beliefs aren't - they're just responses ~ The reasons (to which beliefs are the response to) - no matter how - you - judge them - happened - in one form or another (to be sure - intelligence - education - and exposure - or the lack there of - to other sets of beliefs - plays heavily in the equation)

One form (of reason - not necessarily to be confused with reasoning) - goes something like this = One = I didn't want to do something = Plus one = Authority got all bent out of shape - yelled and swore and threatened punishment = Equals two = I backed down and did what I was told = Three (usually requiring a few more twos to really set) = I believe anger gets things done ~ That's it - reasons - evidence - conviction - pattern - law - the courts adjourned - it doesn't even have to sit anymore.

It's not until - you examine = WHAT - you've been adding up to reach that conviction - that the question = WHY - begins to dig into the = BELIEFS - that have been doing that addition to create more of the same = Begins - to appear.

Remember that distinction we made between the words - yes and no? Which one do you think anger is? Sure = Anger is a most definite - NO = A closed fist ~ Defense is the simplest word to describe anger ~ If you're angry - you're always - defending something = Your body - your property - your rights - your ideas ~ So = In order to be motivated to defend something - you have to believe several things = First = IT (the thing you are defending) - is valuable ~ Second = IT -can be harmed ~ Third = IT - is under threat = Otherwise = You wouldn't bother to defend - IT ~ The next thing = Is how - you choose - to defend IT ~ When you defend something - do you choose the defense - you believe = Won't work? ~ No = Of course not ~ So = If you use anger - does that mean - you believe - it will work?

The point (in case you haven't arrived at it on your own) - is = Is our behavior - always based on - what we believe? In a simplified kind of way - you might say = If we don't believe we can fly - we don't jump off tall buildings ~ Unless - of course - we have some other outcome in mind - which = Would also have to be a result - of our beliefs.

So - the question - truly questioned - of what do you believe - is not just some intellectual exercise - like a conversation you might have at a party ~ What it is = Is taking apart the nuts and bolts - of how we operate ~ So - to follow that line of analogy = What if - beliefs - are like the engine of a car - and = Our experience of the whole car - is entirely based - on the performance of that engine? Experience meaning = Could you even be in a car if you didn't believe in them? Anyway = Is a car - any use - without an engine? True = You could sleep in it - or store things in it ~ But = Can it go anywhere on its own - other than downhill?

What if - to take apart the engine of your beliefs - can dramatically help you - to understand = Why - your life works the way it does? (Which you might say = Means suddenly seeing the whole car) How would that happen? What advantage would there be in knowing - shall we say = How your engine works? That's right = If we were actually talking car engines here - that kind of knowing - would enable you to fix problems - or get the thing running at its best ~ Do you think it could be the same with your beliefs?

Now there's a very good point = To fix your beliefs - would mean = There was something wrong with them - and = That would require changing them - and = The only way to really change them = Would be - to no longer believe them ~ So = What's the problem with that? Sure = You - believe them - because - to you = They don't need fixing = They're true.

Ah - but are they?

[[[[[[[[[Doctor Dude's Dictionary - word nineteen - Awesome:

Words - for all they are printed out in dictionaries as having specific definitions - regularly - change their meanings through time (officially termed - a neologism - which also covers the creation of a brand new word) Most often - and quite appropriately - it's a particular function of youth culture - to implement those changes.

As all of us have gone about the business of inventing ourselves - especially in contrast to the world of our parents (or just the world straight up) - language (which you could call the fabric of culture) - gets cut into new styles (like clothing) - the better to express that invention ~ That's nothing new however = It's been going on for thousands of years - particularly in cities ~ Not a single word we use today - that has not gone through that system of change somehow - and one vital element of that system - is what is called = Colloquialisms ~ Better known as = Slang.

That being said = There is a word - whose reinvention occurred some time in the 1980s –

312

and= Though the action of its regular use has watered down the original meaning considerably - it's always struck me as a very clever adaptation - that = When something strikes you as very cool (meaning truly impressive of course - cool being one of those transformed words) - then it must be = Awesome.

Awesome (if you're sticking to the dictionary) - means = To inspire awe ~ Which is to say = Some characteristic of what you're witnessing or experiencing causes you to feel the emotion of awe ~ So - obviously - awesome is a very cool word indeed ~ But - even more obviously - awe - is the word it's pointing at - and so = Is really the more important one to understand.

Awe - is a unique form of multilayered emotion - in that = In order to experience it - several emotions conspire together to stop you in your tracks - and = Press you to undergo them all simultaneously ~ Wonder is in there (that wide-eyed gasp of barely believe it) Then - there's reverence (which is that raised to another level and blown away by big love feeling - which launches new religions and starry eyed fans at the backstage door) Those two - are tempered (or adjusted to something like ground level) - by humility (which often drags along a bit of self-esteem questioning - a lack of understanding may be apt to poke at us) And that - leads straight into another emotion (that is not necessarily required to complete the experience of awe - except that it also represents another whole use of the word) - which is = Dread ~ The dread that slithers through awe - is the fear of authority kind - where respect - or devotion - or blind obedience - is edged with - or thoroughly squeezed by - fear ~ That's the kind of awe that is all about the use - misuse - or sheer presence - of power ~ Whereas the preceding parts are really about the sheer power of presence.

You've got to admit - there is a lot packed in there for a word with only three letters ~ No wonder it wanted more airplay in the cultural vocabulary ~ Its popularity - may have demoted it from the majestic peaks of linguistic grandeur where it once sat so frighteningly enthroned - but - maybe what's really happened = Is that wealth has now been shared out with the masses - since now - just about anything reasonably good = Can be awesome.]]]]]]]]]

Let's go right back to one of the first things we talked about - which is = The space of question - or the = I don't know ~ Remember that?

Okay - okay = I'm sure you do ~ So - we'll walk right in = Is a belief - something - you know? That is to say - something - your experience holds some kind of proof of? Yes = Very good = There are some beliefs - that are based - on faith - or trust ~ But aren't those beliefs still based on some experience - some persons words - or actions - or a book - some source of information - that - you trust? And - of course - there is some belief present - that allows you - to trust those things too = Isn't there? So - again = Are beliefs - something you know?

Remember that - We Have A Totally Important Function - line? What did I suggest that function might be? That's the one = Happiness ~ What if - the key to happiness - is = To bring to question - every single last belief you possess?

Now - the reason I would say such a thing - is not to claim - that all - or even any - of your beliefs are false ~ But - I can claim - with complete certainty - that = Not one single thing - any of us believe - is based on - total 100% complete across the universe and beyond information ~ To question a belief - is not necessarily - to replace it with another ~ What it is = Is to make room - for a more complete understanding - of the reason - for that belief - and = The results - we get from believing it ~ After all - that's what beliefs are for ~ What would be the point of having them - if it wasn't to do something with them? Just like the engine of that car we talked about = If you don't want to drive somewhere - you don't need an engine.

Okay ~ Enough of that ~ Let's dig into a belief - preferably one that has - issues - connected to it - and find out - how - it affects happiness.

We'll use Michael here.

So Mike = Obviously I'm messing with you - and I do appreciate your good humor about it ~ But - there's a reason for it ~ Do you know what the reason is? Exactly = To get you to examine your beliefs ~ The first question - in such an exam - is always ~ Is it true? So = What do you think?

Alright - I see you've allowed some doubt to seep in - but - basically - what you've been saying = Is people disrespect you when they call you Mike? Alright ~ Again = Is that true?

Yeah = I know you - more or less - still think so ~ So - how about this = Do you know - what - they - think?

No = Most of us don't seem to be capable of that ~ So = You're not really - sure - they disrespect you? Alright = What happens when you - think - they disrespect you? So = Why do you feel bad? Does that mean – ' other people - making - you feel bad - or = A belief - about people calling you Mike (that is - a belief about who Michael is) - that makes you feel bad? What would it be like - if - you didn't have that belief? Yeah = I know you do ~ But = What if - you didn't? Sure = That's it = You wouldn't mind when people called you Mike ~ What if - in fact - some people call you that - because they like you - or - they think it's the friendly thing to do? Again = Can you - know - what's going on in other people's minds?

Alright - that's really a pretty simple example of - exposing - a problem causing belief - and - part of its potential solution ~ Even if it hasn't seemed simple to Michael ~ Until now that is ~ Unless it still doesn't ~ But - a problem (or more like - its solution) - never does appear simple (especially ones we'd be more inclined to label serious) - until = You apply - a different - way of thinking - to solving it - than the one - that created it.

That sounds rather familiar - doesn't it? What if - I'm repeating - that familiar statement (or - the turned around version I just used) - because = It's so true - it's like getting smacked in the face with a shovel? That is - it invites that smack - if - we continue to ignore - it - as a sensible operating system ~ When - we do that ignoring - you might say - we deserve the smack.

314

With that in mind - let me repeat - my reduced version - of Dr. Einstein's' famous statement = **"You can't solve a problem by using the same thinking that created the problem in the first place."**

What if - one way you can get around that - same thinking - is by applying - those same questions (the ones I put to Mike just now) - to absolutely anything that bothers you - any problem - any situation - and so = Open up a new solution - because = That - is a different way - of thinking? That would be pretty useful - wouldn't it?

See - the question is - and always is = Do you want to be happy? Every single moment of our lives is the same question ~ The beliefs we have - that keep us from being happy - are always a judgment - that says = What's going on (or did or could) - is wrong ~ That is - wrong - in the sense - that something else would be better - according to our judgment ~ The real question though - is = How do we know? How can we - know - that - what (did - could) - is going on - is not going to be - the cause - of something better? Do you know what the future holds? Can you say - for instance = That getting your bike stolen - would never - lead you to meeting a person you'd fall in love with? Or = Getting evicted from your apartment - is an impossible way - of finding the job you've always dreamed of? How can you know for sure - what you might learn - or find - or experience - because - of anything? That's right = You can't.

So - the real question is what? Bingo = Do you want to be happy?

|||||||| Self Interest:

If - you have a family - live in a neighborhood - a town - a state - a country - attend a school - belong to a team - a club - have a group of friends - in short = Take part and interact in the lives of other people - or = If you run a business - a school - a government agency - an actual government itself (imagine that) - then = You need to realize (need - being used from a happiness promoting point of view) - that every choice of behavior you make = Affects - influences - impacts - and takes place in connection with - other people ~ Maybe one - maybe millions - maybe (maybe even not maybe) - all of them - all the time.

The condition of this planet is - in a word = Interactive ~ And = As systems of communication - technology - trade - and - more interaction - become increasingly global in scale = It becomes more and more unmistakably seriously valuably necessary (to hazard an opinion or two) - to recognize how no single group - or even individual - operates independent of the rest of the world.

It's easy enough to see how a statement like - what is best for me - multiplies out to all the other people directly - or indirectly - involved ~ When the level of that statement reaches the numbers represented by - what is best for our country - that word - best - is nothing near an accurate measurement - if = It doesn't consider - national well being - as dependent on = Global well-being.

The trouble is = That recognition has yet to become a wholesale purchase - for the very simple reason (like any other form of recognition) = It's an unfamiliar concept - a strange face in the crowd (despite the fact it's been hanging around staring at us for some time now) IT (adopting such a habit of viewing interdependence) - takes practice ~ Just like learning a new language - that practice starts out as a translation - a kind of converting one form of recognition into another - until = The recognition is instant - second nature (as it's called) - no longer a delay between symbol and meaning = You can now - even think - in this new language ~ And = You haven't just increased the number of people you can communicate with - you've opened up to whole new cultures - literature - art - belief systems - opportunities - adventure - friends.

The requirement = IS - to learn that new language (figuratively speaking) - to speak it fluently ~ The alternative = IS - to continue shouting at each other - without ever knowing = Were talking about the same thing.|||||||||

To return to the idea of neural nets = You remember them - don't you? How do they work again? That's right = They construct a kind of cellular map - or memory based navigation system - from the repetition of related experiences - and the thinking that accompanies those experiences - in order to make it easier for us - to know - how to respond - when similar circumstances arise ~ So = How long do you suppose that takes? Not all that long actually ~ In fact = If you consciously - and consistently - repeat a particular idea to yourself - and the behavior that goes with it - say - something like = Declaring ge-sund-heit (that familiar German/Yiddish word/phrase that wishes good health) = Every time you hear someone sneeze = For twenty one days straight = You're well on your way to creating a life long habit ~ Do it for forty = And it's definitely stuck ~ Of course - in that case - it would mean being around a lot of sneezing people ~ So you might want to pick something else ~ But - don't - believe - me = Try it.

The other thing about this mental set up - we call belief - is that = A belief - is always (that's always - no exceptions) = A limitation ~ Meaning = When you believe something - is one way - then = There is no room - for it - to be another.

Now - there is a certain usefulness in that kind of certainty ~ Like when you drive down a highway - believing - the signs that say where it leads - are really accurate ~ At least it's useful - if they are accurate ~ Our lives are full of that kind of belief ~ They would be entirely different if everything had no such certainty to it ~ Of course - that very statement itself - describes a belief structure about the nature of reality and our relationship with it ~ The key word being - EVERYTHING ~ We seldom - if ever - question a belief (or even consider it to be one) - when it fits into the category of governing - a thing relationship - like - hammers and nails - your butt and that chair ~ But - that's not to say that no one does ~ There are some pretty wild experiments going on - out there - that seem to cast some very strong doubts on how well - our beliefs - about reality - do the job of describing it.

So = Why would someone perform an experiment about - how - reality - works? Yeah = We appear - to be surrounded by the stuff - made of the stuff - dependent on the stuff ~ We sure seem to like stuff - buy stuff - eat stuff - want more stuff ~ Could it be - that - we

- believe - that knowing how - stuff - works - will give us power over it? Or - is it that we just - think (that is - believe) - that reality - is - stuff?

Either way - why do people conduct any kind of experiment? Sure = They want to learn about how (I'll use that word one more time) - STUFF - works - what it's made of - what it's capable of doing - and - how that doing - or capability - might be of service to us ~ Very commendable really ~ But actually - before anyone performs an experiment - they have a theory - a hypotheses - or some kind of notion of how the thing will turn out ~ Is a theory a belief? No = It's not - is it? Isn't it more = A belief in question - or - you might say - a possible belief - trying to become - believable? Do you think that maybe that's how we work? Meaning = Do we construct our picture - or experience - of reality - out of theories - we think - we have proof of - and so have forgotten - they are really - just theories? Does that mean = The only thing that can be - real - to us - is what we - believe is real - according to that proof we've collected? Do you think that might be why - we continue to try to solve our problems - by using the thinking - that created them in the first place?

So your assignment is - to question your beliefs ~ No - don't worry ~ I don't mean all of them - just the things that make you angry ~ Next time you find yourself getting angry at someone - ask yourself = Is what I believe to be happening - really true? Which means = Can I prove it? Now - prove - means = Beyond a shadow of a doubt ~ So - open that question just as far as you can stretch it ~ Another question - that might assist that stretch is = Is it possible that the person - that seems to be causing my anger - is really acting on beliefs - different from the one - I believe to be the case? Or = What might those beliefs be? Then = If - or when (keep pushing the - if - and you will arrive at - when) - you find that doubt (the one that may or may not have a shadow) - ask = What would it be like - if I didn't believe the thought - that's causing my anger? And = There you go = That's the real million dollar question = What would - you feel like - if you didn't believe - that thought? Twenty one days of that - and who knows what your life may look like ~ That is - if you keep breathing.

N.P.U. - Chapter Nineteen - Peptides?

So - about that gland in your head - which is to say = That gland - in all our heads - called = The Hypothalamus - which = May sound a bit like some obscure Greek island - but (instead of being somewhere in the Aegean Sea) = It's located a couple of inches behind your eyebrows - just forward of the center of your brain ~ Its job - is to respond - to your responses - as reported to it - by your neurons - which means = Your thoughts - or - what you think about - and - what your thoughts do - with what your senses are telling you ~ In other words = Think something - anything = Oh no - I forgot to do the homework ~ Or = Cool - I aced that quiz ~ Or smell = Chocolate cake baking ~ Hear = Mosquitoes buzzing ~ See = Cute girl or boy walking by ~ The response - the hypothalamus makes - is to match the thought signals it gets - with the corresponding emotional chemical - it then manufactures out of amino acids (better known as proteins) - and proceeds to pump those chemicals into the bloodstream wholesale ~ When those chemicals reach your cells = They dock - or plug into - receptor sites - located on the outer cell walls - to create a physical sensation - exactly the same as psychoactive drugs (such as morphine and heroin) - work at the cellular level - and - what we call these thought prompted sensations - is = Emotions ~ Or - that other word that seems to keep appearing = Feelings (although you might remember there being more to that word - from a previous interruption)

What that means = Are three things = First = Our emotions (physically) - are chemically based ~ Second = Our established neural nets - are responsible for the types of signals that arrive at the hypothalamus - and so = Produce which chemical combinations - to produce which emotions ~ Third = Thoughts (or more accurately - the neural maps laid down by earlier thoughts) - are behind all of it ~ So - by a process of simple addition = It's very clear - that how we feel (is more often than not - if not always) - the result of - what we have thought = In the past.

More than likely - there are deeper levels - to this feeling experience - that science has yet to - and chemicals do not - explain ~ But = That parallel with drugs - is key - to the understanding of this mood pharmacy we're operating ~ To begin with = Studying how the opiate (meaning - derived from the opium poppy) - morphine works in the body was what led neuroscientist - Candace Pert - to isolate and identify these - neuropeptides (peptides for short - or those protein chains produced by the hypothalamus - in case you dozed off there) - which naturally led to the connected discovery = Of the receiving end of the process - or = The hundreds of receptor sites on the outside of cells - which = Are each specifically designed - to accept - only one variety - of peptide - meaning = Each particular chemical match - or trigger - for each particular emotion - has one particular type of receptor (multiplied trillions of times perhaps - but - just as specific as locks and keys) Knowing that - it follows (equally naturally) = That being able to view what kind of peptide receptor sites are most numerous - in any given area of cells (like say… the part of our brain that governs what our eyes focus on - which happen to be covered in a certain kind of pleasure receptor - the same type by the way - that opiates dock on) - makes available - a kind of mapping technique - of the emotions that are - most important - to us (In other words = What are you looking at?)

The reason is = We reproduce those cellular characteristics - that get the most attention ~ Meaning = What's (again) - most important to us - is what gets preference - in that natural process of cellular reproduction that's going on all the time ~ So - what happens is = The new cells - have more of those receptors - that get the most use - and fewer - of the rest ~ What we're talking here (simply identified by numbers) = Is a repetition of that rather ugly word - used earlier = Addiction.

One working definition - of the word addiction - is = A habit - you cannot control ~ In the peptide world - the word habit - could just as easily be replaced by - preference - attraction - compulsion - desire - dependence - and plenty of other words ~ The thing is = At the level of neural net based peptide production signals - and the resulting form of cellular receptors over time = Repetition - is what builds the system - because = That's how the system was designed to be built.

The simple beauty of these incredibly complex bodies of ours - is their awe-inspiring drive - to respond - with life - to what ever they are given ~ They adapt and conform to an endless number of stimuli = Be it on the physical level - as nutrients - chemicals - viruses - pathogens - exercise - abuse - neglect - or - you name it ~ And then = There are (what's appearing more and more to quite possibly be) - the first and foremost level of response producers (if not the entire shebang) - thoughts - beliefs - and attitudes - and still - these bodies arrange themselves around what ever that condition is - as loyal to us (meaning our consciousness) - as paint to a wall.

Of course - you're thinking - that paint chips and peels and fades and has to be repainted - and = You're right - and as such = Our cells follow a similar procedure of renewal ~ Then again = There are those conditions - like cancer and disease - where the paint - apparently - turns against the wall - until one or the other is destroyed ~ Yet - even under such extremes - these bodies still respond and renew ~ In fact - there isn't a single cell (aside from neurons) - in your body - that existed much more than a year ago ~ You don't have a single skin cell you had about a month ago ~ All of your organs have been replaced every few months ~ Even your skeleton participates in that annual renewal program ~ So - actually - at the cellular level - the only (let's call it) - consistent evidence of a physical identity you have retained throughout your life - are parts of your brain - and even that - is still a subject of some debate.

So why - if you've had nearly as many new bodies as birthdays - do you still have things like scars - or limp from old injuries - or have any repetitive physical problems at all? Or - for that matter = Pretty much look the way you did last Summer - especially when you're an adult? And even more mysteriously = Age at all - or - the $64,000 question = Die?

||||||||| Grow young?

What if - we didn't have to grow old? After all - we are constantly producing new cells - and = In experiments with small groups of cells (specifically - guinea pig hearts - which means cells of a type that would normally only live a few weeks or months and be replaced - though granted - they would - normally - do it inside those cute little guinea pigs) - where simple - yet very specific conditions of water pH were maintained = Those cells - lived for decades - and only died - because of an error in maintaining those conditions - rather than some pre-programmed lifespan of their own?

What if - aging - is up to us? Or - in a very particular physical sense (not to ignore the fact of it being entirely dependent on mental conditions) = What if - how we - choose - to maintain the interior terrain of our bodies (most especially pH levels - which completely includes the nature of our thinking) - is key to mastering that process?|||||||||

Well - obviously - or not - genetics are involved - or that DNA stuff - that's usually referred to as - the blueprint for life (not that - we - have gotten anyway near the bottom of figuring out all the mysteries of DNA) So - when cells divide into new cells = They know what they're supposed to do and look like and so on ~ But - those cells (the ones you're carrying around right now) - weren't in that accident you had (provided it was long enough ago) = They weren't there when you sliced your thumb open - or broke your leg ~ So why - would they repeat the symptoms of a condition - they did not participate in?

Okay - you may have noticed - back there - that I mentioned - your neurons (or at least some of them) - have stuck with you - and so = Represent - the only part of your body - that hasn't been replaced continuously ~ However - there is a relatively new scientific conclusion = That neurons are actually being produced from stem cells throughout our lives - which has taken over from the old idea - of one set = Much like adult teeth - which declares just the one shot at reliable chewing into old age ~ Either way - neurons - appear - to be the only cells we carry around - that are capable (according to standard conditions) - of a lifespan resembling our own ~ Which of course = Includes their ability - to expand and contract - connect - and disconnect - or be discarded - as learning and change occur ~ So - that means = The same cells remaining - but - not - those cells - remaining the same.

Certain neural nets - the ones most often relied on to report to us = The True - conditions of reality (you know - money doesn't grow on trees - solid objects are solid - pimples happen - and on and on - in a slightly sarcastic tone - in case you hadn't noticed) - do - remain the same ~ They = Are (in a sense - what we have given permission to be) - the hard wired circuit boards - into which all the rest of those organic electronics of learning have been plugged ~ Those circuits - are what we call = The World ~ And so = Exactly like - the expectation - that biting into your favorite candy bar is going to produce the same results of flavor and texture as the last time you ate one = Those hardwired neural nets - are expecting a certain situation - of reality - from your body - that fits - with the progression of life experiences it has undergone.

‖‖‖‖‖‖‖ Stem What?

You are perhaps already familiar with the term - stem cells - particularly as it is teamed up with those popular buzzwords - research - and - controversy - possibly because of such sources as that great dispenser of pure unbiased truth (tongue firmly jammed in cheek) = The evening news.

But = Do you know what they are? Or = Why - researching them - is good - bad - evil - or miraculous?

The answer (or some part there of) - is = Stem cells - are cells present in the body - which = Have the ability to divide (and so reproduce themselves - the way all cells do) - an unlimited (theoretically) - number of times (very different from other cells) - where each new cell (the product of that division) - has the potential to differentiate as (or change to) - a specialized tissue cell - such as - heart - liver - skin - or intestinal tissues - and even (the ever popular) - neuron.

Stem cells - are broken (to say - divided - might be confusing) - into two categories ~ First = Embryonic - which are the very first cells present in an embryo (that beginning stage in every creature's life - just after the egg is fertilized) - and = Are responsible for generating all the specialized cells required to build that new body ~ Second = Adult stem cells - which are a small number of cells located in various tissues and organs - that = Do the job of maintaining and repairing those same locations in which they are found.

In a sense = Stem cells are the jack of all trades in the cellular world (good name Jack - don't you think?) They - become - what's needed ~ A type of adaptation - or conversion - that is nothing short of amazing - or - one might say = Intelligent ~ Certainly such - fix it abilities - are well respected (and often rewarded) - in this world of keeping technology up and running ~ And that = Is why they are the subject of extensive research.

How do they do it = Is the question ~ Somehow - genetic codes are switched on (or off - as the case may be) - and suddenly = A cell that's been doing little more than just hanging out and absorbing nutrients - splits in half and sends one half off to be a busy little neuron (or what ever else is needed) Work that out - and = A long list of possible health benefits trots right along behind (such as - convincing immune systems to accept tissue and organ transplants - for one)

The other - research goal = Is growing specialized cells - heart - lung - muscle - brain tissues - you name it - and = Patch up people - who otherwise - wouldn't be (for over thirty years now stem cells are the key feature in the leukemia treatment known as a bone marrow transplant) Of course = That's one of those - controversy points - since = That - growing - is basically (or at least perceived to be) - one step away from cloning (or reproducing exact copies of) - whole human beings - and = All the science fiction and belief structure abuses such an ability raises in people's minds - fuels that discord.

Another - unhappy mind element = Is the way in which stem cells for research are - harvested - for the work they do ~ They are grown - the same as you or I were - from the union of an egg and a sperm - only = This happens in a Petri dish in a lab somewhere -

with the necessary ingredients having been willingly donated (most often for the purpose of in vitro fertilization - or the implanting of a living embryo in the uterus of a woman who has been unable to conceive a baby for whatever reason) - and = That use of human life (the embryo is destroyed in the cell gathering process) - is upsetting to some beliefs ~ Oddly enough - some of those - human life protecting believers - are also - great believers - in warfare as a problem-solving technique (go figure)   It's not that I mean to insult anyone's beliefs ~ It's just that = Saving life - is what stem cells are designed to do ~ Beyond that = Slicing up what that means as an idea - is everyone's - choice.||||||||||

See - in theory - all that physical stuff - that makes up your body - is nothing but an out picturing - a projection - like a movie - of what your - learned thinking - has been up to - and your consciousness - has been watching - as the audience of that movie ~ In that world (the one that accepts the theory just described) - it's what you think - or - again = What you've thought = That continues to reproduce your physical form in the shape of its experience.

Now - it may be rather difficult to accept such a theory as reality - or even = That it makes sense to be called a theory at all ~ However - in that - physical out picturing (if you will) - it is rather interesting to note = That the basic rules - that govern the cellular organization of the information access routes in the brain (neural nets) - and - the corresponding chemical emotional reactions - our brains are engaged in delivering this very instant (neuropeptides) - are centered completely on - the thoughts we think - including - our ability - to rearrange - those same systems {{Go ahead read that again}}

It's really only an extension - of that same story (thoughts - or consciousness - directing the organic construction of our brains) - to see our thoughts - as responsible - for more than just thinking and feeling - because = If - they are designing - the physical shape of those two largest elements of our experience - learning - and emotion - then = Why would it be such a great stretch - to recognize them - as the architects - of our health and fitness as well - or even - our entire bodies - full stop?

|||||||||| DNA 101:

The function of DNA - or deoxyribonucleic acid - is (as you yourself probably remember hearing recently) - often described in a shorthand way as = The blueprint for life ~ The reason being = That it contains the design codes - or building plans - for growing and maintaining a body - the way a blueprint illustrates the details of construction involved in creating a building - and as such - the blueprint description fits.

And yet - for all the amazing amount of DNA we contain (there is approximately six feet of it in every cell - which means - stretched end to end - your DNA would wrap around the planet millions of times) - apparently - something like 97% of it - goes unused (and yes - that is a repetition of information delivered previously) - which = Leads to (or connects - gestures at - stumbles around in) - the key oversight in the common understanding of DNA - which = Is the idea - that DNA is the determiner - or decision-maker - of how everything our bodies do on a cellular level - turns out ~ Yes = DNA is the reason you look like your parents ~ Just the same as houses in a suburban neighborhood look basically the same - when the blueprints used in their construction are the same ~ There's no getting around that little bit of design limitation ~ So - in that fashion - DNA provides the guidelines for your growth - and certain physical capabilities or weaknesses - but = It is - not - the cause of those capabilities or weaknesses showing up as conditions in your body's life ~ Instead = It is merely the potential for those conditions ~ Your cells may contain the gene that is associated with obesity (otherwise known as being dangerously over weight) - or developing certain kinds of cancer - or any number of actually desirable traits - and = You may still go through life with none of those conditions ever occurring in your body.

The simplest means of clearing up - the DNA as cause misunderstanding - is the very simple recognition - that = Exactly as is the case on any construction site = The blueprint does not read itself - nor does it deliver the materials - or - build the building.

What - causes - DNA to turn on and off its specific design directions - or codes - are signals from the environment in which cells live (otherwise known as the body - that dynamic community of 50 to 70 trillion cells we go walking around in) - and only then - does that blueprint come into use ~ The signaling devices are proteins - or more specifically = Different combinations of the twenty amino acids that are the ingredients of proteins ~ They work as communicators - both outside (you'll recall those peptide things produced by the hypothalamus gland inside your head) - and inside the cell ~ As well as being the basic material from which new cells are constructed.

Aside from the last few statements hinting that = We all require proper nutrition to provide us with the correct amounts of amino acids to maintain health - they also mean = That communication (that signaling of consciousness to DNA) - is just like any other type of communication that goes on anywhere = It's an interaction ~ And = Like any other kind of interaction - interpretation (which adds up to - perception) - is the (that's - Thee) - key element - of working with what's going on in and around us (which means - that process of experience- or learning - to figure out - what all the sensory information we take in - means) As it turns out (or certainly looks to be turning out) = Perception - is not just a factor - in cellular growth and function - but more like = A giant factor.

Of course - we all know - that in the process of our experience of life - or our learning - certain attitudes - opinions - fears - preferences - desires - prejudices - and - Beliefs - form in our minds ~ It's the product of those thought structures (in the form of proteins sent by the hypothalamus) - that end up as the job site foremen reading the DNA blueprint ~ That is - in the sense of choosing which parts of the blueprint to pay attention to ~ Sure = There are other environmental influences - such as nutrition - toxins - stress - the good - the bad - and the unexpected ~ But - according to emerging understandings of cellular biology = The most consistent cellular reproduction influence (at least in the life of these human organisms) - is the interior environment we call = Perception ~ And that means = What and how we think - may have as much - or more - affect on the ongoing lives of our cells - as those unique double twists of DNA our parents wove together special for us all.||||||||||

You'll notice - I used the phrase - in theory - when I dove into metaphysical physicality a moment ago ~ That is - theoretically - you noticed ~ And now = You're firing the neural nets that will bring that notice to mind ~ Which is to say = You already have ~ So anyway = This now - may be the right now - to examine that word theory a bit deeper - for the sake of noticing - which end of the theoretical funnel - we're looking through.

A theory - is a construction of ideas ~ Therefore = It can be a very flimsy construction - in our skyscraper society that demands solid proof on which to build its hopes (or plans - hopes tending to fall within the same linguistic category as theories) And yet - other flimsy ideas - not called theories - not even called ideas in fact - are in constant circulation among us - quite accepted and unquestioned ~ Paper money makes a prime example ~ Viewed purely as paper - a one dollar note - and a twenty - have an equal value ~ Perhaps even less - if compared to that fresh role of toilet paper you found under the sink sometime earlier ~ At least in that particular circumstance of need ~ But still - the difference of value between - that one - and that twenty - no matter that it's only - an idea of value - make it very simple to choose = Which one you'd rather find laying on the ground ~ The same - ideas of value - hold true for the stock market - the laws that govern us - and - our rights - to personal property.

But theories - it's true - do appear - to be a different kind of idea - within our ideas - because = They have not yet passed the test of entering into acceptable form - usually referred to as = Proven ~ Theories - are like the plans for an expedition - a treasure map - a puzzle - to be solved - by the future ~ All scientific discoveries - advances - breakthroughs - failures - and disasters - begin with one ~ Even if it is as simple as = What if - I put this - on top of this? Because = That is what they are = What ifs = Spaces ~ To begin with at least ~ And then they are generally packed full of - hopes - for solid proof ~ But - it's that beginning - that space - that - what if potential in superposition - which is important right here - because (you guessed it) = It's a feeling.

So - there are two levels - to these strings - these gravitons - these branes - parallel universes - zero point energy - and - form may be nothing but consciousness in action theories - which are - on level one = Just that = Theories - frameworks of ideas - nailed up with other ideas - and plastered over with more - whose only real purpose - or benefit - so far - if not always - are the feelings they produce (which runs us headlong into the theory that feelings are our core motivation in life) Of course - those resulting feelings - to the theories in question - are split along the usual love or fear divide of whether we agree with them or not ~ In that = The stronger we respond with - a yes - or - a no = The more extreme is the difference between which peptides are produced - or the type of electro-magnetic field that is generated ~ So - one of the key words - or points - at this point - is that word = Agree.

One of the main handicaps - all those theories share for being potentially agreeable - is the ability to prove them - is equally theoretical ~ One side of that point is = Technology (which is also dependent on theory) - hasn't caught up yet ~ Which means - the other side is = Our questions - haven't caught up yet ~ Question/theory/technology - move in space - the same as everything else - in the sense of = An ability to expand - to grow ~ It's a type of economy really - a supply and demand interaction ~ When there is a strong enough demand - like say… the Second World War = A whole new technology - based on brand-new theories - spawned by entirely new questions - gets cracked out of the shell of possibility - and - in a very short time = Nuclear weapons appear - where they had been impossible before ~ So (no matter how - you feel - about nuclear weapons) - perhaps now - you feel - the edges of that space - where brand-new experience - is suspended - in potential.

And that - is the other level (the second one - if we stick to my oversimplified suggestion that there are just two - the first being - that they are theories) = The possibility - that those theories (the ones I listed - beginning with strings and ending with form equals consciousness) - are actually describing - how reality works (although there are certain points of competition among them which cause complications to that being the case) And since = Reality - is apparently working all the time - that level offers - the potential - of mastering - how to participate in a relationship with reality - whose benefit is = The possibility - of a more enjoyable reality - all the time ~ Because = That's the demand = That's the call ~ Maybe the faintest jingle in you ~ Maybe ringing off the hook ~ But - either way = It's the question - that's responsible for the demand - because = Change - is the answer - or the result - the supply - the outcome ~ Can't get - IT - without the question - and that = Is really all a theory is = A question.

But - enough of theories - and questions - and space ~ It's time for some real solid chewy evidence = Don't you think?

Class Twenty - Compassion?

BREATHE (Uh-uh-uh = Where you going? This will only take a minute - and = Could last all day - and = Who knows what will happen in that day - that it will improve just spectacularly.)

Okay = Anybody do the assignment? Yes? No? What helped you to do it? What made it difficult to do? So = It requires willingness - to change your mind about being angry? Did you uncover any reasons why you wouldn't have that kind of willingness? Is feeling stronger - or tougher - when you're angry - one of them? What about when it worked - what was that like? What changed? Did it take a kind of weight off you? Did it make you feel freer? Was it up to you - how it worked? Is it still?

While we're thinking about this anger thing = What is the most common reaction - people have - when you get angry at them?

Yup = That's usually the one = They get angry back ~ Why is that?

Well - yeah = It's a kind of attack = It's painful ~ No one really wants anger directed at them ~ Unless they're looking for an excuse for a fight ~ So = If you are responding to anger - with anger - are you defending yourself? But = Didn't we decide (or at least consider) - that anger - is a defense - just on its own? So = Does that make an attack a defense? Or - a defense - an attack?

Yeah - I know = I seem to be twisting words around ~ But - there's always - a different way - of understanding the things that go on in this life - if = You take them out of the order - you habitually observe them in - and = Turn them around.

For instance = When we talked about Michael feeling disrespected by people calling him Mike = What was the way he wanted to feel? Sure = Respected ~ So = What is - the reason - he wants to feel respected? Yup = It's that happy thing again ~ So = He's placed - a condition - on being happy - that says = When people call him Mike - he won't be happy?

I know - this Michael or Mike thing - is getting a bit old ~ Just think how Mike must feel ~ But - hang with me ~ Its very familiarity - will help you see what I'm talking about.

Alright = Is Michael - respecting himself - if he gets unhappy - about the Mike thing?

326

Yeah = You could say = He is demanding respect = It's true ~ But = Is he - respecting - himself? In other words = Is he giving himself - the thing - he wants from other people?

Look at it like this = What is it Michael wants? Respect right? And why? Happiness = Exactly ~ So = If - what he wants is happiness - is he respecting that desire - by making himself - unhappy? Is it up to other people - for him - to feel respect for himself? So = Could it be - what's really going on is = He's giving up his own respect for himself - by making the power to choose how he feels - something that's up to the behavior of others - and then = Being unhappy about it - when they choose the behavior - that uses the power - he's given them?

See = It's turned around that way ~ The cause and effect are reversed ~ The blame = That thing - we use all the time - to take happiness away from ourselves - isn't working the way we thought (that is - the way we are used to thinking) What if - you can turn around any reason - for anger or upset - the same way = If - you are willing - to look into it far enough - to take responsibility - for your own happiness?

In fact = What if - it goes even deeper - and = We actually attract - everything - that happens to us - good - bad - or boring? What if - that's why the subatomic world - appears - so different - because - that's where that attraction interaction - is taking place - and the reason - we don't see it on our level (or readily make sense out of such an idea) = Is that we only see the finished product (so to speak - as I am want to add) - and not = Its raw materials?

[[[[[[[[[**Wise crack:** In reference to living in fear and worry - Mark Twain (Samuel Clemens) - once said = "Some of the worst things in my life never happened"]]]]]]]]]]

While that idea goes pin balling around your neural nets - let's look at another example of upset - a really - severe one - this time ~ I mean - really - really - severe.

Let's say - you were held at knife point by several men and repeatedly raped ~ Now I'm not just talking to you girls either - such things can happen to boys as well ~ But - the point is = What I'm talking about - is something truly terrible - something no one should have to undergo ~ That's what I meant when I said - really severe ~ But = Let's say - it did - happen - to you ~ No shoulds - rights - wrongs - or anything - but = It happened ~ What is your reaction?

Okay = Those are all reactions we'd call normal = Angry - ashamed - disgusted - vengeful - depressed ~ No surprises there ~ And fair enough = You've been through a real nightmare ~ The question is (yup - there's always that question - isn't there) = What are you going - to choose - to feel next?

Yes = I know = It's the kind of experience that doesn't seem to have any other option - but = To go on feeling bad ~ Believe me - I'm not trying to make light of such a thing ~ Perhaps you're even feeling upset or insulted that I've chosen such an example ~ Who is this - this - man - to be questioning reactions to a crime like that?

Of course you'd have such a reaction - according to the world - where such things are possible ~ So - of course - in that same world - it's likely you'd be in a state of shock for some time - or fear - distrust - any number of unhappy (if not miserable) - ways of being ~ But = Do you have to be unhappy? Again = I know the pressure to be unhappy would be huge - or seemingly uncontrollable ~ But = Whose choice is it?

In fact = This seems like the right moment to check in on the idea of what's controllable and what isn't - with an = {{{**Inventory Time**}}}

Let's look at those guys that assaulted you ~ Let's say that you didn't know any of them ~ Or - even if you did = Do you know what went on inside them - that would drive them to such an act? Could they have been brutalized in their own pasts? Were they just following some peer pressure gone out of control - they never would have acted out on their own? Were they full of their own fears and anger - that - they were trying to rise above - by having power over someone else? Were they on drugs? Was it just an unfeeling kind of joke to them - because of any or all or more of those other things?

Now - I'm not saying that any of those things are justifiable excuses for such behavior or remotely any such thing - only that = They could be reasons - or causes - for - why - it happened ~ See - the moment you observe someone - that has (or seems to - have) - done you harm - as just another human being - like yourself - with forces inside of them - the same as inside you - no matter - that they may be far more extreme in some way = You open up a possibility - for your own return - to happiness - because = You step outside the borders - you've constructed - to limit it ~ It's called - to put it into a word - that of course - can't fully cover the whole idea - but will try = COMPASSION.

|||||||||| Doctor Dude's Dictionary - word twenty - Gratitude:

Thank you - is a phrase mirrored in every language ~ Not just because it is the polite thing to say - drilled in by the world's mothers = What do you say to the nice man dear? But - because = That same reflection expresses a universal form of emotional energy known as = Gratitude.

To be grateful (the adjective form of gratitude) - is to be in a state of appreciating - or an awareness - of having benefited from something received - something pleasurable - agreeable - satisfying ~ And yet - that word appreciating - is really an action of judgment - where the quality or value of something - is weighed against other opinions or understandings of quality and value ~ Gratitude - in true full swing - is a momentum - inspired by appreciation - but running on its own steam (as any momentum would - since that word means the force of movement when it's moving) Which is to say - an energy - that is an effect - the product of a cause - which produces - while in the process of being that effect - its own cause - or sustaining energy ~ Simple as rolling a stone down a hill really = Once you get it moving - that is.

As far as gratitude goes (both distance and definition) - it's really all done with mirrors - in that = It moves - as a response to a response to a response ~ Given the inspiration for it is strong enough (a large enough stone) - and the willingness to allow it - is not obstructed by other attitudes (a steep enough hill with a clear path) - it can just roll on and on - one hill to the next - as a cycle of generosity or reciprocation (meaning mutual return) - receiving out of giving and giving out of receiving ~ A gratuity - or tip - is such a thing = Especially if the service it rewards was given gratis - or freely without expectation of payment - which = Is an action of being gratuitous - which = Gratifies - or causes a pleasurable satisfaction on either side of that giving - that anyone would be grateful for.

Gratitude - like every other word - is just a sign post - a symbol ~ It doesn't have a very elegant sound - the way the word pleasure does ~ Perhaps because it's also been associated with obligation and dependence - like the word servitude ~ But - the road sign - and the city - are not the same thing - and the grat in gratitude - including all those other grat words just mentioned - have their roots in an ancient word meaning - pleasing - which = Is obviously a signpost on the road to pleasure ~ So what more can I say but = Thank you.]]]]]]]]]

So - what does that word - compassion - mean to you?

Alright ~ So = It's a kind of - caring feeling? You mean - like being concerned about another person's well being? Does that - well being - more or less mean - their happiness? So = When you see a child - that has been injured or hurt in some way - do you feel compassion for that child?

Do you feel compassion for that gang of rapists? No? Why not? Well sure = They committed a terrible crime against an innocent person ~ Does that mean you can't feel compassion for them? What if - they have had terrible lives themselves - filled with the same - or worse experiences? Would you feel compassion for them then? No? Then again - maybe they've had perfectly easy comfortable lives ~ Does that make it even harder to have compassion for them?

So = What is it you're feeling instead? Okay = Are those feelings of anger and vengeance - about that gang - or - about you?

What I mean is = Is your interest in punishing those people - about changing those people - or = About changing how you feel? Think about this one hard now? Will anything that happens to those people - change - what happened to you?

Don't get me wrong now - preventing somehow - those people from repeating such an act (or anybody else doing the same thing) - only makes sense ~ What I'm talking about - here - is another thing entirely ~ It's a turn around - a view from a completely different angle - a much larger picture.

What if - when you - view - the persons - you have blamed - for what has happened to you (yes - in the rape case - blame hardly seems the appropriate word - but - we'll stick with it just the same) - with compassion - you cannot help - but view yourself - with compassion?

Do you have compassion for yourself? I mean = Do you want your - self - to be happy? To be content? Fulfilled? In love? Do you care about yourself?

Can you feel any of those things - if you are filled with anger or shame?

Ah - there is that old story = How can I help but feel that way when such a terrible thing has occurred? Well = Who is it up to - how you feel? But - but... I know = That kind of compassion seems impossible - or something you would have to be a saint to pull off ~ But = What about the rest - of your life? What about tomorrow? Next month? Next year? What about = Now?

What about another = {{{**Inventory Time**}}}

What if - you don't have to be some amazing great hearted person to be compassionate? You simply have to want to be happy - more - than you want - to hurt yourself - with some other feeling?

When you are angry - who feels your anger the most? No = Not the person you're angry at = You do ~ Does it feel good? Well - yes = Sometimes anger feels like power - and a release of chained up resentment - that can have a certain satisfaction to it - when you let it out ~ Certainly it can be a step up from total depression ~ But = What is the deeper feeling? Why is the anger there? And what is the result - it creates?

Those last three questions are huge really - and = I don't expect you to just answer them ~ What I'm asking you to do = Is ask them ~ Look inside - for the answers ~ Wait for them ~ Don't just jump on the first idea that comes to mind ~ Not to say that those ideas can't be correct - only = Stew them awhile first - feel them - weigh them - try them on.

What if - anger is always a product of fear? Meaning = Fear of losing something - whether that - something - be a solid thing or an invisible idea ~ What if - it is always = Fear?

What are you afraid of?

[[[[[[[[Raging Reality:

Look = I'll be 100% straight up with you right here (not that I have actually been anything other than that with you) Terrible things happen in this world - and - have for thousands of years - and are - right now ~ That's not the point ~ That point - is proven every day a million different ways across the globe ~ You - want to prove it - you can - absolutely no contest.

My point is = The word - has long been = That's how it is = That's how it's always been ~ The reality is - that word - is changing - because = The logic behind it - is no longer logical.

A certain portion of the world has changed in recent decades - and that change - is most noticeable in the speed at which information travels globally ~ Actually - the speed at which many things that are capable of traveling travel - but particularly = Information ~ In such a world - intervention - support - assistance - and above all - education - which all mean change - can also travel at high speed ~ It's where - the choice - that begins the momentum of such change lies - that is the sharp end of my point - because = That end - is pointed directly at all of us.

I chose that example of a gang rape for a specific reason ~ That reason - outweighs the consideration - that my being male and never been raped status - would alienate (or otherwise - piss off) - certain people - notably females - in their thought that I have no right to address the reactions to such an experience ~ And of course - in that sense - they are perfectly correct ~ And still - I have continued with that choice of example - because = It is a savagely violent crime (all too often unreported - ignored - or blamed on the victim) - that leaves its sufferer alive - and = To be alive - is always to be in the location of some kind of choice - or simply - choice itself.

In fact = To be in the position of victim (a condition generally considered powerless - with an intensely powerful belief system written all over the word) - is actually - to be in a position of great personal power - because = The power to choose the course of the rest of your life (and perhaps influence many others) - is so clear cut in that moment (stretched out of course - to many succeeding moments) - that it compares to the decision - to board a ship about to cross the ocean to an entirely new life - or = Remain on the dock.

The question is = Are you - or we - going to react to the product of fear and hate and vengeance and the struggle for power - with the same mirror reflection of fear and hate and on and on - or = With something different? What information will we instant messenger around the world? What picture of that world - will we accept - as its reality?

What is not changed in this world (and so reinforces the conflict of logic mentioned earlier) - is that people - have always desired - to go about their lives - without fear ~ Even the ones wanting to cause fear in others = Still desire to be free of it in themselves ~ Adding all that up - or = As the sum of all the collective knowledge of the species = We know enough now = There is enough research - study - learning - practice - technology - theory - and so = Information = That we could actually make a reasonable go of a thriving world at peace = If - we were to truly do that math.

I'm not trying to push some warm and fuzzy denial smile on anyone who has suffered terribly ~ What I am saying = Is that they/you/we/us have the power of knowledge - to use - what we know as terrible - as a resource - as a means for establishing a clear contrast - from which we can define = What we can envision as wonderful ~ And so = Create that instead ~ Not because that might be a temporary emotional shift - in order to get on with life (even if it is) - but because = It is power.|||||||||

Have you ever seen a bicycle wheel? How do they work? Sure = They spin in a circle - on an axle - and roll along the ground ~ So = Would you say - they're constantly repeating the same motion - in order to accomplish what they do? Okay = Can bicycles fly? Right = They can leave the ground for brief periods - but = Can they - stay airborne? How about cross the ocean? So = Would you say - that bicycle wheels - can only really do one thing?

Alright = What - are you doing - when you get angry? Yeah = You might yell and scream and fight - but = This is more of a - cause - kind of question ~ Those things are actions - or effects - that follow an action - or cause - of mind ~ It's that - action of mind = I'm really looking for here.

I'll repeat the question = What - are you doing - when you get angry?

Okay = That's it = Now you're thinking = You're reacting ~ How about that word reaction then? Doesn't the prefix - re - usually mean to repeat something - like re-apply - re-invest - re-install? So = Does that mean that - re-acting - is repeating - an action - that's happened before? In other words = Isn't every - feeling reaction - programmed by some past experience? And = All we do with that = Is repeat some form of the response - that - our programming - thinks is appropriate? Is that what a reaction is? No? Sort of?

Is a reaction more like a mirror then? In the sense - that your response - mirrors - what has happened to you? Say… anger mirrors anger - violence mirrors violence? Is that how - reaction - works?

Or = Is it both? Meaning = A repetition of a pattern - that mirrors itself? Have you thought about it? Are you thinking about it now? Does it make sense to question it? Does the question make sense?

Okay = Either way - you're reacting ~ That is - when you are ~ Which - yes = Would include - now ~ Although a more emotionally charged moment - is what I had in mind ~ Anyhow = Does that mean - a reaction - is - going through - some set of thoughts and feelings - set in motion - or - because - of someone or something - other than you? So = Does - that mean - you're blaming - that thing or person - for how - you feel? Ah - but = Did they - make - you feel that way?

Alright = Feel angry at me now ~ Did that work? Did I - make you - feel angry at me? No? Why not? Because = I didn't really do anything? Sure I did = I told you to feel angry at me ~ Oh = I have to do something - to - you? So - if I took all your money - poisoned your dog - burned down your house - and - drove off in your car - then you'd feel angry at me? Why?

Yeah = Those are things you don't want to happen = I get that ~ But = Why blame me for how you feel? Am I in charge - of your feelings?

Okay - okay = I know - I'm using some extreme examples there ~ The point is = Is it - ever - up to someone else - how you feel? Or - is it always the ideas - the beliefs - of how things - are - supposed to be - that we use - to make ourselves unhappy - when - things - don't work out - our way? Is it our habit to blame someone else - for what - we've chosen

- to feel? Yes = I know - it doesn't look that way ~ Or even if it does - so what - you'd still get angry?

What I'm asking you - is = To look again.

If you went to the store and bought corn flakes instead of lettuce - would you blame someone else? Yeah = You might try ~ But = Who is really at fault?

What if - it's always the same with our emotions? What if - no matter what - we - are the ones responsible - for how = We feel? And again = What if - it's those feelings - we are choosing - that draw to us - our futures - that make the particle - out of the wave? I know = Truly severe examples - like the one we've just been over - seem impossible to make sense out of in such a fashion - meaning = We being the cause of them ~ That just sounds like a classic case of - blame the victim (mentioned that already haven't I?) Ah - but = What if - in the subatomic world - the quantum field - zero point field (old MacDonald's field) = Its words (meaning the beliefs in ideas - that are represented by words) - like blame - and victim - that do have the power to attract such events - and - keep them in circulation - meaning = Repeat them in one form or another - because = We think - that is how the world is - and = Our thinking - which is our contact with the quantum field = Makes it so?

Alright ~ Your assignment is all about - experimenting - with that responsibility - or - the choice - of how to feel ~ Here's what I want you to do = Think of someone you're upset with for some reason ~ Someone you know well - or you've had a fairly long history with ~ Okay? Have you got that person in mind? Good ~ Now - what you do = Is make a list (yup - on paper) - of everything that person has ever done - that you think - is good ~ Yes = That's everything - from a pat on the back - to giving millions to charity ~ Doesn't matter how big or small - you think - the good thing was - just - write - it - down ~ Then - pick someone else - and do it again ~ Don't slack on this - and only write the first thing that comes to mind and give up ~ There's more = Dig for it = You'll find it = Write it down = Then = When you find yourself getting upset at someone else - try (that's really try) - to think of something good - that person - has done in the past - particularly toward you ~ Okay? And - of course - taking a few deep breaths while you're doing it - especially while you're - considering doing it - will be of great help.

N.P.U. - Chapter Twenty - Random Numbers?

There is a type of machine - whose only purpose - is to generate electrical impulses in random order ~ You could simplify that description (or make some kind of sense of it) - by calling it an electronic coin flipper - but = Instead of coming up with heads or tails - it churns out the numbers - one - and - zero ~ For that reason - they (meaning these machines) - are called - Random Number Generators ~ They are also called - Random Event Generators - because = It's really more of an electrical event - they are generating - than numbers (or bits - to be precise - just like what runs a computer) It's also a more pleasing abbreviation to say - REG - as though it were a name - rather than the three letters - RNG ~ So - for our purposes here (which you may still be questioning) - we'll be using the event name - REG.

Alright - that clarification out of the way = These REGs were developed for the purpose of experimentation - but = Not just any standard accepted type of experimentation - like what test tubes and Bunsen burners represent ~ This high-tech coin flipping device - was aimed at simplifying research into the reality (or non-reality) - of psychokinesis - as it's officially termed - PK for short - mind over matter in common terms - far out woo-woo in popular skeptical slang - or - making physical things happen through the use of the mind alone - in straight forward explanation.

Ah = But - no = It's not the results of the thousands of experiments set up to measure attempts to mentally influence millions of coin tosses that I'm going to reveal ~ Even if they did - consistently nod in favor of PK being real = Sometimes with odds of over a billion to one against chance - and = Have been replicated - or repeated - by more than four dozen independent researchers - involving thousands of people - over the course of five decades ~ What - I want to tell you about = Are the results of an entirely different use of REGs ~ Perhaps no less strange ~ Perhaps even more so ~ But - the biggest news = Is the scale of these next experiments - in that = They involve the entire human population of the Earth (at least they appear to)

First though = I can't help but set the stage - with a remarkable little neuron twister - involving a robot - and a chicken.

So - this robot walks into a bar…

No - no = It's not a joke ~ It was a real robot - created by a Frenchman named Peoch ~ To be sure = It was a very simple one ~ Just a little box on wheels - whose movement was powered by an electric motor - and its direction chosen by an onboard REG ~ So - when it was placed in a box - and turned on - it proceeded to scribble a haphazard route of confused (otherwise known as random) - wanderings and bumpings into the sides of the box - which = Was basically what had been expected ~ Then = When the same procedure was repeated again - and again - and again - expectations were thoroughly confirmed = That the robot never traveled the same pattern twice ~ In other words = Its behavior - was completely random.

Enter the chicken.

It has been essentially confirmed - by the experimentation and observations of a famous animal behaviorist - named Conrad Lorenz (you may recall him talking to duck eggs way back when) - that when baby birds are first hatched - they tend to bond to what ever object is nearby ~ In nature - that object - is most often the mother bird ~ In Peoch's experiment - it was his robot ~ Which means = After 24 hours of being - imprinted (meaning hanging out with the robot as mother hen) - a day old chick was placed in a cage - next to the box - where it could plainly see the robot - and the robot - was switched on ~ This time - while Madame robot still went knocking around in a completely random way - she - never strayed far from the corner of the box - nearest the chick.

Now - of course - in good scientific order - this experiment was repeated multiple times - both - with the same chick - and - dozens of others - who also - went through the exact same drill - again - and again - and again ~ In the end - it was the same effect - with minor variations - all the birds - had on the robot.

So = What was going on?

Well - unless the robot itself - became emotionally attached to the chickens (which seems unlikely at best) - then = The only other explanation = Is that action of consciousness - we've called a bond - on the part of the chickens - exerted a magnetic field (more accurately - electromagnetic field) - or force - that caused the REG to function - less randomly - or - in relative sync - with the desires of the birds ~ Then again - there may be some other property of the psychic abilities of chickens - that science hasn't even begun to dream of ~ All we can really say (from the point of view of solid scientific conclusions) - is = What we're left with - is a mystery - yet = A mystery - with some conclusive proof - there is indeed = A mystery.

On to the next mystery then.

In August of 1997 - a new use for REGs popped out of (or is that - into) - the imagination of field consciousness researchers (you remember that word field - force field - quantum field - electromagnetic field - of course) Well - not exactly new - more like - on a larger scale ~ This inspiration occurred at the time of the car crash death of Princess Diana ~ Hardly a cause for celebration - but = Recognizing - that the live television broadcast of her funeral would be viewed by an estimated audience of hundreds of millions of people around the globe - at the same time (the meaning of live) - an opportunity - to test - if it was possible - to measure - that collective focus of consciousness - had turned up big time ~ Due to the variety of ways REGs had previously been used as measuring devices of conscious coherence (you remember that coherence word too - I'm sure) - it was suddenly an exciting prospect = That perhaps - the tools were on hand for an experiment of truly global proportions ~ And all that need be done = Was turn them on - and watch ~ Then of course = Wade through miles of data in search of patterns.

Again - that first word in REG - is random - so = It means a continuous stream of ones and zeros - bouncing back and forth between the two - with no particular - pattern - or order ~ If you were plotting a graph - with a line that went up representing one - and down representing zero - in the REGs usual output - you'd see a jagged scratching with uneven peaks and valleys - that demonstrated that key word over and over = Random ~ In the case of - coherence - the difference is = Pattern - or the same numbers - either ones or zeros - repeating for a long enough time - to form significant - or defined - peaks or valleys - which means = Less randomness.

When - the data of the twelve REGs that took part in the - funeral - were compared to each other = That's exactly what was found = Less randomness ~ The really exciting part of that - less randomness - is that it occurred - in each machine (all separated by many miles across the US and Europe) - in the same way - at the same time ~ Well - not perfect exact mirror images - but = As compared to the outputs recorded - before and after the funeral - close enough to pour a good deal more fuel on the fire of = A mystery indeed.

[[[[[[[[[Torsion Fields:

Due to certain - unexplainable results - in a variety of scientific experiments = Some scientists have begun to speculate about the existence of another force in the universe - which = Is neither electromagnetism - gravity - or the strong and weak nuclear forces - and instead - is something known as = Torsion fields - or waves.

In a torsion field - like charges (meaning the same - positive-positive or negative-negative) - are attracted to each other - rather than the electromagnetic norm - of opposite charges attracting - and like charges repelling (you've probably all witnessed what that's like with two magnets)

What that means is = An entirely new paradigm (Remember that word?) - in science and technology could be opening up - because = It's possible - that torsion fields can change the rate at which any physical process occurs ~ If indeed - a torsion field - and a gravitational field - operate in different directions of spin (it's all about spin direction with this stuff) - it may be possible to reduce gravity in a given area - and = If time is a vector (a force or influence) - of magnetic fields - then = Controlling a torsion field - might (just might) - allow for distortions of time - that make = Who knows what possible.

There are any number of intriguing possibilities in the torsion world ~ Not the least of which = Is led by the other deal breaker of a characteristic - that these renegade torsion waves seem to possess - which is = Breaking the cosmic speed limit.

Yes = Apparently - torsion waves can travel faster than the speed of light (in a mathematical theory kind of way) - and = They don't dissipate - or break down - or - go slower - as they spread out through the universe ~ What this might mean = Is the possibility of communicating across the galaxy (the universe in fact) - at high speed - without the signal deteriorating ~ Perhaps even - some kind of Star Trek like warp drive is just over the technological horizon as well.

What it comes down to at the moment is (again) = Who knows what it might mean ~ Since - if we knew that = We would know.||||||||||

So - the experiments continued - and = The REGs multiplied ~ By the eve of the millennium (that new century birth - dreaded as the possible opening of Armageddon and worldwide computer crash - known as Y2K) - the network of random generators had grown to dozens of machines spread across every continent and various islands of the world's major oceans - all continuously reporting their blips of randomness to the main collection computer in Princeton New Jersey ~ The big night (01/01/2000) - came (and went of course) - with no disastrous consequences - other than the usual temporary rise in the number of hangovers suffered globally ~ As for the REGs = The analysis of the data - showed very clearly defined periods of coherence - just before - and after - the moment of midnight for each of the world's 19 time zone's - with the actual stroke of midnight - being the peak ~ There was also a notable difference - between time zones of high or low population density (such as New York compared to the widely scattered islands of the Central Pacific) - which also clearly pointed at - the probability - that human collective consciousness - was causing the effect.

Okay - the fire keeps smoldering - with these brief bursts of flame that attract more interest now and then - which = Included REG experiments at seminars - theatrical events - comedy clubs - meditation groups - even pagan rituals and ancient sacred sites and battlefields - where = It was noted that the effects of group coherence were always more powerful than that of an individual ~ But still = It's not all that exciting I admit ~ Then = Something really big happened.

In the early morning hours of September 11 2001 - there were REGs (as I've said) - spread across the globe - and dutifully reporting their collected data in five-minute blocks to command central in New Jersey ~ Now - by = It was early in the morning = I mean - in New Jersey ~ In France - it was late morning ~ In Australia - it was even earlier in the morning ~ Although you could get away with calling it later - since it had just turned September 12th there ~ But - no matter what the local clocks in any of those locations read = At the same time (roughly 6:00 a.m. US Eastern Standard Daylight Time) - all of those REGs - across the globe - began to fall into order - registering less and less - randomness - until = They reached a synchronized peak of coherence (higher than any seen before or after - so far) - a little after 10:00 a.m. in New Jersey ~ Which of course - is in the same time zone as New York City - where = The horror of the World Trade Tower's destruction was being broadcast live - to probably its largest audience by then.

Alright = If you accept - that these devices are being influenced - by the energy of focused human consciousness (and certainly there is abundant reason to lean in that direction) - then why - what - how - and where - did this new twist come from? This twist - just in case you didn't happen to notice - is the fact - that although the first plane crashed into the north tower at 8:45 a.m. - the simultaneous lineup of worldwide REG output - began - nearly three hours earlier.

What does it mean?

[[[[[[[[Dynamic Space:

Is it possible = That space is actually a dynamic creative force - rather than just the room to occupy or move in - required by matter? And - in that possibility (given that space touches everything) = Could that - space - be aware (meaning - conscious) of all it touches - all it fills - and so = Be aware of all events - in relationship to each other (in the sense of how they affect - influence - and respond to each other) - and so = In the case of events which focus (or will focus) - high degrees of attention across the population - the electromagnetic activity of that focus - becomes part of our tangible experience? {{Now reread that – and really think about it}}

In recalling an experiment - previously noted (in the very near future - so keep that in mind) - where images randomly flashed on a computer screen - were physiologically responded to - seconds before - they appeared = Is it possible = That this - non-thing - I've been referring to as - space - is a superconductor - of that premonition ability - where our much denser bodies (or perceptions) - are just that much slower? In taking that on = Could it be = That time - is only relative (meaning - influential) - in the world of objects - whereas - in space - or the world of non-objects (that no thing - thing) = It isn't? And from there = Could it be = Objects - which are actually fluxing in and out of existence at the speed of light (provided that's true) - are not something we can accurately define with the word - real - and instead = Must transfer that definition to - space - as the actual reality? And so = Is it possible = That our definition of space - as the room to move in - and therefore experience our existence - is in fact = The opposite - where we objects - are the experience - by which space - recognizes its existence?

Could it be = This word - space - is just plain the wrong word - for such neuron numbing questions? Or then again…………..]]]]]]]]]

Well - other than the effect of laying an even deeper bed of coals to that mystery fire I keep analogizing about - it means (other than being anyone's guess) = That - if - what we are talking about here is - connection - or levels of connection - then = What we might have uncovered - is a whole new level - of connection ~ Or at least - new - to most people ~ So - while you ponder the possibilities of such findings - or try to explain them away as over imaginative scientists playing with toys they don't really understand - let's look at another experiment - which may not answer any questions - but = Answers have a way of drying up questions - and = Questions - a way of worming into deeper questions - so = Here they come.

A group of scientists - very - carefully chose 40 photographs - all - very - different from each other - but = Each selected for the (yes - that's very) - same reason ~ That being = The high probability of their stimulating a strong emotional response ~ The photos covered the range - from cuddly baby bunnies - to blood soaked murder victims - with sex - joy - disgust - terror - and sloppy kiss reunions in between ~ The experimenters scanned these photos into a computer - and programmed that computer - to flash them on a screen - in random order - at random intervals - for random lengths of time - with nothing but a blank screen separating their appearances.

So again - we're back in the world of random - but this time = The randomness was to - prevent patterns - from being recognizable - because = The purpose of the experiment - was (mostly) - to measure physical emotional response - which = If the participants began to catch on to a pattern - would change the nature of the data collected.

Alright = In come the participants - or subjects - and with them - a whole array of physiological measuring devices ~ There was an EEG - with all its wires and electrodes to graph brain activity ~ An ECG - to measure heart activity ~ Plus = Ways to measure skin temperature - sweat secretion - breathing variation - muscle tension - you name it ~ If there was a physical reaction they could observe and measure - they were going to make a record of it.

And the show begins = Very quickly - it became clear - that particular emotional states - exhibited - equally particular - physical responses - in all the subjects - with variations only in intensity ~ We're talking things such as - sudden drop in skin temperature at the sight of brutality - or relaxed breathing from viewing a gleeful babies face ~ With of course = All the other accompanying system's responses being measured and factored in as well ~ In time (meaning after that diligent scientific method of - repeat - repeat - repeat) - a recognizable signature - of bodily reaction - to each type of emotion - was so clearly defined - that the researchers could describe the nature of the picture being viewed - by looking at the physical data alone.

Well = That's interesting = Sure ~ But hardly something to get you blinking in amazement ~ It's the other finding - all that sophisticated equipment laid out in proper scientific black-and-white - that jumps out of the box of what makes sense ~ Not to mention - the possibly ho-hum of = We could've told you what clammy skin means anyhow ~ What that discovery was = Was timing.

Remember - this whole picture viewing experience - was designed to be totally random in order of appearance - timing of appearance - and duration of appearance ~ Again - that was to ensure - that anticipation - of when - and what - the next image turned up - would not have an effect on the results ~ However - anticipation did play a key role - regardless of how carefully randomness was maintained = Though - not in a guessing kind of way - like betting on the odds of what the next picture would be (despite the fact that such thoughts must have been present) No = What consistently repeated - with all the participants - was = Two - or even three seconds (that's - one Mississippi - two Mississippi - three Mississippi - seconds) - BEFORE - a picture flashed on the screen = The exact signature physical emotional response - appropriate - to that picture - began to take place - in all the systems being measured ~ Again = That's - BEFORE - seeing the picture - and = Not just a response to = I'm about to see a picture - of who knows what - but = The same type of physical response - consistently logged in - as the one - that picture - physically provoked - in all the participants previously measured ~ In other words = The bodies of those people - responded - to what they were going to see - BEFORE - they saw it ~ Which means = Somehow - they KNEW - what they were going to see - BEFORE - they knew it.

SPECIAL BONUS EXERCISE - number ten

Gratitude:

If you were going to research the effects on people's lives - of a particular emotional state - like say… gratitude - how would you go about it?

Luckily (on many levels) - that question has been answered (at least partially) - and the results of such research - point at all kinds of beneficial effects - from more harmonious relationships - expanded generosity - optimism - tolerance - and cooperation - to increased attention span - strengthened dedication to exercise and healthy nutrition - and = Even improved sleep patterns - with all the accompanying health advantages such overall conditions support ~ Wow = All that from a little gratitude.

So - you don't necessarily have to invent your own research project (not to say - that wouldn't be a useful contribution - for which you have my thorough encouragement should you be so inspired) - but instead = You can just repeat the steps of other experimenters in order to test their conclusions yourself (that's what scientists do all the time after all)

As for getting started = There are three techniques to choose from ~ Not that you have to confine yourself to just one ~ Practicing any or all of them - will both simplify and reinforce the practice of either of the rest ~ Not to mention - amplify the results ~ And what's more = They're all really easy to do.

1.**Savoring**: To savor - means to really spend the time enjoying something - while - you're enjoying it ~ Which is to say = Paying attention to enjoyment ~ Such as = Savoring the taste of chocolate melting on your tongue ~ Or = Savoring the texture of warm mud oozing between your toes ~ All you need to do to participate in this technique = Is spend that time - pay attention to anything enjoyable - beautiful - satisfying - or remotely pleasing in any way - and = Savor it ~And then = Express gratitude in your mind for that experience ~ Mustn't forget that part ~ In fact = Savor that gratitude - smile it - hum it - point it out to someone passing by ~ You know = Checkout those clouds man = How cool is that?

2. **Pocket full of gratitude:** Start picking up small objects - interesting stones - pieces of wood - shiny bits of this and that - whatever strikes your fancy - and - as you do = Bring to mind things you're grateful for (such as the things you've been savoring) - any old thing - doesn't matter what - just so long as you're glad it's there - it happened - and = You're grateful for it ~ Then = Put whatever that object is in your pocket ~ Later = When

340

you notice these things in your pockets - do the same thing again = Remember what you're grateful for - and = Dig up more grateful thoughts (savor them) Later again = Start placing these objects where you'll see them regularly - next to the door - in a drawer you use often - on the back of the toilet - anywhere - and when you see them = Find something in your mind to be grateful for ~ Make a kind of game out of it ~ See how many gratitude reminders you can find - how many different places you can plant them - and - no matter what = When you see one - touch one - or even just think of one - if you immediately call to mind a grateful thought - that = Is how you rack up points.

3. **Thank you Journal**: This one is the quickest to explain - but - the most time-consuming to practice ~ However - if you've been doing either or both of the other exercises = It'll be a piece of cake ~ What you do is = At the end of every day - you write down in the special notebook you've chosen for this task - or on scraps of paper you stick in a box - or stuff in a sock (that part's entirely up to you - it's the writing that's important) - at least five things you're grateful for that day - and = That's it ~ Other than you keep those entries - and reread them now and then - just for fun - or perhaps = Gratitude.

The final note - is that you'll need to spend some time at this to make it a really worthwhile experiment ~ So = Start out with seven days - or go for twenty one - maybe a month - all summer ~ Or hey - an afternoon is better than nothing ~ Just - try it ~ See what happens - add your own innovations - inspirations - reminders ~ But - most of all = Pay attention - to how you feel - and act - and notice new things = Like how you feel and act changes - and maybe even - how you sleep at night as well.

Class Twenty One - Re-action?

BREATHE (Yes - yes ~ Didn't even need to remind you ~ It's true isn't it? This is a VERY good thing to do ~ Keep it up - or = Step it up ~ You really will be glad you did)

Did you do it? That is = Did you think of lots of things to write? Did you think of any? What happened as you wrote them down? Did you remain upset? What changed? Is it hard to be angry at someone and praise them at the same time? Did you find that you still wanted - to choose - being angry? Did it become obvious that - you were - choosing to be angry? What about with other people - did you manage to come up with good things about them when - they - upset you? What did doing this exercise tell you about your thinking/feeling relationship?

So = How do you want to feel?

I've said that before haven't I? I'll say it again = How do you want to feel?

It's a question - of now = Not the past = Not the future = Now ~ Fact is - despite all this talking about now we've done - we've also never stopped talking - about the past and the future ~ Especially - in talking about anger - which = Never - exists - unless the past and future - are involved.

Why do you think I asked you about the bicycle wheel? Do you remember me asking? Yeah = I'm a little weird - it's true ~ But - that's not the whole reason ~ I'll help you out = The reason is = Blame - and = Now.

That didn't help huh ~ How about this? What are you doing - when you get angry - at someone else - for how - you feel - that's the same - as the answer to that last question I asked about the bicycle wheel? Which - I'll remind you of my exact words = So - would you say - that bicycle wheels - can only really do one thing?

Bingo = You set in motion - an action - that can only go round and round - doing one thing = And that one thing is? Think about it now.

Yup = It's blame - and = It's now (when it's happening) Perhaps it helped a tad - that I already mentioned that ~ But - in other words = It means = To give away your responsibility - for what - you're actually really responsible for ~ Which is = Your feelings = Right now.

342

See - blame and anger work like a wheel ~ They just do that round and round thing in a circle - or cycle - unless something breaks that cycle ~ History is jammed full of such cycles - that repeat - and repeat - and repeat the same motion - until people decide - to break the cycle somehow ~ Or - die ~ Which of course - has also been very popular.

What happens if you hacksaw a piece out of the rim of a bicycle wheel? Exactly = It won't work anymore.

That's what I'm talking about - when I use the word - compassion ~ Remember that word?

Well = What do you think happens - when - you insert compassion - into that round and round wheel of blame? Yes = It breaks the cycle.

Okay = What do you think happens - when - you practice compassion - as its own cycle? What I mean is = Not as a break in the wheel - but = As the wheel itself - or = Not after you get angry - but = Before - you get angry? What if - such a practice - would not only avoid anger - or defuse anger - but = Draw into your life the opposite of anger ~ In fact = What if - compassion - is just a simple tool - like a switch - that makes anger nothing but a comparison - something that's there only to assist us - in choosing - what we prefer - and then = Empowers us to draw that other thing into our lives?

There's another word - that fills out this idea even more = More - in the sense - that it extends that word compassion - and - by extends - I mean = Expands its size - completes it - and then = Gives it away - or spreads it around - which = Reproduces it - or - makes - more - of it ~ But - like most powerful words - it (this other word) - has different meanings - to different people ~ The word is = Forgiveness.

What does it mean to you?

[[[[[[[[[Vibration Persuasion:

What if - gratitude is one of the highest levels of vibrational energy we produce? In saying highest - I mean = On a parallel with amperage (that being an electrical measurement - roughly meaning - the calculation of how much work a particular unit of electricity is capable of performing) We use the word power - interchangeably with the word - electricity = What would happen - if we did the same thing - with the word = Gratitude?

What if - compassion - like gratitude - is also one of our highest powered electromagnetic vibrational fields? In fact = What if - it is an even more powerful energy source - on a local level (or even - more so - on a non-local one) - in that = It invites all other frequencies to vibrate in tune (or coherence) - with it?

What if - forgiveness - tops both gratitude - and compassion - for electromagnetic potency - because = It removes all friction - all inertia - or the tendency of a - thing - to remain as it is? What if - forgiveness - is the ultimate energy lubricant - accelerator - and

- power booster - because = It taps the power of gratitude - ignites the power of compassion - and opens all boundaries - previously closed - to the expansion of that energy into new forms of experience - even more harmonious - than what inspires the results of those two others combined?

What if - I'm not just playing with metaphor - or philosophy - or even words themselves - in order to make a point - but instead = I'm talking very real forces of energy - as important to our universal quest for happiness - as gravity is - to keeping chairs on the floor? What if - what I'm saying = Makes sense?|||||||||

So - yes = You could put the word pardon in there? Which means what? Okay = Like not punishing someone for something they did? Alright ~ Then there's - letting go - moving on - that kind of thing? Ah = Some of you - feel - that forgiveness says to the world - what a person did - is okay? Is that why it's a hard thing to do? Is that why we drag grudge and blame and vengeance around for years inside us - just in case someone might be confused about - what's okay?

How about this then? What happens - to you - when you forgive someone? Now - I don't mean - say you forgive - but still hang on to resentment = I mean = Really put whatever happened - behind you ~ Have you ever done that? Okay = What happened?

Yeah = That's it isn't it = The thing that was bothering you - stopped bothering you ~ It's kind of like flushing the toilet ~ What happens if you use the toilet - but never flush it? Well = Does the same kind of thing happen - in your head - when you live in a state of anger? What do you suppose happens to your body then? Do you think - there may be a connection - between living in such a state - and the cause of disease - arthritis - heart failure - cancer - and on and on - just the same as it (meaning that state of anger) = Is the cause - of more reasons for anger? Is the idea of such a connection - something you really need scientific proof of (of which there is plenty - by the way) - in order to consider - it may be true?

So = When you forgive someone - what part of time are you forgiving? Exactly = The past ~ Is the past happening now? So = Why is it so hard - to forgive?

Here's a definition for forgiveness you might like ~ It comes from a bumper sticker - that maybe you've already seen ~ It goes = Forgiveness is giving up all hope for a better past.

Very clever - eh? But = What if - there's even more to it? What if - forgiveness - is a hundred doorways opened - for that one door closed ~ Or - to ditch the poetics = What if - forgiveness - is what freedom really is? I mean - break down the verb - forgive - to its parts = For - Give ~ It's all about generosity - giving - and = You can't give what you don't have - so = When you do = You must have had it all along.

What if - you are - in reality (whole 100% mind use reality) - completely free? What if - everything that has happened to you - really doesn't matter - only this present moment does? By which I mean (in case that just messes too much with your relationship with

344

time and identity) = Matters - only in the sense - that you can do whatever you want with it? Would that be a completely different way of experiencing the world - from what you're used to? What would that be like? Why is it - you don't operate that way now?

||||||||| Doctor Dude's Dictionary - word twenty one - Reverberate:

There's a word you can have some fun with (at least I have) - when you play with breaking it down - in the context of things - and the relationships between things - as being energy in motion - or actions creating actions - as a definition of being ~ In short = Verbs (since we are talking about words after all) - but also = Because the word - verb - sits square in the middle of the word = Reverberate.

To reverberate - is to echo or resound - which translates as re-sound or sound again ~ It also means - to be repeatedly reflected - as in = To have the same effect over and over - mirroring itself - the way news travels from one person to the next ~ And that - makes it a repetition word (which explains the re at the beginning) - but = In a kind of bounce back and forth way - rather than completing a task and then repeating it ~ Reverberate's job - is the repetition itself - not the content or story being repeated - just its vibration ~ And like any other vibration (say… in a guitar string) - once it's caused by some force (like the pluck of a fingernail) - it continues to play out the energy of that force = It would not be far off the mark to call that effect - re-vibe-eration.

The really amazing thing about the word = Is that it seems to be both - describing its own meaning - and = Describing the fundamental activity underneath the exterior of all matter ~ No matter what you're looking at - be it rock - paper - scissors - fish - fowl - or grandma - the subatomic levels of that object are in constant motion - even if none of the other - or outer levels - appear to be ~ At that inner level - there is a continuous reproduction process in action - maintaining that action - that vibration - which is the verb = Being ~ So - if being is a verb - then re-verb-erate - is just another - perhaps even more appropriate word - for the same thing - as the verb of what it means to be a verb - or the effect of a cause - that is the cause of an effect ~ Or in other words = A reverberation.|||||||||

Okay = I understand ~ This process - we call living - doesn't seem to work that 100% freedom way ~ Instead = The past sets up things - that happen in the present - and the two of them - set up the future ~ Is that how it works in your mind?

What if - you are mistaken? I mean - in the sense - that there is more to it ~ What if - the only thing - that connects the past and the future - to the present - is - the ideas and beliefs - that you have built up - to tell yourself - they do? And = What if - you were free of those - ideas - you could step right out of time and space - all together - this instant?

Okay = That's pushing it is it? Well - what if - unable to step out of time - you still realized = Your present - is the result - of what your past thoughts - have attracted? In other words = Your now - is the proof - or manifestation - of those thoughts - you asked for proof of - by having them?

Still all sounds a bit farfetched does it? Well = You remember those people five hundred years ago - who had never heard of electricity? What do you suppose they would think - if you went back in time - and tried to explain all the marvels of a world where electricity was as common place as cabbages? That's right = Most of them would think you were nuts ~ Does that mean - you are? Does it mean that what you have experienced - isn't true?

You notice I said - most of them? Do you suppose - that some of them - might believe you? So = What would the rest of those people - think - of the people - that believed you? Sure = They'd probably slot them straight into the - you're nuts - category as well - maybe even use a few for fuel ~ But = Wouldn't - that brave select few - that believed you - be right?

Well - maybe I'm nuts ~ But = I'm not the only one ~ Good chance you're just as nuts (though perhaps differently) - as me ~ Not that I'm trying to insult you ~ We just don't have all the answers ~ Yet - we walk around as though we have - enough - and meanwhile - repeat the same old problems over and over - because = We think - our experience - is the only one - there is to have ~ Well = What if - we're completely wrong - and = Just like those people at the start of the 16th century - we're simply missing some information?

How do you think those words - compassion and forgiveness - tie into those last ideas? Meaning the = You're nuts - and - completely wrong - business.

Could it be - that the answer - fits neatly into one word? Any guesses at what word I have in mind?

What about = Ignorance?

I know = Mostly that word is used harshly - as a kind of superior judgment ~ But = What does it mean?

Yup = Quite simply - it means = Not knowing something - or - the learning - of particular information - hasn't happened yet ~ It doesn't - have - to mean stupid ~ You may be ignorant of how to ask for directions to the bathroom - in Italian - and still hold half a dozen degrees from as many universities ~ And - at the same time = Holding - all those degrees - might be why - if you were to meet someone - from say… 500 years in the future = You might think - what they claim to have experienced - was completely nuts.

See - the thing I'm after here - in tying these ideas together - is = Witnessing ignorance - or - a kind of knowing - that really is - not knowing - without knowing it {{Yeah even I had to read that one a few times}}

What if - the reason - we withhold - compassion and forgiveness - and think people are nuts - is = We don't - know - the whole picture - all the reasons - all the evidence - all the possible solutions - or - what's truly best - for our own peace of mind - or anyone else's - or - the results that may occur - beyond the results we expect - or - want to see -

BECAUSE = What if - what we're doing - is looking at the past - our past - our experience - our ideas - of how everything worked - before - to supply all that stuff (meaning solutions for the future) - as though it could? Does your past supply it? Mine certainly doesn't?

[[[[[[[[Frequencies:

If - you were to hold a device that measures positive and negative charge up to a single atom = You would see the needle wag back and forth between the two polarities on its dial ~ Actually - that wagging action would be taking place too fast to see with standard human vision ~ However - if you are to create a printout - of the action of that needle whipping into a blur - you would see the wavy line that describes the electromagnetic phenomena called = A frequency ~ Because = That is something that can be measured ~ In fact = Every type of atom - generates a signature frequency (meaning - a wavelength unique to that kind of atom) - and = Does so with such strength - that scientists can point sensitive imaging systems (designed to recognize atomic signatures) - at distant stars - and thereby determine those stars chemical and mineral makeup.

What that means (in a picking apart the universe kind of way) - is = Everything - in form - has - or broadcasts - or most simply - is = A frequency ~ And = All interactions between objects - involving energy (and there are no interactions that do not involve energy) - are also frequencies ~ And = The simplest frequency to recognize - as being a frequency - or a movement of energy - is = Sound.

Just tune into a radio station - and you have an immediate demonstration that there are different frequencies ~ Provided you realize that that's what separates one station's broadcast from another ~ But = In order to pass beyond the concept of energy frequencies - and actually physically experience them - just turn the bass on that radio to full blast - and crank up the volume ~ The vibrations you hear - and feel - and maybe even see being produced - are the results of waves of energy (frequencies) - interacting with the other waves of energy - we normally consider to be solid objects - at the energetic level - where they are not solid objects at all.

As you may be aware - certain singers through history - and the present -have been - and are - capable of hitting and sustaining particular notes (that is - frequencies) - that have the power to shatter glass ~ It's not that they are setting up a vibration that fragile glass cannot withstand - but instead = Are projecting the energy wavelength - which matches the one produced by the atomic structure of the glass itself - and = Since it is the atomic structure - or frequency - of the atomic structure of the glass - that maintains its shape as a glass = Overloading those atoms - with too much of their own frequency - causes them to be unable to maintain that structure - and the glass does not simply break - but literally explodes at the atomic level (different from the nuclear level of course - which would destroy everything for miles around)

So = What does paying attention to such facts - mean (by way of practical application that is) - to the frequencies - that are us?
For one (to go directly to that glass shattering trick) - doctors can now treat kidney stones

(which are concretions - just like that word concrete - of mineral salts - that form painful little nuggets in the kidneys) - by directing the correct frequency at the offending organ - and blowing those little bits of internal geology into sand - which = Is much easier to pee out (that being the only exit available) - than the whole rock.

Much more exciting still (medically speaking) - are the new diagnostic machines - which are capable of scanning all the electromagnetic frequencies going on in a body (which happens to be exactly how our bodies are already communicating within themselves) - and thus determine the level of health of all the organs - tissues - and systems - respiratory - digestive - and so on - all in a matter of minutes (about 5 to 90 - depending on the machine) - as well as identify and pinpoint the locations of parasites and unwelcome bacteria (there'll be more on this later)

The question is not = How amazing is that ~ The question is = What will the growing understanding of - Reality - as a set of frequencies - make possible next?|||||||||

So - I'm going to give you a really big = What if? I've already given it to you actually ~ It's really just worded differently this time.

What if - every experience - we - have in this life - is - completely - intentional? Meaning = What if - we - are here - purely - to experience - to feel - all aspects - all possibilities - all potentials - of physical life - and so - we attract them - to us? Meaning = What if - we chose - to do that? Meaning = Have a physical life - for that purpose ~ Which is to say = A - WE - or connected self (that is somehow much larger - and better informed - than the standard issue human level set of choices between vanilla and chocolate) - has made that choice (or choices) - to experience the experience - of physical experience ~ Or - of course = Not.

Told you it was a big - IF ~ But - that's what it is = A question ~ Do you know the answer? I mean - really - know - the answer?

No = I'm not trying to give you the answer - by making it look like a question ~ What I'm giving you = Is the question ~ Which is = The opportunity - for an answer ~ Or more precisely = The opportunity - to ask such questions ~ Perhaps you think it's foolish to ask such questions ~ After all - look around = Is that how - anything - that's happened to you - look like how it happened to you = Like you - chose - it - like… like toppings on a pizza? Yeah - right.

Well - you're just going to make me say it again = How - do - you - know? No = Not what did you read - or somebody told you = How - do - you - know?

Did you know - that the world of atoms - is mostly space - and therefore everything is? That is - before I mentioned it? So = What holds it together? What makes it do what it does? Appear as it does? Live - die - and chew gum as it does? What - is - it? Can you say you know the answer to that other question - when - you don't know the answer - to these?
See - deciding you know an answer - to such a big question - or - that you can't know the

answer (which would be an answer itself) - doesn't have to mean = Your answer - is wrong ~ But - if you have never - asked - the question - then - quite possibly = It is wrong ~ Meaning = It can't ever be a - whole answer (if such a thing can be) - for the simple reason - that = Without questioning past the surface - of any - thing - event - or idea - the only answer available = Is a description of that surface you've - already decided on.

But - you've heard all that before (if you've been listening) - because = The entire point of this course - is one thing ~ And = That one thing is?

You got it = Question!!!

And - why?

Because = What if - the limits to knowledge are - always - artificial? What if - they're made up? What if - all limits - are made up?

Ah = But you can't breathe water - walk through walls - fly?

Okay = What if - you (that more knowledgeable you) - chose - not to? (There I go again) What if - those limits - don't come from the laws of nature - they come from you - as an agreement - to play by the laws of nature? What if - they (or the laws of limitation) - are exactly like the difficulty of forgiving those rapists? What if - the way to change - those limits - is exactly the same - as forgiving those people?

No = I don't mean - saying = What they did was okay ~ I mean = Realizing = It never happened.

But it did happen - you say ~ Well - actually - the thing with the rapists was just a mental exercise I gave you ~ Yeah - yeah = I know = Stuff like that - does happen - as well as everything else (or at least it seems to) - and that's why we were talking about it in the first place = That's right - but....

Remember all that talk about - our experience - always being - an interior one? Or - now - being the only time there really is? If you put those two together - wouldn't it mean = That life - is just something - that's going on - in our minds - right now?

The question - is = Do you know? Or - do you just - think - you know - what's - really - going on? What if - the part of your mind - you're using - to know (say - 15%) - simply doesn't know - the whole picture - because = It - isn't a whole picture?

What if - there's another part of your mind (that is - consciousness) - that does know?

See - when I say - you chose those limits - I don't mean = The you - that has to take Drivers Ed. - or decide what to wear ~ I mean = The you - that's behind - the you - that thinks - you're you.

Alright - I've really run - you - in circles this time - haven't I ~ So - I'm going to make the assignment particularly easy ~ Well - maybe simple is a better word ~ Whether it's easy - or not - is up to you ~ That's sounds familiar - doesn't it?

Okay ~ Here it is ~ It's a question = What is I? Yeah - it sounds like poor English ~ It's not ~ It's a direct question - about that thing - we constantly refer to - when we say = I want to go to the movies = I like bananas = I feel satisfied = I am pissed ~ What is it? What is = I?

Whenever you hear - yourself - use the word - I - ask that self - that's floating around behind the one that said it = What is that? Then = Feel - it = Take your awareness - down into your body - just like we have before - and = Listen - not with your ears - with your feeling - your beingness.

Now - the point - is not to locate the answer ~ The point - is to locate the question ~ Which is to say = Fully participate in the question = Be - the question ~ Forget about answers ~ Just open up the - space - for one ~ You don't need to do anything else = Just ask ~ Of course - breathing will help.

N.P.U. - Chapter Twenty One - The Box?

I apologize - if I left you on the edge of your seat with the results of the last experiment we talked about (you know - the two to three seconds early response to random images on a computer screen one) Of course - I did have my reasons - which = You probably saw coming a good deal longer than three seconds ago - even if you've been quite firmly covering much more than the edge of your seat all along - which - obviously = Is playing with language and has nothing to do with comfortable seating - but = Everything to do - with comfort.

See - what I've done - is laid out the clear systematic information outputs of machines - simply doing the jobs they were designed to do - which = If - were they just performing their usual roles - in hospitals and such = That same output - would appear straightforward enough - and basically uncontestable ~ But - in this case - that information output (which is to say - the timing of that information) - appears - to contradict normal experience - and so = Is apt to cause (regardless of which side of the excitement or rejection fence you fall on) - a feeling of (other than - or) - dis-comfort - meaning = A feeling different from the usual run of middle range feelings we generally experience.

Now - that's not to say - you don't - or can't - enjoy those feelings - and so = Would not be inclined to label them - discomfort ~ What it is to say - is = Where do the boundaries - of that popular buzz phrase - your comfort zone - stand? Because = That - zone - is really just a set of neural nets - or habits - of thought and expectation - we think (not that we have to actually consciously think about them - in order to activate them) = Are comfortable ones ~ The opposite (when those comforts are challenged) - are the jagged edges of the seat - which tends to irritate sensitive areas - and = We don't like that - but = It's there - perched on that edge - where - another modern buzz phrase - or = Pushing the envelope - is most available.

So = Why? What's the buzz - behind those - possibly - overused phrases? What would tie them to (that is - place them in the same conversation as) - electrode covered people staring at computer screens?

Well - yes = It's a recognition ~ A culture wide one in fact - of a natural state ~ A natural state - by the way - as big as - or potentially - unimaginably bigger in bang - than the universe itself = Expansion.

Somewhere - in all of us...

352

Which is another sentence - wearing down further another over worn phrase - as though that somewhere were a real location you could give directions to - like = Take the throat south to Windpipe avenue - turn left at the first bronchial tube and follow the signs for the Pulmonary artery ~ Once you pass the lights at Valve and Ventricle (never mind that you're going against traffic) - take the first right onto the Atrium highway and proceed north till you arrive at the Sinoatrial node ~ Ask for a table near the band.

[[[[[[[[[Setting the Pace:

The sinoatrial node (pronounced - sign - oh - eh - tree - ell - node - rhymes with toad) - is a group of cells (collectively called tissue) - located in the right atrium of the heart ~ Those cells - function as the pace setter - or rhythm stimulator - of cardiac contraction ~ What cardiac contraction means - in simple mechanical terms - is = Every time your heart beats it's double rhythm (often expressed as - lub - dub) - the two sides of that organ - the ventricle and the atrium - contract - first one - then the other - and by doing so - pump your blood - in - out - in - out.

But - you knew that.

As for the pacemaker action (a pacemaker - also being the name of a device that can be surgically implanted for the same purpose) - of the sinoatrial node = It's an electrical impulse - that keeps the beat - or - signals those contractions - generally somewhere between 70 and 100 beats per minute - and in that sense - could be called the electrical dead center of your bodies life (contradictory as it may sound to use the words dead and life in the same sentence)

Now - all heart muscle cells posses the ability to generate electrical impulses that can do the same thing ~ And - in the event of sinoatrial breakdown - that function can be passed on to other similar cells ~ The basic reason for the s node being the drum major - or whip cracker of the cardiac crew = Are its cells ability - to work faster.

Muscle cells in the heart - the same as all other muscle cells - undergo what's known as a - refractory period - following contraction (which is the work muscle cells perform) - when they are unable to contract more - or again - until that period of time (some fraction of a second) - has passed ~ The s node cells - don't require the same (we'll call it a) - recovery period - and so can jump to the electrical charge punch first ~ Of course - it's much more complex a system than what I've sketched out here - with the flow of chemicals - like sodium - calcium - and potassium ions - in and out of cells - creating different polarizations (you know - positive and negative) - and thus - electrical charges - that keep the whole business pumping along.

The truly impressive thing about the sinoatrial node - is not so much what or how - it does what it does - but - that it (or more accurately - they - from a cellular point of view) - just plain is there doing it ~ You have to wonder = If it drives your heart - which drives your body = What drives it?]]]]]]]]]]

Actually - those directions might not be so terribly far off the mark ~ At least from the point of view of locating a position to really start asking questions from ~ But - anyway = In that - IN place - somewhere in all of us (the one a surgeon's knife will never expose - because it's actually more no-where than some-where) - we all (that's - all of us) - recognize a kind of force - whose energy = Is expansion ~ By recognize - I mean = At some point in time (or many points in time - most points in time - or barely the smallest most crushed and oppressed point in time) - we have all - wanted - to be - MORE = More something - trillions of different somethings - but = Whatever it is - was - or will be - its central theme is - MORE ~ Which means = Expansion.

Why such a state is natural - is another - expanding - set of questions ~ And - of course someone - or many someones - are bound to disagree ~ But - raise your hand - if you've ever felt such a drive ~ Then = Answer the question yourself = Is it natural?

If it is - then what else - is natural?

[[[[[[[[[Sleep Silence:

During normal periods of sleep - or something between five and nine hours a night (unless you happen to sleep during the day) - our brains undergo an unexplained phenomenon - where = Millions of neurons will synchronistically (or all at the same time) - participate in a one second burst of electrical activity - after which - the entire brain goes completely silent (no electrical activity at all) - for several seconds.

These electrical storms - are different from the electrical activity of REM (rapid eye movement) - sleep - which is the neuronal action (neurons doing things) - that takes place during intervals of dreaming ~ Nor - is the brain entirely electrically inactive at any other time - except = Following those moments of one second partying just described - which = Take place about a thousand times a night - slowly tapering off in intensity - and then stopping completely before waking.

What do we do in those noisy seconds? Where do we go in those silences? Is that another reason why we have to sleep = So our consciousness can warp drive to the far ends of the universe and back?]]]]]]]]]]

There's another machine - with another three letter abbreviation - that's been put to new uses recently - in probing the nature - of our physically mental natures ~ It's called an - EMG - for electromyography - which means = It can deliver - a sort of electrical information snapshot of motor neuron muscle instructions (that's the outgoing message carrier nerve cell wiring from the brain down) And - that means = EMGs are like a full telephone trunk line wiretap - eavesdropping on what those signals are saying - by seeing what muscles they are delivered to ~ Ordinarily - EMGs are diagnostic tools - or ways of determining what's wrong - when thoughts and muscles aren't cooperating with each other - or = A set of conditions under the umbrella title of neuromuscular disorders - such as Parkinson's disease or Muscular Dystrophy ~ But - in this case - the question put to the machine (figuratively speaking) - is = Does the nervous system - know the difference - between a thought that's directing an action - and - a thought - that's merely thinking about an action?

Yes = It may seem a funny sort of question - when weighed from the perspective of = Of course - you - know the difference between a thought and an action ~ Yet that perspective - is also - the rather comfortable one - that you - and your nervous system - are the same thing ~ Now - that's not saying = That there is a possible separation between you and your nervous system ~ What it is examining = Is the difference - between the awareness you - or consciousness - and the physical mechanism - you also call - you - because = According to the EMG readings - thinking about performing an action - and actually performing that action - appear to be - the same thing.

Athletes of different kinds - like skiers and weightlifters - were hooked up to these machines - then asked to - mentally rehearse - their skills ~ What the EMGs recorded - was = The same electrical impulses - were sent to the same muscles - that are used in the - real - use of those muscles ~ Other research - with EEGs - has upheld the brain end of this claim - by showing that electrical activity in the brain - is identical - for a task performed - and that same task - merely imagined ~ The same neural patterns fire - to produce the same motor skills - meaning = Brain says - biceps flex - abs crunch - quads contract - and all the electrochemical results (which of course are the brain saying those things) - are put through their paces ~ It's as though a nervous system work out were going on - just the same as any form of exercise for any other muscle group ~ Which seems to point in that direction (again) - that the brain - is just another muscle - or shall we say - a physical tool - at - our - service.

Of course - you don't sit there quivering and bouncing around - when you imagine doing something ~ So - yes = You - and that other you - can tell the difference - between imagining and doing ~ Yet - it goes deeper (as you may have suspected) - when compared to the results of other studies - both formal and informal - where = Mental exercise has built real muscle - and far more importantly - unless you are an obsessed bodybuilder = Cured disease.

I imagine you've all heard the phrase - creative visualization - knocked around ~ Or - the more sports fan friendly - psyched up ~ What both those uses of words are about - are uses of mind - to consciously create a particular condition - or outcome - by first - creating it - mentally ~ For decades now - individual athletes - and sports teams all over the world - have employed different forms of those concepts ~ The great pre-game locker room speech - is certainly familiar to everyone through the efforts of Hollywood - if not their own home town coaches ~ And well they should be ~ Truly effective filmmaking (and coaching) - plays the instrument of creative emotion - in order to produce a certain effect ~ The thing is - that more and more - the understanding - expands - that what plays out on the field - or anywhere else - begins - and is controlled by - the mind ~ Therefore - what is expanding - alongside that understanding - is learning - how to cooperate with that principle ~ In other words = Tap into its effectiveness.

The current word in fashion - to boil all those neural exercises down to one game - is = Intention ~ I've - intentionally - used a graphically physical example here (that being sports) - because = It fits pretty smoothly into everyone's (or most everyone's) - comfort zone - of ideas of what effects what - no matter what your relationship with sports may be ~ It's simple enough to stretch to the acceptance - that visualizing the basketball swishing through the net just before a foul shot - will grease up all those motor neuron transmissions in just the right way that every muscle will do exactly what all that practice was all about = And he shoots - it's up - it's up = It's good!!! That's really nothing more than living in the times we do - and absorbing what's out there.

In fact - there's a word - for such culturally accepted and circulated information - which is = Memes ~ Even if it hasn't quite fully stepped into the light of general unscientific use yet ~ It's a word modeled on the word - and concept of - genes - in that = Our genes - or DNA - are passed from one generation to the next - as the design specifications for our personal physical construction ~ Memes - are the same kind of building codes - but = They are applied on a larger scale - capable of being passed on - between - among - and within generations - because = They shape what the culture looks like ~ One of the most obvious illustrations of such transference - is the ongoing adaptation to that acceleration of technology - we talked about long ago - that's now - for better or worse - entered the 21st century ~ Witness the fact - that certain types of electronics - like cell phones - are considered nothing of a novelty or a luxury anymore - but have become almost (if not surpassed almost) - a required accessory ~ The knowledge - that they didn't even exist not so very long ago - is only an abstract idea - in the mind of a twelve-year-old - who can already operate a computer far more skillfully than his grandmother ever will.

But - I've rather left the point behind - haven't I? Or is that = Intentional? See - what I'm talking about here is = The box ~ That box we talk about - stepping outside of - thinking outside of - doing things outside of ~ We like the idea of doing that ~ We praise that idea (well - maybe not all of us) Yet in practice = It's really not very comfortable - outside - the box ~ At least - that's how - it appears - from inside it.

[[[[[[[[[Inside Out:

Generally speaking - the term - thinking outside the box - refers to a creative use of mind known as - innovation ~ To innovate (the verb form of innovation) - is to introduce new ideas to some area of invention - organization - technique - or simply - ideas themselves ~ It's an action of deliberate connection (as that word introduce describes) = So and so - please meet - So and so = An opening - a beginning - an - introduction ~ But - more importantly - it's the willingness to do so - to take the risk of exploring new territory - and - introduce your new acquaintances - to your old ones - who - may not be all that willing to welcome a stranger.

That's why - it's called the box ~ It has sides - a top - a bottom - a containment of - what is = So that - what is - stays predictable.

To return to that - generally speaking - use of the word innovation = It (innovation) - is really just a form of improving the box ~ It steps beyond the boundaries for a moment -

356

only to return and apply what's been learned - inside the same box - which is thereby made slightly different ~ Nothing wrong with that = It's merely looking at it clearly ~ The - general interest - in innovating - isn't in remaining outside - the box ~ It's in = Expanding - predictability.

Again = That - perspective - isn't a question of right or wrong - it's an answer - about our willingness - to question - because = Thinking outside the box - is not innovation ~ Innovation - is its effect ~ Question - is its cause ~ Not that you'd be surprised by now in my saying that ~ However = That repetitive idea bears repeating in any number of forms - because = The practice - of exiting the box - of thinking a way beyond old thoughts - to new experiences (which are only thoughts after they happen) - is exactly that = Practice ~ And practice - is = Repetition.

What are you willing to question?

I repeat = What - are you willing to question?

The sides of the box - are the agreed-upon answers - in their agreed-upon places ~ The thickness of a thought beyond them - is the unknown ~ So = Take something you think - you absolutely unquestionably - know - and = Question it (really absolutely unquestionably question it) - and = You're doing it = You're thinking outside the box.

Take... Your senses for example ~ In this moment - you are collecting and processing huge amounts of sensory information ~ Can you question those systems? Can you consider - that what you feel - and see - and hear - and smell - and taste - is not what's there - is not correct information - is not a function of perceiving your surroundings - it's = Something else?

What else? How far can you take the question? How long can you do it? What happens - when you do?

What about... Money? Can you imagine a world - your life - where money does not exist? Plants and animals seem to be getting along without the stuff ~ Planets and stars and galaxies - don't have bank accounts and credit ratings ~ Yes = Our complex world of specialized tasks and services - does seem to require a form of exchange in order to supply all of our species with the needs of survival - but = Is there another way to do it? Money - is really only a symbol - of value - therefore= An idea ~ Is there another idea - that's better? What is it? Are you willing to look - which means = Ask?

Or... aliens? Here we are in this universe of impossible to count star systems (much less count individual stars - our single galaxy alone containing hundreds of thousands of them) = The idea - that there are no other (so called) - intelligent species - out there (even when you take into account the enormous number of very precise conditions required for a planet to be life supporting) - with the capacity to travel vast distances faster than the speed of light (why not) - is quite simply - against the odds ~ But = That's already something you know (or has passed by your thinking in some way or other that it's not a surprise) - still = What about them then? Do they move inter-dimensionally among us this very moment? Is such movement possible? Are such travel speeds possible? Is an entirely different relationship with space/time reality - not just possible - but - probable? How - far out - are you willing to go with such questioning? How many - old answers - can you loose your hold on?

Don't get me wrong - and think the questions I've suggested - are disguised answers = They're not ~ They're questions that are already floating around - the box - because = The box - really has no sides - but - the ones we agreed to give it ~ We can agree on a question - just as much as agree on an answer - and = Just as there is power in that agreement - to maintain the box - it's possible = There is far more available - in agreeing to question it.||||||||||

Alright - here's a new box to look at ~ One that's well and truly just plain completely outside the box - and = For that reason - may be a somewhat - uncomfortable - idea to swallow - if you don't have a taste for such things ~ But - don't worry - we can't really - step - think - chew - or swallow - outside our collective box ~ We really only can - stretch the sides of it - expand it - because = No matter what - we take all the rest of our ideas - dramatically changed perhaps by the inclusion of new ones - but still - take them - along with us - because = We - the whole thing - that is - We - from unified field - to dysfunctional family - are = The box (but then - maybe you already got that) If you've made it this far - and obviously you have - your part of the box - is ready to expand - whether you agree with that expansion - or not - because = It already has.

Anyway - I really am talking about an actual box - when I say - here's a new box to look at ~ What it is - is a small electronic device (really more just box than electronics) - that has been - imprinted (remember that word from random robot and the chickens) - with a particular intention - by a small group of very experienced meditators.

Before you roll your eyes back too far to see clearly - what you might think is turning into some new age warm and fuzzy time - because of that word - meditators - let me remind you of those ideas of - entrained coherency - we examined back there when Mars looked like a possible vacation site ~ What these - meditators - had been practicing for long years - was that kind of entrainment ~ Meaning = Consciously tuning physical systems - brain waves - respiration - heart rate - electromagnetic fields - and so on - to the same frequency ~ In a word = Coherence ~ To be sure - there's much more to it on the nonphysical level - but = What it means on the level of - imprinting intention - on a little box with a few bits of copper and plastic in it = Is extreme concentration - of coherent focus ~ And what that means - or at least certainly appears connected - is = It worked.

After the imprinting session - the box - was covered in aluminum - and shipped 2,000 miles away to a prepared location - where it was placed next to its - target experiment ~ The target - was nothing more than a container of water - but = Water whose pH level had been measured down to $1/100^{th}$ of a degree ~ The object of the experiment - was to see - if - the intention - imprinted on the device - would affect the water - by causing it to rise at least one full unit of pH ~ Which is really a very significant change - when you can measure down to the hundredth of a degree ~ The reason - why - they wanted to see if such a change would occur - is because = That was exactly the intention - focused on

358

by those meditators - meaning = They intended to raise the targeted waters pH ~ And - like I told you = It was a staggering success.

No - I don't imagine you're the one doing any of that staggering - yet ~ Consider this though = For years now - the same experiment has been repeated - including lowering the pH - plus higher levels of raising and lowering - and = It's been consistently successful ~ What's more = The spaces - where these experiments have taken place - have measurably changed ~ The results - of intention - in those spaces - now happen more powerfully and more quickly - and don't even necessarily require - the device - to be in the room ~ Further experimentation (or measurement) - seems to indicate - that within the condition called - physics gauge symmetry - the magnetic field - has been altered at these locations ~ Which means = Inside the vacuum - or the space - contained in the atoms of the room - new domains of order - have been produced.

[[[[[[[[Vacuum Power:

Without splitting too many scientific hairs = Let's say - this No-thing space we've talked about - is the vacuum level of energy - which - mathematically speaking - is 10 to the 94th grams of mass energy - or - that much (much - much - much) - more energy than is represented by mass ~ To put that into some kind of perspective - it means = If you take the vacuum within a single hydrogen atom - or - 10 to the minus 23 cubic centimeters - and - recognize the latent energy in that (meaning - the energy that's just hanging out not doing anything) - it (vacuum energy) - is a trillion times more energy - than all of the mass of all of the stars and planets out to 20 billion light years away from Earth - give or take a few million light-years ~ And that = Means we exist in a sea of unimaginably powerful energy ~ And that = Means whatever you want it to.]]]]]]]]]

Which probably - means - nothing to you ~ But - to the physicists engaged in this work (prominent among them - Dr. William Tiller) - it means - leaps and bounds - in the journey to discover - if - consciousness affects matter - as well as some small steps toward capturing the prize - that for one - Einstein's $E=mc^2$ - has dangled a possibility before us for a century now = FREE ENERGY.

The Fourth Quarter

Excellent - you've made it to the final stretch ~ Can almost see the light (at the speed it's going) - at the end of the tunnel (as they say - though you'll have to work out why they say it) - from here.

So - take a moment and notice = There are two very amazing phenomenon currently going on in the world - which both qualify to use the phrase - defy explanation ~ The first qualifies - because = So far - there is no conclusive - this is - how and why it happens - explanation ~ The second - is because = The general public - or at least the mainstream media - defies - that is - seemingly - doesn't want to hear - or report - an explanation - of the actual facts that describe the first phenomena.

What I'm referring to are = Crop Circles.

Perhaps you've heard of them ~ Perhaps not ~ What they are (that is - what they look like - what they are - is where that no explanation thing squats) - are shapes - or patterns - most often quite large - pleasingly artistic - and extremely precise - pressed somehow (which is most likely a completely inaccurate verb - it just happens to be what they look like from the air) - the way a footprint is pressed into wet sand - into fields of growing grain - usually wheat or barley or rape seed ~ Unless of course - you're talking about the ones made by human hands - which are generally smaller - rather dull simple shapes - and by detailed comparison - hopelessly sloppy and imprecise.

The strange thing is = A rough majority of people - who have some awareness of crop circles appearing - think - due to the fact that some of them were created by people = That all of them must have been ~ You can't really blame people for being rather narrow on the subject ~ What's called - healthy skepticism - seems to come as standard equipment nowadays (if not all days) - and helps us to cope with only being able to make so much sense out of this crazy world as it is.

But = You'll have to forgive me - while I mirror - a certain dismissive - intelligence questioning tone on the part of the - of course people made them - side of the fence - with my own sarcasm ~ Especially as I say = Go ahead - go out in a field of wheat and trample down a circle - with whatever tool you come up with for the job ~ Make it an exactly perfect circle mind you - and = Don't break a single stalk of that wheat (again - not a single stalk) - and = Make sure that each stalk is bent at precisely the same level - still completely alive and growing ~ While you're at it = Weave the bent down wheat stalks into an interlocking spiral pattern - exactly symmetrical with the shape of the circle you've made ~ And oh yes = Work out some way of drying out the soggy ground only

360

within the exact boundaries of the pattern you've created ~ Of course = You're not allowed to leave any footprints or indication of your coming or going anywhere else in this wheat that so easily bends and breaks ~ And then - there's the next step = Where you create intricate designs of such circles - and lines - and squares - and curves - keeping in mind to represent complex astronomical and mathematical formulas and various other mysterious symbols and such ~ All of which must be directed from ground level ~ Unless of course - you have some type of portable scaffolding - from which to gain a higher view ~ Not that you're allowed to leave any sign of its presence (oh no) - like disrupted soil where you stood it up or took it down ~ But then - you have only a few short hours in the middle of the night to accomplish this task - and are not allowed to show a single light ~ Night vision goggles would be a help certainly - but since this circle thing has been going on for much (much - much) longer than they've been around - that kind of disqualifies you ~ Plus then of course - you have to create hundreds of the things - all over the world - almost never repeating the same design - and = Make certain not a single witness ever sees you doing it (unless you make a particularly shoddy one) - and never a scrap of your presence left behind ~ Oh = And somehow - you have to work it out - that certain electronic equipment doesn't function in the middle of your handiwork - and healings of various kinds occur for people that visit ~ But then - the wild imagination of people who will believe just about anything - should take care of that.

So - sure = Humans can pull all that off = NOT ~ Or = If there are people who can = Those are some folks I really want to meet.

Alright - thanks for indulging me for a moment ~ I'm not saying beings from outer space are behind crop circles (although I can't discount beings from inner space) - or gremlins - or liberal democrats ~ What I am saying is = They happen - and they happen often - and = Why they never appear on the evening news - is a very good question ~ The other - extremely - good question (in fact - never mind the first one - it's just there because it means so many people neglecting to ask the second one) - is = What do they mean? Or = What - is something - somebody - some energy - perhaps the core of what we humans (so busily ignoring these astounding things) - are = Trying to tell us?

Just by way of an after thought = Tell us something - or not = It's possible - that they show us something - about the ability of sonic vibration (more commonly known as sound) - to create patterns - move objects - and who knows what all with the right technology - or - use of mind ~ The science of - cymatics - or the study of wave phenomenon - has for several decades now been experimenting with the effects of vibratory frequencies (again - sound) - on liquids or powders (in the case of powders - or fine particulate materials - such as soil - they were spread out on a metal surface or plate) - by playing different frequencies through those materials - and witnessing the results - which = Are symmetrical geometric shapes - from simple circles at low frequencies - to more and more complex patterns - as the frequencies are raised - often reminiscent of eastern mandala paintings - and (that's right) = Crop circles.

The feature of dry soil (you were earlier challenged to reproduce) - inside the lines of crop circles - where the ground just inches away is anything but (remember - the majority of these things occur in England - which is quite famous for damp) - has been interpreted as another indication of an ultrasonic phenomenon (yes - that's sound again) - happening at high speed (and thus - high temperature) - as the means used to create these formations ~ But - again = Who knows ~ Just has to come down to = What does all this - sound like to you?

And then = All that grain - that was manipulated so by that who knows what - was - and is - harvested and used in all the products - bread to beer - that such crops are grown for ~ If one were to consider the emerging science of homeopathy (where solutions of active chemicals are repeatedly diluted until there is barely even the memory of that substance remaining - and then administered as medicines - which - completely opposite to our normal expectations - actually increases the effectiveness of those drugs ~ But anyway = Considering that science) - then = The world - including the underground waters which flow from rain to oceans through those crops as well - have been being homeopathically treated with the energy of crop circles for some time now - and... it's right back to = Who knows what?

Class Twenty Two - Movie?

BREATHE (Means what? Oxygen - as you may have found now - is only a part of this system of life being life ~ The out - is as important - as the in - because = It's a cycle - a circuit of energy ~ The AH sound - helps to reestablish neuroplasticity - and - circulate that energy coherently - because = By doing so = You are cooperating with the system itself - consciously - which = As you would observe the same cooperation with any other system in nature - results in = A successful system - or = By a certain kind of extension to human terms = Happiness.)

So = How did you go? The you - that thinks it's you - that is? (Sorry - couldn't help that) What about it then? What did you find in there - in that - I - place? Yeah - I know = Words aren't the best tools for the job - but try ~ What does hovering in that question feel like? Is it comfortable? Is it uncomfortable? Does it feel as though there is something much larger being you - than just your body and your thoughts?

Alright ~ I won't load you up with questions this time ~ I'll just say = Keep asking = Keep feeling around inside that question ~ What if - there is something there of more importance to - you - than that - you - that's asking the question - could possibly understand right now? You - wouldn't want to miss out on that would - you? Well - maybe - you - would ~ It is all up to - you - after all.

But really = What if - there is so much more - in that place - than you ever dreamed could be?

Okay enough of this - you - business = I - want to talk about something else.

You've probably heard the term - subconscious? Do you know what it means?

Well now - there's an interesting mix of ideas ~ It makes sense though = That there would be a certain amount of confusion around the meaning of that word - because = There is ~ It's not geology we're talking about when we use it ~ Meaning = There's nothing as solid as rocks to observe when we're talking about consciousness ~ There's all kinds of evidence though - to suggest - that there is - a part - of our consciousness - that we use constantly - yet - are not - conscious of ~ The trouble is = We - still don't fully understand what it is ~ Although - by using the collective - we = I'm referring to a huge number of different understandings - or experiences - which may - or may not - go a long way toward explaining it ~ Yet still = The words "don't fully understand" continue to apply to that - we - as a whole ~ So - when two people are using the word - subconscious - in a conversation - there is - more than likely = Only a limited chance - that they are talking about exactly the same thing.

That disclaimer complete = Generally - what's meant by the word subconscious - is = A part of the mind - that influences - our conscious thinking - and though we are not conscious of that influence - we could - become so ~ Meaning - of course = Become conscious - or aware - of what's going on in that - other - part of consciousness ~ Or not - because - of course = There's bound to be disagreement to that general definition as well - and = Oh well.

So - let's look at one description of - the subconscious - that may - perhaps - be of the most service to becoming = So.

First off = You have to recognize - the subconscious - as only a small portion of - the big picture - of how consciousness operates - and = That's just talking about the limited form of consciousness we call = Living as a Human Being in the world ~ What if = The real Big Picture - makes even that - look microscopic?

But anyway = Let's begin by describing your life - as a movie - which - is constantly in production (that is - being filmed) Now a movie - in its basic form - takes three types - or groups - of experts (or at least people learning to be experts) - to make ~ Of course - modern movies are usually much more complex than that ~ You've all seen the credits that are miles long just for the special effects ~ But never mind that - this is an analogy - so = We're allowed certain liberties.

First = There's the crew ~ They - take care of all the physical requirements ~ They deal with - stuff - on the level of - stuff ~ Put that box over there ~ This thing is broken - fix it ~ Get the food ~ Carry the cameras - operate the cameras - pack them up again ~ You get the picture..

Second = Is the actors ~ They - act - interact - react ~ They - are the main focus of the show ~ Unlike the crew - who are always off camera - in the background - never seen - the actors - are always in plain sight (at least one at a time) The story - or what - appears - most important - to the movie = Is what happens to them.

Then = There's the writers - the producers - and - the director ~ They're - the ones who decide what happens ~ That is - in an overall theme and direction kind of way ~ They designed the thing after all - so it really is their movie ~ Of course - they can't control everything that happens during production (and therefore need to maintain a certain adaptability to the flow) - but = They're still in charge ~ The producers - are also where the money is coming from - only - that's not really important to our analogy (aside from adding another whole level of energy source and all - that you might just store in the back of your mind for now)

Okay = So - you get what the roles of the three groups are?

Good ~ Now we'll tie them into how they describe your life - or = Your movie ~ But first

- we have to change their titles ~ Yet only for the moment - for clarities sake.

The actors = They're = Your conscious self - the - you - that thinks - it's you - or - the person that got up this morning and decided what to wear and is processing these ideas right now - or - thinking about something else ~ Either way = Conscious Self - is their title.

The Director = We'll simplifying it - by cutting out the producers (they're really just concerned with whether the movie is going to make a profit anyway) - and = We'll blend the writers job into a kind of background collaboration that all three groups participate in - which - eliminates the need to mention them again (only really did in the first place for accuracies sake - and to acknowledge the importance of their role in real movie making) So - the Director = Is - that missing 85% and beyond - the higher mind - the place - where those great inspirations come from ~ Which means = Directions - if - you're listening to them ~ So - their title is = Super Conscious Self.

Then - of course - the crew = Yup - they're the working - just do it - part of our mind - that experience has trained - or programmed - to make just those kind of decisions - like how to get through a door - react to danger - sit in a chair without falling out ~ The simple stuff basically - that keeps - things - moving ~ So - their title is - you guessed it = The Subconscious Self.

||||||||| You Feel Sleepy:

Even though the word - hypnosis - is less than 200 years old (coined in 1843 - after the Greek word for sleep - hypnos - by Scottish physician James Braid - who conducted extensive experimentation in its use) - applying its core principles has gone on for thousands of years ~ In ancient India - Egypt - and Greece - what you might call - spiritual clinics - known as sleep temples - were places where sufferers of various ailments went to receive a treatment consisting of an induced trance state (or a slow brain wave pattern brought on by some kind of rhythmic repetition of sound) - and given instructions (or suggestions) - to heal - while in that state ~ There were - of course - several other variables of religious belief and dream experiences woven through the whole procedure - but - those aside = The system had essentially the same working concept as visiting a modern hypnotherapist.

Hypnosis - is described as a sleep like condition - whose key difference from sleep is = One = It is not sleep = And two = The defining feature of that state (or whether you are hypnotized or not) - is a type of - heightened suggestibility - which means = An agreeableness to suggestion - or a willingness to override (ignore - discount - do other than) - your regular behavior or conditioned thinking - and substitute - the suggested ones - such as = I have no desire to smoke - or = You will now run around and squawk like a chicken.

What hypnosis actually is (which is to say - how it works) - remains an incomplete understanding ~ That it does work - particularly in relieving such things as anxiety and insomnia - or managing chronic (long term - ongoing) - pain - and the symptoms of psychosomatic (mental stress caused) - disorders = Is quite well proven ~ It's also been applied with great effect - to habit control (over eating - drug abuse - etc.) - sports performance - treatment of skin diseases - reducing the pain of childbirth - and even - as anesthesia for surgery ~ It may be a mystery - but = It's a real one.

Modern brain imaging (as you might imagine) - has had a go at unraveling that mystery - and = The usual lineup of PET scans - fMRIs - and EEG coherence readings - have pronounced experiences under the influence of hypnosis - to be the same type of brain activity as comparable - real - experiences ~ By way of a specific instance = PET scans - examining a certain part of the brain (the anterior cingulate cortex) - for reactions to sound - found that = The auditory hallucinations - of hypnotized subjects (you now hear the voice of your mother when you were three years old) - displayed an activity equal to that produced for real sounds - and yet = When measuring the same subjects - as they - imagined - hearing sounds - the same area showed little or no activity at all.

Might it be possible = That the unexplained nature of hypnosis (meaning - a lack of scientific understanding) - is because of = A certain dedication (or mind set on the part of scientists) - to solving (let's call it) - a mechanical problem (meaning - designing experimentation from a linear perspective as though the mind were a machine) - which rests on an assumption (or at least a very heavy leaning in one direction) - which has nothing but circumstantial (or indirect) - evidence to back it up - and therefore = Is just as likely - to be false?

Now - there's an intriguing question (if it made any kind of sense to you) What it means is = Science (or systematic investigation which only recognizes - proof - which is delivered in physical form) - may very well be handicapped in its ability to explain hypnosis - because = It's (very generally speaking) - working from the foundational premise (an idea on which a means of persuasion is based) - that consciousness originates - or arises from = The brain ~ And that - is a - truth - floating on nothing - but opinion ~ Certainly - there are all those scientifically witnessed actions up there (under your hair) - of electrochemical high-speed activities - directed blood flow and oxygen absorption - as well as considerable function impairment when damage takes place - but = Is the brain the vehicle - the driver's seat - and - the driver?

{{Perhaps you noticed - that I made you work a bit to squeeze all the meaning out of the last two paragraphs ~ The reason for that = Is the many layers of information processing required for the job (or experience of experiencing experience) - are activated (in your brain - but really more precisely - in your - mind - whatever that really is) - when you take on that job ~ Therefore = If - you didn't particularly cooperate with that activation (and more to the point - feel it) = It's my suggestion = That you do so now}}

You're welcome to your own opinion on that driver analogy of course - but = Perhaps what we're really talking here - is a field of consciousness - a non-local (connected to energies beyond apparent location) - energy - which = Only appears to be housed in a brain = The same as a DJ's voice - appears to be housed in a radio - which = After working out how to observe the radios circuitry in action - would also seem to prove the same thing = If - you were not aware - of the radio's function - as a receiver.

With that in mind = Hypnosis - may be a means of communicating with - that field - more directly - more influentially - because = It is a system of bypassing the middleman ground of established habits - which discount - or are unaware of - its (that field's) - existence ~ Definitely - there is considerable research and experimentation (with astounding results) - using hypnosis to reveal knowledge - which = Could not possibly be information stored somehow by neurons (unless that's not true) - meaning = Past life experiences - or communication with disembodied beings.

Then again = You may consider such wild tangents to be something stored in a cow pasture ~ But - the reason I said = Hypnosis is a mystery - that's real - is because = Its effects - or results - are quite real ~ Picking and choosing among them - doesn't answer the mystery ~ It just defines - what you're willing to consider mysterious.]]]]]]]]]

You may remember (not that you have to - since I'm going to remind you anyway) - that I used the word - basically - back there - while I was outlining the job description of the subconscious self ~ The reason - is - the simple stuff - doesn't have - exactly - hard boundaries - with what you might call - the more complex stuff ~ Sure = Being able to avoid an obstacle on the sidewalk - is simple - or = Not something you want to have to stop and figure out all the time ~ So - that's good ~ The not quite so good - or overlap - or - boundary crossing - that subconscious crew is apt to make (because their experience has trained them to) = Is hook other ideas into the process (or - what we call - emotional triggers) - that of course - drag old reactions into the same process - and = There you have it = The past - deciding - what the present - should feel like - and so = How it should be responded to ~ Kind of like saying = Look out for that dog poop - and - at the same time = Don't you hate and I mean really angry hate dogs and people that own dogs and especially people that own dogs and don't clean up after them and there's one now that lousy no good.....

The trouble is = Well - in its simplest terms = Trouble itself (not dogs and their owners by the way - I love dogs) You see = It's that - ideas are connected to ideas action - in action ~ Trouble - connects - to more trouble ~ Which is that = Train of thought - coupling on more cars - and hauling the cargo that fits so well with the theme of the rest of the train ~ Or - you might just say = Training itself.

If - it - were a real train - then = It'd be coming from somewhere - and going somewhere = Wouldn't it? So = Who - in our on location film production story - is coming and going?

Right = The actors = The conscious self ~ They are the ones - acting out - that reaction - turning it into a movie ~ A movie - by the way - without the benefit of editing = No out takes = No - do that scene over - and over - until we get it right = Just straight footage - 24/7/365.

So = Whose movie is it then - if - the actors - are using the script - provided by - the crew?

368

Exactly = It's the crews (or the past's really) = It's - an old movie - the director isn't having much luck directing.

Okay = You get - the picture ~ But - just to make sure = What kind of - possible reactions - are we talking about here - that subconscious self - might be apt to paste onto - the regular job of simply navigating around it's supposed to get paid for?

There you go ~ Excellent word = Prejudice ~ You can - basically - cover it all - in that one word ~ So = What does it mean?

Yeah - it's most often associated with dislikes between racial groups - or any groups - different from the one - you - or they - he - she - we - identify with ~ Yet - it's full meaning is = Holding (that is - believing) - any idea - that limits our willingness - to allow - any - person - place - or thing - to have a value - based on - its own individual merit - in the present - rather than - as part - or representative - of a group - or set - that some past idea - has determined - is inferior in some way ~ Or - in fewer words = Disliking stuff - just cuz ~ So - you could be prejudiced against leather shoes - a certain color of automobile - or bands whose names start with the word - the.

The - point is = It's the - idea - or prejudice - that sets up - the whole reaction - or script - the crew feeds the actors - instead of just lunch like they're supposed to.

[[[[[[[[[Doctor Dude's Dictionary - word twenty two - Enigma:

What do you get - when you cross quantum physics - with the building techniques of the great pyramid of Giza?

Don't rack your brain too hard now - because = What you get - is not some clever bit of intellectual humor - but a certain word for obscure mystery called = Enigma ~ The reason being = No one really knows how the great pyramid was constructed - to such precise dimensions - with such large blocks of stone - at a time when modern tools and transport and measuring devices - were unavailable ~ Not to ignore the fact = That all that modern stuff is still incapable of reproducing the thing ~ What it is (both the question and the answer) - is a riddle - an obscure and inexplicable puzzle - and so - just like I told you = An enigma   (However = It's also possible - that what might explain the mystery of ancient Egyptian pyramid building - is = An understanding of quantum physics far in advance of anything achieved to date = In our time at least)

No matter how such things do get explained - there is that little word - enigma - around to explain = That something isn't explained ~ It's all about being hidden - unseen - unknown - or obscured ~ Not surprisingly - that word obscure gets tied up in the definition (as it has several times now) - because= It's pointing at the rare and unusual - the hard to find - or little understood - but most literally (or generally - or specifically in the case of the great pyramid) - because = There are other things (that obscure) - in the way - that are difficult or impossible to see through = Such as thousands of years - written records destroyed - conflicting evidence - or - you might say = Just a needle in the haystack lost in the crowd one in a million idea of what's recognizable that never made it to prime time.

Enigma is mystery - ancient as the Greeks who planted its roots in meaning = To speak in riddles ~ And = Just as modern as strange pulsing lights in the skies and intricate patterns appearing in wheat fields in the night ~ It's a feeling as much as a word - or a word for a feeling (to perhaps station it in its more rightful place) Its usefulness - is often to label away a mystery as unsolvable ~ But - like the word riddle (that flirts with the imagination from enigma's definitive core) - it dangles the carrot of finding the answer - of unraveling those threads of the unknown - that tease so tantalizingly unsolved ~ Or not ~ After all - there are plenty of people content to leave unsolved mysteries in their shady corners with little more than a casual glance - or none at all ~ Which of course - you might say = Is another enigma.||||||||||

Okay = That's probably sufficiently hammered on now ~ But - while it's still echoing = You may have noticed that this entire course - is basically - hammering on - essentially - the same - IDEA - just from different angles - or view-points ~ Which - to make it quite plain = Is all the levels - we repeat the same thinking - and the same behavior - thinking - it is different thinking or behavior.

So - what - IDEA - what behavior - what levels - am - I talking about?

That's right = Very good = Ideas - which motivate behavior - in the way of - or - as an obstacle to - happiness ~ That says it all ~ Course I'll add a few more words - for the sake of filling out - the idea - of - in the way - and - levels ~ Which are = Ideas - as obstacles - as limits - as stops - ceilings - boundaries - separations ~ And = From what? Yes = They're in the way of = Yes ~ Which is = Yes to learning - yes to expansion - understanding - harmony - discovery - compassion - love - joy - and yes = Happiness.

So - we've gotten that far ~ It's time for another step then ~ Let's go back to the movie set.

Okay ~ We've looked at the crew's job some - and the actor's ~ So what about the other one = What does a director do?

Yup = Pretty direct - isn't it = They direct ~ Which means? Sure = Point the actors in the - direction - they've designed - the movie to go ~ Steer them - you might say ~ They can't - be - them ~ That is - play their role ~ They - would be the actors at that rate - not - the directors ~ So - the actual roles - are more like - artist - and raw material - or = Director = Artist ~ Actor = Raw material ~ Only - the raw material - in this case - thinks it's also an artist ~ So - it's easy to see how conflicts might arise ~ In our movie however - the biggest conflict - is = Paying no attention to the director at all ~ Even - in fact = Thinking (which is really the reason for that lack of attention) - there is no director - no Super Consciousness - nothing - but other actors.

That being said = Who is this director guy? The other ones are easy enough to get a handle on ~ They're accumulated experience - supporting the action - and - the experiencer - in action - having more experiences ~ Of course - the real experience of experience - is invisible ~ Can't forget that ~ So - this director dude must be doubly so - or - invisibly invisible ~ No wonder so few people are paying attention to him/her - or -

are believing that such a thing - if it does exist - is something - other than - or separate from - them.

Uh oh ~ Possibly sliding into some pretty controversial territory here ~ But - remember = Controversy - is always a conflict between beliefs ~ I'm not asking you to believe ~ I'm asking you to investigate.

Let me add something else right now - just for the sake of clarity (can never have enough of that) I'm not suggesting - in any shape or form - that these movie making analogy parts of you - or - the real - or theoretical - parts of you they represent - are - now - ever have been - or will be - separate from each other ~ What I'm talking about is - one thing - a whole thing - integrated as brown sugar and oatmeal in the spoon headed for your mouth ~ Even - if the thought of that gooey paste turns your stomach ~ Of course - that's the beauty of analogies - you don't have to eat them in order to digest them ~ The point is = I'm talking about one thing - not three ~ The investigation is = Whether one of those things - can become conscious of - being - all three.

[[[[[[[[[**What's in your Genes?**

Humans have - only - 25,000 genes ~ Yes - that does seem like a pretty big number for using the word - only - because = Our bodies are made up of 50 to 70 trillion cells (each of which contain the same DNA made up of those 25,000 genes) So - maybe it really is a huge number when you multiply it out (especially when you consider the millions of miles of length all that stuff adds up to I mentioned at some point earlier) - but = It's also a small number - when you think of all the decision making genes have been (until recently) - considered to be responsible for ~ Especially - when we share 60% - or about 1,500 - of those same genes - with bananas.

See - what it looks like (in that ongoing investigative understanding of the human genome) - is that DNA codes - work as combinations of on or off switches ~ Kind of like a piano keyboard can create any number of musical variations according to the same on or off principle of pressing which keys in what sequence ~ It also looks like = There may be several systems of heredity (or passing on characteristics one generation to the next) - influences on DNA at work in this world - which include = Environmental (what happens in the world around you) - behavioral (how you choose to interact with the world around you) - memory (how you remember happenings and behavior in the world around you) - and even symbolic influences - like language (the words you hear and choose to describe the happenings and behavior in the world around you) - all having an effect on which genes switch on or off in any given moment of cellular reproduction.

The truth is = The jury is still out on how bodies - and species themselves - develop and change over time ~ It's been said = That the on or off actions of genes - and their interactions with proteins - no more explain the shape of physical development - than the stacks of building materials at a construction site - explain the shape of the building they become ~ So - when it comes to humans - the questions got to be = How much of that change - is up to us? And the rest of it (which of course - includes that question) = How in the world - does it work?]]]]]]]]]

371

Alright = What if - the director - is the part of you - that's got the whole picture - the script - if you like? What if - there really is such a part? Meaning = An available knowledge of how everything in your life is set up and working = The why - the when - the where - and how - of all of it ~ What if - this knowledge - is interacting - with the same knowledge - everybody else's directors have - and = Doing it - in a state of total harmony and cooperation - for the sake of delivering to you - the actor - the experiences - your part of the script calls for - and - or because = You knew what the script was about - before - you took on the job of acting it out? {{Yup - definitely read that one again}}

Yeah = That's invisibly invisible alright ~ But = What if - it's true? What if - that idea of - String Theory (just to demonstrate a big picture connectivity notion) - that the universe is entirely made of tiny vibrating strands of energy - that - function together as one harmonious concert of vibrations to make that universe - includes (that's – INCLUDES) - you? Well - yes - of course it would include you - if - it includes everything ~ What I mean - is = Knowingly ~Yes = Knowingly ~ What if - that part (provided it's there) - knows - in a sense - the whole universe? That sense being = It's - in communication with it ~ What if - in fact - that is the understanding - hidden - obvious - or just kind of floating around in the midst of the - Quantum - String - Zero Point - and who invented pizza in the first place - theories = THAT - we - the whole 100% potential WE - knowingly (despite the fact - we small picture minds don't seem to know it) - function in - at that tiny subatomic - yet still - unimaginably enormous level - to - produce - this universe - or - multiple universes - together?

Okay = If - that were true {{Provided you could figure out what that stretched out sentence meant ~ I suggest you read it over a couple more times before proceeding further}} Wouldn't you want - to talk - to this director guy? He/she being - the knower - of all that stuff.

Well = Why don't you? How? Yeah = That does seem to be the big question ~ Funny thing is - it's really kind of a dumb question - since your director - or at least - the idea - I'm talking about - is = You ~ Which means = You want to talk - then talk away ~ Talking really isn't the problem.

So - that's your assignment = Do it = Talk to your director ~ Never mind if you - think - he/she - is not there ~ Just talk ~ Say what you want ~ Meaning = What do you want? Try to stay away from - what you don't want ~ You've probably had plenty of practice with that already ~ Instead = Ask - for - what - you want ~ Just ask ~ Get used to talking to him/her ~ It's really no different from what I've asked you to do all along ~ It's just - stretching it more - is all ~ How far does - you - stretch? How big is - you? Ask that ~ Again = Just ask ~ But - while you're asking = Pay attention to paying attention ~ Feel - the texture - of the whole experience - and - what happens - afterwards ~ Meaning = When will the answers turn up? Be patient - and do plenty of breathing - and = You'll find out.

N.P.U.- Chapter Twenty Two - Television?

Let's return to the quantum world for a moment ~ Not that we ever left it - we just placed our attention on parts of it - we don't refer to as - it ~ We can't actually ever separate ourselves from that world of the less than miniscule super tiny - any more than a bowl of oatmeal can separate itself from being the many individual oats that are in it - not to mention the subatomic action of being those same oats.

The common problem of viewing the quantum world - is attempting to do so - through - the world-world view - where tractor trailer trucks - mountains - oceans - and you get the picture - are so convincingly big - and = Even though fleas and grains of sand and flakes of ground pepper - are also convincingly small - they're still the size of planets - in relation to subatomic particles ~ Again = The quantum leap - of getting a real mental picture of the quantum world = Just ain't happenin' - when it mistakenly involves a kind of shrinking down the images of this big world - to fit the tiny world ~ So - much like some American tourists visiting non-English-speaking countries (as well as other more official representatives of such things as the department of defense) - have found (to their great frustration) - that even when you shout in English - the natives still can't understand you = That shrinking down (big to small) - does not help with translation ~ The big world - and the small world - are just not - the same thing.

Ah = But when you turn that last statement around ~ Which is to say = Reverse the order of small and big = It reverses the ending as well ~ It becomes = The small world - and the big world = Are - the same thing ~ At least in the sense of that bowl of oatmeal being the same as the oats it's made of ~ See = The trick - to avoiding the mistake of trying to understand quantum world on this world's terms - is to see this world - through the eyes - of quantum world.

But = How in the name of particle accelerators do you do that? Or = Is that a more fundamental question - like = Why would you?

Well - by way of suggestion = What if - this big world - we are witnessing with all our senses - is an illusion of solidity and interaction (much like the action on a television screen is the illusion of action - rather than real action) - because = What all that - seemingly solid interaction - is = Is a movie of perception projected on the screen of the quantum field?

In order to make some kind of sense - out of what I just said (even if it does sound oddly familiar already) = You have to = Do - what I said - or = View the quantum world at work in this one ~ The first step = Is to know how a television works ~ No = Not the entire television - just the picture part ~ The advantage you have in this process - is that you've watched TV - and = You're aware that the things happening on the screen - happened - or are happening - somewhere else ~ What is - happening on the screen (more precisely - behind it) - is a beam of electrons striking molecules of phosphorus - which flash momentarily as colored lights - and so create a moving image made of hundreds of tiny dots - called pixels ~ The pixels themselves do not move - any more than the individual lights move in a string of Christmas lights designed to flash in sequence as though the light was traveling from one end of the string to the other.

But - you knew that.

Well - at least in the sense that you - know - the actors - on the TV - are not - in the TV - and = The Christmas lights are just clever electronics ~ I told you - you had an advantage ~ What I'm trying - to get you to do - is use that advantage.

Here's how.

Imagine - that you are standing in the middle of a three-dimensional television screen ~ In other words = You are immersed in an ocean of pixels = Everything - you are seeing and touching - is made of gazillions of tiny dots of light - so many dots in fact = That you don't even notice that they are dots - any more than an episode of your favorite TV show looks like dots (provided the reception is good)

Okay = Now pick up some small round object - a stone - a bead (something that would roll down hill - given there was a hill to roll it down) - and hold it in the palm of your hand ~ Now - look very closely at this object in your hand - and imagine - that suddenly you can see it is made of tiny dots of colored light ~ Roll it around on your palm ~ Watch the dots change color ~ Notice - that just like that string of Christmas lights - the dots appear to move - but = These three dimensional dots are so convincing - they also maintain shape - texture - and even reflect light - and cast shadows - just like the picture on your television set does.

Alright - now = You are about to toss this object into the air ~ But = Before you do - you notice - that time seems to have slowed down to barely a crawl ~ Of course - that isn't actually true ~ What's really happened - is your perception has sped up to Einstein's speed limit (never mind the technicalities - this is imagination remember) So - you toss the object towards the ceiling ~ Which of course appears so slow - it's a bit like tossing an aircraft carrier in the fridge ~ In fact - so slow - that now you can really see that everything - including your hand - and even the air - is made of tiny dots of colored light ~ At last the thing leaves your hand and begins to travel upward ~ But now = Because you can see the dots everywhere - with no hurry at all - you can also see - they're not moving ~ The object headed for the ceiling - slower than a 16-year-old getting out of bed on a Saturday morning - has become obvious - that it's not really an object at all = It's just changes in the color of the dots - exactly like (you guessed it) - a television screen.

What you've just done - is wedge yourself (so to speak) - into the gap between the particle and the wave ~ Not that there really is such a gap (it's just that using the phrase -

so to speak - allows us to get away with stretching words into all kinds of shapes they don't usually cover) But = What if - what you just saw in your imagination - is actually how (with a good deal of poetic license) - everything you're seeing - that you don't think is your imagination - works?

Well = According to quantum physics - that = Is - how it works (aside from the fact - that none of those quantum pixels are solidly fixed in space either) A baseball whacked into left field - is not really the same baseball describing a smooth arc toward the outfielders eager glove - but = A series of speed of light appearances - one after another - of the quantum field reproducing the form of a baseball ~ I know = That's not what it looks like - but then = Sexy beer commercials and the evening news don't look like what they really are either (meaning - momentary flashes of phosphorous)

So = Why? Why would I tell you all this - or you bother to listen? (Actually - a very interesting question - that last bit = Why are you listening?) What does your listening change? Does it - change something? Is change the reason we participate in anything?

Alright ~ There are several reasons (as you've probably guessed) A fairly long list in fact ~ I'll spare you hearing the whole list though - and just give you a couple of key points - by way of inspiration.

The first is = Free Energy.

You remember me using that rather intriguing phrase last time I'm sure ~ Well - it's in there (no - I don't mean the memory - I mean energy) It's - in the atomic vacuum - the space between particles ~ Not a space dividing the particle from the wave mind you - that's not a space ~ It's the space - inside an atom - I'm referring to (which of course - is ringing all those bells in your head) But - yes = You're right = A vacuum means - there's nothing there - and = That's true = There is no - thing - in a vacuum ~ Unless we're talking about cleaning your carpets - then that's another story altogether ~ But - the vacuum I'm talking about - is full - of energy ~ So much energy is packed into the vacuum of just one tiny hydrogen atom ($E=mc^2$ and all that) - that describing its true nature sounds nonsensical in a world that still uses a measurement like - horse power ~ And what's more = That's not even at the top of the list.

What's at the top of the list is = Perspective.

What I mean by - perspective - is = A point of view - a vantage point - a location from which to look at things ~ We tend (and by tend - I mean lean in the direction of - like carrying around a thousand pound weight) - to see - the things we're looking for ~ For example = If you stood a botanist - a farmer - and a building contractor - in the middle of - a so-called - empty field = You would have three entirely different - perspectives - on the importance of that field - and what might be done there.

As for energy (that core fundamental necessity of all action - from breakfast to broadcasting signals to alien species in outer space) - our perspective as earthlings has been mainly confined to the narrow squint of caveman technology ~ Which is to say =

376

Burn things ~ What we have - accomplished - with energy - is another story ~ Not that the two can be disconnected - but = A tiny computer chip that can compute the square root of the circumference of the earth - divide that by 12% - multiply that by the average distance to Mars in 1936 - and subtract the annual cost of school lunches across the USA during the month of September - in a fraction of the time it takes to describe such an absurd equation - does = Make that cave family - warming their toes in front of their fire - appear a shade backward.

The thing is = The vast majority of our - energy needs - that both produce that computer-chip - and deliver your breakfast to you - are still based on = Burning things ~ The predominant fuels being - oil - coal - and natural gas (even nuclear energy requires fuel - in the form of uranium - which then becomes - a very unsafe - form of waste) Now basically - that's not a problem = If you pay no attention to the consequences - which = Has been a very popular - perspective - for the past century or so ~ The trouble is = There are consequences ~ Not the least of which - are dramatic - if not catastrophic - global climate effects - looming energy shortages - and increased armed conflict ~ Not to mention - the entire web of toxic environmental effects - those conditions produce (which - is also not mentioning nuclear energy again - and the dangers of melt down accidents irradiating all of - say... western Europe)

||||||||| **Peak Cheap:**

Not much more than a hundred years ago - an infrastructure (or - underlying framework of basic facilities on which a country or community depends to function) - began to be laid down in these United States (as well as many other parts of the world) - whose central expectation = Was an abundance of cheap energy - in the form of petroleum - or = Oil (due to its amazing concentration of power - just think of the time and the number of people it would take to push your car the distance a gallon of gas does) ~ The difficulty (which was apparently ignored from the get go) - with such an expectation - is that the supply itself = Is finite = It can not be renewed = It will - run out.

Meanwhile = The changes built one on another = Vast highway systems (using billions of tons of oil based asphalt) - were constructed ~ Populations (whose ancestors had moved to cities during the industrialization of the 19th century) - began to move to the outskirts of cities - where communities - based on service economics (maintenance and provisioning businesses - such as automotive repair shops and grocery stores) - which produce none of their own goods (like food) - and are totally dependent on travel for income and sustenance (food - clothing - shelter) - sprang up all over the country ~ Food production (that one commodity no one can survive without) - which had been (up until then) - a relatively local affair - conducted largely by family farmers on small acreages (there are currently tens of thousands more people in prison in this country than there are farmers) - developed into the modern agribusiness - of vast acreages - completely dependent on oil - to till - fertilize (the majority of modern production fertilizers are petroleum-based) - harvest - process - and truck thousands of miles to markets across the country.

At the same time = The automobile was taking over the job of nearly all (far more energy efficient) - public railway transport outside cities ~ The tractor-trailer truck - converted railroads to rust ~ The bus - sent the trolley car to the junkyard - and = More and more - the idea of autonomous (fully independent) - travel - evolved into an unquestioned right (if not necessity) - among Americans - which = Now fills highways with single occupant cars - extremely well designed for speed and comfort - and (by and large) = Even less fuel efficient than vehicles designed 30 years ago - when the first real signs of oil running out began to occur ~ Which adds up to = Burning up oil at higher rates than ever before.

Aside from the very obvious (for some reason - it took all that time for them to become obvious) - short comings of such choices (and I never even touched on the immensely environmental poisonous petroleum feature of modern life everywhere - plastic) - their results - are now beginning to show up in a complex situation - which is simply stated - as the phrase = Peak oil.

Peak oil - means = Arriving at a point in time - where there is still lots of oil in the ground (where there is) - but = The ability to extract and refine that remaining oil - becomes harder and harder - and = More and more expensive.

In 1956 - a man named M. King Hubbert - predicted that US oil production would - peak - in 1970 ~ Mostly - everyone who didn't just outright disagree with him - ignored him ~ 1970 came and went as expected - and = Now that all the numbers and such have been spread out and tallied and juggled and digested - it turns out = He was right.

Hubbert's predictions for a world oil production peak (back in 56) - were for - around the year 2000 ~ This time - it turns out = He was wrong ~ There is still a great deal of controversy - and mathematics - and questionable information about whose got how much surplus - with all the inevitable disagreement involved - but = The fact is = Oil production worldwide - is in a steep decline - and = Had Mr. Hubbert said - around 2008 = He quite likely - would have been correct.

The question (since you've probably heard enough hints of the unavoidable answers) = Is one of consciousness = Choices - are based on what the chooser is conscious of ~ Which - leads as quickly as gasoline catches fire - to the question = Is the generation - who have grown up with the instant global communication network of the Internet (as well as the ones that haven't - which really means - you - me - us - right now) - going to make the same kind of shortsighted - environmentally irresponsible - narrow perspective (polite term for selfish) - use of resources - choices - of how to live on the planet = Or.........]]]]]]]]]

But - that's just the bad news - from a certain perspective ~ The good news is = An opportunity for an entirely new perspective - is already on the table ~ Which means = A whole new set of energy solutions is also sitting on that table ~ It's just a bit fuzzy as yet is all ~ Of course - the reason for that fuzz - is that all perspectives (just like all thoughts - after all that's what they are) - are connected as well - and so continue to influence - our perspective ~ Therefore = You might have a glimpse of a new one - such as = A flying baseball is really just energy traveling across a screen of quantum pixels ~ While at the same time - knowing (of course another matter of perspective) = That if that outfielder catches that ball - your team is going to lose the World Series ~ The beauty of this new opportunity however - is that = It's there ~ It takes a shift in (dare I repeat it one more time) - perspective - but (like I say) = It's there - and already clever minds across the globe are digging into that opportunity - far deeper than you might imagine - and= Actually have been for nearly as long as we've been burning oil.

What if - the role you play - or - the top of the list - in assisting that opportunity to unfold = Is simply - to adopt - the perspective - that = Free energy - is possible (and then of course - that the environmentally responsible use of it - is possible as well)

The parts of this world - and thus - the ideas we have about them - we might be able to pick up and examine - and so = Relate to - as separate things - but = What if - they never are? What if - each one of those atomic pixels (so to speak - since certainly we keep doing that speaking) - are touching each other? What if - the quantum field - no matter who is standing in it - is = One - thing? And so = What if - free energy - is not dependent on whether it exists or not - but merely on - the perspective - we view energy from?

[[[[[[[[[The Law:

Natural laws - are rather more difficult to break than man-made ones ~ Which doesn't stop us trying ~ Only thing is = Breaking a natural law - such as gravity - can only be accomplished by employing another natural law - like thrust - which = Means no law was broken - only transformed to a different kind of energy - because = The ultimate natural law enforcement - is = Energy itself - and - it's unbreakable code of behavior = The law of conservation of energy.

That law states that = Energy cannot be created - or destroyed = It can be transformed from one state to another (like converting the energy of moving water to electricity) - but = The total energy of the universe - remains constant= No matter how many times - or ways - IT (energy) - changes = IT - is never diminished - only recycled = What goes in - must come out.

The question then is = What is energy?

The physical answers - break down to that word - work - or = What amount of what - accomplishes what (gallons of gas - calories - kilowatt hours) Biologically - energy is the word for what provides the means for cells to survive and reproduce ~ Chemically - energy is an attribute (a quality or characteristic) - of structure (atomic or molecular) - and that structure's ability to change - which you might call - stored energy (like the chemical cordite in an artillery shell) There is thermal energy - most simply described as heat ~ Electrical energy - or the jumping of electrons between atoms ~ And - nuclear energy - where the energy holding the nucleus of an atom together - is released.

All those energies - do - measurable work ~ So - in that sense - we are aware of them - employ them - have the ability to predict and rely on them ~ We can also break them down into two parts = Kinetic energy - and - potential energy.

Potential energy - is about systems - such as particles - or systems of particles - being something (say... the spring that shoots the ball in a pinball machine) The energy involved - is described as position (such as that spring - compressed - to shoot the ball - or released - as it does the shooting) Kinetic energy - is (rather more simply) - about motion (or that steel ball flying off on its way to strike the first dinger - which will be another moment of - potential energy)

That - however = Does not answer the question.

What it does answer = Is that - where energy is it interaction with matter (is in fact - being matter) - then energy = Is change ~ Motion is change ~ Work is change - and (as mentioned in an earlier discussion) = History is change - because = All that moving work of transforming one energy into different energies - requires time ~ Therefore = Time - is energy - which then drags along - space - since = There must be space for things to interact in - to move and work and transform and = Change ~ Therefore = Space - is energy.

Adding all that up (ever mindful of the law of conservation of energy) = On this side of energy (the time space continuum) - where things - and doing things - in order to change things - is what it's all about = Energy - is constantly - different ~ On the energy side of energy - where - no matter what amount of change takes place - there is no difference in the amount of energy = Energy - is constantly - the same = It - is always - now ~ In that sense = Energy - never changes - and change (which means time of course) - from that perspective - is an illusion.

The conclusion is = Energy - is permanent - and = We - are not ~ But = The energy - that's what we really are = Is ~ So = What is energy?]]]]]]]]]]

Let me offer you - an entirely connected - yet apparently completely different view of energy - that will perhaps bridge some of the gap between - creating new domains of order in the vacuum field - we talked about last time in the meditators intending pH change experiment (which opens this discussion of free energy) - and = This idea of the importance of perspective ~ It's a story.

A few years back - there was a state mental hospital located In Hawaii - a large portion of which housed - that is locked up - a population of people declared to be criminally insane ~ In short - it was a terrible place to work - dangerous - unclean - unhappy (never mind what it must have been like to be locked up there) So - just keeping the place staffed was a major problem ~ Then - they hired a new psychologist - who claimed he could change things - but = Only if he was allowed to proceed in his own way - which = Was based on an ancient Hawaiian mind discipline called - Ho'Oponopono ~ Desperate for help - the hospital administration agreed to his conditions.

For four years - Dr. Ihaleakala Hew Len dutifully turned up for work - but = He refused to work directly with the patients - or even seen them at all - instead - he reviewed their files - and worked on himself ~ What I mean by "worked on himself" = Is that he looked

380

within himself - his mind - his being - from the perspective - that the cause - or the responsibility - for the patient's illness - was also in there - and as such - so was the cure. Ho'Oponopono is the belief (the perspective) - that everything that touches your life - that is your life - is your responsibility - your creation ~ Dr. Len took on that responsibility - and sat - for days - for weeks - months - years - and looked at patient files while repeating over and over = I'm sorry - and = I love you.

So = What happened - other than a clever psychologist collecting easy money?

Well - a few months later - patients were having their medications reduced or discontinued ~ Shackles (meaning - wrist and ankle chains) - were coming off as no longer needed ~ The whole atmosphere of the place was changing ~ It became a reasonable place to work - even a good one ~ And what's more = They began to release patients ~ People who had been expected to end their lives in that place - were reclassified as healed ~ Today - that part of the hospital is closed.

You may still be wondering what this story has to do with free energy - but all I can say is = It's a matter of - perspective.

SPECIAL BONUS EXERCISE - number eleven

Talking to Chairs:

Given - that quantum mechanics describes all matter - as energy constantly in motion - or vibration - and = Given that vibration - is described as a movement between two points - or poles = Then it is safe to say (safe - from an agreement with quantum mechanics position) = That everything - is a wavelength - or = A frequency.

So far - no surprises in that (provided you've been paying attention) But = Where the idea moves from there - is to say = An electromagnetic interaction - or set of frequencies - is going on in every interaction between - things - because = That's what an interaction is = Electromagnetic frequencies.

Again - that shouldn't be a surprise ~ However - by way of example = Take sitting on that chair there for instance ~ The chair - or any apparently solid object - has a certain range of frequency patterns (wavelengths) - available to interact with - while it's being a chair (particle - rather than wave - you know) Simply used as a butt rest - with no other consideration of its energy (or even its chairness) - the chair's vibration is very slow ~ Dense you might say - solid ~ Which has its benefits - when you want it to hold you up.

You - on the other hand - thighs - back - and all the rest - also have a range of frequencies available to you as a human body ~ However = As a mind - a self-aware consciousness - you - which is to say - we - have a much larger - astonishingly larger - range available to us ~ And = It's there - where that interaction between - things - enters a different kind of potential - because = The chair actually has (meaning - is a part of - or included in) - the very same astonishing range of wavelengths.

Simply put - or questioned = What if - you have the capacity to influence - change - determine - or what have you - how the frequencies of the objects around you are vibrating - simply - by the manner in which you pay attention to them? And = What if - that determination - has the potential - to raise or lower your own vibration correspondingly (or in relation to the thing in question) - because = That's what your attention is already = A range of vibrations?

Okay - yes = That's interesting and all - but = So what? Fast - slow = A chair is a chair ~ What difference does vibration make?

Well - that's the thing = It isn't a chair = It's a frequency pattern ~ And = So are you ~ And = The difference (at least the most immediate one) = Is about feelings.

That correspondence - of raising and lowering - is the action of participating at the electromagnetic level (which you're doing all the time no matter what - as a mood swing kind of dance with the quantum field - which is the matrix of potential for all frequencies - at least as described by quantum physicists) The difference - in doing it consciously - is the recognition - of sharing the energy of that chair - enjoying that energy - and = Expanding that recognition - to include realizing that enjoyment to be an action of consciousness ~ And therefore = Knowing that chair to be a type of consciousness as well (meaning - at the level that it is also energy in interaction with the energy which is your consciousness) And so = The chair - is also - enjoying your energy.

Farfetched as that may sound = It's all been leading up to introducing an exercise - with which = You can test it out yourself ~ Which is to say = Test out - what it feels like.

It's entirely simple = All you do - is greet every object you encounter (or as many as you like) - the same way you would a dear old friend - or even just a friendly stranger ~ The point being = That you alter your usual mental interaction with - objects - animals - plants - minerals - stuff = To a conscious recognition of them as energy = By offering them that recognition ~ You needn't say anything out loud ~ In fact - it may even increase the energy on both ends if you don't ~ But - silently or aloud - to get the most out of it - takes putting the most in ~ Which means = Greeting absolutely everything - no exceptions - every building - tree - leaf - rock - line in the road - screw head - dent - scratch and detail ~ The more you go looking for what you missed - the more you'll see - of what you've been missing ~ And………

Just try it = Feel it = Notice what happens ~ You can take it another step by adding complements - endearments - conversation ~ What do you think would happen - for instance - if you told everything you encounter - that you love it? Go ahead - find out.

Class Twenty Three - Listening?

BREATHE (That's it = That's how you create a new habit ~ Repeat an action enough times (say... 21 days) - especially - with enough enthusiasm and dedication - and = It's stuck in there like blinking - and = How cool is that - when it's actually a really useful habit?)

So = How's your movie going? Any new characters turn up? Is the crew taking directions or giving them? Can you tell the difference? Have you been talking to that director of yours? What did you talk about? Does it feel different inside your head? I mean - has your awareness of its workings changed? Can you explain that difference? Even if you can't explain it - can you feel it? Which really means = {{{**Inventory Time**}}}

Okay - at the end of our last talk - I said = Talking isn't the problem ~ That - would seem to indicate = There's some other problem ~ Any ideas what that problem might be?

Ah - now that's paying attention to paying attention = Yes = Listening = Listening for the answer - is the problem ~ Take this very moment for example ~ Were you just listening? What did I just say? Okay - good = You are listening ~ I appreciate that ~ But = How often - aren't you? How often do you hear a question (wherever you happen to go) - you can't answer - because = You weren't listening - maybe not even to the question itself? Sure = It happens all the time ~ We all do it ~ I'm sure there's plenty getting said - out there (as well as - in here) - you'd probably rather not hear anyway ~ Don't worry = I get it ~ I'm not telling you - you're bad - for doing that ~ The point is = To get you - to see - what you - are doing - instead.

Any ideas - what that - instead - is? Which also means = {{{**Inventory Time**}}}

Bingo ~ Haven't used that word for a while - but anyway = Yes = You - are listening - to something else - instead ~ And what might that something else be? Yup = Your own thoughts ~ Everything - we - hear - has to get past them - either by becoming a part of them (meaning - being of direct interest to us) - or = By shocking them temporarily silent (also - by direct interest to us) That's really the key - to getting information from hearing (or any other sensory function - like say... vision) = Direct interest ~ It comes in different shades of intensity of course ~ It may be about wanting to pass a test - working out how to get your mother off your back - or - getting out of a burning building RIGHT NOW ~ The thing is - without some level - however thin - of direct interest - meaning = Personal = This effects me in some way - attention = Those thoughts of yours - are going to be a

384

distraction - or another whole world going on - quite deaf - to the so called - outside one.

Now - obviously - I've just addressed the kind of listening that's based on ears - which doesn't appear to have much to do with the kind of listening - our problem - is about ~ That being more the inside variety of listening (meaning - hearing super-consciousness - rather than - how interesting the sound coming in the window is) - but = Let's stick to this line for a moment - and see (that is - hear) - what kind of help it might be.

So = What do you think - the key to listening (the ear kind) - is?

Of course = The very same thing = Direct interest ~ Only - from the point of view - of really using that key - it means = Feeling - that interest - consciously choosing to listen - because = It's - important to you ~ Which means = Those thoughts - that are jabbering away all the time - have to be dealt with in the opposite way - in order for them - not - to - be - in the way ~ They have to be ignored - or = Made - unimportant ~ It's actually entirely simple ~ It's remembering to practice it that might seem otherwise.

[[[[[[[[[**The Sight:**

The word hallucination - is defined as = A false perception ~ The false part - being argued from a lack of the proper sensory stimuli - which = Accepted perception - relies upon to conduct business as usual in the physical world ~ In general use - hallucination is the idea of - seeing things - that aren't there - but = It's really designed (by definition) - to cover all the senses - or = It's just as likely to hallucinate the flavor of pumpkin pie - as it is to see your old aunt Gerty - who's been dead these past ten years - sitting in the kitchen ~ That is - if you happen to be susceptible to such experiences.

According to a history as long as human culture itself - such susceptibility - runs in a relatively rare (yet persistent) - portion of the population - quite different from the equally long history of madness and mental disorders - that is the standard corner hallucinations get swept into ~ The difference - is one of clarity - or = A relationship of mind - with what goes on in that mind - that is lucid (a concise little word - meaning - rational or easily understood) - which (naturally enough) = Has its own family of words - intended to describe a talent - rather than a handicap - topped by the roughly umbrella term for them all = Clairvoyant.

That word (clairvoyant) - comes from the 17th century French - meaning = Clear visibility - and is also known - in more folksy terms - as second sight - or - in hushed tones either friendly or gossiping = The Sight ~ The list continues with - clairaudience - which denotes hearing sounds or voices ~ Clairsentience - which is a feeling sense - or ability to physically experience - the vibration (electromagnetic field) - of people - objects - or locations ~ Claircognizance - which is simply - knowing - without benefit of accumulating information ~ Clairalience - which is olfactory - or involving the sense of smell ~ And - clairgustance - the ability to taste things - without putting them in the mouth ~ Not to mention - Clare Jones - the waitress at the local diner - who can tell just by looking at you you're a lousy tipper.

That's a lot of interesting official sounding words (with a certain exoticness when given their French pronunciation) - but = What do they really mean - and = Is that meaning - really true?

To use the word meaning - in a describe the action kind of way = Clairvoyance - is a means of information gathering - same as any other sense - only = Of a non-local source variety - rather like picking up a radio signal far from its point of origin ~ Of course - that's attempting to describe an extremely controversial phenomena - in terms of a well understood one ~ And yet - the intention being = There appear to be - senses - that some people possess (or have developed) - which inform them of things - in a sensory - or awareness kind of way - they could not possibly have realized through the use of their ordinary senses.

Such things as precognition (meaning - advance knowledge of a future event) - or - retro cognition (which is being witness in some form to a past event - you were not present or perhaps even alive to have seen) - are on the menu of documented clairvoyant possibilities ~ Then there is mediumship (not as opposed to a large ship - and likely the most controversial claim of them all) - where a medium (a psychically sensitive person) - moderates or engages in - communication between the living and the dead ~ There are - medical intuitives - who diagnose ailments simply by being in a person's presence ~ Remote viewers - as we touched on long ago ~ And of course - the most popular (in a modern sense) - clairvoyant type out there - the channel - which = Is a person through which direct information from a much larger sphere of knowledge (beings - spirits - extraterrestrials?) - is channeled (meaning - communicated - passed on - delivered) - quite separately from that person's own experience or intellect ~ The very famous Edgar Cayce - known as the sleeping Prophet - was such a one ~ He conducted thousands of - readings - in a trance state - from which he awoke not remembering any of the amazingly detailed and intimate information he had just imparted for people he had never met.

But = Is any of it real?

Science - by and large - does not think so ~ There have been a wide variety of studies and research delving into the question for over a hundred years - with just as varying results ~ Tremendous skepticism - makes for a bit of an obstacle to be sure - as much as unwavering belief - will swallow anything ~ In the end = What we're talking about - is the mystery of the human mind - experiencing itself in a universe so full of mystery - that to define the limits of possibility - as being only those allowed by perception (or science) - adds up - to a possibly even more precise definition - of hallucination.]]]]]]]]]

I'll give you an exercise you can try - that will show you - both = How to concentrate on listening - and = How much - your mind - usually doesn't want to.

It goes like this = Next time someone is talking to you - whether it's - in person - or on the phone - the TV - radio - just someone talking that clearly wants to be listened to - silently - in your head - repeat - every word they say - as soon as you hear it said ~ Just - just - say - say - everything - everything - they - they - say - say ~ Try it - see how it effects your memory of what was said as well - and = How it feels - just to do it.

Alright - again = Although that practice does address the regular day to day action of - hearing - it doesn't seem to cover that listening to the director business - does it? Well - does any part of it help? Yes = Very good = That direct interest thing is still key ~ You have to - think - it's - important - to listen - and = Believe - there's something to hear - that's important ~ The rub (that is - obstacle) - is - not believing enough to listen - and - not listening enough to believe ~ So - here's what you do = You start talking (that is - you continue talking - unless - you haven't started yet) - to your self - by which I mean = Your director ~ I know = That doesn't sound much like a way to listen - but = Stick with me another moment here.

Remember the early assignments about talking to yourself - and then - paying attention to paying attention? Sure = Of course you do ~ Did you do them? Okay = You are well on your way then = You've been looking at your mind in action = You've been interacting with it - and = It's - been listening ~ It doesn't surprise you that your mind is - there - does it? Or your thoughts? But = Did it begin to - feel - as you practiced those forms of attention - that there is a mystery in that relationship - of yourself - with your self? Did it seem somehow larger than you - a sort of constant observer beyond your thoughts - not really affected by them? Or = Did it just piss you off and mess with your skateboarding style? There isn't a - right answer - by the way ~ There's only - yours ~ Or - where - you - are - with - your - own - mind.

However - that mystery - is the thing I'm talking about - talking to ~ And = Because - it is a mystery - it requires a different - way - of listening - in order - to hear it talk back.

Any of you into detective stories? They can be really addictive - can't they? I mean - in a pleasurable way - a sort of - use of the mind - unlike other types of stories - that really engages those gears of interest from a personal involvement place = A - direct interest - you might say ~ Well - that's how = To listen - to your Director ~ Not - from the stand point - of doing a lot of logical deduction work in order to convict the criminal elements of your own mind - but = From the stand point - of watching the story unfold - while still = Knowing - it's not really your story.

Huh what? I know = But don't give up yet.

See - detective work - is centered on two skills - observation - and interpretation of the information gathered through observation ~ It's really just paying attention - then paying attention to paying attention ~ That word - observation - is - directly - in the center though - with bells and whistles on ~ What you need - to listen to - in order to - hear - your Director (remember now - this is the concept of your super conscious self - and although the definition of that is hardly precise - it's still = You - that I'm talking about) - is (that's - IS) = Observing (meaning - precisely paying attention to) - what's going on around you - and = In you = This exact now ~ Which = You've actually had plenty of practice with - having already spent all these years with yourself so far ~ It's just a question (answered as a dedication) - of refinement of technique and purpose - to the kind of focus that really - IS - paying attention - as you continue to practice what will come as entirely familiar to you now when I say = {{{**Inventory Time**}}}

387

||||||||| Doctor Dude's Dictionary - word twenty three - Materialism:

When someone is obsessive about owning things - acquiring more things - hoarding things - protecting their things - or showing them off to everyone in sight - they're displaying a set of values most easily labeled (in a general sense) = Materialism ~ What that means (as a definition - not as a judgment) - is adhering to a belief structure - where - well-being - security - status - purpose - meaning - and what have you - are perceived to come from external - or material - objects (otherwise known as - things) - rather than from nonmaterial - or internal - conditions - considerations - feelings - faith - wisdom - that sort of thing (otherwise known - at least sometimes - as consciousness) No matter how you measure (meaning judge) - such a way of thinking/being/behaving - it's definitely one of the options out there of how to participate in the universe (that is - relate to that participation) - and = The main reason for its availability - is a particular way of viewing - that same universe.

Materialism - as a philosophical opinion (often carried over the blurry border such things share with the world of scientific reasoning) - is the belief that physical matter - and everything it does - or is capable of doing - is the only reality - and so = Everything in the universe - including thought - feeling - mind - and things that go bump in the night - can be - and so must be - explained in terms of physical laws.

In short - that's what the word materialism is all about ~ It's also what you might call - a modern view-point - or - one that has enjoyed an increasing amount of popularity in recent centuries ~ However = There is a very key word used just there - that exposes a somewhat contradictory element of the materialistic philosophy - and that word (or hyphenated word - to be exact) - is view-point.

A view-point - is a perceptual location - or - a mental position from which to view something ~ Which means = What is being viewed must be limited - in the eyes (meaning understanding) - of the viewer - by having to view that thing (concept - attitude - interaction - whatever) - from just one position - or point ~ For example = You may think you look devastatingly attractive as you glance in your car's rear view mirror - but - at the same time = Be utterly unaware of the kick me sign your weasely little brother had taped to the back of your jacket as you were exiting the house.

The point is (and therefore must be included in the definition as much as in the word itself) = That materialism is an - ism - or = A framework of beliefs - decisions - choices - or definitions - of that amazingly adaptable phrase = The truth ~ In that sense - the definition is not concerned with establishing whether materialism as a world view is true or not ~ That point must be left up to your view-point ~ But - let me remind you = That a point - is a very small thing.|||||||||

Remember that - being in communication with everything - addition to String Theory idea I mentioned earlier? What I mean is = If - that is really what the whole you is up to (which is to say - communicating with everything) = Then - everything - is communicating - with you ~ And so = If you want to hear it (it being everything) - you have - to see - it ~ And - by - see it - I mean = Observe the whole interaction of what happens to you - inside and out.

Okay - I know that sounds like too much - or - constantly on your toes and don't miss a detail - but = That's not what I mean ~ What I do mean = Is what I said about - the detective story - not - being yours ~ Just like reading - or watching - a detective story (let's say - a real good one) - you're drawn in - you're convinced - you're participating - emotionally - intellectually - heart rate - adrenaline - hormones ~ BUT = You always - know = It's not your story ~ I know - you - think - your - story - is different = It's = Your story ~ But = What if - you were to watch it differently - observe - it - purely from the point of view - of what - it has to tell you? What if - when you do that = You = Enter into communication with that other part - of you (that super conscious self - or your Director) - because = It's not really - your story - it's just - a story - you're telling yourself - using the whole universe (with its permission - indeed - its full cooperation) - to tell it - in order - to learn = It's - just a story?

Well - that ought to keep you busy {{So do go over that last bit until it makes some kind of sense to you ~ But remember = It's a question}} Let's see if we can narrow it down a little - in order to make it easier to deal with - or - deal with at all.

Here is the question = What - are you paying attention to? I know = You've heard it before ~ But - here's the reason I am repeating it = What if - what you - pay attention to - attracts - more of the same?

I'll break that down for you = First - that word pay = Buy - is what you do - when you pay - right? Okay ~ So - do - you - buy - what's important to you? Sure = Buying feels different ways at different times - but = In order to lay out the cash - there's always - some reason - more important than - not laying it out - right?

Yeah = I know = We've been over this one already ~ Hang in there - there's a reason.

Let's say - paying - is attracting ~ In economic terms - it means - you got the money - and = Someone wants it ~ So - in order to get it - that someone has to have - something - you want - so - you will pay for it ~ Therefore = Your willingness to pay - attracts - the making - of what you're willing to pay for ~ Simple enough?

Okay - yeah = The economics are simple enough - but - in that - communicating with everything story - maybe it appears more complex - or even = That the two ideas (paying money and paying attention) - have nothing to do with each other ~ Well = What if - they are exactly the same? What if - what you are willing to - pay - attention to - creates more of that thing - to buy = A market - if you will? What if - there's actually a natural law - like gravity - and leverage - that governs how your life - anyone's life - works - that's based on attraction? No - I don't mean - wow is she hot or what ~ I mean = Where your thoughts - your attention - dwell - attracts - more of the same ~ Sound familiar?

Here's an example.

Let's say - you're an inventor ~ That is - someone with an inventive designer engineer kind of mind ~ You've been looking around at the way things work (things being - machines and the way people use them) - and = You think - they're mostly stupid - inefficient - wasteful - polluting - and designed more for sustaining profits than sustaining well being ~ Well - you may have quite a good point there ~ But - when you try to design and build a prototype (or a working model) - of one of your own designs = Everything goes wrong - breaks - fails - won't work - frustrates the living manure out of you - and = You've got a serious problem.

Okay = What if - that serious problem - is really - where your attention (your mind and feelings) - has been? And = Where was that attention? Right = It was on - what you think of - as a serious problem - or - all those bad design choices - everyone else - has been making ~ Yes = You want to solve that problem ~ But = What if - your thinking - or - what you're - paying - in attention - has been buying (because - at the crew level of your mind - it's identified as more important) - is - the serious problem - rather than - the solution - so - what you get - is = A serious problem?

[[[[[[[[[Natural law:

As either a reminder - a nudge - or a sharp poke - depending on what you're paying attention to = What we're looking at here - is the possibility - or probability (or who gives a rat's reverse) - of an unknown - or ignored - natural law (or is that - more accurately - a natural habit)

For instance = Childbirth - is a natural law ~ And yet = More often than regularly is referred to as - the miracle of birth ~ Because = Despite the fact - it is an every day occurrence - taken for granted with the same level of expectation as having oxygen to breathe = The moment it is examined in depth (not to mention - witnessed) - it is found to be thoroughly astounding - just plain wow - fantastic - amazingly complex - and it all just = Happens (not that we don't play our role in getting the process started of course)

But - okay = That's natural ~ So - what else is? What controls what controls childbirth? What is the energy that is energy? What brought John and Jane together to give birth to little Muffy?   Are natural laws the effect - or the cause - of nature? What is the difference? Are you paying attention?]]]]]]]]]]

I know - it doesn't - look - like the world works that way ~ But - and I've said it in more ways than I could easily count = What if - it does? What if - what reality looks like - and how it's actually created - are basically opposite from the way we = Perceive - it?

You'd have to keep in mind - of course - that - if - our attention - is creating - or attracting - what happens to us - then it can also - attract - create - serious happiness as well.

The question is = How would you find out? The good news is = If - you've been doing the assignments = You have been (finding out that is) Or at least - you've been - paying -

more attention - to the part of you - that will help - and (hopefully) = Seeing more clearly - the part - that won't.

So here you go - here's another one = First - get some paper and a pen - pencil - crayon - whatever you like ~ Then = Take a deep breath = Take another - and another = Relax - and slip into that alive being energy inside you = Say yes to it - agree with it - until - you - really - feel - it ~ Then (not until then) = Write a letter to your director ~ It's up to you what you say ~ Just like any of this is up to you ~ But = What do you really want to know? To do? To have? Ask about that ~ I know = It's a repetition of that last assignment - but = This time - you're writing it ~ You're taking another step toward really hearing the answer ~ And that - is what you do next = Observe - pay attention - to what your story - your movie - your life - offers you - no matter - from where - what - or whom it comes from - for answers to your questions.

By the way - don't forget that - repeat what you hear listening technique ~ It could make all the difference between - hearing what you're listening to - and - listening to what you're hearing - and = If that doesn't make any sense - don't just breathe - enjoy breathing - because = That always makes sense.

N.P.U - Chapter Twenty Three - Free?

So - I've been knocking around this phrase - free energy - as though it were as simple a concept as free tickets to the baseball game (you know - the one where the ball is just a quantum field image of itself) Well = Maybe it's not quite that simple - or entirely free for that matter - if = How we're defining the word free = Is not spending any money ~ And then = There's not exactly a securely nailed down definition of the concept - energy - either ~ At least when you take a step away from machines and breakfast cereals - or atoms smashed to bits and galaxies spinning - and enter the space where - the concept of energy = Is energy ~ As usual - it comes down to a question - of perspective.

Just the same = What does it mean? What is - free energy?

First off - from a classical physics point of view = There's Water Power - like what's driven water wheels for a couple thousand years or so ~ Then = Wind Power - another technology that's been cranking out free power for centuries ~ Relatively new on the scene - is geothermal power - which taps the energy of rising heat from the Earth's molten depths ~ Next comes = Solar Energy ~ In its most direct form - solar power - will heat water as reliably as the weather ~ Of course - weather is not necessarily the most reliable system going - other than it happens in one form or another no matter what ~ In its more complex form - solar energy produces electricity - as one of the simplest most obvious alternatives to - burning things - available ~ The weak link - in powering the world on sun power - has been the lag behind in evolving battery technology ~ Which means = The capacity to store - and then deliver - power on demand - has not developed to the same light weight long term reliability as the ability of solar voltaic cells to produce electricity has ~ Well - at least that has - appeared - to be the main drawback ~ As it turns out (and battery technology leaps forward with high speed recharge and delivery lithium batteries and research into super cooled super insulators) = The real weak link - is much more a matter of - perspective ~ Our own of course - as in = Not paying attention to it - or = Paying for it - or = Realizing just how important it really is to make such conversions = NOW ~ Then - there are other factors - such as = How are huge multinational corporations going to turn a profit on sunlight?

||||||||| Who - Me?

If you - were going to keep the world (that's the human world - in our standard species-centric way) - supplied with food and water and power = What would you do?

Yes = It's a big question - a planet sized question - which - at that size = Includes everyone (we're all using the stuff after all) - which = Includes you (me - us - we - no breaks on this bus) - so = What would you do?

The question really (as that old space of question goes) - is about = What - you will question - or = How far you can get that old box to stretch in the direction of - not knowing - and = What does that mean?

It means = There are sets of values (or what you might call - what we thought we knew) - that = Govern the decision-making processes - which = Established the systems that are in place now - and = Propel and maintain and preserve those systems - and = The very first of them - is reflected in your reaction to the question I just asked - which = Points the long bony finger of responsibility directly at your squirming little nose (no offense intended - it was just fun to say) - and repeats = What - would - you - do?

The majority of us (here in the US) - don't produce our food or power or do anything to deliver and sustain a water supply other than turn a tap when we want it ~ We - therefore - maintain the value structure of - consumers ~ If - we uphold only that one end of the system = When the system fails (and there are currently a vast number of stresses on the set of systems in question that are undermining their dependability at an ever increasing rate) = We - have real problems.

The questions then - are = What systems do work? And = What changes does that mean for - you?

Just for one = Are you willing to eat differently? Large-scale hamburger lifestyle production (otherwise known as livestock - cattle - or beef - without mentioning the other white meat) - is the least efficient land use (including destructive use - as in the case of overgrazing land to the point of erosion stripping away the soil - or converting oxygen producing rain forest to inadequate pasture with much the same results) - of all food resources ~ Cattle require enormous acreage just for raising their feed - which = Converts pound for pound to a tiny percentage of the nutritive value the same land could produce for direct consumption - plus = Animal waste is one of the largest sources of greenhouse gases (nitrous oxide and methane) - which - spells in a phrase = Global warming.

From there - it moves right on to = Are you willing to use less - own less - share more? The details - are pages and pages of witnessing balance and imbalance between what supports life on this planet - and what poisons it ~ The core question is = What do you need? I mean = Really need? And = How would you go about getting it - if = All the steps involved - were up to you?

You can break that question down = To values ~ Such as the one this world seems to most thoroughly embrace = Competition - and - its mirror image = Cooperation - and possibly arrive (as so many have done before you) - at the conclusion that the later (at least on a large scale) = Is impossible ~ And yet = We all - cooperate - to foster competition ~ Competition isn't a law governing our species = It's an agreement - a cooperative one (just as conflict - is an agreement - to conflict) The only thing - that stands in the way of reversing that status quo (or existing condition - in this case -

competition - or conflict) - is not things - and their value - it's = Ideas.

Of course - having - agreeing on - and employing - new ideas - is what's required - to do - new things ~ So - by way of example = It has been theorized - that turning 0.3% of the Sahara Desert into a solar farm (meaning - covering an area - roughly the size of Ireland - with solar thermal and/or solar voltaic collectors) - would generate enough electrical power to run the world ~ It would take huge finances - tremendous invention - innovation - and imagination - plus = Cooperation - such as the world has never known (barring our historic support of competition) - to achieve - and = Perhaps it's a really bad idea with lots of disastrous environmental effects.

The point (still jabbing that bony finger at you) = Is germinating new ideas themselves ~ New ideas - are new ~ They are connected to old ideas (because ideas are) - but = They are setting foot on foreign soil (so to speak) - which means = Taking risks - such as = The Sahara Forest Project's proposal of huge greenhouses in coastal desert regions - that would be run on concentrated solar power (CSP) - which uses mirrors to focus sun on seawater to create steam to drive turbines to generate electricity ~ Some of that water vapor is pumped through the greenhouses - which creates a cooler (broil you to bones otherwise) - high humidity environment - in which plants just wildly go for it ~ Pilot projects in Tenerife (largest of the Canary islands) - and the countries of Oman and the United Arab Emirates - have already more than proven the technology - and...

Flip to the other side of the planet = Global Seawater Inc. - is developing two plantations on the Gulf of California in Sonora Mexico - whose chief crop thrives in blasting heat on lousy soil with nothing but the occasional dousing of saltwater - and = It's a high protein - high fat vegetable - which can be converted to clean burning fuel - as well as a versatile foodstuff - and - at the same time = Does not compete with arable (fertile) - farmland or sources of fresh water ~ The project includes fish and shrimp farming pools - whose effluent (or waste products) - are used to nourish the salicornia (which is the name of the crop described - also known as sea asparagus) - instead of fouling the ocean (as previous local fish farming concerns have done) - which then = Flows on to man-made inland mangrove wetlands - for the purpose of sequestering (or capturing) - massive quantities of carbon dioxide - as well as providing habitat for wildlife and other forms of edibles ~ The whole thing - also serves as a means of reducing coastal flooding - which is the imminent result of melting ice sheets (one of the drastic results of that global warming thing) - by diverting seawater inland to a useful purpose.

So - there's a few ideas - which circle straight back to = What would you do? The question of consciousness - is not just about states of mind = It's about function - reflecting states of mind ~ It's about = The whole picture.|||||||||

That last remark aside = There are other technologies - rather more complex to explain and understand - than the sticking your head out the window level of description I've offered so far ~ One of them is called - Permanent Magnets ~ It works on the principle - of a tiny amount of electricity - causing a magnetic field to bounce back and forth between two copper wire coils - and so = Produce a much larger (nearly 10 times larger) -

amount of electricity - with no moving parts ~ Then = There's a special metal alloy - patented as long ago as 1957 - that can break down water to hydrogen and oxygen - with no electrical input - that does not chemically change the metal - and so = Is capable of producing hydrogen as fuel - from water - for free - forever ~ At least there is a persistent rumor that such a thing exists ~ It may not be true at all = Perhaps you should look into it.

The list goes on with = Cold Fusion (and the possibility of hot fusion) - which is (seemingly - depending on which sources you listen to) - alive and well - despite all publicity to the contrary - and is capable of revolutionizing the atomic energy industry ~ It's not exactly free - but = It is cheap - possibly even safe - and who knows what else it's capable of doing ~ Not unlike = The Implosion - or Vortex engine - developed as far back as the 1930s - which runs on cooling and suction (much like a tornado does) - rather than the heat and expansion power production of an internal combustion engine like your car - and - unlike your car = Requires no fuel to run.

Of course - getting back to simply sticking your head out of the window (that is if you happen to live near the ocean) - there's = Tidal energy - or a generating system where the movements of the tide (both coming in and going out) - rotate long cylindrical turbines capable of producing a regularly timed - seemingly endless - supply of electric power ~ There's already one such - power plant - off the coast of Portugal - and plans are under consideration for building many more around the globe ~ Also under water = Is the concept of utilizing slow moving ocean floor currents (including large rivers) - which travel at speeds of just a few miles an hour - and could - generate electric power through the vibrations they create in layers of metal rods with their passing ~ Nor do the new ideas stop popping to the surface from there ~ If you go looking = You'll find dozens more - and perhaps come up with a few on your own.

One might think - after studying such a line up - that any looming energy shortage - due to the decades long - fully scientifically predicted - understood - and it's gonna happen baby - knowledge = That the world is running out of oil - would be a cinch to solve ~ However - again - the question drops in the lap of = Perspective ~ What you might say - in this case (or perhaps any case) - involves = Priorities.

You may recall the difficulties encountered by the Biosphere II team - when a certain priority (namely - focusing on harmonious relations) - turned out to be a low priority ~ Well - you might say that = Biosphere Here (better known as Earth) - is undergoing a similar set of difficulties - which = When you add them up - produce the possibility of a very simple explanation - which = Is a repetition of the same priorities (namely - not focusing on harmonious relations) To spell out the perspective in question (for the very direct purpose - that if it is not placed - in a perspective of question - then = There are likely some very uncomfortable answers in store for all of us) = IT - is the condition of thought - that promotes as fact - the idea - that competition for survival - is = The way it is.

To whittle that down to a finer point = IT - is the belief - that things (which of course includes humans - and everything else in the universe - including possible other universes) - are separate from each other.

Now - you may consider - the point I just made - to have nothing to do with belief - but instead = Is just simply the situation we have to deal with and nothing we can do about it ~ To be sure = Such an attitude pretty much nails down exactly - what a belief is ~ Just the same - that little technicality - of the apparent separation between - everything - goes a long way toward explaining why there would be such a perspective as survival being a state of competition rather than cooperation ~ It might even explain = Why the idea of free energy - has basically been viewed as a kind of science fiction fantasy - regardless of the fact it very nearly changed the whole nature of progress over a hundred years ago.

In 1889 - a Croatian born American engineer named Nikola Tesla - was attempting to replicate - or repeat (and so prove) - the results of Heinrich Hertz's experiments (you know - megahertz and all) - that had - seemingly proved - electromagnetic energy to function as a wave ~ Of course - Hertz's work was in part based on Maxwell's - which in turn was based on Faraday's - and so goes the march of science ~ As it worked out - Tesla discovered a rather glaring flaw in Hertz's conclusions - which he personally traveled to Europe to sadly present to his German colleague ~ However - that is the other side of the story ~ It's what Tesla stumbled on - quite by accident (if such a word as accident actually applies) - while working on the electromagnetic wave business - which bears on our context - of free energy ~ I'm afraid - the other side of Tesla's story - leans in the direction of why we're still paying for energy.

To avoid a lot of technical explanation (which for various reasons - none of which are the same as mine - was also something Tesla avoided - and as a result was regularly misunderstood and badly treated) = I'll just sketch out the basics.

Like I said - while attempting to duplicate Hertz's experiments = Tesla made a little experimental detour of his own - by messing around with sudden violent discharges of direct current electricity (that's DC - like a car battery) - and so stumbled into a whole new realm of physics ~ What he found (again - in an extremely simplified version) = Was that electricity can be separated into different parts - and that one of those parts - can be drawn directly from the air (space - the quantum field - the zero point field - or whatever you want to call it - Tesla called it - the ether) - and = By doing so - that power is converted into a form - that can then be sent long distances through the air - much like radio waves ~ What he was proposing - was that any electrical device - anywhere on the planet - could be grounded with a rod pushed into the earth - and then = That same electrical device - would draw energy from the single magnifying transmitter station he had built at Wardenclyffe New York - and = Work - light up - do whatever it was intended to do - without wires - for free.

On top of that - as though that weren't enough - Tesla claimed this same electrical broadcast - which he called - Radiant Energy - would also elevate human consciousness to new levels of ability - clarity - and understanding ~ It would - by his own description - send - intelligence - around the world ~ How he knew - such a fringe benefit was attached - is not so clear ~ Although he did spend a tremendous amount of time around those machines of his - so = One might be led to theorize - it - had that effect - on him ~ Then again - perhaps that remote viewing skill - we talked about in the remote past - was numbered among Tesla's other qualities of genius.

But = Theory shmeory - you may be wondering = If - this Radiant Energy stuff was so great - so easy - and free = Then why - isn't it available right now? Or = Is it all just a load of horse droppings?

Let me first explain - that Tesla - for all his wild notions - was no fly-by-night mad scientist ~ Indeed - he was a flamboyant and controversial character - once the toast of New York society - who gained and lost millions over a lifetime's work spent in trying to improve the lives of humankind (as well as the fame of Nikola Tesla) - and thus - to his credit = Are dozens of electrical innovations and inventions - the most famous of which - is the alternating current system of electrical generating and delivery - the results of which - are likely going on somewhere near you this very instant.

[[[[[[[[[AC/DC or Topsy Turvy:

Beginning in the late 1880s - a series of events took place which are now called - the war of the currents (not to be confused with - the current war) - in which some very famous characters took part (in particular - Thomas Edison - George Westinghouse - and - Nikola Tesla) - and the future form of consumer electricity (from that point in time at least) - was set in motion.

The controversy - was centered on the merits and defects of the (DC) - direct current system of generating and delivering electricity (already in use and heavily invested in) - and = The relatively new innovation of (AC) - alternating current (not to mention huge amounts of money in future profits) Edison - and his company - General Electric - were in the business of that generating and distributing DC power - as well as producing some - and installing all - of the lines and equipment involved in the process~ There were problems however ~ Predominantly = The issue of resistance (or voltage drained away as heat as it moves along a wire) - which = Made long-distance delivery virtually impossible - thereby necessitating the building of a potentially endless number of local power generating stations (a contract Edison's company would have gleefully taken on) - which in many areas was prohibitively expensive ~ There were also = Advantages - such as DC's compatibility (or efficiency of function) - with machinery - battery charging - and incandescent lamps - which were the main electric lighting of the day - and - the major demand for power.

AC - on the other hand - had the advantage of being able to be transmitted at much higher voltage rates (which suffers a lower power loss from resistance - although even still an estimated two thirds of all power generated in the US is lost as resistance) - that could then be stepped down - or reduced - by passing through a transformer (a device which transfers current from one circuit to another - while also effecting a change such as voltage level) That way - the same wires - from the same distant generating source - could supply power for both household use - and heavy industrial motors - and thus avoid the greater expense and complications of the DC system.

Now - that might be quite interesting and all (or completely not - according to your tastes) - but = It's really the drama generated (not the electricity) - that makes for a good story.

It was Tesla - who devised a system for generating - transmitting - and using AC power (the rights to which - he had sold to Westinghouse - Edison's direct competitor in the electricity business) Of course - Edison - who had a long list of patents and considerable cash backing the already up and running DC systems along the East Coast - was anything but happy to give up those interests easily ~ To compound the situation = There was already a certain competitive animosity between the two inventors - with Tesla (an ex-employee of Edison's) - nursing a case of ill-treatment - due to a perceived lack in both scientific respect - and financial compensation ~ And thus = The battle lines were quite well defined.

Edison's main tactic - was a kind of smear campaign - aimed at instilling fear in people about the higher danger of electrocution from AC current (AC does in fact affect heart function differently from DC - although large voltage doses of DC are hardly less dangerous) Aside from a deal of quiet backroom lobbying among state legislatures - there was a very loud display of AC fatalities - conducted by Edison's own technicians - where stray dogs and cats - and even horses and cattle - were publicly electrocuted ~ At the same time = Secretly backed by Edison (despite his published disagreement with capital punishment) - the first electric chair was designed and built for the New York State judicial system - and tested out in August of 1890 - in an ugly little affair that didn't kill the man the first time and had to be repeated to finish the job.

It's perhaps difficult to imagine such spectacles occurring nowadays - but = The final episode - was probably one of the most bizarre incidents of technological history you could hope to find.

Topsy - was a female Indian elephant - approximately twenty eight years old in 1903 ~ She was one of a small group of captive elephants at New York's seedy Coney Island amusement park - where = She had killed three men over a period of three years (one of which was her abusive drunken trainer - who apparently had bought it for feeding her a lit cigarette) - and so = Old Topsy had been judged "a bad elephant" and was condemned to death (they actually considered hanging her - and would have - but for protest by the Humane Society) They tried poisoning her - but that didn't work - so = Along came Thomas and the boys - about 1,500 spectators - and - a film crew - and = It took ten seconds - at 6,600 volts of alternating current - to kill the poor old girl (curious that - that was okay with the Humane Society)

The short film - Electrocuting an Elephant - was widely distributed by Edison - who was still attempting to discredit AC power even then - but = The last straw had really already come - when Westinghouse (using Tesla's AC technologies) - was awarded the contract to generate power from Niagara Falls - which = Was successfully accomplished in November of 1896.

The rest (as they say) - is history ~ And history (as you know) = Is change.|||||||||

The trouble - which is to say - the obstacle - to completing Tesla's vision was - and still is = A matter of perspective.

Agreement - on a whole variety of levels - is what gets things done in this world ~ Agreement on a large scale - requires understanding - which requires attention - which requires not having a lot of reasons - that is beliefs - grievances - arrogance - pride - and on and on ideas - in the way of paying that attention ~ Tesla's difficulty (aside from the technicalities of whether his device would perform on the scale he imagined - for it most certainly did on a small scale) - was in securing that agreement - in a world where his ideas went counter to the accepted "facts" of electrical science (and of course - those "facts" had only very recently gathered enough proof to be stored away in the vaults of - agreed-upon fact) The other agreement in question = Was in obtaining funding - from men - whose chief interest in creating anything - was not in seeing humanity freely benefit - but themselves freely profit ~ In short = It was not an environment supportive of such change - because = It held to the perspective = That free - does not exist.

If you are still wondering - why you have to plug your toaster in to make it work - perhaps you might ask yourself a very simple question = Does - free - exist?

The answer - no matter how educated - informed - considered - or instantly blurted out = Is a perspective - based on past experience ~ It's also = A form of energy.

What if = The real question - behind free energy - is not really - where would it come from - how do you get it - and who's going to pay for finding out - but = How do you free the energy - that's stuck - in ideas?

In this moment - someone out there - is chewing on a new idea that will revolutionize energy generating - use - and - perspectives ~ Maybe even long before these words reach you - such an innovation will be old news ~ Or = Maybe you are that person - and this - is that moment.

[[[[[[[[[Absolute Energy:

If you were to return for a moment - to Einstein's relativity - where Energy equals Mass multiplied by the speed of light squared - and concentrate on that word - equals - then = What's really being said is = Energy and Mass - are not two things = They are one thing - and = When you get right down to it = That one thing - is charge - or = Energy - because = That's what mass - is made of ~ Whereas - energy - is made of - energy - not - mass - which = Is another way of describing an idea repeated by this course in several forms already.

However = Take that repetition of the idea - that everything is energy (repeated into familiarity by now - even if it still remains beyond believing) - and = Convert Einstein's equation - from energy equals mass - to = Energy equals Time - and = You have the beginning comprehension of a source of (another well repeated idea) = Free Energy.

Just as Relativity identifies mass - as compressed - or concentrated energy - a - relatively - new theory - points at Time - as being the same - or - another compression of energy - which = Does not manifest as - things ~ It manifests as - flux - or change - which (as we all know) = Takes time.

All electromagnetic action (and everything's got it going on) - generates an electromagnetic field (no news there) - which flows in longitudinal waves (north - south - or - up - down - as you like) - between positive and negative polls - simply stated as - a dipole ~ A battery produces that field between terminals - an atom - between positive and negatively charged particles - the Earth - between its north and south poles ~ Even the galaxy must be some kind of giant dipole - and = All those fields - are in fact - huge forces of energy (also referred to as - scalar waves - meaning - an energy whose physical quantity is not changed by conditions) - which = Are returning to the vacuum field - zero point field - the no-thing - no-where - sea of energy which generates time (and therefore space) - as the great emptiness - that's really full (you'll be remembering that nearly 100% space at the atomic level information we've been over long ago right about now)

Tapping that energy - capturing - or converting that electromagnetic field - into electricity capable of performing work (lights - refrigeration - you name it) - is the work of moving faster than the equal and opposite reaction of Newtonian physics can respond and cancel out that capture - and = A machine which can do that - is apparently - an accomplished fact ~ At the very least - according to the criteria of the US patent office - which = Does not award patents for devices that do not do what they say they can (in other words = They must work) The Motionless Electromagnetic Generator (MEG) - is the (permanent magnet technology) - machine in question - designed by a small team of clever minds led by retired Army Lt. Col. Tom Bearden - which = Has been independently replicated (meaning - someone else has successfully constructed a working facsimile) - by at least two other inventor teams - who = Entirely endorse its ability to output usable power - far in excess of power input - which = Again declares to a skeptical world = It works.

Trouble is = That patent was awarded back in 2002 - and - as of this moment - in the autumn of 2008 - the machine remains unavailable for public purchase ~ The reasons for that - are also - not exactly public (even though a quick search of the Internet will tell you all about the machine and its inventors) Inadequate financial backing - possible design bugs - conspiracy theories of evil energy conglomerates and secret government interference - rumor around it like flies - but still = When you'll be able to pick one up = Remains to be seen.

The amazing thing is = What remains to be seen - changes every day ~ The cutting edge news contained in this course - could become the dull old scrape of obsolete information with the turn of a newspaper page ~ There are dozens of designs in the works for extracting energy from the vacuum - and = Any moment now - could become the announcement of their availability - and who knows what else.

Most unfortunately = The same energy extraction (in particular the scalar wave technology - Lt Col. Bearden is most anxious to expose) - lends itself to the development of weaponry systems - with destructive powers so sci-fi terrifying - that = The real question is = Are we as a species - capable of using energy (the number one resource in the universe) - responsibly - cooperatively - compassionately = Or.....]]]]]]]]]]

What if = What we are really talking here - are not a multitude of systems - energy -

nations - environments - money - or physicality down to the need to trim your toenails - but = One system - that includes them all?

In the mid1840s - there were buffalo herds across the Great Plains of these (then not quite so) - United States - that numbered in the tens of millions ~ Less than 40 years later - a scientific census conducted across the whole of the country - was hard-pressed to find 200.

And = What does such a detail of history have to do with what we are talking about?

Basically = Nothing - and = Everything = The single most important reason - the buffalo were nearly hunted to extinction = Was so that one culture's way of life - could take over from another.

The point - is not one of right and wrong (despite all the potential there for such judgments) The point is = Are you willing - to be a witness to - the influence - of perspective (particularly your own) - within a system - of interconnected systems?

[[[[[[[[[[**Conscious-mess:**

Conscious - is a state of being - a mind state - a physical state - a knowledge - attention - and better duck now state ~ In this question - of examining - witnessing - and practicing the expansion of all those things = There are some very simple - very direct - questions - about the effect - of that questioning.

How many paper towels - napkins - or sheets of toilet paper did you use today? How much water did you drain down the plumbing? How much electricity did you use - or are using - or don't need to be using? How much fuel have you burned? How much trash have you generated? Where did all that stuff come from in the first place?

No = Those don't sound like questions about consciousness - but = Do know - why they are?]]]]]]]]]]

Class Twenty Four - Practical?

BREATHE (Not so fast there my friend ~ Perhaps you've never done this exercise routine (or then again - perhaps you do it all the time) - and don't ever intend to - and have even stopped reading these little reminder bits until this one caught your eye - and = That's fine - and = Answering the question = Why? May be unnecessary as well - but = You might want to ask it.)

Well - did you write the letter? Did you get a response? Where have you looked for the response? Anything really new - or unusual - happen to you since you wrote it? How about that repeat listening thing - what was that like? Did it affect your ability to understand the people you were listening to in any way? How about - how well you remembered - what they said? What do you feel - right now? How are - listening and feeling - and - right now - related - right now?

Okay - let's start this time with the word - practical ~ Remember me mentioning it right at the start? I said this course would be full of practical tools - but = Those fuzzy edges - of the word - consciousness - might make them appear - not practical? Well - I was entirely serious - and = The ideas presented - the ones that appear the most outrageous - and = Seemingly completely opposite to the word practical - are = What I'm most serious about - as being = The most practical.

But how could that be? How could the totally opposite - of what we observe reality to be - be - what reality really is? I mean - obviously = Reality - is visibly existing - solid - things - that are subject to the - laws - of nature - physics - and - cause and effect - which = We react to - interact with - and are at the mercy of - or - have adapted to cope with - and thereby survive as best we can ~ How could we be mistaken about that?

Well = What if - the reason we are mistaken (if we are) - is that - that world - that universe - that - set of things we think of as reality = Is entirely - a product (only $19.95 if you act now) - of mind - and so = Is - nothing - but - consciousness? Not that - that makes consciousness anything like a - nothing but - mind you ~ It really means = This thing we call - mind - and this thing we call - reality (may) equal each other - much like $E=mc^2$ ~ Which would have to mean = They are not distinct and separate principles of manifestation (or life in a physical world) = They are the expression of one thing ~ Call - that thing - consciousness - or energy - or cosmic poop = What's really at stake = Is a reversal of thinking - that (for all its being somewhat uncomfortable at first) = Is truly exciting.

Yup = I have been saying things like that all along ~ Maybe they've started to make more sense - as you've been looking around that mind of yours ~ Maybe less ~ But - back to that word = Practical.

|||||||| There is no spoon:

You may have heard of a man named Uri Geller - who - during the 1970s became internationally famous for his feats of mind reading - or extra sensory perception (ESP) - and spoon bending (silly as that may sound) - which is officially titled psychokinesis - which means = Producing motion in inanimate (or non-living) - objects - through the use of psychic powers.

One would think that the existence of such scientific sounding names - is proof of diligent research and experimental confirmation ~ However - one - would be relatively incorrect in that assumption ~ There has been a considerable amount of research and experimentation of that nature - but = As was the case in Geller's own story of dealing with the public - there persists a certain stubborn skepticism among scientists - and nonscientists alike - where the word - trickery - is more easily embraced - without proof - than the very real proof (available in large quantities) - that such phenomena are indeed (or can be - dependent on the individuals involved) - quite well proven.

Now that last statement may sound heavily slanted in a certain direction - and = That's because it is ~ I myself have witnessed demonstrations of psychokinesis ~ Which is rather simpler to refer to as - spoon bending - because = That's what it was ~ And - it took place among quite ordinary people - the majority of which did not think they could accomplish it - and yet = The majority - did accomplish it ~ And so = It's not really a slant (or a complaint) - so much as it is a statement of an existing condition - where = Calling Geller a trickster - is basically ignoring all the evidence - because = That's relying on a preference - an opinion based on unquestioned beliefs - rather than a studied conclusion - arrived at by examining all the evidence.

That evidence then = Is extremely impressive (for Geller's psychokinesis that is - we'll ignore the ESP thing here - of course if you're psychic - you already knew that) - with metal bending and twisting and behaving in all kinds of very nonmetallic ways - while = Being witnessed by thousands of people - including presidents and their wives - Cabinet ministers - Generals - nobility - and - the Queen of England ~ Which is not to say - those people make more credible witnesses than you or I - but = They do perhaps have more reputation at stake in verifying the authenticity of something occurring - which = Is supposed to be impossible.

If - you choose to ignore that testimony - then = You might find - the findings - of an electron microscope - slightly more challenging to discard.

Back in the early 90s - a Stanford University professor named William Tiller (a name which appears elsewhere in this course in connection to other remarkable - findings) - examined some of the spoons - bent - by Geller - under the super magnification of just such a microscope - and = He observed something that still remains unexplained by any metallurgical science ~ In the area of the bends - there were something like tiny bubbles of melted metal - which had re-solidified - yet left behind - very real proof - of reacting to an energy - no mechanical device is capable of producing - or for that matter = Explaining.||||||||||

Do you encounter problems as you move through life? Is there ever a time when you finish solving them - and that's that = No more problems? No? They just keep turning up - with varying degrees of intensity? So = Do you approach these problems - with your ideas of - or attempts at - practical solutions? Well - the ones you do anyway - rather than the ones you just complain about? And = Do those practical solutions solve them? Okay - sure = The problem - of being out of gas - is very practically solved - by getting some gas (provided there is any to get) - the same as other - one plus one equals two - kind of solutions ~ Yet still = Do - those - problems - ever really quit?

Could it be = Those laws of - nature - physics - and - cause and effect - are more like - the rules of a club = Rather than the unbreakable principles of how everything works we have no choice but to comply with? Could it be = We have it backwards? Could it be = The results of those laws - are - a type of orderly universe - but = One that endlessly creates - problems (challenges - obstacles - interference - delays - irritants - you know the list) - because = Of the beliefs we have - in those laws? Again = Do your problems in need of solutions - ever stop?

Ah = But problems are just the way life is you say? Well - that makes my point rather clear - don't you think? A universe of problems - in need - of solutions - is exactly what we do believe ~ In other words = That's life ~ Doesn't that - shrug it off statement - we've all used - describe so well our expectation - of problems? What if - it's not those laws of nature we mentioned - that are the basis of that expectation - as we usually assume - but instead = It's the expectation itself - which is working in concert with a different law - that governs what happens out there in the form of - reality? Which - to make it sound official = What if - that mysterious law - is the one that has been called = The law of attraction?

Oh - I know = That may sound like flitting off into a popular new age fancy - where pinning a picture of your dream house on the wall will draw it to you like tacks to a magnet ~ But (and that's a really big - BUT) = What if - those ideas - of like attracts like vibrational magnetism - are really just the first scratches into an understanding of a true function - or natural law - which = Is behind (meaning the organizational features of) - how the vacuum field quantum world - turns energy into stuff - whose reality to us = Is really the interior experience - of what goes on in our minds.

So - again = Still floating around is that word practical (for all it may seem to be floating off instead) It's (that word) - the great problem solver - in our material language ~ But = What if - it's not? That is - how we've defined what it is up until now ~ What if - it's really - the problem maker? Again - what I mean is = Our limited definition of it ~ Because = We've been looking in the wrong direction? We've been interpreting - the reality we see - incorrectly?

404

What if...

But - before we go there = How about - you look at this next question - in the very practical sense - that maybe - just maybe = It could be the means to solving all your problems - forever? Go ahead = Feel - that possibility - as a real - question ~ Only then (meaning - again - only as a true open question) - could you - really - find out - if it's true or not = Okay? Alright then = What if - you're dreaming?

Go ahead - pinch yourself - pinch someone else ~ That's the usual - practical test - isn't it? But = What if - that's how - you - keep - dreaming - because = You - think - a body - and its senses - are - what you are - but = They are really - just - what - you - are dreaming?

Alright ~ You've gotten this far = I guess you're willing to humor me ~ So = What do I mean by dreaming?   Well = What do - you - mean by dreaming? Okay = It's that thing we do in our sleep - where all kinds of weird stuff goes on - but - only in our heads? Well - yeah = That covers my meaning as well ~ To a point anyway ~ The - in our heads bit - would have to be just another part of the dream ~ But basically - that is - what I'm saying ~ Which - to spell it out is = Dreaming - is having an experience - of people - places - objects - and - events - that - while we're having it - we believe it to be real - but = It is only (meaning - really - because only - sounds like trivializing it) - happening - in our minds - or (if you prefer) - consciousness ~ Which (whether you prefer it or not) = In a way - can only return us to square one - or = What is - consciousness?

There is one small difference though - and that is = On this side of square one - you've spent some time paying attention to consciousness ~ So - regardless of - what it is - you know how - some of it at least - feels ~ That - is a huge step - because = What if - that appears - to be - the major - if not possibly = THE - reason - consciousness has a relationship with - or - is the possible cause of - physical form? Which is to say = That reason - is = TO FEEL? At least that's an intriguing way to feel ~ And - or but - or even - wait a minute = You must remember - consciousness - and - feel - are just words ~ There's something much bigger going on here - meaning = The whole energy generating force - of everything - no thing - and what's for dinner - all of which - factor into this thing called consciousness ~ So - don't try too hard to figure out what consciousness is - but - by all means = Keep allowing yourself - to feel it.

[[[[[[[[[Doctor Dude's Dictionary - word twenty four - Entity:

This might be the moment - to look at the word = Entity ~ And - if it's not = Oh well.

An entity - is a being - or something that exists independently from other things - or beings - whose existence is not relative - or related to (meaning - part of - or dependent on) - whether those other things or beings exist or not ~ In language (which is where the word entity is most commonly known to appear) - a person qualifies as being an entity - so does a corporation - a god or a goddess - a monster - or some alien life form ~ All in the sense of being particular units - or individual things - separate and self powered.

The trouble with the word is = It's a concept - whose very definition - falls short of supporting it being what it defines itself to be (now there's a twisty sentence) The difficulty - is non-dependence and existence in the same sentence - or a thing - not being part of or dependent on - other things (that is - in the world of things) It just doesn't hold up - except in the narrowest terms (like the world of things) Even the word - as nothing more than a word - makes no complete sense standing on its own without some supporting words or context to lend it meaning (although it might work well as the title of some creepy sci-fi movie) It's not like good old - who - what - when - where - and why - with their ability to perform alone ~ Yet even they are just go-betweens - pointing out connections already present.

Yes - a person is an entity - just as Zeus - King Kong - and Walt Disney Corporation are entities ~ But = Only in the statement of their being so - in order to distinguish them from other - so called entities ~ As soon as the statement is over - they revert to their interdependent nature (not that they ever left it) - of requiring each other - or other things - in order to exist ~ You might say - the real contradiction going on in the word - is in that distinguishing - that description of differences ~ If - a thing - stands alone - because it is different - it's therefore dependent on differences - to do that standing alone = It's dependent on that description ~ Which means = It's connected by described differences to other things - and so dependent on other things ~ Yes = The differences make it an entity - and in the same breath - cancel out that status.

Perhaps this appears like a harsh treatment for an innocent little word - and it would be if words were capable of being separate entities ~ The real point - is excavating the real meaning of what we're meaning - when we use a word ~ Entity is a perfectly fine word - in that - it fills a language requirement to represent an existing concept in order to be able to refer to that concept when talking about related concepts ~ It's the concept itself in question - that however well-meaning - cannot quite pull off meaning - what it appears to mean.]]]]]]]]]]

So - never mind - the dream thing - for now = I've got another word for you ~ It's = Sentient ~ Anyone know it? How about how to pronounce it? I know - it's not the most popular word in use ~ So it goes like this = Sen - rhymes with hen - and tient - sounds like shent ~ It means = A thing that feels - or - has the power of perception - through its senses ~ It's often teamed with that word - being - meaning = A sentient being ~ Which is - for one = Us - humans ~ Only - it's a description of what we do - not what we are ~ Which is very telling - because = What if - that's exactly - the limiting factor - behind - our less than 100% use of our whole selves?

Let me explain that.

In this world of - doing - things - we can only - do - so much ~ Because of that = We identify our selves - with what we do - or = Butcher - baker - candlestick maker ~ But most of all = We identify ourselves as bodies ~ To be a sentient being - based on perceiving through senses - we need senses - which bodies - if they're not impaired (or damaged in some way) - provide quite nicely ~ But (and I know I've repeated it many times - but) - the real experience of bodies = Is not - locatable in a body - no matter what electrical and circulatory mapping of the brain tells us about - well… electricity and blood in the brain ~ It's still just that = It's electricity and blood in the brain ~ It's not = Experience.

So = What if - the reason I've used the word - dream - and = I've talked about - a limiting factor - or - that 15% - rather than 100% - use of self - and then = This identity as a body thing - all together = Is to be able to relate your growing sense of - and experience of - consciousness - to something you do every day - or - more specifically - in a customary way - every night - and that is = Sleep.

What if - you're asleep? What if - just like sleeping - part of you - is dormant - or - not in use - hibernating - but = Just like in sleep - there's a mental experience going on - that you're - going along with - believing - participating in - and = The reason you are - just like during that - oh so familiar - experience of sleep - is = You haven't woken up to - the real - whole - reality?

Again = I keep saying stuff like that don't I? Now why would I do such a thing?

Alright - I'll take you way back to the start again and = We Have A Totally Important Function ~ What was the function I suggested that might be? Yup = Happiness ~ Okay = That's = WHY.

I'm like all the rest of you = I want to be happy ~ So - I'm talking to me - in the form of talking to you ~ And = What if - that's exactly the same thing? But - before I explain that one - let me finish - which will be very short and simple - because = I've already said it = It's - happiness ~ Our - old ideas - of happiness - are dependent - on contrast - to exist ~ Which means - dependent on problems - or = Problem = Unhappy ~ No problem = Happy ~ In other words = We - think - we can't be happy - unless = There is such a thing as unhappy ~ So - what we are doing here - is digging for - the source - of the idea - of problems - in order - to experience - happiness without contrast.

So as a digestive aid to that idea I'll move to the next ~ Remember me asking you at one point - if you dream at night? And - if you do = Does that mean that all those people and places actually show up at your house to act out that dream? Right = They're just in your head ~ How about when we talked about - the one idea - that if changed - would change everything? Remember that one? How about the - what if - we're all having the same dream question? Kinda sorta? Okay = This dream idea really isn't new then - is it?

Perhaps this one will be though = You've all seen a hologram - haven't you? You know - those weird two dimensional - and yet - three dimensional looking pictures that appear to be floating in space with their own source of light? You see them on stickers - key chains - stuff like that? Anyway - do you know what happens when you smash a glass hologram into a bunch of pieces? That's right = Each fragment - still shows the complete image ~ Pretty amazing huh? Well = What if - we - humans - or sentient beings - are exactly like that - both = In our DNA - those tiny strands of information present in all of our trillions of cells that contain the entire blueprint - or plans - for constructing that same multi trillion cell body - and (pay attention now) = Exactly like that in our consciousness - as a container for the blueprint - the whole image - of everyone - the world - the universe - all in a fragment - or - each individual - just like - that broken hologram? {{Yes - reread that}}

Wow = If that were true (that being the possibility that we are each holograms of the universe) - then = When I'm talking to you - or you to me - or anyone to anyone = We'd really - all - be talking - to our - self?

Hmmmm = That one's pretty out there ~ Well = What if - it's also one of the most practical solutions we've encountered yet?

Alright - alright = You've made it through a lot of talk about - ideas - about practicality - many - if not all of which - probably fit your picture of the world as well as pants on a fish ~ So - how about its time - to do -something practical ~ What do you think?

Are you ready? Here it is = Tell everyone (that's everyone - no exceptions) - that = You love them ~ Yup = You heard me correctly ~ All you have to do is = Whenever you see another person - talk to one - hear one - or just think of one - say - (and no - I don't mean out loud - so you're off the hook there - say) - I love you ~ You don't even have to mean it ~ In fact if you think you have to mean it - most likely - you won't do it ~ So - don't worry about that ~ Just say it - in your head - to everyone ~ And not just once either ~ Try to do it as continuously as possible ~ Each time you look at someone - everyone on the street - in passing cars - anywhere - even just when you turn your head away - when you turn it back - say = I love you - again - and again - and again ~ I know - you don't - feel love - for all those people ~ But - like I said - don't even think about that - just - say it ~ And = If you can remember to take a deep breath every time you say it - who knows what might happen.

THE PERCEPTION PAPERS - number five

Now Hear This:

For only a fraction of a second - the aircraft carrier's public address system - clicks - buzzes - and crackles - and yet = Thousands of ears (there are an average of 3,000 crew members on a carrier - and all of them are required by naval regulation to have two working ears) - instantly tune in to that sound - knowing it will be followed by the words = Now Hear This - which = May have dramatic impact on the next few (or many) - moments of the lives connected to those ears.

And so it has been throughout the history of human kind = Our ears are on constant alert for those signals that warn us = To pay attention now ~ Otherwise= Something might get us (which also describes a mind set - which results in such things as aircraft carriers)

What those signals are = Are wave patterns - or frequencies (what a surprise) - which originate as vibration (friction - impacts - movement - you know - vibration) - which then travel through a matrix (air - water - wallboard - glass - etc.) - as a kind of domino effect of transferring that original vibration from particle to particle at the same rate of vibration (frequency) - so = What reaches our ears - is what we call sound - but = It's really movement - like shoving the guy at the end of the line - in order to get the attention of the one at the front.

When that vibration does reach our ears - it enters the ear canal (those holes on either side of your head) - and encounters the eardrum (a very durable little piece of sensitive membrane stretched across the inside end of the ear canal) The action of that vibration moving towards us - is of course - that wavelength thing - which means a fluctuation between high pressure and low ~ When the high pressure hits the eardrum - it pushes it in ~ When the low follows - it pulls (so to speak) - the drum back out - and thereby = Gets it vibrating at the same frequency as the sound (vibration) - that just arrived.

The vibration of the eardrum - in turn vibrates a series of three tiny bones - imaginatively named - the hammer - the anvil - and the stirrup ~ They - pass that vibration on - by pushing and pulling on the cochlea (cock - lee - ah) - a fluid filled little organ (which looks rather like a snail - spiral shell and all) - lined with 15 to 20,000 hair like receptor cells - differing in length by miniscule amounts and varying in resiliency (or resistance strength) - to the movements of that fluid - which = Explains (at least in part) - how each of those cells has a specialized sensitivity to a particular frequency ~ When the vibration (frequency) - of the fluid matches the tuning (as it were) - of an individual receptor cell - it joins in - and sends an electrical impulse down the auditory nerve to the brain (at least that seems to be the dominant idea of how the physical action of hearing takes place - which doesn't mean it's true) - where = That still mysterious process of experientially prerecorded interpretation networks (also called the brain) - transforms those impulses into the part of perception we call = Hearing.

Take a moment then = And notice all the sounds that are vibrating around you ~ If you put your full attention on it - you'll probably find (depending on where you are) - that there is a complex texture to it all - that the word texture - fits quite well.

The human ear (meaning - the whole auditory system) - is an amazingly powerful information gatherer ~ Its frequency range - is between 20 hertz (Hz) - or cycles per second (a cycle being - the movement from high to low pressure and back again) - and 20,000 Hz ~ Dolphins have us all beat on the ultrasound end (high frequency) - at 200,000 Hz (it's been theorized that they send holographic images to one another through sound) - and elephants on the other end (low frequency - or infrasound) - at 5 Hz ~ But still = We are really good at this hearing thing ~ We (meaning - fully functional ear possessors) - can detect a sound of such low intensity (intensity being a measurement of how much vibrational energy moves through how much space in how much time) - that it displaces particles of air by only one/billionth of a centimeter - and = As high (without doing actual damage) - as more than a billion times stronger ~ We also - have varying numbers of ultra sensitive neurons - located along the auditory nerve - which can detect changes in pitch (or tone shifts - measured in frequency - intensity - and loudness) as fine as one/twelfth of an octave (an octave change is measured as double the rate of a frequency - or - a wavelength vibrating twice as fast) - only bats are better at it than us.

For all we may be taking in the same vibrations = Hearing - is still just as unique to each of us - as the personal use of any of the other four senses ~ We're selective - conditioned

- biased ~ Take language for one = Eavesdropping on our native tongue is a given ~ Whereas chatter in a foreign language - can be ignored (or be entirely fascinating) - as so many crickets on a summer's night - which = Is part of our - seemingly built in - tune out ability ~ White noise (that hum of refrigerators - air conditioners - distant traffic - or those same crickets) - is a constant in many parts of our modern world (not counting the crickets with the word modern) We may have turned the radio on - but that doesn't mean we're listening to it.

Of course - listening - also has automatic cues in our particular wavelength ~ Your name for instance = You could be in a crowded airport - where words are nothing but heavy static - and = The sound of your name will cut through with surgical precision (especially in the form of a familiar voice) The same is true of mothers with babies and young children ~ The sound of their child crying will rouse them from a dead sleep - where other sounds - equally loud or louder - will not - including someone else's child crying.

Go ahead then - have another listen to the sounds around you ~ How much more do you notice - that you weren't a moment ago? Make a sound by moving something - scuffing your feet - tapping on a table ~ How much more complex are those sounds (vibrations) - with attention on them? Close your eyes and do it ~ Tune your whole focus to your ears ~ What does it feel like? Does it seem as though your head is wide open to the world? As far as vibration goes = It is ~ It's just as much a matrix for sound waves as any other atomic structure ~ Feel it then ~ Feel those vibrations moving ~ Notice how you can locate the direction of their source - just by hearing them ~ Notice how much information they carry ~ Notice yourself interpreting that information.

Listening - is a form of attention ~ So - pay it up ~ Make a real investment in it - for an hour - a day ~ Feel yourself hearing ~ Walk around hearing ~ No - no - not to that iPod = To all the vibrating world of sounds out there - the pleasing ones - the irritating ones - the loud - soft - sharp - shout and whisper of it - because = You can.

410

N.P.U - Chapter Twenty Four - Systems?

I asked you - if - you were willing to be a witness last time ~ Which of course = You have been dying to find out what in the world I meant ever since ~ Or - at least maybe you remember I said it ~ Which (also of course) = Makes you a witness to that event ~ Either way = If we were to tax that memory of yours a bit further - you would recall entering one area of the quantum world - through the Copenhagen Interpretation - where - essentially = Reality is said to be the result of an observer - or a measure-er (poor English as that may be) - who - in a word = Is a - witness - to the world of reality.

The sticky bit - in interpreting that interpretation = Is that it seems to suppose (even though it doesn't) - that the observer - and the observed - are separate things ~ Not - that - that is any sort of surprising conclusion - given what looks like the usual state of observing a world that always seems to be there no matter what you do ~ The thing is = That - things observed - are constructed of that subatomic wave world - collapsing from the superposition of possibility - into the particle - when that observation occurs - and = In exactly that same moment - the physical elements - of the observer (which really isn't physical) - are constructed of the very same thing ~ What I'm saying is = We (meaning - our bodies) - are made of the same stuff (or not stuff - as the case may be) - as everything else is ~ So = That would seem to mean = This business of observing - or witnessing - is not one set of things - causing another - or even - two things happening simultaneously - but = One thing - interacting - with itself.

Alright - that probably makes as much sense to you as 1+1=3 ~ Unless of course - you already arrived at three on your own - and in that case = Cool ~ Otherwise = I'll remind you of that witness question - which is = Are you willing to be a witness to the influence of perspective (particularly your own) - within a system of interconnected systems? Because = It's THERE (despite appearances) = IN the world of solid stuff (like buffalo - few as they may be) - that the understanding - of a single - interconnected reality - is actually most easily observed (or is that - witnessed?)

[[[[[[[[[The Vegetable Sisterhood:

In using the word - connection (aside from objects glued - nailed - and bolted together) - we're talking = A state - of interaction (not that glue and nails and bolts are really any different) - just as that fundamental law of physics states = To every action - there is an equal and opposite - reaction = Action - and reaction - are inseparable ~ They do not -

can not - exist - without one another ~ Anymore than an image in the mirror - can do things independently of what it reflects (at least in form - imagination can do anything it likes)

From that understanding - it is simple enough to reflect = That all interactions are connected - as the endless interference pattern of rippling actions and reactions - which = Even though they may appear to cancel each other's energy out (such as catching a pop fly to left field) - they never stop energy - they merely convert it to another form of energy - which = Continues that infinite flow.

Look for a moment then - at an ancient example of deliberate connected interaction - which = Models the kind of balance between action and reaction - that delivers what's known as - a sustainable system (or succotash - depending on your point of view)

It's called = The three sisters of life - the foundational anchor of native American agriculture ~ The sister's names (in English) - are = Corn (originally called maize - and still known by that name outside the US - despite its having originated on this continent) = Beans (the hard - slow cooking - native varieties) - and = Squash (what we call winter squash - such as butternut and pumpkins) They were cultivated together - by virtually every soil tilling tribe between southern Canada and Panama - because = They form a symbiotic relationship of highly complimentary nutritive value.

What that means is = Maize (which was once a variety of wild grass native to the Americas) - grows in the form of a tall stalk (as you've all seen) Beans (which are a form of climbing vine) - grow best when they have something to support them above the ground ~ When planted together - the maize supplies the pole for the beans - and - the beans - which are natural nitrogen fixers (they absorb nitrogen from the air and store it in nodules - or lumps in their roots - where it enters the soil) - provide the heavily nitrogen dependent maize with just what it needs ~ Between the rows of maize and beans - squash plants (which are a creeping ground cover) - furnish a natural mulch with their broad leaves shading the soil - and thereby eliminating weeds and maintaining moisture for the shallow rooted corn (that is - maize) Squash vines - are also uncomfortably spiny - which helps to discourage insects and other vegetable eating critters.

And that = Is a symbiotic (or mutual beneficial) - relationship.

As for complimentary nutritive value = Corn - contains all but two of the essential amino acids that constitute a complete protein ~ Beans (as you may have guessed - or already know) - supply those two aminos (as well as repeating most of the others) - plus riboflavin and niacin (also missing from corn) Squash - is rich in carbohydrates - and vitamin A. - and supplies vegetable fats in its seeds ~ The three eaten in combination (the succotash comment earlier is based on the standard native dish of that name - which is exactly that combination) - is a life-sustaining diet that requires little or no additional foodstuffs to maintain reasonable health (given the same menu doesn't last too long - got to have those leafy greens you know) - and = Has the added benefit of storing well in cold weather.

The most important feature of this tried and true example - is not so much about - what -

we produce to fulfill our needs - but = How - we produce what we need - as a reflection - of the whole understanding - of connected interactions ~ When each part of the picture receives what it needs = There is no such thing as need ~ There is only - cooperative interaction - otherwise known as = Flow.|||||||||

Okay - let's get you up on that witness stand.

Now - if you've ever been in a courtroom - or - witnessed - courtroom scenes on those flashing phosphor pixels of reality illusion called TV = Then you know that a witness stand involves a chair ~ Since this is a far more informal setting (as well as more personal - in a certain sense) - let's say the chair involved this time - is in your kitchen - and - for the purposes of this trial = You just purchased - said chair (exhibit A) - earlier today.

So = What do you observe about this chair?

Okay ~ It's a simple - straight-backed - wooden chair - with a seat and four legs - no padding - no adornment - just a place to sit and that's that?

Alright ~ Will you please tell the court - how this humble object - you call a chair - expresses the total interconnected systems within one system - known as the universe - that you stand accused of being - both the cause - and - effect of.

Huh?

Alright ~ At the risk of appearing to lead the witness - let me assist your ability to answer the question - by reconstructing the event of purchasing this chair - which you claim - to have taken place earlier today ~ Three questions then = Where did you buy it? How did you get there? How did you pay?

Very well ~ You answered = That it came from a furniture store ~ Your friend drove you there ~ And - you paid with a credit card ~ Does that mean you're prepared to answer the question now?

Ahh - right ~ Since you don't appear to fully grasp the question - and = For the sake of speeding up this little episode of cosmic justice - we'll work backwards in time - in literally - a systematic way.

We'll start in the kitchen.

Why did you purchase this chair? So what do you generally do when you're sitting at the kitchen table? Have you eaten today? Do you eat every day? Why? Does that refrigerator have food in it? Where did that food come from? How many different packaging materials are in that fridge? What does that fridge run on? Where does the electricity come from? Did someone invent refrigeration? What's the fridge made of? Where did all those materials come from? Do you suppose all the people involved in all the steps of creating the materials - electricity - packaging - and food - that make up that

414

fridge - also eat food and sit on chairs? How about live in houses? Why? So weather is going on everywhere? What about light and darkness - insects and animals? Does water come out of that faucet? Where does it come from? Where does the drain go? What happens to that water? Have there always been sewer systems? What's this house made of? Who built it? What are those people doing now? Where did all those different materials come from? How did they get here? Were those roads out there always there? Where do they lead? What are they made of? What kind of car does your friend drive? Why? Did you listen to the radio in the car? How did hip-hop music develop? Were the people you passed on the way to the store wearing clothes? What are you wearing? Why that particular style? Does your friend have insurance for his car? How about a drivers license? How do cars work? Where does gasoline come from? What is oil? Are you breathing? What temperature is it? What did you have for lunch? Do you have a cell phone? Can you hear me now? Notice any connections yet?

That's right = We haven't even made it back to the furniture store yet - and we're awash in connections - that = We've barely explored to even the shallowest depth ~ Every last object - idea - relationship - and - system - we've noted - instantly attaches to more - the moment we observe it from that perspective ~ Just think what happens when that credit card comes out ~ And never mind the plastic it's made of - what that magnetic strip can do - the numbers - letters - dates - electronics - phone lines - and cashier involved = What about the local - county - state - national – and global economy directly tapped - billions of people - hundreds of countries - all the work - play - sweat - spit - jokes - tears - and cigarette breaks going on in every landscape - wet - dry - rocky - fertile - barren - and paved over - with every plant - animal - insect - bacteria - and microbe there is on every square millimeter of this planet - and then the solar system - galaxy - universe - right exactly this instant - and...

Perhaps you get the point ~ And there you were thinking that chair was a few pieces of tree - that someone cut down - milled out - constructed - and that was as far as the connections went ~ By the way - have you thought about that furniture store - all those plate glass windows - the acres of carpet - their heating and air-conditioning systems - their catalogs with all their glossy photos - the history of photography - printing - and - furniture styles? How about the manufacturers - the tools - the glues - the stains and finishes - the power used - the pollutants - the forests - the soil - the worms - the nests and burrows and rain and snow and winter and spring and summer and an endless system of systems that cannot exist without = Being connected?

|||||||||| Reproductive systems:

Take a long slow look around you - and = Do you notice any patterns - any repeating shapes - organizations of shapes - and - interactions between those shapes?

In a man-made environment (indoors - city streets - buildings) - you'd probably see lots of right angles - flat planes - straight lines - and movement directed by those shapes and their intended functions ~ In nature - you're more apt to notice the triangle and the circle as dominant forms - and movement - as more random - more opportunistic - directed by a kind of integrated chaos.

Now that you get the point = Take a deep breath - and = Allow the oxygen in it to absorb through you ~ Then = Exhale - and = Think about what you've just done - and - what in the world I might be talking about.

You of course realized - that the subject is = Interactive Geometry (not that you're apt to find that phrase as a subject heading elsewhere) - and your breath - is form and function continuously cycling - connecting you to your environment - reproducing patterns of = Living geometry (expansion - contraction - circulation - cellular sustenance - carbon dioxide exchange)

Now = Do that breathing thing - while - you look around for more patterns interacting ~ Notice - that the walls are in an interaction with each other - trees are interacting with the sky - furniture with the floor - breath with the birds - and - shapes (or geometry) - are everywhere.

The key word in defining a pattern is = Repetition (and that's why I'm repeating it from elsewhere) - which = As a creative process - is called = Reproduction ~ Any system - that reproduces (such as humans) - draws on many repeating systems (fertilization - mitosis - or cellular division - genes - nutrients - which is only the start of the local list - ignoring food and water sources - environmental conditions - or mind itself) - to get the job done ~ The question (in the context of interactive geometry) - is = Is there a pattern - a fundamental structure - of how reality (meaning - form - or that which reproduces) - emerges from the wave - or the vacuum field?

Yes - indeed = On this level of repetition = People - come out of people - as rabbits come out of rabbits - and apples out of apple trees ~ So then - again = If = The vacuum - or the quantum field - is the source of all that repetition reproducing - then = What is - it - repeating?

There are three mathematical forms (to risk a grossly oversimplified statement) - which set out systematic repetition - as (what you might call) - the art form of nature ~ They are = The Golden ratio (also known as phi) - the Fibonacci sequence - and - fractals ~ Detailing them all here = Ain't gonna happen (though I do commend them to your further study) However = The relationship between them (or repeating pattern of behavior - so to speak) - can best be experienced (if not quite accurately described) - by holding a mirror up to another mirror at a slight angle so that the reflection is (or would be - if a finite mirror were infinite) - an endless row of mirror images repeating into the distance.

To continue - with the same menu of rough parallels (for the sake of flavor rather than nutrition necessarily) = The mirror trick - translates those three forms as = Phi (the Golden ratio) - is the proportions of the objects being reflected - in relation to each other - or - the amount they progressively shrink as they appear to get further away ~ The Fibonacci sequence - is the measurement - or rate - of that sequence of shrinkage ~ And fractals - are all of the above - as the same shapes - objects and images - repeated - or contained in each of the frames - no matter how small they get.

416

The reason I hazard this generalized mathematician irritant - is to set the stage for the idea (as yet still theoretical in nature) - that = Yes = There is a geometrical structure to the vacuum - which = Behaves as a fractal type of infinite reproduction formula - mirroring endlessly larger - and endlessly smaller - expressions of energy being - or = Things.

Or at least - there is some truly compelling evidence for that yes (I heartily recommend your looking up the name Nassim Haramein on the net and see where it leads you) And - what's more = That same evidence - points at the understanding of such things - as being something extremely ancient civilizations exploited to build structures (such as the great pyramid of Giza - whose point is only one quarter of an inch off center at the top of over 3,200,000 huge blocks of stone) - which = Modern technology doesn't have a hope of reproducing (sound familiar?) The more (of that what's more) - is what may be possible to accomplish with a whole (or regained) - understanding of that fractal structure (perhaps zero gravity - instantaneous space travel) - or even better = Feel (joy - bliss - union with infinity - that kind of thing)

So = Take another look in that hall of mirrors - and notice = That you're the one being endlessly reflected - and wonder = What does that mean?|||||||||||

What if - our linear view of the world - that 1+1 - ABC - cause and effect - past - present - future - description of reality we base breakfast to dinner on - is simply = A disconnection - like a short circuit in our thinking - that keeps us from seeing the whole picture? What if - how reality - really works - is each being - each mind - each consciousness - is - each and every moment - at the center of a web - the hub of a wheel with infinite spokes - that connects to every other being - form - and event - every moment - as one consciousness?

Yeah = I know it's simpler to just sit on that chair and eat your chicken nuggets with the TV on and who cares what reality is so long as it feels good - and = Who could argue with that? Excepting of course - that maybe it's possible - to feel - really - really - really - good - because = You've consciously - connected - to a more whole experience of reality - rather than just what looks like separate parts ~ So = Let's connect - that possibility - right to your body ~ You don't even have to get up - or stop chewing ~ All you have to do - is have - DNA - and = You do.

DNA - or deoxyribonucleic acid (in case you hadn't heard) - is quite amazing stuff ~ Every last cell in your body has got some - and as such - every one of your cells (that's 50 to 70 trillion) -contains a complete picture of your body - in a blueprint design kind of way - which = If we knew how to do it (we - don't by the way - despite certain dinosaur movies) - we could reproduce an exact physical copy of you from just one of your cells ~ The same thing - is true of a holographic photograph (which you may have recently heard about somewhere) - when it is broken into pieces - or - each fragment - contains the entire picture.

What I'm getting at here - is = What if - we are each such a thing - or - a blueprint of the entire universe - individual - yet = Completely connected? (That ring any other bells?)

Did that interfere with your chewing? (Is that because you still haven't properly digested those ideas from that recent encounter you may have had with them?)

Let me tell you about a couple of experiments then - that won't exactly answer that last question - but certainly = Will give you something different to chew on.

The first - was conducted by the military - who = Are not - generally - a group of people who are interested in proving weird stuff - or universal connectedness for that matter ~ Just the same = They collected DNA from the white blood cells of a number of donors - and placed those samples in separate containers - in which they could measure electrical changes ~ Then = One at a time - each donor was placed in a room away from his/her DNA - where = They were shown a variety of video clips - chosen for their emotional impact (also sound familiar?) While this went on - both the donor - and the donor's DNA - were being electrically monitored ~ What they found = Was in all cases = The DNA exhibited identical electrical responses - at the exact same time - in the exact same way - as the donors themselves were responding to the videos ~ That's = Exact - no time in between - identical ~ Again - just straight up in proper military fashion - exact and identical responses - instantly ~ Then = They began separating donor and DNA by larger distances - and = The same results ~ When they reached a distance of 50 miles - and the same instantaneous transmission occurred - they seem to have concluded that distance was no obstacle - and went no further.

So = What does this mean?

Well - for one = It probably means that all the cells in your body are constantly in communication with each other - instantly ~ It also means - that instant communication - over possibly infinite distances - is possible - if not probable - if not actually proven (you'll be remembering quantum entanglement in this moment I'm sure) And = It means - there is a form of energy - that can do such things - and that energy - is connected to our most fundamental physical design feature - DNA..

What else it means (as well as - if - anything I just said is actually what it means) - is up for anyone's guess - so = I'll describe the next experiment.

A Russian quantum biologist named Vladimir Poponin - created a vacuum in a specialized container - and then measured the locations of the only thing still contained in that container - which were photons - or particles of light (don't ask me how he did such a thing - but he did) - and found that they were distributed in a random way throughout the container ~ Next ≐ A sample of DNA was placed in the container - and = The photon locations - were measured - observed (witnessed) - again ~ This time = The photons aligned exactly with the DNA ~ That is more photons - not - the same photons ~ Standing still is not something photons do.

Okay - that's cool - but = When the DNA was removed - and the photons observed again = They remained - or continued to show up - in an orderly alignment - exactly where - the DNA had been.

418

Alright - is that just uselessly weird stuff going on at such a small scale that you've got to wonder how - or why - anyone has the patience to bother with it? Or = Does it mean - that the physical - and the nonphysical - are in communication (that is - connected) - with each other - and again = That DNA is somehow involved in a way we have yet to understand - or actually - have barely begun to question?

Whatever - It - means - or doesn't mean = It's very clear - that this surface of reality we go skating around on - with our this is that because it isn't that or this - perceptions - is really far deeper than the corner of the rabbit hole we keep that kitchen chair in.

SPECIAL BONUS EXERCISE - number twelve

Cruelty Test:

Are you cruel to others?

Yes = That's a rather pointed question - perhaps even rude in a way ~ But still = Are you?

Now that you've thought about it (if you haven't really - try giving it another go) - let me reverse it = Have others been cruel to you?

What I'm getting at here - is not about pointing blame at you - or away from you = It's about stepping back from the courtroom of blame - and = Looking in the mirror of razor honest self examination - and = Why would we do that?

To start at the beginning (more or less) = All of us - have witnessed some part of the behavior pattern that occurs among children (and - most unfortunately - and most dangerously - among young and old adults as well) - which is usually gathered under the subject heading of = Bullying ~ The pattern takes many forms - such as - insults - humiliation - intimidation - rejection - threats - thievery - violence - but - all of it - adds up to = Cruelty ~ Because = It's all the deliberate inflicting of pain - on someone perceived as weaker or more vulnerable.

The thing is = The cause of cruelty - is also the sum of an emotional (and sometimes physical) - equation ~ Often = Having endured cruelty - equals - behaving cruelly ~ But - more often (or just digging deeper) - it's the simple addition of - ignorance plus judgment - multiplied by fear - equals = Cruelty.

Ignorance - is what ignorance means = Not knowing - not possessing a certain type - or particular piece - of knowledge ~ Not knowing what it's like to inhabit the life of another person - another culture - race - religion - family - body type - intelligence - fashion preference - the list goes on - is not a bad thing ~ It only becomes bad - when it's coupled with a negative judgment - which = Does not take that ignorance into account ~ Of course - judgment - is also a type of addition and subtraction - based on the accumulation of experience - plus = The continual sorting of likes and dislikes that follows close behind ~ All of which determines - not only a personal list of good and bad - but - what's most important to this case = A list of what's most important ~ It's in that list - where fear does its work.

An unbending decision on what's most important - means = Anything that competes - or conflicts - or just plain ignores that decision = Is a threat - something which must be defended against ~ Anything - that carries the requirement to defend - has some element of fear attached ~ According to that math = A bully is not attacking - but = Defending ~ Yes - indeed = That person (the bully) - may be laughing and admired and apparently fearless - but = You do the math = There's no motivation to attack - without fear.

Now - this may seem like trampled ground were on - what with Big Bad Guy and all in the earlier classes - and that's because = It is ~ The reason I've returned to it - is to slide it in another notch deeper at the - ouch - this is really personal level - with the following exercise.

By the way = I know - that more than likely - you're not what anyone would consider a bully ~ That doesn't really matter (unless you are) - because = Ultimately - what this exercise is really about - is the mirror opposite of cruelty - which is = Kindness ~ And - the intended result - which is = Pushing kindness up to the top of the list of what's most important.

As for the exercise = This may not be easy - but = It's extremely simple ~ All it consists of - is asking yourself - when you notice you're having a negative judgment about someone (which of course means - having the presence of mind to realize it's a negative judgment - rather than something you're just right about) = WHY AM I HAVING THIS JUDGEMENT?

Of course - that question could be applied to any form of judgment - and = Be a means of achieving clarity on many levels - if you were to truly pursue it ~ Ah - but - as you've already guessed - it's specifically intended to be about a more specific type of judgment - or - to be that specific = Cruel ones ~ You know - the kind that if they were directed at you - would feel bad.

The question itself - breaks down into parts - many actually - yet essentially - only has two sides - which are = What do I know about this other person? And = What do I know about myself?

How deep are you willing to dig - is the question behind the question of what you'll get out of this exercise of course ~ And that - is where the razor honest self examination kicks in = Are you truly answering the - WHY - part of the question? Or = Are you just repeating the judgment? How much information do you really have about this person's life - their past - their desires - their problems - their dreams - their fears - their own ignorance and why it exists? And - what about you = Why is it so important that you look and dress and act and think and live the way you do? What kind of judgments are you afraid of? Could it be - they are the same ones?

If you appreciate kindness directed toward you - and who doesn't = What if - it's not just

420

important to behave kindly yourself - in order to attract more of it your way - but = To thoroughly examine the reasons why you (or anyone else) - would be unkind?

What can I say - but = Kindly ask the question - and see if you find out.

Class Twenty Five - Empathy?

BREATHE (They say that facing east - is the correct way to do this exercise - and = They may be right ~ What with the rotation of the planet and all - and... I'm not sure what - but = Do you know which way is east from where you are right now? Could you find your location on a map? It's not that the answers are important ~ It's your use of mind that is - and = Rejecting out of hand that the direction matters - well... that's a use of mind that may be worth questioning.)

Well then = Do you love everyone in the world now? No? How far did you get with the assignment? Meaning = First = Did you do it? Second = How much (or often) - did you do it? Third = Did your feelings - about it - and during it - change? Did it start to be habitual - like having a song stuck in your head? Are you doing it now? Have you noticed anything in the rest of your life - your interactions with people - your reactions to them - that - feel - different now?

Okay - I'm going to suggest - you keep that one up ~ Actually = I'd suggest keeping all the assignments up ~ But - if you can (which really means - if you want) - try to continue the - I love you practice ~ See if you can tromp it into a neural pathway - in order = To really find out what happens ~ It's an experiment ~ That's how experiments work after all = You experiment.

In fact = If - you really want to get to the key - the real turn in the lock way in - where = You could actually mean it when you say it = Say it - to yourself = Stand at the mirror and tell your reflection = I love you ~ Smile it - joke it - soft sweet - serious - puckered up or tearful - just repeat it - or = Close your eyes - say your name and = I love you ~ Feel it ~ Allow it ~ No = You don't have to mean it with yourself either - but - different from the other part = Try - if it takes trying - and = Keep trying ~ Never mind any other voice in there contradicting it - just = Say it ~ I won't even go into any detail why you would do such a thing ~ I'll give you straight up credit for already knowing ~ The credit stops there though - if you don't do it ~ Again = It's an experiment ~ Experiments are useless - if all you do is think them up.

Anyway = Let's look at another entrance into the possibility of experiencing = A holographic universe ~ It's a word - and the word is = Empathy ~ Anyone define it?

Yes = It's kind of like sympathy - but = It's more like what comes first - or = Why - you would feel sympathy ~ What it is - is a way of - understanding - the experience - of other people - by mentally placing yourself in their position - or - situation - problems - ambitions - you know = Feelings ~ Standing in someone else's shoes - is how it's often described - despite the fact - it has nothing to do with shoes ~ Underwear would probably be a closer analogy - but that tends to confuse the point ~ Because - the point is = Opening your mind - to the experience - of another mind ~ which I think is a good point for an = {{{**Inventory Time**}}}

So = How do you do that? How do you cross over - the seemingly impossible gap - between your mind - and someone else's? Any ideas?

Excellent = Yes = Through your own experience ~ We've touched on this before - haven't we? Remember when we had Juanita up in front - and we were talking about how we could tell things about how she was feeling and thinking - just by looking at her? How did we do that? Exactly = By recognizing ourselves - in her ~ Which is = Our familiarity with the same experience - or - the location - the common ground of = Similarity ~ Rather than - focusing on = Differences.

[[[[[[[[[It's all done with Mirrors:

Due to the fact - that about three decades ago - some scientists at the University of Parma (in Italy) - were torturing macaque monkeys by sticking wires into their brains and monitoring the actions of individual neurons = We now know (or think we do) - there are processes - in the human brain - where particular neurons fire - for both - an action performed (such as grabbing a peanut) - and = The same action observed (someone else grabbing a peanut) - which = When the electronic reaction to that scenario (peanut grabbing) - was witnessed in Parma - (quite by accident actually) - and repeatedly rewitnessed (bad English as that may be) - it led those Italians to coin the term (translated into English) = Mirror neurons.

A great deal of research since then - has developed a list of theories (though still no exact conclusive proof of their being correct) - of how and why such neuronal systems function - which = Has excited some neuroscientists no end ~ Things like - the original development of language - and/or acquiring language skills as children - the basis for empathy - the Theory of Mind (which is a phrase for the mental mechanism of determining another's state of mind) - and various other learning and socializing processes (such as working out why others do the silly things they do) - have been tagged onto these mimicking mirror cells.

But = We are really talking - interconnected systems of neurons (imagine that) - rather than just individual ones (not to discount the work of individual neurons mind you) Networks - assemblies - pathways - connections - the brain-wide web - are firing away up there as you watch the guy across the aisle yawn and feel that intake of breath ready to stretch your own mouth open almost uncontrollably ~ Not to mention - the tears that ooze as the actor holds his dying lover - or the cringe of pain as the child down the street crashes her bike ~ There's definitely something going on with us - the word mirror - seems a perfect reflection for.

By way of reflection though = It's always popular to isolate things - and parts of things - and place the whole responsibility for some action - on them ~ That's particularly the case with neuroscience = This brain part does this - and that part does that ~ Not - that other kinds of science (or any other linear human endeavor) - are any different with assigning cause-and-effect relationships between this that and the other ~ The particularity bit with that neural nit picking though = Is the assumption - that brain function - is a cause - rather than an effect.

Yes = Neurons in the pre-motor cortex (a matched set of central forward parts of the brain - that have been scientifically assigned partial responsibility for deciding motor commands - or getting what body parts to do what) - do their thing - for both monkey see - and - monkey do - and = That does seem to explain - why we pucker our lips as we watch someone suck a lemon - or - position our bodies in postures that imitate those around us (especially if we're attracted to them) - and even undergo heightened muscle tension while watching sports on TV (the easiest work out going) - and sure = That looks like = The Brain - is the beginning - middle - and end - of information processing - but = Is it?

Flip the coin over (so to speak) - and = In a study in Mexico - two test subjects at a time - were wired up to EEG machines - in separate rooms - and asked to concentrate - on the near by presence of each other ~ Quick enough = Their brain wave patterns began to synchronize - and = Simultaneously - electrical activity between the hemispheres of the brains of each - also synchronized (balanced - or became coherent) - an event that usually only occurs in states such as meditation ~ Plus = It was the person with the more coherent pattern - who dominated that balancing act - with the two brains syncing to that model.

In other experiments - exploring the existence of telepathy and extra sensory perception (how many extra might there be is - again - the real question) - subjects reclined in a soundproof room - their eyes were covered with half ping-pong ball like blindfolds - and their ears with headphones - which played a continuous soft static ~ In that comfortably sensory deprived state - they were asked to just babble away any and all impressions that popped into their minds ~ Meanwhile = Another person - in another room - attempted to mentally send the images they were looking at to that physically damped down person in the next room ~ The object of course - was to compare the babbled imagery - with the sent imagery - and = See how well they matched up for timing and accuracy they were ~ The results = Were consistently higher than chance (chance being measured at 50-50) Those findings - combined with the results of two dozen other studies - all point at the existence of…….

The real addition is = Our measuring ability is based on what we think we are measuring - and so = Our devising means to do that measuring - mirrors - the system of thought we're working with ~ The possibility is = Everything we see and do and think and react to - is an entirely connected field of energy (the zero point - vacuum - wave - no thing - field) - in which = Neurons and telepathy (opposed - or complementary - as you might think them to be) - are merely like the furniture in the room = They're not the whole picture - the whole experience - the meaning - or = Explanation of anything more than where to sit ~ Which actually means = How deep does this empathic bond among the species really go?

424

What if - we're neither - imitating - empathizing - comparing - or - reading each other's minds - and instead = What if - we are - each other's minds? What if - we are all tapping the infinite reservoir of a single energy - and = Our mental mimicry responses to each other - our mirror of feelings - expressions - expansions - contractions - and busy little brain cells buzzing away - is because (like some subatomic magic trick) = It's all done with mirrors = We're just looking at ourselves?|||||||||

What does that phrase - common ground mean?

That's it = It's like jointly owning something - a kind of agreement location - or shared experience ~ Even if - the experience - that's shared - happened in different places - or times - or - is only an idea - or shared belief ~ Of course - ideas - are all the result of experience as well ~ So - what we're really talking about here - is = Experience - and = The experience - of empathy - which takes place on - common ground - is the one I'm trying to get you - to experience the experience of - right now.

There's a point - in most everyone's life - when = The full range of experience it's possible to have on this planet as a human being - has been reached ~ By reached - I mean = Tasted - or - been a witness to - within yourself - physically - emotionally - intellectually - the whole enchilada (experience buffet) - of body based human life ~ Generally it's around the age of 14 or so - younger in some - older in others - or - if there is some kind of handicap present - maybe never - but basically - it's around that age.

Okay = I know that might sound ridiculous = You've never been to war - or skydived - had a car crash - given birth - swam in the Indian Ocean - or held a penguin ~ Unless of course - you have ~ The thing is though = You've tasted (or will taste - if you haven't quite arrived there yet) - all the parts of experience - that make up - all those experiences - and - the great long list of other experiences available to have here on Earth.

Take war - for instance ~ You've probably heard loud noises - explosions even - shouting - been in crowds - smelled smoke - seen blood - meat - dead things - felt pain - been afraid - hungry - dirty - tired - cold - hot - wet - been ordered to do things - gone somewhere unfamiliar - taken a risk ~ It goes on - of course - but you get the idea ~ If you haven't actually been in a war - then you haven't encountered the full extremes of those conditions (and extreme only begins to be the correct word) - or - eaten the entire meal - you might say - but = You've nibbled all its edges - the ingredients - are all present.

That sound familiar?

Yeah = We've chewed on one or two food analogies before - but = The one that comes to mind is "one big restaurant of thought - is how we recognize what's going on - because we've had at least a tiny taste off everyone's plate" = Remember now?

||||||||| Doctor Dude's Dictionary - word twenty five - Sustainability:

In recent times - a word that describes a major shift in consciousness - has moved from relative subculture obscurity - into mainstream media buzz ~ It's a very old word really - whose meaning - you might say - comes in many varieties - or shades - which is basically why - it's the perfect descriptive title for environmental awareness ~ The word is = Green.

Under the canopy of Green (or should I say - in its limelight) - is another word which describes that shift in consciousness from so many different angles (once you dig around in it) - it's a wonder that it has only six syllables ~ That word is = Sustainability.

Sustainability - covers so much ground - because - first = It's a big picture view - a recognition of interconnected systems ~ Which means (which also means - breaking the words down to other words) = Observing - what is dependent on what - how - and why - in order to possess a whole understanding - of how - a condition (say health or well-being) - is sustained (meaning - not used up without creating more of the same) - rather than just blindly achieving a goal at the cost of handicapping or destroying the systems that actually support the condition you want (you know - poisonous pollution for the sake of prosperity - war for the sake of peace) Next comes = Responsibility ~ Which means = Including yourself in the equation - or = Recognizing - that what you do has effects - and = Designing your ongoing role - according to achieving the set of effects - that are the most beneficial - to the condition you want to sustain.

The penultimate (or - just before the end) - completion of defining sustainability (even though I really could go on and on) - is = Connection - or actively - consciously - responsibly - knowing yourself to be an integral part of a dynamic whole (now there's a list of powerful words) Or - more simply = Behaving in a way that promotes cooperation - because - sustaining - is cooperation.

And the last (of that on and on) - definition is = What works - what keeps getting the job done - without putting itself out of a job ~ Sustainability - or moving towards sustainability - is (like I said) - a shift in consciousness - because = It really is describing (and can't even begin to occur without) = Being conscious - and by extension = Being Happy.|||||||||

Anyway = How does that idea - fit into the word - empathy - and where - is this whole thing going?

Alright = It fits - because = It is - IT ~ It's the machinery - of the ability - to empathize ~ We do it all the time actually - talking to our friends - watching movies - TV - reading books - magazines - even advertisements ~ Why else would there be ads - if we couldn't picture ourselves in that new car or wearing those clothes with our minty fresh breath and shiny hair ~ Empathy - is familiarity - connecting - to what's - familiar - beyond - the story - of why - it's familiar ~ In other words (plus why it's an amazing tool) - is = Empathy is a way of dissolving boundaries between people's lives - by recognizing - our own life - in another's.

So yes = That's a good thing - a useful thing in progressing understanding between people and groups and such ~ But = How does it enter into that holographic universe idea? Well

426

= What if - it enters into - it - because - it - comes from - it? What if - the ability - to feel - empathy - to pass beyond the borders of your own experience - into a larger experience - is there - because = The borders don't really exist? What if - empathy is actually = The most - natural thing - your mind is capable of? Other than an = {{{**Inventory Time**}}}

Here = Consider this for a moment.

I imagine you've probably all used the Internet? So = When you go - on line - do you really go somewhere? No = You - connect - to a somewhere - that's connected to a kind of everywhere - that allows you to make that same connection and enter - cyber space ~ Interesting - that we call it a space ~ It doesn't - look - like a space ~ We don't say - television space - or radio space - even though they are the same - in that - we connect to them - for information and entertainment - and they're always going on - available to that connection ~ So = What's the difference between them - and this cyber space thing?

Exactly = Interaction ~ The internet - unlike TV and radio (excepting shows you can call in to) - is set up to be - interactive.

For any possible interaction between two things to take place in this world - what - is always - required?

You guessed it = Space.

It's simple enough if we're talking moving a piano ~ Can't move one if the truck is full - or the road is closed - or there's - no space - to put it in the room where it's going.

It's a bit different - when it's ideas that are interacting - or it seems so ~ Because = Then - it's you - them - he - she - we - all of us - that supply - the space.

Could it be - that's why - we call - cyber space - space - because = It resembles - the space - inside us?

||||||||| **www.communication.bod:**

Communication - is what it's all about (if you disregard the Hokey Pokey) The - it - part of that sentence - means = Function - which means = Movement - action - change - or - all the things that happen to things - through - with - for - and because of - things = That make up this experience of existence in time ~ All of - it = Communicates = Be it sunlight shining on a leaf - a soccer ball whacking into the goal - peptides docking on a cell - chemical changes in a laboratory - an oven - a septic tank - or just your father shouting at the dog again = Every bit of it - is energy - communicating - with energy.

The same - is equally true with human society - as well as being (potentially at least) - that much more obvious a concept to follow ~ Nothing happens in the human world (involving more than one human) - that does not include some form of communication - which then = Spins right around to reflect the original point = That inside each of those humans (no matter how many - or how few) - all functions (covered most succinctly by the word - life) - are - forms of communication.

Peering into the human body then = There are those five senses translating their findings into electrochemical signals our brains can understand - and our brains - zipping all that information through their chattering networks and shooting off reactions to muscles and glands and organs in combinations of coded bits that call up this and shut down that while blood makes deliveries to all those pumping and excreting and expanding and contracting and absorbing and expelling and dividing cellular functions all yakking away (in a manner of - speaking) - as busy in any given moment as the Manhattan telephone exchange on a Friday afternoon.

Given that premise (or a juggling of words attempting to communicate it) - one would probably arrive at another blanket statement - sounding much like = In order to - improve the function - of any system (that's - any - system) - focusing - on improving communication - within that system - or between it and connected systems - would have that effect (improvement)

There are two systems - we deal with every day - that even though they are so closely connected - as to generally be confused as being one and the same thing - there is still a communication gulf possible between them - that even some foreign languages don't suffer between each other ~ They are = Our bodies - and - that thing we call = Ourselves.

In recent decades however - a technique for improving that communication - has been evolving ~ Some people would tell you - it's bunk of the highest order - and others - that it's an information exchange as natural as speech itself ~ Me - I'm just going to tell you about it ~ It - is called - muscle testing - or sometimes - applied kinesiology (though that term is frowned upon by kinesiologists - who practice the study of human movement - which is what the word means)

Muscle testing - consists of a simple physical procedure involving two people (in communication of course) One - the subject - holds a container of a substance in one hand - while extending the opposite arm - either straight out - or to the side (dependent on certain energy flow details) - and = Attempts to hold that arm rigid - as = Two - the practitioner - presses down on it at a given signal ~ The substance in the container - is any number of medicines - herbs - foods - drink - what have you - that are thereby being tested for the correctness of their use (or possible allergic reaction qualities) - by the subject - by consulting = The subject's body.

The idea is = Our bodies know best - and = They signal that knowledge through the strength - or weakness - of a large muscle mass undergoing such a test (any muscle - especially muscles connected to the ailing parts in question - will do - arms just tend to be the most convenient) The results = Are sometimes dramatic - sometimes inconclusive - sometimes contradictory ~ Again = It's a question of which sources you consult - and = Who or what you're willing to believe.

The truly interesting thing about muscle testing (provided it's a truly legitimate phenomenon) - is the larger - field of communication - it represents - because = It would

428

have to be - fields - in communication - identifying one another - analyzing components - compatibilities - requirements - reactions - complete molecular relationships - exchanged - essentially instantaneously - to explain its working ~ No wonder there would be such doubt ~ And yet = Why not? The quantum world is no less astounding ~ Perhaps - we just haven't been listening ~ After all = Communication - is what it's all about.]]]]]]]]]]

What if - the internet - is really just - an out picturing - or projection (you know - like a movie on a screen) - of what our minds are collectively capable of doing - without any electronic equipment - wires - chips - megabytes - gigabytes - any kind of bites at all = We just haven't realized it yet?

In fact = What if - we are already doing it (that's - being connected) - at some invisible level - that's actually orchestrating the working of this reality (which includes the internet) - and the internet - has been created - by us - at that level (meaning - inspired by the invisible one) - in order - to clue us in (that's the - us - still unaware of that level of ourselves) - to the fact - that we are doing it?

Yeah = There I go again ~ But = What if - it's true?

Try this - imagine for a moment - that in your backyard - the street - whatever is outside your door - that there is a tower ~ This tower is so tall that its top is half way to the moon ~ Yeah I know - it couldn't be built - but that's what imagination is for ~ Anyway = This tower has a glass elevator on the outside of it ~ The glass is made in such a way that it magnifies what you see through it - and = The higher up the tower it goes - the stronger the magnification - so that = What you see at ground level - you can still see - just as well - at ten thousand feet - only = A lot more of it ~ So - when you finally reach the top floor (half way to the moon) - you can - not only make out the fingerprints on your kitchen window - but = Everyone else's kitchen widow - and = What the people behind it are having for dinner.

Okay = Did you picture it? How did it feel? Did you allow yourself to really feel it? A bit scary that feeling? Or a new kind of freedom? Well - as you may have guessed = You're going to get a chance to practice it some more.

But first - let me say = What if - that's a picture - an imaginary analogy kind of picture - but = A picture - of your whole 100% mind at work - or a least - the only half way to the moon section? What if - you can rise - or enter - into those other levels (not that they need to be stacked on top of each other the way we usually think of levels - but enter into them - or it) - and find - everyone else's story going on there - the ultimate empathy channel? Would you want to? Would that be frightening - too big - too much? Or would it be something else? Would it - could it = Be fantastically exciting?

Alright = You're assignment - is to try ~ Use the tower image if that helps - or any other of your own that you come up with ~ That doesn't matter ~ It's - OPEN - meaning = How much space will you allow in yourself - that matters ~ You may find that the - I love you exercise - is what really helps ~ The real question - of what helps - is = How much do you want to feel? Of course - a lot of breathing - won't hurt.

N.P.U - Chapter Twenty Five - Responsibility?

There is another experiment - involving DNA - that adds another dimension - to the perspective - of witnessing - energy - to be interconnected (now that's a sentence to chew on - and neatly sliced up for you to boot) In this one - DNA samples were extracted from placenta tissue ~ A placenta (in case you don't know) - is the membrane like lining of the uterus wall in which all mammal babies are enclosed during pregnancy ~ As such - it's also expelled from the mother's body as part of the birthing process - and = Because of the order in which that process occurs - is often referred to as - afterbirth ~ The reason - for using DNA from such a source = Is its pure or uncorrupted state - having not been exposed to the toxins and stresses of life outside the womb ~ Not to say - such things don't make it in there as well - but - in a relative way - that DNA is closer to its original form - and so = Is a kind of clean slate to work with.

Alright = This DNA - from different placentas - was split up among 28 containers in which it could be microscopically observed ~ Those containers were then - one by one as the experiment progressed - placed in the hands of 28 people - all of which had been trained to produce (within themselves) - strong emotional states ~ Yes = It does seem like a strange type of training - but = There's a definite reason for it - which = You could stretch to calling - a cultural need ~ Anyway = What these 28 people did = Was to practice this skill of theirs - while the DNA they were holding - was simultaneously observed for responses ~ As it turned out = Yes = There were definite responses ~ When the focus of emotion was centered on the ideas of gratitude - appreciation - and love = The strands of DNA visibly lengthened - relaxed - and took on a shape where all their codes were fully accessible to use ~ In contrast = When the focus was on anger - fear - and frustration = The DNA strands contracted - rolled up tight - and shut off many of the codes from accessibility ~ That's not to say - they remained that way permanently = When emotional states were reversed - such as - dread to excitement = The same strands of DNA - changed shape accordingly.

Now - there are a couple of very useful (or should I say - practical) - features to the results of this experiment ~ The first - and most obvious - is that our DNA - which supplies the designs for our cellular reproduction - is heavily (that's heavily like tons per square inch) - affected by our emotional states ~ That means = Our physical form - which is expressed as levels of health - fitness - strength - endurance - recovery - aging - that whole picture - is a reflection (at least to a large degree) - of how we feel (which is to say - internally react) - emotionally ~ Which of course means = We have a choice.

[[[[[[[[Gut Feeling:

You've probably heard the phrase - gut feeling ~ Perhaps - it has great meaning to you as a system of navigating through life ~ Maybe - it's no closer an experience to your life than somehow knowing the actor on the big screen is about to take a bullet.

Either way = A gut feeling - is like tapping a source of information - where = You seem to know something - or suspect you do - you don't possess enough information - to know.

It's also a very physical experience (hence the word gut) - and one reason for that - is also very physical = Our guts (otherwise known as our digestive tract) - or more specifically - the cell walls of our large and small intestines - are covered in neuropeptide receptor sites - which means = Chemical signals for emotional responses - have a particularly strong impact in that area of our anatomy ~ In that context - it would also mean = That some thought pattern belief structure neural net (or quantum communication - if you favor that scenario) - is what triggers - or is the cause of that - chemical release   And so = is also the cause of the gut feeling itself.

The problem - with assigning a line of belief structure directed physical cause (or neurons in the brain firing as a habitually linked net that trigger specific peptide production to flow into the bloodstream - that then arrive in the gut - and there you go) - to a border line psychic effect (a gut feeling) - is to wade into a certain set of popular ideas (particularly among females I find) - that feeling occurs faster than thought - or the body knows - before the mind - and can override (bypass or go around) - that neural net business of established reaction routes.

So = The question - really needs to be a deeper excavation into = What is thought? And = What is the mind? And = How does communication work - at the level of energy? And = How does it function - in relation to the body - or cellular communication - and = How fast?

Obviously - conscious thought - or perception arriving at the level of awareness - is only so fast ~ But = what is the precursor (or the event before) - that is - the cause - of feelings (if they do indeed occur first) - and thought (if it doesn't) - and = Are they actually separated by some fraction of time? In other words - or questions = Is thought - the effect of something else - something super fast - something entangled - or connected with all other thoughts - at the quantum level - something instantaneous - that contains far more information than our neural net filters allow us to recognize? Is it true - that our bodies - know things - before we (we - being - an identification with thoughts as a means of understanding) - do? Or - is it a whole function - mind - and body - reacting to energy at the speed of light - which = Still must travel through our belief systems - before arriving - as a feeling - an idea - an itch - a pain - a gut feeling - in that hopelessly slow by comparison place - we call awareness - because = Our awareness - is a belief system?

To remind you - of that physical reaction two or three seconds before seeing the image on a computer screen experiment we talked about some time ago = Is - our whole cellular body/mind/being - continuously scanning the future somehow - that normally - we're not aware of - at least until we encounter = A gut feeling?]]]]]]]]]

The other feature (if it didn't slip past you) - may have you considering the company you keep in a different light ~ You see - the conclusion - that our emotional states change the shape of our DNA - and so = How it functions - is really a bit of an assumption from this experiment (an extremely reasonable assumption I might add - yet still an assumption) - because = The DNA being observed - was not the DNA - of the people experiencing those emotions - it was someone else's ~ What we're really talking here = Is a very effective energy - and - not = A confined energy - but = One being broadcast ~ You might even be tempted to call it - free energy.

What that means - from the constricted fear and anger end of the emotional behavior choice - is = Don't go near anyone that's involved in experiencing such states (perhaps a good reason to unplug your television) But - you'll remember = In the military's DNA experiments - that distance (at least a distance up to 50 miles) - did not change the energy transmission time - or - the nature of what was being transmitted - so = Isolation - probably isn't the answer.

If there is an answer (which of course implies there must be a question) - then = What it must come down to in the end (and no = I'm not going to say perspective - even if it is) - is = Responsibility.

What that responsibility looks like - is = An awareness = An awareness that emotions are not just effects - but causes in themselves ~ How we feel - which ultimately - is about how we have chosen to feel - has (if you accept the different evidences I've placed before you - or perhaps even - your own experience) - a much broader effect - on a system of interconnected systems - than just the personal and social effects of passing moods and reactions ~ What the awareness of that condition pushes forward - is the choice - to be responsible - for the larger effect - you want to see occur - rather than = Just the immediate emotional condition you might be entertaining in yourself - because = You now know (or at least have been informed enough to suspect) - that = That condition (such as - vengeful) - may end up delivering the opposite - of what you really want.

There is a whole layer of human society - belief - behavior - and conditioning - that choice of responsibility - also exposes to view - and that = Is the willingness - or unwillingness = To forgive.

It doesn't really take a list of detailed scientific studies conducted by universities across the country and elsewhere (even though that is the case) - to get someone to connect the dots between not forgiving - and being unhappy ~ Go ahead - think of someone you hold a grudge against - and = Nòtice - how it feels ~ Of course - the extreme end of that same response - is violence - terrorism - warfare - and cycles - of violence - terrorism - and warfare ~ Given the DNA study we just looked at - it appears rather clear - that the constriction emotions - of anger - fear - and vengeance - that are the symptoms of being unwilling to forgive - don't just create today's newspaper headlines - but = The headlines of generations to come ~ Of course - there remains the cycle already in place - of the past dictating the future through our ideas in the present - which = Stews right down to that word - blame - and makes that word - forgiveness - sound like a kind of weakness - or an invitation to further abuse - which = Makes it seem quite reasonable - not to forgive ~

432

But still - that call to responsibility remains - because now = We're playing with a new set of rules ~ Which is to say = We have a better idea - of what the rules actually are.

There have been a number of studies in recent years that have examined this question of forgiveness (or not - to be precise) - from its influence on society as a whole - right down to its influence on sexual function ~ The findings - across the board - point at problems ~ Hardly surprising - but = I'll describe them just the same - by way of reinforcement for that responsibility word I've been trailing around ~ Interestingly - many of the reported - side effects (of not forgiving) - were heart related ~ Such as - heightened blood pressure - increased heart rate - chest pain - irregular heart rhythm - and those = Are just the on the spot measurements of responses of study subjects to being asked - to simply think about - someone who had mistreated them in the past.

The long-term effects of such thinking - are classed under that popular modern term - and way of life = Stress ~ Which immediately draws on much more extensive medical research linking stress with all kinds of heart problems - like heart attack - stroke - and a string of cardiovascular illnesses ~ There is also another stress response involved - right at the ground zero of the brain - which is the neurohormone (brain chemical if you like) - cortisol ~ High levels of cortisol - interfere with the immune system (meaning you get sick easier) - as well as the cardiovascular system already mentioned - and = Has been connected to problems in overall cognitive actions - decision-making - memory - and even (yes - this is the one) = Malfunctions in the reproductive system ~ When it came to studying the effects of forgiveness - or its lack - on romantic partnerships = It's no surprise - that those that tested low for willingness to forgive - also reported more difficulties in getting along - but = Also had higher levels of cortisol present in their blood ~ Likely - more of them also reported having separate bedrooms.

[[[[[[[[[The Singularity:

The term (no matter how out of context it may appear in this moment) - black hole - is well known ~ Almost as well known - are the black hole properties of being super density gravitational vacuums from which - no matter - or even electromagnetic radiation (otherwise known as light) - can escape (hence their blackness) That is - once those things have passed a certain proximity boundary (or - got a little too close) - known as = The event horizon ~ So well known in fact - is the black hole idea - that the category of - theory - barely still applies to them in the popular imagination - and = Has just about almost maybe sort of disappeared as a scientific disclaimer as well - due = To the wealth of circumstantial evidence supporting their existence ~ Specifically (in part) = The orbiting behavior of surrounding stars - and - the gases emitted by those stars - which spirals inward (or black hole-ward) - at increasingly higher temperatures while giving off radiation that is detectable from Earth.

It appears (in that same highly plausible theoretical way) - that black holes are the forces around which galaxies form and spiral in the great gravity dance of the universe ~ We can't see them - but again = The evidence adds up quite convincingly ~ It's all an astronomical mathematics puzzle really - fitted together piece by piece since 1783 - when the idea that such gravitational monsters might exist out there - was first proposed by a

British amateur astronomer named John Michell (Interesting little claim to fame that ~ What might yours be?)

Not so well known - is the term used to describe (despite the fact that is it a concept rather tricky to get perceptual language fully wrapped around) - what lies at the center of a black hole ~ It's called = A singularity - and what it is - is = A kind of point - an area - or region of space - so compressed - that it has no volume (no size - shape - weight - or displacement) - which = Makes it infinitely dense actually - or - impossible to measure - with a potentially limitless capacity to crush star systems.

The same thing (a singularity) - is what's theorized to have been our universe moments before (although presumably - moments did not exist then) - that other popular theory burst on the scene = The Big Bang.

So = Here we have - a beginning singularity (the big bang) - and - what you might call - an ending one (a black hole) - since = Anything that crosses a black hole's event horizon is stretched apart to its gravitational doom (an effect merrily dubbed - spaghettification) Only = It's not a doom = It's a change of energy states (that being a sentence which - theoretically - removes beginning and end from the preceding sentences) What we may really be looking at - is = A cycle - because = A cycle is a circular pattern - a rotation - a spin (if you will) - since = Like I've pointed out in the past - spin is the thing in this universe - and = Some kind of force is responsible for it ~ Quite possibly (or totally not) - what a black hole really is - is = A demonstration of the core of physical creation in action - the power of the vacuum field - which= Is infinitely singular (or one thing) - at the center of all that spin.

What that means (despite it being unorthodox and highly controversial physics) - is = A relationship of forces - or = The fabric of space-time - and - the vacuum field - interacting.

You see = As Einstein described space and time as one thing (a kind of fabric - bending and curving as close to everything as your underwear is to you right now) - that one thing - is constantly shaped by the gravitational fields of objects moving within it = That shape - creates torque - or twist - angular momentum - in short = Spin ~ Just as an engine spins a shaft to turn the wheels of a car = Black holes - may be gravitationally torquing the universe to rotate in all the large and small ways it does - and = At the center of those black holes is the singularity (which is actually the source of all that matter and activity - if - it is the vacuum field - if - that is true) - doing its thing of converting energy from one state to another.

Of course that makes perfect sense to you ~ So = Extend (shrink actually) - those galaxy spinning principles down to the size of an atom - and = Is it possible - that the strong nuclear force (that agreed upon supposition that presumably is the extraordinary power holding protons together - despite the otherwise natural tendency of their shared positive charges to repel each other) - is in fact = The singularity of a black hole? Would that explain then = That why - electrons go flying around in their orbits of the nucleus (barely a hair slower than the speed of light) - is because = Just like the stars outside the

434

perimeter of a black hole's event horizon - they (those stars - and possibly electrons) - are controlled by a singularity's gravity (so that they remain in orbit of it) - but - not sucked in and crushed by it? In other words = Are atoms - mini black holes? Or = Is the fractal repeating nature of matter (which is endlessly reproducing patterns) - based on the same picture (or mystery) - that churns galaxies in circles?

The answer - really isn't a yes or a no ~ Such a definite split - would only reflect opinion in current knowledge terms ~ It's the irresistible gravitational pull of the question itself though - that spins us - that keeps us in an orbit edging ever closer to the center all the time ~ Collectively (despite the disagreement of many individuals) - we just plain know - there are other dimensions of experience available to us beyond our perceived limits ~ We're just looking for them is all ~ So = Why stop now?]]]]]]]]]

So (amazing the power of those two letters - so) - if you're talking - responsibility - for your own health and well-being = Such research does tend to make one think - that hanging onto past wrongs - might just be - hanging onto the wrong thing ~ But = What about the rest of the world? What about all the terrible things that happened - are happening - and so - according to that model - look very much like continuing to happen?

Well - for all it may not look it - on the level of scale - distances - and shear bullheaded human stubbornness = What if - it's still exactly the same responsibility? What I mean is = Centered on you ~ Not to say that anybody else - like me - gets off the hook either - but then - that's forgetting about the possible holographic nature of the universe - where each person - is the universe ~ But anyway....

There was an event a few years back - that you might say = Changed the world ~ Or - you might say = Just created an excuse for the world to continue to involve itself in the conflictive ways it's always used to solve its problems - by creating more of the same ~ I did just say world - and - what I really meant - is = Humanity ~ But = You knew that - because = We as humanity - think of ourselves as the world (certainly a very telling statement - when it comes to recognizing our disregard for interconnected systems... anyway) But = No matter what I - or you - or we - say - September 11, 2001 - was a point in history - where change on a massive scale was presented as a set of = Choices ~ It's clear now - what the choices made were - and = It's becoming more and more clear - what some at least - of the consequences of those choices are ~ What's interesting to consider (especially when you consider - there's really no time limit involved for the - opportunity - for change - at least from the scale of time and the universe as a whole) - what those choices - might have been - from the point of view of a larger responsibility.

[[[[[[[[[**Burning Questions:**

Everyone loves a great mystery (said that before somewhere haven't I) - and = Nothing like a good conspiracy theory (you know - who really killed JFK - did aliens actually crash in Roswell New Mexico - are there...) - to stoke up the flames of that suspicious nature of ours ~ There are any number of possible psychological reasons for the attraction - such as = What's regarded as a natural problem solving drive to reach equilibrium - that balanced state of cause and effect with no puzzle pieces missing - or (speaking of rightful) = The equally (or perhaps disproportionately) - insisted upon - need - to be right - or - just simply = Justifying the tragically stupid - as being the result of the complexly intelligent ~ And then of course = There's the possibility - of real conspiracy.

Slice it up as you like (in the end - it's all about being happy - or not) = There is one key component - on that dangling hook of amateur detective bait - that's guaranteed to get bites - and that is = Anomaly.

An anomaly - is a fact - which does not fit - does not add up with the other facts in a case - to equal (or explain) - the results (or - the interpretation of results) - which identify the case in question (such as the World Trade towers crumbling to the ground) Therefore = An anomaly - is a fact = That should not be a fact - but = Still is.

Disregarding any theories - speculations - politics - or ideological accusations - and purely (or as close as possible with such an emotionally charged subject) - with the object of witnessing the consciousness of our society = There are certain anomalies about the September 11th events - which = Have been explained away - ignored - or skirted over (quite publicly) - in such a way - that no matter what the answers are - the questions sore thumb at that love of mystery like a floodlit billboard - and = Regardless of any other consideration - are about to appear here (or some of them are) - because we're talking one of the most influential events of this century to date - which means = A landmark we can all recognize ourselves as being personally affected by - and so = Extend that recognition - to the understanding - of being a part of the collective consciousness still responding to that effect.

They begin = With explosions - in the lowest levels of both the world trade Towers - before (that's - Before) - the planes struck ~ Explosions - which killed - injured - and knocked down - an unknown number of people - who - nevertheless = Include a large number of surviving witnesses ~ Granted - in the light of following events - that - could - sound like just more confusion - but = What about those events?

When the towers collapsed - they did so at nearly freefall speed - or - the approximate rate of ten floors per second - which = Has been analyzed up down and inside out - but = Never truly accounted for the failure of the 47 massive steel columns at the building's cores - which = At the very least - should - have remained standing hundreds of feet in the air - unless = The completely unaccountable pools of molten metal - found in the basements of all three buildings (yes - that's three) - which were still generating heat of 2000°F (500° hotter than burning jet fuel) - several weeks later - might - have had something to do with it.

Then = There's building seven - a 47 story reinforced concrete office building - that was part of the World Trade Center complex - which = Collapsed - simply fell straight (and quite neatly) - to the ground - just like that - more than six hours after the towers came down ~ The - official explanation - cited fire in the basement - caused by stored diesel fuel (interesting choice of locations for storing large quantities of diesel) - and - structural weakening due to the shockwaves of the falling towers (with some afterthought descriptions of hasty deliberate demolition for the sake of safety - which = Really don't quite cut it from an architectural engineering point of view) And yet = Buildings of essentially the same structural integrity - only a few feet away - remained solidly standing ~ Nor were they particularly damaged even by seven's collapse - which = Fell exactly in the classic pattern of expertly engineered demolition - where all the load bearing framing is dynamited simultaneously - which (presumably) = Takes many hours of careful set up to pull off so efficiently.

Meanwhile = In Washington DC - the facts - of the Pentagon attack quickly disappeared in classified military style ~ Quite possibly (guessing as it may be) - to maintain secrecy of the actual effectiveness of the explosion - with the intention of hiding potential data for a more destructive second attempt - but = The public claim was = That the Boeing 757 - which was flown into the Pentagon (although that very secrecy mentioned has led to controversy over a plane even being involved) - "vaporized on impact" - due to the exploding jet fuel - and = Left not a single trace of itself or any of its contents - excepting = Bits of bodies - including - none other than two of the hijackers (brothers) - who were identified by DNA ~ Which means = An entire aircraft - with its two six ton steel and titanium alloy engines - completely disappeared - and - the soft tissues of two - evildoers - did not?

Overlooking some thinly veiled sarcasm = Again - the only thing I'm doing - is delivering second-hand information - a tiny scratch actually - at the surface of an intricate web of unexplained - although almost entirely public - information - which somehow = Has remained invisible for being too close to our noses ~ Why is that? Is it invisible? What is true - and - what is not?

It's not actually important (at least in this context) - what really happened that day (nor does that mean to ignore all the grief and anger still chewing many hearts) The question here - is = How have you/we used your/our minds? What have we accepted? What have we questioned? What have we allowed to pass by without notice? And = Why?

It's not right - wrong - true - false - or covered up at stake = Its our consciousness - and the way in which we're paying attention to it - that's under the microscope here ~ The real mystery = Is why we would choose - fear - as the information to trust (be it from the right - the left - or the stuck in traffic on the way home from work again middle) - instead = Of trying... something else?|||||||||

September 11th is now a date in the history books - and = It carries great weight ~ It's that very weight however - that overshadows (again - very telling of our cultural valuing of violence) - a potentially even more important date = September 12th ~ Up and down the island of Manhattan on that day - a phenomenon was taking place - that = In comparison to normal working Wednesdays in New York City - would not be stretched too far by using the word - miraculous ~ People of all kinds (and there are certainly all kinds of people in Manhattan) - were talking to each other - crying with each other - hugging - singing - and standing together in large groups silently being one thing ~ It is terribly sad (and again - I'm afraid quite telling of our culture) - that the inspiration for that mass union of hearts and minds (or electromagnetic fields) - was the most devastating grief and shock ~ The difference - in creating a future - from that date - with that form of unity - rather than a form of unity closed in a fearful way to the - outside - is a matter of how a very simple one-word question is approached - and responded to = Why?

Responsibility - dictates the recognition - of what causes what ~ It is hardly very responsible (or productive for that matter) - if when you cut yourself with some tool you are using - you destroy the tool or the work you are engaged in - in order to heal yourself ~ Terrorism - is not a particularly productive way of solving problems either - nor in any way what we would call - excusable ~ It is caused by something though ~ It is part of an interlocking system of systems ~ That question = Why? = Breaks down (in human minds at least) - immediately to = Who - or what - is responsible? The answer to that question - depends entirely on the questioner - because = Of the answers - they've already - brought to the question ~ If - one of those answers - is = Whole responsibility - is wholly shared - including - if not particularly (or even entirely in a holographic universe) - within one's self - then the response = Is to address reaction (whose list is topped by - learning from mistakes) - by using the questions = What are - all - the causes of such a thing? How did the systems involved interact to produce those causes? And = How can an interaction be designed - in order to solve - balance out - or compensate for - the original causes? Rather than = Using the pre-question answers - which just produce an assault on - the symptoms - those causes have created ~ It does not mean that individuals are not held accountable for individual actions ~ It means = That accountability - does not end with individuals ~ It means = A world - may be many things - but = They are all - connected.

{{Now read that paragraph twice more ~ Just as soon as you complete an = {{{**Inventory Time**}}} - and measure it against your own ideas of what makes sense}}

Now don't get me wrong - this is not some political editorial ~ It is a discussion of choice - from the point of view - of knowing - what you are choosing ~ Every day is September 12th - if not a great many of the 1,440 minutes that make up each day ~ What if - the broader a perspective - any of us have - in seeing the probable results of any way of feeling or behaving we might choose - or want to choose = Hands us the advantage - of knowing - how - to choose - happiness? And - what's more = Spread that happiness around?

As for this word forgiveness - it needn't be some holier than thou judgment pedestal - or some meek door mat way of slouching back to our corners ~ Instead - it contains the option to be seen (in your mind that is) - more the way you might view things like vitamins - healthy food - and exercise - as well as - ice cream - chocolate - and big sloppy kisses ~ What if = Forgiveness - from the point of view - of responsibility for survival (and who wants to just plain survive - so lets add joy - which is where the chocolate and kisses figure in) - is not about what happened in the past - but = What you want - the world - of your future - to look like - despite the fact (or perhaps most importantly) - there really is only = Now?

Class Twenty Six - I Self?

BREATHE (Need I say more? That being said = The energy involved - or understood to be available for this super brain thing (and everything else) - is called - Prana (prahn - ah) It's a universal life force vital energy everywhere sort of thing (also known as Qi - which is pronounced - Chee) In Sanskrit - the ancient language of India - the word means - breath - as well as being interchangeable with the life force energy just mentioned - because = That's the intersection ~ Breath is the action of being - where it meets - the being of action ~ It's as simple or complex as you like - believe it or don't ~ Either way = Right in the middle of being alive - is us - breathing ~ So - let's get on with it.)

Well = Did you manage to tune in to the ultimate empathy channel? What happened? Did you have moments of a much larger life than your own? Did you pay attention to your own willingness? What kind of willingness - or space - did you allow? What did it all feel like - the trying - the not trying - the touching another part of mind - and the not being able to? What do you feel - right now?

Alright - I'll start right out with another word ~ It's = Sobriety ~ What does it mean?

Yeah = That's its usual usage - as a kind of contrast - a negative (in a sense) - not drunk - not drugged ~ Why is it used that way? Sure = When drunk or drugged - are realized - to be unhealthy - a problem - an addiction - then (not that it need take that long) = Sobriety - is the cure ~ The thing is - wasn't sobriety the case - before - there were any drugs or alcohol present in someone? But = Does someone - who never uses drugs or alcohol - wake up in the morning and think about sobriety? Not likely - no ~ And yet = There they are - quite sober ~ It's kind of like waking up healthy with no broken bones or blood all over the place = It's really no surprise ~ Unless you went to bed in a condition where - not healthy - was the issue ~ So - perhaps there's more to that word - sober - than getting sober - much like there's more to that word health than - getting - healthy?

Not surprisingly = Yes = There is ~ What sobriety - is really about - is clarity - a movement through living - that's clean ~ Clean - in the sense - that it doesn't pick up lots of attachments to conditions ~ Which means = Dependence - on the obvious things like drugs and alcohol - but also - states of mind - like anger - jealousy - depression - blame - because = Those are also addictions ~ In fact - they are addictions just as chemically physical - as heroine is.

What if - I were to say - that - thinking you're a body - is also an addiction? And then -

add to that - simply thinking itself - is one as well?

Alright = Fair enough = You wouldn't be all that surprised that I asked such a weird question ~ But = What else would you think?

I know = It appears - we really can't get around thinking ~ But = What if - that's the problem? What I mean is = What if - our thinking - we can't get around thinking - is = We think that thinking - is - the definition of our being - our humanness - what sets us apart - from animals - plants - insects - and rocks? In other words = We think - our thoughts - are - who - we are - and = Right along with that thinking - is the thinking = What - we are - are bodies ~ What if - that thinking - is = What limits us to three dimensions - existing - in time - or = Bodies - that think?

Okay = Maybe so ~ Or maybe - NOT ~ But - big deal - right? What do you do with such a notion - when the babies crying - the rent's due - and the car's broke? I know = But try this out.

Is there a ceiling fan where you live - or any kind of fan? If not - then try to get somewhere where there is one ~ Okay? Now - turn on the fan to low speed - if it has one - just on - if it doesn't ~ Then - stare at the fan and blink your eyes rapidly ~ What happened?

Exactly = The blades of the fan - appeared - roughly stopped - rather than a spinning blur ~ This is called - being in phase - with the fan blades ~ In regular time - the fan blades are moving too fast to see clearly ~ In blink time - they're not ~ Because - the effect of blinking - is that you are only seeing a part - of the action taking place ~ So - in effect - you are stopping that action - at least according to the information your visual cortex is processing.

[|[|[[|[[Phase Too:

Going through a phase = Is a description of being in the midst of a temporary state - or - at a particular point - in a sequence - of stages of development - or levels of energy ~ Of course = When you think of that word - stages (the plural form of stage obviously) - it's no very difficult leap to associate it with actors acting - musicians performing = A stage = Is an active - an energetic - location ~ Which means (if you maintain that association) = A phase = Is movement ~ And = Movement = Is change ~ So = Being in a phase (or being in phase - such as electromagnetically - where two wavelengths are in sync) - no matter how much that phase appears to counter - or be opposite to - another phase (such as liquid water - rather than solid ice) - always contains the potential for change - and that containment = Is active.

See = Potential - is never static (meaning - locked in place - no movement) - it always functions (function - is an action) - in a feedback loop - with what is (what is - being apparent existence in any given moment) In this - what is - universe (as compared to the vacuum or wave universe) - things - appear - static (New York doesn't up and visit Los Angeles) - but = The other side (or go-between actually) - of that relationship - is an interaction (call it particle wave if you like) - a continuous gyration (or revolving) - of energy - between what is - and what might be ~ Every instant - that infinite energy source (the vacuum) - feeds its power to the material universe - perfectly balanced in its movement between those opposite poles - and = Spin happens.

As you can see = We've cycled back to the concept of spin (you might say spun - orbited - spiraled - reflected - or… anyway) The reason = Is about examining - the phase of change (evolution - progress - growth) - in which we (humanity) - are currently located - according to our relationship with the dynamic of potential - or = What we do and don't understand - about the structure of reality - and = What is and isn't possible - which = Is a lot of words - but = Go over them again (or several times) - to see the pattern in them - the back-and-forth action of spinning between - where we've been - and where we're going - and there = Is an experience of the fractal nature of space-time - or - as a measurement taking place in time = A frequency.

So - here = Let's see if we can pull all those terms (plus a couple others) - into a form (or pattern) - which can be seen as a whole (or in other words - make sense)

I left you - not so long ago - staring into a mirror of mirrored images of yourself marching off into reflection infinity ~ Let's call - you (the one holding the mirror) - NOW - the present moment ~ Those reflections - are all the potential futures generated by that present - according to an exact structure of perfect equilibrium (or balance) - between each layer of reality (galaxies - planets - creatures - cells - atoms) - stretching out to forever ~ You (that present NOW) - are also = The event horizon of time.

Each moment - the inescapable gravitational pull of the future - drags you toward it - but = You remain in orbit at that horizon - never actually being in the future - always being in now (because existence can only be a now thing) And yet = In each and every of those same moments - you are generating a signal (an electromagnetic picture of now) - to the vacuum field (that singularity energy place where that infinite line of reflections spaghettis out) - which = Responds (the field does) - by feeding back the highest probability reflection (the first one in the mirrored row - so to speak - which is why a standard glance in the mirror is just one image) = As the next nanosecond of your continuing orbit (or reality) - which in turn = Sends out (meaning - you do) - another signal {{What do you think = Reread?}}

A frequency (as you know) - is drawn (or graphed) - as an up and down wavy line ~ That line - represents a fluctuation of charge between positive and negative poles - which = Is actually a loop (the feedback one I just described) - a cycle from one state to the next - which = When you draw it from that perspective - is really a spiral - or = Spin ~ Frequencies exist in time (or define it) - because time = Is the movement = That is change = And all that spin = Equals the same three words = Change = Movement = Time.

To tie the loop then = There is an interaction between the macro (galaxy - solar system - planet) - and the micro (molecules - atoms - particles) - which = Is a continuous structured energy exchange - with - Potential (the vacuum) - which = Creates (or is) - an inward spin - and - an outward one ~ It's really much the same as water going down the

442

drain - requires air coming out - to make room for it - and = Water coming out of a bottle - must have air going in - in order to come out.

We (us humans) - find ourselves on the stage (a phase) - of arriving at a new understanding of all that spiraling activity ~ All of which - may be proven entirely false ~ Which is to say - my description of it - or = If a different - new understanding - is what proves to be true (at least in the temporary way such proving proceeds) Either way = The same phase of arrival remains the case ~ Ignoring of course = That once you arrive in the future = It's just another phase - of now.||||||||||

Okay = What if - it takes as small an action - as blinking rapidly - to come into - phase - with other dimensions of reality?

Yeah - that would be cool ~ But = What would that action be?

Alright = What if - I told you - one way = Is - a single simple question? And the question is = Who am I? Or - in a sense - more accurately = What is I? Which still sounds like improper English - because of how we use that language - which is = Having already decided - what I is ~ It's always = I am tired ~ I have new shoes ~ I am going now ~ There isn't a question of what - I is - because = Our definition of I - is = A body - I call - Me ~ It's - the thing - that's - feeling - doing - possessing - existing ~ But = What is - it?

If - it (this I thing) - were just a body - then = Wouldn't it be - just as visible - as a body? It - isn't though - is it? No = These thoughts - emotions - ideas and such - are all - invisible ~ Yeah = Like I never said that before ~ But - there's really - no way around it ~ The real I - the experiencer - is - invisible ~ It can't be located - in a body - it - just - appears - to be - located - in one ~ So - if we really - want to know - what it is - we have to go beyond - what we - think - it is ~ We have to - question - what it is.

Well = How do you do that?

It's amazingly simple really ~ That's why I used the blink at the fan idea to introduce it ~ You can blink - can't you? Okay - in order to - question - what I is - you - just - do - that ~ No = Not blink = Question ~ Every time you hear yourself use - the word - you ask = What is this I? To what - do these thoughts - these feelings - these ideas - come? Where does the I - come from? Who am I? That's it.

Ah - but you want an answer? Sure = I understand ~ The trouble is - if you got one - it would be the wrong one - because = The I - is the experiencer = It's not - the description - of how - it - experiences ~ Of course - that might sound like some kind of answer - or very confused ~ It's really neither ~ To know - what - the I is - you have to put your attention on - it being - what it is ~ The question - I'm talking about - is not quite like other questions ~ It's not = Define - this thing to me ~ Not even = Show - it to me ~ The closest language can come (mine at least) - is = Be it to me.

I know = I just said = To put your attention on - it being - what it is ~ So = How can you do that - if you don't know - what - IT - is? Don't worry = It's still simple ~ See - the I - is always - being - what it is ~ The - I - that we use - as we describe our experience to ourselves - is a relationship with conditions - or actions - like - hungry - excited - waiting - walking = That's not - the whole I ~ To put our attention on - the whole I - is to remove it (it being our attention) - from those conditions - or actions - and feel - it (the whole I) - beyond those relationships - just being.

Now - maybe that doesn't seem so simple ~ But - that doesn't mean it isn't ~ Maybe - it just means - you're paying attention to the thoughts - that say - it isn't.

[[[[[[[[[Doctor Dude's Dictionary - word twenty six - Synchronicity:

If you synchronize all the clocks in your house - then - when the one in your bedroom says 11:11 - all the rest of them will as well - because - synchronize - means = To happen at the same time ~ Synchronize (in the sense it was used in the previous sentence) - still means the same thing - regardless of whether clocks are involved however - because = It's not a measurement of time = It's the deliberate arrangement of simultaneous occurrences - in time - or - when two (or more) - events of being - are planned to happen - at the same time (like say - whipping open the door just as the pizza guy is reaching out to knock on it)

Synchronize then - is a participatory word - a conscious taking part - in scheduling events ~ That participation changes however - when the word changes to = Synchronicity ~ Synchronicity - is when two (or more) - events occur - unplanned - unscheduled - and therefore apparently out of the blue (or any other color that is available) - all - at the same time.

Another word for such simultaneous events is = Coincidence ~ That is - that's a word which describes those events occurring - but actually - it's really designed to remove participation from the cause of them ~ In other words = Coincidence means - events happening in synchronization - but - randomly (kind of like a hand of cards in a poker game) - rather than as the effect of some action - or force - causing them to be synchronized ~ The difference then - between synchronicity and coincidence - is the idea of including self - or you/me/they/them/us/or something (say... consciousness) - in the equation of - why - events of synchronicity occur (like that poker game for instance) Which means = Instead of removing participation - or some other kind of orderly causation - from the creation of some event - the way coincidence does - synchronicity removes - accident - from that cause ~ Synchronicity doesn't explain why - what happened - happened - it just points at a larger reason - or system of patterns - connections - responses - forces - something other than haphazard bumping around in the dark - that matches one event to another.

You don't have to believe in anything in particular to use the word synchronicity (aside from the use of words themselves - and the objects and relationships they describe) = You - just have to be paying attention.]]]]]]]]]

444

Here's another useful word ~ You might even substitute it for the word - being - I just used - but for the fact it wouldn't make sense grammatically ~ The word is - abstract ~ Who can define it?

Yeah = It's a bit tricky to define - since it basically means - outside of - or not bound by - definition ~ You've probably seen - and heard the term - abstract art? What's that like? Okay = It (abstract art) - doesn't portray - or - represent - what we usually - perceive - as reality? You remember that word perceive of course? Well - in our day to day perception - we mostly relate (there's that relationship thing - I am hungry - I like motorcycles) - to things - in a concrete way ~ That (concrete) - tends to be the word most often used - as a contrast to abstract ~ And = It makes sense = Good old solid - that ain't goin' nowhere stuff - concrete ~ When you get to the other side - the abstract one - stuff is floating around in no apparent order - can't pin it down - can't burn it in the gas tank - dreamy kind of won't pay the rent - stuff - that's not really stuff ~ Of course - now and then - an abstraction - or - an idea - that can't be physically proven - strays into the concrete side ~ The number (that is - concept) - zero - is a prime example ~ Then - there are - mythologies - religious beliefs - paranormal events - miracles - scientific theories ~ Those are all - abstractions - that have concrete effects - whose causes (because they are abstract) - just don't - just won't - talk the bank into giving you a loan ~ Which is not to say - their effects won't ~ But - that's another story.

[[[[[[[[Something for Nothing:

Zero (all on its own) - is not a number ~ Which sounds obvious enough with a moment's thought (go ahead - show me zero elephants) And yet - with just another moment's thought = It is a number - which also occupies a certain amount of the territory of obvious (how else would you account for the lack of elephants- since it's easy to show me zero elephants) - although rather less substantially - because = That's where zero enters its unique numerical value of being a purely conceptual amount - rather than a quantitative amount.

If you have two elephants - and add four more = You then have six - or - a quantity ~ If you have zero elephants - and add zero more = You not only don't have a quantity = You never did ~ Divide - multiply - subtract - or attempt to manipulate zero in any way - and no matter how much you do - all you've accomplished is = Nothing.

Unlike those other nine digits (your fingers are doing such a good job representing) - zero took quite some time to reach its present respectable status ~ It began as a placeholder (the way it works in 20 or 2000) - something like 4000 years ago in Babylonia - only - it was just an empty space then ~ Appropriate enough perhaps - but = Not the whole (except as a hole) - idea ~ That conceptual completion - seems to have taken thousands of years - and (in an old world way) - the credit goes to the mathematicians of India for filling it out (if you can really say such a thing about zero) - by the ninth century CE - which - by the way = Ignores the Mayans of Mexico - who had a working use of it before the first century - derived apparently from an earlier culture which had thrived hundreds of years before that.

Just the same = Nothing - remains an uncomfortable concept ~ Grammatically - the word zero is labeled - an indefinite pronoun ~ Which means = It refers to - something ~ And just so = Is how we tend to relate to it - or = As a contrast to some - or every - thing ~ Things not being there (there are no elephants in the bathroom) - is fine ~ No there (to be being an elephant) - there - is considerably shakier ~ That little zero - is much closer to our hearts as an empty container - because = A container - is something ~ Take away the container - and we are at a loss for reference points - and = Since we ourselves tend to be our own primary reference points - having none at all = Seems to be the basis for feeling that threat.

All that being said = Zero - doesn't actually mean - nothing - because = When you add zero to zero - you don't get nothing - you get = Zero ~ Zero is actually the ultimate even number ~ Divide it by two - and you get zero - there are no fractions - it's perfectly balanced - a whole unto itself ~ Nor can you say - it's neutral ~ No matter how you use it to influence other numbers = It doesn't $(3 + 0 = 3, 18 - 0 = 18)$ Any other function of neutrality - is a nonparticipation - whose effects -cannot be reliably predicted ~ Zero - is completely predictable - in a precisely defined and measurable way.

Zero's other skill - serves as the dividing line between positive and negative numbers ~ Again - not a nothing point - but = An exact boundary (and don't those credit card companies just love it) It's there actually - where its hidden meaning is concealed in plain sight.

Return (if you would) - to that recently revisited image of mirrors reflecting mirrors reflecting mirrors - and recognize yourself - to be holding the position of zero - because = Zero - that boundary between the positive and negative - is = The event horizon.

If - you could reverse that reflection (so to speak) - and instead of (or as well as) - seeing images in front of you - growing progressively smaller - you could also see images - behind you - growing progressively larger ~ And then = Be able to glance back and forth between the two = It would be the simplest thing - to experience the true substance - the heart - of zero ~ Emptiness - is really not - nothing - because = Nothing - is really not - empty.

For all that statement smacks of being a Zen koan (a saying - or teaching parable) = It's not (as far as I know at least) Zero - is a demarcation spot - a point of conversion - an axis - on which contrast spins ~ On one side - things are a certain way - on the other - they are different = Clearly - dramatically - unquestionably - different ~ Your own perspective - poised between the big and the small - is the same = You - intersect (or appear to separate) - the world you see around you - from the unseen quantum world (for all it's just as much around you) - as neatly as zero slices positive from negative.

The one thing left to remember however = Is that zero - is pure concept - an abstraction - and = Such things as that = Are all in your mind.||||||||||

So - this gap - between the concrete and the abstract - seems to be pretty wacking wide ~

Yet - there are a few bridges thrown across - so - it's not exactly an impossible leap ~ Even if those bridges - tend to be - far more like the concrete - than the abstract ~ Which means = They don't actually make it to the other side - because they're still - rooted - in this one.

Anyway = Since that's probably not making much sense (What did you expect from an abstraction?) Here is the - What If - you've suspected was up my sleeve = What if - our - true - natural state - is completely (that's completely - 100% - no additives - no preservatives) - abstract - and - that - is - what - happiness - is?

Yeah = I know ~ How could you even answer - especially - if it is true - other than saying = Whatever ~ Or = What's that got to do with passing my algebra exam? And - you'd be right ~ At least in the world of 15% or less.

The thing is (the concrete thing) = It's up to you ~ The abstract thing is = What if - it's that other part of you - the whole I - the Director - 100% mind - no thing space - that's urged you to go this far - because it (which means you) - wants you (which means it) - to fully remember (which means know) - which means be - who you really are - which means = Happy?

So - no doubt - you've already guessed what your assignment is going to be ~ Yup = It's the I question alright - or = Self inquiry - if you want a more official sounding name ~ Unlike - some of the other assignments - you can do it anywhere - at any time ~ All you do - is ask = What is this I? = Who am I? Or any words that come to you - that explore the same thing ~ And then - feel it ~ Don't - think - about it = Feel it ~ Yes = Those pesky thoughts will want your attention - but = They're not what attention is ~ Give - the feeling - your attention ~ The thoughts will drift off on their own ~ Now - by feeling - I don't mean - your senses ~ I mean = An awareness - a presence - in you ~ You'll feel it ~ It's always been there ~ It's not going anywhere - and will be as patient as it needs to - for you - to consciously - contact it ~ So - like I said = Any where - any time ~ Doesn't matter how long you feel it - only = That you do ~ You know - like any time you take a deep breath.

N.P.U. - Chapter Twenty Six - Intention?

There is a word that acts as a go-between - or connector - between the past and the future ~ Even though it can really only do so in the present ~ It's called = Intention ~ And = Perhaps - it represents more than just communicating a concept of planning - it also = Represents a very real creative force - at the quantum level.

We've nibbled around - the idea - that there could be a natural law (which is also - perhaps - just one of a set of natural laws) - sometimes called - the law of attraction - that arranges this screen of quantum pixels into an order that reflects what we believe - think - or desire - or not desire (as the case may be) - also according to what we think and believe ~ Of course - you may believe - and therefore think - that is crazy ~ But = If - this subatomic world (we've also been nibbling round the edges of) - is actually the ingredient list and fundamental behavioral action of - the real world - we go to the dentist and the movies in - then = What are the rules - that maintain such an amazingly consistent order to it all?

Take this little medical tidbit for example = An article by a usually very orthodox French psychiatrist named Lemoine (orthodox meaning - a follow the rules kind of guy) - described the widespread practice among doctors - of prescribing what he called "impure placebos" ~ You may know the word placebo means (in a medical context anyway) - a pill that doesn't actually do anything - given to a patient - or the subject of an experiment - to fool them into thinking - they really are taking a medication ~ An impure placebo - is one that contains a tiny amount of the active ingredient after which it's named - but - not enough of that ingredient to produce an effect - instead - just enough - that the doctor is not actually lying ~ Lemoine went on to say - a third - or 35 to 40% of all official prescriptions given to patients are such - shall we say - leg pulling.

But why?

Well - basically = Because they work ~ It's extremely well documented - that belief in a placebo will often have the same physical effect - including the side effects cautioned about on the label - that the real drug produces - and sometimes = Even the effects claimed for an entirely imaginary drug - will manifest in the body of an unwitting placebo taker - who was told to expect such effects.

There was one study - where 46,000 heart patients were all taking the same experimental drug ~ That is - they believed they were ~ Half of them were actually taking a placebo ~ The amazing thing - was that the results (which ranged from fair to good) - were essentially the same for both groups.

In another study = A specially recruited group of people - all suffering from a form of arthritis of the knee - were divided into three groups - two of which = Were given a type of surgery designed to relieve pain and improve movement ~ The third group = Were prepared - and placed under anesthesia - and cut - the same as the rest - only no surgery beyond the incision was performed ~ Over the next two years - all three groups reported improvement - but = The placebo group showed the highest overall improvement rate among all of them ~ A point - you might say - which falls rather heavily on indicating = That belief - in the results of that surgery - without actually undergoing it - was a more powerful healing activity in those particular bodies (and minds) - because perhaps = It was belief in such results - that was what worked for all three groups - and not the surgery at all (which of course required recovery - from which the placebo group were spared - other than an external cut) Or then again = Maybe not.

Then = There's another study - where two groups of people - being treated for Parkinson's disease at the University of British Columbia - were told they were receiving doses of synthetic dopamine ~ Now of course - that was only true for one of the groups - since it was an experiment they willingly had signed up for ~ So - half the people were receiving the dopamine - and the other half - a placebo.

Parkinson's - so you know - is a condition where the bodies' system of releasing the real brain chemical (or neurohormone) - dopamine is malfunctioning - and thus = Motor function - or muscle control - which dopamine helps regulate - also malfunctions ~ When those patients who had received the placebo were placed under a PET scan however = It was found that their brains had significantly increased the natural release of the chemical from their bodies own stores - and so counteracted the effects of the disease - as well as - or better than - the subjects receiving the synthetic variety.

If you look at those results long enough - noting that being fooled into - thinking - there was more dopamine available - caused it to be more available - despite having this disease - then = Actually having the disease - becomes suspect ~ In other words = Could it be - that the basis for experiencing disease (or healing for that matter) - is really more a kind of mental agreement - complicated by many levels of thought and belief perhaps - but still = An agreement - to identify ourselves with that condition - rather than a true weakness (or strength) - of the body?

I know - that sounds… well = What ever it sounds like to you ~ One thing it can sound like is = Guilty ~ Meaning = If - it's your mind causing your problems = Then you're screwing up ~ And no one likes that ~ So better to hand it over to someone or something else ~ But = It can also sound like = Power.

There's a woman - you may have heard of - named Brandon Bays - who healed herself of a basketball sized tumor in her abdomen (that's right - basketball sized) - through a certain mind practice technique she now tours and teaches all over the world ~ There are thousands of such cases of healing - all over that same world - involving hundreds of ailments - from terminal cancer - to ingrown toenails - each of which involved = A conscious intention to heal - more powerful than what otherwise might be termed = An unconscious intention - not to.

By extension = That same type of deliberate intention - has been the subject of extensive experimentation - and = Logged huge successes in such oddly diverse areas as - changing the direction small fish swim in a tank - getting gerbils to run faster in exercise wheels - and - keeping red blood cells from exploding (which is what they are inclined to do normally) - in a saline solution to which more and more salt is added ~ Not to mention = Influencing - the growth of plants - bacteria - yeast - the behavior of dogs - cats - rats - chickens - ants - mice - and various human physiological functions - such as enzyme production - and of course - heart rate - and brain waves ~ In some cases - simply wishing for a positive result - such as recovery from an illness - directed by individuals or groups (or participation in groups as a collective agreement for recovery) - has shown measurable results in comparison to control groups (meaning - other suffers of the same conditions - not being focused on so) - or just straight up - as participants beating the statistical odds against such recovery.

Now - that may sound all woo-woo warm and fuzzy - or again = Whatever it sounds like to you ~ One reason for that - is that we seem to live amidst a cultural agreement - to publicly ignore such information (which you may have noticed a certain reoccurring theme of - noticing - throughout this presentation) - and broadcast the information that sounds more like victims at the mercy of germs - genes - bombs - and friendly fire ~ The result - is not that the information I'm offering is inaccurate - but = That it sounds inaccurate - because = Those other sounds - are louder ~ So - let's simply follow along in that theme of language - and talk about = The power of sound itself.

[[[[[[[[[Of Sound Mind:

The famous animal behaviorist - Konrad Lorenz - reported that ducklings that had hatched from eggs he had spent time talking to (a rather interesting habit) - immediately after hatching wobbled toward the sound of his voice - whereas the ones he had not spoken to - did not - which = Is possibly a useful bit of information if you're seeking to bond with ducks (although you've got to wonder what he said to those eggs) - but = It's really more about - how central to the experience of life - sound (or more accurately - vibration) - is.

The ears of human babies - are fully developed - about half way through pregnancy - which means = They can hear - which means = To them - the world (or anything that is not the warm wet movements of Mum) = Is sound (or again - vibration) - and = Just like us (who have survived babyhood) - they are constantly informed by that sound - only = Unlike us (who have categorized that information into representing identifiable things - we think ourselves distanced from the vibrational influence of by - knowing - what they are) - they - are under the direct influence of all and any of the vibrations (frequencies) - they are absorbing - and = Are being formed (at least in part) - by them - which (despite what we may think) = Continues to happen to us.

Sound = Is vibration - both as its cause - and its effect (but you knew that) The effect = Is an oscillation - a swing between extremes (or poles - which create a frequency - can't avoid that word) - whose effect = Is a pulse - which - in the language of sound = Is rhythm ~ The word that describes why we humans are so attracted to rhythms - is = Resonance ~ And the reason = Is because resonance - is = Entrainment - or = The frequency - at which something most naturally vibrates.

If you thump a tuning fork - designed to vibrate at 200 Hz - on your knee - and then hold it near another 200 Hz tuning fork = The second fork - will begin to sing along (vibrate) - merely by being in the same vibrational field ~ That's - entrainment - resonating - because - in essence = Resonance is a cooperative action.

If you buy the idea - that everything - has - or is - a frequency (and why not - it's cheap enough) - then = Everything - has a particular rhythm ~ Of course - everything - comes in all shapes and sizes - and - has all kinds of different effects ~ So - naturally enough - rhythms - have the same range - which means = Resonance (or entrainment) - can also be an action of actively - changing - the vibrational rate (oscillation - rhythm - frequency - wavelength) - of one object (you - for instance) - by exposing it long enough - to another vibration.

Interestingly enough = The Earth's electromagnetic field (the ionosphere) - pulses at right around 7.83 cycles per second - which = Just happens to be the same frequency range - as the human brain's alpha wave state ~ The alpha state - is that slower wavelength (than beta - the standard working pattern of adult minds going about their lives) - which characterizes certain coherence functions - such as occur it relaxed states like meditation and sleep onset ~ They are coherent - in that they synchronize the activities of both hemispheres of the brain - or = A condition of balance - the sum of which is the word - harmony (which perhaps also adds up to the word - review) Alpha - has also been described as a kind of go-between - a mechanism for accessing the subconscious - such as certain processes of memory retrieval and learning ~ It's also the dominant pattern in children up to the age of ten or so - where both imagination (which functions in part with the theta wave pattern - also a strong childhood inclination) - and learning - are highly accelerated processes.

Perhaps not surprisingly then = It is a strongly documented - fact - that children (beginning around the age of five or six) - who are trained in music (playing an instrument - singing - sight reading) - develop a measurably higher (as far as accepted techniques of measuring such a thing go) - intelligence ~ What that has to do with the Earth's magnetic field - is hard to say ~ It is about resonance however - or - actively working with harmonizing vibration ~ It's possible = That the Earth's vibration - is a carrier frequency - quite literally grounding - to a type of natural intelligence (nature to be exact) - or that frequency at which we (meaning - the electromagnetic body/mind experience we're all having) - most naturally vibrate ~ Entraining to that frequency - may (like alpha waves) - be a means of accessing a deeper (meaning - all encompassing) - state of consciousness - and deliver it (so to speak) - to the surface (either mind - or body) - where = Sound - is its echo - its rhythm - its music - its means of communicating ~ Or then again - perhaps not.

Either way = Sound - connects ~ It moves between things - and through things - because = It's moving - and - so are they ~ The next time you hear a piece of music which moves you - it's because = It did.||||||||||

Sound (as you've heard) - is created by - carried by - and perceived - because of = Vibration ~ Musical notes are defined as a particular pitch - meaning = The speed at which they vibrate - or their wavelength - which = Comes down to the word frequency - which = May be reminding you of one or two other things we've already talked about = Say... light for instance ~ Sound is a much slower traveler than light however (which you'll remember - is basically the speed of all electromagnetic energy in that whole particle wave business) - and so = Sonic vibration (that's sound) - and the vibration of the infinitesimally small strands of energy String theory describes (which also requires several extra dimensions in which to do their vibrating) - are not the same thing (by a certain means of measurement) - and yet = They clearly are related - because = Vibration - and patterns of vibration - or movement - are how all those energies function ~ In fact = You might say - that relationship is as close a one as the one between your ears and your brain - meaning = They aren't the same thing (as things are described - until you say the word head - which changes all that) - but = They require each other in order to work (hearing being the work of ears with brains - and everything - at least theoretically - being the work of String theory strings) - so - in that sense = They are the same thing ~ And perhaps - so is the action of = Intention.

The question really - at this point (if not the majority of points leading up to this point) - is = How do these levels of energy interact? And = Where do we (the we - that speak and sing and try to make sense out of what we hear) - come in?

Like I said = Sound is kind of slow in the world of energies ~ But then - so are we - by that same comparison ~ Which probably goes a long way toward explaining why we are so fond of sound ~ Now - hearing - and producing sound - is one of the most normal things going - and at the same time = A force with mysterious properties we have yet to fully understand ~ It's one of the few things we cannot see - and yet can control ~ At least as far as the sounds we personally make ~ Unless you include adjusting the volume knob on your stereo ~ It (sound again) - also offers a whole range of effects - we take for granted for the most part - despite their extraordinary powers - some of which move our ideas - our businesses - our politics - while others move us to tears - to dance - to call the police on the drunken party next door.

All of sound is about movement ~ As for that question of interaction between energies - perhaps sound is also - the missing - or forgotten - tool at our disposal for moving between those levels - and healing this - we - that is still trying to make sense out of what it's hearing (such as that last statement for instance)

You - may not consider sound a mysterious force - or - see yourself in need of healing - but = For many thousands of years - that's exactly how sound has been regarded and used ~ Creation stories from every continent begin with a sound - a song - a word ~ It's the original vibration of communication - and communication is all about connecting one thing to another - or = Bridging that gap that defines things as things (as opposed to - one thing) - moving like a ripple through space to touch everyone and everything in its path - and = Include them in its vibration - so that they know - they are included - because = They were included all along.

Some cultures - like the aboriginals of Australia - hold the belief that the land itself was sung into existence - and to maintain that existence - it must be repeatedly re-sung ~ Perhaps your 21st-century ideas reject such a notion ~ Yet - could it be - that such peoples - who live so close to the earth - have observed the being of that earth and its creatures so intimately - that they recognize a state we call the subatomic world - in their own minds - and in those minds - they view this world - as energy in vibration - that forms itself around intention - in a constantly changing - rather than in a fixed and just there kind of way? In other words = Do they know - and have known for as much as 150,000 years - that their thoughts - their feelings - and so their songs - and the intention of their songs - are fields of vibration - that create - what they see? Is there such a thing to know?

You'll remember that we talked about - entraining systems coherence - some time ago - and that what that means is = Tuning different working frequencies - heart - brain - immune system - cellular communication - and so on = To one harmonious frequency ~ Well - it has been noted by many cultures for centuries - that certain sounds and rhythms - have certain system entraining effects - many of which are as profound as taking strong drugs - or seeing an Earth rise from the surface of the moon ~ Which is actually a way of translating that profundity into our hamburger culture that falls entirely short ~ The real short of it is = It's possible - that sound can do much more than just be heard.

All you need to do to witness one simple - yet remarkable - property of sound - is to take two metronomes (you know - those devices that are used in musical practice to keep a rhythm) - set them at different rhythms - and leave them together in a room ~ In time - a fairly short time in fact (such as over night) - you'll return to find they have synchronized entirely on their own - and are beating the same rhythm - rather than the ones you set them to earlier ~ Pendulum clocks will also perform the same trick.

So = If - vibration affects vibration - and = All our cells and systems - are generating electromagnetic fields - or vibration - then = What are those effects?

[[[[[[[[[[**The Mozart Mystery:**

Music - other than being the art form of popular idols - often more famous than some small countries - is powerful stuff ~ One reason why = Is that neurons (roughly like batteries) - run down - and require vibrational fuel to power them back up ~ One of the ways of accomplishing that - recharge - is listening to high frequency sound - particularly those frequencies between 5000 and 8000 hertz we identify as musical.

Not that just any old music will do ~ As you are well aware - there are innumerable musical forms ~ The specific one - judged to contain the highest level of such frequencies - was written in the 18th century by Wolfgang Amadeus Mozart - and as such = May not be your favorite ~ Nevertheless = It's true.

It's also true (by way of background) = That music - and our bodies - share several organizational patterns (beginning of course - with being based on frequencies) Heartbeat - blood pressure - pulse - and breathing - are all rhythms - tempos - beat - and =

They are always coordinated in the same strict whole number ratios (like two to one and three to one) - known in musical terms as octaves ~ All the other major systems of the body (including brain waves) - are its melody - their individual functions arranged like notes in a score - or - a relationship - a sequencing - with those rhythms - whose simultaneous nature - produce harmony.

So - in concert - with that parallel = Musical rhythms have measurable effects on heart rate - speeding it up - slowing it down - changing muscle tension - skin temperature ~ Certain flows of music - without consistent rhythms - can alter stress (as can certain rhythmic ones) - which influences the hormone producing endocrine system - the oxygen delivering respiration system - connected of course - to the immune system - the nervous system - even digestion - not to mention those brain waves = A metronome set at 60 beats a minute (otherwise known as seconds) - induces an alpha state - ideal for learning and memory retention = Slow baroque music (a style popular in 17th century Europe) - with the same 60 beat rhythmic pattern - does the same thing - as well as contributing to that recharge function mentioned earlier.

In a purely physical way - hearing - or the acoustical nerve - is linked to almost every other cranial nerve (cable like bundles of neuron axons that connect to the brainstem and transmit motor and sensory information for the head and neck region) - which means = That sense (hearing) - is literally connected - to all our others - as well as the mobility of their use - such as turning our head - or blinking ~ The eardrum itself - links hearing to the rest of our bodies through its connection to the vagus nerve (the only one of 12 cranial nerves which extends lower than the neck - whose name is Latin for wanderer) - which communicates between the (so-called) - automatic functions (fight or flight - and - rest and digest - in their most simple terms) - of the internal organs and the brain (another gut feelings connection) It's a physical feature Hollywood soundtracks take full advantage of - because - quite simply (in a sense - the entire argument for the power of sound) = They can.

Returning to Herr Mozart = The complexity of frequencies in his compositions - may act as a kind of brain warm up - stimulating - or getting the attention (as it were) - of the neuronal patterns involved in complex cognitive activities - such as mathematics ~ In an experiment - where college students were given spatial IQ tests (that part of IQ testing which targets the ability to manipulate 3-D objects - such as assembling a puzzle - in your mind) - both before - and after - listening to 10 minutes of Mozart's Sonata for two pianos in D major = Their performance (in the after listening segment) - improved by eight or nine points = An effect which lasted for 10 or 15 minutes and then diminished again - which = Leads one to wonder why they turned the music off at all.

It's not just intelligence though (or even certain types of intelligence) - that's affected by Mozart's work (dependent of course on how you define that word intelligence) Healing systems - that make consistently remarkable use of it - include treating premature infants (which means - creating a vibrational environment in which their development and weight gain is dramatically accelerated) - vocal and hearing handicaps - autism - head injuries - the list goes on - plus = Helping to dissolve the stress of that condition that used to go by the clear causation title of - shellshock (warfare being its most enthusiastic supplier - as you may be recalling from an earlier aside) - now called - post traumatic stress disorder (for having recognized the same symptoms develop from any number of violent sources) And then = There is the brewery in northern Japan - that has found that piped in Mozart increases the yeast density of the saké fermentation process by a factor of ten (who knew?)

Just what it is about Mozart's music that has such diverse power - remains a mystery ~ The fact that people actually like the stuff - may be equally mysterious to you ~ However = Just like broccoli - you don't have to like it (though it does help) - to benefit from it ~ So - now that you know = The menu's bound to sound different.||||||||||

There's one very interesting experiment - inspired by a number of previous investigations into the effects of rhythm and sound - that a high school student (yup - a high school student) - conducted - with surprising (or perhaps not) - indications for certain music fans ~ Well - due to the subjects involved - which were mice - and the lack of that scientific acceptance requirement - repeat - repeat - repeat - you can't exactly call the following results entirely conclusive - in reference to effects on humans of least - but...

This high school student - named David Merrill - got together a bunch of mice (very unscientific measurement - a bunch of - but anyway) He built a fairly intricate maze - and began to train the mice to it by putting them - one at a time - in one end - and some food at the other (in order to inspire them to find their way through) - and off they went ~ After a number of days - the average time for completing the maze for all the mice was 10 minutes ~ Then - he separated the mice into three groups - and started playing music to them ~ That is = For the next three weeks - group number one - listened to classical music - namely Mozart - for 10 hours a day ~ Group two - the control group - heard no music at all ~ Group three - obviously the coolest group - listened to nothing but heavy metal - also for 10 hours a day ~ During those three weeks - David sent each mouse through the maze three times a week ~ At the end of that time - the music-less control group had improved with practice to half the original average - or five minutes ~ The Mozart mice however - had knocked their time down to an astounding - minute and a half ~ Ah - but those rocking mice with their 210 hours of metal mania were the most surprising of all ~ It now took each of them - a solid half hour - to arrive at the feeding end of the maze.

Now - don't take this data as some kind of musical critique ~ It's just how it worked out ~ In fact - it worked out much better than the previous attempt by Merrill - where instead of housing each mouse separately - he had them all together in three cages - and before the experiment was up - the metal mice had killed each other off.

[||||||||| Neuroesthetics:

You could (were you so inclined) - practice that google verb (regardless of the search engine involved) - with the word = Neuroesthetics ~ Its broad range meaning - after you tweeze neurons and aesthetics (that word about the action of taste in beauty and such) -

apart) - is = The science of attempting to understand the impact of music and art at the neurological level.||||||||||

See - it's not a question of taste in music - it's a question of the effects of sound and rhythm ~ You may remember something mentioned early on about the pH effects of different music ~ Well (among other things) = That's also what we're talking about here - or acid verses alkaline ~ I'll let you guess which music has which effect (remembering of course - that acid does just exactly what it sounds like it does) But = There's still that question - of intention ~ What kind of sound and rhythms do our intentions make? Are they a kind of music that echoes back to us in the shape of our world? Is the universe one great symphony of quantum music? Are we jamming with it - or jamming it out? What would happen - if we - intended - to find out?

SPECIAL BONUS EXERCISE - number thirteen

Success List:

What do you think of as success? Is it having an annual income over $100,000? Is it staying awake through math class? Getting into med school? Finding a pair of matching socks under your bed that are still clean enough to wear?

Success - is not a fixed measurement - like a kilometer or a pound ~ It's relative ~ Which means = Related to (or determined and identified by) - all the other measurements we're using to make decisions about how to feel about the circumstances were in ~ Given that room to maneuver - it would be reasonable to say = That a success - is any given outcome - that mirrors - or exceeds the expectations of - any intention - that preceded an action - in quest of that outcome ~ Or - in straight up simple = Getting what you want - in a form that's close enough to what you want - that you want it.

Therefore = When you set your alarm to wake you up at 6:45 a.m. = It was a success = When it did in fact have that effect ~ The other fact - that you didn't actually get out of bed until 7:30 - is another set of measurements ~ Yet still = If you were to be making a list of your successes for the day - you would be entirely accurate including = Woke up at 6:45 as planned.

That - is what we're going to do then (and yes - that includes me - no getting of the hook in this pond) - make a list - keep a tally - an accounting of = Successes ~ It's quite simple ~ All you do - is keep a pen and paper handy - and - every time something takes place - which you consider a success = Write it down.

The criteria - or measurement gauge - for what you consider worth including - is completely personal of course ~ It could range - from successfully taking a shower - to graduating with honors - even - just having a great idea - or an inspiring conversation (hardly the kind of thing to overlook) - can slip very comfortably into such a list.

The trick - which is also the purpose of the exercise - is not to define success - but = To feel it ~ To recognize success in a broader context ~ And so = Blend those recognition moments into one agreement - one vibration - which links loads (of otherwise seemingly separate) - neural reference points - which then say = I'm successful.

And = The way to accomplish that blending - is = To congratulate yourself ~ Pat yourself on the back ~ No = Not some egomaniac better than everyone else rooster strut ~ This isn't a competition ~ It's a construction project ~ And = You're the one under construction - or - what's more to the point = Your happiness is - because = Ultimately - real success - is measured in real happiness ~ So - basically - what you'll be listing - is what you're happy about having done.

Now - you may have noticed that this exercise is very much like - The Winning List exercise at the end of chapter 14 (which of course - you've already filled notebooks with) Maybe even - you might say - this exercise is the mirror image of that exercise ~ The reason for that - is both - you must be paying attention - and = It's true.

This exercise however (but don't you go telling anyone) - is easier - since it's all about noting accomplishments - without planning - or the potential failure or disappointment - involved in anticipating accomplishments ~ Just the same = The Winning List - comes first - because = It sets the stage for realizing - that success - is not really about quantity - or even quality - in the future - or the past ~ It's about follow through - in the present ~ The quantity and quality will take care of themselves when you have trust in your own determination ~ And = Determination - is a much easier thing to fuel - when you derive happiness from it.

So = Start in on that list - and - the first thing you can write is = Began a Success List.

Class Twenty Seven - The G Word?

BREATHE (Now doesn't that feel good? Yoga - boga - or prana - fo fana = It's really not the words and descriptions of larger forces - and beliefs about descriptions and words about larger forces - that matter ~ Or the same of smaller forces and simple systems (complex as some of them may be) It's the experience - the personal what happened when and where - that really counts for us moving around in these minds of ours ~ There's a good deal of research describing the results and benefits of this practice you've been practicing (or can begin to any time you choose) - but = What it comes down to - is = What is your experience? It may be that you think nothing has happened - but = You may be wrong - and = If you stop now = You'll never find out))

Alright ~ I'm not going to ask you a lot of questions this time ~ Only one in fact ~ What - are you doing - in your mind - right now? And = While you're at it - it's = {{{**Inventory Time**}}}

Why do you think I would ask such a question? Which - yes = Is another question ~ But you know me ~ So = Why?

Right = All along - I've been asking you to pay attention to exactly that - your mind ~ So = I'm wondering - if you are?

For thousands of thousands of years - humans - have been exploring these minds of ours - by being in them ~ There seem to be different ways to use them - experience them - and certainly - agree - or not - about the best way to do that ~ There's = How do I get this lawnmower to run? And there's = Wow - how incredibly huge it is inside me here ~ That first one - we label - practical ~ Like we've talked about before ~ The second one - we don't ~ Label practical that is - as we've also touched on.

There's some thinking that happens though - between those two ends - of the human thinking that does that labeling - which tries to cover - both the practical - and the impractical - or = The concrete - and - the abstract - and = In trying to do both - both inspires amazing personal and group experiences - plus - art - music - literature - architecture - and any number of creative expressions - and - causes terrible conflict as well ~ This is where - the G word - shows up ~ That's right = God.

The trouble is (aside from a whole lot of trouble - history - and the present - are filled with - over the word God - which is why - very practically - I've avoided the word until now) - if you are going to talk about consciousness = That word = Is going to come up - and = If you don't refer to it (meaning - the concepts and experiences connected to it) - you're leaving a giant gap (perhaps the biggest one in the universe) - in the potential for understanding (or perhaps more precisely - experiencing) - available to us - from the angles of thinking (or at least some of them) - that use the word (or others like it) - all the time ~ It's kind of like standing in a giant library - wanting to know everything - but then only reading the books in one section ~ Which of course - not only applies to both sides of the practical fence - but also = To history - politics - science - hair care products - or - practically - anything with a label = Information is never complete - if it is gathered according to preconceived notions of what would make it complete (not that - that necessarily makes it complete either - but - hey…)

The other trouble (which is essentially - why - there would be trouble - over the G word) - happens to also be in that angle of thinking - that uses the word all the time ~ All too often - cultures and individuals alike - follow the very human tendency - to separate ideas (which we've discovered to all be connected) - and define - God (or - to use one definition - the source of everything) - as having preferences - for certain parts of everything (namely groups of people who agree on a particular way to relate to the source of everything) - and so = Maintain - the condition - of separating people from each other - and preventing happiness (or peace of mind and harmonious relations) - from being a universal agreement (despite that it's the one thing all of us agree on - wanting)

There's a word - that fits the situation - quite well ~ It's - anthropomorphism ~ That's = Ann - throw - poe - morf - is - em ~ Quite a mouthful eh? What it means - is = Assigning (that is - sticking on - painting over - expecting - or believing in) - human qualities (or conditions of Earth based thinking - behaving - and relating - according to how humans do all that stuff) - to something - that is not human (such as say… energy - what ever that really means ultimately) Children's stories are full of the stuff - cartoons - comics - TV ~ There are all kinds of talking - driving - doing dishes - going to work - animals - cars - toilets - cleaning products - and reptiles out there - which = Is completely harmless - great fun really - so long - as they're not causing hatred or wars.

[[[[[[[[[Heresy:

Five hundred years ago - it was quite clear what sort of ideas would get you burned at the stake ~ These days (now that being burned at the stake is no longer an officially recognized form of behavior modification) - diversity of belief - and it's expression (at least in certain countries) - is a much safer prerogative (a right or privilege) - to practice in public ~ And yet = The pattern (the universe does seem to love patterns) - of establishing - and adhering (the main quality of glue) - to structures of thought that defend against change - remains - unchanged - as a human social pattern (we love patterns as much as the universe does - only differently)

What I'm leading into here - is the word/concept = Heresy - or - an opposing belief - that's highly upsetting to the holders of the beliefs (most often religious ones when the H word is in play - though not exclusively) - that belief opposes ~ It has the ring of an outdated - even barbaric attitude - and yet = The pattern persists ~ Likely - you can find it in your own mind right now - with a moments contemplation of other people's behavior = They - are clearly - wrong ~ Aren't they?

To stand on the razor's edge of heresy then (looking both ways) = Could it be - that the true nature of the universe - including all matter - all organisms - all sentient beings - and all their life cycles - knowledge gathering - and activities of every kind (even - or possibly especially - the driving force of religion) - are in a constant state of = Evolution?

Mr. Charles Darwin - the 19th century botanist who concocted the very famous - Theory of Evolution - withheld publication of his book - Origin of Species - for over 20 years - because = He knew it confronted the dominant worldview (specifically - the Judeo-Christian creation story) - and - would brand him a heretic ~ He also knew - it was a theory - because = It is.

Natural selection - Darwin's central premise - of genetic mutation slowly played out over countless generations in a survival of the fittest design test for successful competition in nature - is based on (and has since accumulated large quantities of) - scientific evidence ~ So much evidence has been revealed in fact - that it has become a dominant belief structure - in direct competition - with the same belief structure Charlie was so hesitant to upset in the first place.

The difficulty (which is to say - the cause - of the difficulty) - is that the extremists on either side of the argument (much like any other argument) - tend to discount the possibility - that some other explanation may actually be - the true one - and = Do not question their own - busy as they are trying to disprove the other ~ Calling such a condition - right or wrong - would only be another result of belief ~ Instead = Noting that it seems to be a recurring pattern among humans - is possibly - much more fertile ground - for evolving - or what's also known as = Emerging.

Darwin's theory - is primarily based on - the fossil record - or the compare and contrast examination of the (converted to minerals) - bones of earlier species ~ As I said = That record is extensive ~ In some cases - it's entirely overwhelming as positive proof that natural selection does in fact occur ~ But = As a complete explanation of life on the planet developing all the way from a single cell organism to office workers - it (as Charlie well knew then - and still is the case) - is woefully incomplete ~ Possibly the most damaging point being = The sudden bloom (appearance - presence) - of life during the so-called Cambrian explosion (about 530 million years ago) - in which 90% of the phyla (or the classification of organisms by their different physical characteristics) - of the current species inhabiting Earth - had their beginnings (again - according to the fossil record) = Simply does not add up to a millions of generations slow adaptation picture.

On the other hand (with its amazing opposable thumb) - the history (or should I say - origin) - of the Bible (the major belief contender in this case) - is often viewed (by believers) - as an irrelevant - or unnecessary consideration - due to the belief (tacked on by more recent centuries) - that it is = The Word of God ~ There's no way to get around such an argument (even if it does appear to ignore the powerful evidence for the hand of many men - over many centuries - compiling its present form - from many sources - for many reasons) - but = There is the complementary (or something which completes) - consideration - that the ancient Jewish culture - from which Genesis (the first of the five books of the Torah - which describes the creation of the world and mankind) - sprang (or was delivered to) - placed immense value on symbolism and metaphor - and in that light = The creation story - was not intended to be taken literally ~ In fact = There is some rather astonishing evidence - that the Torah - is a sort of holographic mathematically-based quantum prophesy software (to put it very roughly) - disguised (in a life on the ground kind of way) - as a set of laws and genealogical stories.

Therefore - leaving you on the edge of that seat = The purpose of delivering these statements (which are themselves entirely up for question) - is not to attack anyone's convictions - but = To point out that = All natural systems - are emergent - or = Always in a state of change - and = Not a single one of them is ever (that's ever) - independent of the whole - plus = To suggest = That there may be far more to - the whole picture - than current (or currently accepted) - explanations supply - and = That those explanations - their history - and even their controversy - are really just more clues - more pieces in a much larger pattern of change - of fine tuning understanding - of achieving conscious coherence with the great mystery of the invisible universe - because = There's always more room - to evolve.|||||||||

See - we are creatures that love stories - especially stories - about other people ~ That's how we understand (to the level we do at least) - our own lives - the lives around us - and the history of the ones before us ~ Stories - are giant for us ~ We live out our lives in stories (is it just me or does this story thing sound strangely familiar) It's when we take those stories (old or new) - of personality - preference - moods - vengeance - and willfulness - and = Use them to define - or make concrete - which is to say - limit - the totally unlimited (or what we've got this word God going for) - that the trouble starts ~ We judge ~ We condemn ~ We blow things up ~ Here we are - one small species - on one isolated planet - in the corner - of an inconceivably vast universe (if not infinite universes) - ready to declare - that our form of relating - to our form of reality - is at the center - of infinity's attention.

Which is not necessarily to say = That - we aren't (at the center that is) What - I am - saying - is = What if - the systems - by which we make those judgments - and so = Cause - the conflicts they support (or even some of the harmonies they support) - is because = We view - everything - through - how - we - experience - this world - as inhabitants of bodies - with personalities - that must compete for survival - in a physical environment? You could call it = Formism - or = The measuring of answers and reality - from the location of locations (meaning space/time/form) - while thinking that such solid (even though they are anything but) - things - and what we call God (or infinite energy) - are different - and thereby hopelessly separated by that difference ~ And so = Because of that = What if - we cannot (meaning - a general theme - rather than an impossibility) - conceive of infinite intelligence (or define what intelligence really is) - or infinite power - or infinite anything - as being something without those limitations - or = Perhaps more importantly = Ourselves without those limitations? What if - we are - indeed - at the center of the great cosmic purpose (with all the above limits to potential understanding applying to the word purpose as well) - it's only = Our ideas - of what we are - where we are - and who we are - that are not?

[[[[[[[[Doctor Dude's Dictionary - word twenty seven - Paradise:

It is often revealing of far more than just a word's current meaning to dig into where it came from ~ Take the word paradise for instance - that luxurious dwelling place of righteous souls after death - or that tropical island just dripping with fruit and friendly natives = Began life in the ancient Middle East as - a walled in enclosure or park ~ Which really means = A safe place from predators or enemies - or = A good place to raise goats ~ In other words = Paradise - in those days - was an excellent goat pasture ~ And = Why wouldn't it be? Health and home have long been dependent on livestock and sturdy walls ~ Safety and freedom from care are the roots of our word paradise ~ Yet - just as tellingly = The word describes its own limits - by way of defining our fundamental fears - and = The hoped-for means for their relief.

What I'm saying is = We tend to view the solution to our problems - as an opposite condition - within the same familiar context ~ Such as - the relief from a flat tire - is a new one - or - soaking wet and freezing - is relieved by becoming warm and dry ~ Our imaginations are limited by the things - we think we don't imagine ~ Meaning = By what we call the real world ~ Imagining that we are rich and famous - is really no great stretch - as would be building a castle - or studying penguins ~ No matter how distant those things may be from our day to day - we have evidence of them - television - magazines - loads of high gloss color photo-shopped and airbrushed representations of what paradise must be like (or at least a new ride and the hotty to go with it) So - when it comes to describing something as unfamiliar as an afterlife or enlightenment - or even perhaps that perfect holiday in the tropics - our toolbox of past experience tends to be rather inadequate ~ Unless - possibly - you can tune your inner radio receiver to the frequency of that first Mesopotamian goatherd to ever lock his gate with such a deep inner assurance of a good night's rest = That his heart sang perfect delight and he never feared the dark again.]]]]]]]]]

Yeah - talk about a mouthful ~ But - it's bites of that mouthful - I've been offering you all along ~ And the reason is = Take a look around you ~ This worlds' got issues (but don't get me wrong - it also has astounding beauty and humor and kindness) - and = They boil down to one of the very first questions I asked you - which is = What is the motivation behind everything we do? Yeah = Happiness ~ Provided you agree with that answer ~ But - even if you don't - you'd be hard pressed to find someone - who doesn't want happiness - no matter how you measure its importance ~ The thing is = We contradict ourselves ~ That is = We do the opposite - of what we want done to us - including - often enough - what we do - to ourselves.

You've heard of - the golden rule? How does it go? Yup = Do unto others as you would have them do unto you ~ How does that ring - with what I just said? Sure = You recognize it = We contradict it (or break it) - all the time ~ Did you know that all five major religions (plus a few more) - have their own version - of the same rule? Well = They do.

There's another rule (a law really) - that three of those - major religions (and we're talking major here) - claim as part of their code of behavior - or = The - Right - way to live - which is = Thou salt not kill ~ All you have to do to witness the breaking (or contradiction) - of that - Rightness - is switch on the evening news.

Wait a minute now ~ I'm not attacking religion ~ Most especially - not yours ~ Religions don't kill people = People kill people ~ The founding principles of religion - are all - about living life in a greater harmony - a state of coherence ~ The killing parts (or the history of fighting for God and country) - are all = About people making up rules - about what harmony is supposed to look like ~ But - I'm not buying or selling morals here ~ I'm still talking the ins and outs of consciousness ~ What I'm really after getting you to look at - is = The way we use these minds - doesn't seem - to get us what we want (= harmony) But - we do get the results - of wanting - to think in those contradictory - or you might say - conflicted ways ~ And - what are those results? Yup = Conflicts.

Which is why another = {{{**Inventory Time**}}} - will instantly illustrate the harmony of functions (even if they include conflicts) - the action of consciously observing perception = Is.

I'm also saying - why - I have been hesitant to use the word - God ~ So = Why am I using it now?

Because = There is - seemingly - encoded - into that mind of ours (the - Wow - how huge it is in here - bit) - a means - or a set of tools - for entering - that larger - unlimited - infinite (and infinitely connected) - space of consciousness (I've been banging on about all this time) - that inspired the creation (or - the use) - of the word God - in the first place ~ And = What if - to neglect - that inspiration - is perhaps to ignore - some of the most practical tools (if not just plain - the tools themselves) - to expanding consciousness (and happiness) - that there are? (As well as the longest list of reference resources imaginable - including ancient understandings mirrored in modern science - which = Even if this course took two more years to complete - would still fall woefully short - and therefore will not even begin to tunnel in that direction) And = What if - the trick is = To avoid - getting caught in the words - the anthropomorphisms - the rightness's - and rules - and = Recognize - those tools - as sign posts - to something inside - you - so abstract - and yet fully available to experience - that no amount of - concrete (or descriptions of belief) - could ever hold it down - or properly describe it?

That being said = We've all heard the statement - God is love ~ Well = What if - that's true? Not in the sense of a someone or something beaming down sweet nothings upon us - but = As a universal organizing principle of ultimate reality (and - to repeat a phrase one more time) - a natural law - a definition (without edges - meaning - a question in search of whole experience) - of what love really is ~ What I mean is = An infinite coherency - structuring this thing we call reality in perfect accord - harmony - symmetry - reflection - and all that good stuff - with however we choose... to choose ~ In other words = What consciousness - just might really be = A single infinite creative force (energy - if you like) - expressing itself in endless forms - and the conscious experience - of those forms - we participate in with every breath and thought and feeling ~ In a word (repeated three times) = Give - give - give - because = At the real core of it all - the 100% whole mind saturation of happiness = We - and God - and love = Are the same thing ~ Or - Not.

[[[[[[[[The Almighty...

Faith is a word that stands for a type of mental possession - an ownership of intangible assets - invisible wealth (unfortunately not the kind of collateral banks tend to recognize) It is generally regarded as the principal commodity of religion - yet actually = It's the main product of any system of belief -which = Assumes the existence - of anything that is not directly physically in your face this very moment (such as tomorrow's sunrise and the continent of Antarctica) Aside from that = The things - we normally categorize as objects (or non-objects - like the G word) - of faith - are regularly the subject of question by someone somewhere - because = That's just the way it is (or seems to be) - since after all - everything - is ultimately up to question of some kind.

There is a belief system out there however - which = Is possibly the most unquestioned form of faith there is - if not the universal religion (by way of a certain power greater than yourself measurement) - of modern humankind = Money.

The remarkable thing about money = Is that everybody's using it - dependent on it - thoroughly tied into the paradigm of its use - but = Very few people - truly understand how the monetary system works - or the consequences (such as war - poverty - crime - greed - corruption - and hunger) - which are built into that system as inevitably as night follows day (speaking as an earthling)

Don't get me wrong now = I'm not moralizing about money being evil ~ It's not ~ It's = Debt.

The Federal Reserve (also known as the Fed) - prints and issues all the money in the US (that's why the bills all say Federal Reserve note on them) It is not - however - a part of the government = It is a privately owned corporation - a bank ~ What the Fed does (and has done since 1913 - or when a central bank monetary system was pushed through Congress – essentially- by the banking interests themselves) - is lend money - at interest - to the government ~ Or more accurately = It hands over paper money - in exchange for paper treasury bonds (essentially contracts to pay the stuff back - plus - a fee) The government - then deposits the Fed's paper into a bank - thereby turning it into legal tender - or - money ~ Of course these days - that's all done electronically - and there isn't even any paper involved.

If that doesn't seem to actually be backed up by real value - hang on - it gets much weirder = Banks - are only required to retain (keep around - save - bank) - 10% of the value of all their deposits ~ The other 90% - is then available to loan out and invest and so on ~ When you take out a loan (to buy a house for instance) - that money (more than likely) - ends up in another bank - where = The same process is repeated ~ Only = From the very start of this number juggling - that 90% - was nothing more than made up (thin air - illusionary) - a number - sort of pasted on top - rather than removed from - the original amount of Fed paper exchanged for Gov. paper - and = Banks repeat the same process - or = Lend out money - they really don't have - over - and over - and over ~ So = In this way - the money supply is increased - and = So is the debt.

You'll recall (just in case you glazed over somewhere back there) = That all the money produced by the Fed - had interest attached - or - a cost for using it (which bank loans - mortgages - and hundreds of millions of credit cards are piling more on the population all the time by the way) - which means = All the money there is (US dollars anyway) - equal less (a great deal less) - than what is owed to the Federal Reserve - because the interest - adds up to more (that great deal more just referred to as less) - and therefore = Can never be paid back in full - and instead = Is an ever increasing spiral of more debt.

Of course = Increasing the money supply - also means spreading the value of money (illusionary as it is already) - over more money - without actually increasing the goods and services that the value of money is supposed to represent - which means = It takes more money to buy less stuff - which = Is known as = Inflation.

Now that you've got all that down = You must realize by now - that this central bank monetary system (or what the Fed is) - potentially (or eventually) - creates (in conjunction with a growth based - rather than a sustainability or resource based - economy) - is a situation in which dept becomes so enormous - and money so devalued by inflation - as to be approaching worthless (one loaf of bread and a quart of milk - that'll be $1249.95) - that the banking system (which presently means the whole economy) - collapses.

For all that may sound like an alarmist stretching of reality = The real reality = Is the state of consciousness - on which the system is built - and which = That same state maintains - and = Like everything else in the universe of matter = Money is energy ~ Only = Since it really is nothing more than a symbol (other than the actual paper stuff) - the energy it really symbolizes - are all the beliefs and relationships between ideas and behavior - which include it as a form of value.

The big-money balance sheet of this world - tips like a mountainside at - 1% of the population - owning 40% of the wealth ~ The condition of mind - which that condition of imbalance - is intimately entangled with - is = Scarcity - or = The belief - that there isn't enough to go around (what ever enough may happen to be) - and therefore = Competing for ownership (or control) - of resources - is the compulsory behavior (or is that faith) - of a global marketplace - where profit and survival - are the opposing teams ~ Anyone - who's ever witnessed any sport - knows = That competition - requires a winner - and - a loser ~ An exchange system based on interest and continuous growth - requires the same = It - cannot rise above its own ceiling - its level of evolution ~ Expecting a different result - is much like hoping World Cup soccer - will turn into a quilting bee.

The truth is (hesitant as I may be to use that word) = There's far more than enough to go around ~ There's plenty - of food - water - energy sources - even - money - and potentially - endlessly so (in a relative way) - at least under the kind of management (consciousness) - which recognizes the well-being of the whole (including the entirety of nature) - to be = What well-being really is ~ What appears to be an enormously complex situation (hence - a problem) - actually hinges on a single core distinction between two ideas (or what generates values - drives behavior - and determines - faith) They are = The almighty dollar - locked and bolted in the treasure chest of - competition - or = Cooperation - pure and simple.

Such a black-and-white choice - may sound naïve - and = By current standards - it practically defines naïveté ~ The thing is (here the word thing - is substituted for the word truth) = The current economic system - is (sooner or later) = Coming apart (a single glance at the national and personal debt in the USA is almost enough alone to back up such a statement) - and so = A new system is required (difficult to imagine perhaps - but then - so was electricity 500 years ago) Sticking to a black-and-white simplification (simply because that's really where the whole thing lands) = It's that one choice - that compete or cooperate - consciousness (it really is - ALL - about consciousness) - that will decide which way it - all - goes.]]]]]]]]]

See - we humans do an interesting thing ~ We take ideas (remember now - how we have determined - that all ideas are connected - and so - all - ideas - are - connected - so - we take these ideas) - that are all connected - no matter what we do - and = We separate them ~ That is - we try ~ And = How do we do it? Well - words are one of our favorite techniques ~ Words like - spiritual - and - scientific (now there's a gaping chasm) We make - garbage collection - and - University - opposite ends of the world ~ But - can you connect them - with a single idea? Pretty simple huh?

What I'm looking at doing here - is = To take all those ideas (meaning - every possible one - you could ever have - about anything) - throw them in a blender - and push liquefy ~ What would you get?

No = Not a big mess = They're invisible - remember ~ What if - what you'd get - is = Mind? And - what you'd see = Is how perfectly - they all fit together - make a whole - like puzzle pieces? Well - maybe more like a fruit smoothie in this analogy ~ The real gulp is = Ideas support each other - smooth as clock work gears meshing ~ The conflicting ones - hold up their opposites - because = What use are they otherwise? Aren't conflicts really agreements - at a deeper level - to conflict? It's that - comparison machine - at work again - light and dark - happy - sad - good - bad ~ Shovel them in ~ Push the button ~ Ta Dah = Mind ~ The whole thing ~ The whole thing that was there all along ~ And yet (how can I resist) - is it?

What if - you discovered - that the world outside you - was a dream - happening only in your mind (not to suggest - there's anything wrong with dreaming) - and = Your body was only part of that dream - and then = When you gave up believing in the dream completely - and even your body - you realized = That your individual mind - was a dream as well? Of course that does beg the question (as they say) = Who's doing the dreaming?

Sounds like a great plot for a science fiction novel - doesn't it? (And a familiar one at this point as well no doubt) Well = What if - you're the main character?

Okay ~ Either way - you are - the main character in that - individual - mind of yours ~ So - here's your assignment ~ It's simple ~ It's another question ~ You can use it with all the rest - with anything really - especially breathing = What is JOY? Just ask it - in your head - in your feet if you like (in fact - try that) - but = Just ask - and see what turns up ~ We've been using that word happiness - but = It's got too many syllables to get right at the core - and maybe = It gets hung up on old ideas now and then - the way that G word does ~ So try this one - in fact - don't stop - any more than you want to stop - breathing.

N.P.U. - Chapter Twenty Seven - Mystical?

If you are going to make a sound = What is the first thing you have to do?

Of course = You have to breathe ~ Which also makes a sound ~ Not much of one perhaps - but still = A sound ~ It's interesting to note - that the deeper and more consciously we breathe - the more sound it makes ~ Such a statement describes a simple principle of physical vibration - but = Perhaps it also describes - a connection - between three things we generally take for granted - or = Breathing - Sound - and - Consciousness ~ Could it be = That our experience of consciousness - could be deepened - by recognizing - and then acting on - the knowledge of that connection?

Such a recognition (you likely won't be surprised to hear) - has been going on in a multitude of cultures for thousands of years ~ The intersection point - or the word - for a type of experience that's located in that connection - of breath - sound - and consciousness - is = Mystical ~ It's a word generally connected to saints and religion - or holy men and women (of various definitions of the word holy) - and - strange goings on in other realms of reality - or imagination - or = Wackoville - if that's what you prefer ~ But = Regardless of preferences - there are huge numbers of accounts and descriptions - stories - anecdotes - and rumors - of people having such experiences (mystical ones) - ever since we worked out ways of telling them to each other ~ So many in fact - from so many different sources - belief structures - practices - and parts of the globe - that one is just about forced to conclude (unless of course your personal choice of force is to ignore all that information) = That a mystical experience - is actually - a very natural thing.

Now I know - the majority of people don't claim to have such experiences ~ Nor am I trying to explain the actual experiences away in a so-called - rational way (like the picture of the UFO was really a Frisbee) What I'm saying - is = What if - it's possible for everyone - to undergo mystical experiences - just as naturally - as we undergo intestinal gas?

Yes - there is often a sound connected with the condition just described - and perhaps - a tendency to want to avoid breathing ~ But - that physical nature aside - again = Are we talking a natural event of consciousness (one that may require a great deal of time and devotion to be sure - but then becoming an master bagpiper doesn't happen overnight either) - a kind of higher order of organization (or coherence) The only difference - from the day to day function of consciousness - being akin to the different skill sets - of whistling Dixie - or - playing Mozart's sonata for piano in B minor - (or perhaps - just as

468

simple a difference - as tying your left shoe from tying your right) - that just maybe =
Breath and sound are intimately connected to?

||||||||| Toning Up:

Before you read this = Turn to chapter 28 and read the section titled - **The Answers** ~ Go
ahead - off you go ~ I'll be right here.

The reasons for such a nonlinear approach - is exactly that = The idea - that chakras - are
a nonlinear approach to a reality that cannot measure them ~ While that same reality -
also = Has no means of measuring the possession (meaning - mental action) - of that idea
(as compared to any other idea) - excepting = The monitoring of certain electrical and
blood flow activities in the brain - which = Still means the same thing = We can't
measure an idea - except = By that invisible process - of having more of them - which =
Just plain drives us around the corner to having to accept = That - real - and - measurable
- are not (at least so far) - the ultimate definitions of each other.

Having spun all that out = There is - a linear set of concepts - relating to the chakra
system (You did read the piece in chapter 28 - didn't you?) - which follow - or connect -
directly to every key concept touched on in this exploration of the power of sound (if not
all the ones in between as well) - which began as = Vibration.

Every vibration = Makes a sound ~ We can't hear them all - any more than we can see
outside the visible (to humans) - light spectrum ~ They are there though - those vibrations
(as well as the much larger spectrum of light) - and no mistake (a turn of phrase meaning
- no mistake) We've called them frequencies - wavelengths - energy - and what ever else
- and now = We'll call them sound as well - because = All those words - describe an
effect - whose cause - is = Movement.

The chakras (according to all descriptions of them) - are vortexes of energy - or little
tornadoes spinning away ~ That's = Movement - or (of course) - vibration ~ Whether you
believe in them or not - the principle - on which they reportedly function - is the same
governing principle - on which the universe - electrons to galaxies - functions = Angular
momentum - or - spin ~ Its influencing - or participating - in that spin - that all activities
in form have in common ~ Everything we do - has its vibrations - its frequencies - and so
= At some level (because of those vibratory frequencies) = Its sound.

Therefore = What it's actually possible to accomplish - with sound - is a whole new (and
possibly very ancient and largely forgotten) - set of sciences - which are only recently
beginning to be recognized and explored.

One of those - sciences - is known as = Sound healing ~ It's arranged around the premise -
that health - is the result of harmonious vibrations - or coherent frequencies - at the level
where - that's true (meaning - the subatomic) - and = Dis-ease - is the result - of inharmonious
vibrations (dissonance - to employ a musical term) The healing part - is in using sound
(vibration) - to restore coherence (harmony) - to that part - or system - of the body - whose
vibration is off - and = One of the means of achieving such a thing - is called = Toning.

Toning - is the very simple action - of intoning (sounding - or singing out) - an extended vowel sound - like Ahhhhh - which = Echoes straight back to the chakras (as well as the exercise at the beginning of each class) - where = There is a specific tone (vowel sound) - associated with each of the seven main ones - and = When used properly (so it's said) - they act as a sort of rotation recharge - which cranks those babies (chakras - and thus - all your energies) - back up to speed - only = Not like some carbonated caffeine adrenaline jolt ~ More in the nature of - tuning in the right station - so the real music (as opposed to static) - can get through ~ In short = Resonance - or cooperation between vibrations - to achieve the same goal.

Take a deep breath then - and exhale it with the lowest pitched (musical note C if you are so inclined - but not to worry otherwise) - Uh sound you can make (pronounced like the u in jug) - for as long a time as you can draw it out ~ And there you go = You've begun to activate the root chakra - which is situated essentially in the spot your body meets a bicycle seat - and = Is connected (meaning - the idea of its area of power) - with the life force - the physical will - to survive.

From there - it's on to the second chakra - which champions the reproductive system - and is located a couple of inches below the navel ~ Its tone - is Ooo (as in who) - rising up the scale (as in doe - ray - me - only stopping at ray - with the musical note D) Number three - is the solar plexus - the seat of personal power - which does its spinning at the sternum (base of the breastbone) - with the Oh sound (as in ho-ho-ho) - another step up the scale (in E) The heart chakra follows - with that classic sound of love and compassion (not to mention - relief) - Ahh (on the note of F) Followed by the throat chakra (singing out a G) - with the sound Eye (as in - I am) - with all the self expression creativity that spot is known for ~ The sixth chakra - is the third eye (confusing as that contradictory numbering may sound) - because it sits just between and slightly above your other two eyes (or lower - according to some traditions) Its note (reaching a much higher pitch now) - is A - and its sound - is the same A (just the way you'd say the letter) - as you spin its power of intuition and farsightedness toward the crown - which = Is the top - the seat of super consciousness ~ The crown is so on top in fact - that it's not even on your head - but hovers just above it in a golden glow (there are individual colors associated with each chakra as well) The Crown's tone - is a high EEE sound on the note of B - which follows a certain logic in its representing ultimate be-ing (corny as that may sound)

So = Now you know ~ You can follow these instructions - and tone your way through the chakras till they're buzzing like nectar drunk bees ~ The idea being - to repeat each tone several times (such as seven) - before moving on - or = Forget all about the idea.

The thing is = This sound and chakra - thing - may be one of the real keys to health and happiness - we've all been searching for ~ If it is - or it isn't - the one thing that's true of any proper search - is = You've got to look everywhere - if you haven't already found it.||||||||||

What is a mystical experience then - and how does it come about?

Well - the most culturally (in this sentence - that's western culture) - accepted mystics (meaning - people who regularly have - or have had - mystical experiences) - are connected to the major - culturally accepted (or at least tolerated) - religions ~ Not that those faiths alone have anything like a monopoly on the phenomena ~ The beliefs and practices of indigenous peoples (that's - native - aboriginal - or just plain got there first people) - of all continents - also include journeys into the mystical ~ Which also tend to be - more culturally accepted - within those cultures ~ Now - that isn't an answer to the question of course - but = It is an introduction to it - in that (despite using words about accepting - which indicates unused words about not accepting - or disagreeing) = Across all those cultural divisions - the strongest theme among the reports of their mystics = Describe oneness - or an uninterrupted connection - between all beings - all things - and - all vibrations ~ In fact - from that point of view - in a whole babble of different languages - the universe has been described over and over as = One great ocean of vibration.

When you examine a number of those traditions (which produce mystics) - you see great diversity - in stories - in customs - dress - diet - relationships with the Earth - and relationships with each other ~ You also see - as the core practices of mystical experience - a number of very definite similarities = Like solitude - fasting - sleep deprivation - prayer - meditation ~ But most often - at the very center of that practical core - are breath - and sound ~ Chanting - singing - intoning prayers or particular sounds - even when practiced silently - all require a direct attention to breathing ~ Breathing - as you know - supplies all our cells with oxygen - which maintains that vibrating verb - life - which in turn is used to create sound - which = Both projects outward - and inward - simultaneously - as certain vibrations - or frequencies - that also affect the vibration of the cells of the entire body and beyond ~ And so = A vibratory feedback loop is created between breath and sound - and sound and breath - with = A universe that could be an ocean of vibration - and = Weird stuff happens.

From a scientific point of view = One of the sound effects - that happen in common - to say - a chanting Tibetan Buddhist monk - and a drumming Native American shaman (both with their heads covered in electrodes hooked to EEG machines) - are changes in brain wave patterns - and = Balanced coherence - or synchronization - between the left and right hemispheres of those same brains ~ Now - what this means is = Moving from the beta wave level of consciousness (or the every day - git-r-done - state of what's called - waking consciousness) - to the more relaxed pattern - called alpha - where a broader range of mental - learning - understanding - remembering - and physical coordination capabilities open up (Speaking of which = Just by balancing on one leg - you will immediately create a burst of alpha activity in your brain) And then - from there it's into = The theta pattern - which is the state of rapid eye movement sleep - or dreaming ~ Of course - the general technique for achieving that brain wave pattern - is to be asleep - which - you may have noticed = Was definitely not the case for either of the two participants mentioned ~ It is true = That at all times - we generate fluctuating frequency levels of all three of those waves - plus a fourth called delta - only = They take turns being the dominant one - or basically - the one in control - which is what we mean when we identify a state as being beta or alpha - etc.

So - what we're talking here - is = Entering a state of consciousness - that is very relaxed - in that it moves (they all move - that's what waves do) - liquidly smooth and evenly -

and = Because the two halves of the brain are in a balanced condition of energy flow in that state - the world of comparison - hot versus cold - good versus bad - or just table versus chair - that the two-sided brain seems to so naturally work from (if not thoroughly represent) - is also relaxed ~ Therefore = It's a state of consciousness - where essentially - as far as the internal world of mind goes = Anything can happen.

|||||||| Levitating Saints:

The word levitate - is defined as = To rise into the air in apparent defiance of gravity ~ Defiance - is defined as = The disposition to resist an opposing force ~ Whereas disposition - means = A being's customary manner of emotional response ~ And then of course - the meaning of definition is = The act of assigning precise meaning to a word or subject.

Circling around those meanings - seems to define a very limited scope of understanding - when it comes to placing meaning on (which is to say - making sense of) - individuals throughout history who have had the talent of being able to float above the ground while in emotional states entirely opposite to any that might be termed defiant ~ Of course - that's just taking the linguistic scenic route to arrive at describing such talented persons ~ However = It's also pointing directly at our habit of craving boundaries of definition - for what we expect from reality (given that - what we call reality - is basically all we ever talk about) - so = When people go floating off the ground for no properly explainable reason - we come up with a word for it - in an attempt to pin it back down somehow to a place where it's not quite so - uncomfortably floating - and = One of our favorite locations for practicing that strategy is = In a dictionary.

The other important reason - for levitation to appear in the dictionary - is the voluminously documented history of its occurrence ~ Which of course means = Lots and lots of written words describing levitation happening.

For one = Take the story of brother Joseph of Copertino - who was a Franciscan monk in 17th century Italy ~ Apparently - hundreds of people witnessed - the hundreds of repetitions - of his rather embarrassing problem of not being able to stay on the ground ~ He was known to just suddenly drift into the air to heights from several inches to several feet - and at least once - to fly between two spots several yards apart in an almost violent manner ~ Most of these events - took place while the good brother was in states of prayer or meditation - but occasionally - they occurred while Joseph was simply performing his regular duties around the monastery.

Although such goings-on were attributed to Joseph's deep religious devotion - they were not considered proper behavior by his brother monks ~ Which - might appear somewhat contradictory - given their own religious calling ~ But = Such was also the case for Sister Teresa of Avila (later called St. Teresa - just as brother Joseph became St. Joseph) - who shared the same difficulty in cooperating with gravity - and even spent some of her time weighted with stones in order to counter act her unnatural buoyancy ~ Nor do she and Joe stand alone in saintly history for displaying such a controversial talent ~ A surprisingly large number of other pious sisters and brothers have humbly laid claim to it as well.

Not that the list ends there either = There are the floating feats (or is that feet) - of several famous psychics of the 19th and 20th centuries - such as Daniel Douglas Homes - who not only could rise into the air without any mechanical assistance (one time outside a window three stories above the ground) - but could also cause heavy pieces of furniture to fly around the room ~ And yes - those abilities were declared quite genuine by several noted scientists of the day - whose original conclusions (characterized by haughty disbelief - I might add) - had been entirely reversed by the experience of studying the man and his aerial tricks firsthand.

The list of such happily gravity defying characters is actually quite long - and includes people from all over the world - particularly India - where = If anything - there is perhaps less of an obstacle in people's minds to marvels of that nature (one reason why they might have worked out the use of zero earlier than others)

And that - quite possibly - defines - how the availability - to what could be a very simple and natural ability we all possess the potential for - is accessed ~ Meaning = By entering a state of consciousness - where those obstacles of mind - we usually regard as natural - are relaxed or temporarily removed - and bingo = We can levitate ~ Now that would certainly be a way to get a party off the ground.

All that being said = Levitation - may be hard enough to imagine as a reality - but = It most certainly has been accomplished uncounted times ~ In fact = I can basically guarantee you that somewhere in the world - at this very moment (or one nearby) - levitation - in one form or another - is taking place.|||||||||

You probably noticed back there - that I said - drumming Native American shaman ~ Which brings up the point = That I neither introduced the instrumental music making element of this mystical business - or described what a shaman is.

Well - as for the music = More than likely - if not definitely - you've heard some of it somewhere - or a lot of it quite regularly ~ What's known as - sacred music - comes from all parts of the globe - and has directly influenced the development of every other musical form ~ Even that mouse muddling metal can trace its roots back to African ritual rhythms imported across the Atlantic in the holds of slave ships ~ All of us have felt the power of music - to influence feelings - imagination - moods - crowds - parades - and football scores ~ There are some who might call music = The universal language ~ Which reversed is = The language of the universe - that great ocean of vibration ~ Of course - the oldest dialect of that cosmic tongue - is percussion - or the more direct description of its favorite tool while in use = Drumming.

From new Guinea in the South Pacific - through the barren hills of Siberia - down to the Congo basin of Central Africa - across to the rainforests of Brazil - up to the Great Plains of North America - and over to the western shores of Ireland (to name just one of a thousand threads) - there are ancient traditions of drumming ~ And tied to those traditions - as much as to those drums - is the legend - the memory - or the presence of = The shaman.

A shaman was - and is - a kind of medicine man - or woman - a healer - an herbalist - a storehouse of myth and legend - or - a witch doctor (in the eyes of fearful or misunderstanding outsiders with other beliefs to defend - not that I wish to defend either side of the question of - rightness - only to describe experience) The experience (to start out with a scientific one) - of an electroencephalogram machine - (that's an EEG) - is that the kind of rhythms used in Shamanic practice - induce - a dominant theta brain wave pattern - which is often referred to as - a trance state ~ In such a state - shamans claim to travel in parallel worlds - as spirits - as animals - fish - birds - you name it - and interact with beings and sources of knowledge and healing - far beyond this gotta pay the mortgage world of ours - and = When they return - they know things - do things - and predict things - they shouldn't be able to ~ At least by the measurements of cultures that say they shouldn't ~ Is their experience real? Is yours? Or is the question still = What is reality?

Well - since I seem to be a human - talking with other humans - about human experience - let me put the following question in those terms = If - as a reference point - you center the brain (the human one) - in the middle of reality - as the tool of perception - and you recognize - that perception is all the levels of measurement - of this - that - and the other thing - which = Are our internal experience of reality - then = What we're talking about as brain waves - are frequencies - or different wavelengths of electromagnetic energy - that function (in a general - oversimplified - yet still roughly parallel way) - like the channels on a TV set ~ What I mean = Is that you can only get the arguing family comedy on one wavelength - the detailed how-to detective documentary on another - the epic historical drama on yet another - and for the last - you have to turn the thing off - yet leave it plugged in ~ If - you continue from that point - and recognize that these wavelengths are the electrical states (or channels) - that govern what types of perceptions we experience - then = Could that mean - that reality - is nothing but changes in frequency of electromagnetic energy - going on in the larger - yet always invisible matrix - of consciousness?

So - there you go - another question about reality - as though dirt and rocks and water and air were something other than dirt and rocks and water and air - and = Where does that get anyone?

Since you asked = There are some new technologies being developed - that use the growing understanding of brain wave activity - to assist in a long list of life changing - neural net establishing practices - from quitting smoking - to none other than inducing mystical experiences.

||||||||| **Quantum Medicine:**

Consciousness and technology - tend to mirror each other ~ What that means is = The tools we invent - and use - and the way we think - about what we think about - are reflections - or echoes - of each other ~ In other words = What's important to us - expected by us - considered necessary to our survival - our well being - our - happiness =

Is the inspiration - the design matrix - the development - maintenance - marketing - spread - acceptance - and - future progress - of our technologies.

It doesn't mean - higher consciousness (that generalized phrase for whole mind coherence) - equals high tech ~ It means = A certain harmony - between thinking (perception - awareness - wisdom - cognition) - and ways of doing things - which = Can just as easily be a stone tool technology society - whose consciousness produces peace - as it can be an atom smashing society - with warfare for a bumper sticker ~ It's complex obviously - with vast quantities of variables and input - and still = It's simple - because = Consciousness and technology - tend to mirror each other.

Fortunately (to place a judged value on it) = Our modern mix of mind and machines - has concentrated on more than just effectively blowing things up ~ The understanding of the subatomic world as being energy - pure and simple (in a complex sort of way) - has led - bit by bit - to an ability (meaning - technology) - to measure that energy in the format known as wavelengths or frequencies (certainly a familiar concept by now) As the technology (ability) - to recognize more and more subtle variations in frequency has progressed - so has the ability (technology) - to distinguish the exact signature frequency emitted by individual types of - things - such as atoms - molecules - cells - or all those things strung together as organisms - and from there = To determine (or locate - in that spot between consciousness and technology - known as mind) - how those - things - are functioning as parts - and - as parts in relationship - or - systems.

The systems relationship - I have in mind here - is the human body - and - the technology = Is a new breed of diagnostic and treatment machinery - filed loosely under the intriguing subject heading = Quantum medicine.

One of these machines (the Introspect Oberon to be exact) - is able to non-invasively (meaning - stay on the outside of the body) - chart out the health (systems relationships) - of the entire body - from physical composition (bone density - water content - pH level - minerals - hormones - etc.) - to organ function (respiratory rate - digestion efficiency - neurotransmission speed - etc.) - plus - pinpoint clogged arteries and blood vessels - tissue inflammation - bacterial populations - parasites - viruses - and cancer cells - as well as locate - measure - and analyze the effect of such things on specific and overall systems (etc.)

How this is all accomplished (technologically) - is by pulsing specific low voltage frequencies at the brain stem (that part of the brain sitting just on top of the spinal column) - which stimulates that organ to radiate a complete electromagnetic spreadsheet (so to speak) - of the body it's being part of - because (apparently) = That's how our bodies communicate with themselves ~ Which means = There is a constant instantaneous exchange of electromagnetic information (frequencies) - flying around in us - all the time - and what we've done (or the parts of we that actually have) = Is learned how to listen in.

The shift (or location) - of consciousness in this techno mirror - is the one most often reflected in nature = Balance ~ And by extension - that musical word that describes cooperation with balance = Harmony.

By way of explanation = There is a treatment end to all of this diagnostic wizardry - which = Having arrived at an exact (more or less) - picture of physical conditions through interpreting frequencies = Can turn around - and broadcast equally exact frequencies - at afflicted parts of that body (sounds like Star Trek - but it's true) - which = Hop the body's own natural (balance) - immune defenses onto the job of healing - in a word = Harmoniously.

To be more exacting (as well as expanding) = In an experiment involving guinea pig hearts kept alive artificially (What's with those guinea pig hearts?) - the signature frequencies of particular coronary drugs (heart medications) - were broadcast at containers of water - which were then poured into the water in which the hearts... lived ~ The resulting effects = Were identical to the effects - that administering the same drugs to heart patients produce.

What quantum medicine is (consciously technically) - capable of (or becoming so) - is precisely identifying imbalance at the level of cause - and counteracting it - at the same level (which is entirely leaving out the connected science/consciousness of natural medicinal and dietary supplements - more effectively researched and prescribed all the time - but hey - can't cover it all) It's a frontier these machines are nosing across - which could not have happened a few short decades ago ~ Not because we couldn't have built them then - because = Consciousness has changed - and so (naturally enough) - has technology ~ The next step - is for more consciousness to catch up - as these machines catch on - and = The image in the mirror changes.]]]]]]]]]

One description of this stuff begins with a term called = Biofeedback ~ Which is a technique of attempting to mentally control some physical function (that's usually considered to be involuntary - like heartbeat or skin temperature) - while using devices that monitor that particular function - in order to know if the mental part is working.

That being said = In the case of brain waves - there's that device we've encountered before - the EEG - for observing what those babies are up to ~ So - the question is = Are brain waves control(ing) - or - control(able)?

In order to save you undo anxiety (despite the fact - that scientists used to think brain waves were an automatic function outside our control - and have yet to actually complete that debate) - there is now sufficient evidence to say with great confidence = What your brain is up to - is up to you ~ Which is to say = That - you - is your mind - rather than - your brain ~ Of course - the two do seem to be kind of stuck together - and = That's where the beauty of a biofeedback process lies.

It has long been known = That practices of meditation calm the mind and produce profoundly still and blissful experiences (too extensive to even begin to outline - if you want this course to ever end) That - has been known for thousands of years ~ For the very much shorter time of about five decades now - a process of uncovering - what goes on in the brain during meditation - has been slowly making itself known ~ The results - as you've already guessed = Are changes in brain wave patterns in different areas of the brain - as well as the balancing of those energies - or - coherence ~ The only drawback to achieving such states through meditation - is that most traditional forms of meditation - require decades of discipline and devoted practice - that our digital attention span culture tends to think is too slow ~ Of course - that is also disregarding the immediate benefits of meditation - or other non- traditional forms of mind training - but = We'll get to that later.

The other difficulty with beginning and maintaining a meditation practice - is receiving limited - or no feedback - as to how you are doing with it - what mistakes you are making - or how to correct them ~ Again - this is not meant to discourage such a practice - it's just laying out the challenges ~ It's all a bit like painting a picture blindfolded - or cooking a meal you can only taste morsels of - which is essentially why it takes so long to perfect ~ Then again - Rome was not built in a day - but = You can now fly there from anywhere in the world in one ~ So = We have thousands of years of meditators to thank for opening the way for a technology (particularly so - if you consider the possibility that they may be the constructors of it at the quantum level) - that could very well have the potential to change the way - everyone - thinks.

In the simplest terms - this is how it works = The person being trained - is hooked up to an EEG machine with electrodes stuck on particular parts of their head ~ They're also hooked to a polygraph machine - or lie detector - as they are commonly referred to (which basically works by measuring changes in sweat secretion by how well a tiny current of electricity is conducted - since electricity travels easily in water - and - we sweat when we lie) The EEG is designed in such a way that different brain waves produce different tones (you know - musical notes - sound) - and varying ranges of those tones ~ The polygraph - records changes in mood (to use an oversimplified - but basically appropriate word) - to be compared later with the EEG results ~ In action - this combination of machinery allows the trainee - to hear = The changes in brain states - as = They are produced - by mind states - and then = To see further documentation of what the relationship between the two was afterwards ~ In essence - it allows a person to tune their mind - much as you would a musical instrument - to a higher functioning state - by literally hearing the results of your thinking ~ You might even say = In the language of the universe.

There are any number of other techno innovations being worked out - or already marketed - out there - that are linking brain and body function to that - in there - phenomenon of mystical mind ~ Virtual reality - other bio-feedback - sound - motion - and stillness - are all getting plugged in to the world of treating mental good - bad - and explorative ~ The thing about technology and mystical experience - is = They transcend (remember that word) - culture and religion - in the sense - that they are universal (another word to remember) - experiences of being ~ Meditative bliss and running a vacuum cleaner - are the same thing for everyone - meaning = Indeed - we bring our own lens to all our experiences - but = There are parts - which are shared - no need for explanations - opinions - descriptions of right or wrong or whether that vacuum sucks or not ~ Machines are not mind - and the other way around - but = It is extremely intriguing to see an evolution of machines (the product of mind) - which may assist in the evolution of understanding and expanding - and healing - that same mind thing (not to mention - the possibility of technology that is the product of highly evolved benignly responsible mind) - call it consciousness or what you like - or (again) = The language of the universe.

Class Twenty Eight - The End?

BREATHE (One more time now = You can do it ~ Of course - by one more time = I mean right now ~ Who knows - you may be doing this for the rest of your life - and = That may be one of the best decisions you ever made ~ So = What do you say = Are you willing to make a commitment to this practice - for say... another week - a month - six months - a year - tomorrow morning? How about = Do it for the first time right now? Is that the condition that actually applies? Don't worry - no push - no guilt - just asking ~ We do what we choose ~ I'm offering a choice ~ Invisible effects are often hard to choose working for ~ But then = Every thought you have is invisible as well ~ Why are they so important?)

So - what - IS - joy? Are - you - what it is? No - no = Not that person that's trying to work all this stuff out - plus everything else - and - look as cool as possible while doing it ~ I'm - not - talking to that person ~ In fact - I'm not talking to - a person ~ I'm talking - to you ~ I know = You think - that person = Is you ~ Well = What if - you're wrong? That is to say = That person - is wrong? What if - that's why = I'm not even going to ask any more questions? (For the moment at least)

Oh - I forgot = Congratulations = You've made it to the final ~ You must be ready for the deep hidden inner secret I've held out until now to tell you - or - maybe not ~ But - I'm going to tell you anyway.

It's simple = I've been lying ~ This entire course - every word - every idea - concept - story - description - practice - question - statement - and - punctuation mark (which you were already aware of) - is a lie ~ Which - is not to say - that none of it was true ~ Actually - all of it was ~ But - it was still a lie ~ Including - calling this - the final class ~ It is - in fact - the first class ~ Except - for the fact = That is also a lie.

So = Does that make a complete pretzel of your thinking?

Good ~ It's supposed to ~ Because = What if - thinking - is - the obstacle - to pure - or - whole - or 100% - consciousness? An = {{{**Inventory Time**}}} - right now - might just give you a feel for what I'm saying.

The thing is - it doesn't matter - that I say - the correct words - in the proper order ~ It hasn't mattered - and it won't - it can't - because = If they (the words) - are what's important - then = They - are in the way as well ~ Language - belongs to the world of

478

thinking ~ Which doesn't mean - it does not serve - that world - with great depth - color - and value = It does ~ And yet = It does so well - it builds an intricate and endlessly fascinating barrier - to stepping beyond - the need of it.

That - is where the lie (who could resist using the word) - lies ~ Throughout this course - I've been using - language - to get you to think - and thinking - to get you to think - and talking about thinking about thinking - to get you to think about thinking - and certainly - questioning thinking (for all that takes some thinking) While all along - I've wanted - to get you to consider - stopping = Thinking that is.

Now - I'm not saying this is a bad thing either (meaning thinking itself - or - how I have approached arriving at this moment) - despite the fact - I've used the word - lying (which is generally regarded as bad behavior) I've only used it - to stress a certain seriousness to the point I'm trying to make ~ The way you might throw in the F. word - when you really want to get someone's attention ~ Not that - that's necessarily - a good way to do it.

|||||||||| **The Gravity of Levity:**

When you stand on your head - up = Is still up - because = It's a word - a description - of a contrast with the most fundamental common denominator of all life on Earth = The planet itself - and = Its gravitational field.

If - there was a super powerful laser strapped to the top of your head (feet still pointing at the ceiling) - which was drilling through the Earth below you = When - that laser pops out somewhere in the southern hemisphere (unless that's where you already are) = It - will no longer be traveling downward - but instead...

Up and down - are possibly the most core experience expressions of physical life there are ~ They're right - up there - with yes and no and love and fear - for reflecting the charge polarities of the universe ~ However = Get far enough into space from old mother Earth - and = There is no up and down ~ There's only - the very clear illustration = That mind - is the gravitational field - of experience - because = In isolation from other reference points - it (mind) - is the central reference - because = It was all along.

Levity (that key portion of the word/action levitate) - is an up word - of the same core antigravity distinction - as up itself - only = It functions equally well in all directions - no matter how far off planet you travel (presumably anyway) - because = It's describing - the force - of mind - that is happiness.

You could start out making sense of that word - force (in the context I just used it) - by describing a relationship with it - a reaction to it - or = The chemistry of happiness ~ But = What the actual chemistry - of happy little neurotransmitters - hormones - amino acids and such - is = Is not what levity is - any more than the great - relief - of taking a breath after rising to the surface of deep water - is relieving oxygen depletion (despite that being what is actually taking place) = It's the relief itself - that is relief.

What levity is = Is buoyancy ~ It is that rise to the surface - like a bubble - lighter than its surroundings = It ascends ~ To take it out of the metaphorical world into a more dictionary oriented one = Its laughter - clowning - silliness - mirth ~ To put it back (with a more scientific twist) = It's an expansive force - naturally permeating a contractive one ~ To suspend it somewhere in the middle = Its release - or - that word already gulped down soaking wet = Relief - because (swimming back to metaphor) = Levity is the breath of our happiness - its successful respiration.

Ultimately (that word that turns up trying to add authoritative finality) = We don't know what levity is - any more than we really know what gravity is ~ Gravity's got that curvature of space time going for it (as far as theory goes) - which perhaps transfers to levity - as a curvature of good time - but (aside from a bit of fun with words) = Do we have the full picture? No.

Therefore - looking at the picture we do have = Let me remind you of this world of nearly 100% subatomic space - where = Gravity - appears to be a force acting on matter ~ However = At nearly 100% space - there really isn't much of the stuff ~ Is that what renders gravity the weakest of the four forces - as it slips through the atomic cracks like wind through bare branches?

No = That doesn't identify what gravity is - but perhaps = It sheds light on the parallel force - of levity.

I use the word parallel (meaning - two lines which do not intersect) - because levity is (or could be - or just metaphorically identifies) - a fifth force - an opposing polarity to gravity - the way electricity and magnetism are polarities - only = Those two make up one force - which means = I could just as easily be describing a unification of gravity and levity - as one force.

As for opposite poles = We're talking ups and downs here - and - as for unification = The word is = Attraction ~ Levity (like gravity) - attracts ~ Laughter - the main effect of (why not - we'll call it) - a levitational field - is infectious ~ A smile - a joke - a bit of witty banter - draws minds together - sets up a cohesive wave pattern between them - where (mentally speaking) = The opposite effect of gravity occurs - and weight - is relieved - pressure dissipated ~ Taken to its extreme (levitation) - and a body leaves the ground ~ In a complete simplification then = Gravity pulls down - and levity = Pulls up.

Does that mean - that gravity - corresponds to - or is the influence - the organizing force - of density = Whereas levity - describes - maintains - connects to - or just is = Spaciousness?

In a sense - this discussion of the gravity of levity - is all a play on words - because = Words are an expression of the experience we call mind - which = Is where the two meet (language and experience) - or - that central reference point mentioned earlier (out in space beyond the up and down) Where they don't meet (or the parallel veers off in different directions) - is in the specific examination (of the general experience) - of levity - when it becomes plainly obvious to be (if not necessarily perfectly controlled - certainly) - invited by = Choice ~ Gravity - doesn't seem to come in the same kind of optional packaging.

480

But then again = Perhaps a more complete understanding - of the force of levity - will confirm gravity - to be a choice as well.|||||||||

So what is the point anyway? Any guesses?

Sure = It's about thinking - or - not thinking ~ But = Beyond that - into that space of question - is where we really need to go ~ So - here's the lead - despite its being expressed in language.

What if -our perception - of how this reality (we appear - to exist in) - works - is completely opposite - to how - it really does work?

I know - I've been juggling such ideas in front of you all along - and = They don't - appear - to be answerable ~ But - that's the point ~ What if - our ability to answer such questions - is big time handicapped - by what we think - an answer - has to do - or in other words = Be - which is = A solution? What if - the real answer is = There are no solutions (I mean - in an ultimate sense - there are still repairs and remedies and such) - because = There are no real problems - because = What we think - is real = Isn't?

Now I know = That goes completely against all your senses - your experience - and even - in a big way - much - if not all - of what I've asked you to do by way of exercises and such ~ But = Again = That's why - I've used the word lying - because = I've known all along - I had something else in mind ~ I've just had to coax you along in steps - in order for you - to get there on your own.

Yeah = Get where? That's what you're wondering - isn't it? Or - maybe not ~ But......

Paying attention = That's the answer ~ I'd even go so far as to call it = The solution = If I didn't know better ~ So instead - I'll call it = The opening ~ Because = What if - that's what this reality - this universe - this world - this body - this story we're all living out - is based on? Meaning = Where - we put - our - attention ~ What if - that's how the subatomic world - organizes - what - it's supposed to be - where - it's supposed to be - and - how it's supposed to be? What if - it's entirely - 100% - the result of - what we (meaning - sub - super and straight up consciousness) -do with our - feeling minds (different - mind you - from just - thinking minds - which is not to say - thinking minds are not included in the equation) - or - what we = Pay for - with our attention? What if - these minds - as whole systems of feelings - beliefs - and expectations (including who knows what kind of cosmic input and potential) - are definitely more powerful than we can imagine - simply because = They can imagine anything - and = That's all they are doing - meaning = Living in an imaginary world - inside - themselves - or better yet = One super mind?

Again = It sure doesn't look that way ~ But - why would it - if that - IS - what we're doing?

481

[[[[[[[[[[Doctor Dude's Dictionary - word twenty eight - Conclusion:

A conclusion is (generally speaking) - what wraps something up - meaning completes - finishes - terminates - and... Cut = The end ~ It's all about arriving at a point in time - where - enough loose threads have been tied together - to weave some sort of reasonable fabric out of many understandings into one whole understanding - or decision - judgment - settlement - opinion - that sort of thing ~ And from there - to move on in time to other situations or ideas.

It all sounds simple enough ~ Common as oxygen molecules even ~ Which is really to say = We expect things to begin and end and make sense and be left behind - and ourselves to form opinions and judgments and what we call knowledge out of all those experiences and information - just as naturally as we take breathing for granted ~ So that (that - being what I just listed in the above sentences) - is not just the definition of the word conclusion - but = The reason for its existence ~ To conclude something - is to draw an imaginary line between the ideas - of what is unfinished or incomplete - and those ideas - that are about finished or complete ~ Its imaginary - regardless of physical conditions changing - such as the faucet not leaking anymore or the lawn been completely mowed - exactly the same as for non-physical changes - like learning how to read or grasping quantum mechanics - because = A conclusion - is a state of agreement - with a perceived outcome ~ In other words = A mental state - a condition - of imagination.

Now - that may seem like slicing an unnecessarily fine line (as if lines were actually involved) - between definition and practice - or thoughts and stuff ~ After all - it's just a word ~ But = Words - are the devices we employ to externalize our interior experience ~ And = As far as interior experience goes = There is no such thing as a dividing line in the ongoing flow of activity that is the nature of being alive (barring death of course - but then our understanding of the experience of death could hardly be called conclusive)

The fact of it is = Our use of the word conclusion - is an extension of the original Latin word from which it developed - which meant = To shut up closely - or confine ~ There's barely a leap left to the word = Imprison ~ A point - which points rather sharply - at a system of order - where what's done - finished - or concluded = Better blanking well stay that way.

In conclusion - I would say = That no matter how we define things - and ideas - and the relationships between things and ideas as being complete or not - there is always the next moment - and the one that follows that - to prove us wrong - or wear out the repair we just made and re-grow the grass ~ It's not exactly orthodox procedure to conclude a definition by prying out the plug of its meaning in order to let its contents go free ~ But then = The best part of going to jail - is getting out.]]]]]]]]]

So - what if - what this - what that - whatever = I know ~ What good is any of this cosmic guessing game?

Well - guess what - I've got another word for you ~ It's = Enlightenment ~ Can someone define it?

Ah = To gain perfect knowledge of inner peace ~ That's lovely ~ Thank you ~ You went directly to - what we might call - the deeper meaning - rather than a rational intellectual gathering of information - the word can also mean.

What if - I were to say - that definition - or - the thinking that would lead to such a definition - is absolute complete horse dung? Would that upset you? What if - I followed that with = No - that horse business isn't really true - but = The inner peace thing only covers as much as pizza alone covers nutrition ~ Would you say = Could you please explain that? Or = How the hell do you know? Are you enlightened or something?

What if - I told you = Yes - I am - and = So are you? What if - it has nothing to do with all the - study - meditation - self denial - raw feet - sore butt - hopeless to achieve - and a fantasy anyway - ideas - you've got stuck to the word? Other than - those are things to occupy yourself with along the way - or = The story of enlightenment (as it were) Of course - playing out stories is what we do in time - and in that sense - all those things are perfectly true - as they apply to your story - but = What if - all enlightenment really is - is remembering - a state of being - we've always contained - every moment - all our lives - nothing to - gain - at all? Kind of like Dorothy's ruby slippers - in the movie The Wizard of Oz ~ Remember that? If not - I would highly recommend seeing it.

But = Yes = A state of being - we've always contained? What if - that state of being - is = Whole happiness - and so = No wonder we would all want it? And what's more = What if - all we have to do - to remember that state - to - be - enlightened - all we have to do - is = Pay - attention - to - happiness - and = Forgive - everything else?

No = You don't - think - so? Well - all I can say is = What are you paying attention to? Which is not to say - the things I've said are right = It's a question ~ All of these are questions ~ I'm not really claiming to be enlightened ~ I'm asking questions = What are you paying attention to? What do you think is right? What is - enlightenment? What if - it's the question - that opens that state - that remembrance - that everything pizza just the sight of is unimaginable bliss?

You know - just to set things straight - I wasn't really lying ~ Well - yes I was ~ No - that's not true - I wasn't ~ Was so ~ Was not ~ Was.......

Okay - that's enough ~ Do you recognize that kind of argument? Rather childish don't you think? Especially if you're having it all by yourself ~ It is an excellent technique for wasting time though (should you happen to need one) The thing is - we all do it - individuals - governments - religions - scientists - you name it ~ It usually doesn't look quite so - juvenile ~ It tends to be more long winded - complex - or even quietly subtle ~ The media - libraries - billboards - bathroom walls - your favorite song - and these words - right here - right now - are all doing it.

So - what is it - we're doing? Of course - another = {{{**Inventory Time**}}} - will answer at least part of that question.

What if - what we are all doing - is generating the friction - the power - if you like - that runs this universe? What if - we're reacting - like a nuclear reactor - according to our - preferences - for particular ideas - beliefs - opinions - what have you - that govern all the different parts of our lives - as though - they - were - different parts - and therefore - in need - of defending - in order - to keep them that way - which is = Different? Or - the ultimate difference = Separate? What if - you are having that - did so - did not - argument - all by yourself - because = There is - only - your self? It really would be that simple you know - because = If - we're not separate - then - there's only one of us.

|||||||| Wrong?

Steering the vehicle of our collective knowledge experience down the road of life - appears - to have only two directional choices (not counting forward - since backward - at least in time - is apparently not an option) - which are = Right - and (no - not left - but) = Wrong ~ With that vague bit of play in the middle - where we attempt to sort the two out (or - get away with what we can)

The problem is = Our knowledge of right and wrong (or more precisely - correct and incorrect - since we're actually not talking morality here - despite how that tends to get mixed up) - is based on - what we've decided - is right or wrong (which includes the determination that there is such a distinction in the first place - including correct and incorrect) - and so = Under a certain level of scrutiny - it's all basically suspect just plain across-the-board.

Take for instance - a bit of stumbling in the dark (recently touched on elsewhere) - which really comes down to admitting full-fledged ignorance = We - don't know - what gravity is.

Sure - Mr. Einstein came up with his fabric of space time being curved by large objects and thereby influencing smaller objects to be drawn toward them - and mathematically - it lines up quite neatly ~ But = Does that mean we know what gravity is = Nope.

Or = How about that elusive force carrier particle - the graviton? Or better yet = The Higgs boson (yes - that is the sound of a vague memory bell ringing) - nicknamed - The God Particle - and fabled to be the basic ingredient in charge of it all ~ Does it make sense to look for such things? Are photons and gluons and muons (the other boson particles - or force carriers) - really what we think they are? Are the forces agreed upon (electromagnetism - gravity - the strong and weak nuclear forces) - just an agreement to cover the behind of (hate to be wrong) - human judgment? Are there smallest parts? Or - do they just go on forever - nested one within the next - infinitely smaller? Or - do they eventually cross the black hole event horizon of this reality - and = Emerge somehow in another universe as... somebody else's oatmeal? Is stringing String theory - between quantum world and relativity world - just adding wrong to wrong? Are they just connecting the dots of old understandings- that are built on more of the same dot drawings - a linear progression of sums and subtractions that seem to explain things - and yet = Perhaps only explain (or more precisely - display) = Our drive to explain?

Indeed - there appears to be an uncontestable line of observation - experimentation - and mathematics to the far reaches of Wahzoo - which = Place the questions just posed - awkwardly - yet firmly - on the - wrong - side of the road (meaning - opposed to what is - considered - right) But = Could it be - might it just be - that all of it = Is wrong?

Look for a moment at the phenomenon of the (so-called) - near death experience = Which is the well-known - leave the body - float around the room - pass through a tunnel of light - encounter dead relatives and benign beings thing - which = Has been recounted by countless numbers of people - who - for whatever reason - spent some time (in some cases actual hours) - clinically (total physical system shut down) - dead - and then = Were revived - or brought back to what we call life ~ The only real - measurable proof - for the authenticity of such things (on this side of the dead line) - is the float around the room bits ~ There are numerous stories told by returned flat liners - which describe the continuing activities in the room they found themselves looking down at their own apparently dead bodies in - as well as their noticing things in obscure corners (such as a tennis shoe on a high window ledge) - that would have been impossible otherwise for them to have seen (or even for others present to have seen) - which were later confirmed as entirely accurate.

You can go round and round with what science thinks - is right - to try to prove those experiences to be - wrong - and = Who knows ~ Knock yourself out ~ But = The evidence in question - is in question - because = It seems to be a demonstration - that mind (or that old word consciousness) - is a non-local event - or - not dependent on the physical container we steer between right and wrong in - and = If that's the case - that our central measurement tool defies all measurement - then = How can we possibly be certain of anything we've measured with it?

Take all this quantum stuff for instance = As a tool for understanding certain functions of our reality (say electromagnetic energy) - it has proven to be - right on - by odds that are absolutely mountainous ~ But = Is it really any better - than opening the window to figure out how weather works? Is a quantum leap (remember that?) - just so many empty words (two actually) - trying to replace = Beats me man? And = What keeps those electrons orbiting? Is it a feedback loop with the zero point field? Momentum left over from the Big Bang? What if - the Big Bang - turns out to be - the Big Flop?

What if (in the end) - it's all really rather silly - what we've chosen to be right about (or wrong about for that matter) - as our local experience (alive) - transitions to a non-local one (dead) - and we find out = Something completely different?|||||||||

Here - let me put that in fewer words = What if - the energy - that runs (which is to say - manifests) - what we call physical life - is - at its core hinge between the wave and the particle = The idea - that = We are separate?

That - is what I mean by - the possibility - of reality - working - completely opposite - to our perception - of working reality.

No = You won't find the answer through that same ability to perceive ~ I'm afraid we can't - think - our way - beyond thinking (at least in such a way that there are no more thoughts to think) And = I'm not exactly serious about giving thinking up either ~ Thinking - is a function of this fantastic mind thing we've got going on - which = Has far greater ability - than anything we normally give it credit for ~ It's achieving a new state - a new dynamic - or system of thought (a system - being a variety of different actions - that function collectively - as one thing) - to use a single word - wisdom - that I'm suggesting here ~ Because = What if - indeed = What if - we were to pay enough attention - enough awareness - enough feeling - to the question = Of what lays beyond the physical experience - beyond bodies - thoughts - and - perception - of bodies - thoughts - and all things physical - and = By employing that system of attention = We were able to experience - what we've always been looking for (I've been calling it happiness mostly - but = What would you call it?) - was never - any distance away - because = There is no such thing - as distance - from that - thing?

Alright ~ If - that's true - or not - you'll have to find out for yourself - just like this next bit - which - by the way = Is definitely true ~ Unless of course - I'm lying ~ But = Yes - this is actually the first class - and - it begins = Right Now ~ After one last = {{{**Inventory Time**}}}

Regardless of how you have reacted - understood - used - or ignored - anything - that has led you to this moment = What if - you - have succeeded in a curiosity - that ultimately = Will feed your happiness beyond anything you could imagine? In the end (even though a continuing progression of unfolding time eliminates the actuality of a real end) = All of our choices of how to think/behave/live - no matter how diverse and seemingly in disagreement they appear - are actually - in complete agreement at the fundamental (conscious - subconscious - and subatomic) - level of = Why we choose them = We want the peace - the health - the resources - the security - the well being - to be = Happy ~ Given that agreement = All that remains to be accomplished - is completing the learning curve - of recognizing - what choices actually provide the conditions - of mind - that support the condition - of happiness.

The math is no mystery = Choosing happiness = Supports happiness.

As for one last assignment then = Don't imagine how your happiness - might be fed = Feed it yourself = Feel it = Pay attention to it = Breathe it = Be - the condition - in which it flourishes ~ Use the tools I've offered ~ You can repeat them all - or = Pick the ones that appeal to you most - or = Find more elsewhere - or = Make up your own - or = Not ~ It's up to you ~ Always was ~ Just pay attention - to what - you're paying attention to - and = You'll see ~ How do I know? Because = If there's a reason for breathing = Then we're all doing it for that reason - and = There really only seems to be - one = We agree on.

N.P.U. - Chapter Twenty Eight - Unified Field?

I talked before about the difficulties - or challenges - of meditation taking too much time - and work - and being a kind of blind groping in the dark (not that I said that last bit exactly) So - let me mention the advantages then - by way of balance - and also because = There's a good deal more to this business of tuning the mind than a week or twos electronic fiddling will set in place ~ Plus - there's also the fact - that meditation does not always mean the same thing - or have the same effects - any more than the word art - describes all art.

First off = Meditation - no matter how it's done - is free ~ Excepting the cost of training in some instances - the actual practice costs nothing ~ The head covered in electrodes gizmo - is big bucks - or a bargain - depending on your relationship with the green stuff - and your mind of course ~ I don't mean to make how you approach your mind an issue of finance (besides - isn't time money?) The issue - is really more a case of the word free itself - and the natural function of the mind to move freely ~ The act of meditation is ultimately (meaning - final result) - not about doing something - or doing nothing - it is about entering a state of movement that produces no friction - and - since that probably makes only so much sense = It is most simply described by the well-worn phrase = Going with the flow.

What if - the natural state of the mind - for all it may not seem so - is a silent observer without opinions or preferences - entirely abstract? (You remember that word abstract don't you?) And yet - within that abstraction = What if - whole mind - is perfectly attuned - to the whole vibration - of all electromagnetic - quantum - string - zero point - and ooh baby energy - there is out there - and = The one way to get there - is to go - in there - and = Meditation is one - of those one ways?

Okay = Yes = There is some complexity to the forms of different meditation practices ~ Such as contemplation of symbols or beings or states of mind like compassion - or repetition of a word or sound called a mantra - or a state called mindfulness - where the practice is continuously allowing thoughts to slip off without connecting them to more - and then there's simply - conscious breathing - but = Ultimately (to use that finalizing word again) - the general goal aimed at in meditation is not complex - nor the sole possession of any certain set of ideas or beliefs - or even really difficult ~ What it is - is = Choosing ~ And - what you are choosing = Is to - freely - step back (figuratively speaking) - and merely be a witness to the being - you are being - on the level of being - that is the harmonious flow - of energy - that being is ~ Yes - maintaining that state for

488

long periods of time - like say… 30 seconds - is where the years of discipline come in ~ However - ultimately again - it's those moments that - it works (meaning - when you're not - working it) - that count - because = The place (not that it really is one) - you're stepping back into - is the one and only place being can be = Now.

[[[[[[[[[Any Where - Any Time:

Just in case this word - meditation - sounds like some mysterious ritual you have to shave your head and twist your legs into some painful position to practice - or whatever you may think it is if you've never done it - I have to point out that = If- you've been doing the assignments - then = You've been practicing different forms of meditation.

Right off the bat - with the conscious breathing exercise - the eyes of a one year old - the alive energy of your body - the mind as radar - and several others (I'll let you identify them) - are forms of meditation.

The only real difference between the every day action of thought - and the action of meditation - is that thought actively involves itself in - what is going on in thought - and meditation (except for the form that is called contemplation) - is simply resting in awareness - with - what is going on in thought - without - participating in it.

Anywhere - any time - you are doing that = You are meditating.]]]]]]]]]

Now - why would you want to do such a thing? That's the real question ~ After all - no one takes on any kind of work - unless they see in doing it - some kind of benefit - to someone - something - or most especially - themselves ~ But - I'm not trying to get you to take on anything - just the question itself ~ It's up to you to sort out the rest ~ But still = Why?

Fundamentally = We've already been all over why ~ It's really just simple addition that's left - or 1+1 = This experience of life seems to break down to two parts - or conditions - or states (you know how words can go on and on) - and they are = Mind and matter ~ What happens - when you begin to break them both down to their - parts - is you go from complex systems - like an entire body - or a whole personality - to progressively simpler systems - like cells - to molecules - to atoms - or - from belief structures - to memories - to thoughts themselves ~ Eventually - if you take the word of ancient wisdom traditions - and - emerging science together - you arrive at a state = Where what appears to separate those two conditions of being (mind and matter) - dissolves - and the two things become one thing - or the so called = Unified field.

So yeah = Talk about abstract - or so what - or whatever ~ But = What I'm talking about - is = A means of accessing that state - and - consciously - influencing - this one.

One technique of meditation - that has been observed scientifically perhaps more thoroughly than the rest - is called = Transcendental Meditation - or TM ~ One of the aspects of that observation - has been to look beyond the personal response to meditating

- and attempt to measure the response of the environment around the meditator ~ Which is to say - the effect it has on the rest of us who happen to be around.

For decades now - very thorough - very systematic - very detailed - and very diligently repeated - reviewed - analyzed - picked apart - and in short = Very scientific studies - have been conducted around how a certain ratio of meditators to population seems to reduce the amount of crime - violence - and other conflicts going on in the area that population lives ~ There are a lot of numbers and statistics and other variables calculated in - but = The results point extremely convincingly at the conclusion = If enough people - or the square root of 1% of a population (which would mean - roughly 8000 people out of the population of Earth) - were practicing TM simultaneously - conflict across the planet would be influenced (from that unified field location) - to lessen - to smooth out - perhaps even (at least temporarily) - to cease altogether.

I know that sounds like La la land - but again = The data involved is truly extensive and minutely examined by multiple independent agencies - and = Repeated over and over ~ Plus = It was gathered in such places as Washington, DC - one of the highest crime rate areas in the US (amazingly enough - or not) - and = In the Middle East - one of the most violent (while Israel and Lebanon were attempting to sort out their long-standing differences a few years back) - as well as dozens of other locations.

What it means = Is that the state of increased coherence (we seem to keep coming across) - which TM has been more than adequately proven to produce (even in people brand new to meditation) - is not confined to brains - or machines that monitor brains - but in fact (apparently) = Influences - or produces - social coherence as well.

{{{Just for the sake of clarity = The above statements are neither advertisement nor biased endorsement of Transcendental Meditation as being more effective than other forms of meditation ~ They are merely recitations of data gathered - and food for thought ~ They do constitute however - a rather appealing buffet of that food - and as such certainly deserve further... chewing?}}}

To return to ideas of sound for a moment = The same type of conscious participation in creating harmonious patterns - as was the case for the meditators in the studies mentioned - is the common experience of billions of people across the globe - when they sit down to make music together ~ Such sound creation occurs in thousands of forms - and is subject to as many variables of belief and personality as all things human - but = There is a key difference in musical interaction - that sets it apart from other types of communication ~ Take the word jam - for one ~ Other than being a popular thing to spread on toast - jamming - is a term for informal musical cooperation - a type of conversation - where the speakers are intent on agreement and mutual compliment ~ Even the wildest - most seemingly formless jazz - takes place in a mental location of agreement - to explore dissonance (remember that word?) - and abstraction outside of melody ~ What we're really looking at here = Is a state called harmony - or a vibratory pattern = That begins as harmony of intention = Extends to harmony of interaction = And completes as harmony of the whole ~ Only - it does it all in a loop - feeding back on itself - and producing more of the same - and = Even though its music that led me into the last pair of statements =

It's not music I'm talking about - other than it's included and offers a wonderful model = It's us = It's life in all its forms - that is the subject here - and = The nature of that unified field we share.

||||||||| Life on Earth:

There's no one - no thing - no plant - animal - mineral - liquid - solid or gas - on Earth - in this moment - that isn't doing one very specific thing - and no exceptions (except perhaps a few metaphysical gray areas due to semantics - or - word choices - but anyway) - and that is = Existing on Earth (or within its atmosphere - that being a more accurate boundary)

No matter how you slice up reality - as an interior experience manifesting an apparently exterior one - a constantly fluxing collapse of the wave function into a particle illusion of solidity and back again - a fractal pattern regeneration in infinite directions - a feedback loop with the vacuum field - or - just a day in day out work and play and eat and poop old world where what you see is what you get = The thing about life on Earth = Is a common reference point - a shared experience - of a single closed system (speaking from a finite physical format) - which = As seen from space - physics - and philosophy - is = One - thing.

Having established that (meaning - laid out a particular viewpoint) = It should be noted = That the odds - for the number of factors required for a planet to support life (meaning - have it appear at all) - all aligning in the same place at the same time - have been roughly estimated to be one chance in 10 to the negative 15th - or one/one thousandth of one/one trillionth ~ Whether those numbers are anything like correct or not - definitely the real ones (what ever they are) - are such = That by comparison - they make winning the lottery sound like a sure thing.

So again = No matter how fine you slice and dice concepts of reality - this planet - with all its profusion of life - particularly - consciously self-aware (or so-called - intelligent) - life (such as ourselves - how ever that description may be up to question) - is a story of the most amazing… list of adjectives you could ever string together.

Having narrowed to that focus = It's that conscious self-awareness thing (threaded so doggedly through this course) - which spirals back to that one specific common denominator of a single planetary experience - and shouts out = Pay attention to the whole picture = It's shared ~ Doesn't matter what you believe ~ One way or another - you're taking part in this Earth story ~ If you want it to be a happy one = That's what you have to share.

That being said (regardless of it being true or not) = There is a different angle from which to visualize this integrated systems system of a planet - which = Can have a subtle - yet profound - influence on approaching the question of how to more harmoniously share it.

It's the movement of the Earth itself - its pattern of motion as it travels through space ~ Our standard - basically two dimensional view of the solar system (even when we project it into animated spheres spinning around the Sun) - looks much like an old phonograph record with all the planets in their appropriate grooves doing the same thing on and on and on ~ The difference - in true three-dimensional spatial dynamics - is not endless circles (or even ellipses - as we've known for a long time now is the more precise shape of planetary orbits) - but = Spirals.

The Sun (our local star) - is also traveling through space - carried along by the great spiraling flow of the Milky Way ~ Earth - and her eight sibling planets (provided you still include Pluto as one) - go chasing after her - only = Not like lettering on a Frisbee with the Sun at the center ~ Instead = More like beads threaded on a coiled wire - or (like I said) = Spirals.

Why that would matter (also like I said) - is subtle - and yet = It adds up to the fact = That this planet of ours (or what represents our wholly connected sharing of experience) - is never in the same place twice ~ It means = At the solar system level - the galactic level - the universe level - and by that lead - every other level = There are patterns that repeat - but = Not one thing in space time - stays in the same place - EVER ~ Where we are (in the universe) - in any given moment - is somewhere we've never been before ~ And that means = We are really not trapped in repetition (and even though I repeat the word - as you can see - it's in a different place) - EVER.||||||||||

What if - the underlying nature of all things - all ideas - all events - is = Harmony? Indeed - one glance at a newspaper front-page is enough to sink that idea in a mile of mud ~ But = What if - that perspective is only true - because = It is so far removed from the location of energy where all the basic parts of this worldly life are manufactured - or - their manifestation is powered - and = Where that's going on (that energy location) - there is complete harmony and cooperation?

Yeah = One more time - such a question falls at the feet of = So what? But - between those toes - lies the fantastic advantage of the moment of history we are sharing - where the experience of knowing an answer (or at least a new set of questions) - to that question - in a global kind of way - draws closer every new moment.

There's another technology - based on manipulating brain waves - with sound as the key feature - that's arisen from the particular intersection of ideas that seems to be fueling - this question answering advantage of present history ~ That busy intersection - is where ancient wisdom - meets modern science ~ Those traditions of wisdom - spiritual - mystical - shamanic - and so on - have been constrained (or limited) - to describe - what cannot be described in words - through metaphor and analogy or myth ~ Lovely stuff - but incomplete in a world of eat and sleep and make money (provided - the experiences described - are not your own) Science - which took over in the view of many people as being more sensible than being governed (often very harshly) - by the interpretation of rules based on metaphor (or that idea of religion that is called - The Church - because others weren't allowed) - has conducted a hands-on dissection of physical reality ~ Of course - that approach is limited (or constrained) - by the requirement of solid proof - which is incomplete in a world of beauty and love and mystical experience (or those experiences from which spirituality sprang) Ah = But like I said - the intersection of the two - is a brand-new vantage. point - because = It opens the power of question in all directions ~ It means = That what ever humans are capable of experiencing = Is attractive and valid material for scientific study - in the hopes (regardless of their validity or not) - of explaining it - and = That willingness to question - expands that other willingness - and the capability - to experience more that we cannot explain - and = FEEL - all of it - dry - dirty - duped - or delicious - along the way.

Anyway = As for describing that new technology (or another low-tech description version) = It's an audio - or listening experience - where = Two tones - of slightly different frequency - are played through headphones into your ears - one tone on the left - the other on the right ~ In the middle - or your brain - a compensation - or adapting reaction - occurs in a place called the olivary nucleus ~ What happens there - is the creation of another frequency - or beat pattern - that is a wavelength exactly in the middle of the two tones entering the ears (or you might say - the difference between the two) - and = That frequency - then acts as a tuning fork for the rest of the brain to vibrate to ~ What this does (other than sound confusing to the parts of your thinking that don't know how to do it) - is = This third tone - generated by the difference between the first two (1+1=3) - has become a carrier frequency - which = Carries (as it were) - the brain of the listener - into the brain wave patterns it vibrates at (sound like entrainment?) So - as these two tones are changed = So are the brain wave patterns of the listener - and = By measured steps - that listener (meaning - his/her brain) - is brought to a wave pattern - that is both the one exhibited in deep dreamless sleep (delta) - and = The deepest states of meditation (as far as electronics have measured anyway)

The benefits claimed for this product (it is a product - and more than one actually - with the whole force of modern marketing techniques behind it - and therefore will remain unnamed here) - are far-reaching (or certainly claim to be) - from a strengthened ability to deal with and release stress - to heightened creativity - awareness - contentment - prosperity - freedom from addiction - the whole show ~ It is also expensive ~ Again = That's according to relative value ~ Currently - the United States spends more on what's known as - defense - than the combined defense budgets of the entire rest of the world ~ In that light - one could perhaps say with relative certainty = That it may be time to reconsider what we consider valuable ~ Have you considered what an army of meditators (an army of one) - might accomplish?

However = The reason I describe this (or these or any form of) - technology - is not to highlight an answer or a solution - but instead = Questions - possibility in action - the exploration of potential - in a word = Change (surprising as that may be) - and = That change - is evolving new forms of interaction with the form-less ~ I mean = Need I really remind you - that the whole of our experience of experience is = An interior one - and = The manufacture and maintenance of form (that old subatomic world) - is = An invisible one ~ Obviously - technology - is neither interior (in the sense of mind) - nor invisible (excepting its production of frequencies and such) - but = It is another of the results of this astounding consciousness of ours - and hey = How cool is that - when you think about using energy - at the level of plug in the wall energy - to access and process energy/information at the level of its source ~ We ain't there yet - but = What if - we could be?

|||||||| The Answers?

Have you worked it all out then? Do you know the answers to = What is consciousness? What is happiness? What is the point?

Before you answer = Let's talk about a circuit of energy - which = Science - has been unable (nor particularly willing) - to prove the existence of - which (in the opinion of hundreds of millions of people) = Proves - beyond a shadow of a doubt - that science - just hasn't got there yet - and perhaps = Can't ~ At least as we currently define the word - as a system of tangible measurement - because = What we're talking here - is another realm of expressing tangible altogether - or = The life force - or spirit - energy centers of the human body = The chakras.

When you drop that word - spirit - in a beaker with the word - science - you tend to get an oil and water suspension effect ~ In other words = They don't mix.

But = Why?

Never mind that question for the moment - and meanwhile = As for the chakras = They are hubs - like a series of spinning transformers - in a system of energy processing - including both physical and psychic health functions (such as happiness) - which has been around as a set of working concepts - or knowledge (you might even be tempted to say - as a science) - for who knows how many thousands of years ~ They are generally familiar as the seven major chakras - spaced along the spinal column from the root (where you sit) - to the crown (you cover with a hat - provided it's tall enough) - but = There are reportedly hundreds of minor ones scattered over the body in a balanced circuitry board - connected by flowing energy channels known as nadis or meridians - complex as the back streets of Calcutta.

Each of the seven (excepting the crown) - is associated with an endocrine gland (such as the pineal gland - roughly in the center of our heads - or the thyroid - in the throat) - as well as a major nerve plexus (or an intersecting network of spinal neurons grouped together to serve a specific region of the body)

It's the glandular/nerve connection - that sidles up most closely with a - scientific basis - of understanding life ~ The glands of the endocrine system - are secretors of hormones - those specialized molecules that travel the bloodstream signaling when to turn on or off particular functions - such as metabolism - growth - reproductive activities and such - as well as playing a role in determining mood (that slightly more fuzzy area between the physical and the psychic) The most familiar of the several nerve plexuses in the body - is the solar plexus - located just below the rib cage and behind the stomach (the area of the third chakra) Its domain of nervous system servicing - are the internal organs (the third chakra - by the way - is associated with intuition - for one - or what you might call - gut feelings) Both the endocrine and nervous systems - are key communicators - in the internal world of the body - or exactly what you describe as = A system of energy processing.

So what does it mean - this word energy - when it's adrift between physical and psychic and scientific and spiritual?

For one = There is the work of Hiroshi Motoyama of Japan (inspired by Chinese medicine - which is directly connected to chakra concepts) In a lead lined recording booth (to screen out any electrical interference) - he measured the electromagnetic fields opposite various chakras - of both - long-term practitioners of chakra-based meditation - and - people with no such experience - and = Found significantly higher levels of energy (actual detectable light in fact) - emanating from the meditators - which = You might call - scientific proof - but = It still remains highly controversial as such (controversy of course - being another form of energy)

Again though = What is this - energy? Where does it come from? Why is it so hard to measure?

One word for it is - kundalini (coon-duh-lean-ee) - the sleeping serpent that lays at the base of the spine (traditionally metaphorically speaking) - awaiting its own awakening (a kind of pre-enlightenment jump start) - which means = Throwing a metaphorical (yet still quite physical) - switch - and opening a spinal circuit to rise to the crown and join with supreme being (super consciousness - the G word - zero point field - your pick) - through the power of Shakti - the dynamic creative forces of the universe ~ Another word is - Qi - or Chi (pronounced - chee - as well as having been pronounced earlier) - which comes from China (the other words come from India) It translates (as simply as possible) - to = Energy flow - the force that is life - and = Is closely connected with the breath - that most obvious demonstration of the balance between Yin and Yang (another Chinese concept - meaning - the forces of contraction and expansion)

As for answers = You've probably worked out - that it's movement - that defines (or at least describes the action of) - consciousness - happiness - life - time - space - penguins and bagpipes - and = Puts them all together in that word = Energy - which = You can reverse - as the definition of movement - life - happiness - and consciousness - which = Is actually no definition at all - but a wheel (which is what the word chakra means) - spinning ~ It's a force (that list of words combined) - because = It will not stand still ~ Measuring it (or attempting to do so) - can only ever look back at its passing - like tire tracks in the mud - and = Describe the tracks as proof of - a thing - without regard to what powered the - thing - without which = There would be no track.

That's the real difficulty - in shaking a blend between science and spirit as lenses to look through ~ The one - has beginnings and endings - while the other - has neither.

They can meet in the middle though - in that word - experience (for which - you can substitute the word - kundalini - if you like) We can argue the ownership of - true and real - until pigs open airports - but experience - quite possibly = IS = The whole point.|||||||||

Either way - we live in a time tumbling over the edge of huge change - environmentally - socially - politically - economically - technologically - personally ~ What we've been looking at here - are options - possibilities for new perspectives - theories - conjecture - mixed up with nuts and bolts and just plain nuts (as the cutting edge of cutting edge is apt to get sliced)   They are not answers (even where they think they are) = They are questions ~ And - we have barely begun to scratch the surface of what generates those questions - and = Where they lead - because = They lead to more questions - as they pass through systems in systems in systems - of extraordinary insights - discoveries - and wisdom - all balanced on that razor of how mind and matter play out their roles so vastly different from adding large fries and a shake ~ The best I could do was point out a few - and leave the rest to you ~ But - since you've arrived at this edge - this frontier - where the end looks like a beginning - just as the beginning looked like an end = There's one more point to consider.

As you work your way down the causation ladder of physical form - from cells to molecules - atoms to particles = Energy - instead of decreasing = Expands ~ Not takes up more space = Takes up less - with more energy ~ Ultimately - it means = All the energy of being - is not in the things that make things - but = In the empty - never empty - nothing - everything - outside - inside - touching it all.

What does that mean?

Keep asking questions.

496

The Final Score

Congratulations - you've made it to the end of this course - that is most recognizable - as being = The End (no matter whether it is or not - or how many times it sounded like it was but wasn't) So - as you step up to the podium to receive your degree - or head for the locker room and a well-deserved shower - or whatever symbol of completion you identify as meaning = Done that - now on to the next thing = Allow me to point out something that has happened to you - which = You may not have noticed.

You (which really means - you and I - which really means - we) - have arrived at = Three.

The two parts of this course (never mind all the other distracting bits) - however distinct - or similar - were separated by an idea (the idea being that they were two parts) - which now = Has arrived by the same transformative action of addition (having both been digested by your mind - to whatever nutritional level that accomplished) - of equaling = One thing - which is = A new thing = Your experience - your thoughts - a different - no matter how minimally = You.

We - as humans - have the wonderfully advantageous benefit of being = Open systems ~ Which means = We are energy exchangers ~ As opposed to closed systems - such as car engines - which = Are energy users - or at best - converters ~ A car engine uses (or converts) - fuel like gasoline - to a controlled explosion (energy) - whose effect is mechanical motion - and off they go ~ The problem - with being a closed system - is an inability to change - to adapt - to learn how to do new things ~ Closed systems wear out - because = They cannot renew themselves - and = When they are faced with a crisis - such as running out of oil (a phrase you could interpret on a couple of different levels) - they can't reorganize their function and exchange energy differently = They seize up - and become useless.

We - on the other hand (which is one reason we have two) - can use crisis - or chaos - or complete Oh my God breakdown = To learn - to evolve - to reorganize at a higher level of functioning ~ At the cellular level - we do it continuously ~ We are designed - from top to bottom - to change = We - are = Open systems.

The information we have examined - and explored the experience of together - is all about that reorganization ~ Whatever was new to you in that process (especially what did not make sense - or you actively resisted) - was (or is) = A kind of threshold - a doorway - to a new experience of your own functioning ~ You may have encountered it in quantum mechanics - String theory - forgiveness - Crop Circles - black holes - or just this weird twist on punctuation I've forced you to endure ~ Which is not to claim - the label of truth - or rightness - for any idea or format presented here - only = That those are locations of overwhelm - where you have made that leap from an old system of being who you are - to a new one - even if it took you reaching this page to do it - or some page years from now.

The timing is not the point ~ The point is = You - are to be congratulated - for looking - for asking - for allowing = Change - to occur ~ There are any number of changes you may have undergone in this time we've spent together - new habits you may have formed - and certainly have the opportunity to go on forming ~ You won't have even noticed some - or even all of them - but = I'll place in your notice right now = That from now on (and of course - there never really is anything but - now) = The word - **Inventory** - is changed for you = You'll hear it = You'll notice that you hear it - and = It will direct you instantly to a state of attention to your own experience - which = Will cause you to smile - because = Now you know just how rich that experience is - and that (just as natural as rolling down hill) = Will lead you to that space of question - which asks = How much more to this experience of consciousness is there?

We learn - we grow - we expand - into = The Unknown ~ Anything else = Is just a repetition of what we think we know ~ We can't plan the unknown - intend it - visualize it - or even imagine it ~ The only way in = Are questions ~ The only answers = Are the ones - we're going - to find out ~ The ones we already - agree with - will (or might) - get us to the door - on whose other side is the unknown - but not through it ~ How could they? This - space of question - we're beginning and ending with - is not a state of weakness = It's one of power ~ Just like that vacuum field out there - in here - everywhere - it's not the least bit empty - and contains infinitely more energy than any apparently solid object (or answer) - that perception can describe or lay claim to understanding.

There is a word tossed around these days - with many levels of association and meaning (yet only one very simple reference to experience) - which = Makes it the perfect universal symbol (translated into different languages of course) - of an action we all recognize ~ The word is = Awakening.

It means = That transition - from unconscious - to conscious - to move out of sleep - where we are limited - inactive - and vulnerable (never mind dreams - which are a whole different set of symbols) = To awareness - where we are involved - responsible - and = Powerful ~ No matter how you categorize - or bemoan the present world of humanity - there is an awakening in progress that you are an important - even essential - part of - which = Is evolving an entirely different perspective on (hence - a new relationship with) - reality - than we collectively (as far as I know - and quite possibly incorrectly) - have ever known before - and = It is my great privilege and honor - to welcome you to it.

And now - you can exhale - because = For all the times I've reminded you to breathe = I've never mentioned how important the action of completely exhaling is - and = Since it's the last point I'll make = You're bound to remember it.

Our normal - not conscious of breathing - breath - only empties our lungs to a certain percentage - or something like 60 to 40% - which means (much the same as not breathing deeply) = That the lower cells of our lungs are not absorbing oxygen efficiently - and instead = Are sitting in the byproduct of breathing = Carbon dioxide ~ All you have to do to change that condition however = Is contract your stomach muscles as you exhale - and force the air out of your lungs - by consciously - squeezing yourself empty - and then of course = Remember - to breathe.

Jack

3418610